DATE DUE

MR 25-05			
06-19-06			

DEMCO 38-296

HUMAN DEVELOPMENT REPORT 2001

Making new technologies work for human development

Published
for the United Nations
Development Programme
(UNDP)

New York   Oxford
Oxford University Press
2001

Oxford University Press
Oxford   New York
Athens   Auckland   Bangkok   Calcutta
Cape Town   Chennai   Dar es Salaam   Delhi
Florence   Hong Kong   Istanbul   Karachi
Kuala Lumpur   Madrid   Melbourne
Mexico City   Mumbai   Nairobi   Paris
Singapore   Taipei   Tokyo   Toronto

and associated companies in
Berlin   Ibadan

Copyright ©2001
by the United Nations Development Programme
1 UN Plaza, New York, New York, 10017, USA

Published by Oxford University Press, Inc.
198 Madison Avenue, New York, New York, 10016

Oxford is a registered trademark of Oxford University Press

ISBN 0-19-521836-1 (cloth)
ISBN 0-19-521835-3 (paper)

9 8 7 6 5 4 3 2 1
Printed in the United States of America on acid-free, recycled paper, using soy-based ink.

Cover and design: Gerald Quinn, Quinn Information Design, Cabin John, Maryland

Editing, desktop composition and production management: Communications Development Incorporated,
Washington, DC

Foreword

Development and technology enjoy an uneasy relationship: within development circles there is a suspicion of technology-boosters as too often people promoting expensive, inappropriate fixes that take no account of development realities. Indeed, the belief that there is a technological silver bullet that can "solve" illiteracy, ill health or economic failure reflects scant understanding of real poverty.

Yet if the development community turns its back on the explosion of technological innovation in food, medicine and information, it risks marginalizing itself and denying developing countries opportunities that, if harnessed effectively, could transform the lives of poor people and offer breakthrough development opportunities to poor countries.

Often those with the least have least to fear from the future, and certainly their governments are less encumbered by special interests committed to yesterday's technology. These countries are more willing to embrace innovations: for example, shifting from traditional fixed line phone systems to cellular or even Internet-based voice, image and data systems. Or to jump to new crops, without an entrenched, subsidized agricultural system holding them back.

So with the Internet, agricultural biotechnology advances and new generations of pharmaceuticals reaching the market, it is time for a new partnership between technology and development. *Human Development Report 2001* is intended as the manifesto for that partnership. But it is also intended as a source of cautionary public policy advice to ensure that technology does not sweep development off its feet, but instead that the potential benefits of technology are rooted in a pro-poor development strategy. And that in turn means, as the *Human Development Reports* have argued over 11 editions,

that technology is used to empower people, allowing them to harness technology to expand the choices in their daily lives.

In India, for example, there are two development faces to harnessing information technology. One is the beginning of Internet connectivity in isolated rural villages—allowing critical meteorological, health and crop information to be accessed and shared. But the second is growing regional information technology–based economic clusters, as skills demand by successful start-ups drives the opening of new universities and the rapid expansion of an extensive ancillary service sector. In other words, technology itself has become a source of economic growth.

While it is undeniable that many of the high-tech marvels that dazzle the rich North are inappropriate for the poor South, it is also true that research and development addressing specific problems facing poor people—from combating disease to developing distance education—have proved time and again how technology can be not just a reward of successful development but a critical tool for achieving it.

That has never been more true than today. We live at a time of new discovery, with the mapping of the human genome, enormous structural shifts in the way science is carried out and unprecedented networking and knowledge-sharing opportunities brought about by the falling costs of communications. But it is also a time of growing public controversy on issues ranging from the possible risks of transgenic crops to providing access to lifesaving drugs for all who need them.

Our challenge now is to map a path across this fast-changing terrain. Not just to put to rest the debate over whether technological advances can help development but to help identify the global and national policies and institutions that can best accelerate the benefits of technological advances while carefully safeguarding against the new risks that inevitably accompany them.

As the Report details, emerging centres of excellence throughout the developing world are already providing hard evidence of the potential for harnessing cutting-edge science and technology to tackle centuries-old problems of human poverty. Many countries are making huge strides in building the capacity to innovate, adapt and regulate technology for their needs. They are negotiating for their interests in international agreements, drawing up comprehensive science and technology policies that reflect local needs and tapping the new opportunities of the network age to help create a critical mass of entrepreneurial activity that can generate its own momentum.

But the Report also shows how many other countries are failing to keep pace. And with limited resources, their governments have to be increasingly strategic and selective if they are to have any hope of bridging the technology divide and becoming full participants in the modern world. Worse, there is no simple blueprint. Technological progress is not a simple hand-me-down in an appropriate form and cost to developing country users. Rather, it must also be a process of knowledge creation and capacity building in developing countries. Needs, priorities and constraints inevitably vary widely by region and country—hence the importance of a strategy for every country.

Nevertheless, a critical foundation for success includes, at a minimum, some combination of unshackled communications systems, sustained support for research and development in both the private and public sectors, education policies and investments that can help nurture a sufficiently strong skills base to meet local needs and sufficient regulatory capacity to sustain and manage all these activities. And these domestic initiatives need to be supported by far-sighted global initiatives and institutions that help provide resources and lend support to the capacity of developing countries—and that pay more attention to neglected areas, from treating tropical diseases to helping developing countries better participate in and benefit from global intellectual property regimes.

In short, the challenge the world faces is to match the pace of technological innovation with real policy innovation both nationally and globally. And if we can do that successfully, we can dramatically improve the prospects for developing countries of meeting the key development goals set out in last year's historic United Nations Millennium Declaration. I believe this Report helps set us firmly in the right direction.

Mark Malloch Brown
Administrator, UNDP

The analysis and policy recommendations of this Report do not necessarily reflect the views of the United Nations Development Programme, its Executive Board or its Member States. The Report is an independent publication commissioned by UNDP. It is the fruit of a collaborative effort by a team of eminent consultants and advisers and the *Human Development Report* team. Sakiko Fukuda-Parr, Director of the Human Development Report Office, led the effort, with extensive advice and collaboration from Nancy Birdsall, Special Adviser to the Administrator.

Team for the preparation of
Human Development Report 2001

Director and Lead Author
Sakiko Fukuda-Parr

Special Adviser
Nancy Birdsall

Core team
Selim Jahan (Deputy Director), Haishan Fu (Chief of Statistics), Omar Noman and Kate Raworth with Ruth Hill, Claes Johansson, Petra Mezzetti, Laura Mourino-Casas, Andreas Pfeil, Richard Ponzio, David Stewart and Emily White.

Statistical advisor: Tom Griffin

Principal consultants
C. P. Chandrasekhar, Joel Cohen, Meghnad Desai, Calestous Juma, Devesh Kapur, Geoffrey Kirkman, Sanjaya Lall, Jong-Wha Lee, Michael Lipton, Peter Matlon, Susan McDade, Francisco Sagasti.

Editors: Bruce Ross-Larson, Justin Leites
Design: Gerald Quinn

Acknowledgements

The preparation of this Report would not have been possible without the support and valuable contributions of a large number of individuals and organizations.

CONTRIBUTORS

Many background studies, papers and notes were prepared on thematic issues in technology and human development as well as analyses of global trends in social and economic development. These were contributed by Amir Attaran, Christian Barry, Nienke Beintema, David E. Bloom, C. P. Chandrasekhar, Ha-Joon Chang, Joel I. Cohen, Carlos Correa, Meghnad Desai, Francois Fortier, José Goldemberg, Carol Graham, Nadia Hijab, Thomas B. Johansson, Allison Jolly, Richard Jolly, Calestous Juma, Devesh Kapur, Geoffrey Kirkman, Paul Kleindorfer, Michael Kremer, Sanjaya Lall, Jong-Wha Lee, Michael Lipton, James Love, Peter Matlon, Susan McDade, Suppiramaniam Nanthikesan, Howard Pack, Phil G. Pardey, Stefano Pettinato, Pablo Rodas-Martini, Andrés Rodríguez-Clare, Francisco Sagasti, Joseph E. Stiglitz, Michael Ward, Jayashree Watal, Shahin Yaqub and Dieter Zinnbauer.

Many organizations generously shared their data series and other research materials: the Carbon Dioxide Information Analysis Center, Center for International and Interarea Comparisons (University of Pennsylvania), Food and Agriculture Organization, International Institute for Strategic Studies, International Labour Organization, International Telecommunication Union, Inter-Parliamentary Union, Joint United Nations Programme on HIV/AIDS, Luxembourg Income Study, Organisation for Economic Co-operation and Development, Stockholm International Peace Research Institute, United Nations Children's Fund, United Nations Conference on Trade and Development, United Nations Department of Economic and Social Affairs, United Nations Educational, Scientific and Cultural Organization, United Nations High Commissioner for Refugees, United Nations Interregional Crime and Justice Research Institute, United Nations Population Division, United Nations Statistics Division, World Bank, World Health Organization, World Intellectual Property Organization and World Trade Organization. The team also gratefully acknowledges data received from numerous UNDP country offices.

ADVISORY PANELS

The Report benefited greatly from intellectual advice and guidance provided by the external Advisory Panel of eminent experts, which included Gabriel Accascina, Carlos Braga, Manuel Castells, Lincoln Chen, Denis Gilhooly, Shulin Gu, Ryokichi Hirono, H. Thaweesak Koanantakool, Emmanuel Lallana, Mirna Lievano de Marques, Patrick Mooney, Jay Naidoo, Subhi Qasem, Gustav Ranis, Andrés Rodríguez-Clare, Vernon W. Ruttan, Frances Stewart, Doug Sweeny and Laurence Tubiana. An advisory panel on statistics included Sudhir Anand, Lidia Barreiros, Jean-Louis Bodin, Willem DeVries, Lamine Diop, Carmen Feijo, Andrew Flatt, Paolo Garonna, Leo Goldstone, Irena Krizman, Nora Lustig, Shavitri Singh, Timothy Smeeding, Soedarti Surbakti, Alain Tranap and Michael Ward.

UNDP READERS

Colleagues in UNDP provided extremely useful comments, suggestions and input during the drafting of the Report. In particular, the authors would like to express their gratitude to Anne-Birgitte Albrectsen, Håkan Björkman, Stephen Browne, Marc Destanne de Bernis, Djibril Diallo, Moez Doraid, Heba El-Kholy, Sally Fegan-Wyles, Enrique Ganuza, Rima Khalaf Hunaidi, Abdoulie Janneh, Bruce Jenks, Inge Kaul, Radhika Lal, Justin Leites, Kerstin Leitner, Carlos Lopes, Jacques Loup, Khalid Malik, Elena Martinez, Saraswathi Menon, Kalman Mizsei, Hafiz Pasha, Jordan Ryan, Jennifer Sisk, Jerzy Szeremeta, Modibo Toure, Jens Wandel, Eimi Watanabe and Raul Zambrano.

CONSULTATIONS

Many individuals consulted during the preparation of the Report provided invaluable advice, information and materials. We thank all of them for their help and support. Lack of space precludes naming everyone here, but we would like to especially recognize the contributions of Yasmin Ahmad, Bettina Aten, Dean Baker, Julia Benn, Seth Berkley, Ana Betran, Yonas Biru, Thomas Buettner, Luis Carrizo, Paul Cheung, S. K. Chu, David Cieslikowski, Patrick Cornu, Sabrina D'Amico, Carolyn Deere, Heloise Emdon, Robert Evenson, Susan Finston, Kathy Foley, Maria Conchetta Gasbarro, Douglas Gollin, Jean-Louis Grolleau, Emmanuel Guindon, Bill Haddad, Andrew Harvey, Peter Hazell, Huen Ho, Ellen 't Hoen, Eivind Hoffmann, Hans Hogerzeil, Mir Asghar Husain, Edwyn James, Lawrence Jeff Johnson, Gareth Jones, Robert Juhkam, Vasantha Kandiah, Jan Karlson, Alison Kennedy, John van Kesteren, Jenny Lanjouw, Georges LeMaitre, Nyein Nyein Lwin, Farhad Mehran, Ana Maria Mendonça, Zafar Mirza, Scott Murray, Per Pinstrup-Andersen, Christine Pintat, William Prince, Agnes Puymoyen, Jonathan Quick, Kenneth W. Rind, Simon Scott, Sara Sievers, Josh Silver, Anthony So, Petter Stålenheim, Eric Swanson, Geoff Tansey, Joann Vanek, Chinapah Vinayagum, Neff Walker, Tessa Wardlaw, Wend Wendland, Patrick Werquin, Siemon Wezeman, Frederick Wing and Hania Zlotnik.

A consultation meeting with UN organizations included Brian Barclay, Shakeel Bhatti, Henk-Jan Brinkman, Duncan Campbell, K. Michael Finger, Murray Gibbs, Mongi Hamdi, Cynthia Hewitt de Alcantara, Tim Kelly, Anthony Marjoram, Adrian Otten, Philippe Quéau, Frédéric J. Richard, Kathryn Stokes and German Velasquez.

STAFF SUPPORT

Administrative support for the Report's preparation was provided by Oscar Bernal, Renuka Corea-Lloyd and Maria Regina Milo. Other Human Development Report Office colleagues provided invaluable input to the Report: Sarah Burd-Sharps, Francois Coutu, Geneve Mantri, Stephanie Meade, Marixie Mercado and Sharbanou Tadjbakhsh. The Report also benefited from the dedicated work of interns: Altaf Abro, Sharmi Ahmad, Mohammad Niaz Asadullah, Elsie Attafuah, Yuko Inagaki, Safa Jafari, Demetra Kasimis, Vadym B. Lepetyuk, Chiara Rosaria Pace and Aisha Talib.

The Environmental Division of the United Nations Office for Project Services provided the team with critical administrative support and management services.

EDITING, PRODUCTION AND TRANSLATION

As in previous years, the Report benefited from the editing and pre-press production of Communications Development Incorporated's Bruce Ross-Larson, Fiona Blackshaw, Garrett Cruce, Terrence Fischer, Wendy Guyette, Paul Holtz, Megan Klose, Molly Lohman, Susan Quinn, Stephanie Rostron and Alison Strong. The team also thanks Mike Elliot and David Major for their editorial inputs.

The Report also benefited from the translation, design and distribution work of Elizabeth Scott Andrews, Maureen Lynch and Hilda Paqui.

•   •   •

The team expresses sincere appreciation to Lincoln Chen, Denis Gilhooly, Sanjaya Lall, Jessica Matthews, Lynn Mytelka and Doug Sweeny for their advice to the Administrator. And to peer reviewers Meghnad Desai and Calestous Juma as well as Paolo Garonna, Irena Krizman and Ian Macredie.

Last but not least, the authors are especially grateful to Mark Malloch Brown, UNDP Administrator, for his leadership and vision.

Thankful for all the support they have received, the authors assume full responsibility for the opinions expressed in the Report.

AIDS	acquired immunodeficiency syndrome
ASEAN	Association of South-East Asian Nations
CAT	Convention Against Torture and Other Cruel, Inhuman or Degrading Treatment or Punishment
CD-ROM	compact disc with read-only memory
CEDAW	Convention on the Elimination of All Forms of Discrimination Against Women
CFC	chlorofluorocarbon
CGIAR	Consultative Group for International Agricultural Research
CIS	Commonwealth of Independent States
CRC	Convention on the Rights of the Child
DDT	dichlorodiphenyltrichloroethane
DNA	deoxyribonucleic acid
DNS	domain name system
DVD	digital versatile disk
EU	European Union
GDI	gender-related development index
GDP	gross domestic product
G-8	Group of 8 industrial countries
GEM	gender empowerment measure
GNP	gross national product
HDI	human development index
HIV	human immunodeficiency virus
HPI	human poverty index
ICANN	Internet Corporation for Assigned Names and Numbers
ICCPR	International Convention on Civil and Political Rights
ICERD	International Convention on the Elimination of All Forms of Racial Discrimination
ICESCR	International Convention on Economic, Social, and Cultural Rights
NASDAQ	National Association of Securities Dealers Automated Quotations
NGO	non-governmental organization
OECD	Organisation for Economic Co-operation and Development
ORT	oral rehydration therapy
PPP	purchasing power parity
R&D	research and development
TAI	technology achievement index
TRIPS	Trade-Related Aspects of Intellectual Property Rights
UNDP	United Nations Development Programme
WAP	wireless application protocol
UNESCO	United Nations Educational, Scientific and Cultural Organization
UNICEF	United Nations Children's Fund

Contents

OVERVIEW

Making new technologies work for human development   1

CHAPTER 1

Human development—past, present and future   9

Thirty years of impressive progress—but a long way still to go   9

Unequal incomes   16

Human development—at the heart of today's policy agenda   20

The Millennium Declaration's goals for development and poverty eradication   21

CHAPTER 2

Today's technological transformations—creating the network age   27

Technology can be a tool for—not only a reward of—development   27

Today's technological transformations combine with globalization to create the network age   29

The new technological age brings new possibilities—for still greater advances in human development   35

The network age is changing how technologies are created and diffused—in five ways   37

The opportunities of the network age exist in a world of uneven technological capacity   38

Turning technology into a tool for human development requires effort   43

Annex 2.1   The technology achievement index—a new measure of countries' ability to participate in the network age   46

CHAPTER 3

Managing the risks of technological change   65

Risky business: assessing potential costs and benefits   66

Shaping choices: the role of public opinion   68

Taking precautions: different countries, different choices   70

Building the capacity to manage risk   71

Challenges facing developing countries   73

National strategies to deal with the challenges of risk   73

Global collaboration for managing risks   76

CHAPTER 4

Unleashing human creativity: national strategies   79

Creating an environment that encourages technological innovation   79

Rethinking education systems to meet the new challenges of the network age   84

Mobilizing diasporas   91

CHAPTER 5

Global initiatives to create technologies for human development   95

Creating innovative partnerships and new incentives for research and development   97

Managing intellectual property rights   102

Expanding investment in technologies for development   109

Providing regional and global institutional support   112

Endnotes   118
Bibliographic note   120
Bibliography   122

SPECIAL CONTRIBUTIONS

Human resource development in the 21st century: enhancing knowledge and information capabilities *Kim Dae-jung*   24

The *antyodaya* approach: a pathway to an ever-green revolution *M. S. Swaminathan*   75

Insisting on responsibility: a campaign for access to medicines *Morten Rostrup*   117

BOXES

1.1   Measuring human development   14

1.2   Why inequality matters   17

1.3   International comparisons of living standards—the need for purchasing power parities   20

2.1   Technology and human identity   27

2.2   Modern science creates simple technology—oral rehydration therapy and vaccines adapted
        to village conditions   28

2.3   Breaking barriers to Internet access   35

2.4   The new economy and growth paradoxes   36

2.5   India's export opportunities in the new economy   37

2.6   Combining traditional knowledge and scientific methods to create breakthrough treatment
        for malaria in Viet Nam   39

3.1   Historical efforts to ban coffee   68

3.2   DDT and malaria: whose risk and whose choice?   69

3.3   "Use the precautionary principle!" But which one?   70

3.4   Miracle seeds or Frankenfoods? The evidence so far   72

3.5   Strengthening institutional capacity in Argentina and Egypt for dealing with genetically modified commodities   75

4.1   Technology foresight in the United Kingdom—building consensus among key stakeholders   80

4.2   Attracting technology-intensive foreign direct investment in Costa Rica—through human skills, stability
        and infrastructure   81

4.3   Strategies for stimulating research and development in East Asia   83

4.4   A push for education quality in Chile—measuring outcomes and providing incentives   85

4.5   Orientation and content as important as resources—lessons from education strategies in East Asia   86

4.6   Providing incentives for high-quality training in Singapore   89

4.7   Taxing lost skills   92

5.1   Tropical technology, suffering from an ecological gap   96

5.2   Homemade but world class: research excellence for an alternative agenda   98

5.3   From longitude to long life—the promise of pull incentives   100

5.4   Hidden costs of drug donation programmes   101

5.5   IAVI's innovation in networked research   102

5.6   Lessons from the history of intellectual property rights   103

5.7   Making the global intellectual property rights regime globally relevant   105

5.8   Paper promises, inadequate implementation   109

5.9   ASARECA and FONTAGRO—promoting regional collaboration in public agricultural research   113

5.10   Who administers the Internet? ICANN!   116

TABLES

1.1   Serious deprivations in many aspects of life   9

1.2   Countries suffering setbacks in the human development index, 1999   10

1.3   Countries where girls' net secondary enrolment ratio declined, 1985–97   15

1.4   Trends in income distribution in OECD countries   19

2.1   Technology as a source of mortality reduction, 1960–90   29

2.2   High-tech products dominate export expansion   31

2.3   The private sector leads technology creation   37

2.4   Venture capital spreads across the world   38

2.5   Investing in domestic technology capacity   39

2.6   Competing in global markets: the 30 leading exporters of high-tech products   42

2.7   High rates of return to investing in agricultural research   44

A2.1   Technology achievement index   48

A2.2   Investment in technology creation   52

A2.3   Diffusion of technology—agriculture and manufacturing   56

A2.4   Diffusion of technology—information and communications   60

3.1   Policy stances for genetically modified crops—the choices for developing countries   71

4.1   Telecommunications arrangements in various countries by sector, 2000   82

4.2   Enterprises providing training in selected developing countries   88

4.3   Average public education spending per pupil by region, 1997   91

5.1   Who has real access to claiming patents?   104

FIGURES

1.1   Income growth varies among regions   10

1.2   Different paths of human progress   13

1.3   No automatic link between income and human development   13

1.4   No automatic link between human development and human poverty   15

1.5   Comparing incomes—developing regions and high-income OECD   16

1.6   Widening income gap between regions   17

1.7   Income inequality within countries   18

2.1   Links between technology and human development   28

2.2   Oral rehydration therapy reduces child mortality without income increase   29

2.3   Enrolments reflect uneven progress in building skills   43

4.1   The cost of being connected   81

5.1   The rise of networked research: international co-authorship of published scientific articles   97

5.2 Research and development spending in OECD countries   109

5.3 Public investment in agricultural research   110

5.4 Priorities for energy research and development in major industrial countries   110

5.5 Whose voices are heard in international negotiations?   116

5.6 Industry's influence over public policy   117

FEATURES

1.1 Progress in the past 30 years has been impressive . . .   11

1.2 . . . but the pace of the progress and the levels of achievement vary widely among regions and groups   12

1.3 Millennium Declaration goals for 2015   22

2.1 The promise of today's technological transformations for human development—information and communications technology   32

2.2 The promise of today's technological transformations for human development—biotechnology   34

2.3 Uneven diffusion of technology—old and new . . . between countries . . . and within countries   40

5.1 Easing access to HIV/AIDS drugs through fair implementation of TRIPS   106

MAP

2.1 The geography of technological innovation and achievement   45

HUMAN DEVELOPMENT INDICATORS

Note on statistics in the Human Development Report   133

MONITORING HUMAN DEVELOPMENT: ENLARGING PEOPLE'S CHOICES . . .

1 Human development index   141

2 Human development index trends   145

3 Human and income poverty: developing countries   149

4 Human and income poverty: OECD countries, Eastern Europe and the CIS   152

. . . TO LEAD A LONG AND HEALTHY LIFE . . .

5 Demographic trends   154

6 Commitment to health: access, services and resources   158

7 Leading global health crises and challenges   162

8 Survival: progress and setbacks   166

. . . TO ACQUIRE KNOWLEDGE . . .

9 Commitment to education: public spending   170

10 Literacy and enrolment   174

. . . TO HAVE ACCESS TO THE RESOURCES NEEDED FOR A DECENT STANDARD OF LIVING . . .

11 Economic performance   178

12 Inequality in income or consumption   182

13 The structure of trade   186

14 Flows of aid from DAC member countries   190

15 Flows of aid, private capital and debt   191

16 Priorities in public spending   195

17 Unemployment in OECD countries   199

... WHILE PRESERVING IT FOR FUTURE GENERATIONS ...

18   Energy and the environment   200

... PROTECTING PERSONAL SECURITY ...

19   Refugees and armaments   204

20   Victims of crime   208

... AND ACHIEVING EQUALITY FOR ALL WOMEN AND MEN

21   Gender-related development index   210

22   Gender empowerment measure   214

23   Gender inequality in education   218

24   Gender inequality in economic activity   222

25   Women's political participation   226

HUMAN AND LABOUR RIGHTS INSTRUMENTS

26   Status of major international human rights instruments   230

27   Status of fundamental labour rights conventions   234

28   BASIC INDICATORS FOR OTHER UN MEMBER COUNTRIES   238

Technical notes

1   Calculating the human development indices   239

2   Calculating the technology achievement index   246

3   Assessing progress towards the Millennium Declaration goals for development and poverty eradication   247

Statistical references   248

Definitions of statistical terms   250

Classification of countries   257

Index to indicators   261

Countries and regions that have produced human development reports   264

Making new technologies work for human development

This Report, like all previous *Human Development Reports,* is about people. It is about how people can create and use technology to improve their lives. It is also about forging new public policies to lead the revolutions in information and communications technology and biotechnology in the direction of human development.

People all over the world have high hopes that these new technologies will lead to healthier lives, greater social freedoms, increased knowledge and more productive livelihoods. There is a great rush to be part of the network age—the combined result of the technological revolutions and globalization that are integrating markets and linking people across all kinds of traditional boundaries.

At the same time, there is great fear of the unknown. Technological change, like all change, poses risks, as shown by the industrial disaster in Bhopal (India), the nuclear disaster in Chernobyl (Ukraine), the birth defects from thalidomide and the depletion of the ozone layer by chlorofluorocarbons. And the more novel and fundamental is the change, the less is known about its potential consequences and hidden costs. Hence there is a general mistrust of scientists, private corporations and governments—indeed, of the whole technology establishment.

This Report looks specifically at how new technologies will affect developing countries and poor people. Many people fear that these technologies may be of little use to the developing world—or that they might actually widen the already savage inequalities between North and South, rich and poor. Without innovative public policy, these technologies could become a source of exclusion, not a tool of progress. The needs of poor people could remain neglected, new global risks left unmanaged. But managed well, the rewards could be greater than the risks.

At the United Nations Millennium Summit, world leaders agreed on a set of quantified and monitorable goals for development and poverty eradication to achieve by 2015. Progress the world has made over the past 30 years shows that these goals are attainable. But many developing countries will not achieve them without much faster progress. While 66 countries are on track to reduce under-five mortality rates by two-thirds, 93 countries with 62% of the world's people are lagging, far behind or slipping. Similarly, while 50 countries are on track to achieve the safe water goal, 83 countries with 70% of the world's people are not. More than 40% of the world's people are living in countries on track to halve income poverty by 2015. Yet they are in just 11 countries that include China and India (with 38% of the world's people), and 70 countries are far behind or slipping. Without China and India, only 9 countries with 5% of the world's people are on track to halve income poverty. New technology policies can spur progress towards reaching these and other goals.

1. The technology divide does not have to follow the income divide. Throughout history, technology has been a powerful tool for human development and poverty reduction.

It is often thought that people gain access to technological innovations—more effective medicine or transportation, the telephone or the Internet—once they have more income. This is true—economic growth creates opportunities for useful innovations to be created and diffused. But the process can also be reversed: investments in technology, like investments in

People all over the world have high hopes that new technologies will lead to healthier lives, greater social freedoms, increased knowledge and more productive livelihoods

education, can equip people with better tools and make them more productive and prosperous. Technology is a tool, not just a reward, for growth and development.

In fact, the 20th century's unprecedented gains in advancing human development and eradicating poverty came largely from technological breakthroughs:

• In the late 1930s mortality rates began to decline rapidly in Asia, Africa and Latin America, and by the 1970s life expectancy at birth had increased to more than 60 years. In Europe that same gain took more than a century and a half starting in the early 1800s. The rapid gains of the 20th century were propelled by medical technology—antibiotics and vaccines —while progress in the 19th century depended on slower social and economic changes, such as better sanitation and diets.

• The reduction in undernutrition in South Asia from around 40% in the 1970s to 23% in 1997—and the end of chronic famine—was made possible by technological breakthroughs in plant breeding, fertilizers and pesticides in the 1960s that doubled world cereal yields in just 40 years. That is an astonishingly short period relative to the 1,000 years it took for English wheat yields to quadruple from 0.5 to 2.0 tonnes per hectare.

These examples show how technology can cause discontinuous change: a single innovation can quickly and significantly change the course of an entire society. (Consider what an affordable vaccine or cure for AIDS could do for Sub-Saharan Africa.)

Moreover, technology-supported advances in health, nutrition, crop yields and employment are usually not just one-time gains. They typically have a multiplier effect—creating a virtuous cycle, increasing people's knowledge, health and productivity, and raising incomes and building capacity for future innovation— all feeding back into human development.

Today's technological transformations are more rapid (the power of a computer chip doubles every 18–24 months without cost increase) and more fundamental (genetic engineering breakthroughs) and are driving down costs (the cost of one megabit of storage fell from $5,257 in 1970 to $0.17 in 1999). These transforma-

tions multiply the possibilities of what people can do with technology in areas that include:

• *Participation.* The Internet, the wireless telephone and other information and communications technology enable people to communicate and obtain information in ways never before possible, dramatically opening up possibilities to participate in decisions that affect their lives. From the fax machine's role in the revolutions of 1989 to the email campaigns that helped topple Philippine President Joseph Estrada in January 2001, information and communications technology provides powerful new ways for citizens to demand accountability from their governments and in the use of public resources.

• *Knowledge.* Information and communications technology can provide rapid, low-cost access to information about almost all areas of human activity. From distance learning in Turkey to long-distance medical diagnosis in the Gambia, to information on market prices of grain in India, the Internet is breaking barriers of geography, making markets more efficient, creating opportunities for income generation and enabling increased local participation.

• *New medicines.* In 1989 biotechnological research into hepatitis B resulted in a breakthrough vaccine. Today more than 300 biopharmaceutical products are on the market or seeking regulatory approval, and many hold equal promise. Much more can be done to develop vaccines and treatments for HIV/AIDS and other diseases endemic in some developing countries.

• *New crop varieties.* Trangenics offer the hope of crops with higher yields, pest- and drought-resistant properties and superior nutritional characteristics—especially for farmers in ecological zones left behind by the green revolution. In China genetically modified rice offers 15% higher yields without the need for increases in other farm inputs, and modified cotton (Bt cotton) allows pesticide spraying to be reduced from 30 to 3 times.

• *New employment and export opportunities.* The recent downturn in the Nasdaq has quieted the hyperbole, but the long-term potential for some developing countries remains tremendous as electronic commerce breaks barriers of distance and market information. Revenues

The 20th century's unprecedented gains in advancing human development and eradicating poverty came largely from technological breakthroughs

from India's information technology industry jumped from $150 million in 1990 to $4 billion in 1999.

All this is just the beginning. Much more can be expected as more technologies are adapted to the needs of developing countries.

---

2. The market is a powerful engine of technological progress—but it is not powerful enough to create and diffuse the technologies needed to eradicate poverty.

Technology is created in response to market pressures—not the needs of poor people, who have little purchasing power. Research and development, personnel and finance are concentrated in rich countries, led by global corporations and following the global market demand dominated by high-income consumers.

In 1998 the 29 OECD countries spent $520 billion on research and development—more than the combined economic output of the world's 30 poorest countries. OECD countries, with 19% of the world's people, also accounted for 91% of the 347,000 new patents issued in 1998. And in these countries more than 60% of research and development is now carried out by the private sector, with a correspondingly smaller role for public sector research.

As a result research neglects opportunities to develop technology for poor people. For instance, in 1998 global spending on health research was $70 billion, but just $300 million was dedicated to vaccines for HIV/AIDS and about $100 million to malaria research. Of 1,223 new drugs marketed worldwide between 1975 and 1996, only 13 were developed to treat tropical diseases—and only 4 were the direct result of pharmaceutical industry research. The picture is much the same for research on agriculture and energy.

Technology is also unevenly diffused. OECD countries contain 79% of the world's Internet users. Africa has less international bandwidth than São Paulo, Brazil. Latin America's bandwidth, in turn, is roughly equal to that of Seoul, Republic of Korea.

These disparities should come as no surprise. After all, electric power generation and grid delivery were first developed in 1831 but are still not available to a third of the world's people. Some 2 billion people still do not have access to low-cost essential medicines (such as penicillin), most of which were developed decades ago. Half of Africa's one-year-olds have not been immunized against diphtheria, pertussis, tetanus, polio and measles. And oral rehydration therapy, a simple and life-saving treatment, is not used in nearly 40% of diarrhoea cases in developing countries.

Inadequate financing compounds the problem. High-tech startups in the United States have thrived on venture capital. But in many developing countries, where even basic financial services are underdeveloped, there is little prospect of such financing. Moreover, the lack of intellectual property protection in some countries can discourage private investors.

The global map of technological achievement in this Report shows huge inequalities between countries—not just in terms of innovation and access, but also in the education and skills required to use technology effectively. The Report's technology achievement index (TAI) provides a country-by-country measure of how countries are doing in these areas.

Technology is also unevenly diffused within countries. India, home to a world-class technology hub in Bangalore, ranks at the lower end of the TAI. Why? Because Bangalore is a small enclave in a country where the average adult received only 5.1 years of education, adult illiteracy is 44%, electricity consumption is half that in China and there are just 28 telephones for every 1,000 people.

---

3. Developing countries may gain especially high rewards from new technologies, but they also face especially severe challenges in managing the risks.

The current debate in Europe and the United States over genetically modified crops mostly ignores the concerns and needs of the developing world. Western consumers who do not face food shortages or nutritional deficiencies or work in fields are more likely to focus on food safety and the potential loss of biodiver-

Technology is created in response to market pressures—not the needs of poor people, who have little purchasing power

sity, while farming communities in developing countries are more likely to focus on potentially higher yields and greater nutritional value, and on the reduced need to spray pesticides that can damage soil and sicken farmers. Similarly, the recent effort to globally ban the manufacture of DDT did not reflect the pesticide's benefits in preventing malaria in tropical countries.

Moreover, while some risks can be assessed and managed globally, others must take into account local considerations. The potential harms to health from mobile phones or to unborn children from thalidomide are no different for people in Malaysia than in Morocco. But gene flow from genetically modified corn would be more likely in an environment with many corn-related wild species than in one without such indigenous plants.

Environmental risks in particular are often specific to individual ecosystems and need to be assessed case by case. In considering the possible environmental consequences of genetically modified crops, the example of European rabbits in Australia offers a warning. Six rabbits were introduced there in the 1850s. Now there are 100 million, destroying native flora and fauna and costing local industries $370 million a year.

If new technologies offer particular benefits for the developing world, they also pose greater risks. Technology-related problems are often the result of poor policies, inadequate regulation and lack of transparency. (For instance, poor management by regulators led to the use of HIV-infected blood in transfusions during the 1980s and to the spread of mad cow disease more recently.) From that perspective, most developing countries are at a disadvantage because they lack the policies and institutions needed to manage the risks well.

Professional researchers and trained technicians are essential for adapting new technologies for local use. A shortage of skilled personnel—from laboratory researchers to extension service officers—can seriously constrain a country's ability to create a strong regulatory system. Even in developing countries with more advanced capacity, such as Argentina and Egypt, biosafety systems have nearly exhausted national expertise.

Just as the steam engine and electricity enhanced physical power to make possible the industrial revolution, digital and genetic breakthroughs are enhancing brain power

The cost of establishing and maintaining a regulatory framework can also place a severe financial demand on poor countries. In the United States three major, well-funded agencies—the Department of Agriculture, Food and Drug Administration and Environmental Protection Agency—are all involved in regulating genetically modified organisms. But even these institutions are appealing for budget increases to deal with the new challenges raised by biotechnology. In stark contrast, regulatory agencies in developing countries survive on very little funding. Stronger policies and mechanisms are needed at the regional and global levels, and should include active participation from developing countries.

---

4. The technology revolution and globalization are creating a network age—and that is changing how technology is created and diffused.

Two simultaneous shifts in technology and economics—the technological revolution and globalization—are combining to create a new network age. Just as the steam engine and electricity enhanced physical power to make possible the industrial revolution, digital and genetic breakthroughs are enhancing brain power.

The industrial age was structured around vertically integrated organizations with high costs of communications, information and transportation. But the network age is structured along horizontal networks, with each organization focusing on competitive niches. These new networks cross continents, with hubs from Silicon Valley (United States) to São Paulo to Gauteng (South Africa) to Bangalore.

Many developing countries are already tapping into these networks, with significant benefits for human development. For instance, new malaria drugs created in Thailand and Viet Nam were based on international research as well as local knowledge.

Scientific research is increasingly collaborative between institutions and countries. In 1995–97 scientists in the United States co-wrote articles with scientists from 173 other countries, scientists in Brazil with 114, in Kenya with

81, in Algeria with 59. Global corporations, often based in North America, Europe or Japan, now typically have research facilities in several countries and outsource production worldwide. In 1999, 52% of Malaysia's exports were high-tech, 44% of Costa Rica's, 28% of Mexico's, 26% of the Philippines's. Hubs in India and elsewhere now use the Internet to provide real-time software support, data processing and customer services for clients all over the world.

International labour markets and skyrocketing demand for information and communications technology personnel make top scientists and other professionals globally mobile. Thus developing country investments in education subsidize industrial country economies. Many highly educated people migrate abroad even though their home country may have invested heavily in creating an educated labour force. (For instance, 100,000 Indian professionals a year are expected to take visas recently issued by the United States—an estimated resource loss for India of $2 billion.) But this migration can be a brain gain as well as a brain drain: it often generates a diaspora that can provide valuable networks of finance, business contacts and skill transfer for the home country.

—————————

5. Even in the network age, domestic policy still matters. All countries, even the poorest, need to implement policies that encourage innovation, access and the development of advanced skills.

Not all countries need to be on the cutting edge of global technological advance. But in the network age every country needs the capacity to understand and adapt global technologies for local needs. Farmers and firms need to master new technologies developed elsewhere to stay competitive in global markets. Doctors seeking the best care for their patients need to introduce new products and procedures from global advances in medicine. In this environment the key to a country's success will be unleashing the creativity of its people.

Nurturing creativity requires flexible, competitive, dynamic economic environments. For most developing countries that means build-ing on reforms that emphasize openness—to new ideas, new products and new investment, especially in telecommunications. Closed-market policies, such as telecommunications laws that favour government monopolies, still isolate some countries from global networks. In others a lack of proper regulation has led to private monopolies with the same isolating effects. In Sri Lanka competition among providers of information and communications technology has led to increased investment, increased connectivity and better service. Chile offers a successful model for pursuing privatization and regulation simultaneously.

But open markets and competition are not enough. At the heart of nurturing creativity is expanding human skills. Technological change dramatically raises the premium every country should place on investing in the education and training of its people. And in the network age, concentrating on primary education will not suffice—the advanced skills developed in secondary and tertiary schools are increasingly important.

Vocational and on-the-job training also cannot be neglected. When technology is changing, enterprises have to invest in training workers to stay competitive. Smaller enterprises in particular can benefit from public policies that encourage coordination and economies of scale and that partly subsidize their efforts. Studies in Colombia, Indonesia, Malaysia and Mexico have shown that such training provides a considerable boost to firm productivity.

Market failures are pervasive where knowledge and skills are concerned. That is why in every technologically advanced country today, governments have provided funding to substitute for market demand with incentives, regulations and public programmes. But such funding has not been mobilized to do the same for most developing countries, from domestic or international sources.

More generally, governments need to establish broad technology strategies in partnership with other key stakeholders. Governments should not try to "pick winners" by favouring certain sectors or firms. But they can identify areas where coordination makes a difference because no single private investor will act alone (in building in-

In the network age, every country needs the capacity to understand and adapt global technologies for local needs

frastructure, for example). Costa Rica has been successful in implementing such a strategy.

---

6. National policies will not be sufficient to compensate for global market failures. New international initiatives and the fair use of global rules are needed to channel new technologies towards the most urgent needs of the world's poor people.

Policy, not charity, will determine whether new technologies become a tool for human development everywhere

No national government can single-handedly cope with global market failures. Yet there is no global framework for supporting research and development that addresses the common needs of poor people in many countries and regions.

What is the research needed for? The list is long and fast changing. Some top priorities:
• Vaccines for malaria, HIV and tuberculosis as well as lesser-known diseases like sleeping sickness and river blindness.
• New varieties of sorghum, cassava, maize and other staple foods of Sub-Saharan Africa.
• Low-cost computers and wireless connectivity as well as prepaid chip-card software for ecommerce without credit cards.
• Low-cost fuel cells and photovoltaics for decentralized electricity supply.

What can be done? Rich countries could support a global effort to create incentives and new partnerships for research and development, boosted by new and expanded sources of financing. Civil society groups and activists, the press and policy-makers could nurture public understanding on difficult issues such as the differential pricing of pharmaceuticals and the fair implementation of intellectual property rights. The lesson of this Report is that at the global level it is policy, not charity, that will ultimately determine whether new technologies become a tool for human development everywhere.

Creative incentives and new partnerships. At a time when universities, private companies and public institutions are reshaping their research relationships, new international partnerships for development can bring together the strengths of each while balancing any conflicts of interest. Many approaches to creating incentives are possible—from purchase funds and prizes to tax credits and public grants.

One promising model is the International AIDS Vaccine Initiative, which brings together academics, industry, foundations and public researchers through innovative intellectual property rights agreements that enable each partner to pursue its interests while jointly pursuing a vaccine for the HIV/AIDS strain common in Africa.

Dedicated funds for research and development. At the moment it is not even possible to track how much each government or international institution contributes to research and development to deal with global market failures. For instance, it is relatively easy to find out how much a donor spends to promote health in a given country—but much harder to determine how much of that goes for medical research. A first step towards increased funding in this area would be establishing a mechanism for measuring current contributions.

Private foundations, such as Rockefeller, Ford and now Gates and Wellcome, have made substantial contributions to research and development targeted at the needs of developing countries. But these contributions are far from sufficient to meet global needs, and at least $10 billion in additional funds could be mobilized from:
• *Bilateral donors.* A 10% increase in official development assistance, if dedicated to research and development, would put $5.5 billion on the table.
• *Developing country governments.* Diverting 10% of Sub-Saharan Africa's military spending in 1999 would have raised $700 million.
• *International organizations.* In 2000 about $350 million of the World Bank's income was transferred to its interest-free arm for lending to the poorest countries. A much smaller amount dedicated to technology development for low-income countries would go a long way.
• *Debt-for-technology swaps.* In 1999 official debt service payments by developing countries totalled $78 billion. Swapping just 1.3% of this debt service for technology research and development would have raised more than $1 billion.
• *Private foundations in developing countries.* Developing countries could introduce tax incentives to encourage their billionaires to set up foundations. Rich individuals from Brazil

to Saudi Arabia to India to Malaysia could help fund regionally relevant research.

- *Industry.* With their financial, intellectual and research resources, high-tech companies could make bigger contributions than they do now. The head of research at Novartis has proposed that these companies devote a percentage of their profits to research on non-commercial products.

Differential pricing. From pharmaceuticals to computer software, key technology products are in demand worldwide. An effective global market would encourage different prices for them in different countries, but the current system does not.

A producer seeking to maximize global profits on a new technology would ideally divide the market into different income groups and sell at prices that maximize profits in each. With technology, where the main cost to the seller is usually research rather than production, such tiered pricing could lead to an identical product being sold in Cameroon for just one-tenth—or one-hundredth—the price in Canada.

But in the network age segmenting the international market is not easy. With increasingly open borders and growing Internet sales, producers in rich countries fear that re-imports of heavily discounted products will undercut the higher domestic prices charged to cover overhead and research and development. And even if products do not creep back into the home market, knowledge about lower prices will—creating the potential for consumer backlash. Without mechanisms to deal with these threats, producers are more likely to set global prices (for AIDS drugs, for instance) that are unaffordable for the citizens of poor countries.

Part of the battle to establish differential pricing must be won through consumer education. Civil society groups and activists, the press and policy-makers could help the citizens of rich countries understand that it is only fair for people in developing countries to pay less for medicines and other critical technology products. Without higher prices in rich countries, companies would have far less incentive to invest in new research and development.

The broader challenge for public, private and non-profit decision-makers is to agree on

ways to segment the global market so that key technology products can be sold at low cost in developing countries without destroying markets—and industry incentives—in industrial countries. This goal should be high on the agenda in upcoming international trade negotiations.

Fair use of intellectual property rights and fair implementation of TRIPS. Intellectual property rights are being tightened and increasingly used worldwide. The World Intellectual Property Organization's Patent Co-operation Treaty accepts a single international application valid in many countries; the number of international applications rose from 7,000 in 1985 to 74,000 in 1999. In the midst of this boom, there are two new hurdles for developing countries and poor people.

First, intellectual property rights can go too far. Some patent applications disclose their innovations with great obscurity, stretching patent officers' capacity to judge and the ability of other researchers to understand. In 2000 the World Intellectual Property Organization received 30 patent applications over 1,000 pages long, with several reaching 140,000 pages. From patents on genes whose function may not be known to patents on such ecommerce methods as one click purchasing, many believe that the criteria of non-obviousness and industrial utility are being interpreted too loosely.

In particular, patent systems lay open indigenous and community-based innovation to private sector claims. Ill-awarded patents, granted despite prior art, obviousness or lack of innovation—such as a US patent on the Mexican enola bean—are contributing to the silent theft of centuries of developing country knowledge and assets.

Second, current practices are preventing the fair implementation of the World Trade Organization's agreement on Trade-Related Aspects of Intellectual Property Rights (TRIPS). As signatories to the 1994 TRIPS agreement, developing countries are implementing national systems of intellectual property rights following an agreed set of minimum standards, such as 20 years of patent protection. A single set of minimum rules may seem to create a level playing field, since one set of rules applies to all. But as currently practiced, the game is not fair be-

The broader challenge is to agree on ways to segment the global market so that key technology products can be sold at low cost in developing countries

cause the players are of such unequal strength, economically and institutionally.

For low-income countries, implementing and enforcing intellectual property rights put stress on scarce resources and administrative skills. Without good advice on creating national legislation that makes the most of what TRIPS allows, and under intense external pressure to introduce legislation beyond that required by TRIPS, countries can legislate themselves into a disadvantageous position. Moreover, the high costs of disputes with the world's leading nations are daunting, discouraging developing countries from asserting their rights.

If the game is to be played fairly, at least two changes are needed. First, the TRIPS agreement must be implemented in a way that enables developing countries to use safeguard provisions that secure access to technologies of over-riding national importance.

For instance, under a range of special conditions TRIPS allows governments to issue compulsory licenses for companies to manufacture products that have been patented by others. Such licenses are already in use from Canada and Japan to the United Kingdom and the United States for products including pharmaceuticals, computers and tow trucks. They are used particularly as antitrust measures to prevent reduced competition and higher prices. But so far these provisions have not been used south of the equator. Developing countries, like other countries, should be able to do in practice what TRIPS allows them to do in theory.

Second, commitments under TRIPS and many other multilateral agreements to promote technology transfer to developing countries are paper promises, often neglected in implementation. They must be brought to life.

The heart of the problem is that although technology may be a tool for development, it is also a means of competitive advantage in the global economy. Access to patented environmental technologies and pharmaceuticals, for example, may be essential for combating global warming and for saving lives worldwide. But for countries that own and sell them, they are a global market opportunity. Only when the two interests are reconciled—through, say, adequate

public financing—will fair implementation of the TRIPS agreement become a real possibility.

Policy—not charity—to build technological capacity in developing countries

Global arrangements can only be as effective as national commitments to back them. The first step is for governments to recognize that technology policy affects a host of development issues, including public health, education and job creation.

There are many successful examples of international corporate philanthropy involving technology. For instance, in-kind donations by pharmaceutical companies have saved many lives, and the agreement to give poor farmers access to vitamin A–enhanced rice could help reduce global malnutrition. These initiatives have tremendous appeal—they can be a win-win proposition in which a country gets access to vital new technologies and a company get good public relations and sometimes tax incentives.

But these kinds of industry initiatives are no substitute for structural policy responses from governments. High-profile projects may gain such support from industry, but less newsworthy research cannot depend on it. When HIV/AIDS drugs and golden rice are no longer in the news every day, will Chagas disease and mosaic virus–resistant cassava motivate the same global public support?

Developing countries should not forever be held hostage to the research agendas set by global market demand. If any form of development is empowering in the 21st century, it is development that unleashes human creativity and creates technological capacity. Many developing countries are already taking up the challenge to make this happen. Global initiatives that recognize this will not only provide solutions to immediate crises but also build means to cope with future ones.

The ultimate significance of the network age is that it can empower people by enabling them to use and contribute to the world's collective knowledge. And the great challenge of the new century is to ensure that the entire human race is so empowered—not just a lucky few.

Commitments under TRIPS to promote technology transfer to developing countries are paper promises, often neglected in implementation. They must be brought to life.

CHAPTER 1

Human development—past, present and future

Human development is about much more than the rise or fall of national incomes. It is about creating an environment in which people can develop their full potential and lead productive, creative lives in accord with their needs and interests. People are the real wealth of nations. Development is thus about expanding the choices people have to lead lives that they value. And it is thus about much more than economic growth, which is only a means—if a very important one—of enlarging people's choices.

Fundamental to enlarging these choices is building human capabilities—the range of things that people can do or be in life. The most basic capabilities for human development are to lead long and healthy lives, to be knowledgeable, to have access to the resources needed for a decent standard of living and to be able to participate in the life of the community. Without these, many choices are simply not available, and many opportunities in life remain inaccessible.

This way of looking at development, often forgotten in the immediate concern with accumulating commodities and financial wealth, is not new. Philosophers, economists and political leaders have long emphasized human well-being as the purpose, the end, of development. As Aristotle said in ancient Greece, "Wealth is evidently not the good we are seeking, for it is merely useful for the sake of something else."

In seeking that something else, human development shares a common vision with human rights. The goal is human freedom. And in pursuing capabilities and realizing rights, this freedom is vital. People must be free to exercise their choices and to participate in decision-making that affects their lives. Human development and human rights are mutually reinforcing, helping to secure the well-being and dignity of all people, building self-respect and the respect of others.

THIRTY YEARS OF IMPRESSIVE PROGRESS—BUT A LONG WAY STILL TO GO

Human development challenges remain large in the new millennium (tables 1.1 and 1.2). Across the world we see unacceptable levels of deprivation in people's lives. Of the 4.6 billion people in developing countries, more than 850 million are illiterate, nearly a billion lack access to improved water sources, and 2.4 billion lack access to basic sanitation.[1] Nearly 325 million boys and girls are out of school.[2] And 11 million children under age five die each year from preventable causes—equivalent to more than 30,000 a day.[3] Around 1.2 billion people live on less than $1 a day (1993 PPP US$),[4] and 2.8 billion on less than $2 a day.[5] Such deprivations are not limited to developing countries. In

Development is about expanding the choices people have to lead lives that they value

---

TABLE 1.1
Serious deprivations in many aspects of life

Developing countries

Health
968 million people without access to improved water sources (1998)
2.4 billion people without access to basic sanitation (1998)
34 million people living with HIV/AIDS (end of 2000)
2.2 million people dying annually from indoor air pollution (1996)

Education
854 million illiterate adults, 543 million of them women (2000)
325 million children out of school at the primary and secondary levels, 183 million of them girls (2000)

Income poverty
1.2 billion people living on less than $1 a day (1993 PPP US$), 2.8 billion on less than $2 a day (1998)

Children
163 million underweight children under age five (1998)
11 million children under five dying annually from preventable causes (1998)

OECD countries

15% of adults lacking functional literacy skills (1994–98)
130 million people in income poverty (with less than 50% of median income) (1999)
8 million undernourished people (1996–98)
1.5 million people living with HIV/AIDS (2000)

Source: Smeeding 2001b; UNAIDS 2000a, 2000b; UNESCO 2000b; World Bank 2000d, 2001b, 2001c, 2001f; WHO 1997, 2000b; OECD and Statistics Canada 2000.

TABLE 1.2

Countries suffering setbacks in the human development index, 1999

HDI lower than in 1975	HDI lower than in 1980	HDI lower than in 1985	HDI lower than in 1990	HDI lower than in 1995
Zambia	Romania Russian Federation Zimbabwe	Botswana Bulgaria Burundi Congo Latvia Lesotho	Belarus Cameroon Kenya Lithuania Moldova, Rep. of South Africa Swaziland Ukraine	Malawi Namibia

Source: Indicator table 2.

FIGURE 1.1

Income growth varies among regions

GDP per capita annual growth rate (percent), 1975–99

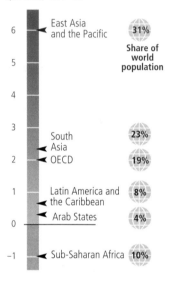

Source: Indicator table 11.

OECD countries more than 130 million people are income poor,[6] 34 million are unemployed, and adult functional illiteracy rates average 15%.

The magnitude of these challenges appears daunting. Yet too few people recognize that the impressive gains in the developing world in the past 30 years demonstrate the possibility of eradicating poverty. A child born today can expect to live eight years longer than one born 30 years ago. Many more people can read and write, with the adult literacy rate having increased from an estimated 47% in 1970 to 73% in 1999. The share of rural families with access to safe water has grown more than fivefold.[7] Many more people can enjoy a decent standard of living, with average incomes in developing countries having almost doubled in real terms between 1975 and 1998, from $1,300 to $2,500 (1985 PPP US$).[8]

The basic conditions for achieving human freedoms were transformed in the past 10 years as more than 100 developing and transition countries ended military or one-party rule, opening up political choices. And formal commitment to international standards in human rights has spread dramatically since 1990. These are only some of the indicators of the impressive gains in many aspects of human development (feature 1.1).

Behind this record of overall progress lies a more complex picture of diverse experiences across countries, regions, groups of people and dimensions of human development. The indicator tables in this Report provide a rich array of data on many indicators of human development for 162 countries, as well as aggregates for countries grouped by region, income and human development level. Feature 1.2 provides a snapshot.

REGIONAL CONTRASTS IN THE PACE OF PROGRESS

All regions have made progress in human development in the past 30 years, but advancing at very different paces and achieving very different levels. East Asia and the Pacific has made rapid, sustained progress in most areas, from expanding knowledge to improving survival to raising standards of living. South Asia and Sub-Saharan Africa lag far behind other regions, with human and income poverty still high. The adult literacy rate in South Asia is still 55% and in Sub-Saharan Africa 60%, well below the developing country average of 73%. Life expectancy at birth in Sub-Saharan Africa is still only 48.8 years, compared with more than 60 in all other regions. And the share of people living on less than $1 a day is as high as 46% in Sub-Saharan Africa and 40% in South Asia, compared with 15% in East Asia and the Pacific and in Latin America.[9]

The Arab States also lag behind in many indicators, but have been making the most rapid progress. Since the early 1970s life expectancy at birth has improved by 14 years and the infant mortality rate by 85 per 1,000 live births, and since 1985 the adult literacy rate has risen by 15 percentage points—faster progress than in any other region.

Differences among regions and countries are particularly marked in economic growth, which generates public resources to invest in education and health services and increases the resources people have to enjoy a decent standard of living and improve many other aspects of their lives. In 1975–99 per capita income quadrupled in East Asia and the Pacific, growing 6% a year (figure 1.1). The growth rate in South Asia exceeded 2%. Two countries that together account for a third of the world population did well: per capita income in China grew at an impressive 8% a year, and in India at an average rate of 3.2%. OECD countries had average growth of 2% a year, raising already high incomes to an average of more than $22,000 (PPP US$).

But in the Arab States and Latin America and the Caribbean growth has been slower, averaging less than 1%. Most devastating has been the performance of Sub-Saharan Africa, where

PROGRESS IN THE PAST 30 YEARS HAS BEEN IMPRESSIVE...

The structure of human development in the world has shifted

1975 Predominantly low and medium human development

Human development

High — 650 million
Medium — 1.6 billion
Low — 1.1 billion

1999 Predominantly medium and high human development

High — 900 million
Medium — 3.5 billion
Low — 500 million

Number of people

Note: Data refer only to countries for which data are available for both 1975 and 1999.
Source: Based on indicator tables 2 and 5.

Stronger recognition of human rights

Countries ratifying the 6 major human rights conventions and covenants

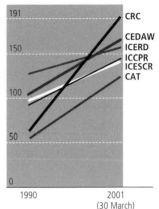

CRC
CEDAW
ICERD
ICCPR
ICESCR
CAT

1990 — 2001 (30 March)

Note: For full names of conventions see the list of abbreviations.
Source: UN 2001b.

People are living longer, healthier lives...

Life expectancy at birth	Infant mortality rate	Under-5 mortality rate	Under-nourished people
1970–75 to 1995–2000 (years)	1970–99 (per 1,000 live births)	1970–99 (per 1,000 live births)	1975–99 (millions)

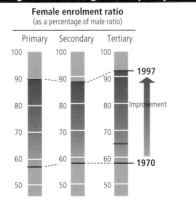

Improvement

Source: Indicator table 8 and FAO 2000b.

...are more literate and better educated...

Adult literacy rate	Gross enrolment ratio 1970–97 (percent)		Children out of school
1970–2000 (est.) (percent)	Primary	Secondary	1970–2000 (est.) (millions)

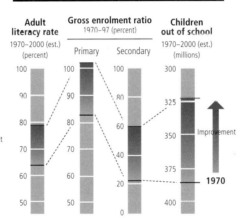

Improvement
1970

Source: UNESCO 2000b.

...and have higher incomes

Developing countries

Income	Income poverty
1975–98 (GDP per capita, 1985 PPP US$)	1990–98 (percent)

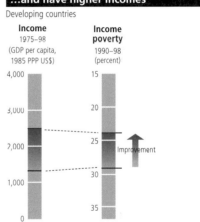

Improvement

Note: The poverty data refer to the share of the population living on less than $1 a day (1993 PPP US$).
Source: Human Development Report Office calculations based on World Bank 2001g, 2001h.

Progress towards gender equality...

Female enrolment ratio
(as a percentage of male ratio)

Primary	Secondary	Tertiary

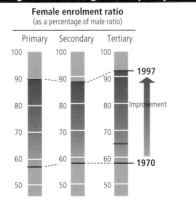

1997
Improvement
1970

Source: Based on UNESCO 2001a.

...environmental sustainability...

Carbon dioxide emissions (tonnes of carbon per capita)	Energy efficiency (GDP in PPP US$ per kg of oil equivalent)

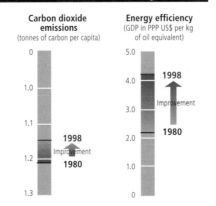

1998
Improvement
1980

1998
Improvement
1980

Source: UNDP, UNDESA and WEC 2000; indicator table 18.

...and democracy

Countries with multiparty elections
(percent)

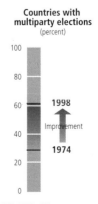

1998
Improvement
1974

Source: IMF, OECD, UN and World Bank 2000.

FEATURE 1.2

...BUT THE PACE OF THE PROGRESS AND THE LEVELS OF ACHIEVEMENT VARY WIDELY AMONG REGIONS AND GROUPS

Regional variations in human survival, education and income

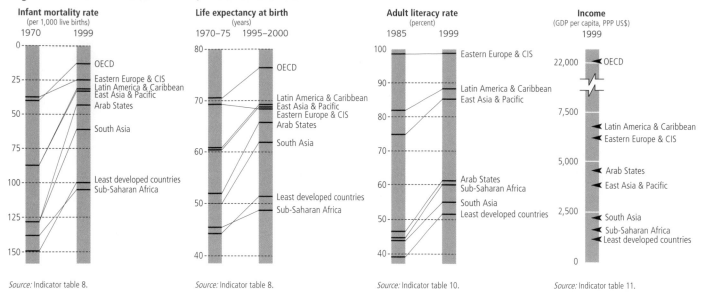

Source: Indicator table 8. *Source:* Indicator table 8. *Source:* Indicator table 10. *Source:* Indicator table 11.

Regional variations in income and human poverty

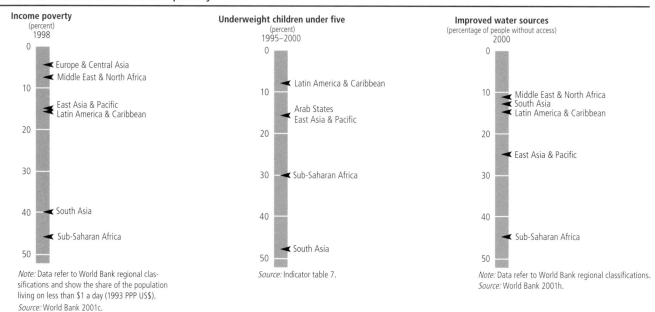

Urban-rural disparity in achievements and deprivations

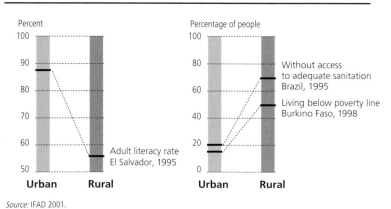

Source: IFAD 2001.

Across the world, women's achievements lag, deprivations are greater

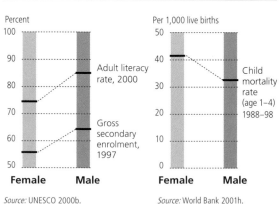

Source: UNESCO 2000b.   *Source:* World Bank 2001h.

already low incomes have fallen; in 1975–99 GDP per capita growth in the region averaged –1%. Madagascar and Mali now have per capita incomes of $799 and $753 (1999 PPP US$)— down from $1,258 and $898 (1999 PPP US$) 25 years ago. In 16 other Sub-Saharan countries per capita incomes were also lower in 1999 than in 1975. In Eastern Europe and the Commonwealth of Independent States (CIS) too, incomes have dropped sharply. Since 1990 per capita incomes have declined in 16 countries —in 4 by more than half.

NEW CHALLENGES AND SETBACKS

The course of human development is never steady. The changing world always brings new challenges, and the past decade has seen serious setbacks and reversals.

• At the end of 2000 about 36 million people were living with HIV/AIDS—95% of them in developing countries and 70% in Sub-Saharan Africa. More than 5 million became newly infected in 1999 alone.[10] In Sub-Saharan Africa, mainly because of HIV/AIDS, more than 20 countries experienced drops in life expectancy between 1985–90 and 1995–2000. In six countries—Botswana, Burundi, Namibia, Rwanda, Zambia and Zimbabwe—life expectancy declined by more than seven years.[11] The spread of HIV/AIDS has multiple consequences for development. It robs countries of people in their prime, and leaves children uncared for. By the end of 1999, 13 million children were AIDS orphans.[12]

• In Eastern Europe and the CIS the disruptive impact of the transition has exacted a heavy toll on human lives, with adverse effects on income, school enrolment and life expectancy, particularly of males.

• Personal security continues to be threatened by crime and conflicts. Globalization has created many opportunities for cross-border crime and the rise of multinational crime syndicates and networks. In 1995 the illegal drug trade was estimated at $400 billion,[13] and an estimated 1.8 million women and girls were victims of illegal trafficking.[14] And because of conflict, the world now has 12 million refugees and 5 million internally displaced people.[15]

• Democracy is fragile and often suffers reversals. Elected governments have been toppled in such countries as Côte d'Ivoire and Pakistan.

WHAT THE HUMAN DEVELOPMENT INDEX AND HUMAN POVERTY INDEX REVEAL

This year's Report presents estimates of the human development index (HDI) for 162 countries, as well as trends in the HDI for 97 countries having data for 1975–99 (box 1.1; see indicator tables 1 and 2). The results show a substantial shift of the world's people from low to medium levels of human development and from medium to high levels (see feature 1.1).

As a summary measure of human development, the HDI highlights the success of some countries and the slower progress of others. For example, Venezuela started with a higher HDI than Brazil in 1975, but Brazil made much faster progress (figure 1.2). The Republic of Korea and Jamaica had similar HDI rankings in 1975, but today Korea ranks 27 and Jamaica 78.

Rankings by HDI and by GDP per capita can be quite different, showing that countries do not have to wait for economic prosperity to make progress in human development (see indicator table 1). Costa Rica and Korea have both made impressive human development gains, reflected in HDIs of more than 0.800, but Costa Rica has achieved this human outcome with only half the income of Korea. Pakistan and Viet Nam have similar incomes, but Viet Nam has done much more in translating that income into human development (figure 1.3). So, with the right policies, countries can advance faster in human development than in economic growth. And if they ensure that growth favours the poor, they can do much more with that growth to promote human development.

The HDI measures only the average national achievement, not how well it is distributed in a country. Disaggregating a country's HDI by region and population group can spotlight stark disparities, and in many countries the results have sparked national debate and helped policy-makers assess differences in human development between rural and urban areas and among regions and ethnic and income groups. In South Africa in 1996 the HDI for the North-

FIGURE 1.2
Different paths of human progress

Human development index

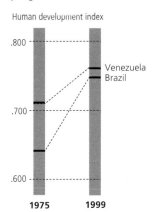

Source: Indicator table 2.

FIGURE 1.3
No automatic link between income and human development

Similar income, different HDI, 1999

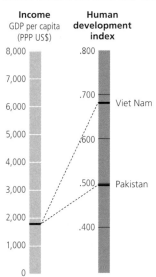

Source: Indicator table 1.

BOX 1.1

Measuring human development

Human Development Reports, since the first in 1990, have published the human development index (HDI) as a composite measure of human development. Since then three supplementary indices have been developed: the human poverty index (HPI), gender-related development index (GDI) and gender empowerment measure (GEM). The concept of human development, however, is much broader than the HDI and these supplementary indices. It is impossible to come up with a comprehensive measure—or even a comprehensive set of indicators—because many vital dimensions of human development, such as participation in the life of the community, are not readily quantified. While simple composite measures can draw attention to the issues quite effectively, these indices are no substitute for full treatment of the rich concerns of the human development perspective.

Human development index

The HDI measures the overall achievements in a country in three basic dimensions of human development—longevity, knowledge and a decent standard of living. It is measured by life expectancy, educational attainment (adult literacy and combined primary, secondary and tertiary enrolment) and adjusted income per capita in purchasing power parity (PPP) US dollars. The HDI is a summary, not a comprehensive measure of human development.

As a result of refinements in the HDI methodology over time and changes in data series, the HDI should not be compared across editions of the *Human Development Report* (see indicator table 2 for an HDI trend from 1975 based on a consistent methodology and data). The search for further methodological and data refinements to the HDI continues.

Human poverty index

While the HDI measures overall progress in a country in achieving human development, the human poverty index (HPI) reflects the distribution of progress and measures the backlog of deprivations that still exists. The HPI measures deprivation in the same dimensions of basic human development as the HDI.

HPI-1

The HPI-1 measures poverty in developing countries. It focuses on deprivations in three dimensions: longevity, as measured by the probability at birth of not surviving to age 40; knowledge, as measured by the adult illiteracy rate; and overall economic provisioning, public and private, as measured by the percentage of people not using improved water sources and the percentage of children under five who are underweight.

HPI-2

Because human deprivation varies with the social and economic conditions of a community, a separate index, the HPI-2, has been devised to measure human poverty in selected OECD countries, drawing on the greater availability of data. The HPI-2 focuses on deprivation in the same three dimensions as the HPI-1 and one additional one, social exclusion. The indicators are the probability at birth of not surviving to age 60, the adult functional illiteracy rate, the percentage of people living below the income poverty line (with disposable household income less than 50% of the median) and the long-term unemployment rate (12 months or more).

Gender-related development index

The gender-related development index (GDI) measures achievements in the same dimensions and using the same indicators as the HDI, but captures inequalities in achievement between women and men. It is simply the HDI adjusted downward for gender inequality. The greater is the gender disparity in basic human development, the lower is a country's GDI compared with its HDI.

Gender empowerment measure

The gender empowerment measure (GEM) reveals whether women can take active part in economic and political life. It focuses on participation, measuring gender inequality in key areas of economic and political participation and decision-making. It tracks the percentages of women in parliament, among legislators, senior officials and managers and among professional and technical workers—and the gender disparity in earned income, reflecting economic independence. Differing from the GDI, it exposes inequality in opportunities in selected areas.

HDI, HPI-1, HPI-2, GDI—same components, different measurements

Index	Longevity	Knowledge	Decent standard of living	Participation or exclusion
HDI	Life expectancy at birth	1. Adult literacy rate 2. Combined enrolment ratio	GDP per capita (PPP US$)	—
HPI-1	Probability at birth of not surviving to age 40	Adult illiteracy rate	Deprivation in economic provisioning, measured by: 1. Percentage of people not using improved water sources 2. Percentage of children under five who are underweight	—
HPI-2	Probability at birth of not surviving to age 60	Percentage of adults lacking functional literacy skills	Percentage of people living below the income poverty line (50% of median disposable household income)	Long-term unemployment rate (12 months or more)
GDI	Female and male life expectancy at birth	1. Female and male adult literacy rates 2. Female and male combined primary, secondary and tertiary enrolment ratios	Estimated female and male earned income, reflecting women's and men's command over resources	—

ern Province was only 0.531, compared with 0.712 for Gauteng.[16] In Cambodia in 1999 the HDI for the poorest 20% was 0.445, well below the national average of 0.517 and, more important, nearly one-third less than that for the richest 20%, at 0.623.[17] In Guatemala in 1998 the rural HDI, at 0.536, was well below the urban HDI, at 0.672.[18] In the United States in 1999 the HDI for white Americans was 0.870, ahead of the 0.805 for African Americans and well ahead of the 0.756 for people of Hispanic origin.[19] The HDI for untouchables in Nepal, at 0.239 in 1996, was almost half that for Brahmins, at 0.439.[20]

Another way to look at the distribution of national achievements in human development is to estimate the human poverty index (HPI), a multidimensional measure of poverty introduced in 1997. The United Republic of Tanzania and Uganda, for example, have very similar HDI rankings (140 and 141), but Uganda has higher human poverty (figure 1.4; see indicator table 3). Similarly, the 17 OECD countries for which the HPI has been estimated have nearly identical HDIs, yet their HPIs range from 6.8% in Sweden to 15.8% in the United States (see indicator table 4).

Disaggregating a country's HPI by region can identify concentrations of impoverishment. In the Islamic Republic of Iran in 1996 the disaggregated HPI showed that human deprivation in Tehran was only a quarter that in Sistan and Baluchestan.[21] The HPI for urban Honduras in 1999 was less than half that for rural areas.[22] For English speakers in Namibia in 1998 the HPI was less than one-ninth that for San speakers.[23]

Similar differences exist in the developed world. In the United States the HPI for Wisconsin in 1999 was less than half that for Arkansas.[24]

GENDER INEQUALITIES IN CAPABILITIES AND OPPORTUNITIES

Because the HDI assesses only average achievements, it masks gender differences in human development. To reveal these differences, the gender-related development index (GDI), introduced in 1995, adjusts the HDI for inequalities in the achievements of men and women. This year the GDI has been estimated for 146 countries (see indicator table 21).

With gender equality in human development, the GDI and the HDI would be the same. But for all countries the GDI is lower than the HDI, indicating the presence of gender inequality everywhere. The extent of the inequality varies significantly, however. For example, while in many countries male and female literacy rates are similar, in 43 countries—including India, Mozambique and Yemen—male rates are at least 15 percentage points higher than female rates. And while there has been good progress in eliminating gender disparities in primary and secondary enrolments, with the ratio of girls to boys in developing countries 89% at the primary level and 82% at the secondary level in 1997,[25] in 27 countries girls' net enrolment declined at the secondary level between the mid-1980s and 1997 (table 1.3).

The gender empowerment measure (GEM), also introduced in 1995, helps to assess gender inequality in economic and political opportuni-

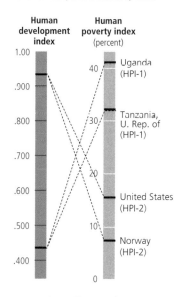

FIGURE 1.4

No automatic link between human development and human poverty

Similar HDI, different HPI, 1999

Source: Indicator tables 1, 3 and 4.

TABLE 1.3
Countries where girls' net secondary enrolment ratio declined, 1985–97

Arab States	Asia and the Pacific	Eastern Europe and the CIS	Latin America and the Caribbean	Sub-Saharan Africa
Bahrain	Mongolia	Bulgaria	Bolivia	Angola
Iraq		Croatia	Ecuador	Cameroon
Kuwait		Estonia	Haiti	Central African Republic
Qatar		Georgia	Honduras	Congo
Syrian Arab Republic		Kyrgyzstan		Côte d'Ivoire
		Latvia		Equatorial Guinea
		Romania		Guinea
		Russian Federation		Lesotho
				Mozambique

Note: Refers to declines of 5% or more.
Source: UNIFEM 2000.

ties. This year it has been estimated for 64 countries (see indicator table 22). Some observations:

• The GEM values range from less than 0.300 to more than 0.800, showing the great variation across the world in empowering women.

• Only 3 of the 64 countries—Iceland, Norway and Sweden—have a GEM of more than 0.800. As many as 25 countries have a GEM of less than 0.500. So, many countries have far to go in extending economic and political opportunities to women.

• Some developing countries outperform much richer industrial countries. The Bahamas and Trinidad and Tobago are ahead of Italy and Japan. Barbados has a GEM 30% higher than Greece's. The message: high income is not a prerequisite to creating opportunities for women.

• Disaggregations of the GEM in national human development reports show that differences within a country can also be large. For example, the GEM for the Puttalam district in Sri Lanka in 1994 was less than 8% of that for Nuwara Eliya.[26]

There is much to improve in women's economic and political opportunities. Women's share of paid employment in industry and services has increased in most countries, yet in 1997 women working in these sectors typically earned 78% of what men earned. In only eight countries do women hold 30% or more of the seats in par-

Income growth has varied considerably among countries in recent decades, more so than trends in many human development indicators

liament. And in only four—Denmark, Finland, Norway and Sweden—have there been simultaneous achievements in the female secondary enrolment ratio (to 95% or more), in women's share of paid employment in industry and services (to around 50%) and in their share of parliamentary seats (to at least 30%).[27]

UNEQUAL INCOMES

Income is a very important means of enlarging people's choices and is used in the HDI as a proxy for a decent standard of living. Income growth has varied considerably among countries in recent decades, more so than trends in many human development indicators. The distribution of the world's income, and the way this is changing, are thus a vital issue deserving special consideration.

Income levels across countries have been both diverging and converging—with some regions closing the income gap and others drifting away (figure 1.5). In 1960 there was a bunching of regions, with East Asia and the Pacific, South Asia, Sub-Saharan Africa and the least developed countries having an average per capita income around ⅛ to ¹⁄₁₀ of that in high-income OECD countries. Latin America and the Caribbean fared better, but still had just ⅓ to ½ of the per capita income of these OECD countries.

The impressive growth in East Asia and the Pacific is reflected in the improvement in the ratio of its income to that of high-income OECD countries, from around ¹⁄₁₀ to nearly ⅕ over 1960–98. The relative income in Latin America and the Caribbean stayed about the same. Income in South Asia—after worsening in the 1960s and 1970s, then improving significantly in the 1980s and 1990s—remains about ¹⁄₁₀ of that in OECD countries. In Sub-Saharan Africa the situation has worsened dramatically: per capita income, around ⅑ of that in high-income OECD countries in 1960, deteriorated to around ¹⁄₁₈ by 1998.

Despite a reduction in the relative differences between many countries, absolute gaps in per capita income have increased (figure 1.6). Even for East Asia and the Pacific, the fastest growing region, the absolute difference in income with high-income OECD countries

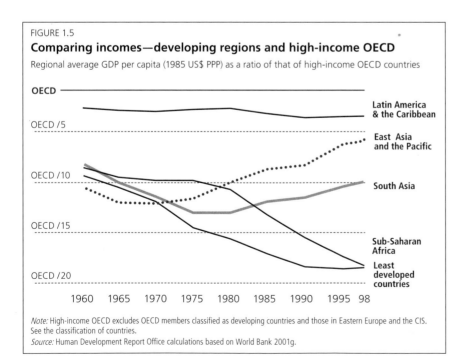

FIGURE 1.5

Comparing incomes—developing regions and high-income OECD

Regional average GDP per capita (1985 US$ PPP) as a ratio of that of high-income OECD countries

Note: High-income OECD excludes OECD members classified as developing countries and those in Eastern Europe and the CIS. See the classification of countries.

Source: Human Development Report Office calculations based on World Bank 2001g.

widened from about $6,000 in 1960 to more than $13,000 in 1998 (1985 PPP US$).

WITHIN-COUNTRY INEQUALITY—WHAT'S HIDING BEHIND AVERAGE INCOMES?

Also important is income inequality within countries, which may affect long-term prosperity (box 1.2). Although there are reasonable data on within-country inequality for points in time, the data are not based on uniform surveys across countries and so comparisons must be treated with care (see indicator table 12).[28] But even very rough comparisons reveal a lot about within-country inequality. The variation is vast, with Gini coefficients ranging from less than 20 in Slovakia to 60 in Nicaragua and Swaziland (figure 1.7).

Has the situation been improving or deteriorating? Not clear. A study of 77 countries with 82% of the world's people shows that between the 1950s and the 1990s inequality rose in 45 of the countries and fell in 16.[29] Many of the countries with rising inequality are those in Eastern Europe and the CIS that suffered low or negative growth in the 1990s. In the remaining 16 countries either no clear trend emerged or income inequality initially declined, then levelled off.

Latin American and Caribbean countries have among the world's highest income inequality. In 13 of the 20 countries with data for the 1990s, the poorest 10% had less than ½₀ of the income of the richest 10%. This high income inequality places millions in extreme poverty and severely limits the effect of equally shared growth on

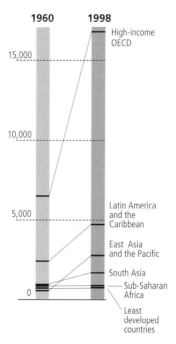

FIGURE 1.6
Widening income gap between regions
GDP per capita (1985 PPP US$)

Source: Human Development Report Office calculations based on World Bank 2001g.

BOX 1.2
Why inequality matters

Whether and why inequality matters is an old issue—going back to the time of Karl Marx and before. For development economists concerned primarily with the world's poor countries, the central issues have been growth and poverty reduction, not inequality. And for mainstream economists during most of the postwar period of the 20th century, inequality was at worst a necessary evil—helping to enhance growth by concentrating income among the rich, who save and invest more, and by creating incentives for individuals to work hard, innovate and take productive risks.

But income inequality does matter. It matters in itself if people—and nations—care about their relative income status. It may also matter for instrumental reasons—that is, because it affects other outcomes.
• Inequality can exacerbate the effects of market and policy failures on growth and thus on progress against poverty. That makes inequality a special problem in poor countries, where imperfect markets and institutional failures are common. For example, where capital markets are weak, poor people, lacking good collateral, will be unable to borrow. Their potential to start small businesses will be limited—reducing overall growth and limiting opportunities for poor people. Though growth is not always sufficient to advance human development and reduce income poverty, the experiences of China, the Republic of Korea and other countries of East Asia suggest that it makes a big contribution. Finally, there is the arithmetic reality. Even if there is growth and poor people gain proportionately from that growth, the same growth rate buys less poverty reduction where inequality is high to start with.

• Concentration of income at the top can undermine the kinds of public policies—such as support for high-quality universal public education—that are likely to advance human development. Populist policies that generate inflation hurt poor people in the long run. Artificially low prices for water and sanitation mean that bankrupt public utilities never expand to poor neighbourhoods. If rich people support industrial subsidies or cheap loans for large landowners, that may reduce growth directly as well. Developing and implementing good social policies is especially difficult where inequality takes the form of concentration at the top combined with substantial poverty at the bottom—and thus the absence of a middle class that demands accountable government.
• Inequality is likely to erode social capital, including the sense of trust and citizen responsibility that is key to the formation and sustainability of sound public institutions. It can undermine participation in such common spheres of community life as parks, local sports leagues and parent-teacher associations of public schools. Street crime undermines communal life, and differences in income inequality across countries are closely associated with differences in rates of crime and violence.
• Inequality may over time increase a society's tolerance for inequality. If global pressures lead to increases in wage differences (for example, as the salaries of the most skilled and internationally mobile people rise), the social norm for what wage gap is acceptable may eventually shift. If inequality matters for any of the reasons above, the possibility that it can worsen matters too.

Source: Birdsall forthcoming.

poverty. So Latin America and the Caribbean can reach the Millenium Declaration's development target of halving poverty by 2015 only if the region generates more growth and that growth disproportionately benefits poor people.[30]

All five South Asian countries with data have fairly low Gini coefficients, in the 30s. While the Arab States show more variation, they also have fairly low income inequality. Countries in East Asia and the Pacific exhibit no clear pattern—varying from the fairly equal Korea and Viet Nam to the much less equal Malaysia and the Philippines.

China and India—two countries with low but rapidly growing per capita incomes and large populations—deserve special consideration. In China inequality has followed a U-shaped pattern, with inequality falling until the mid-1980s and rising since. The story is better in India, with inequality falling until recently, and then coming to a halt.[31]

Many countries in Sub-Saharan Africa have high levels of income inequality. In 16 of the 22 Sub-Saharan countries with data for the 1990s, the poorest 10% of the population had less than $\frac{1}{10}$ of the income of the richest 10%, and in 9 less than $\frac{1}{20}$. Despite the pressing need to understand what is happening to income inequality over time in this poor region, trend data on income distribution remain too limited to draw conclusions.

Most countries in Eastern Europe and the CIS have relatively low inequality—though there are notable exceptions, such as Armenia and the Russian Federation.[32] Before the transition to market economies the countries of Eastern Europe and the CIS were bunched closely, with Gini coefficients in the low- to mid-20s. Changes in inequality during the transition were modest in Eastern European countries such as Hungary and Slovenia, but much more dramatic in countries of the former Soviet Union. Russia saw its Gini coefficient jump by an astonishing 24 points, Lithuania by 14.[33]

Among OECD countries there is also diversity in income inequality, from the low levels in Austria and Denmark to the relatively high levels in the United Kingdom and the United States. Still, in global terms income inequality among these countries is relatively low.[34] What about trends over time? Results from a variety of country and cross-country studies suggest that income inequality increased in many OECD countries between the mid- to late 1980s and mid- to late 1990s (table 1.4). While data for earlier periods are more limited, these countries seem to have experienced a U-shaped change in inequality, with declines in the 1970s changing to increases in the 1980s and 1990s. The constant level in Canada and slight improvement in Denmark are exceptions to the apparent trend.

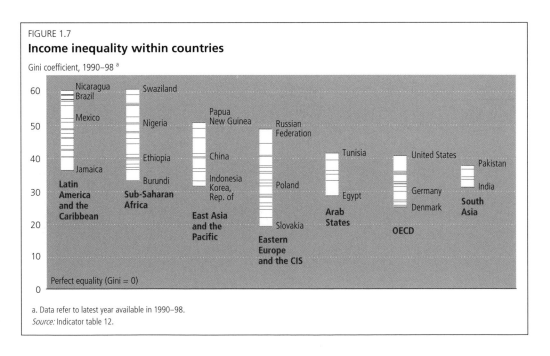

FIGURE 1.7
Income inequality within countries

Gini coefficient, 1990–98 [a]

a. Data refer to latest year available in 1990–98.
Source: Indicator table 12.

Another measure of inequality looks both between and within countries—lining up all the world's people from richest to poorest (in real purchasing power) regardless of national boundaries (box 1.3). A recent study by Milanovic compares the poorest and richest people across the globe, giving a much more complete picture of world inequality than a simple comparison of country averages would. Based on household surveys for 1988–93, the study covers 91 countries (with about 84% of the world's population) and adjusts income levels using purchasing power parity conversions.[35] The disadvantage is that the study relies entirely on household budget survey data that are not necessarily comparable and are limited in their scope. Nevertheless, the study produced some powerful results:[36]

• World inequality is very high. In 1993 the poorest 10% of the world's people had only 1.6% of the income of the richest 10%.

• The richest 1% of the world's people received as much income as the poorest 57%.

• The richest 10% of the US population (around 25 million people) had a combined income greater than that of the poorest 43% of the world's people (around 2 billion people).

• Around 25% of the world's people received 75% of the world's income (in PPP US$).[37]

INEQUALITY AND MOBILITY

Two societies with the same income inequality could differ greatly in the mobility and opportunity facing individual members—and in the mobility and opportunity that children have relative to their parents. A focus on mobility helps to identify the factors that block the opportunities of poor people and contribute to the intergenerational transmission of poverty. This approach is well suited to evaluating the effects of policy changes on poverty and inequality.

The problem is that mobility is difficult to measure accurately. Still, the few studies that examine it are suggestive.[38]

• In South Africa 63% of households in poverty in 1993 were still there in 1998, while 60% of households in the highest income cate-

gory in 1993 were still there in 1998, indicating limited income mobility.

• In Russia downward mobility was extreme in the late 1990s. Among households in the top income quintile in 1995, nearly 60% slid to lower quintiles by 1998—and 7% fell to the bottom quintile.

• In Peru there has been a great deal of movement up and down the income ladder. Opportunities are increasing with market reforms, but so are insecurities. Between 1985 and 1991, 61% of households had income increases of 30% or more and 14% had income drops of 30% or more. Overall, downward mobility dominated in 1985–91, and upward mobility in 1991–97.

In every country family background significantly influences the length of children's schooling. Children with wealthier, better-educated

The richest 1% of the world's people received as much income as the poorest 57%

TABLE 1.4
Trends in income distribution in OECD countries

Country	Early to mid-1970s to mid- to late 1980s	Mid- to late 1980s to mid- to late 1990s
Australia	0	+
Austria	0	+ +
Belgium	0	+
Canada	–	0
Denmark	..	–
Finland	–	+
France	–	..
Germany	–	+
Ireland	–	+
Italy	– –	+ +
Japan	0	+ +
Netherlands	0	+ +
New Zealand	0	+ + +
Norway	0	+ +
Sweden	–	+
Switzerland	..	+
United Kingdom	+ +	+ +
United States	+ +	+ +

Note: The results are based on the percentage change in Gini coefficients and reflect the general trends reported in national and comparative studies. However, trends are always sensitive to beginning and ending points as well as to other factors. The following symbols denote the change in income inequality:

+ + + Increase of more than 15%.
+ +   Increase of 7–15%.
+   Increase of 1–7%.
0   Change between –1% and 1%.
–   Decrease of 1–7%.
– –   Decrease of 7–15%.
– – – Decrease of more than 15%.
..   No consistent estimate available.
Source: Smeeding 2001a, forthcoming.

parents are always likely to do better. But there is substantial variation across countries and periods, depending on macroeconomic conditions and public education policies.

An emphasis on basic schooling in public spending enhances intergenerational mobility in Latin America.[39] There, a person needs at least 10 years of schooling to have a 90% or higher probability of not falling into poverty or of moving out of poverty. And having just 2 years less schooling means 20% less income for the rest of a person's active life.[40]

With globalization and technology-led growth, how will the determinants of mobility change?

HUMAN DEVELOPMENT—AT THE HEART OF TODAY'S POLICY AGENDA

More than 360 national and subnational human development reports have been produced by 120 countries, in addition to 9 regional reports. The reports have injected the human development concept into national policy dialogues—not only through human development indicators and policy recommendations, but also through the country-led process of consultation, data collection and report writing.

Botswana's 2000 human development report focuses on how HIV/AIDS is reducing economic growth and increasing poverty, and provides policy guidance for political action at the highest levels.[41] The report spurred public discussion on the accessibility of antiretroviral drugs and whether the government should be responsible for providing them. Botswana's minister of health then asked the Bank of Botswana to explore the financial viability of such an approach. Meetings were convened at UNDP with key stakeholders, including the National AIDS Coordinating Agency, the ministries of health, finance and development and major insurance companies. Those consultations led to a decision in March 2001 by the pres-

National human development reports have injected the human development concept into national policy dialogues

---

BOX 1.3

International comparisons of living standards—the need for purchasing power parities

To compare the incomes of people in different countries, the incomes must first be converted into a common currency. Until 1999 the *Human Development Report* used income measures based on exchange rate conversions in assessing global income inequality (as in the comparison of income for the richest 20% and the poorest 20% in the world). But exchange rate conversions do not take into account price differences between countries, which is vital when comparing living standards. To take account of these price differences, purchasing power parity (PPP) conversion rates are used to convert incomes into a common currency in which differences in national price levels have been eliminated.

The two approaches to measuring inequality produce very different results. Using exchange rates not only produces much higher measures of inequality, but also affects trends in inequality.

With the exchange rate measure, the ratio of the income of the richest 20% to that of the poorest 20% grew from 34 to 1 in 1970 to 70 to 1 in 1997. With the PPP measure, the ratio fell, from 15 to 1 to 13 to 1. Although both measures show increasing inequality between the richest 10% and poorest 10%, the exchange rate measure shows a much larger increase than the rise in real living standards.

While PPPs are the best way to convert income when comparing living standards, they are not without theoretical and practical problems. These problems point to the need for greater support—financial and institutional—for the collection of PPP data.

Income inequality between the world's richest and poorest, based on country averages, 1970 and 1997

Measure	Richest 10% to poorest 10%		Richest 20% to poorest 20%	
	1970	1997	1970	1997
Exchange rate	51.5	127.7	33.7	70.4
Purchasing power parity	19.4	26.9	14.9	13.1

Source: UN 2000b; Melchior, Telle and Wiig 2000; Human Development Report Office calculations based on World Bank 2001h and 2001g.

ident of Botswana to provide antiretroviral drugs for free to the 17% of the country's people with HIV.

The Philippines's 2000 report analyses the education issues and challenges facing the Filipino society in coming years.[42] It calls for the country to take advantage of the network age and today's technological transformations. The report spurred major debates on education reform in the country's Senate and Executive Cabinet. The country's 1997 report helped catalyse a presidential directive requiring all local governments to devote at least 20% of domestic revenue to human development priorities.[43]

Many of India's 25 states rival medium-size countries in size, population and diversity. The government of Madhya Pradesh was the first to prepare a state report on human development, in 1995, to bring the subject to political discourse and investment planning.[44] By 1998 social services accounted for more than 42% of planned investment, compared with 19% in the previous plan budget.[45] Human development reports have also been prepared in Gujarat, Karnataka and Rajasthan and are under way in Arunachal Pradesh, Assam, Himachal Pradesh and Tamil Nadu.[46] The states' preparation of the reports has made human development priorities an important part of political discourse and development strategies.

Kuwait's first human development report, in 1997, raised awareness of the human development concept and its relevance to the country's struggle to shift from dependence on oil towards a knowledge-based economy.[47] The report's production and promotion helped advance new thinking in academia, research institutions and the government. The Ministry of Planning has started to monitor human development and to incorporate the human development approach in its indicators for strategic planning. Given the success of the first report, the ministry is following up with a second.

Colombia's 2000 report looks at human rights as an intrinsic part of development and shows how they bring principles of accountability and social justice to the development process.[18] Exposing weaknesses in the interpretation and implementation of some constitutional rights, the report has moved debates and dialogues on human rights to a new level, with a vigorous focus on economic, social and cultural rights. The report stresses basic social services, discusses social exclusion and revisits labour rights under globalization, providing a new lens for viewing development in Colombia.

Bulgaria's 2000 report, analysing the socioeconomic situation in each of the country's 262 municipalities, initiated a healthy competition among neighbouring municipalities to do better in human development.[49] The report has been used in determining the target locations for a large government programme for small-business job creation. It has also sparked constructive debates, in the media and among mayors, governors and ministers, about such issues as decentralization, municipal budgets and educational attainment and subsidies.

After the *Atlas of Human Development in Brazil*—an electronic database with human development indicators for all 5,000 Brazilian municipalities—was launched in 2000,[50] the central government's budgetary law for 2000 was revised to make the HDI mandatory in focusing social programmes. Encouraged by that move, the state of São Paulo has produced a new index reflecting both human development and social responsibility. Having decided to institutionalize the index, the state legislative body intends to issue a decree making production of the index mandatory for city administrations.

THE MILLENNIUM DECLARATION'S GOALS FOR DEVELOPMENT AND POVERTY ERADICATION

As the world entered the new millennium, heads of state and government gathered at the United Nations General Assembly to lay out their vision for the world. The leaders of the summit adopted the United Nations Millennium Declaration, recognizing their "collective responsibility to uphold the principles of human dignity, equality and equity at the global level". Among the many objectives set out by the declaration are specific, quantified and monitorable goals for development and poverty eradication by 2015:

• To halve the proportion of the world's people living on less than $1 a day.

The Millennium Declaration recognizes the "collective responsibility to uphold the principles of human dignity, equality and equity at the global level"

MILLENNIUM DECLARATION GOALS FOR 2015

A balance sheet of human development—goals, achievements and unfinished path

Goals	Achievements	Unfinished path
Halve the proportion of people living in extreme poverty.	Between 1990 and 1998 the proportion of people living on less than $1 (1993 PPP US$) a day in developing countries was reduced from 29% to 24%.	Even if the proportion is halved by 2015, there will still be 900 million people living in extreme poverty in the developing world.
Halve the proportion of people suffering from hunger.	The number of undernourished people in the developing world fell by 40 million between 1990–92 and 1996–98.	The developing world still has 826 million undernourished people.
Halve the proportion of people without access to safe water.	Around 80% of people in the developing world now have access to improved water sources.	Nearly one billion people still lack access to improved water sources.
Enrol all children in primary school. Achieve universal completion of primary schooling.	By 1997 more than 70 countries had primary net enrolment ratios over 80%. In 29 of the 46 countries with data, 80% of children enrolled reach grade 5.	In the next 15 years provision must be made for the 113 million children now out of primary school and the millions more who will enter the school-age population.
Empower women and eliminate gender disparities in primary and secondary education.	By 1997 the female enrolment ratio in developing countries had reached 89% of the male ratio at the primary level and 82% at the secondary level.	In 20 countries girls' secondary enrolment ratios are still less than two-thirds of boys' enrolment ratios.
Reduce maternal mortality ratios by three-quarters.	Only 32 countries have achieved a reported maternal mortality ratio of less than 20 per 100,000 live births.	In 21 countries the reported maternal mortality ratio exceeds 500 per 100,000 live births.
Reduce infant mortality rates by two-thirds.[a] Reduce under-five mortality rates by two-thirds.	In 1990–99 infant mortality was reduced by more than 10%, from 64 per 1,000 live births to 56. Under-five mortality was reduced from 93 per 1,000 live births to 80 in 1990–99.	Sub-Saharan Africa has an infant mortality rate of more than 100 and an under-five mortality rate of more than 170—and has been making slower progress than other regions.
Halt and begin to reverse the spread of HIV/AIDS.	In a few countries, such as Uganda and possibly Zambia, HIV/AIDS prevalence is showing signs of decline.	Around 36 million people are living with HIV/AIDS.
Provide access for all who want reproductive health services.[a]	Contraceptive prevalence has reached nearly 50% in developing countries.	Around 120 million couples who want to use contraception do not have access to it.
Implement national strategies for sustainable development by 2005 to reverse the loss of environmental resources by 2015.[a]	The number of countries adopting sustainable development strategies rose from fewer than 25 in 1990 to more than 50 in 1997.	Implementation of the strategies remains minimal.

a. International development goal.

Millennium Declaration goals for development and poverty eradication: how are countries doing?

Legend (bar categories): Achieved | On track | Lagging | Far behind | Slipping

NUMBER OF COUNTRIES

Goal (for 2015)	Achieved	On track	Lagging	Far behind	Slipping	Total	LDCs	Sub-Saharan Africa
Gender equality								
Eliminate disparity in primary education	15	57	2	13	1	14	9	9
Eliminate disparity in secondary education	39	25	3	16	2	18	10	12
Infant and child mortality								
Reduce infant mortality rates by two-thirds [a]		63	14	73	9	82	27	35
Reduce under-five mortality rates by two-thirds		66	17	66	10	76	26	34
Maternal mortality								
Reduce maternal mortality ratios by three-quarters	13	49	46	37		37	27	31
Basic amenities								
Halve the proportion of people without access to safe water	18	32	42	41		41	27	26
Hunger								
Halve the proportion of people suffering from hunger	6	37	3	23	17	40	16	21
Universal education								
Enrol all children in primary school	5	27	4	13	9	22	9	10
Achieve universal completion of primary schooling	8	32	28	15		15	11	11
Extreme income poverty								
Halve the proportion of people living in extreme poverty — Business-as-usual growth pattern	11	4	39	31		70	14	17
Halve the proportion of people living in extreme poverty — Pro-poor growth pattern		29	6	19	31	50	9	13

(Number of countries far behind or slipping shown in Total, LDCs, Sub-Saharan Africa columns.)

Note: This analysis excludes high-income OECD countries. See technical note 3 for an explanation of the assessments of progress and for information on the data sources used. LDCs are least developed countries.

a. International development goal.

Millennium Declaration goals: how are people doing?

Percentage of world population[a]

Goal (for 2015)	Achieved or on track	Lagging, far behind or slipping	No data
Gender equality			
Eliminate disparity in primary education	58	5	22
Eliminate disparity in secondary education	42	22	21
Infant and child mortality			
Reduce infant mortality rates by two-thirds[b]	23	62	(.)
Reduce under-five mortality rates by two-thirds	23	62	(.)
Maternal mortality			
Reduce maternal mortality ratios by three-quarters	37	48	(.)
Basic amenities			
Halve the proportion of people without access to safe water	12	70	3
Hunger			
Halve the proportion of people suffering from hunger	62	11	12
Universal education			
Enrol all children in primary school	34	5	46
Achieve universal completion of primary schooling	26	13	46
Extreme income poverty			
Halve the proportion of people living in extreme poverty — Business-as-usual growth pattern	43	34	8
Halve the proportion of people living in extreme poverty — Pro-poor growth pattern	54	23	8

Note: Population shares do not sum to 100% because the analysis excludes high-income OECD countries.

a. Refer to sum of country population in respective categories as a percentage of world population.

b. International development goal.

Source: FAO 2000b; UNICEF 2001b, 2001c; World Bank 2000c, 2001h; UNESCO 2000b; UNFPA 2001; UNAIDS 1998, 2000b; IMF, OECD, UN and World Bank 2000; Hanmer, Healey and Naschold 2000.

- To halve the proportion of the world's people suffering from hunger.
- To halve the proportion of the world's people without access to safe drinking water.
- To achieve universal completion of primary schooling.
- To achieve gender equality in access to education.
- To reduce maternal mortality ratios by three-quarters.
- To reduce under-five mortality rates by two-thirds.
- To halt and begin to reverse the spread of HIV/AIDS, malaria and other major diseases.

These goals build on the international development goals, which include three more targets—namely, to reduce infant mortality rates by two-thirds, to provide access for all who want reproductive health services and to implement national strategies for sustainable development by 2005 to reverse the loss of environmental resources by 2015.[51]

What are the prospects for achieving these goals? The good news is that for universal primary education and gender equity in education, many developing countries have already achieved the goals or are on track to do so (feature 1.3). Because of the importance of educa-

---

SPECIAL CONTRIBUTION

Human resource development in the 21st century: enhancing knowledge and information capabilities

We are living in an age of knowledge and information, fraught with both opportunities and dangers. There are opportunities for the underprivileged and poor to become rich and strong. But at the same time there is a danger that the gap between rich and poor nations could widen. The message is clear. We must continue to develop our human resources. The success or failure of individuals and nations, as well as the prosperity of mankind, depends on whether we can wisely develop our human resources.

During the 20th century such tangible elements as capital, labour and natural resources were the driving force behind economic development. But in the new century such intangible elements as information and creativity will give nations a competitive edge. Consequently, if we succeed in developing the potential of our citizens by fostering a creative spirit of adventure, individuals and nations will become rich, even if they are without much capital, labour or natural resources.

The Republic of Korea is not endowed with sufficient natural resources and capital, but its people have the spirit of challenge and the confidence that they can become a first-rate advanced country in the new century. The source of their confidence lies in their innate potential and their determination to develop themselves to the fullest. With their long-standing enthusiasm for education, the Korean people have built up an impressive knowledge base. The percentage of high school seniors who go on to college in Korea is 68 percent, one of the highest rates in the world. Koreans also have a rich tradition in creativity, trans-

forming imported cultures into their own, as exemplified by their own schools of Buddhism and Confucianism.

Based on this tradition, we are making a concerted effort to develop our human resources in order to take the lead in the age of knowledge and information. We are offering educational opportunities to all citizens, including students, farmers, fishermen, men and women in uniform and prison inmates, to enhance their information capabilities. We have completed the construction of a nationwide information superhighway network and now provide high-speed Internet access to most elementary, middle and high schools for free. We are combining conventional industries, such as automobile manufacturing, shipbuilding, textiles and even the agricultural industry, with information capabilities.

The number of Internet users in Korea recently topped 20 million, and some 28 percent of the population, or 4 million households, have high-speed Internet access. And we plan to produce some 200,000 specialists in information and technology by 2005. All of this is part of our efforts to forge Korea into a nation with advanced knowledge and information capabilities in the 21st century.

I believe that developing nations that lagged behind in their industrialization during the 20th century can overcome poverty and achieve economic growth by successfully developing their human resources. And to do so, assistance and cooperation from the international community are vital.

Enhancement of information capabilities can bring affluence to us by increasing efficiency. But it is also widening the digital divide

between the information technology haves and have-nots. The whole world must cooperate to close the gap and seek co-prosperity. To that end, we must take "globalization of information" a step further to "globalization of the benefits of information". Developing nations should be able to participate in the process of furthering information capabilities and to receive their fair share of the benefits. We must make a joint effort, both regionally and globally, so that all of humanity can share the benefits of advanced information and communications technologies.

Korea's proposals for the joint development of leading-edge industries were adopted at various multilateral forums, including ASEM, APEC and ASEAN+3. Furthermore, Korea hosted a forum on South-South Cooperation in Science and Technology in Seoul in February 2000, in conjunction with the United Nations Development Programme, to help build a cooperative network for technological development among developing nations.

Korea will continue to support developing nations through the official development assistance programme, while actively participating in international efforts to help these countries enhance their information capabilities. It is the belief of this government that only through such efforts can all humanity share peace and prosperity.

Kim Dae-jung

Kim Dae-jung
President of the Republic of Korea

tion to so many areas of development, these bright prospects strengthen the possibilities for accelerating progress towards the other goals (see the special contribution by President Kim Dae-jung of the Republic of Korea). Furthermore, over 60% of the world's people live in 43 countries that have met or are on track to meet the goal of halving the number of people who are hungry.

The bad news is that in other areas more than half the countries for which data are available will not achieve the goals without a significant acceleration in progress. Many of these are least developed countries in Sub-Saharan Africa. While 50 countries have achieved or are on track to achieve the safe water goal, 83 countries with 70% of the world's people are lagging or far behind. And while 62 countries are on track to reduce maternal mortality by three-quarters, 83 are lagging or far behind. In income poverty, more than 40% of the world's people live in countries that are on track to meet the goal. But they are concentrated in 11 countries, including India and China, while 70 countries are far behind or

slipping. Though these countries contain only a third of the world's people, they constitute more than half of all developing countries. Without China and India, 9 countries, with 5% of the world's people, would be on track to halve the proportion of people living in extreme income poverty. The situation is perhaps most serious for under-five mortality. While 66 countries are on track to meet the goal, 83 countries with around 60% of the world's people are lagging or far behind—and in 10 under-five mortality rates are increasing. While there is not comparable trend data on the prevalence of HIV/AIDS to do a full analysis, the global prevalence of HIV/AIDS among adults is still on the rise, with only a handful of countries, such as Uganda and possibly Zambia, showing signs of decline.[52]

Human progress in the past 30 years shows what is possible. So does this year's Report. One of its main messages is that technological advance has contributed greatly to the acceleration of human progress in the past several centuries. Those contributions have the promise of even greater acceleration.

Technological advance has contributed greatly to the acceleration of human progress in the past several centuries

CHAPTER 2

Today's technological transformations—creating the network age

Technological innovation is essential for human progress. From the printing press to the computer, from the first use of penicillin to the widespread use of vaccines, people have devised tools for improving health, raising productivity and facilitating learning and communication. Today technology deserves new attention. Why? Because digital, genetic and molecular breakthroughs are pushing forward the frontiers of how people can use technology to eradicate poverty. These breakthroughs are creating new possibilities for improving health and nutrition, expanding knowledge, stimulating economic growth and empowering people to participate in their communities.

Today's technological transformations are intertwined with another transformation—globalization—and together they are creating a new paradigm: the network age. These transformations expand opportunities and increase the social and economic rewards of creating and using technology. They are also altering how—and by whom—technology is created and owned, and how it is made accessible and used. A new map of innovation and diffusion is appearing. Technology growth hubs—centres that bring together research institutes, business startups and venture capital—are dotted across the globe, from Silicon Valley (United States) to Bangalore (India) to El Ghazala (Tunisia), linked through technology development networks. But these new networks and opportunities are superimposed on another map that reflects a long history of unevenly diffused technology, both among and within countries.

No individual, organization, business or government can ignore these changes. The new terrain requires shifts in public policy—national and global—to harness today's technological transformations as tools for human development.

TECHNOLOGY CAN BE A TOOL FOR—NOT ONLY A REWARD OF—DEVELOPMENT

Technology is not inherently good or bad—the outcome depends on how it is used. This Report is about how people can create and use technology to improve human lives, especially to reduce global poverty.

Some people argue that technology is a reward of development, making it inevitable that the digital divide follows the income divide. True, as incomes rise, people gain access to the benefits of technological advance. But many technologies are tools of human development that enable people to increase their incomes, live longer, be healthier, enjoy a better standard of living, participate more in their communities and lead more creative lives. From the earliest times, people have fashioned tools to address the challenges of existence, from war to health care to crop production (box 2.1). Technology is like education—it enables people to lift themselves out of poverty. Thus technology is a tool for, not just a reward of, growth and development.

Today's technological transformations are intertwined with another transformation—globalization—and together they are creating the network age

---

BOX 2.1

Technology and human identity

Technology has been at the heart of human progress since earliest times. Our prehuman ancestors fashioned sticks to reach for food, used leaves to sop up water and hurled stones in anger, just as chimpanzees do today. The first human species is named *Homo habilis*—the "handy man". Its fossils from some 2.5 million years ago lie with chipped pebbles, the first unequivocal stone tools. Early *Homo* may have used the perishable technologies of gourds to drink water and leather slings to carry infants. About half a million years ago, *Homo erectus* fashioned elegant leaf-shaped hand axes throughout Africa, Asia and Europe and was apparently using fire. Our own species, *Homo sapiens*—the "wise man" from some 40,000 years ago in Europe, the Middle East and Australia—made tools of stone, bone and antler as well as necklaces for adornment, and drew symbolic art on rock walls—technology in the service of ideas and communication.

Source: Jolly 2000.

FIGURE 2.1

Links between technology and human development

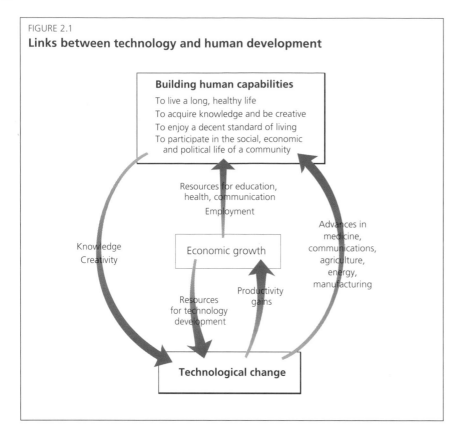

Building human capabilities
To live a long, healthy life
To acquire knowledge and be creative
To enjoy a decent standard of living
To participate in the social, economic and political life of a community

Resources for education, health, communication
Employment

Knowledge Creativity

Economic growth

Advances in medicine, communications, agriculture, energy, manufacturing

Resources for technology development

Productivity gains

Technological change

BOX 2.2

Modern science creates simple technology—oral rehydration therapy and vaccines adapted to village conditions

When oral rehydration therapy was developed at Bangladesh's International Centre for Diarrhoeal Disease Research, the *Lancet,* a leading medical journal, hailed it as possibly the most important medical discovery of the 20th century. Until then the only effective remedy for dehydration caused by diarrhoea was providing sterilized liquid through an intravenous drip—costing about $50 per child, far beyond the budgets, facilities and capacities of most developing country health centres. But scientists found that giving a child sips of a simple sugar-salt solution in the right proportions led to a 25-fold increase in the child's rate of absorption of the solution compared with water alone. During the 1980s packets of oral rehydration salts were manufactured by the hundreds of millions, with most selling for less than 10 cents apiece.

Adaptation to developing country conditions of vaccines for the killer communicable diseases—measles, rubella, whooping cough, diphtheria, tetanus,

tuberculosis—was another major breakthrough. The antigens to tackle these six diseases had long been known. But they required sterile conditions and a reliable cold chain—a system of well-maintained refrigerators and cold transport from the point of vaccine production to clinics and village health centres thousands of miles away. Important advances came with technological improvements: a polio vaccine that requires only a drop on the tongue, freeze-dried and more heat-stable vaccines that do not require refrigeration and the development of vaccine cocktails in a single shot.

For both oral rehydration therapy and new immunization methods, advances in technology had to go hand in hand with advances in organization. Massive campaigns were developed to spread awareness. Politicians, churches, teachers and non-governmental organizations were enlisted to underscore the facts and help organize the efforts.

Source: Jolly 2001; UNICEF 1991; WHO 1998.

Technological innovation affects human development in two ways (figure 2.1). First, it can directly enhance human capabilities. Many products—drought-tolerant plant varieties for farmers in uncertain climates, vaccines for infectious diseases, clean energy sources for cooking, Internet access for information and communications—directly improve people's health, nutrition, knowledge and living standards, and increase people's ability to participate more actively in the social, economic and political life of a community.

Second, technological innovation is a means to human development because of its impact on economic growth through the productivity gains it generates. It raises the crop yields of farmers, the output of factory workers and the efficiency of service providers and small businesses. It also creates new activities and industries—such as the information and communications technology sector—contributing to economic growth and employment creation.

Human development is also an important means to technology development. Technological innovation is an expression of human potential. Higher levels of education make especially powerful contributions to technology creation and diffusion. More scientists can undertake research and development, and better-educated farmers and factory workers can learn, master and use new techniques with greater ease and effectiveness. In addition, social and political freedom, participation and access to material resources create conditions that encourage people's creativity.

So, human development and technological advance can be mutually reinforcing, creating a virtuous circle. Technological innovations in agriculture, medicine, energy, manufacturing and communications were important—though not the only—factors behind the gains in human development and poverty eradication documented in chapter 1. These innovations broke barriers to progress, such as low incomes or institutional constraints, and made possible more rapid gains.

Survival and health. Medical breakthroughs such as immunizations and antibiotics resulted in faster gains in Latin America and East Asia in the 20th century than Europe achieved through better nutrition and sanitation in the 19th century. Human health and survival began to improve dramatically in both regions in the 1930s.[1] By the 1970s life expectancy at birth had climbed to more than 60 years, achieving in four decades an increase that took Europe a century and a half starting in the early 1800s.

The 1980s saw the impact of two new breakthroughs—oral rehydration therapy and vaccines better adapted to conditions in developing countries. These technologies, diffused through a major global campaign, enabled major reductions in child mortality (box 2.2). In developing countries deaths from major childhood diseases and from diarrhoea-related illnesses were cut by about 3 million between 1980 and 1990—an especially impressive achievement given that it came during that "lost decade" of economic growth, when income growth was stagnant or negative (figure 2.2).[2] Moreover, under-five mortality rates were cut by nearly half between 1970 and 1999, from 170 to 90 per 1,000.

The importance of technology is quantified in a recent World Bank study showing that technical progress accounted for 40–50% of mortality reductions between 1960 and 1990—making technology a more important source of gains than higher incomes or higher education levels among women (table 2.1).[3]

Food production and nutrition. Technological progress has played a similar role in accelerating food production. It took nearly 1,000 years for wheat yields in England to increase from 0.5 tonnes per hectare to 2, but only 40 years to go from 2 tonnes per hectare to 6.[4] Starting in 1960 a green revolution of plant breeding, fertilizer use, better seeds and water control transformed land and labour productivity around the world. This had dynamic ef-

fects on human development: increased food production and reduced food prices eliminated much of the undernutrition and chronic famine in Asia, Latin America and the Arab States. Because the poorest families rely on agriculture for their livelihood and spend half their incomes on food, this also contributed to huge declines in income poverty.

Participation. Like the printing press of earlier centuries, the telephone, radio, television and fax of the 20th century opened up communications, reducing isolation and enabling people to be better informed and to participate in decisions that affect their lives. Tied to these technologies is the free media, a pillar of all functioning democracies. The advent of the fax machine in the 1980s enabled much more rapid popular mobilization both nationally and globally.

Employment and economic growth. In the 1970s the acquisition and adaptation of manufacturing technology brought rapid gains in employment and incomes to the Republic of Korea, Malaysia and Singapore. The industrial revolution was triggered by technological change, and economists argue that technological progress plays a pivotal role in sustained long-term economic growth.[5] Cross-country studies suggest that technological change accounts for a large portion of differences in growth rates.[6]

TODAY'S TECHNOLOGICAL TRANSFORMATIONS COMBINE WITH GLOBALIZATION TO CREATE THE NETWORK AGE

Today's technological advances are faster (Moore's law) and more fundamental (break-

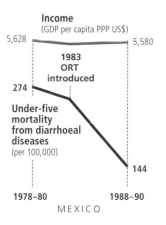

FIGURE 2.2
Oral rehydration therapy reduces child mortality without income increase

Income
(GDP per capita PPP US$)
5,628 — 5,580
1983 ORT introduced
274
Under-five mortality from diarrhoeal diseases
(per 100,000)
144
1978–80   1988–90
MEXICO

Source: Gutierrez and others 1996; World Bank 2001q.

TABLE 2.1
Technology as a source of mortality reduction, 1960–90
(percent)

Improvement in	Contribution of gains in income	Contribution of gains in education level of adult females	Contribution of gains in technical progress
Under-five mortality rate	17	38	45
Female adult mortality rate	20	41	39
Male adult mortality rate	25	27	49
Female life expectancy at birth	19	32	49

Source: Wang and others 1999.

throughs in genetics). They are driving down costs (computing and communications) at a pace never before seen. Leading these transformations are the accelerated developments in information and communications technology, biotechnology and just-emerging nanotechnology.

INFORMATION AND COMMUNICATIONS TECHNOLOGY—CREATING NETWORKS WITH GROWING REACH, FALLING COSTS

Information and communications technology involves innovations in microelectronics, computing (hardware and software), telecommunications and opto-electronics—microprocessors, semiconductors, fibre optics. These innovations enable the processing and storage of enormous amounts of information, along with rapid distribution of information through communication networks. Moore's law predicts the doubling of computing power every 18–24 months due to the rapid evolution of microprocessor technology. Gilder's law predicts the doubling of communications power every six months—a bandwidth explosion—due to advances in fibre-optic network technologies.[7] Both are accompanied by huge reductions in costs and massive increases in speed and quantity (feature 2.1).

In 2001 more information can be sent over a single cable in a second than in 1997 was sent over the entire Internet in a month.[8] The cost of transmitting a trillion bits of information from Boston to Los Angeles has fallen from $150,000 in 1970 to 12 cents today. A three-minute phone call from New York to London that in 1930 cost more than $300 (in today's prices) costs less than 20 cents today.[9] E-mailing a 40-page document from Chile to Kenya costs less than 10 cents, faxing it about $10, sending it by courier $50.[10]

Linking computing devices and allowing them to communicate with each other creates networked information systems based on a common protocol. Individuals, households and institutions are linked in processing and executing a huge number of instructions in imperceptible time spans. This radically alters access to information and the structure of communication

—extending the networked reach to all corners of the world.

BIOTECHNOLOGY—TRANSFORMING LIFE SCIENCES

Modern biotechnology—recombinant DNA technology—is transforming life sciences. The power of genetics can now be used to engineer the attributes of plants and other organisms, creating the potential for huge advances, particularly in agriculture and medicine. The cloning of Dolly the sheep and the mapping of the human genome open scientific frontiers and will transform technology development for years to come (feature 2.2). Genetics is now the basis of life sciences, with much research in pharmaceuticals and plant breeding now biotechnology based.

AND PERHAPS SOON, NANOTECHNOLOGY

To these two new technologies may soon be added a third, nanotechnology. Nanotech is evolving from scientific breakthroughs enabling engineering and science at the molecular level. (A nanometer is one-billionth of a meter.) Nanotechnologies rearrange atoms to create new molecular structures. Few areas of human activity will not be touched by nanotech. Nanoscale robots will heal injured human tissue, remove obstructions in the circulatory system and take over the function of subcellular organelles. Solar nanotechnologies will provide energy to an ever-growing population. In the bionic world, where nanotech and biotech merge, look forward to biocomputers and biosensors able to monitor everything from plant regulators to political rallies. For now, research on nanotechnology remains limited relative to other technologies—some $500 million a year in the United States in 2000, with Japan and Europe following—but investment has been almost doubling each year.[11]

TECHOLOGICAL TRANSFORMATIONS AND GLOBALIZATION—MUTUALLY REINFORCING

Today's technological transformations are intertwined with another major historic shift—

The cost of transmitting a trillion bits of information from Boston to Los Angeles has fallen from $150,000 in 1970 to 12 cents today

economic globalization that is rapidly unifying world markets. The two processes are mutually reinforcing. The late 20th century integration of world markets was driven by trade liberalization and other dramatic policy changes around the world—privatization, the fall of communism in the former Soviet Union. The new tools of information and communications technology reinforced and accelerated the process.

Globalization propels technological progress with the competition and incentives of the global marketplace and the world's financial and scientific resources. And the global marketplace is technology based, with technology a major factor in market competition.

High-tech manufacturing has been the fastest-growing area of world trade (table 2.2), and now accounts for one-fifth of the total. A study of 68 economies accounting for 97% of global industrial activity shows that in 1985–97 high-tech production grew more than twice as fast as total production in all but one country.[12]

FROM THE INDUSTRIAL TO THE NETWORK AGE—A HISTORIC SHIFT

Structures of production and other activities have been reorganized into networks that span the world. In the industrial age—with its high costs of information access, communications and transportation—businesses and organizations were vertically integrated. In the network age, with the costs of communications and information down to almost zero, horizontal networks make sense. Production is increasingly organized among separate players—subcontractors, suppliers, laboratories, management consultants, education and research

institutes, marketing research firms, distributors. Their complex interactions, with each playing a niche role, create the value chains that drive the technology-based global economy.

The new age is giving rise to global networks in many areas of activity. When these networks reach a critical mass of members and interactions, they become an important new force in shaping the path and spread of technology.

• Scientific research and innovation—the original networked communication between universities that breathed life into the Internet—is increasingly collaborative between institutions and countries. From 1995–97, scientists in the United States co-authored articles with scientists from 173 other countries; scientists in Brazil with 114, in Kenya with 81, in Algeria 59.[13]

• Production—global corporations, often headquartered in North America, Europe or Japan, but with research facilities in several countries and outsourced production worldwide, drawing many new countries into creating their global value chains. In 1999 in Costa Rica, Malaysia and Singapore, high-tech exports exceeded 40% of the total.

• E-business—only now emerging as a future commerce network, business-to-business e-commerce is projected to rise.

• Diaspora—skyrocketing demand for information and communications technology personnel makes top scientists and technologists globally mobile. When they come from developing countries, their global dispersal creates diaspora that can become valuable networks of finance, business contacts and skill transfer for their home country.

• Advocacy—the globalization of civil society concerns—from Jubilee 2000 to the ban-

The new age is giving rise to global networks in many areas of activity— an important new force in shaping the path and spread of technology

TABLE 2.2
High-tech products dominate export expansion
(average annual percentage growth in exports, 1985–98)

Area	High-tech manufactures	Medium-tech manufactures	Low-tech manufactures	Resource-based manufactures	Primary products
World	13.1	9.3	9.7	7.0	3.4
Developing countries[a]	21.4	14.3	11.7	6.0	1.3
High-income OECD[b]	11.3	8.5	8.5	7.0	4.4

a. Includes Eastern Europe and the Commonwealth of Independent States.
b. Includes Cyprus, Israel and Malta.
Source: Lall 2001.

THE PROMISE OF TODAY'S TECHNOLOGICAL TRANSFORMATIONS FOR HUMAN DEVELOPMENT

INFORMATION AND COMMUNICATIONS TECHNOLOGY

Information technology timeline

3000 BC Abacus developed

1823–40 Automatic calculating machine designed by Charles Babbage

1946 First high-speed electronic computer, ENIAC, runs a thousand times faster than previous computing machines

1947 Transistor invented by Gordon Bell

1959 Integrated circuit invented by Robert Noyce, putting an entire electronic circuit on a tiny silicon chip

1966 First disk storage introduced by IBM

1971 Microprocessor invented by Marcian Hoff

1975 First personal computers introduced—programmable machines small and inexpensive enough to be used by individuals

1980 QDOS (Quick and Dirty Operating System) introduced by Seattle Computer Products, later renamed MS-DOS by Microsoft

1984 Macintosh introduced by Apple Computers, setting the standard for point and click graphical environments. Windows operating system (rudimentary version) followed in 1985

1980s Mobile computing (laptops) introduced

1993 Palm Pilot developed and marketed—the emergence of sophisticated handheld computing devices

1994 Disk drive with transfer rate of more than 100 megabytes a second introduced by Seagate

1995 Digital Versatile Disk (DVD) standardized, capable of storing more than eight times the information of a compact disc (CD)

2000 AMD Gigahertz microprocessor introduced

The future research agenda: natural language input and output, artificial intelligence, wearable computers, nanocomputing, distributed systems computing

The rapid growth of the Internet
Internet hosts (thousands)

	1995	2000
Brazil	26.8	1,203.1
China	10.6	159.6
Korea, Rep. of	38.1	863.6
Macedonia, TFYR	0.1	3.8
Uganda	0.1	0.9
Ukraine	2.4	59.4

Rapid advances in two technologies—digital storage and processing of information (information) and satellite and optical fibre transmission of information (communications)—are creating new and faster ways of storing, handling, distributing and accessing information. More than that, these advances are dramatically lowering costs.

BENEFITS FOR HUMAN DEVELOPMENT ARE JUST BEGINNING

These new technologies dramatically increase access to information and communications, breaking barriers to knowledge and participation. But can these tools reach poor people? The potential is only beginning to be explored. Initiatives are mushrooming and hint at tremendous possibilities.

Political participation is being redefined by the creative use of two-way communications. In the Philippines an electronic advocacy network was set up in early 2001 in response to the impeachment trial of former President Joseph Estrada, collecting more than 150,000 petition signatures and coordinating a letter-writing campaign that targeted senators to vote with their consciences, not with their vested interests. In Honduras an organization of small-scale fishermen has sent Congress a video of the illegal destruction of their mangroves by politically powerful commercial farmers, raising awareness of and protesting against the loss of their livelihoods and habitat. In the future, virtual committee rooms could allow citizens to testify on various issues, further expanding the Internet's possibilities for enhancing participation.

Greater transparency in planning and transactions is making markets and institutions work better. In Morocco the ministries of finance and planning have used information and communications technology to make the budget process more efficient, creating a common platform to share data on tax revenue, auditing and spending management. The time required to prepare a budget has been halved, and budgets better reflect actual revenue and spending. In the Indian state of Gujarat, dairy farmers are paid based on the weight and fat content of their milk, which can be tested instantly using low-cost equipment. Such transparent and accurate measures reduce the risk of underpayment, and farmers' accounts are matched with databases of their cattle, keeping a record of inoculation requirements—helping cooperatives to better manage input requirements and veterinary services.

Income Inventive use of the Internet is increasing incomes in developing countries. In Pondicherry, India the MS Swaminathan Research Foundation has set up rural information centres for local communication and Internet access using solar and electric power and wired and wireless communications. Farmers are getting information such as market prices, enabling them to negotiate better with intermediaries. Fishermen can download satellite images that indicate where fish shoals are. Internet connections with other villages have encouraged local dialogue on farming techniques, microcredit management, business

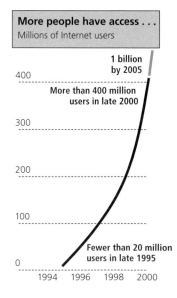

More people have access . . .
Millions of Internet users

1 billion by 2005

More than 400 million users in late 2000

Fewer than 20 million users in late 1995

. . . to more information . . .
Number of Websites

20 million Websites in late 2000

First large-scale cyber war coincides with Serbia-Kosovo conflict

First banner ads appear on hotwired.com

First Internet shopping malls

Fewer than 200 Websites in mid-1993

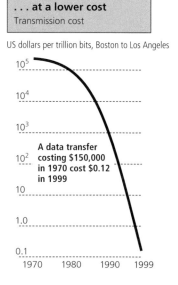

. . . at a lower cost
Transmission cost

US dollars per trillion bits, Boston to Los Angeles

A data transfer costing $150,000 in 1970 cost $0.12 in 1999

Communications technology timeline

1833 Morse Code developed by Samuel Morse, allowing the transmission of signals through wires. First telegraph introduced in 1837

1876 Telephone introduced by Alexander Graham Bell

1895 Wireless transmission and reception demonstrated by Gugllelmo Marconi

1920s Television experimenters and demonstrators shown around the world

1947 Mathematical theory of communications established by Claude Shannon, providing the basic theory for all modern digital communications

1966 Satellite telecommunications developed (Telestar)

1977 First mobile telecommunications network established by Ericsson in Saudi Arabia

1977 First fibre optic communication system installed by AT&T and GTE

1979 First computer modem introduced by Hayes

1982 Basic networking protocol adopted as a standard, leading to one of the first definitions of the Internet

1989 Concept of the World Wide Web developed by Cern

1993 Mosaic introduced—the first popular graphical interface for the World Wide Web

1995 Public Internet with high-speed backbone service linking supercomputing centres established by the US National Science Foundation

1995 MP3, Real Audio and MPEG enable Internet distribution of audio and video content services such as Napster and Real Player

1997 Wireless Application Protocol (WAP) developed

The future High-speed connection to every home, Internet coupling with game devices, merger of cellular phones and personal digital assistants

Source: Fortier and Trang 2001; Chandrasekhar 2001; Hijab 2001; Tamesis 2001; UNDP, Accenture and Markle Foundation 2001; Zakon 2000, ITU 2001b; Nua Publish 2001; Cox and Alm 1999; Archive Builders 2000; Universitiet Leiden 1999; W3C 2000; Bell Labs 2000; Bignerds 2001; Telia Mobile 2000.

and education opportunities, traditional medicine and religious events. About one-third of the users are from assetless households, and about 18% are women.

Grameen Telecom provides telephones throughout Bangladesh, allowing individuals, schools and health centres to get the information they need easily and cheaply. Studies suggest that a single call provides real savings of 3–10% of the average family's monthly income, benefiting poor households that use village phones for calls that replace the need to collect information through more expensive channels.

Health Where health problems are rooted in lack of information, new solutions are emerging. In Ginnack, a remote island on the Gambia river, nurses use a digital camera to record patients' symptoms. The pictures are sent electronically to a nearby town to be diagnosed by a local doctor, or sent to the United Kingdom if a specialist's opinion is required.

The Healthnet Project is a network of networks launched in 1989 for health care professionals—especially in remote areas—in Africa, Asia and Latin America. It enables them to procure equipment efficiently, cooperate with medical institutions worldwide and provide information on emerging outbreaks. Nepal's Healthnet has 150 user points around the country, reaching 500 health professionals and getting 300 hits a day on its Website.

These examples are just the beginning. Tapping the potential of these new technologies will depend on adaptations to the conditions in developing countries, especially for poor users. Much will depend on innovations—technological, institutional and entrepreneurial—to create low-cost, easy to use devices and to set up access through public or market centres with affordable products.

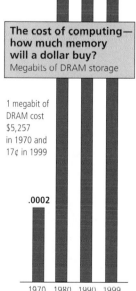

Petronas Tower
Tallest building in the world
Kuala Lumpur, Malaysia

1999
5.9 mb

1990
.13 mb

.002

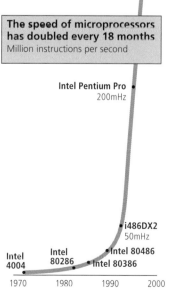

The cost of computing— how much memory will a dollar buy?
Megabits of DRAM storage

1 megabit of DRAM cost $5,257 in 1970 and 17¢ in 1999

.0002

1970 1980 1990 1999

The speed of microprocessors has doubled every 18 months
Million instructions per second

Intel Pentium III
500mHz

Intel Pentium II
333mHz

Intel Pentium Pro
200mHz

i486DX2
50mHz

Intel 80486

Intel 80386

Intel 80286

Intel 4004

1970 1980 1990 2000

THE PROMISE OF TODAY'S TECHNOLOGICAL TRANSFORMATIONS FOR HUMAN DEVELOPMENT

BIOTECHNOLOGY

Biotechnology timeline

1856 Gene established as the functional unit of inheritance by Gregor Mendel

1871 DNA discovered by Frederich Miescher

1909 The word gene introduced by Wilhelm Jorgenson, replacing Mendelian factors

1944 Oswald Avery, Colin MacLeod and Mclyn MacCartey determine that genes are encoded by DNA

1953 A structure for DNA—the double helix—introduced by James Watson and Francis Crick

1960s Proteins responsible for cutting DNA (restriction enzymes) discovered by Werner Arber, Hamilton Smith and Daniel Smith

1972 First recombinant DNA technology constructed by Paul Berg

1973 Herb Boyer and Stanley Cohen are the first to use a plasmid to clone DNA, allowing the replication and use of recombinant DNA modules

1982 First biotechnology drug released for use

1982 First transgenic plants introduced experimentally

1996 First transgenic plants available commercially

1996 Dolly the sheep cloned at the Roslin Institute, Edinburgh

2000 Celera Genomics and the US National Institute of Health's Human Genome Project announce the assembling of a working draft of the human genome

Biotech information

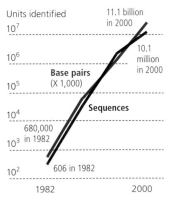

Recombinant DNA technology—a group of technologies that enhances our ability to manipulate genetic material—is often what is referred to as biotechnology. Since the discoveries of the 1960s, the introduction of recombinant DNA molecules into organisms has become more efficient and effective—making it possible to use the power of genetics to engineer the attributes of an organism. More precise techniques have emerged, enabling the genetic modification of most crops and food plants. Biotechnology has also been applied to seemingly intractable health issues, determining which genes are responsible for creating or enabling disease processes, how these genes control these processes and what might be done to stop them.

BENEFITS FOR HUMAN DEVELOPMENT ARE JUST BEGINNING

Breakthrough applications in medicine and agriculture have huge potential for accelerating human development. But this potential will be truly tapped only if biotechnology is used to address the key health and agriculture challenges of poor countries—tropical diseases and the crops and livestock of the marginal ecological zones left behind by the green revolution. And only if this is done with a systematic approach to assessing and managing risks of harm to human health, environment and social equity.

In health, pharmaceutical companies are moving from drug discovery and development based on medicinal chemistry to designing and developing drugs based on information provided by genomics and related technologies. Nearly 300 biopharmaceuticals have been approved for use or are being reviewed by the US Food and Drug Administration. The genomics-based pharmaceutical market is projected to grow from $2.2 billion in 1999 to $8.2 billion in 2004. These products offer treatment for diseases that was not possible before. Insulin as a tool to fight diabetes was made possible through recombinant DNA technology, as was a vaccine for hepatitis B. But that is just the beginning. Biotechnological knowledge has the potential to develop better treatment and vaccines for AIDS, malaria, cancer, heart disease and nervous disorders. Gene therapy and antisense technologies will forever change the treatment of disease by actually curing diseases rather than treating symptoms. Five gene therapy drugs for various forms of cancer are expected to hit the market by 2005. Researchers at Cornell University in the United States have created transgenic tomatoes and bananas that contain a hepatitis B vaccine. Just one dried banana chip or one portion of tomato paste inside a wafer contains enough of the needed medication to act as a dose—costing less that one cent to make, in contrast to the usual $15. PowderJect Pharmaceuticals, a British company, has created DNA-based vaccines with a needle-free way to deliver them. The handheld device pumps a microscopic powdered vaccine painlessly into the skin in a jet of gas, making it far easier and safer to use than syringes and eliminating the need for refrigeration. Biotechnical knowledge could also be used to modify organisms that transmit diseases—for example, creating the "perfect" mosquito, unable to carry malaria.

In agriculture, plant breeding promises to generate higher yields and resistance to drought, pests and disease. Traditional cross-breeding takes a long time, typically 8–12 years. Biotechnology speeds the process of producing crops with altered traits by using a specific genetic trait from any plant and moving it into the genetic code of any other plant. More significantly, the modification of plants is no longer restricted by the characteristics of that species. Cacti genes responsible for tolerating drought can be used to help food crops survive drought. Dwarfing genes used to increase cereal yields have been shown to have the same effect on other crops, so dwarfing could increase yields in crops previously unable to benefit from these genes. Genetic control of the rice yellow mottle virus shows what transgenics can do where conventional approaches failed. And farmers in China have been able to control the cotton bollworm, which can no longer be controlled by chemicals or host plant protection, by growing cotton expressing the Bacillus thuringiensis toxin.

New treatment for livestock diseases appears to be the most significant area for product development. Diagnostic tests and recombinant DNA vaccines for rinderpest, cowdriosis (heartwater), theileriosis (East coast fever) and foot-and-mouth disease are reportedly ready for large-scale testing or product development.

Source: Cohen 2001; Bloom, River Path Associates and Fang 2001; CDI 2001; BCC Research 2000; Biopharma 2001; Powderjet 2001; Doran 2001; NCBI 2001.

ning of land mines—puts advantage on globally networked advocacy. Technology concerns are likewise addressed with countervailing pressure and alternative opinions, from access to HIV/AIDS drugs and intellectual property rules to the risks of genetically modified foods.

THE NEW TECHNOLOGICAL AGE BRINGS NEW POSSIBILITIES—FOR STILL GREATER ADVANCES IN HUMAN DEVELOPMENT

Today's technological advances can accelerate human development in many areas.

Biotechnology provides a way forward in medicine and agriculture where earlier methods were less successful. Designing new drugs and treatments based on genomics and related technologies offers potential for tackling the major health challenges facing poor countries and people—possibly leading, for example, to vaccines for malaria and HIV/AIDS. Genomics can speed up plant breeding and drive the development of new crop varieties with greater drought and disease resistance, less environmental stress and more nutritional value. Biotechnology offers the only or the best 'tool of choice' for marginal ecological zones—left behind by the green revolution but home to more than half of the world's poorest people, dependent on agriculture and livestock.

There is a long way to go before biotechnology's potential is mobilized. Transgenic crops increased from 2 million hectares planted in 1996 to 44 million hectares in 2000. But 98% of that is in just three countries—Argentina, Canada and the United States.[14] Moreover, all governments must devise new institutional and scientific policies to manage the health, environmental and social risks of this new innovation (chapter 3).

Applications in *information and communications technology* are farther ahead of those in biotechnology. The *Internet* has grown exponentially, from 16 million users in 1995 to more than 400 million users in 2000—and to an expected 1 billion users in 2005.[15] Connectivity is rising at spectacular rates in Europe, Japan, the United States and many developing countries (see feature 2.1). In Latin America Internet use is growing by more than 30% a year—though that still means that only 12% of individuals will be connected by 2005. Broader expansion is limited by low household incomes.[16]

Connecting a major portion of the population will be a challenge in developing regions. But the digital divide need not be permanent if technological adaptations and institutional innovations expand access. Creativity and entrepreneurship in Brazil, India, Thailand, Niger and elsewhere have already developed software for illiterate users and low-cost, solar-powered wireless devices (box 2.3). Community access—public and private—is proliferating in urban and rural settings. From South Africa to Bangladesh, innovations like prepaid phone cards are expanding access to information and communications technology. Multiple uses are made from health to education to political participation, not to mention raising the incomes of poor families.

What is new and different about information and communications technology as a means for eradicating poverty in the 21st century? First, it is a pervasive input to almost all human activities: it has possibilities for use in an almost endless range of locations and purposes. Second, information and communications technology breaks barriers to human development in at least three ways not possible before:

• *Breaking barriers to knowledge.* Access to information is as central as education to building human capabilities. While education de-

The digital divide need not be permanent if technological adaptations and institutional innovations expand access

---

BOX 2.3

Breaking barriers to Internet access

The World Wide Web is too expensive for millions of people in developing countries, partly because of the cost of computers that are the standard entry point to the Web: in January 2001 the cheapest Pentium III computer was $700—hardly affordable for low-income community access points. Further, the text-based interface of the Internet puts it out of reach for illiterate people.

To overcome these barriers, academics at the Indian Institute of Science and engineers at the Bangalore-based design company Encore Software designed a handheld Internet appliance for less than $200. Based on the Linux open source operating system, the first version of the Simputer will provide Internet and email access in local languages, with touch-screen functions and microbanking applications. Future versions promise speech recognition and text-to-speech software for illiterate users. The intellectual property rights have been transferred for free to the non-profit Simputer Trust, which is licensing the technology to manufacturers at a nominal fee—and the device is soon to be launched.

Source: PC World 2000; Simputer Trust 2000; Kirkman 2001.

velops cognitive skills, information gives content to knowledge. The Internet and the World Wide Web can deliver information to the poor and the rich alike.

• *Breaking barriers to participation.* Poor people and communities are often isolated and lack means to take collective action. Global Internet communications have powered many global civil society movements in recent years: the agreement to ban land mines, initiatives to provide debt relief to poor countries and efforts to provide HIV/AIDS drugs in poor countries. The Internet is just as powerful in mobilizing people locally. E-mail campaigns against corruption influenced Korea's 1999 elections and gave rise to the recent movement that deposed Philippine President Joseph Estrada. The world over, citizens are increasingly able to use the Internet to hold governments more accountable.

• *Breaking barriers to economic opportunity.* Despite the recent drops in technology stocks and the demise of many dot-coms, information and communications technology and related industries are among the most dynamic sectors of the global economy (box 2.4). They offer the potential for developing countries to expand exports, create good jobs and diversify their economies. The information and communications technology sector requires less initial investment in capital and infrastructure than do more traditional sectors—which may explain why high-tech industries are growing faster than medium-tech industries in developing countries. Moreover, such industries are labour-intensive, providing new jobs and wages for educated workers. Wages are high for Indian software professionals, but competitive in the global market (box 2.5).[17]

What does the future hold? Global spending on information and communications technology is projected to grow from $2.2 trillion in 1999 to $3 trillion by 2003—providing many niche opportunities for service providers in developing countries.[18] There are now about 2.5 billion unique, publicly accessible Web pages on the Internet, and 7.3 million new ones are added every day.[19] With Internet access through wireless devices, including mobile phones, expected to outstrip personal computer access by 2005,[20] people and businesses in developing countries will become increasingly able to access valuable Internet-based information. Global business to consumer e-commerce is projected to grow from $25 billion in 1999 to $233 billion by 2004;[21] business to business e-commerce projections range from $1.2 to $10 trillion by 2003.[22]

Developing countries that can develop the requisite infrastructure can participate in new global business models of intermediation, business process outsourcing and value chain integration. In developing countries, as the user base expands, costs fall and technologies are adapted to local needs, the potential of information and communications technology will be limited only by human imagination and political will.

BOX 2.4

The new economy and growth paradoxes

Proponents of the new economy claim that today's technological revolution has created a new growth paradigm that will allow US GDP to keep expanding at well over 4% a year—a new engine of higher long-term growth comparable to the railway or electricity. But a dismissive contingent, bolstered by the downturn in dot-coms and NASDAQ share prices, claims that increases in productivity have been confined to the computer sector, helped along by the economic cycle—and that computers and the Internet do not rate with the industrial revolution. Has everything changed, or nothing? The reality is that the growth of the new economy has not defied the laws of economics (overinvestment still overheats the economy). But it has contributed to the recent rapid growth of the US economy.

What has happened? First, the fast growth of the computer sector—hardware, software, the Internet—has directly contributed to US growth, accounting for about a quarter of output growth in the 1990s. Second, since the mid-1990s the use of computers and the Internet has affected other parts of the economy, raising productivity in traditional manufacturing and services. After 20 years of annual productivity growth averaging about 1%, since 1995 productivity growth has risen as much as 3% a year—and has sustained that level even as the economy slowed in 2000–01.

This recent US experience seems to resolve the so-called productivity paradox that led Robert Solow to remark in the late 1980s, "you can see the computer age everywhere but in the productivity statistics". But that is not the case in all OECD countries. In much of Europe and in Japan productivity growth has not accelerated.

Why? Some have argued that the benefits of the computer and the Internet come only when they reach, say, 50% penetration and begin reducing costs in other parts of the economy. That rate was reached in the United States only in 1999. It is not the number of computers that triggers higher productivity but overall change in the way the economy works—whether labour is mobile from one location and type of job to another, whether some businesses fail while others start up, whether investors shift their money from one new idea to another, whether relationships among firms and their traditional suppliers break up and realign, whether organizations change. In a recent US survey a quarter of firms reported that they had made organizational changes in response to the emergence of the Internet.

Source: President of the United States 2001; Bassanini, Scarpetta and Visco 2000; Solow 1987; Jorgenson and Stiroh 2000; David 1999; OECD 2000a; *The Economist* 2000.

The network age is changing how technologies are created and diffused—in five ways

Several contours of this new age must be understood if poor countries and poor people are to take advantage of the new opportunities.

First, skills matter more than ever in today's more competitive global market. Technology transfer and diffusion are not easy. Developing countries cannot simply import and apply knowledge from outside by obtaining equipment, seeds and pills. Not every country needs to develop cutting-edge technologies, but every country needs domestic capacity to identify technology's potential benefits and to adapt new technology to its needs and constraints. To use a new technology, firms and farmers must be able to learn and develop new skills with ease. In Thailand four years of education triples the chance that a farmer will use fertilizer effectively. In India educated farmers are more likely to use irrigation and improved seeds. In this era of rapid technological advance, mastering new technology is a continuous process. Without continuous upgrading of skills, countries cannot stay competitive (chapter 4).

Second, new global rules giving value to technology also matter more. New rules endorsed by almost all countries have brought tighter intellectual property protection worldwide. These raise the market value of technology, increasing incentives to invest in research and development. But they also imply new choices for developing countries in accessing technology and shifts in costs for consumers (chapter 5).

Third, the private sector is leading global research and development, and has much of the finance, knowledge and personnel for technological innovation. Among most OECD countries the private sector finances 50–60% of research and development. Firms play an even bigger role in research and development in Ireland, Japan, Korea and Sweden. In most countries corporations implement more research than they fund, indicating that there is some government funding of corporate research and development. Universities typically undertake 15–20% of national research and development,

while public research institutions account for about 10% in North America and the Nordic countries, slightly more than 15% in the European Union (table 2.3).[23]

New forms of private financing of high-risk research are part of the story. Small, technology-based startups carry high risks, making them unlikely candidates for conventional financing. Venture capital, central to the technology boom in the United States and backing new technology companies in Europe and Japan, allows the market to pick a winner. It is emerging elsewhere—including China, India, Israel and Singapore (table 2.4).

Corporations dominate research and development in the information and communi-

---

BOX 2.5

India's export opportunities in the new economy

What real promises does the new economy hold for developing countries? The explosive expansion of global information and communications technology has triggered new opportunities for niche activities. In India the industry generated 330 billion rupiah ($7.7 billion) in 1999, 15 times the level in 1990, and exports rose from $150 million in 1990 to nearly $4 billion in 1999. One study estimates that this could rise to $50 billion by 2008, leading information technology to account for 30% of India's exports and 7.5% of its GDP. Employment in the software industry is projected to rise from 180,000 in 1998 to 2.2 million in 2008, to account for 8% of India's formal employment.

Information and communications technology has created new outsourcing opportunities by enabling services to be provided in one country and delivered in another. Delivered by telecommunication or data networks, the services include credit card administration, insurance claims, business payrolls and customer, financial and human resource management. The global outsourcing market is worth more than $100 billion, with 185 Fortune 500 companies outsourcing their software requirements in India alone. India now has 1,250 companies exporting software.

India shows why public policy is important. By providing education for information technology—India's English-language technical colleges turn out more than 73,000 graduates a year—and investing in infrastructure (especially high-speed links and international gateways with sufficient bandwidth), the government has ensured India's place in the new economy. These efforts will deliver long-term benefits for human development and equitable economic growth.

Source: Landler 2001; Reuters 2001; Chandrasekhar 2001.

TABLE 2.3

The private sector leads technology creation
(percentage of research and development spending, 1995)

Source	North America	European Union	Nordic countries
Private sector financing	59	53	59
Private sector carrying out	71	62	67
Universities carrying out	16	21	23
Public sector carrying out	10	16	10

Note: Excludes research and development by non-profit organizations.
Source: Lall 2001.

cations technology and biotechnology that matter so much for human development. Worldwide, the pharmaceutical and biotechnology industries spent $39 billion on research and development in 1998. Research-based pharmaceutical companies in the United States invested $24 billion in 1999, increasing to $26.4 billion in 2000. Since the mid-1990s the top 20 pharmaceutical companies have doubled their spending on research and development. If that trend continues, average spending per company could rise to $2.5 billion by 2005.[24]

Fourth, a global labour market has emerged for top technology professionals. Propelled by skill shortages in Europe, Japan and the United States, such workers are increasingly mobile across countries. In 2000 the United States approved legislation allowing 195,000 more work visas each year for skilled professionals. Of the 81,000 visas approved between October 1999 and February 2000, 40% were for individuals from India and more than half were for computer-related occupations, a sixth for sciences and engineering.[25] A secondary effect has emerged: a new kind of business or brain diaspora. A strong link between Silicon Valley and Bangalore is built on the Indian diaspora in economic networks as they invest at home, but is also facilitating contacts for market access.

Fifth, startup companies, research labs, and financiers and corporations are converging in new global hubs of innovation, creating a dynamic environment that brings together know-how, finance and opportunity. Top scientists and eager entrepreneurs from around the world congregate in these hubs, attracting investors. *Wired* magazine has identified 46 top hubs and ranked them by importance and vitality based on the presence of corporate offices, venture capitalists, business startups and universities and research labs.[26] The United States has 13 hubs, Europe has 16, Asia 9, South America 2, Africa 2, Australia 2, Canada 1 and Israel 1. Other hubs may soon make the list—Hyderabad in India or Beijing and Shanghai in China.

THE OPPORTUNITIES OF THE NETWORK AGE EXIST IN A WORLD OF UNEVEN TECHNOLOGICAL CAPACITY

The uneven diffusion of information and communications technology—the digital divide—has caught the attention of world leaders. Bridging this divide is now a global objective. But the uneven diffusion of technology is nothing new (feature 2.3). There have long been huge differences among countries. As a result the world's 200 or so countries face the challenges of human development in the network age starting from very different points. The technology achievement index introduced in this Report presents a snapshot of each country's average achievements in creating and diffusing technology and in building human skills to master new innovations (see map 2.1, p. 45; and annex 2.1, p. 46).

In addition to the differences across countries, the index reveals considerable disparities within countries. Consider India, home to one of the most dynamic global hubs—Bangalore, which *Wired* rated 11th among the 46 hubs. Yet India ranks 63rd in the technology achievement index, falling among the lower end of dynamic adopters. Why? Because of huge variations in technological achievement among Indian states. The country has the world's seventh largest number of scientists and engineers, some 140,000 in 1994.[27] Yet in 1999 mean years of schooling were only 5.1 years and adult illiteracy was 44%.

The uneven diffusion of technology is nothing new—there have long been huge differences among countries

TABLE 2.4
Venture capital spreads across the world
(millions of current US dollars in investment)

Country or area	1995	2000
United States	4,566	103,170
United Kingdom	19	2,937
Japan	21	1,665
Germany	13	1,211
France	8	1,124
Hong Kong, China (SAR)	245	769
Singapore	5	651
Sweden	—	560
Israel	8	474
India	3	342
Finland	—	217
China	—	84
Korea, Rep. of	1	65
Philippines	2	9
South Africa	—	3

Note: Data for Finland and Sweden represent private equity.
Source: Thomson Financial Data Services 2001.

The technology achievement index focusses on three dimensions at the country level:

• Creating new products and processes through research and development.

• Using new technologies—and old—in production and consumption.

• Having the skills for technological learning and innovation.

TECHNOLOGY CREATION

New invention and product development, mostly the result of systematic investments in research and development, are carried out almost exclusively in high-income OECD countries and a handful of developing countries in Asia and Latin America.[28] OECD countries, with 14% of the world's people, accounted for 86% of the 836,000 patent applications filed in 1998 and 85% of the 437,000 scientific and technical journal articles published worldwide.[29] These countries also invest more in both absolute and relative terms—an average of 2.4% of their GDP in research and development, compared with 0.6% in South Asia (annex table A.2.2). Innovation also means ownership. Of worldwide royalty and license fees in 1999, 54% went to the United States and 12% went to Japan.[30]

Still, this picture of concentration in OECD countries masks developments and dynamism in many developing countries. There are hubs of innovation in Brazil, India, South Africa, Tunisia and elsewhere, and several other Asian and Latin American countries are increasingly engaged in technology creation. Brazil is developing low-cost computers, Thailand has developed treatments for dengue fever and malaria (see box 5.2) and Viet Nam has developed treatment for malaria using traditional knowledge (box 2.6). Argentina, China, Korea, Mexico and Thailand are filing substantial numbers of patents. In Korea spending on research and development amounts to 2.8% of GDP, more than in any other country except Sweden (table 2.5).

TECHNOLOGY USE

The use of new and old technologies is, not surprisingly, uneven—an obvious function, among other things, of income. What is surprising is the rapid diffusion of new technologies in some countries and the diverse trends among them.

In Hong Kong (China, SAR), Iceland, Norway, Sweden and the United States the Internet

---

BOX 2.6

Combining traditional knowledge and scientific methods to create breakthrough treatment for malaria in Viet Nam

Viet Nam has dramatically reduced malaria deaths and cases using locally produced, high-quality drugs. Between 1992 and 1997 the death toll from malaria was slashed 97%, and the number of cases fell almost 60%. What made such great gains possible?

In the early 1990s the Vietnamese government took advantage of an upturn in the economy, increasing its investment in malaria control and identifying the drive against malaria as a national priority. The first major breakthrough was the development and manufacture of a new drug —artemisinin—to treat severe and multidrug-resistant cases of malaria. The drug, extracted from the indigenous thanh hao tree, has been used in traditional Chinese and Vietnamese medicine for centuries. Collaboration between industry and researchers led to local production of high-quality artemisinin and other derivatives at low cost.

Source: WHO 2000a.

TABLE 2.5
Investing in domestic technology capacity

Country or group	Gross tertiary enrolment ratio (percent)		Share of tertiary enrolment in science (percent)	Research and development spending (percentage of GNP)
	1980	1997	1995–97	1987–97
Korea, Rep. of	15	68	34.1	2.8
Singapore	8	43	62.0	1.1
Sweden	31	55[a]	30.6	3.8
Thailand	15	22[a]	20.9	0.1
United States	56	81[a]	17.2	2.6
Developing countries	7	9[a]	27.6	..
High-income OECD	39	64[a]	28.2	2.4

a. Refers to earlier year.
Source: Human Development Report Office calculations based on UNESCO 1999 and 2001a and World Bank 2001h.

UNEVEN DIFFUSION OF TECHNOLOGY—OLD AND NEW . . .

INTERNET USERS—STILL A GLOBAL ENCLAVE

The large circle represents world population.
Pie slices show regional shares
of world population.
Dark wedges show Internet users.

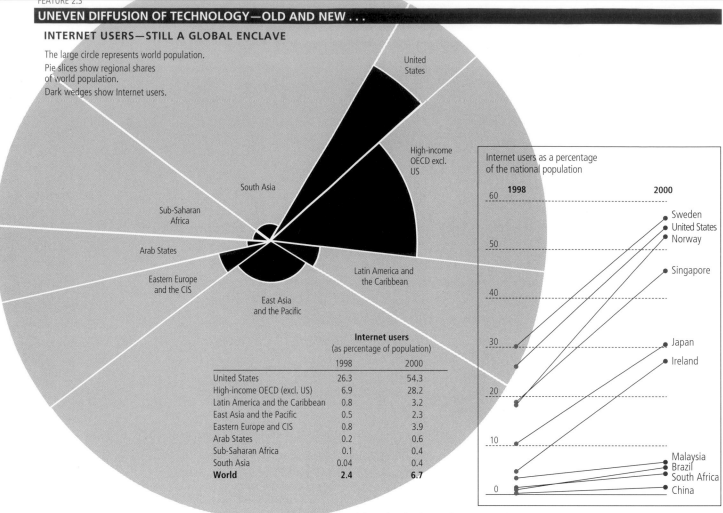

Internet users (as percentage of population)		
	1998	2000
United States	26.3	54.3
High-income OECD (excl. US)	6.9	28.2
Latin America and the Caribbean	0.8	3.2
East Asia and the Pacific	0.5	2.3
Eastern Europe and CIS	0.8	3.9
Arab States	0.2	0.6
Sub-Saharan Africa	0.1	0.4
South Asia	0.04	0.4
World	**2.4**	**6.7**

Internet users as a percentage of the national population

Source: Human Development Report Office calculations based on data supplied by Nua Publish 2001 and UN 2001c.

The divide narrows—but ever so slowly

More than three-quarters of Internet users live in high-income OECD countries, which contain 14% of the world's people

World population — High-income OECD — 14%

Internet user population

High-income OECD 88% in 1998

79% in 2000

Source: Human Development Report Office calculations based on data supplied by Nua Publish 2001 and UN 2001c.

The digital divide within countries

Though data are limited on the demography of Internet users, Internet use is clearly concentrated. In most countries Internet users are predominantly:

• *Urban and located in certain regions.* In China the 15 least connected provinces, with 600 million people, have only 4 million Internet users—while Shanghai and Beijing, with 27 million people, have 5 million users. In the Dominican Republic 80% of Internet users live in the capital, Santo Domingo. And in Thailand 90% live in urban areas, which contain only 21% of the country's population. Among India's 1.4 million Internet connections, more than 1.3 million are in the five states of Delhi, Karnataka, Maharashtra, Tamil Nadu and Mumbai.

• *Better educated and wealthier.* In Bulgaria the poorest 65% of the population accounts for only 29% of Internet users. In Chile 89% of Internet users

have had tertiary education, in Sri Lanka 65%, and in China 70%.

• *Young.* Everywhere, younger people are more apt to be online. In Australia 18–24-year-olds are five times more likely to be Internet users than those above 55. In Chile 74% of users are under 35; in China that share is 84%. Other countries follow the same pattern.

• *Male.* Men make up 86% of users in Ethiopia, 83% in Senegal, 70% in China, 67% in France and 62% in Latin America.

Some of these disparities are easing. For example, the gender gap seems to be narrowing rapidly—as in Thailand, where the share of female users jumped from 35% in 1999 to 49% in 2000, or in the United States, where women made up 38% of users in 1996 but 51% in 2000. In Brazil, where Internet use has increased rapidly, women account for 47% of users.

Source: UNDP, Country Offices 2001; Nanthikesan 2001.

The digital divide is nothing new. Diffusion of decades-old inventions has slowed

ELECTRICITY
Kilowatt-hours per capita

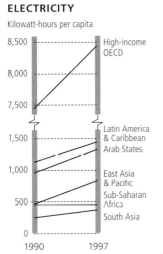

TRACTORS
Per 1,000 hectares
of permanently cropped land

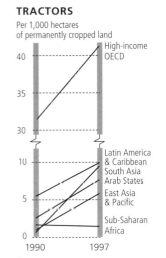

TELEPHONES
Telephone mainlines per 1,000 people

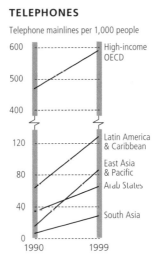

Source: Human Development Report Office calculations based on World Bank 2001h, FAO 2000a and ITU 2001b.

MODERN CROP VARIETIES

Percentage of permanently cultivated agricultural land

Type	Latin America				Asia				Middle East and North Africa				Sub-Saharan Africa			
	1970	1980	1990	1998	1970	1980	1990	1998	1970	1980	1990	1998	1970	1980	1990	1998
Wheat	11	46	83	90	19	49	74	86	5	16	38	66	5	22	32	52
Rice	2	22	52	65	10	35	55	65					0	2	15	40
Maize	10	20	30	46	10	25	45	70					1	4	15	17
Sorghum					4	20	54	70					0	8	15	26
Millet					5	30	50	78					0	0	5	14
Cassava	0	1	2	7	0	0	2	12					0	0	2	18

Note: Shaded areas indicate less than 30% of land is planted with modern crop varieties.
Source: Evenson and Gollin 2001.

... AND WITHIN COUNTRIES

Indian state/territory	Access to electricity (percentage of households) 1994	Telephones (per 1,000 people) 1999	Internet connections (per 1,000 people) 1999	Secondary gross attendance ratio (percent) 1996
Maharashtra	59.7	43	8.21	66
Punjab	83.5	47	1.24	64
Kerala	61.1	43	0.87	83
Karnataka	63.0	29	2.73	52
West Bengal	15.6	16	2.51	44
Orissa	18.8	9	0.12	54
Uttar Pradesh	20.1	10	0.12	43

Source: Human Development Report Office calculations based on NCAER 1999; UNDP, India Country Office 2001; Chandrashekar 2001: Government of India, Department of Education 2001.

has reached more than half the population, and in other OECD countries close to one-third.[31] In the rest of the world the shares are much smaller, reaching only 0.4% of Sub-Saharan Africans. Even in India, home to a major global hub of innovation, only 0.4% of people use the Internet. From these levels it will take years for the digital divide to be bridged. Today 79% of Internet users live in OECD countries, which contain only 14% of the world's people.

Still, Internet use is exploding in many countries—in OECD countries excluding the United States the share of Internet users quadrupled from 7% to 28% between 1998 and 2000. Even in developing countries the increase was dramatic: from 1.7 million to 9.8 million users in Brazil, from 3.8 million to 16.9 million in China and from 2,500 to 25,000 in Uganda.[32] Yet because they are starting from very low bases, the portion of the population reached remains small.

TABLE 2.6
Competing in global markets: the 30 leading exporters of high-tech products

Rank	Country or area	Billions of US dollars, 1998–99	Index (1990=100)
1	United States	206	250
2	Japan	126	196
3	Germany	95	206
4	United Kingdom	77	255
5	Singapore	66	420
6	France	65	248
7	Korea, Rep. of	48	428
8	Netherlands	45	310
9	Malaysia	44	685
10	China	40	1,465
11	Mexico	38	3,846
12	Ireland	29	535
13	Canada	26	297
14	Italy	25	177
15	Sweden	22	314
16	Switzerland	21	231
17	Belgium	19	296
18	Thailand	17	591
19	Spain	11	289
20	Finland	11	512
21	Denmark	9	261
22	Philippines	9	1,561
23	Israel	7	459
24	Austria	7	172
25	Hungary	6	..
26	Hong Kong, China (SAR)	5	111
27	Brazil	4	364
28	Indonesia	3	1,811
29	Czech Republic	3	..
30	Costa Rica	3	7,324

Source: Human Development Report Office calculations based on data from Lall 2000 and UN 2001a.

The diffusion of the Internet has also been uneven within countries, concentrated in urban areas, among young men and among people with higher incomes and more education. In a positive sign, the gender gap seems to be closing in several countries, while the spread of access sites such as Internet cafes and community information centres is increasing use by lower-income groups.

Many countries are using the latest technology competitively in manufacturing industries, as shown by their success with high-tech exports. Of the 30 top exporters, 11 are in the developing world—including Korea, Malaysia and Mexico (table 2.6). But in Sub-Saharan Africa, the Arab States and South Asia high-tech exports still account for less than 5% of the total (annex table A2.3).

Yet many inventions that are decades old have not been adopted around the world despite their enormous value as tools of human progress. With many of these old technologies, diffusion has stagnated or stalled, apparently hitting the limits of income, infrastructure and institutions.

• *Electricity* has not reached some 2 billion people, a third of the world's population. In 1998 average electricity consumption in South Asia and Sub-Saharan Africa was less than one-tenth that in OECD countries.

• The *telephone* has been around for more than a hundred years. While there is more than 1 mainline connection for every 2 people in OECD countries, there is just 1 for every 15 in developing countries—and 1 for every 200 in the least developed countries. Such disparities impede Internet access and hinder connections to the network age. Recently, however, infrastructure investments, institutional reforms, innovations in marketing and technological progress have accelerated the spread of telephone connections. Between 1990 and 1999 mainline density increased from 22 to 69 per 1,000 people in developing countries. Mobile telephones have overcome infrastructure constraints, spreading as widely as mainlines in some countries. South Africa has 132 cellular subscribers compared with 138 phone lines per 1,000 people, and Venezuela has 143 cellular subscribers and 109 mainlines per 1,000 people (annex table A.2.4). Until recently, though, mobile phones have actually widened the gap because they have been diffused more rapidly in OECD countries.

• *Agrotechnical transformations* of plant breeding, better seeds, fertilizer, water control and mechanization started in Europe in the mid-18th century and spread to the rest of the world. With the green revolution, world cereal yields doubled between the early 1960s and late 1990s, growing especially fast in Asia and Latin America. But Sub-Saharan Africa lags far behind in the use of modern seed varieties, tractors and fertilizer.[33] Climate and soils help explain such differences, but lower yields also reflect lower technological inputs.

• *Medical advances* that have driven huge gains in survival are still out of reach for many. Some 2 billion people do not have access to essential medicines such as penicillin. Oral rehydration therapy is still not used in 38% of diarrhoea cases in developing countries. And half of 1-year-old Africans have been immunized against diphtheria, pertussis, tetanus, polio and measles.[34]

HUMAN SKILLS

Developing countries that rank high in the technology achievement index have made spectacular gains in human skills in the past few decades. Tertiary gross enrolment rates in Korea rose from 15% to 68% between 1980 and 1997, and 34% of that enrolment is in science and mathematics—well ahead of 28%, the OECD average.[35] But most developing countries lag far behind OECD countries in school enrolment (figure 2.3).

TURNING TECHNOLOGY INTO A TOOL FOR HUMAN DEVELOPMENT REQUIRES EFFORT

At the end of the 19th century the application of science to manufacturing techniques or to agricultural practices became a basis of production systems, eventually increasing most workers' incomes. In the 20th century investments in research and development transformed knowledge into a critical factor of production, and industrial laboratories began producing inventions that soon found their

way to the shop floor. Entrepreneurship and market incentives accelerated technological progress to meet consumer demand. In just the past 10 years the store of indigenous knowledge has begun to reach people more widely. Its value can be enhanced when developed with modern methods, diffused and marketed (see box 2.6).

But the market is not enough to channel technological development to human needs. The market may produce video games and palliatives for baldness, but it will not necessarily eliminate the ill health, malnutrition, isolation and lack of knowledge that afflict poor people. Many 20th century successes required deliberate efforts to develop technological solutions to human problems, adapt them to developing countries and diffuse them widely to poor people. The green revolution required mobilizing the international community in a massive programme of agricultural research to prevent global famine, along with scientific research and adaptation at local levels. Oral rehydration therapy emerged from state-of-the-art research, but its dissemination required a major public effort (see box 2.2). And though penicillin was discovered in 1928, it was not marketed until 15 years later. Why? The untapped demand for antibiotics was undoubtedly huge, but pharmaceutical companies were not interested. It took a war to crystallize this demand into a viable market.[36]

So, turning technology into a tool for human development often requires purposive effort and public investment to create and diffuse innovations widely. Investment in creating, adapting and marketing products that poor people can afford or need is inadequate because their incomes are too low and do not present a market opportunity for the private sector. In developing countries national capacities are also limited. Intellectual property rights can stimulate innovation, but in today's world of very uneven demand and capacity, they are not enough to stimulate innovation in many developing countries. At the global level, potentially huge benefits require difficult coordination. Yet public investment in technology development can have enormous returns. For example, some 1,800 public research programmes on wheat, rice,

FIGURE 2.3
Enrolments reflect uneven progress in building skills

SECONDARY ENROLMENT

Gross enrolment ratio (percent)

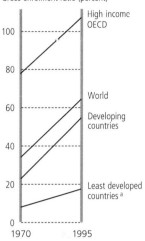

TERTIARY ENROLMENT

Gross enrolment ratio (percent)

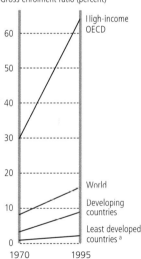

a. Data refer to 1970 and 1994.
Source: Human Development Report Office calculations based on UNESCO 1999.

TABLE 2.7

High rates of return to investing in agricultural research
(percent)

Location	Internal rate of return, 1958–98
All known locations	44
Sub-Saharan Africa	33
Asia and the Pacific	48
Latin America and the Caribbean	41
West Asia and North Africa	34
Multinational or international	35

Note: Regional classifications differ from those used elsewhere in the Report. Shows average of 1,809 public sector programmes.
Source: Lipton, Sinha and Blackman 2001.

maize and other food crops—occurring in all regions and spanning four decades from 1958—are estimated to have had an average internal real rate of return of 44% (table 2.7).

The rest of this Report explores how national and global public policy can address the fundamental constraints to creating and diffusing technology for poor people and countries. Chapter 3 focuses on managing risks, chapter 4 on building national capacity and chapter 5 on fostering global initiatives.

MAP 2.1

THE GEOGRAPHY OF TECHNOLOGICAL INNOVATION AND ACHIEVEMENT

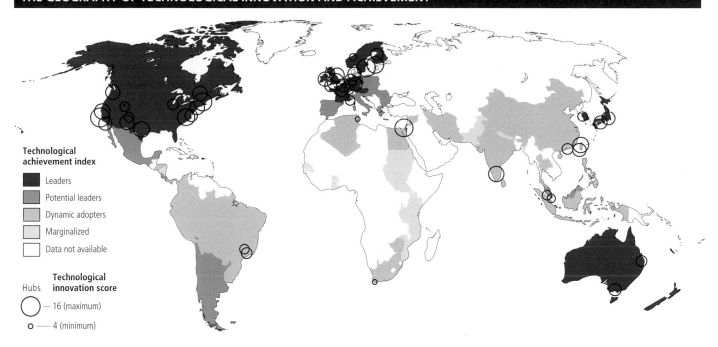

Technological achievement index

- Leaders
- Potential leaders
- Dynamic adopters
- Marginalized
- Data not available

Hubs **Technological innovation score**
- — 16 (maximum)
- — 4 (minimum)

Global hubs of technological innovation   In 2000 *Wired* magazine consulted local sources in government, industry and the media to find the locations that matter most in the new digital geography. Each was rated from 1 to 4 in four areas: the ability of area universities and research facilities to train skilled workers or develop new technologies, the presence of established companies and multinational corporations to provide expertise and economic stability, the population's entrepreneurial drive to start new ventures and the availability of venture capital to ensure that the ideas make it to market. Forty-six locations were identified as technology hubs, shown on the map as black circles

Score				
16 Silicon Valley, US	13 Taipei, Taiwan (province of China)	11 Malmo, Sweden–Copenhagen, Denmark	10 Paris, France	8 Santa Fe, US
15 Boston, US	13 Bangalore, India	11 Bavaria, Germany	10 Baden-Wurttemberg, Germany	8 Glasgow-Edinburgh, UK
15 Stockholm-Kista, Sweden	12 New York City, US	11 Flanders, Belgium	10 Oulu, Finland	8 Saxony, Germany
15 Israel	12 Albuquerque, US	11 Tokyo, Japan	10 Melbourne, Australia	8 Sophia Antipolis, France
14 Raleigh-Durham-Chapel Hill, US	12 Montreal, Canada	11 Kyoto, Japan	9 Chicago, US	8 Inchon, Rep. of Korea
14 London, UK	12 Seattle, US	11 Hsinchu, Taiwan (province of China)	9 Hong Kong, China (SAR)	8 Kuala Lumpur, Malaysia
14 Helsinki, Finland	12 Cambridge, UK	10 Virginia, US	9 Queensland, Australia	8 Campinas, Brazil
13 Austin, US	12 Dublin, Ireland	10 Thames Valley, UK	9 Sao Paulo, Brazil	7 Singapore
13 San Francisco, US	11 Los Angeles, US		8 Salt Lake City, US	6 Trondheim, Norway
				4 El Ghazala, Tunisia
				4 Gauteng, South Africa

Source: Hillner 2000.

Four categories of the technology achievement index (see annex 2.1, p. 46; and annex table A2.1, p. 48)

LEADERS	POTENTIAL LEADERS	DYNAMIC ADOPTERS		MARGINALIZED
Finland (2 hubs)	Spain	Uruguay	Tunisia (1 hub)	Nicaragua
United States (13 hubs)	Italy	South Africa (1 hub)	Paraguay	Pakistan
Sweden (2 hubs)	Czech Republic	Thailand	Ecuador	Senegal
Japan (2 hubs)	Hungary	Trinidad and Tobago	El Salvador	Ghana
Korea, Rep. of (1 hub)	Slovenia	Panama	Dominican Republic	Kenya
Netherlands	Hong Kong, China (SAR)	Brazil (2 hubs)	Syrian Arab Republic	Nepal
United Kingdom (4 hubs)	Slovakia	Philippines	Egypt	Tanzania, U. Rep. of
Canada (1 hub)	Greece	China (3 hubs)	Algeria	Sudan
Australia (2 hubs)	Portugal	Bolivia	Zimbabwe	Mozambique
Singapore (1 hub)	Bulgaria	Colombia	Indonesia	
Germany (3 hubs)	Poland	Peru	Honduras	
Norway (1 hub)	Malaysia (1 hub)	Jamaica	Sri Lanka	
Ireland (1 hub)	Croatia	Iran, Islamic Rep. of	India (1 hub)	
Belgium (1 hub)	Mexico			
New Zealand	Cyprus			
Austria	Argentina			
France (2 hubs)	Romania			
Israel (1 hub)	Costa Rica			
	Chile			

THE TECHNOLOGY ACHIEVEMENT INDEX—A NEW MEASURE OF COUNTRIES' ABILITY TO PARTICIPATE IN THE NETWORK AGE

This Report introduces the technology achievement index (TAI), which aims to capture how well a country is creating and diffusing technology and building a human skill base—reflecting capacity to participate in the technological innovations of the network age. This composite index measures achievements, not potential, effort or inputs. It is not a measure of which country is leading in global technology development, but focuses on how well the country as a whole is participating in creating and using technology. Take the United States—a global technology powerhouse—and Finland. The United States has far more inventions and Internet hosts in total than does Finland, but it does not rank as highly in the index because in Finland the Internet is more widely diffused and more is being done to develop a technological skill base throughout the population.

A nation's technological achievements are larger and more complex than what this or any other index can capture. It is impossible to reflect the full range of technologies—from agriculture to medicine to manufacturing. Many aspects of technology creation, diffusion and human skills are hard to quantify. And even if they could be quantified, a lack of reliable data makes it impossible to fully reflect them. For example, important technological innovations occur in the informal sector and in indigenous knowledge systems. But these are not recorded and cannot be quantified. Thus the TAI is constructed using indicators, not direct measures, of a country's achievements in four dimensions. It provides a rough summary—not a comprehensive measure—of a society's technological achievements.

Why a composite index?

The TAI is intended to help policy-makers define technology strategies. This Report argues that development strategies need to be redefined in the network age. It calls on policy-makers to take a new look at their current technology achievements as a first step. A composite index helps a country situate itself relative to others, especially those farther ahead. Many elements make up a country's technological achievement, but an overall assessment is more easily made based on a single composite measure than on dozens of different measures. Like other composite indices in *Human Development Reports* (such as the human development index), the TAI is intended to be used as a starting point to make an overall assessment, to be followed by examining different indicators in greater detail.

The design of the index reflects two particular concerns. First, to focus on indicators that reflect policy concerns for all countries, regardless of the level of technological development. Second, to be useful for developing countries. To accomplish this the index must be able to discriminate between countries at the lower end of the range.

Components of the index

The TAI focuses on four dimensions of technological capacity that are important for reaping the benefits of the network age. The indicators selected relate to important technology policy objectives for all countries, regardless of their level of development:

• *Creation of technology.* Not all countries need to be at the leading edge of global technological development, but the capacity to innovate is relevant for all countries and constitutes the highest level of technological capacity. The global economy gives big rewards to the leaders and owners of technological innovation. All countries need to have capacity to innovate because the ability to innovate in the use of technology cannot be fully developed without the capacity to create—especially to adapt products and processes to local conditions. Innovation occurs throughout society, in formal and informal settings, though the current trend is towards increasing commercialization and formalization of the process of innovation. In the absence of perfect indicators and data series the TAI uses two indicators to capture the level of innovation in a society. The first is the number of patents granted per capita, to reflect the current level of invention activities. The second is receipts of royalty and license fees from abroad per capita, to reflect the stock of successful innovations of the past that are still useful and hence have market value.

• *Diffusion of recent innovations.* All countries must adopt innovations to benefit from the opportunities of the network age. This is measured by diffusion of the Internet—indispensable to participation—and by exports of high- and medium-technology products as a share of all exports.

• *Diffusion of old innovations.* Participation in the network age requires diffusion of many old innovations. Although leapfrogging is sometimes possible, technological advance is a cumulative process, and widespread diffusion of older innovations is necessary for adoption of later innovations. Two indicators used here—telephones and electricity—are especially important because they are needed to use newer technologies and are also pervasive inputs to a multitude of human activities. Both indicators are expressed as logarithms and capped at the average OECD level, however, because they are important at the earlier stages of technological advance but not at the most advanced stages. Thus while it is important for India to focus on diffusing electricity and telephones so that all its people can participate in the technological revolution, Japan and Sweden have passed that stage. Expressing the measure in logarithms

ensures that as the level increases, it contributes less to the index.

• *Human skills.* A critical mass of skills is indispensable to technological dynamism. Both creators and users of new technology need skills. Today's technology requires adaptability—skills to master the constant flow of new innovations. The foundations of such ability are basic education to develop cognitive skills and skills in science and mathematics. Two indicators are used to reflect the human skills needed to create and absorb innovations: mean years of schooling and gross enrolment ratio of tertiary students enrolled in science, mathematics and engineering. Though it would be desirable to include indicators of vocational training, these data are not available.

Data sources and limitations

The data used to construct the TAI are from international series that are the most widely used in analyses of technology trends, and so are considered the most reliable of available sets, as shown below. The range of appropriate indicators is limited to those with reasonable coverage.

Limitations in data series must be taken into account in interpreting TAI values and rankings. Some countries will have undervalued innovations because patent records and royalty payments are the only systematically collected data on technological innovation and leave out valuable but non-commercialized innovations such as those occurring in the informal sector and in indigenous knowledge systems. Moreover, national systems and traditions differ in scope and criteria. High numbers of patents may reflect liberal intellectual property systems. Diffusion of new technologies may be understated in many developing countries. Internet access is measured by Internet hosts because these data are more reliable and have better coverage than Internet user data at the country level.

Weighting and aggregation

The methodology for constructing the TAI is presented in detail in the technical note. Each of the four dimensions has equal weight. Each of the indicators that make up the dimensions also has equal weight.

TAI values and rankings

TAI estimates have been prepared for 72 countries for which data are available and of acceptable quality. For others, data were missing or unsatisfactory for one or more indicators, so the TAI could not be estimated. For a number of countries in the developing world, data on patents and royalties are missing. Because a lack of data generally indicates that little formal innovation is occurring, a value of zero for the missing indicator was used in these cases.

Dimension	Indicator	Source
Creation of technology	Patents granted per capita	World Intellectual Property Organization (WIPO 2001a)
	Receipts of royalty and license fees from abroad per capita	World Bank (World Bank 2001h)
Diffusion of recent innovations	Internet hosts per capita	International Telecommunication Union (ITU 2001a)
	High- and medium-technology exports as a share of all exports	United Nations Statistical Division (calculated based on data from Lall 2001 and UN 2001a)
Diffusion of old innovations	Logarithm of telephones per capita (mainline and cellular combined)	International Telecommunication Union (ITU 2001b)
	Logarithm of electricity consumption per capita	World Bank (World Bank 2001h)
Human skills	Mean years of schooling	Barro and Lee (Barro and Lee 2000)
	Gross enrolment ratio at tertiary level in science, mathematics and engineering	United Nations Educational, Scientific and Cultural Organization (calculated based on data from UNESCO 1998, 1999 and 2001a)

The results show three trends: a map of great disparities among countries, diversity and dynamism in technological progress among developing countries and a map of technology hubs superimposed on countries at different levels of development.

The map of great disparities shows four group of countries (see map 2.1), with TAI values ranging from 0.744 for Finland to 0.066 for Mozambique. These countries can be considered leaders, potential leaders, dynamic adopters or marginalized:

• *Leaders (TAI above 0.5)*—topped by Finland, the United States, Sweden and Japan, this group is at the cutting edge of technological innovation. Technological innovation is self-sustaining, and these countries have high achievements in technology creation, diffusion and skills. Coming fifth is the Republic of Korea, and tenth is Singapore—two countries that have advanced rapidly in technology in recent decades. This group is set apart from the rest by its higher invention index, with a marked gap between Israel in this group and Spain in the next.

Source: Desai and others 2001.

• *Potential leaders (0.35–0.49)*—most of these countries have invested in high levels of human skills and have diffused old technologies widely but innovate little. Each tends to rank low in one or two dimensions, such as diffusion of recent innovations or of old inventions. Most countries in this group have skill levels comparable to those in the top group.

• *Dynamic adopters (0.20–0.34)*—these countries are dynamic in the use of new technology. Most are developing countries with significantly higher human skills than the fourth group. Included are Brazil, China, India, Indonesia, South Africa and Tunisia, among others. Many of these countries have important high-technology industries and technology hubs, but the diffusion of old inventions is slow and incomplete.

• *Marginalized (below 0.20)*—technology diffusion and skill building have a long way to go in these countries. Large parts of the population have not benefited from the diffusion of old technology.

These rankings do not shadow income rankings and show considerable dynamism in several

countries with rising technological achievement—for example, Korea ranks above the United Kingdom, Canada and other established industrial economies. Ireland ranks above Austria and France. Large developing countries—Brazil, China, India—do less well than one might expect because this is not a ranking of "technological might" of a country.

Finally, technology hubs have a limited effect on the index because of disparities within countries. If the TAI were estimated only for the hubs, such countries would undoubtedly rank as leaders or potential leaders.

Technological achievement and human development

Although technological achievements are important for human development, the TAI measures only technological achievements. It does not indicate how well these achievements have been translated into human development. Still, the TAI shows a high correlation with the human development index (HDI), and it correlates better with the HDI than with income.

TAI rank		Technology achievement index (TAI) value	Technology creation		Diffusion of recent innovations		Diffusion of old innovations		Human skills	
			Patents granted to residents (per million people) 1998 [a]	Receipts of royalties and license fees (US$ per 1,000 people) 1999 [b]	Internet hosts (per 1,000 people) 2000	High- and medium-technology exports (as % of total goods exports) 1999	Telephones (mainline and cellular, per 1,000 people) 1999	Electricity consumption (kilowatt-hours per capita) 1998	Mean years of schooling (age 15 and above) 2000	Gross tertiary science enrolment ratio (%) 1995–97 [c]
Leaders										
1	Finland	0.744	187	125.6	200.2	50.7	1,203 [d]	14,129 [e]	10.0	27.4
2	United States	0.733	289	130.0	179.1	66.2	993 [d]	11,832 [e]	12.0	13.9 [f]
3	Sweden	0.703	271	156.6	125.8	59.7	1,247 [d]	13,955 [e]	11.4	15.3
4	Japan	0.698	994	64.6	49.0	80.8	1,007 [d]	7,322 [e]	9.5	10.0 [g]
5	Korea, Rep. of	0.666	779	9.8	4.8	66.7	938 [d]	4,497	10.8	23.2
6	Netherlands	0.630	189	151.2	136.0	50.9	1,042 [d]	5,908	9.4	9.5
7	United Kingdom	0.606	82	134.0	57.4	61.9	1,037 [d]	5,327	9.4	14.9
8	Canada	0.589	31	38.6	108.0	48.7	881	15,071 [e]	11.6	14.2 [f]
9	Australia	0.587	75	18.2	125.9	16.2	862	8,717 [e]	10.9	25.3
10	Singapore	0.585	8	25.5 [h, i]	72.3	74.9	901	6,771	7.1	24.2 [h]
11	Germany	0.583	235	36.8	41.2	64.2	874	5,681	10.2	14.4
12	Norway	0.579	103	20.2 [i]	193.6	19.0	1,329 [d]	24,607 [e]	11.9	11.2
13	Ireland	0.566	106	110.3	48.6	53.6	924 [d]	4,760	9.4	12.3
14	Belgium	0.553	72	73.9	58.9	47.6	817	7,249 [e]	9.3	13.6 [f]
15	New Zealand	0.548	103	13.0	146.7	15.4	720	8,215 [e]	11.7	13.1
16	Austria	0.544	165	14.8	84.2	50.3	987 [d]	6,175	8.4	13.6
17	France	0.535	205	33.6	36.4	58.9	943 [d]	6,287	7.9	12.6
18	Israel	0.514	74	43.6	43.2	45.0	918 [d]	5,475	9.6	11.0 [f]
Potential leaders										
19	Spain	0.481	42	8.6	21.0	53.4	730	4,195	7.3	15.6
20	Italy	0.471	13	9.8	30.4	51.0	991 [d]	4,431	7.2	13.0
21	Czech Republic	0.465	28	4.2	25.0	51.7	560	4,748	9.5	8.2
22	Hungary	0.464	26	6.2	21.6	63.5	533	2,888	9.1	7.7
23	Slovenia	0.458	105	4.0	20.3	49.5	687	5,096	7.1	10.6
24	Hong Kong, China (SAR)	0.455	6	..	33.6	33.6	1,212 [d]	5,244	9.4	9.8 [f, g]
25	Slovakia	0.447	24	2.7	10.2	48.7	478	3,899	9.3	9.5
26	Greece	0.437	(.)	0.0 [j]	16.4	17.9	839	3,739	8.7	17.2 [f]
27	Portugal	0.419	6	2.7	17.7	40.7	892	3,396	5.9	12.0
28	Bulgaria	0.411	23	..	3.7	30.0 [i]	397	3,166	9.5	10.3
29	Poland	0.407	30	0.6	11.4	36.2	365	2,458	9.8	6.6 [f]
30	Malaysia	0.396	..	0.0	2.4	67.4	340	2,554	6.8	3.3 [f]
31	Croatia	0.391	9	..	6.7	41.7	431	2,463	6.3	10.6
32	Mexico	0.389	1	0.4	9.2	66.3	192	1,513	7.2	5.0
33	Cyprus	0.386	..	..	16.9	23.0	735	3,468	9.2	4.0
34	Argentina	0.381	8	0.5	8.7	19.0	322	1,891	8.8	12.0 [g]
35	Romania	0.371	71	0.2	2.7	25.3	227	1,626	9.5	7.2
36	Costa Rica	0.358	..	0.3	4.1	52.6	239	1,450	6.1	5.7 [g]
37	Chile	0.357	..	6.6	6.2	6.1	358	2,082	7.6	13.2
Dynamic adopters										
38	Uruguay	0.343	2	0.0 [j]	19.6	13.3	366	1,788	7.6	7.3
39	South Africa	0.340	..	1.7	8.4	30.2 [k]	270	3,832	6.1	3.4
40	Thailand	0.337	1	0.3	1.6	48.9	124	1,345	6.5	4.6
41	Trinidad and Tobago	0.328	..	0.0 [i]	7.7	14.2	246	3,478	7.8	3.3
42	Panama	0.321	..	0.0	1.9	5.1	251	1,211	8.6	8.5
43	Brazil	0.311	2	0.8	7.2	32.9	238	1,793	4.9	3.4
44	Philippines	0.300	(.)	0.1	0.4	32.8	77	451	8.2	5.2 [f]
45	China	0.299	1	0.1	0.1	39.0	120	746	6.4	3.2
46	Bolivia	0.277	..	0.2	0.3	26.0	113	409	5.6	7.7 [f, g]
47	Colombia	0.274	1	0.2	1.9	13.7	236	866	5.3	5.2
48	Peru	0.271	..	0.2	0.7	2.9	107	642	7.6	7.5 [f]
49	Jamaica	0.261	..	2.4	0.4	1.5 [i]	255	2,252	5.3	1.6
50	Iran, Islamic Rep. of	0.260	1	0.0 [i]	(.)	2.0	133	1,343	5.3	6.5

TAI rank	Technology achievement index (TAI) value	Technology creation		Diffusion of recent innovations		Diffusion of old innovations		Human skills	
		Patents granted to residents (per million people) 1998 [a]	Receipts of royalties and license fees (US$ per 1,000 people) 1999 [b]	Internet hosts (per 1,000 people) 2000	High- and medium-technology exports (as % of total goods exports) 1999	Telephones (mainline and cellular, per 1,000 people) 1999	Electricity consumption (kilowatt-hours per capita) 1998	Mean years of schooling (age 15 and above) 2000	Gross tertiary science enrolment ratio (%) 1995–97 [c]
51 Tunisia	0.255	..	1.1	(.)	19.7	96	824	5.0	3.8
52 Paraguay	0.254	..	35.3	0.5	2.0	137	756	6.2	2.2
53 Ecuador	0.253	..	..	0.3	3.2	122	625	6.4	6.0 [f,g]
54 El Salvador	0.253	..	0.2	0.3	19.2	138	559	5.2	3.6
55 Dominican Republic	0.244	..	..	1.7	5.7 [i]	148	627	4.9	5.7
56 Syrian Arab Republic	0.240	..	..	0.0	1.2	102	838	5.8	4.6 [g]
57 Egypt	0.236	(.)	0.7	0.1	8.8	77	861	5.5	2.9
58 Algeria	0.221	..	..	(.)	1.0	54	563	5.4	6.0
59 Zimbabwe	0.220	(.)	..	0.5	12.0	36	896	5.4	1.6
60 Indonesia	0.211	..	..	0.2	17.9	40	320	5.0	3.1
61 Honduras	0.208	..	0.0	(.)	8.2	57	446	4.8	3.0 [g]
62 Sri Lanka	0.203	..	..	0.2	5.2	49	244	6.9	1.4
63 India	0.201	1	(.)	0.1	16.6 [i]	28	384	5.1	1.7

Marginalized

TAI rank	Technology achievement index (TAI) value	Patents granted to residents	Receipts of royalties and license fees	Internet hosts	High- and medium-technology exports	Telephones	Electricity consumption	Mean years of schooling	Gross tertiary science enrolment ratio
64 Nicaragua	0.185	..	..	0.4	3.6	39	281	4.6	3.8
65 Pakistan	0.167	..	(.) [j]	0.1	7.9	24	337	3.9	1.4 [f,g]
66 Senegal	0.158	..	0.0 [j]	0.2	28.5	27	111	2.6	0.5 [f,g]
67 Ghana	0.139	(.)	..	(.)	4.1	12	289	3.9	0.4 [f,g]
68 Kenya	0.129	(.)	(.)	0.2	7.2	11	129	4.2	0.3 [f]
69 Nepal	0.081	..	0.0	0.1	1.9 [i]	12	47	2.4	0.7
70 Tanzania, U. Rep. of	0.080	..	(.)	(.)	6.7	6	54	2.7	0.2
71 Sudan	0.071	..	0.0	0.0	0.4 [i]	9	47	2.1	0.7 [f,g]
72 Mozambique	0.066	..	..	(.)	12.2 [i]	5	54	1.1	0.2

Others

TAI rank	Technology achievement index (TAI) value	Patents granted to residents	Receipts of royalties and license fees	Internet hosts	High- and medium-technology exports	Telephones	Electricity consumption	Mean years of schooling	Gross tertiary science enrolment ratio
Albania	..	..	..	0.1	4.2 [i]	39	678	..	2.7
Angola	..	..	..	(.)	..	10	60	..	..
Armenia	..	8	..	0.9	11.7	158	930	..	4.0
Azerbaijan	..	..	..	0.1	6.3	118	1,584	..	7.3 [f]
Bahamas	..	..	..	..	..	422	..	..	..
Bahrain	..	..	..	3.6	5.7 [i]	453	7,645	6.1	6.7 [f]
Bangladesh	..	(.)	(.)	0.0	2.9 [i]	5	81	2.6	..
Barbados	..	..	0.8	0.5	31.3	538	..	8.7	6.1
Belarus	..	50	0.1	0.3	46.5	259	2,762	..	14.4
Belize	..	..	0.0 [i]	2.2	0.2 [i]	182	..	..	..
Benin	..	..	..	(.)	..	..	46	2.3	0.5
Bhutan	..	..	..	2.1	..	18	..	..	..
Botswana	..	1	(.)	2.7	..	150	..	6.3	1.6
Brunei Darussalam	..	..	..	8.0	..	451	7,676	..	0.4
Burkina Faso	..	..	..	(.)	..	5	..	..	0.2
Burundi	..	..	0.0	0.0	..	3	..	..	..
Cambodia	..	..	..	(.)	..	11	..	..	0.2
Cameroon	..	..	..	(.)	2.2 [i]	..	185	3.5	..
Cape Verde	..	..	(.) [i]	0.1	..	131	..	..	..
Central African Republic	..	..	..	(.)	13.6 [i]	..	..	2.5	..
Chad	..	..	..	(.)	..	..	..	..	0.1
Comoros	..	..	..	0.1	..	10	..	..	..
Congo	..	..	0.0 [j]	(.)	..	..	83	5.1	..
Congo, Dem. Rep. of the	..	..	..	(.)	..	..	110	3.0	..
Côte d'Ivoire	..	..	..	0.1	..	33	..	..	..
Denmark	..	52	..	114.3	41.0	1,179	6,033	9.7	10.1
Djibouti	..	..	..	0.1	..	14	..	..	..
Equatorial Guinea	..	..	..	0.0	..	..	..	..	..
Eritrea	..	..	..	(.)	..	7	..	..	..
Estonia	..	1	1.2	43.1	31.9	624	3,531	..	13.4

TAI rank	Technology achievement index (TAI) value	Technology creation		Diffusion of recent innovations		Diffusion of old innovations		Human skills	
		Patents granted to residents (per million people) 1998 [a]	Receipts of royalties and license fees (US$ per 1,000 people) 1999 [b]	Internet hosts (per 1,000 people) 2000	High- and medium-technology exports (as % of total goods exports) 1999	Telephones (mainline and cellular, per 1,000 people) 1999	Electricity consumption (kilowatt-hours per capita) 1998	Mean years of schooling (age 15 and above) 2000	Gross tertiary science enrolment ratio (%) 1995–97 [c]
Ethiopia	..	..	..	(.)	..	3	22	..	0.3
Fiji	..	..	..	0.9	..	130	..	8.3	..
Gabon	..	..	..	(.)	0.9 [i]	39	749	..	..
Gambia	..	1	..	(.)	..	27	..	2.3	..
Georgia	..	67	..	0.4	..	142	1,257	..	20.2
Guatemala	..	(.)	..	0.5	16.0	86	322	3.5	..
Guinea	..	..	..	(.)	..	9	..	..	0.4
Guinea-Bissau	..	..	..	(.)	..	..	..	0.8	..
Guyana	..	..	..	0.1	..	78	..	6.3	2.7
Haiti	..	..	..	0.0	3.2 [i]	12	33	2.8	..
Iceland	..	15	..	232.4	9.8	1,297	20,150	8.8	7.4
Jordan	..	..	..	0.2	..	105	1,205	6.9	..
Kazakhstan	..	55	..	0.6	15.0	111	2,399	..	13.7
Kuwait	..	..	..	4.4	6.8	398	13,800	6.2	4.4
Kyrgyzstan	..	14	..	1.1	10.9	77	1,431	..	3.3 [f]
Lao People's Dem. Rep.	..	..	..	0.0	..	8	..	..	..
Latvia	..	71	4.3	13.4	12.4	412	1,879	..	9.5
Lebanon	..	..	..	2.3	..	..	1,820	..	4.5
Lesotho	..	..	6.5	0.1	..	..	..	4.2	0.3
Libyan Arab Jamahiriya	..	..	..	(.)	1.8 [i]	..	3,677	..	..
Lithuania	..	27	(.)	7.5	29.2	401	1,909	..	11.7
Luxembourg	..	202	272.6	49.5	34.0	1,211	12,400	..	..
Macedonia, TFYR	..	19	1.1	1.9	23.8 [i]	258	..	..	7.6
Madagascar	..	..	(.) [i]	0.1	3.0	..	..	..	0.4
Malawi	..	..	..	0.0	..	6	..	3.2	..
Maldives	..	..	0.0 [i]	1.7	..	90	..	..	..
Mali	..	..	..	(.)	..	..	..	0.9	..
Malta	..	18	0.0	19.5	72.0	609	3,719	..	3.9
Mauritania	..	..	0.0 [i]	(.)	..	6	..	..	..
Mauritius	..	..	0.0	5.2	4.3	312	..	6.0	1.0
Moldova, Rep. of	..	42	(.)	0.7	6.2	131	689	..	12.0
Mongolia	..	56	0.4	0.1	3.2 [i]	53	..	..	4.2
Morocco	..	3	0.2	0.1	12.4 [i]	66	443	..	3.2
Myanmar	..	..	(.)	0.0	..	6	64	2.8	2.3
Namibia	..	..	3.5 [i]	3.7	..	82	..	..	0.4
Niger	..	..	..	(.)	..	..	..	1.0	..
Nigeria	..	..	..	(.)	0.4	..	85	..	1.8
Oman	..	..	..	1.4	13.2	139	2,828	..	2.4
Papua New Guinea	..	..	..	0.1	..	14	..	2.9	..
Qatar	..	..	..	..	..	406	13,912	..	..
Russian Federation	..	131	0.3	3.5	16.0	220	3,937	..	19.7 [g]
Rwanda	..	..	0.0	0.1	..	3	..	2.6	..
Samoa (Western)	..	..	..	5.3	..	..	..	..	..
Saudi Arabia	..	(.)	0.0	0.3	5.2 [i]	170	4,692	..	2.8
Sierra Leone	..	..	..	0.1	..	..	..	2.4	..
Suriname	..	..	0.0 [i]	0.0	1.0 [i]	213	..	..	..
Swaziland	..	..	0.2	1.4	..	45	..	6.0	1.3
Switzerland	..	183	..	82.7	63.6	1,109	6,981	10.5	10.3
Tajikistan	..	2	..	0.1	..	35	2,046	..	4.7
Togo	..	..	..	0.1	0.4	12	..	3.3	0.4

A2.1 Technology achievement index				Technology creation		Diffusion of recent innovations		Diffusion of old innovations		Human skills	
				Patents granted to residents (per million people)	Receipts of royalties and license fees (US$ per 1,000 people)	Internet hosts (per 1,000 people)	High- and medium-technology exports (as % of total goods exports)	Telephones (mainline and cellular, per 1,000 people)	Electricity consumption (kilowatt-hours per capita)	Mean years of schooling (age 15 and above)	Gross tertiary science enrolment ratio (%)
TAI rank			Technology achievement index (TAI) value	1998 a	1999 b	2000	1999	1999	1998	2000	1995–97 c
Turkey			..	(.)	..	2.5	26.7	384	1,353	5.3	4.7
Turkmenistan			..	10	..	0.3	..	83	859	..	..
Uganda			..	..	0.0 j	(.)	2.2	5	..	3.5	0.3
Ukraine			..	84	..	1.2	..	203	2,350	..	..
United Arab Emirates			..	..	..	20.9	..	754	9,892	..	3.2
Uzbekistan			..	25	..	(.)	..	68	1,618	..	..
Venezuela			..	..	0.0	1.2	6.2	253	2,566	6.6	..
Viet Nam			..	..	..	(.)	..	31	232	..	..
Yemen			..	..	..	(.)	..	18	96	..	0.2
Zambia			..	(.)	..	0.2	..	12	539	5.5	..

a. For purposes of calculating the TAI a value of zero was used for countries for which no data were available.

b. For purposes of calculating the TAI a value of zero was used for non-OECD countries for which no data were available.

c. Data refer to the most recent year available during the period specified.

d. For purposes of calculating the TAI the weighted average value for OECD countries (901) was used.

e. For purposes of calculating the TAI the weighted average value for OECD countries (6,969) was used.

f. Data refer to the most recent year available during the period 1989–94.

g. Data are based on preliminary UNESCO estimates of the gross tertiary enrolment ratio.

h. Data are from national sources.

i. Data refer to 1998.

j. Data refer to 1997.

k. Data refer to the South African Customs Union, which comprises Botswana, Lesotho, Namibia, South Africa and Swaziland.

l. Data refer to medium-technology exports only.

Source: Column 1: calculated on the basis of data in columns 2–9; see technical note 2 for details; column 2: WIPO 2001a; column 3: unless otherwise noted, World Bank 2001h; column 4: ITU 2001a; column 5: calculated on the basis of data on exports from Lall 2001 and UN 2001a; column 6: ITU 2001b; column 7: World Bank 2001h; column 8: Barro and Lee 2000; column 9: calculated on the basis of data on gross tertiary enrolment ratios and tertiary science enrolment from UNESCO 1998, 1999 and 2001a.

HDI rank	Mean years of schooling (age 15 and above)				Research and development (R&D) expenditures		Scientists and engineers in R&D (per 100,000 people) 1987–97 [a]
	1970	1980	1990	2000	As % of GNP 1987–97 [a]	In business (as % of total) 1987–97 [a]	
High human development							
1 Norway	7.2	8.2	11.6	11.9	1.6	49.9	3,664
2 Australia	10.2	10.3	10.4	10.9	1.8	45.7	3,357
3 Canada	9.1	10.3	11.0	11.6	1.7	50.7	2,719
4 Sweden	8.0	9.7	9.5	11.4	3.8	62.9	3,826
5 Belgium	8.8	8.2	8.9	9.3	1.6	64.8	2,272
6 United States	9.5	11.9	11.7	12.0	2.6	59.4	3,676
7 Iceland	6.6	7.4	8.1	8.8	..	34.6	4,131
8 Netherlands	7.8	8.2	8.8	9.4	2.1	44.7	2,219
9 Japan	7.5	8.5	9.0	9.5	2.8	81.7	4,909
10 Finland	6.1	7.2	9.4	10.0	2.8	57.7	2,799
11 Switzerland	8.5	10.4	10.1	10.5	2.6	67.4	3,006
12 Luxembourg	..	..	..	..	..	..	..
13 France	5.7	6.7	7.0	7.9	2.3	48.7	2,659
14 United Kingdom	7.7	8.3	8.8	9.4	2.0	51.9	2,448
15 Denmark	8.8	9.0	9.6	9.7	2.0	49.8	3,259
16 Austria	7.4	7.3	7.8	8.4	1.5	49.0	1,627
17 Germany	..	..	9.9	10.2	2.4	61.4	2,831
18 Ireland	6.8	7.5	8.8	9.4	1.6	63.4	2,319
19 New Zealand	9.7	11.5	11.3	11.7	1.0	33.9	1,663
20 Italy	5.5	5.9	6.5	7.2	2.2	43.7	1,318
21 Spain	4.8	6.0	6.4	7.3	0.9	40.3	1,305
22 Israel	8.1	9.4	9.4	9.6	2.4	35.7	..
23 Greece	5.4	7.0	8.0	8.7	0.5	20.2	773
24 Hong Kong, China (SAR)	6.3	8.0	9.2	9.4	..	2.8	..
25 Cyprus	5.2	6.5	8.7	9.2	..	13.1	209
26 Singapore	5.1	5.5	6.0	7.1	1.1	62.5	2,318
27 Korea, Rep. of	4.9	7.9	9.9	10.8	2.8	84.0	2,193
28 Portugal	2.6	3.8	4.9	5.9	0.6	18.9	1,182
29 Slovenia	..	..	6.6	7.1	1.5	49.1	2,251
30 Malta	..	..	..	..	..	..	..
31 Barbados	9.7	6.8	7.9	8.7	..	..	..
32 Brunei Darussalam	4.8	6.0	..	..	..	..	..
33 Czech Republic	..	..	9.2	9.5	1.2	63.1	1,222
34 Argentina	6.2	7.0	8.1	8.8	0.4	11.3	660
35 Slovakia	..	..	8.9	9.3	1.1	60.4	1,866
36 Hungary	8.1	9.1	8.9	9.1	0.7	79.6	1,099
37 Uruguay	5.7	6.2	7.1	7.6	..	..	..
38 Poland	7.9	8.8	9.5	9.8	0.8	31.8	1,358
39 Chile	5.7	6.4	7.0	7.6	0.7	15.2	445
40 Bahrain	2.8	3.6	5.0	6.1	..	..	..
41 Costa Rica	3.9	5.2	5.6	6.1	0.2	..	532
42 Bahamas	..	..	..	..	..	..	..
43 Kuwait	3.1	4.5	5.8	6.2	0.2	64.3	230
44 Estonia	..	..	9.0	..	0.6	7.7	2,017
45 United Arab Emirates	..	..	..	..	..	..	..
46 Croatia	..	..	5.9	6.3	1.0	19.0	1,916
47 Lithuania	..	..	9.4	..	0.7	..	2,028
48 Qatar	..	..	..	..	..	..	..
Medium human development							
49 Trinidad and Tobago	5.3	7.3	7.2	7.8	..	..	..
50 Latvia	..	..	9.5	..	0.4	20.5	1,049

| HDI rank | | Mean years of schooling (age 15 and above) | | | | Research and development (R&D) expenditures | | Scientists and engineers in R&D (per 100,000 people) |
		1970	1980	1990	2000	As % of GNP 1987–97 [a]	In business (as % of total) 1987–97 [a]	1987–97 [a]
51	Mexico	3.7	4.8	6.7	7.2	0.3	17.6	214
52	Panama	4.8	6.4	8.1	8.6	..	..	..
53	Belarus	..	..	..	..	1.1	27.9	2,248
54	Belize	..	..	..	..	..	..	..
55	Russian Federation	..	..	..	..	0.9	15.5	3,587
56	Malaysia	3.9	5.1	6.0	6.8	0.2	8.3	93
57	Bulgaria	6.6	7.3	9.2	9.5	0.6	60.5	1,747
58	Romania	6.2	7.8	9.4	9.5	0.7	23.1	1,387
59	Libyan Arab Jamahiriya	..	..	..	..	..	..	..
60	Macedonia, TFYR	..	..	..	..	..	28.2	1,335
61	Venezuela	3.2	5.5	5.0	6.6	0.5	..	209
62	Colombia	3.1	4.4	4.7	5.3	..	..	..
63	Mauritius	4.2	5.2	5.6	6.0	0.4	2.4	361
64	Suriname	..	..	..	..	..	..	..
65	Lebanon	..	..	..	..	..	..	..
66	Thailand	4.1	4.4	5.6	6.5	0.1	12.2	103
67	Fiji	5.5	6.8	7.9	8.3	..	..	..
68	Saudi Arabia	..	..	..	..	..	..	..
69	Brazil	3.3	3.1	4.0	4.9	0.8	40.0	168
70	Philippines	4.8	6.5	7.3	8.2	0.2	1.9	157
71	Oman	..	..	..	..	..	..	..
72	Armenia	..	..	..	..	..	..	1,485
73	Peru	4.6	6.1	6.2	7.6	..	27.2	233
74	Ukraine	..	..	..	..	..	46.3	2,171
75	Kazakhstan	..	..	8.9	..	0.3	1.0	..
76	Georgia	..	..	..	..	..	..	..
77	Maldives	..	..	..	..	..	..	..
78	Jamaica	3.2	4.1	4.7	5.3	..	..	..
79	Azerbaijan	..	..	..	..	0.2	..	2,791
80	Paraguay	4.2	5.1	6.1	6.2	..	..	..
81	Sri Lanka	4.7	5.6	6.1	6.9	..	..	191
82	Turkey	2.6	3.4	4.2	5.3	0.5	32.9	291
83	Turkmenistan	..	..	..	..	..	..	..
84	Ecuador	3.5	6.1	5.9	6.4	(.)	..	146
85	Albania	..	..	..	..	..	..	..
86	Dominican Republic	3.4	3.8	4.4	4.9	..	..	..
87	China	..	4.8	5.9	6.4	0.7	..	454
88	Jordan	3.3	4.3	6.0	6.9	0.3	..	94
89	Tunisia	1.5	2.9	3.9	5.0	0.3	..	125
90	Iran, Islamic Rep. of	1.6	2.8	4.0	5.3	0.5	..	560
91	Cape Verde	..	..	..	..	..	..	..
92	Kyrgyzstan	..	..	..	..	0.2	24.8	584
93	Guyana	4.5	5.2	5.7	6.3	..	..	..
94	South Africa	4.6	3.8	5.4	6.1	0.7	54.4	1,031
95	El Salvador	2.7	3.2	4.3	5.2	..	..	20
96	Samoa (Western)	6.4	5.9	..	..	..	..	..
97	Syrian Arab Republic	2.2	3.7	5.1	5.8	0.2	..	30
98	Moldova, Rep. of	..	..	9.2	..	0.9	51.4	330
99	Uzbekistan	..	..	..	..	..	..	1,763
100	Algeria	1.6	2.7	4.3	5.4	..	..	..

TODAY'S TECHNOLOGICAL TRANSFORMATIONS—CREATING THE NETWORK AGE

HDI rank		Mean years of schooling (age 15 and above)				Research and development (R&D) expenditures		Scientists and engineers in R&D (per 100,000 people)
		1970	1980	1990	2000	As % of GNP 1987–97 [a]	In business (as % of total) 1987–97 [a]	1987–97 [a]
101	Viet Nam	..	..	3.8	..	..	..	..
102	Indonesia	2.9	3.7	4.0	5.0	0.1	76.4	182
103	Tajikistan	..	..	9.8	..	..	..	666
104	Bolivia	4.8	4.6	5.0	5.6	0.5	..	172
105	Egypt	..	2.3	4.3	5.5	0.2	..	459
106	Nicaragua	2.9	3.2	3.7	4.6	..	..	204
107	Honduras	2.2	2.8	4.2	4.8	..	..	..
108	Guatemala	1.7	2.7	3.0	3.5	0.2	0.5	104
109	Gabon	..	..	..	..	..	..	234
110	Equatorial Guinea	..	..	..	..	..	..	..
111	Namibia	..	..	..	..	..	..	..
112	Morocco	..	..	..	..	..	..	..
113	Swaziland	2.5	3.9	5.3	6.0	..	..	..
114	Botswana	2.0	3.1	5.3	6.3	..	..	..
115	India	2.3	3.3	4.1	5.1	0.7	24.0	149
116	Mongolia	..	..	..	..	..	..	910
117	Zimbabwe	2.0	2.1	5.0	5.4	..	..	..
118	Myanmar	1.4	1.6	2.5	2.8	..	..	..
119	Ghana	3.3	3.4	3.6	3.9	..	..	..
120	Lesotho	3.4	3.8	3.9	4.2	..	..	..
121	Cambodia	..	..	..	..	..	..	..
122	Papua New Guinea	1.1	1.7	2.3	2.9	..	..	..
123	Kenya	2.2	3.4	3.7	4.2	..	..	..
124	Comoros	..	..	..	..	..	..	..
125	Cameroon	1.9	2.4	3.1	3.5	..	..	..
126	Congo	..	..	5.1	5.1	..	25.5	..
Low human development								
127	Pakistan	1.5	2.1	4.2	3.9	0.9	..	72
128	Togo	0.8	2.3	2.9	3.3	0.5	..	98
129	Nepal	0.2	0.9	1.6	2.4	..	..	..
130	Bhutan	..	..	..	..	..	..	..
131	Lao People's Dem. Rep.	..	..	..	..	..	..	..
132	Bangladesh	0.9	1.9	2.2	2.6	(.)	..	52
133	Yemen	..	0.3	1.5	..	..	..	..
134	Haiti	1.2	1.9	2.9	2.8	..	..	..
135	Madagascar	..	..	..	..	0.2	..	12
136	Nigeria	..	..	..	..	0.1	..	15
137	Djibouti	..	..	..	..	..	..	..
138	Sudan	0.6	1.1	1.6	2.1	..	..	..
139	Mauritania	..	..	2.4	..	..	..	..
140	Tanzania, U. Rep. of	2.8	2.7	2.8	2.7	..	..	..
141	Uganda	1.4	1.8	3.3	3.5	0.6	2.2	21
142	Congo, Dem. Rep. of the	1.2	2.0	2.8	3.0	..	..	..
143	Zambia	2.8	3.9	4.2	5.5	..	..	..
144	Côte d'Ivoire	..	..	..	..	..	..	..
145	Senegal	1.7	2.2	2.3	2.6	(.)	..	3
146	Angola	..	..	..	..	..	..	..
147	Benin	0.5	1.1	2.0	2.3	0.0	..	176
148	Eritrea	..	..	..	..	..	..	..
149	Gambia	..	0.9	1.6	2.3	..	..	..
150	Guinea	..	..	..	..	..	..	..

HDI rank	Mean years of schooling (age 15 and above)				Research and development (R&D) expenditures		Scientists and engineers in R&D (per 100,000 people)
	1970	1980	1990	2000	As % of GNP 1987–97 [a]	In business (as % of total) 1987–97 [a]	1987–97 [a]
151 Malawi	1.9	2.7	2.7	3.2	..	..	..
152 Rwanda	1.1	1.7	2.1	2.6	(.)	..	35
153 Mali	0.3	0.5	0.7	0.9	..	..	..
154 Central African Republic	0.8	1.3	2.4	2.5	..	..	56
155 Chad	..	..	..	..	..	..	..
156 Guinea-Bissau	..	0.3	0.7	0.8	..	..	..
157 Mozambique	0.6	0.8	0.9	1.1	..	..	..
158 Ethiopia	..	..	..	..	..	..	..
159 Burkina Faso	..	..	..	..	0.2	..	17
160 Burundi	..	..	1.4	..	0.3	..	33
161 Niger	0.3	0.6	0.8	1.0	..	..	..
162 Sierra Leone	0.9	1.6	2.1	2.4	..	..	..
Developing countries	..	3.9	4.9	..	..	..	..
Least developed countries	..	..	..	..	..	..	..
Arab States	..	..	..	..	..	..	..
East Asia and the Pacific	..	4.7	5.7	..	1.3	..	..
Latin America and the Caribbean	3.8	4.4	5.3	6.1	0.6	..	..
South Asia	2.1	3.0	3.9	4.7	0.6	..	152
Sub-Saharan Africa	..	..	..	..	..	..	..
Eastern Europe and the CIS	..	..	..	..	0.9	..	2,437
OECD	7.3	8.6	9.1	9.6	2.3	..	2,585
High-income OECD	7.7	9.2	9.5	10.0	2.4	..	3,141
High human development	7.6	8.9	9.4	9.9	2.3	..	2,827
Medium human development	..	4.1	5.1	..	0.6	..	..
Low human development	..	1.8	2.8	..	..	..	..
High income	7.7	9.1	9.5	10.0	2.4	..	3,127
Middle income	..	4.8	5.9	..	1.0	..	687
Low income	..	..	..	..	0.9	..	..
World	..	5.2	6.0	..	2.2	..	959

a. Data refer to the most recent year available during the period specified.

Source: Columns 1–4: Barro and Lee 2000; *columns 5 and 7:* World Bank 2001h, based on data from UNESCO; *column 6:* UNESCO 1999.

HDI rank	Fertilizer consumption (kg per hectare of arable and permanently cropped land)		Tractors in use (per hectare of arable and permanently cropped land)		Low-technology exports (as % of total goods exports)		Medium-technology exports (as % of total goods exports)		High-technology exports (as % of total goods exports)	
	1970	1998	1970	1998	1980	1999	1980	1999	1980	1999
High human development										
1 Norway	244.3	225.8	110.6	163.0	5	4	18	14	3	5
2 Australia	23.2	39.1	7.8	5.8	4	5	7	11	2	5
3 Canada	18.4	58.0	13.6	15.6	5	9	25	38	6	11
4 Sweden	164.6	100.6	59.0	59.3	16	12	39	34	11	26
5 Belgium	511.2 [a]	365.4 [a]	97.8 [a]	127.5 [a]	20 [a]	15	30 [a]	37	6 [a]	11
6 United States	81.6	110.5	27.7	26.8	..	10	..	34	..	32
7 Iceland	3,335.4	3,100.0	1,411.7	1,753.2	5	2	3	8	(.)	2
8 Netherlands	749.3	494.2	156.0	164.7	11	12	22	25	9	26
9 Japan	337.2	289.5	48.0	450.6	16	8	59	51	14	30
10 Finland	188.8	140.6	60.2	89.7	19	9	21	24	4	27
11 Switzerland	383.1	749.4	189.6	255.1	16	15	40	38	16	26
12 Luxembourg	..	..	..	..	..	37	..	24	..	10
13 France	243.5	247.5	64.4	65.1	17	14	36	37	11	22
14 United Kingdom	263.1	330.4	62.1	79.3	12	11	33	33	15	29
15 Denmark	223.4	169.8	65.3	59.0	16	19	24	22	9	19
16 Austria	242.6	170.4	148.1	238.3	29	23	34	38	8	12
17 Germany	384.4	242.7	121.5	88.6	16 [b]	13	48 [b]	46	12 [b]	18
18 Ireland	306.7	519.9	61.1	123.3	15	10	17	12	12	42
19 New Zealand	128.1	201.7	27.6	23.2	8	8	4	10	1	5
20 Italy	89.6	157.9	41.2	133.7	32	30	37	40	8	11
21 Spain	59.3	110.4	12.7	44.1	23	16	31	43	5	10
22 Israel	140.1	277.1	40.0	56.1	..	12	..	16	..	29
23 Greece	86.1	123.3	15.8	61.2	26	26	12	13	1	5
24 Hong Kong, China (SAR)	..	..	..	..	63	56	22	10	9	24
25 Cyprus	120.9	143.0	27.2	118.9	32	24	12	11	2	12
26 Singapore	250.0	2,350.0	1.7	65.0	8	7	18	17	14	58
27 Korea, Rep. of	245.0	457.6	(.)	82.7	47	18	25	34	10	33
28 Portugal	41.8	96.1	10.4	60.1	35	36	16	34	8	7
29 Slovenia	..	268.7	..	367.5	..	28	..	38	..	12
30 Malta	45.6	90.9	10.2	45.1	..	19	..	11	..	61
31 Barbados	335.3	176.5	24.4	34.4	28	16	9	22	13	9
32 Brunei Darussalam	..	..	0.6	10.3	..	..	..	..	..	..
33 Czech Republic	..	90.3	..	25.5	..	26	..	40	..	12
34 Argentina	3.3	29.8	6.5	10.3	9	9	9	16	2	3
35 Slovakia	..	66.3	..	15.6	..	24	..	42	..	7
36 Hungary	149.7	90.3	12.1	18.3	24	17	11	40	26	24
37 Uruguay	48.5	102.0	20.7	25.2	..	24	..	12	..	2
38 Poland	167.8	113.2	14.7	91.1	18	31	36	28	10	8
39 Chile	31.6	194.6	8.3	23.5	..	3	..	5	..	1
40 Bahrain	..	100.0	..	2.0	..	4 [c]	..	5 [c]	..	(.) [c]
41 Costa Rica	100.1	391.9	10.3	13.9	..	13	..	8	..	44
42 Bahamas	133.3	30.0	5.9	11.0	..	..	..	..	..	..
43 Kuwait	..	300.0	9.0	11.7	..	1	..	6	..	(.)
44 Estonia	..	28.5	..	44.9	..	26	..	15	..	17
45 United Arab Emirates	..	390.1	11.7	3.4	..	..	..	..	..	..
46 Croatia	..	127.7	..	1.7	..	27	..	33	..	8
47 Lithuania	..	46.5	..	28.2	..	30	..	22	..	7
48 Qatar	..	58.8	25.0	4.4	..	..	..	..	..	..
Medium human development										
49 Trinidad and Tobago	88.0	86.9	18.5	22.1	1	11	1	13	(.)	1
50 Latvia	..	23.8	..	28.5	..	32	..	6	..	6

		Fertilizer consumption (kg per hectare of arable and permanently cropped land)		Tractors in use (per hectare of arable and permanently cropped land)		Low-technology exports (as % of total goods exports)		Medium-technology exports (as % of total goods exports)		High-technology exports (as % of total goods exports)	
HDI rank		1970	1998	1970	1998	1980	1999	1980	1999	1980	1999
51	Mexico	23.2	62.5	3.9	6.3	..	16	..	39	..	28
52	Panama	38.7	49.2	4.4	7.6	..	9	..	3	..	2
53	Belarus	..	145.0	..	15.2	..	22	..	42	..	5
54	Belize	73.3	52.8	12.7	12.9	..	12	..	(.)	..	..
55	Russian Federation	..	8.5	..	6.7	..	6	..	13	..	3
56	Malaysia	43.6	184.9	1.0	5.7	3	9	4	16	10	52
57	Bulgaria	141.1	37.5	11.8	5.5	..	23 c	..	24 c	..	6 c
58	Romania	56.5	36.5	10.2	16.8	..	48	..	21	..	4
59	Libyan Arab Jamahiriya	6.2	23.8	1.9	16.1	..	2 c	..	2 c	(.) c	(.) c
60	Macedonia, TFYR	..	69.3	..	85.0	..	40 c	..	21 c	..	3 c
61	Venezuela	17.0	69.6	5.5	14.0	..	3	..	6	..	(.)
62	Colombia	28.7	152.4	4.5	5.1	10	11	4	11	1	2
63	Mauritius	209.5	312.3	2.7	3.5	21	67	2	3	3	1
64	Suriname	56.3	82.1	24.2	19.9	..	(.) c	..	1 c	..	(.) c
65	Lebanon	135.4	196.4	7.7	18.2	..	..	..	..	..	..
66	Thailand	5.9	81.5	0.5	10.8	11	19	9	19	1	30
67	Fiji	40.7	77.2	15.1	24.6	(.)	..	(.)	..	..	..
68	Saudi Arabia	3.3	84.1	0.4	2.5	(.)	1 c	(.)	5 c	(.)	(.) c
69	Brazil	79.5	88.0	4.9	12.4	..	12	..	24	..	9
70	Philippines	26.9	62.8	0.9	1.2	12	7	3	7	1	26
71	Oman	..	95.2	0.9	2.4	..	3	..	11	..	2
72	Armenia	..	..	..	31.3	..	9	..	8	..	4
73	Peru	30.0	45.7	3.9	3.2	11	12	3	2	1	1
74	Ukraine	..	15.4	..	10.3	..	..	..	..	..	..
75	Kazakhstan	..	1.5	..	2.1	..	5	..	12	..	3
76	Georgia	..	32.7	..	15.5	..	..	..	..	..	..
77	Maldives	..	..	..	..	..	..	..	..	..	..
78	Jamaica	87.3	85.6	7.0	11.2	3	18 c	2	1 c	(.)	(.) c
79	Azerbaijan	..	12.2	..	17.1	..	2	..	5	..	1
80	Paraguay	9.8	26.9	5.2	7.2	..	9	..	1	..	1
81	Sri Lanka	55.5	123.4	7.1	3.9	12	64	1	2	(.)	3
82	Turkey	15.7	80.9	3.8	32.4	..	47	..	20	..	7
83	Turkmenistan	..	89.1	..	29.5	..	..	..	..	..	..
84	Ecuador	13.3	57.5	1.2	3.0	1	3	1	2	(.)	1
85	Albania	73.6	35.8	10.0	11.7	..	61 c	..	2 c	..	2 c
86	Dominican Republic	33.4	61.6	1.7	1.5	..	2 c	..	5 c	..	(.) c
87	China	43.0	258.8	1.2	5.2	..	44	..	18	..	21
88	Jordan	8.7	60.1	8.8	12.3	..	..	..	..	..	..
89	Tunisia	7.6	24.7	4.7	7.2	20	52	10	16	(.)	3
90	Iran, Islamic Rep. of	6.0	66.6	1.3	12.1	..	5	..	2	..	(.)
91	Cape Verde	..	..	0.1	0.4	3	..	2	..	(.)	..
92	Kyrgyzstan	..	39.7	..	13.3	..	5	..	7	..	4
93	Guyana	27.0	32.7	9.0	7.3	..	..	..	..	..	..
94	South Africa	42.2	49.7	11.8	5.6	4 d	11 d	5 d	26 d	(.) d	4 d
95	El Salvador	104.0	102.0	4.0	4.2	..	28	..	13	..	6
96	Samoa (Western)	..	..	0.1	0.6	1	..	1	..	..	..
97	Syrian Arab Republic	6.8	60.0	1.5	17.0	4	6	2	1	(.)	(.)
98	Moldova, Rep. of	..	55.5	..	20.2	..	20	..	4	..	2
99	Uzbekistan	..	177.2	..	35.1	..	..	..	..	..	..
100	Algeria	16.3	11.7	5.9	11.4	(.)	(.)	(.)	1	(.)	(.)

HDI rank	Fertilizer consumption (kg per hectare of arable and permanently cropped land)		Tractors in use (per hectare of arable and permanently cropped land)		Low-technology exports (as % of total goods exports)		Medium-technology exports (as % of total goods exports)		High-technology exports (as % of total goods exports)	
	1970	1998	1970	1998	1980	1999	1980	1999	1980	1999
101 Viet Nam	50.7	268.6	0.5	17.0	..	..	..	..	..	..
102 Indonesia	9.2	89.5	0.3	2.3	1	23	(.)	11	1	7
103 Tajikistan	..	65.4	..	33.7	..	..	..	..	..	..
104 Bolivia	0.9	3.4	1.3	2.6	1	10	1	5	(.)	21
105 Egypt	131.2	337.2	6.1	27.3	..	24	..	7	..	2
106 Nicaragua	21.5	19.2	0.4	1.0	..	3	..	3	..	(.)
107 Honduras	15.6	68.4	1.1	2.5	..	11	..	7	..	1
108 Guatemala	29.8	116.7	2.0	2.3	..	14	..	12	..	4
109 Gabon	..	0.8	2.7	3.0	..	(.) c	..	(.) c	..	1 c
110 Equatorial Guinea	8.4	..	0.3	0.4	..	..	..	..	..	..
111 Namibia	..	..	3.1	3.8	..	..	..	..	..	..
112 Morocco	11.7	35.1	1.4	4.3	11	22 c	3	12 c	(.)	(.) c
113 Swaziland	39.6	30.6	7.6	16.2	..	..	..	..	..	..
114 Botswana	4.2	12.1	4.0	17.3	..	..	..	..	..	..
115 India	13.7	99.1	0.6	9.1	33	38 c	10	11 c	3	5 c
116 Mongolia	2.2	3.8	7.4	5.3	..	7 c	..	3 c	..	(.) c
117 Zimbabwe	43.7	52.1	6.2	6.9	..	11	..	11	..	1
118 Myanmar	2.1	16.9	0.5	0.8	..	..	..	..	..	..
119 Ghana	1.0	2.9	0.8	0.7	..	7	..	2	..	2
120 Lesotho	1.0	18.5	1.0	6.2	..	..	..	..	..	..
121 Cambodia	1.2	3.3	0.4	0.3	..	..	..	..	..	..
122 Papua New Guinea	4.3	22.4	2.9	1.7	..	..	..	..	..	..
123 Kenya	12.5	28.2	1.8	3.2	4	10	2	6	1	2
124 Comoros	..	2.5	..	..	..	..	..	..	..	..
125 Cameroon	3.4	5.5	(.)	0.1	1	3 c	1	2 c	(.)	1 c
126 Congo	48.3	22.9	4.2	3.2	(.)	..	(.)	..	(.)	..
Low human development										
127 Pakistan	14.6	111.7	1.1	14.5	..	76	..	7	..	1
128 Togo	0.2	7.5	(.)	(.)	2	5	2	(.)	(.)	(.)
129 Nepal	2.7	40.9	0.4	1.5	..	74 c	..	2 c	..	(.) c
130 Bhutan	..	0.6	..	..	..	..	..	..	..	..
131 Lao People's Dem. Rep.	0.3	11.9	0.4	1.0	..	..	..	..	..	..
132 Bangladesh	15.7	140.5	0.2	0.6	64	87 c	2	3 c	(.)	(.) c
133 Yemen	0.1	13.5	1.2	3.6	10 e	..	32 e	..	2 e	..
134 Haiti	0.4	8.9	0.2	0.2	..	72 c	..	(.) c	..	3 c
135 Madagascar	6.1	2.8	1.0	1.1	3	34	(.)	1	2	2
136 Nigeria	0.2	6.1	0.1	1.0	..	(.)	..	(.)	..	(.)
137 Djibouti	..	..	..	..	..	..	..	..	..	..
138 Sudan	2.8	2.2	0.4	0.6	..	2 c	..	(.) c	..	(.) c
139 Mauritania	1.1	4.2	0.4	0.8	..	..	..	..	..	..
140 Tanzania, U. Rep. of	5.1	6.0	5.8	1.6	..	4	..	5	..	2
141 Uganda	1.4	0.3	0.3	0.7	..	1	..	2	..	(.)
142 Congo, Dem. Rep. of the	0.6	..	0.1	0.3	..	..	..	..	..	..
143 Zambia	7.3	7.6	0.6	1.1	..	..	..	..	..	..
144 Côte d'Ivoire	6.4	15.4	0.4	0.5	..	..	..	..	..	..
145 Senegal	3.4	11.8	0.1	0.2	3	8	9	22	2	7
146 Angola	3.3	1.5	2.1	2.9	(.)	..	(.)	..	..	..
147 Benin	4.4	20.4	0.1	0.1	..	..	..	..	..	..
148 Eritrea	..	13.0	..	1.2	..	..	..	..	..	..
149 Gambia	2.3	7.5	0.3	0.2	..	..	..	..	..	..
150 Guinea	2.7	2.2	(.)	0.4	..	..	..	..	..	..

HDI rank	Fertilizer consumption (kg per hectare of arable and permanently cropped land)		Tractors in use (per hectare of arable and permanently cropped land)		Low-technology exports (as % of total goods exports)		Medium-technology exports (as % of total goods exports)		High-technology exports (as % of total goods exports)	
	1970	1998	1970	1998	1980	1999	1980	1999	1980	1999
151 Malawi	8.5	25.1	0.7	0.7	6	..	(.)	..	(.)	..
152 Rwanda	0.3	0.3	0.1	0.1	..	..	..	..	..	..
153 Mali	3.1	11.3	0.3	0.6	1	..	(.)	..	(.)	..
154 Central African Republic	1.2	0.3	(.)	(.)	(.)	(.) c	(.)	13 c	(.)	(.) c
155 Chad	0.7	4.7	(.)	(.)	..	..	..	..	..	..
156 Guinea-Bissau	..	1.7	(.)	0.1	..	..	..	..	..	..
157 Mozambique	2.2	1.5	1.4	1.7	..	3 c	..	11 c	..	1 c
158 Ethiopia	0.4	15.5	0.2	0.3	(.)	..	(.)	..	..	..
159 Burkina Faso	0.3	14.6	(.)	0.6	3	..	2	..	1	..
160 Burundi	0.5	1.9	(.)	0.2	..	..	..	..	..	..
161 Niger	0.1	0.2	(.)	(.)	1	..	1	..	(.)	..
162 Sierra Leone	5.7	5.6	0.3	0.2	..	..	..	..	..	..
Developing countries	19.2	100.7	1.9	7.7	..	20	..	20	..	25
Least developed countries	3.4	18.1	0.6	0.7	..	..	..	..	..	..
Arab States	16.6	44.9	2.6	7.4	..	10	..	7	..	1
East Asia and the Pacific	33.9	193.3	1.0	5.9	..	24	..	20	..	33
Latin America and the Caribbean	21.8	71.3	5.1	9.7	..	12	..	26	..	16
South Asia	13.6	98.6	0.7	9.5	..	31	..	3	..	1
Sub-Saharan Africa	7.4	13.8	1.8	1.5	..	8	..	12	..	2
Eastern Europe and the CIS	..	..	..	..	..	18	..	26	..	8
OECD	94.4	113.6	27.4	39.6	17	14	37	38	10	21
High-income OECD	99.8	118.3	31.4	40.6	16	13	37	38	10	20
High human development	97.1	114.6	28.7	40.2	17	13	36	37	10	22
Medium human development	24.4	118.1	2.2	8.7	..	21	..	19	..	19
Low human development	4.5	28.8	0.5	2.6	..	..	..	..	..	..
High income	99.8	118.5	31.4	40.6	17	13	36	37	10	21
Middle income	39.2	129.6	4.3	12.6	..	21	..	22	..	20
Low income	9.9	65.6	0.6	5.4	..	21	..	7	..	4
World	50.1	105.4	12.3	18.6	..	15	..	33	..	22

a. Includes Luxembourg.

b. Data refer to the Federal Republic of Germany before unification.

c. Data refer to 1998.

d. Data refer to the South African Customs Union, which comprises Botswana, Lesotho, Namibia, South Africa and Swaziland.

e. Data refer to the former Yemen Arab Republic.

Source: Columns 1–4: calculated on the basis of data on fertilizer consumption and land use from FAO 2000a; *columns 5–10:* calculated on the basis of data on exports from Lall 2000 and UN 2001a.

HDI rank	Telephone mainlines (per 1,000 people)		Cellular mobile subscribers (per 1,000 people)		Internet hosts (per 1,000 people)		Cost of a three-minute local call		Waiting list for mainlines (per 1,000 people)	
							PPP US$	Index (1990 = 100)		
	1990	1999	1990	1999	1995	2000	1999	1999	1990	1999
High human development										
1 Norway	503	712	46	617	20.1	193.6	0.07	51	0	0
2 Australia	456	520	11	343	17.7	125.9	0.18	..	0	0
3 Canada	565	655	22	227	17.5	108.0	..	..	0	0
4 Sweden	681	665	54	583	18.6	125.8	..	..	0	0
5 Belgium	393	502	4	314	3.5	58.9	0.16	77	2	..
6 United States	545	682	21	312	21.1	179.1	..	..	0	0
7 Iceland	510	677	39	619	31.3	232.4	0.10	188	0	0
8 Netherlands	464	606	5	435	12.2	136.0	0.13	77	1	0
9 Japan	441	558	7	449	2.3	49.0	0.06	91	0	0
10 Finland	534	552	52	651	42.2	200.2	0.12	93	0	0
11 Switzerland	574	699	18	411	12.9	82.7	0.10	80	1	0
12 Luxembourg	481	724	2	487	5.7	49.5	0.10	67	8	0
13 France	495	579	5	364	3.1	36.4	0.11	83	0	0
14 United Kingdom	441	575	19	463	8.4	57.4	0.17	..	0	0
15 Denmark	567	685	29	495	11.4	114.3	0.09	86	0	0
16 Austria	418	472	10	514	7.1	84.2	0.16	84	4	0
17 Germany	441	588	4	286	6.3	41.2	0.10	..	(.)	0
18 Ireland	281	478	7	447	4.2	48.6	..	..	1	..
19 New Zealand	434	490	16	230	15.1	146.7	0.00	..	(.)	0
20 Italy	388	462	5	528	1.6	30.4	..	..	1	0
21 Spain	316	418	1	312	1.8	21.0	0.11	221	7	(.)
22 Israel	343	459	3	459	5.4	43.2	..	..	4	..
23 Greece	389	528	0	311	0.8	16.4	0.08	..	107	2
24 Hong Kong, China (SAR)	450	576	24	636	5.2	33.6	0.00	..	1	0
25 Cyprus	428	545	5	190	0.6	16.9	0.03	..	35	6
26 Singapore	349	482	17	419	7.4	72.3	0.02	..	(.)	0
27 Korea, Rep. of	310	438	2	500	0.8	4.8	0.06	94	(.)	0
28 Portugal	243	424	1	468	1.3	17.7	0.14	121	23	3
29 Slovenia	211	378	0	309	2.9	20.3	..	..	36	3
30 Malta	360	512	0	97	0.2	19.5	0.20	453	57	2
31 Barbados	281	427	0	111	(.)	0.5	..	..	11	3
32 Brunei Darussalam	136	246	7	205	0.5	8.0	..	..	52	..
33 Czech Republic	158	371	0	189	2.2	25.0	0.36	146	30	7
34 Argentina	93	201	(.)	121	0.2	8.7	..	..	24	..
35 Slovakia	135	308	0	171	0.6	10.2	0.35	..	21	13
36 Hungary	96	371	(.)	162	1.6	21.6	0.30	111	59	8
37 Uruguay	134	271	0	95	0.2	19.6	0.24	266	29	0
38 Poland	86	263	0	102	0.6	11.4	0.15	339	62	..
39 Chile	66	207	1	151	0.7	6.2	..	..	24	..
40 Bahrain	192	249	11	205	0.2	3.6	..	..	(.)	..
41 Costa Rica	101	204	0	35	0.6	4.1	0.05	24	16	9
42 Bahamas	274	369	8	53	5.1	..	..	..	..	..
43 Kuwait	247	240	15	158	0.7	4.4	..	..	..	0
44 Estonia	204	357	0	268	2.4	43.1	0.14	..	..	27
45 United Arab Emirates	206	407	17	347	0.2	20.9	..	..	1	(.)
46 Croatia	172	365	(.)	66	0.5	6.7	..	..	39	..
47 Lithuania	212	311	0	90	0.1	7.5	0.13	..	55	20
48 Qatar	190	263	8	143	0.0	..	..	..	1	..
Medium human development										
49 Trinidad and Tobago	141	216	0	30	0.2	7.7	..	..	1	8
50 Latvia	234	300	0	112	0.5	13.4	0.27	..	..	8

HDI rank		Telephone mainlines (per 1,000 people)		Cellular mobile subscribers (per 1,000 people)		Internet hosts (per 1,000 people)		Cost of a three-minute local call		Waiting list for mainlines (per 1,000 people)	
								PPP US$	Index (1990 = 100)		
		1990	1999	1990	1999	1995	2000	1999	1999	1990	1999
51	Mexico	65	112	1	79	0.2	9.2	0.22	86	13	..
52	Panama	93	164	0	86	0.3	1.9	..	..	6	..
53	Belarus	153	257	0	2	(.)	0.3	0.06	..		43
54	Belize	92	156	0	26	(.)	2.2	0.12	..	14	..
55	Russian Federation	140	210	0	9	0.2	3.5	0.09	..	74	44
56	Malaysia	89	203	5	137	0.3	2.4	0.06	44	5	..
57	Bulgaria	242	354	0	42	0.1	3.7	..	..	67	40
58	Romania	102	167	0	61	0.1	2.7	..	..	42	33
59	Libyan Arab Jamahiriya	48	..	0	..	0.0	(.)	..	..	54	15
60	Macedonia, TFYR	148	234	0	24	0.1	1.9	0.02	..	..	..
61	Venezuela	82	109	(.)	143	0.1	1.2	..	..	32	..
62	Colombia	75	160	0	75	0.1	1.9	..	..	14	..
63	Mauritius	52	224	2	89	0.0	5.2	0.10	..	52	25
64	Suriname	92	171	0	42	(.)	0.0	..	..	23	88
65	Lebanon	118	..	0	194	0.1	2.3	..	..	..	..
66	Thailand	24	86	1	38	0.1	1.6	0.23	..	18	7
67	Fiji	57	101	0	29	0.1	0.9	0.13	80	17	..
68	Saudi Arabia	77	129	1	40	0.1	0.3	..	..	8	..
69	Brazil	65	149	(.)	89	0.2	7.2	..	..	3	..
70	Philippines	10	39	0	38	(.)	0.4	0.00	..	9	..
71	Oman	60	90	2	49	(.)	1.4	..	..	3	..
72	Armenia	157	155	0	2	(.)	0.9	0.49	..	..	20
73	Peru	26	67	(.)	40	(.)	0.7	..	..	17	1
74	Ukraine	136	199	0	4	(.)	1.2	..	..	69	52
75	Kazakhstan	80	108	0	3	(.)	0.6	..	..	45	11
76	Georgia	99	123	0	19	(.)	0.4	..	..	53	19
77	Maldives	29	80	0	11	0.0	1.7	0.19	..	4	2
78	Jamaica	45	199	0	56	0.1	0.4	..	..	39	..
79	Azerbaijan	86	95	0	23	(.)	0.1	..	..	..	11
80	Paraguay	27	55	0	81	(.)	0.5	..	..	2	..
81	Sri Lanka	7	36	(.)	12	(.)	0.2	0.18	137	3	12
82	Turkey	121	265	1	119	0.2	2.5	..	..	25	7
83	Turkmenistan	60	82	0	1	0.0	0.3	..	..	24	13
84	Ecuador	48	91	0	31	0.1	0.3	0.03	351	15	..
85	Albania	12	36	0	3	( )	0.1	0.06	86	77	26
86	Dominican Republic	48	98	(.)	50	0.1	1.7	..	..	..	..
87	China	6	86	(.)	34	(.)	0.1	0.06	..	1	..
88	Jordan	58	87	(.)	18	0.1	0.2	0.06	197	15	5
89	Tunisia	38	90	(.)	6	(.)	(.)	0.07	27	15	9
90	Iran, Islamic Rep. of	40	125	0	7	(.)	(.)	0.03	..	9	18
91	Cape Verde	24	112	0	19	0.0	0.1	0.11	..	..	14
92	Kyrgyzstan	72	76	0	1	0.0	1.1	..	..	22	14
93	Guyana	20	75	0	3	0.0	0.1	0.02	35	29	88
94	South Africa	87	138	(.)	132	1.2	8.4	0.21	..	3	..
95	El Salvador	24	76	0	62	(.)	0.3	0.13	..	14	..
96	Samoa (Western)	26	..	0	17	0.0	5.3	..	..	6	..
97	Syrian Arab Republic	40	102	0	(.)	0.0	0.0	0.02	35	124	179
98	Moldova, Rep. of	106	127	0	4	(.)	0.7	0.17	..	49	27
99	Uzbekistan	69	67	0	2	(.)	(.)	..	..	17	2
100	Algeria	32	52	(.)	2	(.)	(.)	..	..	27	..

HDI rank	Telephone mainlines (per 1,000 people)		Cellular mobile subscribers (per 1,000 people)		Internet hosts (per 1,000 people)		Cost of a three-minute local call		Waiting list for mainlines (per 1,000 people)	
							PPP US$	Index (1990 = 100)		
	1990	1999	1990	1999	1995	2000	1999	1999	1990	1999
101 Viet Nam	1	27	0	4	0.0	(.)	0.37	..	..	..
102 Indonesia	6	29	(.)	11	(.)	0.2	0.08	44	2	..
103 Tajikistan	45	35	0	(.)	0.0	0.1	0.03	..	..	..
104 Bolivia	28	62	0	52	(.)	0.3	0.20	..	..	1
105 Egypt	30	70	(.)	7	(.)	0.1	0.07	..	22	19
106 Nicaragua	13	30	0	9	(.)	0.4	0.43	..	7	22
107 Honduras	17	44	0	12	0.0	(.)	0.17	223	24	27
108 Guatemala	21	55	(.)	30	(.)	0.5	0.19	127	22	..
109 Gabon	22	32	0	7	0.0	(.)	..	..	3	..
110 Equatorial Guinea	4	..	0	..	0.0	0.0	..	..	..	..
111 Namibia	39	64	0	18	(.)	3.7	0.16	..	..	3
112 Morocco	16	53	(.)	13	(.)	0.1	0.22	..	8	..
113 Swaziland	17	31	0	14	(.)	1.4	0.17	83	10	..
114 Botswana	21	75	0	75	(.)	2.7	..	..	6	..
115 India	6	27	0	2	(.)	0.1	0.09	45	2	4
116 Mongolia	32	39	0	13	0.0	0.1	0.08	..	26	15
117 Zimbabwe	12	21	0	15	(.)	0.5	..	..	6	..
118 Myanmar	2	6	0	(.)	0.0	0.0	..	..	..	2
119 Ghana	3	8	0	4	(.)	(.)	0.34	131	1	..
120 Lesotho	7	..	0	..	(.)	0.1	..	..	5	..
121 Cambodia	(.)	3	0	8	0.0	(.)	0.15	..	..	..
122 Papua New Guinea	8	13	0	2	0.0	0.1	..	..	..	..
123 Kenya	8	10	0	1	(.)	0.2	0.14	..	4	4
124 Comoros	8	10	0	0	0.0	0.1	0.62	..	1	..
125 Cameroon	3	..	0	..	0.0	(.)	..	..	..	..
126 Congo	7	..	0	..	0.0	(.)	..	..	1	..
Low human development										
127 Pakistan	8	22	(.)	2	(.)	0.1	0.08	41	6	..
128 Togo	3	8	0	4	0.0	0.1	0.40	60	1	4
129 Nepal	3	11	0	(.)	(.)	0.1	0.08	31	4	12
130 Bhutan	4	18	0	0	0.0	2.1	..	..	..	..
131 Lao People's Dem. Rep.	2	7	0	2	0.0	0.0	..	..	..	..
132 Bangladesh	2	3	0	1	0.0	0.0	0.14	65	1	1
133 Yemen	11	17	0	2	0.0	(.)	0.04	318	4	7
134 Haiti	7	9	0	3	0.0	0.0	..	..	..	..
135 Madagascar	2	3	0	..	0.0	0.1	0.25	91	..	(.)
136 Nigeria	3	..	0	..	0.0	(.)	..	..	3	..
137 Djibouti	11	14	0	(.)	0.0	0.1	..	..	(.)	0
138 Sudan	3	9	0	(.)	0.0	0.0	0.10	..	..	12
139 Mauritania	3	6	0	0	0.0	(.)	0.37	84	(.)	18
140 Tanzania, U. Rep. of	3	5	0	2	0.0	(.)	0.17	300	4	1
141 Uganda	2	3	0	3	(.)	(.)	0.64	..	1	(.)
142 Congo, Dem. Rep. of the	1	..	0	..	0.0	(.)	..	..	..	..
143 Zambia	9	9	0	3	(.)	0.2	0.11	111	7	1
144 Côte d'Ivoire	6	15	0	18	(.)	0.1	0.15	69	1	..
145 Senegal	6	18	0	10	(.)	0.2	0.32	..	1	3
146 Angola	8	8	0	2	0.0	(.)	0.20	..	..	2
147 Benin	3	..	0	..	0.0	(.)	..	..	..	..
148 Eritrea	..	7	..	0	0.0	(.)	0.12	..	..	5
149 Gambia	7	23	0	4	0.0	(.)	1.34	484	6	13
150 Guinea	2	6	0	3	(.)	(.)	0.40	125	..	..

HDI rank	Telephone mainlines (per 1,000 people)		Cellular mobile subscribers (per 1,000 people)		Internet hosts (per 1,000 people)		Cost of a three-minute local call		Waiting list for mainlines (per 1,000 people)	
							PPP US$	Index (1990 = 100)		
	1990	1999	1990	1999	1995	2000	1999	1999	1990	1999
151 Malawi	3	4	0	2	0.0	0.0	0.12	122	1	3
152 Rwanda	2	2	0	2	0.0	0.1	..	..	(.)	1
153 Mali	1	..	0	..	0.0	(.)	..	..	..	..
154 Central African Republic	2	3	0	..	0.0	(.)	..	..	..	..
155 Chad	1	1	0	..	0.0	(.)	..	..	(.)	..
156 Guinea-Bissau	6	..	0	..	0.0	(.)	..	..	..	..
157 Mozambique	3	4	0	1	0.0	(.)	..	..	2	2
158 Ethiopia	3	3	0	(.)	(.)	(.)	0.15	47	2	4
159 Burkina Faso	2	4	0	(.)	0.0	(.)	0.37	..	..	..
160 Burundi	2	3	0	(.)	0.0	0.0	..	..	(.)	..
161 Niger	1	..	0	..	0.0	(.)	..	..	(.)	..
162 Sierra Leone	3	..	0	..	0.0	0.1	0.10	21	4	..
Developing countries	22	69	(.)	34	0.1	1.0	..	..	..	..
Least developed countries	3	5	0	1	(.)	(.)	..	..	..	..
Arab States	34	69	(.)	17	(.)	0.4	..	..	..	..
East Asia and the Pacific	17	85	(.)	45	0.1	0.6	..	..	..	..
Latin America and the Caribbean	63	131	(.)	82	0.2	5.6	..	..	..	..
South Asia	7	29	(.)	2	(.)	0.1	..	..	..	..
Sub-Saharan Africa	..	..	..	..	0.1	0.6	..	..	..	..
Eastern Europe and the CIS	125	205	(.)	35	0.3	4.7	..	..	..	..
OECD	392	509	10	322	8.4	75.0	..	..	..	..
High-income OECD	473	594	13	371	11.0	96.9	..	..	..	..
High human development	416	542	11	347	9.0	80.5	..	..	..	..
Medium human development	28	79	(.)	28	(.)	1.0	..	..	..	..
Low human development	4	9	(.)	2	(.)	(.)	..	..	..	..
High income	470	591	13	373	10.8	95.2	..	..	..	..
Middle income	45	122	(.)	55	0.1	2.1	..	..	..	..
Low income	11	27	(.)	3	(.)	0.1	..	..	..	..
World	102	158	2	85	1.7	15.1	..	..	..	..

Source: Columns 1–4, 9 and 10: ITU 2001b; *columns 5 and 6:* ITU 2001a; *column 7:* calculated on the basis of data on call costs from ITU 2001b and data on purchasing power parity conversion factors from World Bank 2001h; *column 8:* calculated on the basis of data on call costs from ITU 2001b and data on GDP deflators and purchasing power parity conversion factors from World Bank 2001h.

CHAPTER 3

Managing the risks of technological change

Every technological advance brings potential benefits and risks, some of which are not easy to predict. The benefits of technologies can be far greater than what their creators foresaw. When Guglielmo Marconi invented the radio in 1895, he intended it for two-way private communication, not for broadcasting. Today the transistor is heralded as one of the most significant inventions ever—but on its invention in 1947 foreseers could think of few uses beyond developing better hearing aids for deaf people. In the 1940s IBM thought that the market for computers would never amount to more than a few unit sales a year.

At the same time, the hidden costs of technologies can be devastating. Bovine spongiform encephalitis—mad cow disease—almost certainly owes its origin and spread to cost-cutting techniques used to make cattle feed. Nuclear power, once believed to be a limitless source of energy, came to be seen as a dangerous threat to health and the environment after the accidents at Three Mile Island (United States) and Chernobyl (Ukraine). Some harms are revealed quickly and removed. Thalidomide, first marketed in 1957 to treat morning sickness in pregnant women, resulted in horrific birth defects in thousands of children around the world and was banned by the early 1960s. But other harms are hidden for decades. Chlorofluorocarbons (CFCs), invented in 1928, were widely used in refrigerators, aerosol cans and air conditioners. Only in 1984—more than 50 years later—came conclusive evidence of their connection with the depletion of the ozone layer and increased skin cancer for people in countries exposed to more ultraviolet light. Still used in many countries, CFCs are to be phased out by 2010.

Societies respond to these uncertainties by seeking to maximize the benefits and minimize the risks of technological change. Doing so is not easy: managing such change can be complex and politically controversial. Though the agricultural technology of the green revolution more than doubled cereal production in Asia between 1970 and 1995,[1] the impacts on farm workers' income and on the environment are still hotly debated.

As in previous eras of change, today's technological transformations raise concerns about their possible ecological, health and socio-economic impacts. Genetically modified plants are suspected of introducing new sources of allergens, of creating "super weeds" and of harming species such as monarch butterflies. Cutting-edge biotechnological research has raised ethical concerns about the possibility of human cloning and the easy manufacture of devastating biological weapons. Information and communications technology facilitates international crime, supports drug trade networks and assists the dissemination of child pornography.

In the face of such concerns, why adopt new technologies? For three reasons.

- *Potential benefits.* As chapter 2 describes, the possibilities for promoting human development through today's technological transformations are tremendous in developing countries. In some cases the expected benefits are at least as great as the risks.
- *Costs of inertia versus costs of change.* New technologies often improve on the ones they replace: the modern jet, for example, is safer and faster than the propeller aeroplane. Had the Luddites succeeded in prohibiting the adoption of spinning jennies, Britain would have forgone the productivity growth that al-

Every technological advance brings potential benefits and risks, some of which are not easy to predict

lowed employment and incomes to increase so dramatically.

• *Means of managing risks.* Many potential harms can be managed and their likelihood reduced through systematic scientific research, regulation and institutional capacity. When these capacities are strong, countries are far more able to ensure that technological change becomes a positive force for development.

Yet out of these reasons for embracing change comes a dilemma for many developing countries: the potential benefits of change may be great and the costs of inertia significant—but the institutional and regulatory capacity needed to manage the concurrent risks may be too demanding. The trade-offs of technological change vary from country to country and use to use: societies expect different benefits, face different risks and have widely varying capacities to handle those risks safely.

From this perspective, most developing countries are at a disadvantage in the face of technological change because they lack the regulatory institutions needed to manage the risks well. But there can be advantages to being technological followers. Unlike front-runners, followers do not incur the first-mover risks of using new technologies: they can instead observe how those risks play out in other countries. They can also learn from others in designing their regulations and institutions. Moreover, for some technologies they may be able to establish low-cost regulatory systems that build on, or even rely on, the regulatory standards of early adopters.

Societies ultimately face choices in the timing and extent of embracing technological change. Given the importance of getting it right, and the risks of getting it wrong, developing countries need to build national policies, and need international support, to create the capacity that will enable them to embrace new opportunities. But which criteria should be used in adopting technologies, and whose voices should be heard in the debate? How can countries develop systematic approaches to assessing technological risks? What policies and practices—nationally and internationally—are needed? These questions are the focus of this chapter.

Societies expect different benefits, face different risks and have widely varying capacities to handle those risks safely

RISKY BUSINESS: ASSESSING POTENTIAL COSTS AND BENEFITS

Some risks of technological change are rooted in human behaviour and social organization. Biotechnological research can be turned into weapons if governments or terrorists choose that path—hence the need for multilateral bans against the creation of biological weapons and for inspections to monitor compliance. Information and communications technology could lead to an invasion of privacy and an increase in money laundering and in trade in arms and drugs—hence the importance of domestic and international regulation to block these harms.

Other risks are directly associated with technologies. Could the genes flowing from genetically modified organisms into non-target organisms endanger non-target populations? It depends on how genetically modified organisms interact with their environment. Could using mobile telephones cause brain or eye cancer? It depends on how radiation from the handset affects human tissue. Whether or not these harms could possibly occur is a matter of science—but if the possibilities are real, the extent to which they become risks depends on how the technologies are put to use. Constructing agricultural buffer zones around genetically modified crops cuts the likelihood of gene flow and super weeds; raising public awareness and changing the design of mobile telephones reduce the likelihood of cancer.

The first kind of risk has long been handled through economic, social and political institutions and policies that shape and regulate the way technologies are used in and by societies. But managing the second kind calls for sound science and strong regulatory capacity as well. And many concerns voiced about this technology revolution, particularly biotechnology, are focused on risks such as these—hence the growing attention worldwide to the role that science and regulation must play in managing this era of technological change.

Two potential harms are under scrutiny:
• *Possible harms to human health.* Technologies have long posed threats to human health. Some pollute air and water: power plants using fossil fuels produce sulphur dioxide, which

in high concentrations can irritate the upper respiratory tract. Others can introduce harmful substances to the body through medicines, such as thalidomide, or through the food chain. New biotechnology applications in health care—from vaccines and diagnostics to medicines and gene therapy—could have unexpected side effects. With genetically modified foods, the two main concerns are that the introduction of novel genes could make a food toxic and that they could introduce new allergens into foods, causing reactions in some people.

• *Possible harms to the environment.* Some claim that genetically modified organisms could destabilize ecosystems and reduce biodiversity in three ways. First, transformed organisms could displace existing species and change the ecosystem. History shows the danger: six European rabbits introduced in Australia in the 1850s soon multiplied into 100 million, destroying habitats and native flora and fauna. Today the rabbits cost Australian agricultural industries $370 million a year.[2] The question is whether genetically modified organisms could overrun ecosystems in a similar way. Second, gene flow among plants could transfer the novel genes into related species, leading, for example, to super weeds. Third, the novel genes could have unintended harmful effects on non-target species. Laboratory studies have shown that the pollen of Bt corn, designed for pest control against stemborers, can also kill monarch butterflies if enough is consumed.

Some of these risks are the same in every country: potential harms to health from mobile phones or to unborn children from thalidomide are no different for people in Malaysia than in Morocco—though the ability to monitor and handle them may vary considerably. But other risks vary significantly: gene flow from genetically modified corn would be more likely to happen in an environment with many corn-related wild species than in one without. For this reason, the environmental risks of biotechnology are often specific to individual ecosystems and need to be assessed case by case. Risks to human health are more common across continents.

These risks deserve attention—but cannot be the only consideration in shaping choices of technologies: an approach to risk assessment that looked only at potential harms would be flawed. A full risk assessment needs to weigh the expected harms of a new technology against its expected benefits—and compare these to:

• The expected value of harms and benefits of existing technologies that would be replaced.

• The expected value of harms and benefits of alternative technologies that might be preferable to new or existing technologies.

People make these assessments all the time, often unconsciously, choosing the benefits of activities such as travelling in cars and aeroplanes over their potential dangers. Debates today, however, sometimes proceed as if risks about specific products can be isolated from the context in which they occur.

Opponents of new technologies often ignore the harms of the status quo. A study highlighting the risk to monarch butterflies of transgenic pest-resistant corn pollen received worldwide attention, but lost in the protest was the fact that such crops could reduce the need to spray pesticides that can harm soil quality and human health. Sustained exposure to pesticides can cause sterility, skin lesions and headaches. One study of potato farm workers using pesticides in Ecuador found that chronic dermatitis was twice as common among them as among other people.[3]

Similarly, proponents of new technologies often fail to consider alternatives. Nuclear power, for example, should be weighed not just against fossil fuels but also against third—possibly preferable—alternatives such as solar power and hydrogen fuel cells. And many people argue that the use of genetically modified organisms should be weighed against alternatives such as organic farming, which in some situations could be a more suitable choice.

But even when societies and communities consider all sides, they may come to different decisions because of the variety of risks and benefits they face and their capacity to handle them. European consumers who do not face food shortages or nutritional deficiencies see few benefits of genetically modified foods; they are more concerned about possible health effects. Undernourished farming communities in developing countries, however, are more likely to

A full risk assessment needs to weigh the expected harms of a new technology against its expected benefits

focus on the potential benefits of higher yields with greater nutritional value; the risks of no change may outweigh any concerns over health effects. Choices may differ even between two developing countries that need the nutritional benefits of genetically modified crops, as one may be better able to handle the risks.

Conducting these debates in a global context alters the issues that dominate and changes the voices that shape decision-making.

Views that dominate the global debate can lead to decisions not in the best interest of local communities

SHAPING CHOICES: THE ROLE OF PUBLIC OPINION

In democratic systems public opinions of risk trade-offs are often key determinants of whether a technology is promoted or prohibited. Public preferences matter, since it is ultimately individuals and communities that stand to gain from change or to bear its costs. But views that dominate the global debate can lead to decisions that are not in the best interest of local communities.

DRIVING THE DEBATE: PUBLIC FEAR AND COMMERCIAL INTERESTS

At least two factors have been important in shaping debates.

Public trust in regulators. Poor management of health and environmental crises in Europe has undermined confidence in public health and environmental regulators. In the United Kingdom mad cow disease has resulted in the slaughter of millions of cattle and the deaths of dozens of people from a related brain-wasting disease.[4] HIV-infected blood used in transfusions infected more than 3,600 people in France in the mid-1980s.[5] In these and other cases a lack of transparency about what was known and delays in policy responses damaged the reputations of regulators. This mistrust spread to attitudes towards new technologies. In a 1997 survey asking Europeans whom they trusted most to tell the truth about genetically modified crops, 26% named environmental organizations—while just 4% named public authorities and 1% named industry.[6]

Claims from competing interests. Public perceptions of risk can also be strongly influenced by the claims and counter-claims of interest groups, sometimes magnified through media hype. Scientific evidence can be presented selectively or distorted outright. This tactic is hardly new: when coffee drinking in the 17th and 18th centuries began to threaten vested economic and political interests, fears about its health effects were stirred up to protect them (box 3.1). Likewise today, both supporters and opponents of technological change try to shape public perceptions.

In the case of transgenic crops the commercial lobby overstates the near-term gains to poor people from the genetically modified organisms it develops. Meanwhile, the opposing lobby overstates the risk of introducing them and downplays the risk of worsening nutrition in their absence. Some European farmers have used public fear of the risk from genetically modified organisms to protect domestic markets; some political parties and non-governmental organizations have exploited this public fear to generate support and mobilize resources. Language itself has become a political weapon. "Miracle seeds" and "golden rice" exaggerate the positive, while "traitor technologies", "Frankenfoods" and "genetic pollution" deliberately engender fear and anxiety.

Under these conditions objective, well-informed debate is difficult. The opinions of those most vociferous, rather than those who stand to gain or lose the most, can drive decision-making.

BOX 3.1

Historical efforts to ban coffee

Many of the crops that dominate today's global market went through long periods of rejection because of perceived risks. For example, coffee, now the world's second largest traded commodity by value, has a history marked by episodes of vilification and outright bans. In London in 1674 the Women's Petition Against Coffee protested "the grand inconveniences accruing to their sex from the excessive use of the drying and enfeebling liquor". Opposition to coffee-houses often had a political foundation—King Charles II of England tried to ban them in 1675 because they were hotbeds of revolution.

In 1679, when coffee was perceived to be competing with wine in France, physicians attacked the drink. One physician suggested that coffee dried up brain fluids, leading to exhaustion, impotence and paralysis. In Germany, where coffee was equally controversial, physicians claimed that it caused female sterility and stillbirths. In 1732 Johann Sebastian Bach composed his Kaffee-Kantate partly as an ode to coffee and partly as a protest against the movement to stop women from drinking it. Concerned about the draining effect of green coffee imports on Prussia's wealth, in 1775 Frederick the Great condemned the increase in coffee consumption as "disgusting" and urged his people to drink beer, like their ancestors.

Source: Pendergrast 2000; Roast and Post Coffee Company 2001.

Where it once took years to disseminate technological change worldwide, today a new software package can be instantaneously introduced to markets everywhere. Communication about the perceived risks and benefits of new technologies is likewise global. Activists are organized globally and principles of democratic governance have taken hold in the international arena, opening policy debates to wider participation. When highly mobilized and vociferous communities promote their views and values worldwide, the local roots of their preferences can end up having global reach, influencing communities that may face very different trade-offs.

Debates on emerging technologies tend to mirror the concerns of rich countries. The opposition to yield-enhancing transgenic crops in industrial countries with food surpluses could block the development and transfer of those crops to food-deficit countries. Electronic books may not do much for workers in the world's major publishing houses, but they could be a boon for education programmes in poor countries. For industrial countries, banning the use of the chemical DDT (dichlorodiphenyl-trichloroethane) may have been an easy trade-off. But extending that ban to development assistance programmes, despite DDT's unique value in malaria control, turned out to be an imposition of one society's trade-offs and values on others' needs and preferences (box 3.2).

Developing countries have distinct concerns about and interests in the biotechnological revolution. Some have feared that biotechnology could displace their traditional products, for example, by using tissue culture to make low-cost laboratory-grown substitutes for gum arabic and vanilla. Others have wanted to use new tools to raise productivity, reduce chronic malnutrition and convert their abundant bio-resources into value added products. But the dominant debate between Europe and the United States over transgenic foods has focused attention on issues of allergies and toxic health effects.

It is not just public opinion that can have global influence. Developing countries can come under pressure from donor agencies, non-profit foundations, multinational companies and international organizations to adopt either prohibitive or permissive policies, to fall in line behind either Europe or the United States. When European countries provide assistance in designing biosafety legislation, for example, they may model the legislation on the precautionary standards set in Europe, even though that might not be the preferred stance of the country receiving the assistance.

If developing countries are to make the best possible informed choices on technological change, the imbalance of voices and influences needs to be rectified and their own choices need to drive decision-making. As Nigeria's minister of agricultural and rural development recently stated, "Agricultural biotechnology, whereby seeds are enhanced to instill herbicide tolerance or provide resistance to insects and disease, holds great promise for Africa....We don't want to be denied this technology because of a misguided notion that we don't understand the dangers of the future consequences."[7]

*The imbalance of voices
and influences needs
to be rectified*

BOX 3.2

DDT and malaria: whose risk and whose choice?

Conservationists have demonstrated to Western governments that DDT is an irremediable pollutant, causing every industrial country to stop using it. Good: persistent and extensive use of DDT as an agricultural pesticide has substantial environmental consequences—bioaccumulated DDT causes thinning of eggshells and reproductive failure in birds—and rich countries have little to gain from its use.

In developing countries, in contrast, DDT is one of the few affordable and effective tools for tackling malaria and is used in far smaller quantities, without such severe environmental impacts. A malaria eradication campaign using DDT, launched in the 1950s and 1960s, had impressive early results. In less than 20 years Sri Lanka's annual burden of malaria fell from 2.8 million cases and 7,300 deaths to 17 cases and no deaths; similar reductions occurred in India and Latin America. In contrast to rich countries, some malaria-prone developing countries have much to gain from the use of DDT.

A treaty of the United Nations Environment Programme signed in May 2001 bans the manufacture and use of DDT for all purposes—but with an exception for public health use because of its advantages in fighting malaria. Yet despite this exception, some donor agencies and governments will not fund its use.

DDT could pose harms to health: it may be a carcinogen, and it could interfere with lactation, though neither of these harms has been conclusively confirmed. But it is up to developing countries to weigh these considerations against the benefits of DDT as often the only affordable, effective tool against a disease that kills more than 1 million people a year, mainly children in poor areas of the tropics. In the absence of a better alternative, at least 23 tropical countries use DDT to fight malaria, yet they may be prevented from continuing to do so.

Source: Attaran and others 2000.

TAKING PRECAUTIONS: DIFFERENT COUNTRIES, DIFFERENT CHOICES

The precautionary principle is still evolving

Every country must take a stance on risk assessment. One much-discussed tool for decision-making is the precautionary principle—often interpreted as the rule that a country can or should reject the products of new technologies when full scientific certainty that such products will not cause harm is lacking. In fact, the precautionary principle is a fairly new concept with many different formulations, not one clear, immutable principle with standing in international law (box 3.3). A range of formulations—from soft to strong—are used in different circumstances because different technologies and situations require different degrees of precaution. At least six elements might differ between soft and strong formulations:

• *Consideration of benefits and risks in current technology.* Soft formulations guide regulatory action by considering not only the harmful risks of technological change but also the potential benefits, as well as the risks of technology that would be removed. Strong formulations, in contrast, often examine only the direct risks of the new technology.

• *Cost-effectiveness of prevention.* Soft formulations emphasize the need to balance the costs of preventing potential environmental harms associated with a new technology against the costs of those harms. Strong formulations often do not weigh the costs of prevention.

• *Certainty of harm or certainty of safety.* Soft formulations state that the absence of certainty of harm does not prevent regulatory action. Strong formulations often require certainty of safety to avoid regulatory action, which in complex and dynamic systems is often impossible to achieve.

• *Burden of proof.* Soft formulations place the burden of proof on those who claim that harm will occur if a new technology is introduced. Strong formulations may shift the burden of proof to the producers and importers of a technology, requiring that they demonstrate its safety.

• *Optional or obligatory action.* Soft formulations permit regulators to take action, while strong formulations often require action.

• *Locus of decision-making.* Soft formulations place authority in regulators, while strong formulations may vest power in political leaders.

The precautionary principle is still evolving, and its final character will be shaped by scientific and political processes. Even individual formulations are often vaguely worded—some say deliberately—to permit multiple interpretations for adaptation to local circumstances and different interests. When used to cover for discriminatory practices in trade, the principle loses its usefulness other than as a political ploy. Any formulation of the principle that does not start with well-established, knowledge-based risk assessment and management will be reduced to a rhetorical statement with little operational value.

Ultimately, countries will make different choices—and for good reasons. They face different potential costs and benefits from new technologies. Their citizens may have different attitudes towards taking risks and vary widely in their capacities to handle potential outcomes. Developing countries are taking very different stances towards genetically modified organisms —from preventive to promotional—through

---

BOX 3.3

"Use the precautionary principle!" But which one?

A variety of precautionary principles are in use, ranging from soft to strong formulations. A relatively soft formulation appears in the 1992 Rio Declaration on Environment and Development, where it says that "to protect the environment, the precautionary approach shall be widely applied by states according to their capability. Where there are threats of serious or irreversible damage, lack of full scientific certainty shall not be used as a reason for postponing cost-effective measures to prevent environmental degradation." That is, regulators can take cost-effective steps to prevent serious or irreversible harm even when there is no certainty that such harm will occur.

A strong formulation is set out in the 1990 Third Ministerial Declaration on the North Sea, which requires governments to "apply the precautionary principle, that is to take action to avoid potentially damaging impacts of [toxic] substances . . . even where there is no scientific evidence to prove a causal link between emissions and effects." This formulation requires governments to take action without considering offsetting factors and without scientific evidence of harm.

Between these two declarations lie a wide range of positions. For example, the 2000 Cartagena Protocol on Biosafety states that "lack of scientific certainty due to insufficient…knowledge regarding the extent of the potential adverse effects of a living modified organism on the conservation and sustainable use of biological diversity in the Party of import, taking also into account risks to human health, shall not prevent that Party from taking a decision, as appropriate, with regard to the import of the living modified organism in question…to avoid or minimize such potential adverse effects." This formulation drops the requirement that prevention be cost-effective and shifts the burden of proof for safety onto exporting countries. At the same time, refusing import is optional, not obligatory, and countries can decide to accept the risks on the basis of other factors that they consider relevant, such as potential benefits and the risks inherent in the technologies that would be replaced.

Source: UNEP 1992a; Matlon 2001; Juma 2001; Soule 2000; SEHN 2000.

---

their policies on biosafety, food safety and consumer choice, investment in public research and trade (table 3.1).

BUILDING THE CAPACITY TO MANAGE RISK

Safe use of new technologies is best ensured by creating a systematic approach to risk assessment and management. This calls for clear regulatory policies and procedures—not just writing legislation but implementing, enforcing and monitoring its provisions. For the introduction of genetically modified crops, every country needs to create a biosafety system with clear and coherent guidelines, skilled personnel to guide decision-making, an adequate review process and mechanisms for feedback from farmers and consumers.

USING SCIENTIFIC INFORMATION: TURNING UNCERTAINTY INTO RISK

In the absence of information, there is uncertainty. Scientific research generates information about the likely impacts of a new technology, turning that uncertainty into risk—the estimated probability that a certain harmful impact will occur. With more and better information, risk can be more accurately predicted and better managed.

When technologies are familiar in a given environment, information on their impact already exists. The conventional breeding of new crop varieties, for example, embodies techniques that have been used for years, so its benefits and potential harms are well known. So, when the international centres of the Consultative Group for International Agricultural Research (CGIAR) plan research, they use impact analysis results from similar research to guide projected assessments.

But when a technology is genuinely new or being introduced in a new environment, the resulting uncertainty must be turned into informed probability through research. The novelty of genetically modified organisms has rightly motivated extensive research for this reason (box 3.4).

ENSURING PUBLIC PARTICIPATION THROUGH RISK COMMUNICATION

Recent debates on the commercialization of agricultural biotechnology have underscored the importance of public participation and education on its risks—because the public ulti-

Safe use of new technologies is best ensured by a systematic approach to risk assessment and management

---

TABLE 3.1

Policy stances for genetically modified crops—the choices for developing countries

Policy area	Promotional	Permissive	Precautionary	Preventive
Biosafety	No careful screening, only token screening or approval based on approvals in other countries	Case-by-case screening primarily for demonstrated risk, depending on the product's intended use	Case-by-case screening for scientific uncertainties owing to novelty of development process	No careful case-by-case screening; risk assumed because of development process
Food safety and consumer choice	No regulatory distinction made between modified and unmodified foods when testing or labelling for food safety	Distinction made on some food labels but not so as to require segregation of market channels	Comprehensive labelling of all modified foods required and enforced with segregated market channels	Sales of genetically modified food banned, or warning labels required that stigmatize modified foods as unsafe
Investment in public research	Treasury resources spent on development and local adaptation of modified crop technology	Treasury resources spent on local adaptation of modified crop technology but not on development of new transgenes	No significant treasury resources spent on modified crop research or adaptation; donors allowed to finance local adaptation of modified crops	Neither treasury nor donor funds spent on adapting or developing modified crop technology
Trade	Genetically modified crops promoted to lower commodity production costs and boost exports; no restrictions on imports of modified seeds or plant materials	Imports of modified commodities limited in the same way as unmodified commodities in accordance with World Trade Organization standards	Imports of modified seeds and materials screened or restrained separately and more tightly than unmodified ones; labelling required for imports of modified foods and commodities	Imports of genetically modified seeds and plants blocked; unmodified status maintained in hopes of capturing export market premiums

Source: Paarlberg 2000.

mately produces and consumes the products of new technology. A recent survey in Australia highlights the need for better education: 49% of respondents feel that the risks of agricultural biotechnology outweigh its benefits, but 59% could not name a specific risk.[8]

BOX 3.4

Miracle seeds or Frankenfoods? The evidence so far

Few health or environmental risks from the use of genetically modified crops in agriculture have been observed. But many of the much-needed long-term studies on potential environmental risks have not yet been done. What is the evidence so far?

Health risks

Allergies. There is a worry that the introduction of novel gene products with new proteins will cause allergic responses. The expression of Brazil nut protein in soybeans confirmed that genetic engineering can lead to the expression of allergenic proteins.

Toxicity. The possible introduction or increase of toxic compounds might increase toxicity. Further testing is needed—the potential for human toxicity of novel proteins produced in plants should be kept under scrutiny.

Pleiotropic effects. Previously unknown protein combinations may have unforeseen secondary effects in food plants. While further monitoring is needed, no significant secondary effects have been found from commercially available transgenic plants or products.

Antibiotic resistance. Concern has been raised about antibiotic markers, such as kanamycin, used in plant transformation. These antibiotics are still used to treat infections in humans, and increased exposure to them might cause infections to become resistant to antibiotics, rendering these medicines ineffective. While no definitive evidence has been found that the use of antibiotic markers harms humans, alternatives are rapidly becoming available and are increasingly useful for food crop development.

Environmental risks

Unintended effects on non-target species. Although laboratory studies have reported damage to monarch butterfly larvae feeding on pollen from Bt plants, as a specific case of effects on non-target species, no studies have shown an actual negative effect on butterfly densities in the wild. Again, further research is needed.

Effects of gene flow to close relatives. Pollen dispersal can lead to gene flow, but only trace amounts are dispersed more than a few hundred feet. The transfer of conventionally bred or transgenic resistance traits to weedy relatives could worsen weed problems, but such problems have not been observed or adequately studied.

Increased weediness. Some new traits introduced into crops—such as pest or pathogen resistance—could cause transgenic crops to become problem weeds. This could result in serious economic and ecological harm to farm or wildlife habitats.

Development of pest resistance to pest-protected plants. Insects, weeds and microbes have the potential to overcome most of the control options available to farmers, with significant environmental impacts. But management approaches can be used to delay pest adaptations.

Concerns about virus-resistant crops. Engineered plants containing virus resistance may facilitate the creation of new viral strains, introduce new transmission characteristics or cause changes in susceptibility to other, but related, viruses. Engineered plants are unlikely to present problems different from those associated with traditional breeding for virus resistance.

Threats to biodiversity. Gene exchange could spread to wild relatives that are rare or endangered—especially if the exchange happens in centres of crop diversity. Scientists must increase their awareness of these and other problems arising from potential gene flow from genetically modified crops.

Source: Cohen 2001, drawing on Altieri 2000; Royal Society of London, US National Academy of Sciences, Brazilian Academy of Sciences, Chinese Academy of Sciences, Indian National Science Academy, Mexican Academy of Sciences and Third World Academy of Sciences 2000; National Research Council 2000.

Risk communication—the exchange of information and opinions on risk between all stakeholders in the risk management process—helps to develop transparent, credible decision-making and instil public confidence in policy decisions. Many countries undertake risk communication through public consultation, including France, Norway, Spain, Sweden and the United States. Some countries require labelling of genetically modified products so that consumers can choose whether to buy them—as in Australia, Brazil, Japan and the United Kingdom. There is pressure for other countries to follow suit. In the United States, where there is no labelling, surveys show that 80–90% of consumers want it.[9]

CREATING FLEXIBLE INSTITUTIONS AND DIVERSE TECHNOLOGIES

If societies are to manage technology safely, they need flexible and responsive institutions but also a range of technology options for creating alternative solutions—hence the need to invest in building institutional and research capacity.

The former Soviet Union's rigid dependence on nuclear power highlighted the dangers of inflexibility. In the 1980s the grid in Kiev relied solely on nuclear power generated in Chernobyl, so the reactor was generating unusually high output in 1986 even while undergoing tests. This overload, combined with errors made during the tests, resulted in a fatal explosion. Because there were no alternative energy sources, the Chernobyl station was reopened just six months after the accident. Technological diversity and institutional flexibility would have allowed other energy sources to be used—potentially averting the initial accident and preventing the need to reopen the power station under such hazardous conditions.

In some cases vested economic interests inhibit the development of alternative technologies. The oil and gas industries, for example, have traditionally viewed alternative energy and transportation technologies as a threat. But incentives and regulations can overcome such obstacles. For example, high gasoline prices and new emission criteria in Europe have changed the way cars are produced for that market, making them increasingly efficient.

CHALLENGES FACING DEVELOPING COUNTRIES

Though all countries must find ways to deal with the risks of technological change, developing countries face several specific challenges that can add to the costs, increase the risks and reduce their ability to handle change safely.

• *Shortage of skilled personnel.* Professional researchers and trained technicians are essential for adapting new technologies for local use. Yet even in developing countries with more advanced capacity, such as Argentina and Egypt, biosafety systems have nearly exhausted available expertise. A shortage of skilled personnel, from laboratory researchers to extension service officers, can seriously constrain a country's ability to create a strong regulatory system.

• *Inadequate resources.* The cost of establishing and maintaining a regulatory framework can be a severe financial demand on poor countries. In the United States three major, well-funded agencies—the Department of Agriculture, Food and Drug Administration and Environmental Protection Agency—are all involved in the regulation of genetically modified organisms. Even these institutions are appealing for budget increases to deal adequately with the new challenges raised by biotechnology. Research institutes in developing countries, in stark contrast, survive on little funding and are often financed largely by donor assistance—a risky dependence if local sources of funding are not also secured.

• *Weak communications strategies.* The extent of public awareness about genetically modified organisms varies among developing countries, but in many there is no official communications strategy for informing the public about them and about how biosafety is being handled. The typical difficulties of mounting effective public information campaigns are compounded by high rates of illiteracy in some countries and the lack of a tradition of public empowerment and of consumer activists demanding information and asserting their right to know. As a result, when media campaigns raise fears and create public opposition to technological change, the institutions responsible for managing biosafety often lack the plan and the means to respond with an alternative perspective.

• *Inadequate feedback mechanisms.* Technology is ultimately put to use not in laboratories but in homes and schools, on farms and in factories. A user's ability to follow safety procedures determines whether the benefits of technology can be reaped or will be lost. But mechanisms for providing information to and gathering feedback from users may not be well developed. In the United States, where farmers have multiple sources of support and advice on safety procedures, a survey in 2000 found that 90% of farmers planting transgenic maize crops believed they were following the correct safety procedures—but only 71% of them actually were.[10] In developing countries such mechanisms for providing information and gathering feedback are typically weaker.

Such barriers are a critical bottleneck to the use of biotechnology for the sake of development. Kenya, for example, introduced fairly tight biosafety legislation in 1998, with assistance from the Dutch government. But far less assistance in building the scientific and technical capacity and infrastructure needed to implement those policies followed. Biosafety administrators working in such situations know they will be criticized by non-governmental organizations and the media if they fail to meet the high standards set down on paper. As a result they tend to move slowly and make as few decisions as possible. In Kenya it took 18 months to approve the research use of transgenic sweet potatoes, despite the very low risks involved. To enable developing countries to benefit from the opportunities of new technology, these challenges need to be overcome through national policies and global support.

NATIONAL STRATEGIES TO DEAL WITH THE CHALLENGES OF RISK

Despite the challenges, developing countries can create strategies for building the capacity to manage risk that take advantage of their being technology followers and make the most of regional collaboration.

Several specific challenges can add to the costs, increase the risks and reduce the ability to handle change safely

LEARN FROM TECHNOLOGY LEADERS

Developing countries can take advantage of being technology followers by learning from the experiences and best practices of first-movers. Regulatory frameworks, for example, can be based on those established by early adopters. Argentina and Egypt drew up their guidelines for ensuring the environmental safety of releases of genetically modified organisms by examining the regulatory documents of Australia, Canada, the United States and others, then adapting them to national agricultural conditions.

Developing countries can also establish low-cost regulatory systems that build on, or even rely on, the regulatory standards of early adopters. Some industrial countries use mutual recognition agreements, accepting each other's approvals of products when they share common standards. Such agreements can help facilitate trade by eliminating redundant testing and bringing new products to the marketplace more quickly.[11] The European Union and the United States adopted this approach in 2001 for a variety of products, such as medical devices and telecommunications equipment. The arrangement is expected to save industry and consumers as much as $1 billion a year.[12] Developing countries could likewise take advantage of the regulatory expertise and experience of other—often industrial—countries. For example, the impact of medicines on people's health tends to vary little from one country to another. This enables developing countries to choose to accept the regulatory approvals of medicines granted in countries with much greater capacity to undertake such reviews—such as the United States, whose principal consumer protection agency, the Food and Drug Administration, has an annual budget exceeding $1 billion.

HARMONIZE STANDARDS THROUGH REGIONAL COLLABORATION

One of the first steps in promoting trust in technology is to develop health and environmental standards and harmonize those being developed independently in different countries. Divergence in safety norms between environmental and trade rules threatens to create conflict in addressing the safety of foods derived from biotechnology. Differences in planting and regulating genetically modified crops are already causing trade frictions. Consistent approaches, where they are possible, would reduce such conflicts, and harmonization could make more information available to the public and so promote accountability.

Regional cooperation in sharing knowledge, best practices, research findings, biosafety expertise and regulatory approvals across similar environments and ecosystems could achieve major efficiencies—laying the information base for regionally harmonized risk assessment and management. The Association for Strengthening Agricultural Research in Eastern and Central Africa (ASARECA) has begun to do just this, enabling regional expertise to be pooled and member countries with less regulatory capacity to benefit from the more advanced scientific capabilities in the region. Given the informal movement of plant materials across national borders within the region, such coordinated research and regulation will be critical to ensuring the safe use of biotechnology.

DEVELOP NATIONAL SCIENTIFIC AND EXTENSION CAPACITIES

It is crucial for countries to develop their adaptive or applied research capacities. For poor countries, adaptive research is more relevant—enabling them to borrow and adapt technologies generated elsewhere. For countries with a stronger scientific base, developing applied research capacity may be possible—allowing them to generate new technology for local conditions. In either case the scientific capacity should be directed towards improving understanding of the potential risks associated with technology, whether borrowed or "home grown". The social risk of marginalizing poor people from the benefits of new technologies can be avoided by ensuring that their participation is central to field-level trials and dissemination strategies (see the special contribution from M.S. Swaminathan).

STRENGTHEN REGULATORY INSTITUTIONS

Effective implementation of safety measures requires human and institutional capacity at the national level. Science and technology policy analysis is still a nascent field, and non-existent in most developing countries. Building capacity in this field would put the developing world in a better position to manage the benefits and risks associated with emerging technology. But discussions on introducing regulatory measures have been accompanied by concerns about the costs of such regulation. Argentina and Egypt provide good examples of how regulation for safely introducing genetically modified organisms has been incorporated into existing regulation (box 3.5).

A number of countries have launched programmes aimed at involving the public in assessing technology. This is essential if the views of farmers and consumers in developing countries are to influence national policy-making and bring more diverse voices to global debates. The non-governmental organization ActionAid set up a citizens jury in India, involving a range of farmers who could be affected by genetically modified crops. Experts from universities, farmers unions, non-governmental organizations, state and national governments

SPECIAL CONTRIBUTION

The *antyodaya* approach: a pathway to an ever-green revolution

Ecological and social setbacks from new crop production techniques are often due to monoculture, the excessive application of mineral fertilizers and chemical pesticides and the unsustainable exploitation of soil and groundwater. At the same time, population expansion—coupled with enhanced purchasing power—leaves most developing countries with no option except to produce more under conditions of diminishing per capita arable land and irrigation water resources. Taking the seemingly easy option of importing food would aggravate rural unemployment in countries where the livelihood security of more than 60 percent of rural families depends on agriculture. How then can we achieve a continuous rise in biological productivity without associated ecological and social harm?

Fortunately, we have entered the age of the Internet, genomics and proteomics. The past three decades indicate that the technological transformation of small farm agriculture—if rooted in the principles of ecology, economics, social and gender equity and livelihood generation—can contribute significantly to both poverty eradication and social integration. To be sure, technology has been an important factor in enlarging the rich-poor divide since the onset of the industrial revolution in Europe. But we have uncommon opportunities today to enlist technology as an ally in the movement for economic and gender equity. Recent advances in biotechnology and space and information technologies are helping to initiate an ever-green revolution capable of enabling small farm families to achieve sustainable advances in productivity and profitability per unit of land, time, labour and capital.

The new genetics, involving molecular mapping and modification, is a powerful tool for fostering ecofarming as well as for enhancing the productivity of rainfed and saline soils. Genes have been transferred by scientists in India from *Amaranthus* to potato for improving protein quality and quantity, and from mangroves to annual crops for imparting tolerance to salinity. Mapping based on geographic information systems (GIS) and progress in short- and medium-term weather forecasting, coupled with advanced markets and pricing information, are helping farmers strike a proper balance between land use and ecological, meteorological and marketing factors. The advances are crucial, given that agriculture provides the largest avenue for new employment through environmental enterprises—such as the recycling of solid and liquid waste and bioremediation, ecotechnologies developed by blending traditional knowledge with modern science and community-centred food and water security systems.

Our experience in Pondicherry, India, has shown that women-managed and user-driven, computer-aided and Internet-connected rural knowledge centres help bridge simultaneously the gender and digital divides. Synergies between technology and public policy on the one hand, and public and private partnership on the other, will lead to rapid progress in creating new on-farm and non-farm livelihoods. But it is important to realize that if the market is the sole determinant of research investment decisions, "orphans will remain orphans" and economic and technological divides will grow.

How can we ensure that an ever-green revolution movement based on genetic and digital technologies is characterized by social and gender inclusiveness? The answer to this question was given by Mahatma Gandhi more than 70 years ago when he said, "Recall the face of the poorest and the weakest person you have seen, and ask yourself, if the steps you contemplate are going to be of any use to him." An *antyodaya* approach—that is, development based on attention to the poorest people—to bridging the digital, genetic and gender divides, adopted in our biovillages in India, has proven very effective in including the excluded in technological and skill empowerment.

My nearly 40 years' experience—starting with the National Demonstration programme in wheat and rice in India in 1964, as well as my later experience in several Asian and African countries with the Sustainable Rice Farming systems and the Women in Rice Farming Networks of the International Rice Research Institute—have led me to postulate two basic guidelines in the design of technology testing and dissemination programmes:
• If demonstrations and testing are organized in the fields of resource-poor farmers, all farmers benefit. The reverse may not happen.
• If women are empowered with technological information and skills, all members of a family benefit. The reverse may not happen.

The antyodaya pathway should be the bottom line in all development planning and technology dissemination programmes if we are to avoid inequity-driven growth and unsustainable environmental practices in the future.

M. S. Swaminathan

M. S. Swaminathan
Recipient of the 1987 World Food Prize

and Monsanto, the largest producer of commercial transgenic crops, presented evidence for and against the use of transgenic seeds to the jury of farmers. The jury members then discussed whether such crops would improve their livelihoods or increase their poverty and insecurity and formed their own position on the issue. Such public discussions can also be organized by national and local governments or by community-based organizations.

Restoring or maintaining public trust is central to building robust national regulatory systems

GLOBAL COLLABORATION FOR MANAGING RISKS

Beyond national borders, some challenges of managing risk affect and influence communities worldwide. More research is needed into the possible impacts of biotechnology to increase understanding of its risks everywhere. The effects from mismanaging health and environmental safety risks can rapidly cross borders through trade and travel. And poor regulation of technology in one country can prompt public mistrust in science internationally. It is in the interest of all countries that each country manage the risks well.

BOX 3.5

Strengthening institutional capacity in Argentina and Egypt for dealing with genetically modified commodities

Argentina and Egypt are among the developing countries that have advanced furthest in current and intended use of genetically modified crops and products. Egypt has approved field test releases and is on the verge of commercializing its first genetically modified crop. Argentina has been exporting genetically modified commodities since 1996.

The two countries share several successes in the way they have strengthened their capacity to handle biosafety issues:
• National guidelines for ensuring the environmental safety of genetically modified organisms were formulated by examining regulations from countries with expertise in this area, then adapting the regulations to national agricultural conditions.
• Application, review and approval procedures for food safety and seed registration were built on existing laws. The procedures

evolved over time, allowing regulatory procedures to be coordinated among ministries and regulators.
• Advanced research institutes conduct state-of-the-art biotechnology research, and their highly skilled personnel are called on to serve on biosafety committees or as technical advisers.
• Clear standards have been established for evaluating the risks of a proposed release. Evaluations compare predicted impacts of the genetically modified organism with those of the equivalent unmodified variety. Genetically modified varieties that present no greater risk are deemed acceptable for testing and eventual commercial release.

Such policies show that, even when facing initial disadvantages, developing countries can create biosafety systems that enable them to move forward in managing technological safety.

Source: Cohen 2001.

CONDUCT MORE, AND LONGER-TERM, RESEARCH

The current debate on biotechnology lacks consolidated, science-based assessments to provide rigorous, balanced evidence on the health and environmental impacts of emerging technology. More peer-reviewed and transparent assessments would provide a basis for dialogue and help build confidence in these technologies. Such assessments could also help ground public perceptions in scientific and technical findings. In 2000 the national science academies of Brazil, China, India, Mexico, the United Kingdom and the United States and the Third World Academy of Sciences jointly reviewed the evidence and called for more research: "Given the limited use of transgenic plants worldwide and the relatively constrained geographic and ecological conditions of their release, concrete information about their actual effects on the environment and on biological diversity are still very sparse. As a consequence there is no consensus to the seriousness, or even the existence, of any potential environmental harm from GM [genetic modification] technology. There is therefore a need for a thorough risk assessment of the likely consequences at an early stage in the development of all transgenic plant varieties, as well as for a monitoring system to evaluate these risks in subsequent field tests and releases."[13]

RESTORE PUBLIC TRUST IN SCIENCE

Given the uncertainties surrounding technology, a loss of trust in regulatory institutions can be disastrous. Restoring or maintaining public trust in their judgements and policies is central to building robust national regulatory systems that draw on public consultation. As the report by the six national science academies and the Third World Academy of Sciences states, "Ultimately, no credible evidence from scientists or regulatory institutions will influence popular public opinion unless there is public confidence in the institutions and mechanisms that regulate such products."[14]

In some countries, especially in Europe, science has lost the public's trust—and that affects the prospects for technological progress worldwide. But sometimes that mistrust is misplaced. Poor policies, inadequate regulation and lack of transparency—not science—are often the cause of harm. Scientific methods, when combined with public deliberation, provide the foundation for managing technological risk; regulators must put them to good use. Most countries use scientifically based case-by-case hazard characterization and risk assessment, develop regulations that build on existing institutions rather than establish new ones and reduce regulation for products considered low risk.

Some observers question whether science is making the contribution it should, for several reasons. First, scientists, like all other people, approach problems with a particular methodology and have interests and incentives that shape their work. As a result not all relevant investigations are pursued. Consider the analysis of industrial hazards. Scientific research generally analyses the effects of single substances, but many of the most serious industrial hazards involve interactions between substances. For example, when fluoride is added to water, it increases the absorption of lead from pipes—a danger that would not come to light by studying lead or fluoride alone. For lack of funding, however, few comprehensive studies of multisubstance hazards have been undertaken.

Second, the complexity of the issues means that scientists who undertake such studies may arrive at inconclusive results—but clear results in a narrower field bring more recognition. Third, scientific evidence of hazard or harm is sometimes ignored, suppressed or attacked by powerful lobbies: the tobacco industry suppressed evidence on the carcinogenic effects of tobacco for decades before the information was finally forced into the public domain. These pressures make some scientists less willing to undertake such studies because of the possible effects on their careers.[15] These concerns highlight the importance of publicly funding research and of finding new ways to recognize scientists who strive to discover harms and hazards in the interests of society.

Information and communications technology is important for sharing information and experience with risk assessment. But other things are also needed if such information is to be disseminated to those who need it most. Safety information clearinghouses within national and international agencies can perform a useful role here.

The Cartagena Protocol on Biosafety, adopted in 2000 under the Convention on Biological Diversity, establishes a biosafety clearinghouse for countries to share information about genetically modified organisms. Countries must inform the clearinghouse within 15 days of approving any crop varieties that could be used in food, animal feed and processing. Exporters are required to obtain an importing country's approval, through a procedure known as advance informed agreement, for initial shipments of genetically modified organisms—such as seeds and trees—intended for release into the environment. Genetically modified organisms intended for food, feed and processing—in other words, commodities—are exempted from this requirement. But they must be labelled to show that they "may contain" genetically modified organisms, and countries can decide, on the basis of a scientific risk assessment, whether to import those commodities. Other clearinghouses could share and disseminate experience on technological safety between public, private and academic communities and between nations and regions.

These discussions of risk must involve developing countries. The European Union and the United States have established a consultative forum on biotechnology that touches on issues of interest to developing countries. Yet the forum does not include any members representing the developing world.

EXPAND DONOR ASSISTANCE FOR BUILDING CAPACITY

The past 10 years have seen more programmes aimed at creating the human capacity needed for technological safety regulation, through training as well as workshops, seminars and techni-

The freedom to innovate—and to take risks—will continue to play a central role in global development

cal meetings. International organizations have played a key role in supporting such activities. But more formal and sustained efforts are needed. Support has often been given for drawing up legislation and creating biosafety systems—but not for implementing them.

•   •   •

Breakthroughs in technology in the second half of the 20th century have opened new avenues for human development. These advances offer many benefits but also pose risks, increasing the demand for systems of governance that bring the management of technology under the control of democratic institutions. The freedom to innovate—and to take risks—will continue to play a central role in global development. The challenge facing us all is to ensure that those exercising this essential freedom do so in a way that promotes good science, builds trust in science and technology and expands their role in human development.

CHAPTER 4

Unleashing human creativity: national strategies

The technology revolution begins at home—yet no country will reap the benefits of the network age by waiting for them to fall out of the sky. Today's technological transformations hinge on each country's ability to unleash the creativity of its people, enabling them to understand and master technology, to innovate and to adapt technology to their own needs and opportunities.

Nurturing creativity requires flexible, competitive, dynamic economic environments. For most developing countries this means building on reforms that emphasize openness—to new ideas, new products and new investments. But at the heart of nurturing creativity is expanding human skills. For that reason, technological change dramatically raises the premium every country should place on investing in the education and skills of its people.

Many developing countries are in a good position to exploit the opportunities of the technology revolution and advance human development. Others face significant hurdles, lacking the kind of economic environment that encourages innovation, lacking the skills and institutions to adapt new technologies to local needs and constraints.

But sound public policy can make a difference. The key is to create an environment that mobilizes people's creative potential to use and develop technological innovations.

CREATING AN ENVIRONMENT THAT ENCOURAGES TECHNOLOGICAL INNOVATION

Creating an environment that encourages innovation requires political and macroeconomic stability. Take the Asian success stories, built on a strong commitment to education and health coupled with low inflation, moderate fiscal and balance of payments deficits and high levels of savings

and investment. It is not just big firms that demand stability. Small businesses and family farms also depend on a stable financial setting where savings are safe and borrowing is possible. And they are where innovation and adaptation often start.

While such stability is necessary, it is not enough. Proactive policies are required to stimulate innovation.
- Technology policy can help to create a common understanding among key actors about the centrality of technology to economic diversification.
- Reforms to make telecommunications competitive are vital for giving people and organizations better access to information and communications technology.
- To stimulate technology-oriented research, governments can promote links between universities and industry—and provide fiscal incentives for private firms to conduct research and development.
- Stimulating entrepreneurship is also essential, and venture capital can be important in fostering technology-based start-up businesses.

CREATING A VISION FOR TECHNOLOGY

Governments need to establish a broad technology strategy in partnership with all key stakeholders. Several governments have promoted technology development directly. Some have subsidized high-technology industries—with industrial policies that have been widely criticized because government does not always do a good job of picking winners. But what government can do is identify areas where coordination will make a difference because no private investor will act alone—say, in building infrastructure. Here, some governments have done a credible job.

No country will reap the benefits of the network age by waiting for them to fall out of the sky

Many countries are conducting "foresight studies" to create more coherent science and technology policy and to identify future demands and challenges, linking science and technology policy to economic and social needs. The process creates awareness among stakeholders about the state of technological activity in the country, emerging trends worldwide and the implications for national priorities and competitiveness. Involving civil society in areas relating to new technological developments with potentially strong social and environmental impacts helps build consensus on a response. India, the Republic of Korea, South Africa, Thailand and several Latin American countries are now involved in such exercises. In the United Kingdom the exercise has led to resource allocations and incentives to promote new technologies in a mature economy (box 4.1).

Governments have not always led the process. In Costa Rica businesses took the lead in the effort that led to Intel's decision to invest there. Costa Rica was able to attract technology-intensive foreign direct investment because of its social and political stability, its proximity to the United States and its highly skilled labour force, built up through decades of emphasis on education (box 4.2).

MAKING TELECOMMUNICATIONS SERVICES COMPETITIVE

Telecommunications and Internet costs are particularly high in developing countries. Monthly Internet access charges amount to 1.2% of average monthly income for a typical US user, compared with 614% in Madagascar,[1] 278% in Nepal, 191% in Bangladesh and 60% in Sri Lanka (figure 4.1).[2]

With high costs and low incomes, community access is key to Internet diffusion in much of the developing world. Computers, email accounts and Internet connections are often shared by several individuals or households. Telecentres, Internet kiosks and community learning centres make telephones, computers and the Internet more accessible and more affordable for more people.

In the United Republic of Tanzania Adesemi Communications International is providing the first reliable telephone service. It has installed durable, user-friendly units capable of connecting local, long-distance and international calls. The company's wireless system allows the flexibility to install payphones where they are most needed, regardless of whether landlines exist. Small businesses dependent on communications have reaped tremendous benefits.[3] In Peru Red Científica Peruana, the largest provider of Internet access in the country, has set up a national network of 27 telecentres.[4]

A big part of the reason for the high costs is that most countries have had state monopolies for telecommunications services. Without competition, their prices remain high—true for

---

BOX 4.1

Technology foresight in the United Kingdom—building consensus among key stakeholders

The UK technology foresight programme, announced in 1993, is forging a closer partnership between scientists and industrialists to guide publicly financed science and technology activity. More market oriented and less science driven than similar efforts elsewhere, the programme has had three phases.

First it set up 15 panels of experts on the markets and technologies of interest to the country, each chaired by a senior industrialist. Each panel was charged with developing future scenarios for its area of focus, identifying key trends and suggesting ways to respond. In 1995 the panels reported to a steering group, which synthesized the main findings and identified national priorities.

Next the steering group produced a report distilling its recommendations under six themes: social trends and impacts of new technologies; communications and computing; genes and new organisms, processes and products; new materials, synthesis and processing; precision and control in management, automation and process engineering; and environmental issues.

The steering group assigned priorities to three categories: key technology areas, where further work was vital; intermediate areas, where efforts needed to be strengthened; and emerging areas, where work could be considered if market opportunities were promising and world-class capabilities could be developed.

Now the recommendations from the exercise are being implemented. For ex-

ample, research in the four priority areas—nanotechnology, mobile wireless communications, biomaterials and sustainable energy—is being supported through a research award scheme. Another example is its application in Scotland. Scottish Enterprise hosts the Scottish foresight coordinator, who focuses on promoting foresight as a tool for business to think about and respond to future change in a structured way. The coordinator works with a wide range of public, private and academic actors. While a key goal is to help individual companies better manage change, this is being achieved by channelling efforts through a range of trusted business intermediaries—industry bodies, networks and local delivery organizations—that have a sustainable influence on company activities. All panels and task forces address two underpinning themes: sustainable development and education, skills and training.

On education and skills, the ethos of the foresight programme is captured in one of its statements: "The roots of our learning systems—classrooms and lecture theatres—can be traced back to the needs of the 19th century industrial age. At the start of the 21st century we need to re-engineer the learning process. While many existing educational institutions will remain, they will look very different to those of today. They will become more social environments in which to support effective learning, and will perform new functions and have different responsibilities."

Source: UK Government Foresight 2001; Lall 2001.

BOX 4.2

Attracting technology-intensive foreign direct investment in Costa Rica— through human skills, stability and infrastructure

Costa Rica exports more software per capita than any other Latin American country. Two recent decisions by Intel have contributed to the development of the domestic industry. First, Intel decided to invest in a centre to develop software for the company and to contribute to semiconductor design, moving beyond the limits of an older assembly and testing plant. Second, through its venture capital fund, Intel invested in one of the country's most promising software companies. Reinforcing these activities is the presence of internationally recognized centres of research, training and education.

How did Costa Rica achieve such success? The country's long commitment to education has been critical. But human skills, while important, need to be complemented by other factors.

After the economic crisis of the early 1980s, it became clear that the country had to abandon import substitution. So it moved to promote exports (and improve access to the US market) through two systems of fiscal incentives:

• A system of export processing zones allowed companies to import all their inputs and equipment tax free and avoid paying income tax for eight years. This system became key in attracting high-technology multinational companies.

• To help domestic companies become export oriented, firms were given an income tax holiday, the right to import equipment and inputs tax free and a subsidy equal to 10% of the value of their exports. The subsidy was meant to compensate exporters for inefficiencies in such public services as ports, electricity and telecommunications and for the high costs of financial services like banking and insurance.

Technology foresight—through a non-governmental organization

The new export promotion model was supported from the beginning by the Costa Rica Investment and Development Board (CINDE), a private non-profit organization founded in 1983 by prominent businesspeople, supported by the government and financed by donor grants. Its broad aim was to promote economic development, but attracting foreign direct investment was always a top priority.

In the early 1990s CINDE realized that the country was losing competitiveness in industries relying on unskilled labour and that the North American Free Trade Agreement (NAFTA) would give Mexico better access to the US market. So it decided to focus its efforts to attract investment only on sectors that were a good match for Costa Rica's relatively high education levels. It chose electronics and related activities, rapidly growing industries that required skilled labour.

Meantime, Intel was starting to look for a site for a chip assembly and testing plant. CINDE campaigned for Costa Rica, and in 1996 Intel decided to locate its plant there. Four factors were key:

• Costa Rica had political and social stability, the rule of law and a low level of corruption; relatively liberal rules relating to international trade and capital flows; a relatively well-educated and technically skilled but low-cost workforce with acceptable knowledge of English; a "pro-business" environment with a favourable attitude towards foreign direct investment; a good package of incentives; and good location and transportation logistics.

• The country's growing emphasis on attracting high-technology foreign direct investment gave credibility to the case that it had the human resources Intel required.

• An aggressive, effective and knowledgeable foreign investment promotion agency (CINDE), with links to the government, arranged successful meetings between Intel executives and public authorities.

• The government understood the importance of an Intel investment in the country. The president met with Intel executives and encouraged the rest of the government to help Intel.

Spillover benefits

Intel's investment has had a big impact on Costa Rica's ability to attract other foreign direct investment in high-technology industries—and on the economy's general competitiveness in skill-intensive industries. Intel's reputation for rigorous site selection has given other companies the confidence to invest in the country.

Intel has also contributed by training its own workforce and supporting universities. The Instituto Tecnológico de Costa Rica (ITCR) has gained "Intel Associate" status and several new degree programmes. And Intel's presence has increased awareness of career opportunities in engineering and other technical fields. At the ITCR enrolment in engineering grew from 9.5% of students in 1997 to 12.5% in 2000.

Today the country is following a strategy that appears to enjoy strong support from key stakeholders: recognizing the need to liberalize telecommunications, improving infrastructure through private sector participation, improving the protection of intellectual property rights and improving access to foreign markets through free trade agreements with such countries as Canada, Chile and Mexico. Some reforms have met with resistance and open expressions of disagreement—all part of the policy debate in a pluralistic society.

Source: Rodriguez-Clare 2001.

FIGURE 4.1
The cost of being connected

Monthly Internet access charge
as a percentage of average monthly income

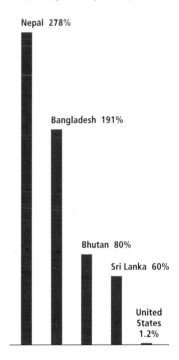

Nepal 278%

Bangladesh 191%

Bhutan 80%

Sri Lanka 60%

United States 1.2%

Source: Human Development Report Office calculations based on ITU 2000 and World Bank 2001h.

leased telephone lines, Internet service provision and local and long-distance telephone calls. Breaking those monopolies makes a difference. After the US long-distance monopoly provider AT&T was broken up in 1984, the rates for long-distance telephone calls fell by 40%.[5]

In the midst of the Asian crisis the Korean mobile telephony market saw the number of subscribers double each year in 1996–98 despite falling consumer demand.[6] What made the fast growth possible? The entry of five competitive providers into the market, offering easy credit and subsidies for handsets. In Sri Lanka too, competition has led to more investment, more connectivity and better quality service.[7]

Internet service provision is competitive in the majority of countries surveyed in a recent study (table 4.1). But despite the benefits from competitive telecommunications markets, monopolies and duopolies continue to dominate for leased telephone lines and for local and long-distance telephony. And much remains to be done in such newer markets as paging, cable television and digital cellular telephony.

Privatization can make these markets more competitive. But alone, it does not produce a liberalized, competitive sector. In many countries private monopolies have replaced state monopolies. And while many countries have privatized telecommunications quickly, they have built up regulatory capacity much more slowly. The nature and scope of regulatory reform greatly affect performance in telecommunications. For example, by pursuing regulation and privatization simultaneously, Chile has done much better than the Philippines, which put in place a regulatory system at a later stage.[8]

Encouraging links between universities and industry can stimulate innovation

STIMULATING RESEARCH AND DEVELOPMENT

Governments have a responsibility to promote research and development (R&D). Some R&D needs to be undertaken by the public sector, especially for people's needs that may not be met through the market. But governments are not responsible for doing all the R&D—and they can create incentives for other actors. Two mechanisms have been particularly important in promoting technology-oriented research—links between universities and industry, and fiscal incentives to promote R&D by private firms.

Encouraging links between universities and industry can stimulate innovation. High-technology companies thrive on state-of-the-art knowledge and creativity as well as the scientific and technical expertise of universities. Hubs are created as entrepreneurs purposely establish their businesses near universities.

Tampere University of Technology in Finland links Nokia, the Technical Research Centre of Finland and firms in the wood processing industry. Industrialists in science and technology spend 20% of their time at universities, giving lectures to students in their areas of expertise. The "adjunct professors" work on a challenging interface between industry and academia, and students learn the relevance of technology to industry.[9]

In China too, institutions of higher education support the technological work of enterprises. Tsinghua University established the Chemical Engineering and Applied Chemistry Institute jointly with Sino Petrochemical Engineering Company, which has given more than $3.6 million to support the university's research activities and recruited more than 100 of its graduates.[10] The State Torch Programme encourages enterprises to strengthen their ties with research institutions, to accelerate the commercialization of research results. Chinese universities have also established science parks. The Shanghai Technology Park acts as an incubator for the rapid application of scientific and technological work in industry.

In the 1990s China emphasized the development of high-technology industry through a variety of government programmes to support R&D. Now China is also using R&D to improve the productivity of traditional activities in agriculture. The Spark Programme propagates

TABLE 4.1
Telecommunications arrangements in various countries by sector, 2000

Sector	Number of countries			Total surveyed
	Monopoly	Duopoly	Competition	
Local telephony	121	19	44	184
National long distance	134	12	36	182
International long distance	129	16	38	183
Digital cellular	47	28	79	154
Mobile satellite market	32	12	65	109
Fixed satellite market	61	14	59	134
Internet service	13	3	81	97

Source: Center for International Development at Harvard University analysis of 2000 ITU data, as cited in Kirkman 2001.

technologies to the countryside and assists farmers in using them for agricultural development.[11]

Governments use a range of policy options to stimulate enterprise R&D (box 4.3). One is to provide matching funds for R&D. The Malaysian government contributes matching funds equivalent to 125% of the resources committed by private firms.[12] Another is to co-finance R&D through a technology fund. Such funds allocate resources as a conditional loan, to be repaid if ventures succeed and written off otherwise.

STIMULATING ENTREPRENEURSHIP

Beyond promoting R&D, strong ties between industry and academia can also stimulate entrepreneurship. The Center for Innovation and Entrepreneurship, an autonomous unit at Linköping University in Sweden, linked to the city's Foundation for Small Business Development, has applied technical know-how and financial resources to stimulate the growth and development of technology-based firms.[13]

BOX 4.3

Strategies for stimulating research and development in East Asia

East Asian governments have used a variety of incentives to stimulate R&D by the private sector, drawing on a mix of public funding and tax breaks to encourage in-firm R&D as well as collaboration among government agencies, universities and the private sector.

Republic of Korea

The Korean government has directly supported private R&D through incentives and other forms of assistance. It awarded firms tax-exempt funds for R&D activities (though the funds were subject to punitive taxes if not used within a specified period). The funds could also be invested in Korea's first venture capital fund, the Korea Technology Development Corporation, or in collaborative R&D efforts with public research institutes. The government has given tax credits, allowed accelerated depreciation for investments in R&D facilities and cut taxes and import duties on research equipment. It has also used other tax incentives to promote technology imports. And the government has given grants and long-term, low-interest loans to companies participating in R&D projects and tax privileges and public funds to private and government R&D institutes.

But the main stimulus to industrial R&D in Korea came less from specific incentives than from the overall strategy—creating large conglomerates (*chaebol*), awarding them finance, protecting markets to allow them room to master complex technologies and then forcing them into export markets by removing protective barriers. Korea's strategy for promoting technology has given the chaebol a strong base for entering into demanding mass production. While many aspects of the chaebol system fostered inefficiencies and are being reformed, Korea is nonetheless one of the most dramatic examples of rapid technological transformation.

Taiwan (province of China)

As in Korea, the main impetus for rising R&D in Taiwan (province of China) came from an export orientation combined with measures to guide enterprises into more complex activities and reduce their dependence on technology imports. But the Taiwanese government did not promote the growth of large private conglomerates. While the "lighter" industrial structure in Taiwan (province of China) meant less growth in private sector R&D compared with that in Korea, it was also a source of strength—leading to innovative capabilities that are more flexible, more responsive to markets and much more broadly spread in the economy.

The government started to support local R&D capabilities in the late 1950s, when a growing trade dependence reinforced the need to upgrade and diversify exports. A science and technology programme, started in 1979, targeted energy, production automation, information science and materials science technologies for development. In 1982 biotechnology, electro-optics, hepatitis control and food technology were added to this list. A science and technology development plan for 1986–95 continued strategic targeting, aiming for R&D totalling 2 percent of GDP by 1995.

Around half the R&D is financed by the government. But enterprise R&D has risen as some local firms have expanded to become significant multinationals. The government has used a variety of incentives to encourage such R&D over the years, including providing venture capital and financing for enterprises that develop strategic industrial products. The tax system provides full tax deductibility for R&D expenses, accelerated depreciation for research equipment and special incentives for enterprises based in the Hsinchu Science Park. The government also requires large firms to invest 0.5–1.5 percent of their sales in R&D and has launched large-scale research consortiums, co-funded by industry, to develop critical products such as new-generation automobile engines and more sophisticated computer memory chips.

Singapore

The Singapore government launched a $1.1 billion, five-year technology plan in 1991 to promote development in such sectors as biotechnology, microelectronics, information technology, electronic systems, materials technology and medical sciences. The plan set a target for R&D spending of 2% of GDP by 1995. A new plan, launched in 1997, doubled expenditure for science and technology, directing the funds to strategic industries to ensure future competitiveness.

Singapore uses several schemes to promote R&D by the private sector. The Cooperative Research Programme gives local enterprises grants (with at least 30% local equity) to develop their technological capabilities through work with universities and research institutions. The Research Incentive Scheme for Companies gives grants to set up centres of excellence in strategic technologies, open to all companies. The R&D Assistance Scheme gives grants for specific product and process research that promotes enterprise competitiveness. And the National Science and Technology Board initiates research consortiums to allow companies and research institutes to pool their resources for R&D. Together these schemes have raised the share of private R&D to 65% of the total.

Source: Lall 2001.

Venture capital can also stimulate entrepreneurship. It is no surprise that the United States dominates in this. But other countries where innovation has become important, such as Israel and India, also have vibrant venture capital markets.[14]

In 1986 Israel had only two venture capital funds, with less than $30 million in total investable assets. Today about 150 venture capital firms manage up to $5 billion in venture capital and private equity. The market took off in the early 1990s when the government set up a venture capital company, Yozma, to act as a catalyst for the emerging industry. With a budget of $100 million, Yozma invested in local companies and attracted foreign capital from Europe and the United States. The Yozma fund is a model for the state-led emergence of a venture capital and high-technology industry.

In India annual venture capital investments reached $350 million in 1999, with most concentrated in the technology hubs in the country's south and west. The government has developed policy guidelines to encourage venture capital, and the National Association of Software and Service Companies projects that up to $10 billion of venture capital may be available by 2008.

In both India and Israel the government played an important role in establishing the venture capital industry and stimulating innovation, but a sophisticated financial sector was a precondition for attracting venture capital. Also key were strong ties to entrepreneurs and venture capitalists in the United States, and education systems that produce a significant number of highly skilled people, generating a critical mass for innovative activity.

RETHINKING EDUCATION SYSTEMS TO MEET THE NEW CHALLENGES OF THE NETWORK AGE

To bring life to an environment of technological creativity, people need to have technical skills, and governments need to invest in the development of those skills. Today's technological transformations increase the premium on such skills and change the demand for different types of skills. This calls for a rethinking of education and training policies. In some countries systems need an overhaul. In others, a redirection of public funds. How much for public education? For science? For formal education? For vocational training? Tough choices, indeed.

INCREASING THE EMPHASIS ON QUALITY

Greater resources and higher enrolments alone are not enough. The quality and orientation of education at each level, and the link with the demand for skills, are critical for mastering technology.

Primary education for all is essential. It develops some of the most basic capabilities for human development. And it creates a base of numeracy and literacy that enables people to be more innovative and productive. Although most countries in the low human development category have net primary enrolment ratios below 60%, most other developing countries have achieved nearly universal primary enrolment (see indicator table 10).

Secondary and higher education are also crucial for technology development. University education creates highly skilled individuals who reap the benefits through higher salaries. But it is also at the heart of creating national capacity to innovate, to adapt technology to the country's needs and to manage the risks of technological change—benefits that touch all of society. In 1995 gross enrolment ratios averaged just 54% at the secondary level and 9% at the tertiary level in developing countries, compared with 107% and 64% in high-income OECD countries.[15]

Increasing the quantity of education is not enough, for it is the low quality of secondary schools that leads to low completion rates in many countries—and then low university enrolments. Korea and Singapore built high university enrolments on high secondary completion rates in good schools. In internationally comparable tests in mathematics, students in Singapore, Korea, Japan and Hong Kong (China, SAR) show the highest achievements. South Africa and Colombia, by contrast, performed significantly lower than the international average.[16] Some differences across countries reflect differences in incomes. But that is not the whole story. Korea ranks

The quality and orientation of education at each level are critical for mastering technology

higher in test scores than countries with twice the GDP per capita, such as Norway.

International comparisons, despite their problems, have two important advantages. First, they move the debate towards an assessment of outcomes rather than inputs, such as education budgets. Second, they force policy-makers to seek more refined measures to capture the quality of skills. Several countries, for example, have established national and local standards for assessing outcomes. These may not be internationally comparable, but they set important benchmarks. Assessments based on these standards make it clear that at the primary and secondary levels developing countries need to increase instruction time in science and mathematics, critical in improving students' achievement in these subjects.[17]

Chile is taking important strides to improve the quality of education, measuring the quality of outcomes and providing resources and incentives (box 4.4). And East Asia has shown that the technology orientation and content of education are as important as the expansion of resources (box 4.5).

In advanced economies education reform has placed new emphasis on helping people adapt to the new skill demands that come with shifting employment patterns. Students are encouraged to keep their education and career options open. In Denmark general courses in vocational programmes have opened new pathways to higher education. In the United Kingdom examination systems allow students to choose subjects from both general and vocational programmes. In Finland the government has raised the status of vocational education and increased public resources for on-the-job learning. Since 1999 all three-year vocational courses have had to offer six months' work experience to every student.[18]

USING TECHNOLOGY TO IMPROVE QUALITY

With the rapid development of information and communications technology, it has become critical to teach basic computer skills to children. The biggest concern for developing countries is the lack of resources—both physical and human—to ensure adequate equipment and efficient teaching of such skills in schools. A computer costs more than the annual income of most people in developing countries, and teachers need to be trained to use new instructional material.

Yet information and communications technology also provides new possibilities for improving the quality of education at low cost. And there has been a proliferation of imaginative attempts in developing countries to spread new technology to education institutions in cost-effective ways.

- Costa Rica launched a "computers in education" programme in 1998, aimed at raising the quality of education in primary schools. The programme uses an imaginative pedagogical approach to encourage interaction among children and raise cognitive skills. The goal is to help transform education through changes in learning and teaching brought about by the use of

---

BOX 4.4

A push for education quality in Chile—measuring outcomes and providing incentives

Chile is making a concerted effort to improve the quality of education. The key measures mark a shift in its education policies from a focus on inputs to a concern with outcomes:

- *National evaluation.* A comprehensive standardized testing system—Sistema de Medición de la Calidad de la Educación (SIMCE)—assesses Spanish and mathematics skills every two years for students in grades 4 and 8 and monitors schools' progress in improving outcomes.
- *Positive discrimination.* A government programme known as the P900 Programme targets assistance—from new textbooks and materials to professional support for teachers—to the 900 poorest primary schools..
- *Rewards.* A national system of performance evaluation for government-funded schools—Sistema Nacional de Evaluación del Desempeño de los Establecimientos Educacionales Subvencionados (SNED)—provides bonuses to all teachers in a school on the basis of student outcomes.

Made widely available and published in national newspapers, the SIMCE testing results have several uses:

- Policy-makers use the results to compare school performance nationally and identify schools needing special help.
- Schools use good results to market themselves and attract more students.
- Parents use the results to help them select the best school for their children.

SIMCE data are also used to assess the pace of progress among children attending the schools in the P900 Programme. Schools improving their results enough to "graduate" become part of the mainstream reform efforts for primary school and are replaced in the programme by other schools.

SNED has established competition between schools roughly comparable in student population and socio-economic levels. Around 31,000 teachers received bonuses in each of the first two rounds of SNED awards.

Many parents, teachers and school administrators believe that this system of external standards and evaluation provides a good yardstick for measuring schools' performance. Others think that SIMCE is unfair, especially to schools and students in poor neighbourhoods. Despite the controversy, Chile is clearly moving towards a more quality-oriented education system.

Source: Carlson 2000; King and Buchert 1999; OECD 2000c; Chile Ministry of Education 2001.

---

computers, the training of teachers and the excitement generated by children's self-directed learning, knowledge creation and problem solving. The programme was designed to reach one-third of the country's primary school children, providing some 80 minutes of access to computers each week. Teacher surveys confirm that student performance has improved.[19]

• In Brazil a community schools programme is equipping young people in poor communities to use computers. The Committee for Democ-

racy in Information Technology (CDI), a non-profit organization, is helping communities develop self-sufficient "information technology and citizenship schools". Communities that want to start a school must go through a rigorous process to ensure that they can sustain the school once CDI assistance ends. CDI provides free technical assistance for three to six months, trains the instructors, works with the school to procure an initial donation of hardware and then helps the school install the computers. After a school

---

BOX 4.5

Orientation and content as important as resources—lessons from education strategies in East Asia

Over the past four decades the East Asian "tigers"—Hong Kong (China, SAR), Republic of Korea, Singapore and Taiwan (province of China)—achieved rapid development of human skills, equipping them for rapid progress in adapting technologies. Their success suggests strategies that less developed countries could consider and adapt to their own circumstances.

One key lesson: the orientation and content of education are as important as resource allocation. These countries not only invested in basic education but also emphasized a technology-oriented curriculum at higher levels. These investments in skills were part of an export-led development strategy, which provided demand signals for the skills required for improving competitiveness.

Public education spending had been fairly low in East Asia, around 2.5% of GNP in 1960 for most countries. In 1997 the regional average was still only 2.9%, far less than the 3.9% average for all developing countries and the 5.1% average for Sub-Saharan African. But as the region's countries grew rapidly, so did the absolute level of spending on education. And education spending has also expanded as a share of national income, partly through increased private spending.

Evolving priorities in education strategies

At an early stage of development East Asia gave priority to basic education, achieving universal primary schooling in the late 1970s. That made it easier to concentrate on improving quality and increasing resources in upper secondary and tertiary education. At the tertiary level enrolment ratios remained below 10% until 1975, contrasting unfavourably with those in Latin America. But as countries advanced, they needed more skilled and educated workers—and higher education expanded rapidly, especially after

1980. In Korea the tertiary enrolment ratio soared from 16% in 1980 to 39% in 1990 and then to 68% in 1996.

Private funding for post-basic education

East Asia has taken a unique approach to financing education, relying on private sources for a relatively large share of spending, especially at the upper secondary and tertiary levels. And some countries have depended largely on the private sector to provide higher education. In Korea in 1993 private institutions accounted for 61% of enrolments in upper secondary education and 81% in tertiary education.

A large private role in providing education raises important questions about equity in access. Countries have used different approaches to address this issue. Korea targets public resources to basic education and is more selective about the mix of private and public resources at higher levels. Singapore maintains relatively strong government involvement in the operation and financing of education at all levels.

Evidence shows that privately financed institutions have lower unit operating costs. Not all developing countries can rely on private funding, but combining private and public funding at higher levels of education with public spending for primary and lower secondary levels is an option—as long as adequate access to higher education is assured for poor children. Here, grants, loans and subsidies can play a useful role.

High pupil-teacher ratios but attractive salaries for teachers

Both small class sizes and high teacher quality have been shown to enhance student achievement. East Asian governments opted for a strategy in which highly qualified, well-paid teachers

work with more students. In Korea in 1975 pupil-teacher ratios exceeded 55 at the primary level and 35 at the secondary level, compared with developing country averages of 36 and 22. But Korea also pays teachers starting and mid-career salaries that are higher relative to per capita GNP than those in any other OECD country.

Lifelong learning

Continuous training was considered a key to developing human skills in the context of rapid technological change. As East Asian countries became more sophisticated, pressures emerged for governments and firms to provide effective education and training systems. In Korea, following enactment of the Vocational Training Law in 1967, the government established well-equipped public vocational training institutes and subsidized in-plant training programmes. In the 1970s, when the government was seeking to develop the heavy and chemical industries, it promoted vocational high schools and junior technical colleges to satisfy the rising demand for technicians. The government also established public education and research institutions to supply high-quality scientists and engineers, such as the Korea Institute of Science and Technology in 1967 and the Korea Advanced Institute of Science and Technology in 1971.

The government of Singapore took similar initiatives, launching a series of training programmes—Basic Education for Skill Training in 1983, Modular Skills Training in 1987 and Core Skills for Effectiveness and Changes in 1987. In the 1990s the government also led the development of the information and communications technology industry by supporting study in this area in tertiary institutions and building specialized training institutes as well as joint-venture institutes with private companies.

Source: World Bank 1993; Lee 2001; Lall 2001.

---

has been selected, CDI serves as a partner and consultant but does not manage the programme. CDI has adapted its method to reach such diverse communities as street children and indigenous groups. As a result of its work in partnership with community associations, more than 35,000 children and young people, in 208 schools in 30 cities, have been trained in basic computer literacy. Most schools charge the students a symbolic fee of $4 a month, equivalent to the cost of five roundtrip metro rides in Rio de Janeiro, to ensure their commitment.[20]

An interesting approach to improving Internet access and use relies on school networking initiatives, or "schoolnets". A few developing countries have established broad Internet access for schools through nationwide networks, among them Chile, Thailand and South Africa.

• The Enlaces project in Chile has linked 5,000 basic and secondary schools to its network. Schools receive equipment, training, educational software and ongoing support from a technical assistance network of 35 Chilean universities organized by the Ministry of Education. The aim is to connect all secondary schools and half the basic education institutions. The Enlaces network provides access to email and educational resources through the public telephone network, taking advantage of low overnight call charges. And La Plaza, a customized software interface developed locally, provides a virtual "meeting place" for teachers and students.[21]

• Thailand has developed the first nationwide, free-access network for education in South-East Asia, SchoolNet@1509. With only 120 dial-in telephone lines, the network was obliged to establish a system to optimize the use of the lines: it gave each school one account for Web browsing and no more than two for Web development, limiting total access to 40 hours a month. It also created a Website to increase schools' awareness of the network and make Thai content available on the Internet.[22]

• The South African School Net (SchoolNetSA) is an interesting example for its structure and partnerships. SchoolNetSA, which is spread across several provinces, provides Internet services to local schools: connectivity, domain administration, email and technical support. SchoolNetSA has also developed on-line

educational content, and many schools have developed their own Web pages.[23]

Technologies such as CD-ROM, radio and cable television—or a mix of technologies—can be combined with the Internet to extend its reach. The Kothmale Community Radio in Sri Lanka uses radio as a gateway to the Internet for its listeners in remote rural communities. Children or their teachers send requests for information about school topics for which no local resources exist; other listeners may also submit requests. The broadcasters search for the information on the Internet, download it and make it available by constructing a broadcast around the information, mailing it to the school or placing it in the radio station's open-access resource centre. The resource centre provides free Internet access and a library with computer databases, CD-ROMs, downloaded literature and print materials. This mediated access brings the Internet's resources to rural and underserved communities. And community rebroadcasting can relay the information in local languages rather than English, the dominant language of the Internet.[24]

Regional and global cooperation can reduce the cost of access to the Internet. Indeed, the development of information and communications technology provides the tools for learning through a global network. And wireless technologies enable developing countries with little telecommunications infrastructure to connect to the network. A pan-African satellite system, to be launched later in 2001, is expected to provide cheaper and better network service to African countries. Satellite-based distance education systems can provide poor nations access to higher-quality education and training in advanced countries. Such initiatives can be part of cost-effective solutions for bridging the "digital divide" between countries.

Many universities in developing countries are testing or implementing Web-based education systems.

• The University of Botswana evaluated two distance education methods: an Internet-based course, free of charge, that ran three months, and a video-based course that ran one week. The Internet course boosted test results by 49%, and

Many universities in developing countries are testing or implementing Web-based education systems

the video technology by a similar amount, suggesting to the evaluators that both technologies have potential for distance learning.[25]

• The Indira Gandhi National University, established in 1985, has extended its communications capabilities to impart lifelong education and training, particularly to those living in rural and remote areas. Its sophisticated media centre has a satellite-based communications system, and all its education centres are equipped with computers and email access. Its Website provides general information and course material for all programmes. The Internet is serving a growing number of learners, though it is still only a small part of a system using a wide range of communications technologies, including radio, television, cable television and teleconferencing.[26]

Other communities have developed the concept of the "virtual university", using the Internet as a place for students, teachers and researchers to "meet". Working with universities in developing countries, the Francophone Virtual University supports distance education through advice, assistance and educational materials. A first call for proposals in 1998 resulted in the funding of 26 projects, mostly based on the Internet, and 132 more proposals from 16 countries are under consideration.[27]

PROVIDING ON-THE-JOB TRAINING FOR LIFELONG LEARNING

Formal education is only part of the skill creation system. Vocational and on-the-job training are just as important. When technology is changing, enterprises have to invest in worker training to remain competitive. They are more likely to do

so when their workers are better educated to start with, since that lowers the cost of acquiring new skills.

Several studies—in Colombia, Indonesia, Malaysia and Mexico—have shown the high impact of enterprise training on firm productivity. Such training can be an effective and economical way to develop the skills of a workforce, particularly where employers are well informed about the skills needed. Some may also have the expertise and resources to provide training in both traditional and emerging skills. The costs of enterprise training tend to be low compared with those of formal training, though employers lose part of the benefit if employees leave. Studies suggest that enterprise-based training yields higher private returns than other post-school training, in both developing and industrial countries.[28]

Enterprise training is also an essential complement to new investment in technology, plants and equipment. Many studies in industrial countries suggest that the shortage of appropriate worker skills is a major constraint to the adoption of new technologies, while well-trained workers accelerate their adoption.[29]

Despite the demonstrated gains in productivity from training, not all employers provide it. Training involves costs—in materials, time and forgone production. In Colombia, Indonesia, Malaysia and Mexico a sizable share of enterprises provide no worker training (table 4.2). Among small and medium-size enterprises, more than half provide no formal, structured training, and more than a third no informal training. Weak management, high training costs, inability to exploit scale economies in training, poor information about the benefits of training, market imperfections and the absence of competitive pressures—all are reasons that firms provide too little training.

CHOOSING POLICIES FOR BETTER QUALITY TRAINING

Skill development requires policy intervention —in many forms. Governments can establish training centres that involve the private sector. Or they can use fiscal incentives or matching grants to encourage industry associations to es-

When technology is changing, enterprises have to invest in worker training to remain competitive

TABLE 4.2
Enterprises providing training in selected developing countries
Percent

Country, year	Informal training	Formal training
Colombia, 1992	76	50
Indonesia, 1992	19	19
Malaysia, 1994	83	35
Mexico, 1994	11	11

Source: Tan and Batra 1995, cited in Lall 2001.

tablish and manage such centres. In East Asia industry associations provide many valuable training and technical services. Also worth considering are generous tax allowances to smaller firms for investing in training (Malaysia and Thailand give a 200% tax deduction).[30] And governments can sponsor coordination units to support interaction, with majority representation by the private sector to ensure that industry needs are addressed in the design of the training curriculum.

A comprehensive strategy for skill creation needs to address the entire range of market failures through a mix of institutional and other policies. Examples of such failures include a lack of information on education needs in industry and on student demands, inadequate incentives for trainers, low educational qualifications among employers and managers, low absorptive capacity among poorly educated workers and an inability to form efficient training programmes in line with changing skill and technology needs. Consider Singapore's public funding and incentives for lifelong skill development, which try to overcome market deficiencies (box 4.6).

What are some of the key policies developing countries should consider for upgrading skills?

• Conduct comprehensive audits of skill provision and needs, not just once but on a regular basis. International benchmarking can be used to assess skill needs. And there may be a case for targeted development of new skills likely to be critical for future competitiveness, in such areas as food processing, capital-intensive process industries and electrical and electronics engineering. Such exercises can be undertaken by industry associations, academic institutions and government, working together.

• Target special information and incentive programmes to small and medium-size enterprises to encourage them to invest in training. Governments can build on apprenticeship systems, in which craftspeople teach young workers traditional methods, upgrading the systems by setting up training centres and subsidizing training by small and medium-size enterprises.

• Provide recent secondary school graduates with partially financed training in accredited private centres, both encouraging skill acquisition and helping to create a market for private training.

• While most of these examples relate to training in the urban, industrial and service sectors, similar lessons apply in agriculture, where extension workers, researchers and others involved in technological upgrading also need training.

FINANCING EDUCATION—TOUGH CHOICES

Public investments in learning yield high returns to society as a whole. But where should each country direct its investments? Have today's technological transformations made the returns to secondary and tertiary education as high as those to primary education—or even higher? If so, how should spending be distributed across primary, secondary and tertiary systems? And are there ways to increase resource flows to education, beyond simply expanding public spending?

Skill development requires policy intervention in many forms

BOX 4.6

Providing incentives for high-quality training in Singapore

The Singapore government has invested heavily in developing high-level skills. It expanded the country's university system and directed it towards the needs of its industrial policy, changing the specialization from social studies to technology and science. In the process the government exercised tight control over the content and quality of curriculum, ensuring its relevance for the industrial activities being promoted. The government also devoted considerable efforts to developing the industrial training system, now considered one of the world's best for high-technology production.

The Skill Development Fund, established in 1979, collected a levy of 1 percent of payroll from employers to subsidize training for low-paid workers. Singapore's four polytechnics, which meet the need for mid-level technical and managerial skills, work closely with business in designing courses and providing practical training. In addition, with government assistance under the Industry-Based Training Programme, employers conduct training courses matched to their needs. And the Economic Development Board continuously assesses emerging skill needs in consultation with leading enterprises and mounts specialized courses. National investment in training reached 3.6 percent of annual payroll in 1995, and the government plans to raise it to 4 percent. Compare this with an average of 1.8 percent in the United Kingdom.

The programme's initial impact was felt mostly in large firms. But efforts to increase small firms' awareness of the training courses and to support industry associations have increased the impact on smaller organizations. To expand the benefit, a development consultancy scheme has been introduced to provide small and medium-size enterprises with grants for short-term consultancies in management, technical know-how, business development and staff training.

As a result of all these efforts the workforce has shifted significantly towards more highly skilled jobs, with the share of professional and technical workers rising from 15.7% in 1990 to 23.1% in 1995.

Source: Lall 2001.

The social benefits of primary education—such as lower fertility and improved health for mothers and children—have made universal primary education a worldwide goal. But developing countries cannot ignore secondary and post-secondary education, though the social benefits from investments at these levels are less well documented. Getting the balance right is difficult. What indicators can countries use to help them choose the best policy?

The share of national income spent on education relative to, say, defence and health, is only a start. This indicator needs to be supplemented with others, such as teachers' salaries relative to average incomes. Countries differ enormously in what they pay teachers. In Uruguay, for example, the statutory salary of an experienced teacher at a public lower secondary school is just 80% ($7,458 PPP US$) of average income. In Jordan a teacher with the same experience would earn almost 3.5 times ($11,594 PPP US$) the country's average income.[31] Offering starting salaries that are around the average income, or even lower, makes it difficult to attract enough qualified teachers.

An important indicator for higher education is the rate of enrolment in technical subjects such as science, engineering, mathematics and computing. Some developing countries have had great success in raising such enrolments. For example, of the 3 million students enrolled in college in the four East Asian "tigers"—Hong Kong (China, SAR), Republic of Korea, Singapore and Taiwan (province of China)—in 1995, more than 1 million were in technical fields. China and India both have more than a million students enrolled in technical subjects.[32] These large enrolments generate a critical mass of skilled personnel. But there are stark disparities between nations. While gross tertiary enrolment in science and technical subjects was 23.2% in Korea in 1997, it was only 1.6% in Botswana and 0.2% in Burkina Faso in 1996 (see annex table A2.1 in chapter 2).

Tertiary education is expensive—too expensive for many poor countries. That leads to some difficult policy questions. Which skills should countries acquire by sending students abroad? Which subjects require public resources, and which can be privately financed?

The logic of government financing for secondary education is indisputable. Nor can governments neglect the post-secondary level. But public financing does need to be targeted to science, public health, agriculture and other fields in which technological innovation and adaptation will generate large spillover benefits for society as a whole. For some developing countries, participating in regional and global networks of universities will make sense for several decades. But in the long run most will want to establish their own universities and research centres.

Most developing countries already devote substantial public resources to education (table 4.3). But countries around the world find that they need to finance skill development through a mix of public resources, private finance and the direct contributions of individuals. Some policy choices:

- Retain public responsibility for funding basic education, with mandatory primary education the responsibility of government. Out of 196 countries, 172 have passed laws making primary education compulsory.[33] These laws have not always been fully implemented.
- Reconsider the extent to which individuals should pay for some courses at the tertiary level. For courses that generate high private returns, there may be a case for cost recovery. Courses in business and law, for example, could be priced to reflect the market value of these degrees.
- Encourage private supply of some education services, particularly at the post-secondary level. The extent of private spending on education varies enormously across countries. In Korea, for example, private spending is equivalent to 2.5% of GDP.[34]
- Rely more on private funding for vocational and on-the-job training, through private firms or trade associations. Use subsidies and tax allowances for training to encourage individuals and firms to invest in skills.

Public policy in developing countries thus has to focus on increasing resources and, in many, on changing the orientation of education systems. Financing education calls for a mix of public and private responsibility. The public sector must retain responsibility for universal primary education and for secondary and some tertiary education. But countries should consider allowing greater scope for private supply of some education services—and rely more on payments from individuals for advanced professional courses with strong market rewards.

MOBILIZING DIASPORAS

Rich countries are opening their doors to developing country professionals—at a high cost to the home countries. About 100,000 Indian professionals a year are expected to take new visas recently issued by the United States. The cost of providing university educations to these professionals represents a resource loss for India of $2 billion a year (box 4.7).

This "brain drain" makes it more difficult for developing countries to retain the very people critical for technological development, people whose wages are increasingly set in the global marketplace. How can a diaspora contribute to the home country? What can supplier countries do to get some "compensation" for generating skills that have an international market? Can countries sustain and improve their domestic education institutions? What can they do to persuade talented people to return? Many countries have adopted strategies to encourage links between the diaspora and the home country.

INDIA'S DYNAMIC DIASPORA NETWORK

Diasporas can enhance the reputation of the home country. The success of the Indian diaspora in Silicon Valley, for example, appears to be influencing how the world views India, by creating a sort of "branding". Indian nationality for a software programmer sends a signal of quality just as a "made in Japan" label signals first class consumer electronics. India's information technology talent is now being courted not just by companies in the United States but by those in other countries.

The worldwide network of Indian professionals has been investing in skill development at home. The network has worked to raise the endowments and bolster the finances of some of India's institutions of higher education. And an effort is under way to establish five global institutes of science and technology.

The Indian diaspora is also having important effects in the information technology sector. Firms increasingly have operations in both the United States—the "front office"—and India—the "manufacturing facility". At a time that talent in information technology has been scarce, Indian-launched firms in the United States have had a competitive advantage stemming from an unusual factor: they are up and running faster than their rivals simply because they can hire technical people faster, drawing as they do from a large transnational network. This has led to rapidly growing demand for information technology specialists from India and thus to a rapid expansion of information technology training, increasingly by the private sector.[35]

Many countries have adopted strategies to encourage links between the diaspora and the home country

TABLE 4.3
Average public education spending per pupil by region, 1997
(estimated)

	Average		Primary and secondary[a]		Tertiary	
	US$	Percentage of GNP per capita	US$	Percentage of GNP per capita	US$	Percentage of GNP per capita
World	1,224	22	999	18	3,655	66
Advanced countries	5,360	21	4,992	20	6,437	25
Developing countries	194	16	150	12	852	68
Sub-Saharan Africa	252	11	190	8	1,611	68
Middle East	584	22	494	19	1,726	66
Latin America	465	14	392	12	1,169	35
East Asia	182	14	136	11	817	64
South Asia	64	15	44	11	305	73
Transition countries	544	26	397	19	603	33

a. Includes pre-primary.
Source: Lee 2001 using UNESCO 2000b.

Korea and Taiwan (province of China) have focused more on encouraging their diasporas to return than on encouraging them to invest at home. Taiwan (province of China) set up a government agency—the National Youth Commission—to coordinate efforts to encourage return. The commission acts as an information clearinghouse for returning scholars seeking employment and for potential employers. Korea has focused on upgrading its research institutions, such as the Korea Institute for Science and Technology (KIST), as a way to attract returnees. Those who join KIST are given a great deal of research and managerial autonomy.

Both Korea and Taiwan (province of China) have tried hard to attract scholars and researchers. Intensive recruiting programmes search out older professionals and scholars and offer them salaries competitive with overseas incomes, better working conditions and help with housing and children's schooling. Visiting professor programmes allow the countries to tap the expertise of those uncertain about returning home for good.

In the 1960s just 16% of Korean scientists and engineers with doctorates from the United States returned to Korea. In the 1980s that share jumped about two-thirds.[36] A large part of the difference was due to Korea's improved economic prospects.

Today, rather than focusing only on the physical return of their pools of technological talent living abroad, the two countries are working to plug their diasporas into cross-national networks. They are organizing networks of professionals overseas and linking them with the source country.

AFRICA'S ATTEMPTS TO REVERSE ITS BRAIN DRAIN UNDER ADVERSE CONDITIONS

Many African countries have suffered from internal conflicts and stagnant economies. Many skilled people have left this hostile environment. The Return of Qualified African Nationals Programme, run by the International Organization for Migration, has tried to encourage qualified nationals to return and helped them reintegrate. It reintegrated 1,857 nationals in 1983–99, slightly more than 100 a year.[37] Given the high level of brain drain from Africa, this effort is unlikely to make much of a difference.

•   •   •

Can countries do anything to get compensation for the skills lost through brain drain? One

---

BOX 4.7

Taxing lost skills

The brain drain from skill-poor countries to skill-rich countries is likely to continue in the foreseeable future. What are the resources at stake for the skill-supplying countries? And how might these countries recover some of the resources they lose through the brain drain?

Consider the drain of software professionals from India to the United States. Under new legislation introduced in October 2000, the United States will issue about 200,000 H-1B visas a year over the next three years. These visas are issued to import specific skills, primarily in the computer industry. Almost half are expected to be issued to Indian software professionals. What resource loss will this represent for India?

Consider just the public spending on students graduating from India's elite institutes of technology. Operating costs per student run about $2,000 a year, or about $8,000 for a four-year programme. Adding in spending on fixed capital, based on the replacement costs of physical facilities, brings the total cost of training each student to $15,000–20,000. Multiply that by 100,000, the number of professionals expected to leave India each year for the next three years. At the high end, it brings the resource loss to $2 billion a year.

How might India begin to recover this loss? The simplest administrative mechanism would be to impose a flat tax—an exit fee paid by the employee or the firm at the time the visa is granted. The tax could be equivalent to the fees charged by headhunters, which generally run about two months' salary. Assuming annual earnings of $60,000, this would amount to a flat exit tax of $10,000, or about $1 billion annually (and $3 billion over three years).

Public spending on education by India's central and state governments amounts to about 3.6% of GDP. The share going to higher education (including technical education) is 16.4%, or 0.6% of GDP—around $2.7 billion in 1999. Exit tax revenues—whether collected through unilateral or bilateral mechanisms—could easily raise public spending in higher education by a fifth to a third.

But estimates of the revenue potential of an exit tax need to take into account behavioural responses: people might try to evade the tax by leaving as students at an early age and then staying on. How would one tax this group of (potential) immigrants, who are likely to be the "cream of the crop" for a developing country? Moreover, if the children of the elite do not enrol in a country's education institutions, the political support for ensuring that the institutions are run well will wither.

Beyond the exit tax, there are several alternatives for taxing flows of human capital:
• A requirement for loan repayment, where each student in tertiary education is given a loan (equivalent to the subsidy provided by the state) that would have to be repaid if the student leaves the country.
• A flat tax, where overseas nationals pay a small fraction of their income, say, 1%.
• The US model, where individuals are taxed on the basis of nationality, not residence. This would require negotiating bilateral tax treaties.
• The cooperative model, where a multilateral regime would allow automatic intergovernmental transfers of payroll taxes or income taxes paid by nationals of other countries.

As with all taxes, each of these involves trade-offs between administrative and political feasibility and revenue potential.

Source: Kapur 2001; Bhagwati and Partington 1976.

---

possibility is to use tax policy to generate resources for institutions that create skills relevant for both international and domestic markets . Various tax proposals—from a one-time exit tax to longer-term bilateral tax arrangements—have been around for some time (see box 4.7). In light of the increased migration of skills in recent years, such proposals deserve serious consideration.

The contrasting experiences noted above point to an obvious reality: countries with substantial diasporas have a potential resource. A diaspora's expertise and resources can be in-valuable, but effectiveness depends on the state of affairs in the home country. That means that it must have an environment conducive to economic development, with political stability and sound economic policies. The diaspora's attitude towards returning to the home country is likely to change as the country develops and its prospects improve. Both the Indian and Korean diasporas responded to improving domestic conditions. Timing and chance play a part in this, but in the end diaspora networks can be effective only when countries get their houses in order.

CHAPTER 5

Global initiatives to create technologies for human development

Today's technological transformations are pushing forward the frontiers of medicine, communications, agriculture, energy and sources of dynamic growth. Moreover, such advances have a global reach: a breakthrough in one country can be used around the world. The human genome, mapped primarily by researchers in the United Kingdom and the United States, is equally valuable for biotechnological research the world over. The Internet was created in the United States, but its cost-slashing consequences for information and communications enhance people's opportunities in every country.

But technologies designed for the wants and needs of consumers and producers in Europe, Japan or the United States will not necessarily address the needs, conditions and institutional constraints facing consumers and producers in developing countries. Some technologies can be adapted locally, but that takes resources. Others essentially need to be reinvented. Developing countries can do a lot to exploit the benefits and manage the risks of new technologies—but global initiatives are also crucial. Why global? Because the value of research and development crosses borders, and few countries will invest enough on their own to provide global public goods. Moreover, the global impact of technological advance hinges on the weakest links in the chain. For example, insufficient monitoring of the impacts of genetically modified crops in the poorest countries can ultimately affect the richest.

At the global level, two things are needed. First, more public funding spent in new ways, with public policy motivating creative partnerships among public institutions, private industry and non-profit organizations. Second, a reassessment of the rules of the game and their implementation, ensuring that international

mechanisms—from the agreement on Trade-Related Aspects of Intellectual Property Rights (TRIPS) to the allocation of domain names by the Internet Corporation for Assigned Names and Numbers—are not loaded against latecomers or implemented to the disadvantage of those already behind.

On the one hand, today's technological transformations have tremendous potential to help eradicate poverty. Though they do not replace the need to mobilize and make better use of existing technologies, they offer new ways of overcoming old constraints. Possibilities include:

- Vaccines for malaria, HIV and tuberculosis as well as lesser-known diseases like sleeping sickness and river blindness.
- Drought-tolerant and virus-resistant varieties of the staple crops in Sub-Saharan Africa and of farmers on marginal lands.
- Low-cost computers, wireless connectivity, low-literacy touch screens and prepaid chipcard software for e-commerce without credit cards.
- More efficient fuel cells for transportation, power and heat generation; modernized biomass technologies for producing liquid and gaseous fuels and electricity; and cheaper and more efficient solar and wind power technologies.

On the other hand, much stands in the way:

Different climates, different demands. Many of the technologies needed to make progress in agriculture, health and energy differ significantly in temperate and tropical climates—contrast, for example, their diseases, pests, soils and energy resources, each of which calls for context-specific technologies. Some technologies can be adapted to cross the ecological divide—especially information and communications technology—but others cannot. A measles vaccine cannot be turned into a

A breakthrough in one country can be used around the world

malaria vaccine, and irrigated rice varieties are of little use in arid zones. Over the past two centuries temperate zone technologies have left tropical needs far behind (box 5.1).

Because technological advance is cumulative, the long-standing concentration of scientific research and technological innovation has opened a yawning gap between rich and poor countries, with global markets driving a technological trajectory that is not suited to the needs of developing countries. Research agendas are driven by the interests of scientists and inventors in research hubs and motivated by the needs and desires of high-income consumers in Europe, Japan and North America—and the developing world elite.

Low incomes, weak institutions. Human poverty and weak institutions widen the gap between technologies suited to the incomes and capacities of rich and poor countries. Low incomes, low literacy and skill levels, unreliable power supplies, weak administrative infrastructures—all are barriers to diffusing and using technologies designed for rich countries in poor ones. As a result diffusion can stall, and poor people can end up paying more than rich for the same services—such as buying kerosene when there is no electricity supply. In addition, weak institutions can slow innovation as well as diffusion of products specific to developing countries—sometimes because insecure intellectual property rights discourage private investors who cannot be sure that competition will not come in, copy the technology and undercut their profits.

Public goods, private producers. Innovations have many valuable benefits that cannot be captured by the innovator, even with intellectual property rights, and so will be underinvested in by private producers. Furthermore, the benefits of new technologies cross borders: an effective cholera vaccine developed in any one country—whether through public or private investment—will be of value to many. But without an effective way of coordinating this latent demand and capturing these external benefits, neither private investors nor national public agencies will be motivated to invest in innovation at socially optimal levels or in the most important areas.

Global markets, global pricing. Some products of new technologies—from pharmaceuticals to computer software—are in demand worldwide. But when they are protected by intellectual property rights and produced under a temporary monopoly, pricing strategies and global market mechanisms can hold them out of reach. A monopoly producer seeking to maximize global profits on a new technology would ideally divide the market into different income groups and sell at prices that maximize revenue in each, while still always covering marginal costs of production. Such tiered pricing could lead to an identical product being sold in Cameroon for just one-tenth—or one-hundredth—the price in Canada. But seg-

---

BOX 5.1

Tropical technology, suffering from an ecological gap

Given the varied political, economic and social histories of the world's regions, it seems more than coincidence that almost all the tropics remain underdeveloped at the start of the 21st century. Some argue that the North-South divide of latitude misses the point: the real gap is the temperate-tropical divide of ecology. In 1820 at the start of the modern growth era, the tropical world had a per capita income roughly 70% of that in the temperate world. By 1992 the gap had widened, with per capita incomes in the tropical zone just one-quarter of those in the temperate zone.

How did physical ecology, social dynamics, economic growth and technology trajectories interact to create this divide? Five possible explanations:
- *Ecological specificity.* Technologies for promoting human development, especially in health, agriculture and energy, are ecologically specific—determined by soils, pests, diseases and energy endowments—and cannot be transferred from one zone to another merely through tinkering.
- *Head start.* By 1820 temperate zone technologies were more productive than tropical zone technologies in these critical areas. They were also economically integrated in an international market of innovation and diffusion across the temperate zone, but with little cross-over into the tropical zone.

- *Returns to scale.* Technological innovation offers increasing returns to scale. With richer populations in temperate countries, market demand coupled with increasing returns has tremendously amplified the gap between temperate and tropical zones in the past two hundred years.
- *Social dynamics.* Urbanization and demographic transition—processes largely complete in temperate countries—further fuelled economic growth. But in tropical countries they have been held back, in a vicious circle, by low food productivity and poor public health.
- *Geopolitical dominance.* Temperate countries historically dominated tropical regions through colonialism, neglecting education and health care and suppressing local industry. Today temperate countries continue to dominate through the institutions of globalization, writing the rules of the game for international economic life.

Of course, ecology is just one of many factors: some tropical countries have bucked the trend, and some temperate countries have not met their promise. But if these five explanations lie behind a broad ecological divide, they call for policy solutions—from nations and from the global community—that focus on finding new ways to harness technology to tackle the challenges of tropical health, agriculture, energy and environmental management.

Source: Sachs 2000b.

---

menting the market is not easy. With increasingly open borders, producers in rich countries fear that re-imports of heavily discounted products will undercut the higher prices charged to cover overhead and research and development costs. And even if products do not creep back into the more expensive market, knowledge about lower prices will, creating consumer backlash. Without mechanisms to deal with these threats, producers are more likely to set global prices that are unaffordable in poor countries.

Weak technological capacity in many developing countries. Building technological capacity in developing countries is central to forging long-term solutions because technologies for development have not, cannot and will not be supplied through the global marketplace alone. Though the past 20 years have seen an important rise in research excellence in some developing countries, others still lack adequate research and development capacity. Without it, they cannot adapt freely available global technologies to their needs—let alone set their own research agendas for new innovations. Inadequate national policies are partly responsible, but the loss of highly skilled migrants, the lack of supporting global institutions and unfair implementation of global trade rules create additional barriers.

This Report calls for global action on four fronts:

• *Creating innovative partnerships and new incentives for research and development*—motivating the private sector, government and academia to combine their strengths in research and development, both within developing countries and through international collaboration.

• *Managing intellectual property rights*—striking the right balance between private incentives to innovate and public interests in providing access to innovations.

• *Expanding investment in technologies for development*—ensuring the creation and diffusion of technologies that are urgently needed but neglected by the global market.

• *Providing regional and global institutional support*—with fair rules of the game and with strategies that build the technological capacity of developing countries.

CREATING INNOVATIVE PARTNERSHIPS AND NEW INCENTIVES FOR RESEARCH AND DEVELOPMENT

Incentives to match technology to the needs of poor people have to suit the times. A new terrain of interaction is emerging, requiring a rethink of policies in developing countries and in the international community on the incentives and opportunities for research.

The low cost of communications makes virtual research communities far more feasible across countries. The Multilateral Initiative on Malaria, for example, exchanges information from malaria research worldwide to reduce duplication and maximize learning across projects. Virtual communities offer ways of drawing on the skills and commitment of the science diaspora from developing countries.

Moreover, over the past 20 years some developing countries have created centres of world-class research for a range of new technologies (box 5.2). This move allows developing countries to set priorities for research and generates potential for regional cooperation. Efforts to build on these research centres will benefit doubly from regional relevance and world-class collaboration.

The benefits of low-cost communications and new research centres are reflected in the growth of international research collaboration. Over the past 15 years it has grown worldwide, with researchers in both industrial and developing countries co-authoring research articles with scientists from an ever-growing number of countries, establishing a truly global research community. In 1995–97 scientists in the United States wrote articles with scientists from 173 other countries, scientists in Japan with 127, in Brazil with 114, in Kenya with 81, in Tunisia with 48 (figure 5.1).

Roles in research communities have changed dramatically, creating new ways of working. Think of the double helix, the structure that creates life—two ribbons of DNA, intertwined but not entangled. Can that same balance be struck among private industry, university researchers and public institutes—in both developing and industrial countries—to create a "triple helix" that pursues research driven by the needs

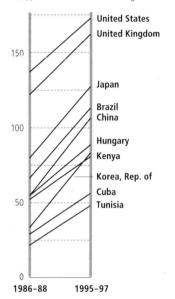

FIGURE 5.1

The rise of networked research: international co-authorship of published scientific articles

Number of other nationalities among co-authors

Source: NSF 2001.

BOX 5.2

Homemade but world class: research excellence for an alternative agenda

With the emergence of world-class research capacity in some developing countries comes new sources of technological excellence. Research in developing countries focuses on problems specific to their contexts, whether local diseases or low incomes. Four examples:

Thailand's drug to fight malaria. Thailand has the world's highest resistance to antimalarial drugs, so treatment is limited. But scientists at Thailand's Clinical Research Management Coordinating Unit are optimistic about a drug they are developing especially for local conditions. Hailed by the World Health Organization as one of the most important developments in malaria treatment, the new drug, dihydro-artemisinin (DHA), will be combined with mefloquine in a single tablet—making it easier for patients to follow dosage instructions and providing a new edge against resistance. If trials are successful and DHA passes rigorous testing, it will be the first home-grown pharmaceutical licensed in Thailand. With the possibility of local manufacture of its plant-based raw materials, DHA has the potential to be a widely available and highly effective treatment in Thailand and beyond.

Cuba's meningitis vaccine. Each year meningitis B kills 50,000 children worldwide. For years Western scientists struggled in vain to develop a vaccine. Now Cuba's heavy investment in medical research has paid off. In the mid-1980s a deadly outbreak of meningitis B prompted the publicly funded Finlay Institute to invest in research—and it succeeded, producing a vaccine, providing national immunization by the late 1980s and selling the vaccine throughout Latin America. Still unavailable in Europe and the United States due to regulatory barriers and US trade sanctions, the vaccine is now to be licensed to GlaxoSmithKline, a UK-based pharmaceutical giant. In return Cuba will be paid a license fee and royalties—part in cash and part in kind, food and medicines because of the US sanctions.

Brazil's computer breakthrough. Providing Internet access to low-income users is stalled by computer costs. In the global market multinational computer companies focus on doubling computing power, not halving costs. So in 2000 the government of Brazil commissioned a team of computer scientists at the Federal University of Minas Gerais to

do the reverse: produce a basic computer for around $300. "We realized this was not a First World problem—we were not going to find a Swedish or a Swiss company to solve this for us. We would have to do it ourselves", said the mastermind of the project.

In just over a month a prototype was made, with a modem, colour monitor, speakers, mouse, Internet software and options for adding printers, disk drives and CD-ROM drives. The government is now seeking a manufacturer, offering tax incentives to push the project forward. Plans include installing the device in public schools to reach 7 million children and selling it on credit to low-wage earners. The potential market extends worldwide.

India's wireless Internet access. Internet access is typically provided through telephone lines, but the cost of installing telephones in India means that only 2–3% of the population can afford them. To increase access from the current 15 million to, say, 150–200 million, costs would need to fall 50–65%. The technologies being offered by multinational companies cannot meet that challenge—but a home-grown alternative can.

In 1999 the Indian Institute of Technology in Madras created a low-cost Internet access system that needs no modem and eliminates expensive copper lines. At its core is a wireless local system developed in collaboration with Midas Communication Technologies in Madras and US-based Analog Devices. The result is faster and cheaper access: ideal for providing access to low-income communities throughout India and beyond. Licensed to manufacturers in India, Brazil, China and France, the technology is already in use internationally, from Fiji and Yemen to Nigeria and Tunisia. This is proof—according to the chairman of Analog Devices—that "Indian engineers are fully capable of designing and deploying world-class products for the Internet age".

All these initiatives were supported by national public funding and incentives. Global initiatives must reinforce such efforts and help realize the full potential of research institutes and enterprises in developing countries by encouraging international collaboration and providing incentives that draw them into international research projects.

Source: Cahill 2001; Lalkar 1999; Pilling 2001a; SiliconValley.com 2001; Rediff.com 1999; Anand 2000; Rich 2001.

and responsive to the feedback of the ultimate users—farmers and patients, households and businesses? Striking such a balance requires understanding each actor.

Private research is growing—and with it comes private ownership of the tools and findings of research. Much basic research is still publicly funded and licensed to the private sector. But it is often in the private sector that technological applications are developed, responding to market demand. New incentives are needed to motivate industrial research and development to address the technological needs of developing countries, not just the demands of the global marketplace. It is no longer easy to develop many technologies without the involvement of the private sector.

University research—mandated to serve the public interest—has been increasingly commercialized, especially in the United States. The 1980 Bayh-Dole Act allows universities to patent and license their federally funded research results, earning royalties. In 1985 only 589 utility patents—patents for inventions, not designs—were granted to US universities; in 1999, 3,340 were.[1] A more commercial orientation has helped bring HIV/AIDS treatments and cancer drugs to market. But closer industry ties can direct more research towards corporate rather than public interests, and towards commercial rather than open-ended basic research. In 1998 industry funding for academic research in the United States, though still a fraction of the total, was nearly five times the level of 20 years before.[2]

Public research, still the main source of innovation for much of what could be called poor people's technology, is shrinking relative to private research. Gaining access to key patented inputs—often owned by private firms and universities in industrial countries—has become an obstacle to innovation, sometimes with prohibitive costs. Especially in developing countries, public institutions often lack the negotiation, legal and business skills for licensing and cross-licensing proprietary research tools and products. And long-standing mutual suspicion and even hostility between public researchers and private developers impede many valuable avenues of work. In a 1996 survey of the malaria research community, half the respondents said they knew of promising results that were not followed up—one reason being the gap between the different stages and actors involved in turning research into a product.[3]

What does this new terrain mean for turning proprietary research to public interests? How can partnerships draw on the strengths of different actors? At a time of such technological and institutional flux, it would be premature to settle on one approach. Across different fields of technology, the options within these complex arrangements are under intense discussion—and most likely will be for years as policies and strategies evolve.

OPTIONS FOR PUBLIC INSTITUTIONS

With proprietary ownership of tools and technologies concentrated in industry and universities, public institutions are exploring new means of gaining access. Cross-licensing—exchanging rights to use patents—is common in industry, but the public sector has largely been blocked out of this strategy because its research results are not usually patented. Some controversial propositions are under debate. Will public institutions need to claim intellectual property rights for their innovations to generate bargaining chips? Should developing countries allow their universities to obtain patent rights for government-funded research? Would doing so increase secrecy, create conflicts of interest and divert research from non-commercial national priorities? Are there alternatives to the scramble for patents, or is this the inevitable way forward?

To access cutting-edge agricultural technologies, some public institutes are entering joint ventures with corporations in adaptive research. The Applied Genetic Engineering Research Institute (AGERI), an Egyptian public research institute, worked with Pioneer Hi-Bred International to develop a new variety of maize. By collaborating, AGERI was able to train staff through contact with world-class researchers and develop the local strain of the maize. Pioneer Hi-Bred secured the rights to use the new strain for markets outside Egypt. Such agreements to segment markets are increasingly used, with segmentation by:

- *Crop and region.* Insect-resistant maize using patented genetic material from Novartis has been transferred from the International Maize and Wheat Improvement Center (better known as CIMMYT) to Africa, but it can only be used within the region.
- *Variety.* Monsanto and the Kenyan Agricultural Research Institute's agreement to transfer genes patented by Monsanto to create virus resistant sweet potatoes is restricted to selected varieties grown by small farmers in central Kenya.
- *Country income.* The International Rice Research Institute negotiated with Plantech to get the rights to use the stemborer resistance gene in all developing countries.

These partnerships can produce win-win outcomes, but they may also face longer-term conflicts over market interests—especially if farmers undertake their own adaptive research and if developing countries plan to expand their markets and export their crops.

PUBLIC POLICY INITIATIVES

Basic research is usually promoted by giving government funding to researchers whose findings are then put in the public domain, promoting the sharing of knowledge and supporting the exploratory and cumulative nature of scientific understanding. Then that basic research must be transformed into a final product through extensive tests, trials, scaling up and packaging. How can product development to meet specific human development needs be promoted?

Two approaches are possible. "Push" incentives pay for research inputs by putting public money into the most promising research in public institutes. "Pull" incentives promise to pay only for a result, such as a vaccine for tuberculosis or a drought-tolerant variety of maize, whether it is produced by a private company or a public institute. One current pull proposal is to commit in advance to buying, say, a tuberculosis vaccine that meets specified requirements and to make it available to those who need it. Such a commitment could create strong incentives for applied research that results in viable products, while spending no public money

Partnerships can produce win-win outcomes, but they may also face longer-term conflicts over market interests

until the product is created. This mechanism could work for vaccine development because the desired product and quantity are relatively easy to specify (box 5.3).

Combining push and pull, Australia, the European Union, Japan, Singapore and the United States have each introduced orphan drug legislation to facilitate the development of drugs for rare diseases—usually those afflicting fewer than 500,000 patients a year—which are unlikely to be profitable for pharmaceutical companies. The legislation typically provides tax incentives for research and development as well as patent protection. In the United States in 1973–83, before the legislation was adopted, fewer than 10 drugs and bioproducts for rare diseases entered the market. Since the 1983 Orphan Drug Act more than 200 such drugs have been produced.[4]

In a similar way, a global orphan drug initiative could provide a much-needed push for research on tropical diseases, which also represent small commercial markets—not because they are rare but because they afflict poor peo-

ple. But such tax credits can have drawbacks. A tax credit for research on products for developing countries could be claimed by companies pursuing research not appropriate for developing countries—such as a company doing research on a short-term malaria vaccine appropriate for travellers—or research not actually aimed at developing the desired technology. One solution could be to award modest tax credits retroactively if a private firm produced a new product that was then purchased for use in developing countries.

INDUSTRY INITIATIVES

Public attention to the powerful influence of the private sector has prompted industry initiatives. One approach—already practised by one of the agribusiness giants—is to allow company scientists to use part of their time (say, 15%) for self-directed research using company resources. Such efforts could be linked to the agendas of public research institutes, strengthening the links between private and public research.

Some corporations have donated their proprietary technologies for public research. Consider the case of vitamin A–enhanced rice. It was developed entirely with public funding but, it was later discovered, drew on 70 proprietary research tools belonging to 32 companies and universities. After much negotiation and high-profile media attention, all the license holders agreed to grant free use of their intellectual property for distributing the rice to farmers who will earn less than $10,000 from growing it.[5]

In terms of providing access to the products of proprietary technologies, drug donation programmes have become the primary means of corporate philanthropy in the pharmaceutical industry: the combined product donations of five major pharmaceutical companies rose from $415 million in 1997 to $611 million in 1999.[6] Among the best known are Merck's mectizan programme for onchocerciasis (river blindness), started in 1987, and Pfizer's zithromax programme for trachoma, started in 1998. Such donations can be a winwin proposition where a country gets a free supply of the needed drugs and the company

Public attention to the powerful influence of the private sector has prompted industry initiatives

BOX 5.3

From longitude to long life—the promise of pull incentives

Vaccine markets are notoriously weak: research is long and expensive but the market is not secure. Health budgets in developing countries can cover only a fraction of a vaccine's social value. And once a vaccine has been produced, major buyers may pressure the developers to offer low prices, creating an uncertain return. Incentives are needed to guarantee the market, and purchase commitments—promising a set price and quantity to be purchased for a specific product—offer a way of doing that. The basic idea is not new. In 1714 the British government offered 20,000 pounds—a fortune at the time—to whoever could invent a way of measuring a ship's longitude at sea. The offer worked: by 1735 the clockmaker and inventor John Harrison had produced an accurate maritime chronometer.

Such an incentive could also work for vaccines. Public money would be spent only when the vaccine was produced, and developers (rather than governments) would choose which projects to pursue. A purchase com-

mitment requires clear conditions to make it credible. Vaccine developers must trust the market guarantee, so legally binding contracts would be needed. Setting the price and effectiveness criteria in advance would insulate the evaluators of vaccines from political and corporate pressure and enhance credibility. The need for credibility and clear rules was a lesson learned by Harrison, who despite his chronometer's accuracy was denied the cash prize during many years of political wrangling and redefining of rules.

But on its own a purchase commitment would not be sufficient to address the concentration of pharmaceutical research and development in industrial countries. While the incentives generated by a commitment would not be limited to the residents of any country, developing country researchers often lack the capital to finance research up front. Building local research capacity with other mechanisms would continue to be essential for developing countries to have the ability to create medicines for their own needs.

Source: Kremer 2000a, 2000b; Business Heroes 2001; Baker 2000; Bloom, River Path Associates and Fang 2001.

gets good public relations and sometimes tax incentives.

For countries, however, drug donations are still just one element in a sensible long-term plan for increasing access. The framework for their use needs to ensure that they do not undermine existing or potential market-driven access (box 5.4). And if donations are conditional on not using provisions in the TRIPS agreement—such as compulsory licensing and parallel importing—they could inhibit local initiatives and capacity building.

Industry initiatives of these kinds—donations of time, of patents and of products—provide one-off solutions, but are no substitute for good public policy. The recent backlash against pharmaceutical companies over HIV/AIDS drugs illustrates the need for policy-makers to provide a framework that ensures structural and market-driven, not only charitable, access to lifesaving medicines. The challenge for governments and the international community is to create incentives and regulations that form the right framework.

MULTIACTOR ALLIANCES

A promising new strategy is to create technology alliances that draw together diverse actors with a common interest—including government agencies, industry, academia, civil society and committed individuals who can make specific contributions to the task at hand. Such alliances are bringing new momentum to research, particularly in health. But coordinating the diverse interests of actors is a challenge, especially in handling the intellectual property rights of any resulting products.

A pioneering example is the non-profit International AIDS Vaccine Initiative (IAVI), with major funding from private foundations and several governments. By drawing together academia, industry, foundations and public researchers with win-win intellectual property rights agreements, IAVI's setup enables each partner to pursue its own interests—while jointly pursuing a vaccine for the HIV strain common in Africa (box 5.5). IAVI's success can be judged only by its results, but the initiative has inspired rethinking in many other fields. Could a similar initiative be launched in agriculture? In renewable energy? Now is the time to try.

BUILDING THE TRIPLE HELIX

The intertwining of public, university and private efforts is at the heart of new approaches to creating technology. But it needs to be carefully balanced, with each partner focusing on its mandate and comparative advantage. To capture the benefits, interactions should be based on clear principles, including:

- Ensuring transparency and accountability in decision-making and governance.
- Agreeing beforehand on an assignment of intellectual property that ensures public rights to use the inventions equitably or inexpensively.
- Making the end products affordable and accessible to those who need them.
- Contributing whenever possible to local capacity, for example, by collaborating with researchers in developing countries and with the ultimate users of technologies.

The intertwining of public, university and private efforts is at the heart of new approaches to creating technology

---

BOX 5.4

Hidden costs of drug donation programmes

Good drug donation programmes can be highly effective. In 1987 Merck introduced a programme to provide free "wherever needed for as long as needed" the drug mectizan to eradicate onchocerciasis (river blindness). In 1998 an estimated 25 million people in 32 countries were treated. This was a great success, both in corporate policy and in impact—but it is not always replicable. Onchocerciasis, found in a limited geographic area, can be eradicated and has a simple treatment. These features make an open-ended donation feasible for Merck to guarantee. But most diseases are not so containable. One danger of drug donation programmes is that they may be seen as a solution to access, when in fact they cannot address the problem adequately. Drawbacks include:

- *Sustainability.* Donations cannot be a long-term solution for a disease that persists. As the current chief executive officer of Merck admits, "giving our medicines away in general is an unsustainable and unrealistic answer because, at the end of the day, we must earn an adequate return on our investment in order to fund future research".

- *Scale.* The volume of corporate donations cannot meet demand. Of the 36 million people with AIDS, 95% are in developing countries. Companies clearly could not donate for free to every person in need a treatment sold for $10,000–12,000 a year in the United States.

- *Restrictions.* Drug donations are often restricted to a certain number of patients, limited to certain regions, available for a restricted time or supplied only to treat certain diseases—excluding, for administrative reasons, some people equally poor and in need.

- *Burden on public health structures.* Some donation programmes require establishing separate disbursement systems to keep drugs from being diverted. But this only draws staff away from the existing health care structure, stretching other services too thin.

- *Delay.* Because donations tend to be more complex than standard commercial transactions, access to the medicine can be delayed by protracted negotiations. Pfizer's fluconazole donation to South Africa was announced in April 2000, but by February 2001 no patients had received the drug.

Source: Guilloux and Moon 2000; Kasper 2001.

The new arrangements and incentives being explored make it possible for public interests to be served during this rush to own the tools of research. But the future is far from secure. Whether these alliances and incentives ultimately ensure that technologies are developed for poor people's needs is the vital test—and the fundamental standard for judging their success.

Managing intellectual property rights

Intellectual property rights lie at the heart of a highly polarized debate on technology and development. Why the uproar? Intellectual property rights—from trade marks and patents to copyrights and geographic indications—offer an incentive to research and develop technologies because they make it easier for innovators to reap returns on their investment. With patents, for example, inventors are given a temporary monopoly in the market, during which time they can charge prices that more than cover the initial cost of investment. Once the patent expires, competition can enter, pushing prices closer to production costs. The ideal regime of intellectual property rights strikes a balance between private incentives for innovators and the public interest of maximizing access to the fruits of innovation.

This balance is reflected in article 27 of the 1948 Universal Declaration of Human Rights, which recognizes both that "Everyone has the right to the protection of the moral and material interests resulting from any scientific, literary or artistic production of which he is the author" and that "Everyone has the right . . . to share in scientific advancement and its benefits". Likewise, the World Trade Organization's TRIPS agreement invokes a balance between "the promotion of technological innovation and . . . the transfer and dissemination of technology".

The transfer of technology, as well as innovation, played a key role in the history of industrialization. But whether that transfer occurred through formal or informal routes varied greatly. Industrialization has traditionally created national capacity by reproducing the technologies of advanced economies. But many of today's advanced economies refused to grant patents throughout the 19th and early 20th centuries, or found legal and illegal ways of circumventing them—as illustrated by the many strategies used by European countries during the industrial revolution (box 5.6). They formalized and enforced intellectual property rights gradually as they shifted from being net users of intellectual property to being net producers; several European countries—including France, Germany and Switzerland—completed what is now standard protection only in the 1960s and 1970s.

BOX 5.5

IAVI's innovation in networked research

Global spending on developing an AIDS vaccine is $300 million—just 10% of what Europe and the United States spend annually on drugs to treat HIV/AIDS. To rectify this extreme imbalance, in 1994 the Rockefeller Foundation launched a programme that was spun off in 1996 as the International AIDS Vaccine Initiative (IAVI). The mission is to accelerate the development, manufacture and distribution of AIDS vaccines at affordable prices to the public sectors of developing countries. IAVI is doing this by creating partnerships between industry, academia and the public sector. The objective: to get a dozen vaccines through early development and then get two or three into big clinical trials. Already some success is evident: in January 2001 clinical trials began in Kenya to test IAVI's first AIDS vaccine.

The initiative is breaking new ground in several ways. First, research is focused on the A strain of HIV and so is targeted at developing country needs—unlike most AIDS research, which focuses on the strains common in rich countries. Second, IAVI shows that research networks can work: scientists at Oxford University and the University of Nairobi and manufacturers in Germany and the United Kingdom have moved the leading vaccine from concept to clinical trials in record time. Third, through these networks IAVI has encouraged the buildup of local capacity by working with developing country researchers and using local doctors to conduct trials.

But the most important experiment is the intellectual property terms that IAVI has agreed to with its public and private partners. IAVI's expectation is that a company (or one of its strategic partners) will be the ultimate manufacturer and distributor of the vaccine. But if the company is later unwilling or unable to deliver the vaccine to the public sectors of developing countries at affordable prices, thus losing the time and money in the new technology, IAVI is free to seek alternate suppliers. IAVI would have rights to a non-exclusive license to find an alternative manufacturer to produce the vaccine for sale only to the public sector and only in developing countries.

Though this arrangement is appealing, there are additional complications, such as agreeing on affordable pricing or on the handling of proprietary intellectual property that industry partners may bring with them. There are real possibilities of blocking patents and cross-licensing agreements that could thwart the use of IAVI's opt-out options. These details, to be worked out case by case, will be the test of whether such public-private partnerships can deliver success for all sides.

The prospects look good. Academic research centres have been attracted by IAVI's proposition. A few biotechnology companies—with ideas but little capital—have also joined the collaboration, such as Alphavax in North Carolina and its partners in South Africa. Aventis, one of the world's "big four" vaccine producers, has also expressed an interest in partnerships with IAVI when the time comes to do large clinical trials in developing countries.

Source: Berkley 2001; IAVI 2000; *The Economist* 2001.

Today, however, intellectual property rights are being tightened worldwide. As signatories to the TRIPS agreement, developing countries are now implementing national systems of intellectual property rights following an agreed set of minimum standards, such as 20 years of patent protection; the least developed countries have an extra 11 years to do so.

In this new global regime two problems are creating new hurdles for progress in human development. First, consensus is emerging that intellectual property rights can go too far, hampering rather than encouraging innovation and unfairly redistributing the ownership of knowledge. Second, there are signs that the cards are stacked against fair implementation of TRIPS.

WHEN INTELLECTUAL PROPERTY RIGHTS GO TOO FAR

Intellectual property rights have increased private investment in industries such as agribusiness, pharmaceuticals and software by enabling the gains of research to be captured. The number of patents claimed has risen dramatically over the past 15 years—in the United States from 77,000 in 1985 to 169,000 in 1999.[7] The World Intellectual Property Organization's Patent Cooperation Treaty accepts a single international application valid in many countries; the number of international applications rose from 7,000 in 1985 to 74,000 in 1999.[8] Much of this increase reflects a boom in innovative activity, but some reflects less benign change.

First, the scope of patent claims has broadened—especially in the United States, the trendsetter on patent practice. From patents on genes whose function may not be known to patents on such e-commerce methods as one-click purchasing, many believe that the criteria of non-obviousness and industrial utility are being interpreted too loosely. Patent authorities have been accused of acting as service providers to patent applicants, not as rigorous watchdogs of the public domain.

Second, the strategic use of patents has also become more aggressive, because they are recognized as a key business asset. Minor changes to products at the end of the patent life—especially for medicines—are used to evergreen

the monopolist's rights. Moreover, some patent applications disclose their innovations with great obscurity, stretching patent officers' capacity to judge and the ability of other researchers to understand. In 2000 the World Intellectual Property Organization received 30 patent applications over 1,000 pages long, with several reaching 140,000 pages.

These two trends hamper innovation and shift traditional knowledge into private hands:
- *Hampering innovation.* Patents are not just an output of research, they are also an input. And when used in excess, they can bind up product development in licensing negotiations and transaction costs, creating uncertainty and

---

BOX 5.6

Lessons from the history of intellectual property rights

Technology transfer played a central role in the industrial revolution but intellectual property protection was by no means the only route, nor was it always respected. Until the mid-19th century the most important means of technology transfer was hiring skilled workers who brought needed technological knowledge. Skilled workers from industrially advanced countries were in high demand, resulting in government action. In 1719 French and Russian attempts to recruit British workers—especially those skilled in wool, metal and watch-making industries—prompted the British government to ban skilled worker migration, making it punishable by fine or even imprisonment. Emigrant workers who failed to return home within six months of warning could lose their land, property and citizenship.

As technologies became embodied in machines, the focus shifted to controlling their export. In 1750 Britain banned the export of "tools and utensils" in wool and silk industries, then in 1781 widened that to "any machine, engine, tool, press, paper, utensil or implement whatsoever". But in response, entrepreneurs and technicians in Belgium, Denmark, France, the Netherlands, Norway, Russia and Sweden devised new ways to get the technologies, often with explicit state consent or even active encouragement, including offers of bounty for specific technologies.

By the mid-19th century key technologies were too complex to acquire by hiring workers and importing machines, and li-

censing patents became increasingly important. Most of today's industrial countries introduced patents by 1850, followed by copyright and trade mark laws. But there were important exceptions. Swiss patent law was weak until 1907—when Germany threatened trade sanctions—and did not cover chemicals and pharmaceuticals until 1978. The United States, despite being a strong proponent of patent rights, did not recognize copyrights for foreigners until 1891.

Despite the emergence of international intellectual property rights among these countries, they continued to break the rules. In the late 19th century German manufacturers found ways of infringing on British trade mark laws, producing counterfeit Sheffield cutlery with fake logos and placing the stamp of country of origin only on packaging, or hidden out of sight—as on the bottom of sewing machines.

What implications does this history have today? First, tight and uniform intellectual property rights were not the only way technologies were transferred between today's industrial countries—despite arguments often made by these countries about the importance of the TRIPS agreement. Second, each country crafted its own path, at its own pace, in introducing intellectual property protection—highlighting the importance of countries creating their own strategies today, even within the multilateral regime.

Source: Chang 2001.

---

the risk of "submarine patents"—prior claims that surface only when research is under way. Without better information on patent claims and easier exchange of patented inputs, researchers risk wasting time inventing around proprietary technology and being blocked out of whole avenues of research.

• *Shifting traditional knowledge to private owners.* Existing patent systems lay open indigenous and community-based innovation in private sector claims. Infamous cases of falsely claimed patents include those on the properties of the Neem tree, turmeric and, more recently, the Mexican enola bean. Claiming, using and defending patents is easier for private industry than for public institutes and innovative communities (table 5.1). Recognizing the need to correct the resulting imbalance of access to patents, the World Intellectual Property Organization has launched an initiative to provide alternative forms of protection (box 5.7).

THE CURRENT IMPLEMENTATION OF TRIPS: NEW HURDLES FOR HUMAN DEVELOPMENT

Views vary tremendously on the expected impact of the TRIPS agreement on developing countries. For several reasons the likely outcomes are not yet clear:

• *Diverse national situations.* The impact of TRIPS will vary according to each country's economic and technological development. Middle-income countries like Brazil and Malaysia are likely to benefit from the spur to local innovation. Poorer countries, where formal innovation is minimal, are likely to face higher costs without the offsetting benefits.

• *Diverse national legislation.* TRIPS's minimum standards for intellectual property must be reflected in national legislation. But there is good scope for appropriate national strategies within that multilateral framework. The impact of TRIPS will partly depend on whether countries choose the strategies that best suit their interests.

• *Too recent to assess.* The TRIPS agreement entered into force in most developing countries in January 2000; the least developed countries have until 2006. With implementation still under way and industries still adjusting, little empirical evidence is available on the effects of legislative change.

• *Determined by case law.* TRIPS, like other World Trade Organization agreements, is an agreement on a legal framework. Its implications will be decided by resolving disputes. That makes case law and the power of the parties involved of great importance.

The game is hardly fair when the players are of such unequal strength, economically and institutionally

TABLE 5.1
Who has real access to claiming patents?

Issue	Multinational corporations	Public research institutes	Farming communities
Under intellectual property law the inventor must be named	Employee contracts ensure that inventors surrender most or all rights to the company	Employee contracts can ensure that inventors surrender most or all rights to the institute	The concept of an individual inventor is alien to many communities and can cause conflict
The criteria for patents include novelty and an inventive step	Companies' focus on small improvements usually meets the criteria	Focused more on basic research, institutes often cannot meet the criteria	Since these criteria have little to do with the process of community invention, they are hard to meet
Legal advice from specialized patent lawyers is expensive	Companies have in-house legal departments and ready access to expert consultants	Institutes have little in-house capacity and limited access to expensive expertise	Communities usually cannot afford or obtain either basic or expert advice
Patent holders must defend their patents under civil law	Companies employ aggressive tactics, using patent claims to stake out their market turf	Institutes often lack strong patent defence and give in to political pressure not to challenge the private sector	Communities find it almost impossible to monitor— let alone confront— patent infringements around the world.

Source: UNDP 1999a.

A single set of minimum rules may seem to create a level playing field, since one set of rules applies to all. But the game is hardly fair when the players are of such unequal strength, economically and institutionally. For low-income countries, implementing and enforcing the intellectual property rights regime put stress on already scarce resources and administrative skills. Without good advice on creating national legislation that makes the most of what TRIPS allows, and under intense pressure from some leading countries to introduce legislation beyond that required by TRIPS, many countries have legislated themselves into a disadvantageous position. Moreover, the high costs of disputes with the world's leading nations are daunting, discouraging countries from asserting their rights—hence the importance of ensuring that adequate legal aid is provided through the World Trade Organization.

If the game is to be fairly played, at least two critical shifts must take place. First, the TRIPS agreement must be implemented fairly. And second, commitments under this and other multilateral agreements to promote technology transfer must be brought to life.

Ensuring fair implementation of the TRIPS agreement. Under TRIPS countries can use compulsory licensing—permitting the use of a patent without the consent of the patent holder—in a number of circumstances, which they must embody in their own legislation. Typical uses are for public health emergencies and as antitrust measures to maintain competition in the market. TRIPS also allows countries to choose whether or not to permit patented goods to be imported from other countries where they are sold by the same company but more cheaply. Many industrial countries include these measures in their law and practice as part of their national strategy for using intellectual property rights. Yet under pressure and without adequate advice, many developing countries have not included them in their legislation, or are challenged when they try to put them to use. These legal provisions rarely grab public attention—but the development consequences of their unfair implementation can. The strongest example is the recent high-profile debate on developing countries' access to HIV/AIDS drugs. It has in-

creased public awareness of the far-reaching implications of intellectual property rights and highlighted the urgent need for fair implementation of TRIPS (feature 5.1).

Taking technology transfer from provisions to practice. Beyond the negotiating room, provisions for technology transfer written into many international agreements have often turned out to be paper promises. Consider three examples. The 1990 Montreal Protocol on Substances that Deplete the Ozone Layer, despite its overall success, ran into conflicts over commitments to ensure fair and favourable access for developing countries to chlorofluorocarbon (CFC) substitutes protected by intellectual property rights. The 1992 Convention on Biological Diversity aims to ensure fair and equitable use of genetic resources partly through technology cooperation, but its technological provisions have received little attention or have been downsized. And the 1994 TRIPS agreement calls for

The TRIPS agreement must be implemented fairly

BOX 5.7

Making the global intellectual property rights regime globally relevant

Genetic resources, traditional knowledge and expressions of folklore have all gained new scientific, economic and commercial value for developing countries. But the impact of intellectual property rights on the conservation, use and benefit sharing of these resources has been controversial.

A regime for global intellectual property rights is not fair if it is global in enforcement but not in the tools it provides. Intellectual property law—patents, copyright, trade marks, industrial design, geographic indications—arose from the needs of inventors in the industrial revolution. But the keepers of genetic resources, traditional knowledge and folklore have different customs, institutions, needs and ways of working that are not yet adequately reflected in this framework.

In response, in 1998 the World Intellectual Property Organization (WIPO) launched an initiative to make intellectual property rights more relevant. Efforts include sponsoring workshops for indigenous people and others on protecting traditional knowledge, providing information on how traditional knowledge can become part of the searchable prior art (to reduce the chances

of patents being granted for "inventions" already well-known in traditional communities), publishing information on customary laws and regimes, and recording experiences of indigenous people using intellectual property rights to protect their traditional knowledge.

In 2000 WIPO's member states established an Intergovernmental Committee on Intellectual Property and Genetic Resources, Traditional Knowledge and Folklore. By establishing this body, member states signalled that the time has come for intergovernmental discussions of these issues. Central to the committee's work will be better understanding and managing the relationships between intellectual property and the conservation, use and sharing of benefits from genetic resources, traditional knowledge and folklore. The goal will be to develop internationally accepted intellectual property standards for regulating access to and sharing the benefits of genetic resources and for protecting traditional knowledge and expressions of folklore. The challenge is ensuring that the international intellectual property system becomes relevant to and adequate for all communities.

Source: WIPO 2001b; Wendland 2001.

EASING ACCESS TO HIV/AIDS DRUGS THROUGH FAIR IMPLEMENTATION OF TRIPS

Worldwide, 36 million people are living with HIV/AIDS. Some 70% of them are in Sub-Saharan Africa—one in seven adult Kenyans, one in five South Africans, one in four Zimbabweans and one in three Batswana. This epidemic has been likened to the 14th-century plague that swept through Europe—except this time, lifesaving treatment exists. Since 1996 a three-drug combination of antiretrovirals has dramatically cut AIDS deaths in industrial countries.

These lifesaving drugs are produced under patent by a handful of US and European pharmaceutical companies. Prior to the Uruguay Round of the General Agreement on Tariffs and Trade (GATT) negotiations, during which the agreement on Trade-Related Aspects of Intellectual Property Rights (TRIPS) was adopted, 50 countries did not provide patent protection for pharmaceutical products, enabling them to produce or import low-cost generic versions of patented drugs. Such patenting was introduced in France only in 1960, Germany in 1968, Japan in 1976 and Italy, Sweden and Switzerland in 1978. Yet the TRIPS agreement requires 20-year product patents from all World Trade Organization members.

At the same time, the agreement allows countries to include in national legislation safeguards against patent monopolies that might harm extraordinary cases of public interest. The agreement does not prevent countries from importing brand name drugs that are sold more cheaply in other countries—known as parallel imports. And in some cases it allows countries to use patents without the permission of the patent holder, in return for a reasonable royalty on sales—known as compulsory licensing. The question is whether these provisions can become practice when they are most needed.

Providing access to drugs is just one part of tackling AIDS—but it is an important part. It can significantly increase the quality and length of life of people already infected as well as aid prevention by encouraging others to get tested and reducing mother-to-child transmission of the virus. In addition, such drugs can provide a much-needed motive to improve health care distribution systems in developing countries. Yet in December 2000 antiretrovirals were priced globally at $10,000–12,000 a patient a year, far from affordable for governments in countries where most affected people live. At that price in 1999 it would have cost Kenya at least twice its national income, Zambia more than three times, to provide treatment (see table). As a result just 0.1% of the 25 million people with HIV/AIDS in Sub-Saharan Africa have access to these lifesaving drugs.

Two connected responses to this urgent situation are being pursued: tiered pricing of brand name drugs and the production of generic drugs.

Several initiatives are under way to create tiered pricing for brand name drugs. The Accelerating Access initiative was launched in May 2000 by the Joint UN Programme on HIV/AIDS and five major pharmaceutical companies: Boehringer Ingelheim, Bristol-Myers Squibb, F. Hoffman-La Roche, GlaxoSmithKline and Merck. Price cuts have been negotiated by company and by country, and by April 2001 Cameroon, Côte d'Ivoire, Mali, Rwanda, Senegal and Uganda had negotiated prices believed to be $1,000–2,000 a person a year. But this process has not lived up to expectations: slow negotiations run counter to the urgency of the AIDS crisis and, with terms of agreements kept secret, some critics suspect that price cuts are conditional on introducing even tighter intellectual property legislation. They have called for deeper, across-the-board, publicly announced price cuts. Merck, Abbott Laboratories, Bristol-Myers Squibb and GlaxoSmithKline took steps in that direction in March 2001—the promising start of what urgently needs to become a general trend.

At the same time, generic versions of antiretrovirals are being produced far below global prices by manufacturers in Brazil, Cuba, India and Thailand. In February 2001 the Indian company Cipla offered three-drug combination therapy at $600 a person a

The affordability gap of treating AIDS in 1999

	Switzerland	Kenya	Uganda	Zambia
Population	7 million	30 million	23 million	10 million
People with HIV	17,000	2,100,000	820,000	870,000
Cost of treating all infected people with antiretroviral drugs at global market prices, about $12,000 a person a year ($)	204 million	25 billion	10 billion	10 billion
Cost of treatment as % of GDP	0.08	238	154	336
Public health care spending as % of GDP, 1998	7.6	2.4	1.9	3.6
Total health care spending as % of GDP, 1998	10.4	7.8	6.0	7.0

Source: UN 2001c; Hirschel 2000; World Bank 2001h; UNAIDS 2000b.

year to governments and $350 to Médecins Sans Frontières and other non-governmental organizations; many believe that with time and competition, generic drug prices will fall to $200–250. The price breakthrough made possible by generics has dramatically opened up treatment possibilities in developing countries, as shown by Brazil's pioneering policy. In 1993 Brazil began producing generic antiretrovirals and has distributed them for free, saving lives and money. Since 1996 deaths have fallen by half; in 1997–99 the government saved $422 million in hospitalization costs and a further $50 million in reduced costs of treating opportunistic diseases.

These two responses are connected: industry prices have often fallen in response to actual or potential competition from generic producers. But though this creates competition, it also creates controversy. From Thailand to Brazil to South Africa, companies producing brand name pharmaceuticals have opposed developing countries' strategies to combat HIV/AIDS by producing or importing low-cost generic drugs—yet these companies have been slow in creating global access to their drugs. Three arguments are put forward for such opposition: fears of re-imports, the scope of the TRIPS agreement and incentives for research and development.

Fears of re-imports
Pharmaceutical companies fear that both cut-price brand name drugs and generic drugs could be re-imported into their primary markets, undercutting their major sales base. Even if cheaper drugs do not leak into the home market, information about the dramatically lower prices abroad will, potentially leading domestic consumers to demand the same. These fears demand policies to tackle them. Educating consumers and purchasing agencies on the reasons for different prices in the developing world could build understanding and acceptance of the tiered system. Export controls in developing countries and demand forecasting by suppliers could stop re-export markets from emerging. And renaming and repacking cut-price drugs in different shapes and colours could make their origins more transparent.

Scope of the TRIPS agreement
Some patent holders claim that generic AIDS drugs violate their rights under the TRIPS agreement. But in some circumstances, such as for national emergencies, public non-commercial use and antitrust measures, the agreement allows governments to issue compulsory licenses to domestic or overseas producers of generic drugs. First introduced in British intellectual property legislation in 1883, compulsory licensing has been part of the law and practice of many industrial countries for more than a century—including Australia, Canada, Germany, Ireland, Italy, New Zealand, the United Kingdom and the United States.

Until joining the North American Free Trade Area (NAFTA) in 1992, Canada routinely issued compulsory licenses for pharmaceuticals, paying a 4% royalty rate on the net sales price. Between 1969 and 1992 such licenses were granted in 613 cases for importing or manufacturing generic medicines. In 1991–92 alone this practice saved Canadian consumers an estimated $171 million in drug costs. Since the adoption of the TRIPS agreement, compulsory licenses have been used in Canada, Japan, the United Kingdom and the United States for products such as pharmaceuticals, computers, tow trucks, software and biotechnology—particularly as antitrust measures to prevent reduced competition and higher prices. In the United States compulsory licensing has been used as a remedy in more than 100 antitrust case settlements, including cases involving antibiotics, synthetic steroids and several basic biotechnology patents.

In contrast, not one compulsory license has been issued south of the equator. Why? Pressure from Europe and the United States makes many developing countries fear that they will lose foreign direct investment if they legislate for or use compulsory licenses. In addition, attempts to use such licenses could result in long, expensive litigation against the pharmaceutical industry. But alternative legislative models can be used to avoid the emphasis on litigation and to create provisions suited to the needs of developing countries.

Turning compulsory license provisions into feasible policy options means creating a legal structure suited to developing countries. Five recommended features:
• *Administrative approach.* Any system that is overly legalistic, expensive to administer or easily manipulated is of little use; the best option is an administrative approach that can be streamlined and procedural.
• *Strong government use provisions.* The TRIPS agreement gives governments broad powers to au-

EASING ACCESS TO HIV/AIDS DRUGS THROUGH FAIR IMPLEMENTATION OF TRIPS (continued)

Pharmaceutical sales in the global market, 2002

Percentage of forecast revenues

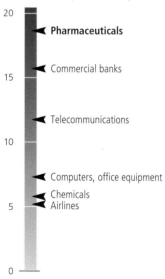

North America 41.8

Europe 24.8

Japan 11.3

Latin America & Caribbean 7.5

South-East Asia/China 5.0

} Middle East 2.6
Eastern Europe 1.8
Indian subcontinent 1.8
Australasia 1.3
Africa 1.3
CIS 0.8

Source: IMS HEALTH 2000.

Profitable industry— pharmaceuticals top the list

Median return on revenue for Fortune 500 companies, 1999 (percent)

20 —

◄ **Pharmaceuticals**

◄ Commercial banks

15 —

◄ Telecommunications

10 —

◄ Computers, office equipment

◄ Chemicals
◄ Airlines

5 —

0 —

Source: Fortune 2000.

thorize the use of patents for public non-commercial use, and this authorization can be fast-tracked, without the usual negotiations. No developing country should have public use provisions weaker than German, Irish, UK or US law on such practice.

• *Allow production for export.* Legislation should permit production for export when the lack of competition in a class of drugs has given the producer global market power that impedes access for alternative drugs, or when the legitimate interests of the patent owner are protected in the export market—as when that market provides reasonable compensation.

• *Reliable rules on compensation.* Compensation needs to be predictable and easy to administer; royalty guidelines reduce uncertainty and speed decisions. Germany has used rates from 2–10%, while in Canada the government used to pay royalties of 4%. Developing countries could award an extra 1–2% for products of particular therapeutic value and 1–2% less when research and development has been partly covered by public funds.

• *Dispute demands disclosure.* The onus should fall on the patent holder to back up claims that the royalty rate is inadequate. This will help promote transparency and discourage intimidating but unjustified claims.

Incentives for research and development

Companies producing brand name pharmaceuticals claim that generic competition will erode their incentives to invest in long, costly research and development, which can take 12–15 years and cost $230–500 million for each drug. But the threats of generic competition are disputed. Africa is expected to account for just 1.3% of pharmaceutical sales in 2002—hardly a market share likely to influence global investment decisions (see figure on top left).

Furthermore, the high profitability of the pharmaceutical industry has prompted deeper exploration of the costs incurred (see figure on bottom left). Many AIDS drugs were publicly funded through basic and applied research and even through clinical trials. But once transferred under exclusive license

to pharmaceutical companies for development, they have been patented and marketed at monopoly prices. Understanding the true costs of research and development to the pharmaceutical industry is crucial to assessing the impact of generic drugs on incentives to invest. Value chain analysis can be used to break down the costs of each stage, but the lack of transparent industry data creates conflicting assessments. An alternative to debating over data is creating a public or non-profit drug development entity to carry public research through the final stage and place the resulting drugs in the public domain, to be produced competitively and sold close to marginal cost.

Between December 2000 and April 2001 the possibility of treatment was transformed for people with AIDS in the developing world. The price of treatment fell from at least $10,000 to less than $600 a person a year. This opportunity must be translated into action. In March 2001 the government of Botswana seized this opportunity, announcing that it would provide free national access to antiretrovirals. Globally, resources need to be mobilized to create an HIV/AIDS prevention and treatment trust fund, which could be administered by the United Nations, drawing on drug supplies—including generics—offered at the best world price. In April 2001 UN Secretary-General Kofi Annan called for a major campaign to raise $7–10 billion a year as a global fund dedicated to battle HIV/AIDS and other infectious diseases.

A longer-term solution involves building the pharmaceutical manufacturing capacity of developing countries. In March 2001 the European Parliament supported the use of compulsory licensing and called for technology cooperation to strengthen production capacity in developing countries. Wider support for these measures, followed up with action, will be essential to ensure that such a crisis of access does not occur again for HIV/AIDS or future health epidemics.

Source: Correa 2001 and 2000; Harvard University 2001; Médecins Sans Frontières 2001a; Love 2001; Oxfam International 2001; Weissman 2001.

technology transfer to the least developed countries, yet that provision has scarcely been translated into action (box 5.8). From the UN Framework Convention on Climate Change to the Convention to Combat Desertification, commitments to technology transfer have been given short shrift.

The heart of the problem is that although technology may be a tool for development, it is also a means of competitive advantage in the global economy. Access to patented environmental technologies and pharmaceuticals, for example, may be essential for protecting the ozone layer and saving lives worldwide. But for countries that own and sell them, they are a market opportunity. Only when the two interests are reconciled—through, say, adequate public financing—will fair implementation of the TRIPS agreement become a real possibility.

EXPANDING INVESTMENT IN TECHNOLOGIES FOR DEVELOPMENT

Missing technologies are not just a matter of imperfect intellectual property rights protection in developing countries. Some markets are too economically or ecologically small to motivate private research—local or international—even when intellectual property is protected. Who would invest in lengthy research for a vaccine to be sold to governments of countries where public health spending is as low as $10 a person a year? Who would undertake costly biotechnological research for a variety of cassava to be sold to subsistence farmers on marginal land in a handful of African countries? Where markets are too small to motivate private research, public funding is essential—and policy-makers must take the lead, working closely with industry.

Research on and development of technologies for poor people's needs have long been underfunded. Despite the possibilities of technological transformations, this continues to be the case. Without a mechanism for global transfers, there is no dedicated source of funding. And voluntary public funding, national and international, has long been inadequate.

In 1998 the 29 OECD countries spent $520 billion on research and development[9]—more than the combined economic output of the world's 30 poorest countries.[10] Over the past 10 years a growing portion of that research has been funded by the private sector (figure 5.2). Yet despite such high investment, research remains woefully inadequate for the technologies most needed for development. Limited data are available on exactly how much is spent on development needs—a sign of the lack of attention paid to this problem.

In 1992 less than 10% of global spending on health research addressed 90% of the global disease burden. Just 0.2%, for example, was dedicated to research on pneumonia and diarrhoea—11% of the global disease burden.[11] This funding gap creates research and medicine gaps. In 1995 more than 95,000 therapy-relevant scientific articles were published but only 182—0.2% of the total—addressed tropical diseases. And of 1,223 new drugs marketed worldwide between 1975 and 1996, only 13 were developed to treat tropical diseases—and

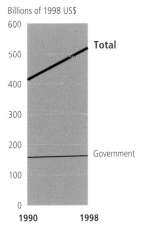

FIGURE 5.2
Research and development spending in OECD countries

Billions of 1998 US$

Source: Bonn International Center for Conversion 2000.

BOX 5.8
Paper promises, inadequate implementation

Commitments to technology transfer are central to many international agreements. But once the negotiations are over, many of these provisions are ignored or implemented only superficially.

The World Trade Organization's TRIPS agreement calls for developed country members to "provide incentives to enterprises and institutions in their territories for the purpose of promoting and encouraging technology transfer to least-developed country members in order to enable them to create a sound and viable technological base". Yet the obligations that this entails have received inadequate attention and action.

The Montreal Protocol on Substances that Deplete the Ozone Layer commits industrial countries to take every practical step to ensure that the best available environmentally safe substitutes and related technologies are quickly transferred to the protocol's signatories, and that the transfers occur under fair, favourable conditions. Yet DuPont, holder of the patents on CFC sub-

stitutes, refused to license production of those substitutes to manufacturers in developing countries such as India and the Republic of Korea, where the high cost of importing these chemicals limited the widespread diffusion of an environmentally sound technology.

The Convention on Biological Diversity seeks to conserve biodiversity, sustainably use its components and promote the fair sharing of the benefits arising from the use of genetic resources—including through appropriate funding and the appropriate transfer of relevant technologies. The convention established a subsidiary body to identify innovative, efficient, state-of-the-art technologies and know-how relating to the conservation and sustainable use of biodiversity and advise on ways of promoting the development and transfer of such technologies. But most of the focus has been on biosafety—important, but just one of many functions needed to make technology support the preservation of biodiversity.

Source: WTO 1994; UNEP 1992a and 1998; Juma and Watal 2001; Mytelka 2000.

FIGURE 5.3
Public investment in agricultural research

Percentage of agricultural GDP

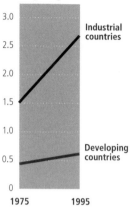

Source: Pardey and Beintema 2001.

FIGURE 5.4
Priorities for energy research and development in major industrial countries

Shares of public spending on energy R&D, 1985–99 (percent)

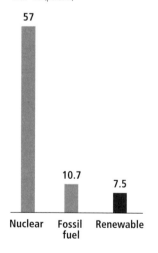

Note: Refers to 23 major industrial countries.
Source: IEA 2000.

only 4 were the direct result of pharmaceutical industry research.[12] Reallocating just 1% of global spending on health research would provide an additional $700 million for priority research on poor people's maladies.[13]

Though agricultural research offers tremendous potential for productivity improvements, in developing countries it is lagging behind. For every $100 of agricultural GDP in 1995, industrial countries reinvested $2.68 in public agricultural research and development; developing countries, just $0.62 (figure 5.3).[14] Agricultural research is neglected by both national governments and the international community. Why?

First, because of the perception that the world's food surplus means research on productivity is no longer needed. But that surplus is not in the hands of the people who need it: productivity increases for low-income farmers are still essential for increasing food security and eradicating poverty. Second, with declining global food prices, protectionist agricultural policies—particularly in the European Union—are resulting in food dumping in developing countries, so local markets are being undermined. Third, increases in private agricultural research in industrial countries have obscured the need to maintain public investment for the crops and needs of developing countries.

International public agricultural research is also in trouble, despite clear evidence of its high returns. Funding for the Consultative Group for International Agricultural Research has stagnated: it rose from less than $300 million a year in the 1970s to a peak of $378 million in 1992 but by 2000 had fallen to $336 million.[15] At the same time, the number of research centres in the network has grown and its mandate broadened. The effect? Resources for research to raise crop productivity fell from 74% of the total in 1972–76 to 39% in 1997–98.[16]

New energy technologies are also underfunded. Research and development spending is low relative to both the direct value of energy spending and the negative environmental impacts of conventional energy sources. Since funding jumped in the wake of the 1979 energy crisis, energy research and development has been falling: for 23 of the main industrial countries, public spending fell from $12.5 billion in 1985 to $7.5 billion in 1999 (in 1999 prices).[17] Just nine OECD countries account for more than 95% of the world's publicly supported energy research and development,[18] and the focus is not on technologies compatible with the resource endowments, needs and capabilities of developing countries. Renewable energy, a potential boon for developing countries, receives little attention. Although its share in energy research and development in the major industrial countries doubled after 1975, it was on average just 7.5% of the total between 1985 and 1999 (figure 5.4).

The result: a glaring contrast between the world's research agenda and the world's research needs.

• In 1998 global spending on health research was $70 billion; just $300 million was dedicated to vaccines for HIV/AIDS and about $100 million to malaria research.[19]

• Private agricultural research exceeded $10 billion in 1995; the Consultative Group for International Agricultural Research estimates it will need just $400 million annually to fulfil its research agenda in the coming years, but has not yet been able to raise it.[20]

• In 1998 OECD countries invested $51 billion in defence research—a stark comparison of priorities.[21]

Why is public funding of research for human development needs so low? Partly because investment in technology has rarely been seen as a central tool for development. Among bilateral and multilateral agencies there has long been a lack of institutional commitment to research programmes:

• *National rather than global focus.* The notion of global programming is still unfamiliar in many agencies, and country interventions do not focus on such global public goods as a tuberculosis vaccine or basic germ plasm research.

• *No clear accounting for such resource use.* The Development Assistance Committee's reporting system for donor assistance does not include a budget line for resources committed to research and development. Such a line is needed to provide information on such efforts and to encourage greater attention to them.

- *Too many small initiatives.* Small initiatives can be experimental and innovative, but too many fragmented efforts—rather than strategically coordinated investments—neglect bigger investment needs.

- *Short-term demand for results.* Successful technology-based development programmes require long experiments. But the politics and short-term planning horizons of much bilateral and multilateral assistance have limited investments that take 15-20 years to show results.

Private foundations, mostly in the United States, have been taking up some of the slack, from the Rockefeller and Ford foundations funding the green revolution in the 1960s and 1970s to the Gates Foundation with its tremendous boost to public health research today. But the amounts they provide are still small. Traditional sources of finance need to be renewed and new sources secured.

- *Bilateral donors.* If donor governments increased official development assistance by 10% and dedicated that to technology research, development and diffusion, there would be $5.5 billion on the table (based on 1999 assistance). They could go further and take seriously the agreed standard for official development assistance of 0.7% of GNP. Doing so in 1999 would have increased official development assistance from $56 billion to $164 billion[22]—and dedicating 10% of that to technology would have generated more than $16 billion.

- *Developing country governments.* Some developing countries are funding sophisticated research projects, an essential input into making global efforts locally relevant. Even for governments with limited budgets, investment in local adaptation of research is essential and can have high returns. But sometimes the problem is not a lack of funds. In 1999 the governments of Sub-Saharan Africa dedicated $7 billion to military spending.[23] Was that the right choice of priorities for a continent with such urgent technology needs in other areas? Diverting just 10% would have raised $700 million, more than double current spending on HIV/AIDS vaccine research.

- *International organizations.* Member governments of international organizations have not matched the rhetoric of concern about global

problems with serious commitment. Many of these problems—the spread of disease, environmental risks—are caused by or can be addressed by technological applications. UN agencies such as the World Health Organization and Food and Agriculture Organization have a mandate to help developing countries exploit the benefits and manage the risks of technology. But to do so, they need inspired leadership and adequate funding from their members. Donor government members of the World Bank and regional development banks have established trust funds for agricultural research and environmental programmes. The same approach could be used to raise funds that the banks could deploy (including to private groups) to ensure that developing countries benefit from new technological possibilities. Shareholders could also agree to use some of the banks' income for these global initiatives—though that would require broad consensus among borrowers and non-borrowers. In 2000 about $350 million of the World Bank's income was transferred to its interest-free arm for lending to the poorest countries.[24] A much smaller amount dedicated to technology development for low-income countries would go a long way.

- *Debt-for-technology swaps.* In 2000 official debt service payments by developing countries amounted to $78 billion.[25] A swap of just 1.3% of this debt service for technology research and development would have raised over $1 billion.

- *Private foundations.* A handful of foundations have made exemplary commitments to investing in long-term research; many others could follow that lead. And developing countries could introduce tax incentives to encourage their own billionaires to set up foundations with a regional focus. In 2000 Brazil had 9 billionaires with a collective worth of $20 billion, India 9 worth $23 billion, Malaysia 5 worth $12 billion, Mexico 13 worth $25 billion, Saudi Arabia 5 worth $41 billion.[26] Such foundations could make important contributions to regionally relevant research agendas.

- *Industry.* With its financial, intellectual and research resources, industry could make an invaluable contribution by committing a portion of profits to research on non-commercial products—a suggestion made by the head of re-

There is a glaring contrast between the world's research agenda and the world's research needs

search of Novartis, a major Swiss pharmaceuticals company. In the pharmaceutical industry alone, if the top nine Fortune 500 companies had dedicated just 1% of their profits to such research in 1999, they would have raised $275 million.[27]

Funds raised from these diverse sources could be distributed in a variety of ways to take advantage of new partnerships and institutional structures. Regional groups such as the revived East Africa Community could pool national funds to create regional science foundations—modelled on the US National Science Foundation—to focus on regional needs and channel grants to the regional and global institutions best equipped to work in the new research environment. Donor funds could add to these to build up strong regional centres that set their own research priorities and agendas.

PROVIDING REGIONAL AND GLOBAL INSTITUTIONAL SUPPORT

Without international cooperation, many public goods will be undersupplied in national markets or missed altogether. Both regional and global initiatives are needed.

REGIONAL COOPERATION: FORMING ALLIANCES

Large, consistent, accessible markets better stimulate technology investment by making it easier to cover the costs of research and infrastructure. Small countries can overcome the barriers of size by building regional alliances to undertake research, make joint purchases and build infrastructure.

Alliances in researching and diffusing technologies can be effective if they address a common regional concern and pool expertise and resources. In agricultural research, for example, local adaptation of international research is always needed. But for small countries in ecologically similar regions, autonomous agricultural research systems—each researching a range of crops and problems—may not make sense because of overlapping overhead costs and duplicated research. The Internet makes collaborative networks easier than ever. Initia-

tives in East and Central Africa and in Latin America show the potential for such collaboration (box 5.9).

Likewise, alliances to lower the costs of technology-rich products can reap tremendous savings. After personnel costs, pharmaceuticals are usually the largest item in public health budgets. So, in 1986 the nine governments of the Organisation of Eastern Caribbean States pooled their procurement of pharmaceuticals. Buying in bulk made for far lower prices: by 1998 regionally contracted prices were 38% lower than individual country prices.[28]

Regional alliances are also being used to build infrastructure to bridge the digital divide. The Association of South-East Asian Nations (ASEAN) launched the e-ASEAN Task Force in 1999. As ASEAN's first public-private advisory body, the task force is developing a comprehensive regional action plan for competing in the global information economy, with private investment focused on creating infrastructure and public policy focused on creating the best legal and regulatory environment. A landmark agreement on regional policies has since received the commitment of member governments, on issues ranging from extending connectivity and building content to creating a seamless regulatory environment and a common e-marketplace.

GLOBAL INITIATIVES: PROVIDING SUPPORT

Formal and informal mechanisms of governance can help to fill missing markets, protect common resources, promote common standards and provide information. Some examples follow.

Filling missing markets. Weak financial institutions in developing countries can block the diffusion of highly effective technologies. There is enormous potential demand for electricity in off-grid markets, especially in rural areas, and photovoltaic solar home systems offer a reliable, cost-effective, environmentally clean way to meet that need. Yet they have reached far less than 1% of the potential market. Three reasons are financial: a lack of medium-term funding that would allow households to repay the $500–1,000 cost of installation over time,[29] a lack of understanding of photovoltaic markets by conven-

Regional groups could pool national funds to create regional science foundations to focus on regional needs

tional financial intermediaries and weak capitalization of many photovoltaic companies. To fill this gap on a global scale, the World Bank, the International Finance Corporation and several non-profits have established the Solar Development Corporation. By providing financing, working capital and business advice to photovoltaic dealers in developing countries, the initiative will help the market take off.

Protecting common resources. Biodiversity provides farmers and scientists with the raw materials—plant genetic resources—to make more robust, nutritious, productive crops. Protecting and preserving traditional crop varieties makes an essential contribution to agricultural development, yet many such crops have been replaced by new varieties and can no longer be found in farmers' fields. Today more than 6 million samples of plant genetic resources are held in nearly 1,300 national, regional, international and private collections. But as a result of the extensive duplication between collections, 11 Future Harvest Centres collectively maintain as much as 60% of the world's unique samples in their gene banks.[30] In 1996, 150 countries agreed on a Global Plan of Action for Plant Genetic Resources, pledging to develop a rational global gene bank system to eliminate unnecessary duplication and better coordinate the world's collections. To implement this plan will cost an estimated $1 billion—equivalent to just 3% of annual spending on global agricultural research in 1993–95.[31]

There are also common resources to protect and add to in computing. Open source software is the outcome of myriad voluntary contributions from around the world. The details of how the software works cannot be hidden, as with proprietary software, but must be kept open for all to see—making it ideal for learning software development and well suited to local adaptation, a benefit in developing countries. It is low-cost, often free, enabling governments to make their information and communications technology budgets go much further.

Open source software could speed the information and communications technology revolution if its use takes off on a sufficiently wide scale. What global initiatives could help? For a start, the UN's Information and Communica-

tions Technology Task Force could advertise its benefits in stimulating local research and development in poor countries. Initiatives could fund research into applications for developing countries, raise awareness of open source software among policy-makers and champion its use in the public sector—an option already taken up in countries such as Brazil, China and Mexico.

Promoting common standards. Common standards are essential to globally diffused innovation and production of technologies. Without them, uncertainty and unreliability fragment the market and cut into demand. Until recently the cells, converters and batteries that make

---

BOX 5.9

ASARECA and FONTAGRO— promoting regional collaboration in public agricultural research

Each of the 10 countries of East and Central Africa has a small system for national agricultural research. In 1998 these systems employed the equivalent of 2,300 full-time scientists—compared with 2,000 in Indonesia and 40,000 each in China and India. Given the region's size and ecological diversity, no country alone could address all its research needs. Hence in 1994 the Association for Strengthening Agricultural Research in Eastern and Central Africa (ASARECA) was founded to improve the management of national agricultural research systems, increase efficient use of scarce resources, reap economies of scale and make research more accountable to farmer needs and market demands. ASARECA also provides a way of channelling support from international agricultural research centres, advanced research institutes, the private sector and donors.

The association coordinates 18 networks, programmes and projects, focused on commodities like maize, wheat, root crops and bananas, as well as cross-cutting issues like information and communications, post-harvest processing and plant genetic resources. The results have been impressive. The potato network, for example, was established in 1994 because each country had only one or two scientists focused on potatoes and sweet potatoes. Pooling expertise created a critical mass of expertise: a network equivalent to 22 scientists working full time on potatoes and 15 on sweet potatoes. Since 1998 this network has released 14 new varieties of potatoes and

16 of sweet potatoes throughout the region. The new varieties are disease resistant, tolerant of acidic and marginal soils and have better post-harvest qualities. Moreover, the yields of these improved varieties are at least three times those of local varieties. Funded 30% by the US Agency for International Development and 70% by the national research systems, the potato network is providing good results for research money.

In Latin America and the Caribbean the Regional Fund for Agricultural Technology (FONTAGRO) was established in 1998 to promote agricultural research of cross-country interest in the region and throughout the Americas. A target fund of $200 million is being raised from member countries. FONTAGRO disburses grants to public research institutes and companies, universities and non-governmental organizations working with regional and international research organizations. Research projects, selected competitively and transparently, focus on priority issues identified across the region's agroecosystems. Twenty diverse projects are currently being funded, ranging from potatoes, papaya and Andean fruit trees to coffee, bananas and rice. By supporting research of relevance throughout the region, FONTAGRO is promoting applied and strategic research in national research centres. And by networking researchers, it is helping transfer and build technical capacity of most relevance to the region.

Source: Mrema 2001; Moscardi 2000; FONTAGRO 2001.

---

up photovoltaic energy systems followed no global product or system standards—causing quality problems and consumer frustration and jeopardizing the reputation of the entire technology. In response, in 1997 industry, financial institutions and government agencies formed the Global Approval Program for Photovoltaics. This non-profit organization promotes international standards, quality management processes and organizational training in the design, manufacture, sale, installation and service of photovoltaic systems.

Similarly, common standards are essential to the unity and spread of the Internet. Protocols such as the Transmission Control Protocol/Internet Protocol (TCP/IP)—designed to maximize connectivity between computer systems—are shaped and refined by the Internet Engineering Task Force, the main global forum for software developers, operators and vendors. As Internet standards evolve, dominant industry players will push for their proprietary standards to be used, providing them with market advantage but threatening to hamper competitive innovation. The task force will have to withstand that pressure and ensure that the building blocks of the Internet are openly negotiated and available to developers worldwide.

Providing information. Accurate and timely information on global market opportunities is crucial for giving policy-makers in developing countries choices in acquiring, adapting and using technologies. The Internet provides the ideal vehicle for ensuring that such information is available to policy-makers everywhere. What kind of information is needed?

• *Medical supplies.* Data on suppliers, prices and patent status of quality-approved medicines, both generic and brand name, are essential to enable policy-makers to make the most of their overstretched health budgets. This function has been mandated by the World Health Assembly because of its importance in empowering governments in their purchase negotiations.

• *An intellectual property clearinghouse.* Identifying and accessing individual patent claims for research in agricultural biotechnology is complex. A fairer and more efficient global trade in patented genetic materials, germ

plasm and applied technologies would be made possible through a clearinghouse. By identifying all relevant intellectual property for a given technology, indicating what is available for use and how, establishing a pricing scheme and monitoring and enforcing contracts, the clearinghouse could be an important step towards solving the collective problem of agricultural research.

• *Internet connection costs.* Worldwide, people pay very different prices to access the Internet, often because of discriminatory tariffs charged by the US backbone or because of high costs for domestic phone calls. One valuable service would be to provide data online for every country showing the comparative costs of international tariffs, Internet service providers and local phone calls. Greater knowledge of the unjustified discrepancies would empower policy-makers and consumer groups to demand flat monthly tariffs from Internet service providers, transparent and non-discriminatory international phone tariffs and flat-rate, cheap local phone calls.

REORIENTING INTERNATIONAL INSTITUTIONS AND INITIATIVES

International institutions are struggling to cope with the challenges of technology transformations. Because new challenges of infectious diseases, ecological degradation, electronic crimes, biosafety and biological weapons will continue to emerge, new attitudes and approaches are needed to create the institutional frameworks that can tackle them. As the meeting place for the world's governments, the United Nations has a role to play, but institutional innovations in governance are needed. What can be done?

Recognize that global technology governance starts at home. Global governance of technology is largely an expression of the collective will—often imbalanced—of governments and other actors to recognize the importance of science and technology in development. Global arrangements can only be as effective as governments are committed to making them. The first step is for countries to recognize that public health, food and nutrition, energy, communications and the environment are public policy

International institutions are struggling to cope with the challenges of technology transformations

issues deserving serious attention through technology policy. The recognition by the US State Department, for example, of HIV/AIDS as a national security issue helped raise the profile of global public health. Very few developing countries have followed suit, though ill health and hunger are the greatest threats to human security in many of them. Giving greater national priority to science and technology can bring new momentum to articulating those threats at the global level.

Launch fresh thinking on technology and development. Inadequate attention to the role of science and technology in human development is one of the main shortcomings of the global system governing technological change. Despite the widespread recognition that knowledge is central to development, traditional programming by the main development organizations has yet to take the new thinking on board. The United Nations could turn this around and become a forum for bringing together the world's leading science and technology institutions to identify new research areas that could bring science and technology to the core of development thinking.

Improve coordination in providing technology cooperation and assistance. When development assistance to build technology infrastructure and capacity comes from a variety of sources, it can be inefficient, creating duplication and incompatibility between technological systems. Better coordination among donors is essential to ensure that their assistance helps rather than hampers technological development.

The Group of Eight (G-8) countries are at the forefront of producing information and communications technology. At the Okinawa Summit in July 2000, the leaders of the G-8 created the Digital Opportunities Task Force, or DOT Force, to coordinate their diverse plans to bridge the global digital divide. The DOT Force includes members from the public, private and non-profit sectors in each G-8 country as well as government representatives from nine developing countries, including Brazil, China and India. The collaboration aims to ensure that assistance focuses on providing the most coherent information and communica-

tions technology infrastructure for developing countries by increasing coherence among diverse initiatives, promoting innovative forms of public-private partnership to address the issues and mobilizing additional official development assistance for this international effort.

Build capacity for policy analysis. Developing country policy-makers must be equipped to get the best technologies for their countries. But the issues are of unprecedented complexity. Bilateral and multilateral donors could support far more training for policy-makers to undertake technology policy analysis, launching a new professional cadre—much needed to clarify the role of science and technology in development. National science academies could identify training needs and encourage universities to develop appropriate curriculums.

The capacity is needed both domestically and internationally. It is widely accepted that local priorities should determine development assistance. But in practice that is often still the exception: many development strategies are still driven by donor interests, from the choice of how to tackle malaria to which crops should be researched. Greater national policy advocacy is central to reversing these roles.

Internationally, capacity is needed to undertake negotiations. Recent experience in negotiations on biosafety and on the TRIPS agreement shows that only a handful of developing countries have the resources to negotiate positions that reflect their people's interests. Increased understanding will help produce fairer agreements than those now causing such acrimonious debate. Given the likely impact of new rules on the prospects for technologies in developing countries, a more active role in global negotiations is crucial. The attention paid to these debates has increased over the past few years, but developing countries still have too few delegates relative to their populations. In negotiations on the future of plant genetic resources, for example, countries with low and medium human development are consistently underrepresented (figure 5.5). These and many other negotiations continue to be driven by a few industrial countries. Funding for developing country participation is not guaranteed, so delegates are often uncertain about participating

Inadequate attention to the role of science and technology in human development is one of the main shortcomings of the global system governing technological change

until the last minute, arrive underprepared and are stretched among too many meetings. The effects on the resulting rules of the game are inevitable.

Create fair rules of the game. The institutions governing technology issues tend to be founded and led by countries or groups already engaged. But these institutions can have a tremendous influence on the prospects for others of using the technology, potentially building bias against latecomers to the game. As in all areas of governance, transparency and balanced participation are needed. The system for allocating Internet domain names exemplifies the challenge of providing such balance—and is an unprecedented experiment in doing so (box 5.10).

International negotiations have often failed to produce fair rules of the game or fair implementation of those rules, creating great controversy about the interpretation of global agreements and the resolution of international disputes. Civil society groups offer an important countervailing pressure and sometimes take the lead in calling for change. Drawing global attention to an issue is the first step, as shown by the dramatic developments and shifts in positions on access to HIV/AIDS drugs. The spotlight has fallen on pharmaceutical companies, partly because they seem to be the only actors involved. But if their strategies fly in the face of the public interest, the rules of the game need to be changed—and that is a matter for public policy. Industry responds to regulations and incentives, which are shaped by governments. It seems simple, but there are several complications.

First, industry is important to national economic growth. In Britain, for example, the pharmaceuticals industry accounts for nearly one-quarter of research and development spending and 60,000 jobs. Governments fear that supporting policies counter to such industries' interests could drive them overseas.[32]

Second, industrial financing of politics holds great sway. Industrial contributions to US campaigns, for example, have doubled since 1991–92. In 1999–2000 the main industrial sectors gave $400 million in campaign contributions—including $130 million from the communications and electronics industry, $65 million from energy and natural resources, $58 million from agribusiness, $55 million from transportation and $26 million from pharmaceuticals (figure 5.6).

Third, governments gain leverage in the global economy on the coattails of their most powerful corporations, so they have a vested interest in their success. As a result industry has tremendous influence on the framing of regulations and incentives, with industrial representatives accompanying government delegates to negotiate agreements like TRIPS. Combined, these forces create a status quo in the way governments set the rules of business—a status quo that is hard to change even when the public knows something is wrong. Ultimately, the excessive influence of industry means that public policy has failed the public, both in national governments and in international institutions.

Of course, industry also responds to consumers, and democratic governments respond to voters. Consumers can use their market power and voters their political clout to push for pol-

FIGURE 5.5
Whose voices are heard in international negotiations?
Representation in negotiations, 1998

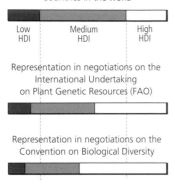

Countries in the world

| Low HDI | Medium HDI | High HDI |

Representation in negotiations on the International Undertaking on Plant Genetic Resources (FAO)

Representation in negotiations on the Convention on Biological Diversity

Source: Mooney 1999a; UNDP 2000d.

BOX 5.10

Who administers the Internet? ICANN!

Global Internet governance is in the making. The Internet Corporation for Assigned Names and Numbers (ICANN), a US-based private non-profit, has been entrusted with managing core Internet infrastructure resources. For data on the Internet to find its way from sender to receiver, a complex addressing system of names (domain names) and corresponding numbers (Internet protocol or IP numbers) is deployed. These names and numbers, known as the Domain Name System (DNS), make up the core of the Internet.

Internet governance used to be rooted in the US research community and administered rather informally. But the Internet's explosive growth, worldwide diffusion and intensified commercialization make informal governance inappropriate. Thus in 1998 the US government initiated a process for formalizing governance structures—giving birth to ICANN.

Assessments of ICANN vary. Its mandated self-organizing process has proven extraordinarily painstaking, leading to a complex system of advisory committees and supporting organizations. In a highly publicized exercise, in late 2000 ICANN chose some of its board members through global online elections; others were appointed under less transparent rules. Some observers emphasize the importance of ICANN as an unparalleled historical experiment in new forms of governance for a global multistakeholder phenomenon. Others voice concerns about potential capture by narrow interest groups.

To guarantee accountability in Internet governance and to accommodate latecomers from developing countries, an open debate needs to address:
• *Transparency*—open debate and information for all stakeholders.
• *Representation*—include governments, information technology developers, current and future Internet users and countries from all regions. Online ICANN elections are innovative but limited to those with Internet access, overlooking future users with different needs and interests.

Source: Zinnbauer 2001d.

icy changes. Civil society groups fighting for fairer outcomes play an important role in informing citizens and voters. In the absence of better public policy, such groups have stepped in, in a role made possible—and powerful—by globalization and information and communications technology. It is largely thanks to the committed work of non-governmental organizations (NGOs) worldwide that the crisis surrounding HIV/AIDS drugs has gained so much global attention, forcing corporations, governments and international agencies to rethink what is possible (see the special contribution from Médecins Sans Frontières).

NGOs can create change because they can raise awareness: they can create pressure with informal regulation in corporate codes of conduct, and they can use high-profile campaigns to highlight the activities of corporations. As long as public interest is focused on these issues, corporations have an incentive to change their policies to protect their bottom line from consumer backlash or the threat of more formal regulation.

But public interest has a habit of fading—be it in war, in famine or in health crises, let alone in the complexities of intellectual property legislation. When will access to HIV/AIDS drugs become yesterday's news—and what will happen to prices and patents then? The momentum created by civil society activism must be translated into structural policy change. Several key policy-makers have hinted at their support for this—the test is to see what change they will create. And structural policy change is needed beyond HIV/AIDS drugs. This crisis should be seen as an entry point into broader reflection on the rules of the game, not the exceptional case that gets special treatment.

• • •

The challenge is tremendous: to turn today's technological transformations to the goals of human development. The genius of what can be done through technology is astounding. But the collective failure to turn that genius to the technology needed for development is indefensible. As the potential of what can be done continues to unfold, will innovations in science and technology be matched by innovations in policy to turn global technological advance into a tool for development? This will be the ultimate test of public policy in the new technology era.

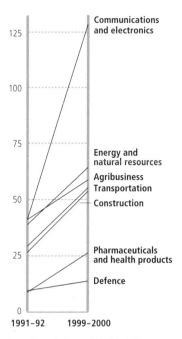

FIGURE 5.6

Industry's influence over public policy

Contributions to federal candidates and political parties in the United States (millions of 2000 US$)

Source: Centre for Responsive Politics 2001.

SPECIAL CONTRIBUTION

Insisting on responsibility: a campaign for access to medicines

Médecins Sans Frontières (MSF) is known by the world for its emergency action, whether in delivering medical supplies by mule into war-torn Afghanistan, or in treating malnourished children in southern Sudan. But in recent years, we have witnessed a different kind of disaster: our patients are dying not only from floods, hunger or land mines, but increasingly, because they cannot get the medicines they need.

One-third of the world's population does not have access to essential medicines; in the poorest parts of Africa and Asia, this figure rises to one-half. Too often in the countries where we work, we cannot treat our patients because the medicines are too expensive or they are no longer produced. Sometimes, the only drugs we have are highly toxic or ineffective, and nobody is looking for a better cure.

This is no coincidence. The growing power of commercial interests, the declining role of governments and a general retreat from responsibility have combined to create the current crisis.

MSF doctors refuse to accept this situation. In the name of personal medical ethics and the principles on which MSF was founded, we launched the Access to Essential Medicines Campaign to insist on change. MSF's role has always been to speak out about the injustices we witness in the lives of our patients. So we are demanding that international trade rules treat medicines as fundamentally different from other commodities; that international health organizations prioritize treatment alongside prevention; that pharmaceutical companies lower their prices to affordable levels; and that national governments fulfil their responsibilities to protect public health. In short, we are demanding a system in which public health is protected, rather than sacrificed to the laws of the market.

The response has been encouraging. The price of AIDS drugs has plummeted from 1999 levels. Abandoned drugs are coming back into production. Donors in wealthy countries are discussing funding new research and development. Activists in developing countries are demanding more from their governments. And finally—though too slowly—more drugs are reaching patients. But these are small, temporary successes in what remains an uphill battle. They cannot replace real political solutions. MSF remains committed to pushing for improved access to medicines, but also challenges governments, companies, international organizations and civil society to make it happen.

[signature]

Morten Rostrup, M.D., Ph.D.
President of the International Council Médecins Sans Frontières, recipient of the 1999 Nobel Peace Prize

Endnotes

Chapter 1

1. World Bank 2001f; UNESCO 2000b.
2. UNESCO 2000b.
3. WHO 1997.
4. World Bank 2001c.
5. World Bank 2001b.
6. Smeeding 2000b.
7. Cairncross and Jolly 2000.
8. Human Development Report Office calculations based on World Bank 2001g.
9. World Bank 2001c.
10. UNAIDS 2000a.
11. UN 2001d.
12. UNAIDS 2000b.
13. UNDCP 1997.
14. USAID 1999.
15. UNHCR 2000.
16. UNDP 2000f.
17. UNDP 2000c.
18. UNDP 1999e.
19. Human Development Report Office calculations based on US Census Bureau 1999.
20. Nepal South Asia Centre 1998.
21. UN and Islamic Republic of Iran, Plan and Budget Organization 1999.
22. UNDP 1999b.
23. UNDP with UN Country Team 1998.
24. Human Development Report Office calculations based on US Census Bureau 1999.
25. UNESCO 2000b.
26. UNDP 1998b.
27. UNIFEM 2000.
28. Comparing income inequalities between countries must be done cautiously. Surveys can differ according to whether they measure income or consumption, how and if publicly provided services—such as health care and education—are included, if taxes and transfers are included, and in terms of population coverage and adjustments for household sizes. Trend data can also be problematic, because collection methods can vary across periods even in the same survey. Furthermore, due to the cyclical nature of economies, trends are sensitive to beginning and end points.
29. Cornia 1999.
30. Hanmer, Healy and Naschold 2000.
31. Cornia 1999.
32. Indicator table 12.
33. Milanovic 1998.
34. Indicator table 12.
35. Milanovic forthcoming.
36. Castles and Milanovic 2001.
37. As with all empirical innovations, these results must be treated with caution. The chief concerns are the quality, comparability and timeliness of the country income surveys on which the study is based. Other issues also arise, such as the problem of normalizing the income and consumption data from different surveys, the non-inclusion of publicly financed health and education (for which data are not available) and discrepancies between household survey and GDP data. While Milanovic's (forthcoming) study is a breakthrough in measuring inequality among the world's people, these concerns point to further avenues for research and to the urgent need for more and better data on within-country income distribution and within-country inequality.
38. Graham 2001.
39. Birdsall, Behrman and Szekely 2000.
40. Graham 2001.
41. UNDP 2000a.
42. UNDP and HDN 2000.
43. UNDP and HDN 1997.
44. Government of Madhya Pradesh, India 1995.
45. Government of Madhya Pradesh, India 1998.
46. Grinspun 2001.
47. UNDP and Kuwait Ministry of Planning 1997.
48. UNDP 2000e.
49. UNDP 2000b.
50. UNDP, IAR, JPF and BBS 2000.
51. OECD, DAC 1996; IMF, OECD, UN and World Bank 2000.
52. UNAIDS 2000b.

Chapter 2

1. Chen 1983.
2. WHO 1998.
3. Wang and others 1999.
4. Hazell 2000.
5. Romer 1986, 1990; Lee 2001; Aghion and Howitt 1992.
6. Lee 2001.
7. Gilder 2000.
8. Gilder 2000.
9. Chandrasekhar 2001.
10. Human Development Report Office calculations based on UNDP, Country Offices 2001; UPS 2001; Andrews Worldwide Communications 2001.
11. National Nanotechnology Initiative 2001; Smalley 1995; Mooney 1999b.
12. Lall 2001.
13. NSF 2001.
14. James 2000.
15. Angus Reid 2000.
16. Jupiter Communications 2000a.
17. Chandrasekhar 2001.
18. International Data Corporation 2000.
19. School of Information Management and Systems, University of California at Berkeley 2001.
20. Reuters 2000.
21. US Internet Council and ITTA 2000.
22. US Internet Council and ITTA 2000.
23. Lall 2001.
24. Arlington 2000.
25. Kapur 2001.
26. Hillner 2000.
27. UNESCO 1999.
28. Throughout this chapter, OECD refers to high-income OECD countries.

29. Human Development Report Office calculations based on WIPO 2000 and World Bank 2001h.

30. Human Development Report Office calculations based on World Bank 2001h.

31. Human Development Report Office calculations based on Nua Publish 2001.

32. Nua Publish 2001; UNDP 1999a.

33. Lipton, Sinha and Blackman 2001; FAO 2000a.

34. UNICEF 2001e.

35. UNESCO 1999.

36. Bloom, River Path Associates and Fang 2001.

Chapter 3

1. Hazell 2000.

2. Global Network of Environment and Technology 1999.

3. Lipton, Sinha and Blackman 2001.

4. CNN 2000.

5. CNN 2001.

6. Haerlin and Parr 1999.

7. Quoted in Cohen 2001

8. Biotechnology Australia 2001.

9. Consumers Union 1999.

10. *New Scientist* 2001.

11. US Food and Drug Administration 2000b.

12. TIA 2001.

13. Royal Society of London, US National Academy of Sciences, Brazilian Academy of Sciences, Chinese Academy of Sciences, Indian National Science Academy, Mexican Academy of Sciences and Third World Academy of Sciences 2000, p. 20.

14. Royal Society of London, US National Academy of Sciences, Brazilian Academy of Sciences, Chinese Academy of Sciences, Indian National Science Academy, Mexican Academy of Sciences and Third World Academy of Sciences 2000, p. 17.

15. University of Sussex, Global Environmental Change Programme 1999.

Chapter 4

1. Nanthikesan 2001.

2. Human Development Report Office calculations based on ITU 2000 and World Bank 2001h.

3. Readiness for the Networked World 2001.

4. Readiness for the Networked World 2001.

5. Singh 2000.

6. Choi, Lee and Chung 2001, p.125.

7. Singh 2000.

8. Galal and Nauriyal 1995, cited in Wallsten 2000.

9. Jones-Evans 2000.

10. Yu 1999; Yingjian 2000.

11. Yu 1999.

12. Lall 2001.

13. Jones-Evans 2000.

14. Pfeil 2001.

15. UNESCO 1999.

16. Lall 2001.

17. Lall 2001.

18. CERI 2000.

19. Perraton and Creed 2000.

20. CDI 2001.

21. Enlaces 2001, cited in Perraton and Creed 2000.

22. SchoolNet Thailand Project 2001, cited in Perraton and Creed 2000.

23. SchoolNetSA 2001, cited in Perraton and Creed 2000.

24. Perraton and Creed 2000.

25. Kumar 1999, cited in UNESCO 2000a.

26. Chaudhary 1999, cited in UNESCO 2000a.

27. Agence Universitaire de la Francophonie 2001.

28. Tan and Batra 1995, cited in Lall 2001.

29. Lall 2001.

30. Lall 2001.

31. OECD 2000c.

32. UNESCO 1999.

33. UNESCO 2000b.

34. World Bank 2000b.

35. Kapur 2001; Saxenian 1999 and 2000.

36. Kapur 2001.

37. Kapur 2001.

Chapter 5

1. US Patent and Trademark Office 2000a.

2. NSF 2001.

3. Anderson, MacLean and Davies 1996.

4. US Food and Drug Administration 2000a.

5. Potrykus 2001.

6. Guilloux and Moon 2000.

7. US Patent and Trademark Office 2000b.

8. WIPO 2001a.

9. Bonn International Center for Conversion 2000.

10. Indicator table 1.

11. Global Forum for Health Research 2000.

12. Trouiller and Olliaro 1999.

13. de Francisco 2001.

14. Pardey and Beintema 2001.

15. CGIAR 2001.

16. Pardey and Beintema 2001.

17. IEA 2001.

18. McDade and Johansson 2001.

19. de Francisco 2001; *The Economist* 2001; Attaran 2001.

20. Pardey and Beintema 2001; CGIAR 2001.

21. Bonn International Center for Conversion 2000.

22. Indicator table 15.

23. SIPRI 2000.

24. World Bank 2000a.

25. World Bank forthcoming.

26. *Forbes* 2001.

27. *Public Citizen* 2000.

28. Burnett 1999.

29. SDC 1998.

30. FAO 1998.

31. Pardey and Beintema 2001.

32. McBride 2001.

Bibliographic note

Chapter 1 draws on the following: Atkinson and Brandolini 1999, Birdsall 2000 and forthcoming, Birdsall, Behrman and Szekely 2000, Bourguignon 2000, Cairncross and Jolly 2000, Canberra Group 2001, Castles and Milanovic 2001, Cornia 1999, Clymer and Pear 2001, FAO 2000b, First Nations and Inuit Regional Health Survey National Steering Committee 1999, Gardner and Halwell 2001, Government of Madhya Pradesh, India 1995 and 1998, Graham 2001, Grinspun 2001, Gwatkin and others 2000a and 2000b, Hanmer and Naschold 2000, Hamner, Healy and Naschold 2000, Hill, AbouZahr and Wardlaw 2001, IFAD 2001, IMF, OECD, UN and World Bank 2000, International IDEA 2000, ILO 1998 and 2001, Lee 2001, Malaysia Economic Planning Unit 1994, Matthews and Hammond 1997, Melchior, Telle and Henrik Wiig 2000, Milanovic 1998 and forthcoming, Nepal South Asia Centre 1998, OECD and Government of Canada Central Statistical Office 2000, OECD, DAC 1996, Pettinato 2001, Scholz, Cichon and Hagemejer 2000, Shiva Kumar 1997, Smeeding 2001a, 2001b and forthcoming, UN 1996, 2000a, 2000b and 2000d, UN and Islamic Republic of Iran, Plan and Budget Organization 1999, UNAIDS 1998, 2000a and 2000b, UNDCP 1997, UNDESA 2000b, UNDP 1998a, 1998b, 1998c, 1999a, 1999b, 1999c, 1999d, 2000a, 2000b, 2000c, 2000e and 2000f, UNDP, Regional Bureau for Europe and the CIS 1997, 1998 and 1999, UNDP and HDN 1997 and 2000, UNDP, IAR, JPF and BBS 2000, UNDP and Kuwait Ministry of Planning 1997, UNDP and UNAIDS 1997, UNDP with UN Country Team 1998, UNDP, UNDESA and World Energy Council 2000, UNESCO 1999, 2000b, 2001a and 2001b, UNFPA 2001, UNHCR 2000, UNICEF 2001a, 2001c, 2001d and 2001e, UNICEF, Innocenti Research Centre 1999 and 2000, UNIFEM 2000, UNOCHA 1999, USAID 1999, US Census Bureau 1999, van der Hoeven 2000, Vandermoortele 2000, Water Supply and Sanitation Collaborative Council 1999, WHO 1997 and 2000b, World Bank 2000c, 2000d, 2001a, 2001b, 2001c, 2001d, 2001e, 2001f, 2001g and 2001h, WRI 1994, Yaqub 2001 and Zhang 1997.

Chapter 2 draws on the following: AAAS 2001, Aghion and Howitt 1992, Analysys 2000, Andrews Worldwide Communications 2001, Angus Reid 2000, Archive Builders 2000, Arlington 2000, Barro and Lee 2000, Bassanini, Scarpetta and Visco 2000, BCC 2000, Bell Labs 2000, Bignerds 2001, Biopharma 2001, Bloom, River Path Associates and Fang 2001, Brown 2000, Brynjolfsson and Kahin 2000, Castells 1996 and 2000, Chandrasekhar 2001, Chen 1983, Cohen 2001, Cohen, DeLong and Zysman 1999, Cox and Alm 1999, David 1999, Desai, Fukuda-Parr, Johansson and Sagasti 2001, Doran 2001, The Economist 2000, El-Osta and Morehart 1999, Evenson and Gollin 2001, FAO 2000a, Fortier and Trang 2001, G-8 2000, Gilder 2000, Goldemberg 2001, Government of India, Department of Education

2001, Gu and Steinmueller 1996, Gutierrez and others 1996, Hazell 2000, Hijab 2001, Hillner 2000, ILO 2000 and 2001, Intel 2001, International Data Corporation 2000, ITDG 2000, ITU 2001a and 2001b, James 2000, Japan Ministry of Foreign Affairs 2000, A. Jolly 2000, R. Jolly 2001, Jorgenson and Stiroh 2000, Juma and Watal 2001, Jupiter Communications 2000a and 2000b, Kapur 2001, Lall 2000 and 2001, Landler 2001, Lee 2001, Lipton, Sinha and Blackman 2001, Mansell 1999, Matlon 2001, McDade and Johansson 2001, Mooney 1999b, Nanthisekan 2001, National Nanotechnology Initiative 2001, NCAER 1999, NCBI 2001, NSF 2001, Nua Publish 2001, OECD 2000a, 2000d, 2000f and 2000h, Pardey and Bientema 2001, PC World 2000, Pfeil 2001, PowderJect 2001, President of the United States 2001, Reuters 2000 and 2001, Romer 1986 and 1990, Sachs 2000a, Sagasti 2001, School of Information Management and Systems, University of California Berkeley 2001, Simputer Trust 2000, Smalley 1995, Solow 1970 and 1987, Tamesis 2001, Telia Mobile 2000, Tomson Financial Data Services 2001, UN 2000c, 2000d, 2001a and 2001b, UNCTAD 2000, UNDP 1999a, 1999e and 1999f, UNDP, Country Offices 2001, UNDP India Country Office 2001, UNDP and Government of Karnataka 1999, UNDP, Accenture and the Markle Foundation 2001, UNESCO 1998, 1999 and 2001a, UNICEF 1991, 1999 and 2001e, Universitiet Leiden 1999, UPS 2001, US Internet Council and ITTA 2000, W3C 2000, Wang and others 1999, WHO 1998 and 2000a, WIPO 2000, World Bank 1999 and 2001g, World Economic Forum 2000, Zakon 2000 and Zinnbauer 2001a.

Chapter 3 draws on the following: Attaran and others 2000, Barry 2001, Biotechnology Australia 2001, Bonn International Center for Conversion 1999, CNN 2000 and 2001, Cohen 2001, Consumers Union 1999, Dando 1994, Global Network of Environment and Technology 1999, Graham and Weiner 1995, Haas, Keohane and Levy 1993, Haerlin and Parr 1999, Hawken, Lovins and Lovins 1999, Hazell 2000, Holmes and Schmitz 1994, Jordan and O'Riordan 1999, Juma 2000 and 2001, Lally 1998, Lipton, Sinha, and Blackman 2001, Matlon 2001, Naray-Szabo 2000, New Scientist 2001, Novartis Foundation for Sustainable Development 2001, Paarlberg 2000, Pendergrast 2000, Physicians for Social Responsibility 2001, Roast and Post Coffee Company 2001, Royal Society of London, US National Academy of Sciences, Brazilian Academy of Sciences, Chinese Academy of Sciences, Indian National Science Academy, Mexican Academy of Sciences and Third World Academy of Sciences 2000, SEHN 2000, SIPRI 2000, Soule 2000, UNDP, UNDESA and WEC 2000, UNEP 1992a and 1992b, University of Sussex, Global Environmental Change Programme 1999, US Food and Drug Administration 2000b and Wolfenbarger and Phifer 2000.

Chapter 4 draws on the following: Agence Universitaire de la Francophonie 2001, Asadullah 2000, Asian Venture

Capital Journal 2000, Bhagwati and Partington 1976, Birdsall 1996 and forthcoming, Buchert 1998, Carlson 2000, CDI 2001, CERI 1998, 1999a, 1999b and 2000, CERI and IMHE 1997, Chaudhary 1999, Chile Ministry of Education 2001, Chinapah 1997, Choi, Lee and Chung 2001, DACST 1998, Enlances 2001, Evenson and Gollin 2001, Galal and Nauriyal 1995, ILO 2001, ITU 2000, Jones-Evans 2000, Kapur 2001, Kimbell 1997, King and Buchert 1999, Kumar 1999, Lall 2001, Lee 2001, Nakamura 2000, Nanthikesan 2001, National Electronics and Computer Technology Center 2001, OECD 2000b, 2000c, 2000e, 2000g and 2000h, Owen 2000, Perraton and Creed 2000, Pfeil 2001, Readiness for the Networked World 2001, Rodríguez-Clare 2001, Saxenian 1999 and 2000, SchoolNETSA 2001, SchoolNet Thailand Project 2001, Singh 2000, Tallon and Kremer 1999, Tan and Batra 1995, UK Government Foresight 2001, UNDESA 2000a, UNESCO 1999, 2000a and 2000b, Wallsten 2000, Wang, Qin and Guan 2000, Watkins 2000, Winch 1996, World Bank 1993, 1999, 2000b, 2000d and 2001h, Yingjian 2000 and Yu 1999.

Chapter 5 draws on the following: Anand 2000, Anderson, MacLean and Davies 1996, Attaran 2001, Baker 2000, Berkley 2001, Bonn International Center for Conversion 2000, Bloom, River Path Associates and Fang 2001, Bonn International Center for Conversion 2000, Burnett 1999, Business Heroes 2001, Brazil Ministry of Health 2000, Byerlee and Fischer 2000, Cahill 2001, Centre for Responsive Politics 2001, CGIAR 2001, Chang 2001, Correa 2000 and 2001, de Francisco 2001, DOT Force 2001, The Economist 2001, FAO 1998, FONTAGRO 2001, Forbes 2001, Fortune 2000, Fox and Coghlan 2000, Global Forum for Health Research 2000, Guilloux and Moon 2000, Harvard University 2001, Hirschel 2000, IAVI 2000, IEA 2000 and 2001, IMS HEALTH 2001, Juma and Watal 2001, Kasper 2001, Kirkman 2001, Kremer 2000a, 2000b and 2001, Lalkar 1999, Lipton 1999, Lipton, Sinha and Blackman 2001, Love 2001, McBride 2001, MacDade and Johansson 2001, Medecins Sans Frontieres 2001a and 2001b, MIM 2001, Mooney 1999a, Moscardi 2000, Mrema 2001, Mytelka 2000, NSF 2001, Oxfam International 2001, Pardey and Beintema 2001, Pearce 2000, Philips and Browne 1998, Pilling 2001a and 2001b, Potrykus 2001, Press and Washburn 2000, Public Citizen 2000, PV GAP 1999, Rediff.com 1999, Rich 2001, Sachs 2000b, SDC 1998, SiliconValley.com 2001, SIPRI 2000, Stiglitz 2001, Trouiller and Olliaro 1999, UN 1948, UNAIDS 2000b, UNDP 1999a, UNDP, UNDESA and WEC 2000, UNEP 1992a and 1998, UNPOP 2000, US Department of the Treasury 2000, US Food and Drug Administration 2000a, US Patent and Trademark Office. 2000a and 2000b, Weissman 2001, Wendland 2001, WHO 2001, WIPO 2001a and 2001b, World Bank. 2000a, 2001h and forthcoming, WTO 1994 and Zinnbauer 2001a and 2001d.

Bibliography

Background papers

Attaran, Amir. 2001. "The Scientific Omissions of International Aid: Why Human Development Suffers."

Barry, Christian. 2001. "Ethics and Technology: The Lay of the Land."

Bloom, David, River Path Associates and Karen Fang. 2001. "Social Technology and Human Health."

Chandrasekhar, C. P. 2001. "ICT in a Developing Country: An India Case Study."

Chang, Ha-Joon. 2001. "Intellectual Property Rights and Economic Development—Historical Lessons and Emerging Issues."

Cohen, Joel I. 2001. "Harnessing Biotechnology for the Poor: Challenges Ahead Regarding Biosafety and Capacity Building."

Correa, Carlos. 2001. "The TRIPS Agreement: How Much Room for Manoeuvre?"

Desai, Meghnad, Sakiko Fukuda-Parr, Claes Johansson and Francisco Sagasti. 2001. "How Well Are People Participating in the Benefits of Technological Progress? Technology Achievement Index (TAI)."

Fortier, Francois, and Tran Thi Thu Trang. 2001. "Use of Information and Communication Technologies and Human Development."

Goldemberg, José. 2001. "Energy and Human Well-Being."

Graham, Carol. 2001. "Mobility, Opportunity and Vulnerability: The Dynamics of Poverty and Inequality in a Global Economy."

Hijab, Nadia. 2001. "People's Initiatives to Bridge the Digital Divide."

Juma, Calestous. 2001. "Global Technological Safety."

Juma, Calestous, and Jayashree Watal. 2001. "Global Governance and Technology."

Kapur, Devesh. 2001. "Diasporas and Technology Transfer."

Kirkman, Geoffrey. 2001. "Out of the Labs and into the Developing World."

Kliendorfer, Paul. 2001. "The Economics of New Energy Technologies."

Kremer, Michael. 2001. "Spurring Technical Change in Tropical Agriculture."

Lall, Sanjaya. 2001. "Harnessing Technology for Human Development."

Lee, Jong-Wha. 2001. "Education for Technology Readiness: Prospects for Developing Countries."

Lipton, Michael, Saurabh Sinha and Rachel Blackman. 2001. "Reconnecting Agricultural Technology to Human Development."

Love, James. 2001. "Access to Medicine and the Use of Patents without Permission of the Patent Owner: Models for State Practice in Developing Countries."

McDade, Susan, and Thomas B. Johansson. 2001. "Issues and Priorities in Energy."

Nanthikesan, S. 2001. "Trends in Digital Divide."

Pack, Howard. 2001. "Industrialisation Options for the Poorest Countries."

Pardey, Phil G., and Nienke M. Beintema. 2001. "Losing Ground? What's Happened with Agricultural Research Regarding Less Developed Countries."

Pettinato, Stefano. 2001. "Inequality: Currents and Trends."

Pfeil, Andreas. 2001. "The Venture Capital Revolution: New Ways of Financing Technology Innovation."

Rodas-Martini, Pablo. 2001a. "Has Income Distribution Really Worsened in the South? And Has Income Distribution Really Worsened between the North and the South?"

———. 2001b. "Income Distribution and Its Relation to Trade, Technological Change and Economic Growth: A Survey of the Economic Literature."

Rodríguez-Clare, Andrés. 2001. "Costa Rica's Development Strategy Based on Human Capital and Technology: How It Got There, the Impact of Intel, and Lessons for Other Countries."

Sagasti, Francisco. 2001. "The Knowledge Explosion and the Knowledge Divide."

Stiglitz, Joseph E. 2001. "Knowledge of Technology and the Technology of Knowledge: New Strategies for Development."

Ward, Michael. 2001. "Purchasing Power Parity and International Comparisons."

Yaqub, Shahin. 2001 "Intertemporal Welfare Dynamics."

Zinnbauer, Dieter. 2001a. "The Dynamics of the Digital Divide: Why Being Late Does Matter."

———. 2001b. "E-commerce and Developing Countries: An Introduction."

———. 2001c. "Internet and Political Empowerment—A Double Edged Sword."

———. 2001d. "Societal Implications of Internet Governance: An Introduction."

Background notes

Lipton, Michael, Saurabh Sinha and Rachel Blackman. 2001a. "The Developing Water Crisis: Implications for Technology."

———. 2001b. "Ecosustainability."

———. 2001c. "The Impact of Agricultural Technology on Human Health."

———. 2001d. "Integrated Pest Management."

———. 2001e. "Participatory Technology Development."

———. 2001f. "Potential for Public-Private Partnerships in Agricultural Research."

Matlon, Peter. 2001. "Outstanding Issues in Global Agricultural Technology Development."

References

AAAS (American Association for the Advancement of Science). 2001. "Guide to R&D Data—Total U.S. R&D (1953-)." [www.aaas.org/spp/dspp/rd/guitotal.htm]. 1 February 2001.

Adaptive Eyecare. 2001. "Adaptive Eyecare—The Technology." [www.adaptive-eyecare.com/technology.htm]. 2 April 2001.

Agence Universitaire de la Francophonie. 2001. "Histoire." [www.aupelf-uref.org/UVF/]. 27 March 2001.

Aghion, Phillippe, and Peter Howitt. 1992. "A Model of Growth through Creative Destruction." *Econometrica* 60 (2): 323–51.

Alitieri, M.A. 2000. "International Workshop on the Ecological Impacts of Transgenic Crops." Executive summary of a workshop organized by the Consultative Group for International Agricultural Research's NGO Committee, University of California at Berkeley.

Analysys. 2000. "The Network Revolution and the Developing World." Report 00-194. Cambridge.

Anand, M. 2000. "Professor Wireless." *Business World India.* [www.businessworldindia.com/archive/200522/Infotech2.htm]. April 2001.

Anderson, J., M. MacLean and C. Davies. 1996. "Malaria Research: An Audit of International Activity." PRISM Report 7. Wellcome Trust, Unit for Policy Research in Science and Medicine, London.

Andrews Worldwide Communications. 2001. "International Calling." [www.andrews.com/click/international.htm]. 10 April 2001.

Angus Reid. 2000. "Face of the Web Study Pegs Global Internet Population at More than 300 Million." [www.angusreid.com/media/content/displaypr.cfm?id_to_view=1001]. 20 February 2001.

Archive Builders. 2000. "Evolution of Intel Microprocessors." [www.archivebuilders.com/whitepapers/22016h.html]. February 2001.

Arlington, Steve. 2000. "Pharma 2005: An Industrial Revolution in R&D." *Pharmaceutical Executive* 20 (1): 74.

Asadullah, Niaz. 2000. "Governing Industrial Technology Development in the LDCs: A Technology Policy Approach." Oxford University, Queen Elisabeth House.

Asian Venture Capital Journal. 2000. *The 2001 Guide to Venture Capital in Asia.* Hong Kong, China.

Atkinson, A.B., and A. Brandolini. 1999. "Promise and Pitfalls in the Use of 'Secondary' Data-sets: Income Inequality in OECD Countries." Oxford University, Nuffield College.

Attaran, Amir. 2001. Correspondence on current research spending on malaria. Harvard University, Center for International Development. 16 January. Cambridge, Mass.

Attaran, Amir, Donald R. Roberts, Chris F. Curtis and Wenceslaus L. Kilama. 2000. "Balancing Risks on the Backs of the Poor." *Nature Medicine* 6 (7): 729–31.

Baker, Dean. 2000. Correspondence on critiques of pull incentives for vaccine development. Centre for Economic and Policy Research. 18 December. Washington, DC.

Barro, Robert J., and Jong-Wha Lee. 2000. "International Data on Educational Attainment: Updates and Implications." NBER Working Paper 7911. National Bureau of Economic Research, Cambridge, Mass.

Bassanini, Andrea, Stefano Scarpetta and Ignazio Visco. 2000. "Knowledge, Technology and Economic Growth: Recent Evidence from OECD Countries." Paper presented at the 150th anniversary conference of the National Bank of Belgium, 11–12 May, Brussels.

BCC (Business Communications Company) Research. 2000. "Genomics Market Soaring in the Next Decade." [www.bccresearch.com/editors/RB-142.html]. 1 March 2001.

Bell Labs. 2000. "Bell Labs Early Contribution to Computer Science." [www.bell-labs.com/history/unix/blcontributions.html]. 7 February 2001.

Berkley, Seth. 2001. Correspondence on intellectual property in research agreements on the International AIDS Vaccine Initiative. 30 January. New York.

Bhagwati, Jagdish N., and Martin Partington, eds. 1976. *Taxing the Brain Drain.* Amsterdam: North-Holland.

Bignerds. 2001. "History of the Computer Industry in America: America and the Computer Industry." [www.bignerds.com/science/history.txt]. 5 February 2001.

Biopharma. 2001. "Biopharmaceutical Products in the U.S. Market." [www.biopharma.com/pr.html]. 3 April 2001.

Biotechnology Australia. 2001. "Most Australians Unable to Name Benefits or Risks of Genetically Modified Foods." [www.biotechnology.gov.au/sydney_backgrounder_27_Mar-web1.doc]. 27 March 2001.

Birdsall, Nancy. 1996. "Public Spending on Higher Education in Developing Countries: Too Much or Too Little?" *Economics of Education Review* 15 (4): 407–19

———. 2000. "Why Inequality Matters: The Developing and Transition Economies." Paper presented at a conference on the world economy in the 21st century: challenges and opportunities, 18–19 February, Mount Holyoke College, South Hadley, Mass.

———. Forthcoming. "Why Inequality Matters: Some Economic Issues." *Ethics and International Affairs.*

Birdsall, Nancy, Jere Behrman and Miguel Szekely. 2000. "Intergenerational Mobility in Latin America: Deeper Markets and Better Schools Make a Difference." In Nancy Birdsall and Carol Graham, eds., *New Markets, New Opportunities? Economic and Social Mobility in a Changing World.* Washington, DC: Brookings Institution and Carnegie Endowment for International Peace.

Bonn International Center for Conversion. 1999. *Conversion Survey 1999.* Oxford: Oxford University Press.

———. 2000. *Conversion Survey 2000: Global Disarmament, Demilitarization and Demobilization.* [www.bicc.de/r&d/frame.html]. 3 April 2001.

Bourguignon, Francois. 2000. "Crime, Violence and Inequitable Development." In Boris Pleskovic and Joseph E. Stiglitz, eds., *Annual World Bank Conference on Development Economics 1999.* Washington DC: World Bank.

Brazil Ministry of Health. 2000. "AIDS Drugs Policy." [www.aids.gov.br/assistencia/aids_drugs_policy.htm]. April 2001.

Brown, Paul. 2000. "Vaccine in GM Fruit Could Wipe out Hepatitis B." *The Guardian.* 8 September.

Brynjolfsson, Erik, and Brian Kahin, eds. 2000. *Understanding the Digital Economy.* Cambridge, Mass.: MIT Press.

Buchert, Lene, ed.1998. *Education Reform in the South in the 1990s.* Paris: United Nations Educational, Scientific and Cultural Organization.

Burnett, Francis. 1999. "OECS (Organisation of Eastern Caribbean States) at Work: Eastern Caribbean Drug Service." *The Montserrat Reporter On-Line.* [www.montserratreporter.org/news0200-4.htm]. April 2001.

Business Heroes. 2001 "John Harrison: The Maritime Chronometer." [www.businessheroes.com/Pages/history/history.htm]. April 2001.

Byerlee, Derek, and Ken Fischer. 2000. "Accessing Modern Science: Policy and Institutional Options for Agricultural Biotechnology in Developing Countries." [wbln0018.worldbank.org/essd/susint.nsf/research/iprs]. March 2001.

Cahill, Laurena. 2001. "Thailand Developing Drug to Fight Malaria." *The Nation.* [www.nationmultimedia.com/byteline/stories/Mar20/st11.shtml]. April 2001.

Cairncross, Sandy, and Richard Jolly. 2000. Correspondence on the compilation of data on access to water and sanitation for the World Health Organization and United Nations Children's Fund. London School of Hygiene and Tropical Medicine. 20 January. London.

Canberra Group. 2001. *Expert Group on Household Income Statistics: Final Report and Recommendations.* Ottawa.

Carlson, Beverly A., ed. 2000. *Achieving Educational Quality: What Schools Can Teach Us. Learning from Chile's P900 Primary Schools.* Santiago: Comisión Económica para América Latina (CEPAL).

Castells, Manuel. 1996. *The Rise of the Network Society.* Oxford: Blackwell.

———. 2000. "Information Technology and Global Capitalism." In Will Hutton and Anthony Giddens, eds., *On the Edge: Essays on a Runaway World.* London: Jonathan Cape.

———. 2001. "The Internet Galaxy." The 2000 Clarendon Lectures in Management, Oxford University.

Castles, Ian, and Branko Milanovic. 2001. Correspondence on data issues in Milanovic (1998b). World Bank. February. Canberra and Washington, DC.

CDI (Comitê para Democratização da Informática). 2001. "Institutional Information." [www.cdi.org.br/]. 28 February 2001.

Centre for Responsive Politics. 2001. "Industry Profiles." [www.opensecrets.org/industries/index.asp]. April 2001.

CERI (Centre for Educational Research and Innovation). 1998. *Making the Curriculum Work.* Paris: Organisation for Economic Co-operation and Development.

———. 1999a. *Education Policy Analysis 1999.* Paris: Organisation for Economic Co-operation and Development.

———. 1999b. *Innovating Schools.* Paris: Organisation for Economic Co-operation and Development.

———. 2000. *Motivating Students for Lifelong Learning.* Paris: Organisation for Economic Co-operation and Development.

CERI (Centre for Educational Research and Innovation) and IMHE (Programme on Institutional Management in Higher Education). 1997. *Information Technology and the Future of Post-Secondary Education.* Paris: Organisation for Economic Co-operation and Development.

CGIAR (Consultative Group for International Agricultural Research). 2001. *CGIAR Annual Report 2000: The Challenge of Climate Change: Poor Farmers at Risk.* Washington, DC.

Chandrashekar, C. P. 2001. Correspondence on state-level Internet data for India. Jawaharlal Nehru University. March 2001. New Delhi.

Chaudhary, Sohanvir S. 1999. "Communication Technology for Enhancement and Transformation of Open Education: The Experience at the Indira Gandhi National Open University in India." Paper presented at the PAN Commonwealth Forum on Open Learning, 1–5 March, Brunei-Darussalam. [www.col.org/forum/PCFpapers/Chaudhary.pdf]. 27 March 2001.

Chen, Lincoln. 1983. "Child Survival: Levels, Trends, and Determinants." In Rudolfo A. Bulatao and Ronald D. Lee with Paula E. Hollerbach and John Bongaarts, eds., *Determinants of Fertility in Developing Countries: Supply and Demand for Children.* vol. 1. New York: Academic Press.

Chile Ministry of Education. 2001. "Gobierno de Chile, Ministerio de Educacion, Educatión Básica [Government of Chile, Ministry of Education, Primary Education]." [www.mineduc.cl/]. 30 March 2001.

Chinapah, Vinayagum. 1997. *Handbook on Monitoring Learning Achievement: Towards Capacity Building.* Paris: United Nations Educational, Scientific and Cultural Organization.

Choi, Seon-Kyou, Myeong-Ho Lee and Gya-Hwa Chung. 2001. "Competition in Korean Mobile Telecommunications Market: Business Strategy and Regulatory Environment." *Telecommunications Policy* 25: 125–38.

Clymer, Adam, and Robert Pear. 2001. "Congress Begins Planning for Increased Number of Uninsured as Economy Slows." *The New York Times.* 27 March.

CNN (Cable News Network). 2000. "Mad Cow Report Criticizes British Officials." [www.cnn.com/2000/WORLD/europe/UK/10/26/bse.report/index.html]. 9 April 2001.

———. 2001."Verdicts in France Tainted-Blood Trail 'Intolerable' for Victims." [www.cnn.com/WORLD/europe/9903/09/france.blood.02/]. 2 April 2001.

Cohen, Stephen, Bradford DeLong and John Zysman. 1999. "An E-conomy?" [www.j-bradford-delong.net/OpEd/virtual/technet/An_E-conomy]. 6 April 2001.

Consumers Union. 1999. "Summary of Public Opinion Surveys Related to Labeling of Genetically Engineered Foods." [www.consumersunion.org/food/summpollny699.htm]. 31 March 2001.

Cornia, Andrea G. 1999. "Liberalization, Globalization and Income Distribution." Working Paper 157. United Nations University, World Institute for Development Economics Research, Helsinki.

Correa, Carlos. 2000. "Intellectual Property Rights and the Use of Compulsory Licenses: Options for Developing Countries." [www.southcentre.org/publications/complicense/toc.htm]. April 2001.

Cox, W. Michael, and Richard Alm. 1999. *The New Paradigm: Federal Reserve Bank of Dallas Annual Report 1999.* Dallas: Federal Reserve Bank of Dallas.

Dando, Malcolm. 1994. *Biological Warfare in the 21st Century.* London: Brassey's.

David, Paul A. 1999. "Digital Technology and the Productivity Paradox: After Ten Years, What Has Been Learned?" Paper presented at a US Department of Commerce conference on understanding the digital economy: data, tools and research, 25–26 May, Washington, DC.

DACST (Department of Arts, Culture, Science and Technology). 1998. "The National Research and Technology Foresight Project." South Africa. [www.dacst.gov.za/science_technology/foresight/pamphlet.htm]. 27 March 2001.

de Francisco, Andres. 2001. Correspondence on estimates by the Global Forum for Health Research of resource flows into health research in the 1990s. Global Forum for Health Research. 9 March. Geneva.

Doran, James. 2001. "PowderJect Makes Third World Pledge." *The Times.* 24 February.

DOT Force (Digital Opportunity Task Force). 2001. "Addressing the Global Digital Divide." [www.dotforce.org]. April 2001.

The Economist. 2000. "The New Economy." 23 September.

———. 2001. "AIDS Vaccines on Trial." 3 February.

El-Osta, Hisham S., and Mitchell J. Morehart. 1999. "Technology Adoption Decisions in Dairy Production and the Role of Herd Expansion." *Agricultural and Resource Economics Review* 28 (1): 84–95.

Enlaces. 2001. "El Portal Educativo de Chile." [www.enlaces.cl/]. 28 March 2001.

Evenson, Robert E., and Douglas Gollin, eds. 2001. *Crop Variety Improvement and Its Effect on Productivity: The Impact of International Research.* Wallingford, UK: CAB International.

FAO (Food and Agriculture Organization). 1998. "The State of the World's Plant Genetic Resources for Food and Agriculture." Rome.

———. 2000a. "FAOSTAT Agriculture Data." [apps.fao.org/]. December 2000.

———. 2000b. *The State of Food Insecurity in the World 2000.* Rome.

First Nations and Inuit Regional Health Survey National Steering Committee. 1999. *First Nations and Inuit Regional Health Survey: National Report 1999.* St. Regis, Canada.

FONTAGRO (Regional Fund for Agricultural Technology). 2001. "About the Fund." [www.fontagro.org/about.htm]. April 2001.

Forbes. 2001. "Forbes World's Richest People 2000." [www.forbes.com/tool/toolbox/billnew/]. April 2001.

Fortune. 2000. "How the Industries Stack Up." 17 April.

Fox, Barry, and Andy Coghlan. 2000. "Patently Ridiculous." New Scientist. 9 December.

Galal, Ahmed, and Bharat Nauriyal. 1995. "Regulating Telecommunications in Developing Countries." Policy Research Working Paper 1520. World Bank, Washington, DC. Cited in Wallsten 2000.

Gardner, Gary, and Brian Halwell. 2001. "Escaping Hunger, Escaping Excess." *World Watch* 13 (4): 24–35.

G-8 (Group of Eight). 2000. "G-8 Communiqué Okinawa 2000." 23 July.

Gilder, George. 2000. *Telecosm: How Infinite Bandwidth Will Revolutionize Our World.* New York: Free Press.

Global Forum for Health Research. 2000. "10/90 Report on Health Research." [www.globalforumhealth.org/report.htm]. March 2001.

Global Network of Environment and Technology. 1999. "Rabbits Threaten Australia." [www.gnet.org/ColdFusion/News_Page1.cfm?NewsID=6024&start=771]. 31 March 2001.

Government of India, Department of Education. 2001. "Educational Statistics Compiled by IAMR (Institute of Applied Manpower Researcher)." [www.education.nic.in/html web/iamrstat.htm]. 3 April 2001.

Government of Madhya Pradesh, India. 1995. *The Madhya Pradesh Human Development Report 1995.* Bhopal: Directorate of Institutional Finance, Project Office.

———. 1998. *The Madhya Pradesh Human Development Report 1998.* Bhopal: Directorate of Institutional Finance, Project Office.

Graham, John D., and Jonathan Baert Weiner, eds. 1995. *Risk versus Risk: Tradeoffs in Protecting Health and the Environment.* Cambridge, Mass.: Harvard University Press.

Grinspun, Alejandro, ed. 2001. *Choices for the Poor: Lessons from National Poverty Strategies.* New York: United Nations Development Programme.

Gu, Shulin, and Edward Steinmueller. 1996. *Information Revolution and Policy Implications for Developing Countries.* Maastricht: United Nations University, Institute for New Technologies.

Guilloux, Alain, and Suerie Moon. 2000. "Hidden Price Tags: Disease-Specific Drug Donations: Costs and Alternatives." Médecins Sans Frontières, Geneva.

Gutierrez, G., R. Tapia-Conyer, H. Guiscafre, H. Reyes, H. Martinez and J. Kumate. 1996. "Impact of Oral Rehydration and Selected Public Health Interventions on Reduction of Mortality from Childhood Diarrhoeal Diseases in Mexico." *Bulletin of the World Health Organization* 74 (2): 189–97

Gwatkin, Davidson R., Shea Rutstein, Kiersten Johnson, Rohini P. Pande and Adam Wagstaff. 2000a. *Socio-Economic Differences in Health, Nutrition and Population in Ecuador.* Washington, DC: World Bank.

———. 2000b. *Socio-Economic Differences in Health, Nutrition and Population in Indonesia.* Washington, DC: World Bank.

Haas, Peter, Robert Keohane and Marc Levy, eds. 1993. *Institutions for the Earth.* Cambridge, Mass: MIT Press.

Haerlin, Benny, and Doug Parr. 1999. "How to Restore Public Trust in Science." [www.gene.ch/genet/1999/Aug/msg00019.html]. 31 March 2001.

Hanmer, Lucia, and Felix Naschold. 2000. "Attaining the International Development Targets: Will Growth Be Enough?" *Development Policy Review* 18 (March): 11–36.

Hanmer, Lucia, John Healy and Felix Naschold. 2000. "Will Growth Halve Global Poverty by 2015?" ODI Poverty Paper 8. Overseas Development Institute, London.

Harvard University. 2001. "Consensus Statement on Antiretroviral Treatment for AIDS in Poor Countries." [aids.harvard.edu/overview/news_events/events/consensus.html]. April 2001.

Hawken, Paul, Amory Lovins and L. Hunter Lovins. 1999. *Natural Capitalism: Creating the Next Industrial Revolution.* London: Earthscan.

Hazell, Peter B. R. 2000. "The Green Revolution." Prepared for the *Oxford Encyclopaedia of Economic History.* Oxford.

Hill, Kenneth, Carla AbouZahr and Tessa Wardlaw. 2001. "Estimates of Maternal Mortality for 1995." *Bulletin of the World Health Organization* 79 (3): 182–93.

Hillner, Jennifer. 2000. "Venture Capitals." *Wired.* 7 August.

Hirschel, Bernard. 2000. "HIV/AIDS Roundtable—How Large Is the Gap?" Fondation du Présent/Treatment-Access. [www.hivnet.ch:8000/topics/treatment-access/viewR?875]. 1 April 2001.

Holmes, Thomas J., and James Schmitz, Jr. 1994. "Resistance to Technology and Trade between Areas." Staff Report 184. Federal Reserve Bank of Minneapolis, Research Department, Minnesota.

IAVI (International AIDS Vaccine Initiative). 2000 "IAVI's Intellectual Property Agreements." IAVI Backgrounder Publication. [www.iavi.org]. March 2001.

IEA (International Energy Agency). 2000. *World Energy Outlook 2000.* [www.iea.org/weo/index.htm]. April 2001.

———. 2001. "Energy Technology R&D Statistics, 1974–1998." [data.iea.org/iea/link_wds.asp]. April 2001.

IFAD (International Fund for Agricultural Development). 2001. *Rural Poverty Report 2000: The Challenge of Ending Rural Poverty.* Rome: Oxford University Press.

ILO (International Labour Organization). 1998. World Employment Report 1998/1999. Geneva: International Labour Office.

———. 2000. "Healthcare: The Key to Decent Work?" [www.ilo.org/public/english/bureau/inf/pkits/wlr2000/wlr00 ch4.htm]. 5 April 2001.

———. 2001. *World Employment Report 2001.* Geneva: International Labour Office.

IMF (International Monetary Fund), OECD (Organisation for Economic Co-operation and Development), UN (United Nations) and World Bank. 2000. *A Better World for All: Progress towards the International Development Goals.* Washington, DC.

IMS HEALTH. 2001. "Health Market Report: Five Year Forecast of the Global Pharmaceutical Markets." [www.imsglobal.com/insight/report/global/report.htm]. April 2001

Intel. 2001. "Moore's Law, Overview." [www.intel.com/research/silicon/mooreslaw.htm]. February 2001.

International Data Corporation. 2000. *Digital Planet 2000: The Global Information Economy.* Vienna, Va.: World Information Technology and Services Alliance.

International IDEA (Institute for Democracy and Electoral Assistance). 2000. *Voter Turnout from 1945 to Date: A Global Report on Political Participation.* Stockholm.

ITDG (Intermediate Technology Development Group). 2000. *Technology . . . Is Only Half the Story.* Rugby, UK.

ITU (International Telecommunication Union). 2000. *The Internet from the Top of the World: The Nepal Case Study.* [www.itu.int/ti/casestudies/nepal/material/nepal.pdf]. 4 April 2001.

———. 2001a. *World Internet Reports: Telephony.* Geneva.

———. 2001b. *World Telecommunication Indicators.* Database. Geneva.

James, Clive. 2000. "Global Review of Commercialized Transgenic Crops: 2000." Brief 21: Preview. International Service for the Acquisition of Agribiotech Applications, Ithaca, NY.

Japan Ministry of Foreign Affairs. 2000. "Report of the International Symposium on Information Technology and Development Co-operation." Tokyo.

Jolly, Alison. 2000. *Lucy's Legacy: Sex and Intelligence in Human Evolution.* Cambridge, Mass: Harvard University Press.

Jolly, Richard. 2001. Correspondence on oral rehydration therapy and vaccines for communicable diseases. February. Sussex.

Jones-Evans, Dylan. 2000. "Entrepreneurial Universities: Policies, Strategies, and Practice." In Pedro Conceicao, David Gibson,

Manuel V. Heitor and Syed Shariq, eds., *Science, Technology and Innovation Policy: Opportunities and Challenges for the Knowledge Economy.* Westport, Conn.: Quorum Books.

Jordan, Andrew, and Timothy O'Riordan. 1999. "The Precautionary Principle in Contemporary Environmental Policy and Politics." In C. Raffensperger and J. Tickner, eds., *Protecting Public Health and the Environment: Implementing the Precautionary Principle.* Washington, DC: Island Press.

Jorgenson, Dale W., and Kevin J. Stiroh. 2000. "Raising the Speed Limit: US Economic Growth and the Information Age." Brookings Papers on Economic Activity 2. Washington, DC: Brookings Institution.

Juma, Calestous. 2000. "Biotechnology in the Global Economy." *International Journal of Biotechnology* 2 (1/2/3): 1–6.

———. 2001. Correspondence on the precautionary principle. Harvard University. March. Cambridge, Mass.

Jupiter Communications. 2000a. *Latin America: Online Projections.* Jupiter Analyst Report. New York.

———. 2000b. "US Online Demographics: Fundamentals and Forecasts, Spring 2000." Jupiter Consumer Survey 4. New York.

Kasper, Toby. 2001. Correspondence on Pfizer's fluconazole donation to South Africa. Médecins Sans Frontières. 1 April. Johannesburg.

Kimbell, Richard. 1997. *Assessing Technology: International Trends in Curriculum and Assessment: UK, Germany, USA, Taiwan, and Australia.* Buckingham, UK: Open University Press.

King, Kenneth, and Lene Buchert, eds. 1999. *Changing International Aid to Education.* Paris: United Nations Educational, Scientific and Cultural Organization.

Kremer, Michael. 2000a. "Creating Markets for New Vaccines: Part I: Rationale." NBER Working Paper 7716. National Bureau of Economic Research, Cambridge, Mass.

———. 2000b. "Creating Markets for New Vaccines: Part II: Design Issues." NBER Working Paper 7717. National Bureau of Economic Research, Cambridge, Mass.

Kumar, Krishan Lall. 1999. "Teacher Education Via Internet and Video Tele-teaching: An Effectiveness Study." Paper presented at the nineteenth world conference on open learning and distance education, International Council for Open and Distance Education, 20–24 June, Vienna. [www.fernuni-hagen.de/ICDE/final/s_lists/abstract/u1b00585.htm].

Lalkar. 1999. "Cuba Vaccine Will at Last Become Available against Meningitis." [www.lalkar.demon.co.uk/issues/contents/sep1999/cuba.html]. April 2001.

Lall, Sanjaya. 2000. "The Technological Structure and Performance of Developing Country Manufactured Exports, 1985–98." *Oxford Development Studies* 28 (3): 337–69.

Lally, A. P. 1998. "ISO 14000 and Environmental Cost Accounting: The Gateway to the Global Market." *Law and Policy in International Business* 29 (4): 501–38.

Landler, Mark. 2001. "Opportunity Knocks: India's High-Tech Bull Is Ready for Bear." *International Herald Tribune.* 14 March.

Lipton, Michael. 1999. "Reviving Global Poverty Reduction: What Role for Genetically Modified Plants?" Sir John Crawford Memorial Lecture at the Consultative Group for International Agricultural Research International Centers Week, 28 October, Washington, DC.

Malaysia Economic Planning Unit. 1994. "Poverty Eradication, Expansion of Productive Employment and Social Integration in Malaysia, 1971–94." Prime Minister's Department, Kuala Lumpur.

Mansell, Robin. 1999. "Global Access to Information and Communication Technologies: Priorities for Action." Paper prepared for the International Development Research Centre. Science and Technology Policy Research, Brighton.

Matlon, Peter. 2001. Correspondence on the precautionary principle. United Nations Development Programme. March. New York.

Matthews, Emily, and Allen Hammond. 1997. "Natural Resource Consumption." Background paper prepared for *Human Development Report 1998.* United Nations Development Programme, Human Development Report Office, New York.

McBride, Janet. 2001. "UK Sides with Drugs Industry over Developing World." [www.biz.yahoo.com/rf/010328/l28252121.html]. 28 March.

Médecins Sans Frontières. 2001a. "AIDS Triple Therapy for Less than $1 a Day: MSF Challenges Pharmaceutical Industry to Match Generic Prices." [www.accessmed-msf.org/msf/accessmed/accessmed.nsf/html/4DTSR2?OpenDocument]. April 2001.

———. 2001b. "Letter from European Commissioner Pascal Lamy re: South Africa, 2 March." [www.accessmed-msf.org/msf/accessmed/accessmed.nsf/html/4DTSR2?OpenDocument]. April 2001.

Melchior, Arne, Kjetil Telle and Henrik Wiig. 2000. "Globalisation and Inequality: World Income Distribution and Living Standards, 1960–1998." Studies on Foreign Policy Issues Report 6b. Norwegian Institute of International Affairs, Oslo.

Milanovic, Branko. 1998. *Income Inequality and Poverty during the Transition from Planned to Market Economy.* Washington, DC: World Bank.

———. Forthcoming. "True World Income Distribution, 1988 and 1993: First Calculations Based on Household Surveys Alone." *Economic Journal.*

MIM (Multilateral Initiative on Malaria). 2001. "Objectives." [mim.nih.gov/english/about/objectives.html]. March 2001.

Mooney, Pat Roy. 1999a. "The ETC Century: Erosion, Technological Transformation and Corporate Concentration in the 21st Century." *Development Dialogue* 1–2: 123–24.

———. 1999b. "Technological Transformation: The Increase in Power and Complexity Is Coming Just as the Raw Materials Are Eroding." *Development Dialogue* 1–2: 25–74.

Moscardi, Edgardo. 2000. "Successful Research Partnerships." Paper prepared for a conference on agricultural research for development sponsored by the Global Forum on Agricultural Research, 21–23 May, Dresden.

Mrema, Geoffrey. 2001. Correspondence on the Association for Strengthening Agricultural Research in Eastern and Central Africa. 27 March. Entebbe, Uganda.

Mytelka, Lynn. 2000. "Knowledge and Structural Power in the International Political Economy." In Thomas Lawton, James Rosenau and Amy Verdun, eds., *Strange Power: Shaping the Parameters of International Relations and International Political Economy.* Burlington, Vt.: Ashgate.

Nakamura, Leonard I. 2000. Education and Training in an Era of Creative Destruction. Working Paper 00-13. Federal Reserve Bank of Philadelphia, Philadelphia.

Naray-Szabo, Gabor. 2000. "The Role of Technology in Sustainable Consumption." In B. Heap and J. Kent, eds., *Towards Sustainable Consumption: A European Perspective.* London: Royal Society.

National Electronics and Computer Technology Center. 2001. "Network Design and Resource Management Scheme in SchoolNet Thailand Project." [www.nectec.or.th/users/paisal/inet99/]. 27 March 2001.

National Nanotechnology Initiative. 2001. "National Nanotechnology Initiative: The Initiative and Its Implementation Plan." [www.nano.gov/nni2.htm]. 23 March 2001.

National Research Council. 2000. *Genetically Modified Pest-protected Plants: Science and Regulation.* Washington, DC: National Academy Press.

NCAER (National Council of Applied Economic Research). 1999. *India Human Development Report.* New Delhi: Oxford University Press.

NCBI (National Centre for Biotechnology Information). 2001. "GenBank Growth." [www.ncbi.nlm.nih.gov/Genbank/genbankstats.html]. 8 February 2001.

Nepal South Asia Centre. 1998. *Human Development Report of Nepal 1998.* Kathmandu: United Nations Development Programme.

New Scientist. 2001. "Breaking the Rules: Almost a Third of US Farmers Broke Rules for Planting GM Maize Last Year." 5 February.

Novartis Foundation for Sustainable Development. 2001. "The Political Economy of Agricultural Biotechnology for the Developing World." [www.foundation.novartis.com/political_economy_agricultural_biotechnology.htm]. 5 January 2001.

NSF (National Science Foundation). 2001. *Science and Engineering Indicators 2000.* [www.nsf.gov/sbe/srs/seind00/start.htm]. 1 February 2001.

Nua Publish. 2001. "Nua Internet Surveys: How Many Online, Worldwide." [www.nua.ie/surveys/how_many_online/world.html]. 13 February 2001.

OECD (Organisation for Economic Co-operation and Development). 2000a. *A New Economy? The Changing Role of Innovation and Information Technology in Growth.* Paris.

———. 2000b. *Education at a Glance.* OECD Indicators. Paris.

———. 2000c. *Investing in Education: Analysis of the 1999 World Education Indicators.* Paris.

———. 2000d. *Measuring the ICT Sector.* Paris.

———. 2000e. *OECD Economic Outlook.* Paris.

———. 2000f. *OECD Information Technology Outlook 2000.* Paris.

———. 2000g. *Schooling for Tomorrow: Learning to Bridge the Digital Divide.* Paris.

———. 2000h. *Science, Technology and Industry Outlook 2000.* Paris.

OECD (Organisation for Economic Co-operation and Development), DAC (Development Assistance Committee). 1996. *Shaping the 21st Century: The Contribution of Development Co-operation.* Paris.

OECD (Organisation for Economic Co-operation and Development) and Statistics Canada. 2000. *Literacy in the Information Age: Final Report of the International Literacy Survey.* Paris: OECD.

Owen, Arthur. 2000. "Barbados: Budget Includes Phased Liberalization of Telecommunications Sector." *BBC Monitoring Americas—Economic.* 26 October.

Oxfam International. 2001. "Fatal Side Effects: Medicine Patents under the Microscope." Policy Paper 02/01. [www.oxfam.org.uk/cutthecost/indepth.html]. April 2001.

Paarlberg, Robert L. 2000. "Governing the GM Crop Revolution: Policy Choices for Developing Countries." Food, Agriculture and the Environment Discussion Paper 33. International Food Policy Research Institute, Washington, DC.

PC World. 2000. "'Simputer' Aims at the Developing World." [www.pcworld.com/resource/printable/article/0,aid,17401,00.asp]. 2 April 2001.

Pearce, Fred. 2000. "Sold to the Highest Bidder." *New Scientist.* 16 December.

Pendergrast, Mark. 2000. *Uncommon Grounds: The History of Coffee and How It Transformed Our World.* New York: Basic Books.

Perraton, Hilary, and Charlotte Creed. 2000. *Applying New Technologies and Cost-Effective Delivery Systems in Basic Education.* Cambridge. Mass.: International Research Foundation for Open Learning.

Philips, Michael, and Brooks H. Browne. 1998. "Accelerating PV Markets in Developing Countries." [www.repp.org/articles/pv/7/7.html]. April 2001.

Physicians for Social Responsibility. 2001. "Nuclear Security: Health and Environmental Effects." [www.psr.org/ncomplex.htm]. 6 April 2001.

Pilling, David. 2001a. "Cuba's Medical Revolution." *Financial Times.* 13 January.

———. 2001b. "Patents and Patients." *Financial Times.* 17 February.

Potrykus, Ingo. 2001. "Golden Rice and Beyond." [www.plantphysiol.org/cgi/content/full/125/3/1157]. March 2001.

PowderJect. 2001. "PowderJect and GlaxoSmithKline Initiate DNA Vaccine Clinical Study in Field of Hepatitis B Immunotherapy." [www.powderject.com/mains/press_releases/230201.html]. 2 April 2001.

President of the United States. 2001. *Economic Report of the President Transmitted to the Congress January 2001.* House Document 107-2. Washington, DC: US Government Printing Office.

Press, Eyal, and Jennifer Washburn. 2000. "The Kept University." *Atlantic Monthly* 285 (3): 39–54.

Public Citizen. 2000. "Analysis of Corporate Profits 1999." [www.citizen.org/congress/drugs/factshts/corporate$.htm]. March 2001.

PV GAP (Global Approval Program for Photovoltaics). 1999. "Quality Management In Photovoltaics." In *PV Manufacturers Quality Control Training Manual.* Geneva.

Readiness for the Networked World. 2001. "ICTs in Action." In *A Guide for Developing Countries.* Harvard University, Center for International Development, Information Technologies Group. [www.readinessguide.org/vignettes.html]. April 2001.

Rediff.com. 1999. "Internet Unplugged." [www.rediff.com/computer/1999/jun/16jhunjh.htm]. April 2001.

Reuters. 2000. "Mobile Web Users Seen Outstripping PC Users by 2005." 12 July.

———. 2001. "Big Scope Seen for India in Biotech Research Business." 13 March.

Rich, Jennifer. 2001. "Compressed Data: Brazilians Think Basic to Bridge the Digital Divide." *The New York Times.* 12 February.

Roast and Post Coffee Company. 2001. "The History of Coffee, Coffee in Europe." [www.realcoffee.co.uk/Article.asp?Cat=History&Page3]. 22 March 2001.

Romer, Paul. 1986. "Increasing Returns and Long-Run Growth." *Journal of Political Economy* 94 (5): 1002–37.

———. 1990. "Endogenous Technological Change" *Journal of Political Economy* 70 (1): 65–94.

Royal Society of London, US National Academy of Sciences, Brazilian Academy of Sciences, Chinese Academy of Sciences, Indian National Science Academy, Mexican Academy of Sciences and Third World Academy of Sciences. 2000. *Transgenic Plants and World Agriculture.* Washington, DC: National Academy Press.

Sachs, Jeffrey. 2000a. "A New Map of the World." *The Economist.* 24 June.

———. 2000b. "Tropical Underdevelopment." Paper presented at the Economic History Association's 60th annual meeting, 8 September, Los Angeles.

Saxenian, AnnaLee. 1999. "Silicon Valley's New Immigrant Entrepreneurs." [www.ppic.org/publications/PPIC120/PPIC120.pdf/index.html]. 30 April 2001.

———. 2000. "Bangalore: The Silicon Valley of Asia?" Paper presented at a conference on Indian economic prospects: advancing policy reform, Center for Research on Economic Development and Policy Reform, May, Stanford, Calif. [dcrp.ced.berkeley.edu/faculty/anno/Papers.htm].

Scholz, Wolfgang, Michael Cichon and Krzystof Hagemejer. 2000. *Social Budgeting.* Geneva: International Labour Office and International Social Security Association.

SchoolNetSA. 2001 "About the SchoolNetSA." [www.school.za/]. April 2001.

SchoolNet Thailand Project. 2001. "Network Design and Resource Management Scheme in SchoolNet Thailand Project." [www.nectec.or.th/users/paisal/inet99/]. 27 March 2001.

School of Information Management and Systems, University of California at Berkeley. 2001. "How Much Information? World Wide Web." [www.sims.berkeley.edu/research/projects/how-much-info/internet.html#www]. 2 April 2001.

SDC (Solar Development Corporation). 1998. "Project Brief." [www.gefweb.org/wprogram/Oct98/Wb/solar.pdf]. March 2001.

SEHN (Science and Environmental Health Network). 2000. "The Precautionary Principle in International Treaties and Agreements." [www.sehn.org/ppta.htm]. 30 April 2001.

Shiva Kumar, A. K. 1997. "Poverty and Human Development: The Indian Experience." Background paper prepared for *Human Development Report 1997*. United Nations Development Programme, Human Development Report Office, New York.

SiliconValley.com. 2001. "Brazil Attacks Digital Divide with $300 Volkscomputer." [www.siliconvalley.com/docs/news/tech/082944.htm]. April 2001.

Simputer Trust. 2000. "The Simputer Project." [www.simputer.org/]. March 2001.

Singh, J. P. 2000. "The Institutional Environment and Effects of Telecommunication Privatization and Market Liberalization in Asia." *Telecommunications Policy* 24: 885–906.

SIPRI (Stockholm International Peace Research Institute). 2000. *SIPRI Yearbook 2000: Armaments, Disarmament and International Security.* Oxford: Oxford University Press.

Smalley, R. E. 1995. "Nanotechnology and the Next 50 Years." Speech presented at the University of Dallas, Tex. [cnst.rice.edu/dallas12-96.html]. 2 April 2001.

Smeeding, Timothy. 2001a. Correspondence on income distribution in OECD countries. Luxembourg Income Study. 26 March. New York.

———. 2001b. Correspondence on income poverty in industrial countries. Luxembourg Income Study. 20 January. New York.

———. Forthcoming. "Changing Income Inequality in OECD Countries: Updated Results from the Luxembourg Income Study (LIS)." In R. Hauser and I. Becker, eds., *The Changing Distribution of Income.* Berlin: Springer-Verlag.

Solow, Robert M. 1970. *Growth Theory: An Exposition.* Oxford: Oxford University Press.

———. 1987. "We'd Better Watch Out." *New York Review of Books.* 12 July.

Soule, Edward. 2000. "Assessing the Precautionary Principle." *Public Affairs Quarterly* 14 (4): 309–28.

Tallon, Paul. P., and Kenneth L. Kremer. 1999. "Information Technology and Economic Development: Ireland's Coming of Age with Lessons for Developing Countries." University of California, Center for Research on Information Technology and Organizations and Graduate School of Management, Irvine.

Tamesis, Pauline. 2001. Correspondence on Elagda campaign. United Nations Development Programme. 16 February. New York.

Tan, Hong W., and Geeta Batra. 1995. *Enterprise Training in Developing Countries: Incidence, Productivity Effects, and Policy Implications.* Washington, DC: World Bank.

Telegeography. 2000. "Hubs and Spokes. A Telegeography." Washington, DC.

Telia Mobile. 2000. "Mobile Telephony—The Dream of the Century." [www.teliamobile.se/articles/00/00/0a/0c/01]. 3 April 2001.

Thomson Financial Data Services. 2001. Correspondence on venture capital data for selected countries. 28 March. Newark, NJ.

TIA (Telecommunications Industry Association). 2001. "US-EU Mutual Recognition Agreement." [http://www.tiaonline.org/international/global/type/us_eu_mra.cfm]. 23 April 2001.

Trouiller, Patrice, and Piero Olliaro. 1999. "Drug Development Output: What Proportion for Tropical Diseases?" [www.accessmed-msf.org/msf/accessmed/accessmed.nsf/html/4DTSR2?OpenDocument]. April 2001.

UK Government Foresight. 2001. "Foresight." [www.foresight.gov.uk]. 30 March 2001.

UN (United Nations). 1948. "The Universal Declaration of Human Rights." [www.unhchr.ch/html/intlinst.htm]. March 2001.

———. 1996. "Women and Violence: The Work of the Special Rapporteur." Department of Public Information. [www.un.org/rights/dpi1772e.htm]. April 2001.

———. 2000a. "Millennium Declaration." Millennium Summit, 6–8 September, New York.

———. 2000b. *Report of the Friends of the Chair of the Statistical Commission: An Assessment of the Statistical Criticisms Made of Human Development Report 1999.* United Nations Statistical Commission. E/CN.3/2001/18. New York.

———. 2000c. *World Economic and Social Survey.* New York.

———. 2001a. Correspondence on technology exports. Statistics Division. 25 January. New York.

———. 2001b. "Multilateral Treaties Deposited with the Secretary-General." [untreaty.un.org]. March 2001.

———. 2001c. *World Population Prospects 1950–2050: The 2000 Revision.* Database. Department of Economic and Social Affairs, Population Division, New York.

———. 2001d. *World Population Prospects 1950–2050: The 2000 Revision: Comprehensive Tables.* Department of Economic and Social Affairs, Population Division, New York.

UN (United Nations) and Islamic Republic of Iran, Plan and Budget Organization. 1999. *Human Development Report of the Islamic Republic of Iran 1999.* Tehran.

UNAIDS (Joint United Nations Programme on HIV/AIDS). 1998. *Report on the Global HIV/AIDS Epidemic.* Geneva.

———. 2000a. *AIDS Epidemic Update: December 2000.* Geneva.

———. 2000b. *Report on the Global HIV/AIDS Epidemic.* Geneva.

UNCTAD (United Nations Conference on Trade and Development). 2000. *Building Confidence: Electronic Commerce and Development.* Geneva.

UNDCP (United Nations Drug Control Programme). 1997. *World Drug Report.* Vienna.

UNDESA (United Nations Department of Economic and Social Affairs). 2000a. *World Economic and Social Survey 2000.* New York.

———. 2000b. *The World's Women 2000: Trends and Statistics. Social Statistics and Indicator Series K 16.* New York.

UNDP (United Nations Development Programme). 1998a. *Latvia Human Development Report 1998.* Riga.

———. 1998b. *National Human Development Report of Sri Lanka: Regional Dimensions of Human Development.* Colombo.

———. 1998c. *Zambia Human Development Report 1998.* Lusaka.

———. 1999a. *Human Development Report 1999.* New York: Oxford University Press.

———. 1999b. *Informe sobre Desarrollo Humano Honduras 1999: El Impacto Humano de un Huracan [Human Development Report for Honduras 1999: The Human Impact of a Hurricane].* Tegucigalpa.

———. 1999c. *Latvia Human Development Report 1999.* Riga.

———. 1999d. *Lithuanian Human Development Report 1999.* Vilnius.

———. 1999e. *National Human Development Report for Guatemala: El Rostro Rural del Desarrollo Humano 1999.* Guatemala.

———. 1999f. *National Human Development Report for Thailand 1999.* Bangkok.

———. 2000a. *Botswana Human Development Report: Towards an AIDS-Free Generation.* Gaborone.

———. 2000b. *Bulgaria 2000: Human Development Report: The Municipal Mosaic.* Sofia.

———. 2000c. *Cambodia Human Development Report: Children and Employment.* Phnom Penh.

———. 2000d. *Human Development Report 2000.* New York: Oxford University Press.

———. 2000e. *Informe de Desarrollo Humano para Colombia 2000 [Colombia Human Development Report 2000].* Bogotá.

———. 2000f. *South African National Human Development Report: Transformation for Human Development.* Pretoria.

UNDP (United Nations Development Programme), Country Offices. 2001. Correspondence on demographics of Internet use within countries. January and February. Aguilla and St. Lucia, Argentina, Belarus, Bolivia, Bhutan, Brazil, Bulgaria, Chile, China, Dominican Republic, Guinea, Lebanon, Lithuania, Madagascar, Mauritius, Montserrat, Pakistan, Palestine, Russia, São Tomé and Principe, South Africa, Sri Lanka, Thailand, Turkey and Uruguay.

UNDP (United Nations Development Programme), India Country Office. 2001. Correspondence on state-level communication, education, energy and electricity data for India. March. New Delhi.

UNDP (United Nations Development Programme), Regional Bureau for Europe and the CIS. 1997. *The Shrinking State: Governance and Sustainable Human Development.* New York.

———. 1998. *Poverty in Transition?* New York.

———. 1999. *Central Asia 2010: Prospects for Human Development.* New York.

UNDP (United Nations Development Programme) and Government of Karnataka. 1999. *Human Development in Karnataka 1999.* Bangalore, India.

UNDP (United Nations Development Programme) and HDN (Human Development Network). 1997. *Philippine Human Development Report 1997.* Manila: United Nations Development Programme.

———. 2000. *Philippine Human Development Report 2000.* Manila: United Nations Development Programme.

UNDP (United Nations Development Programme) and Kuwait Ministry of Planning. 1997. *Human Development Report: The State of Kuwait 1997.* Kuwait City: United Nations Development Programme.

UNDP (United Nations Development Programme) and UNAIDS (Joint United Nations Programme on HIV/AIDS). 1997. *HIV/AIDS and Human Development: South Africa.* Pretoria: Amabukhu Publications.

UNDP (United Nations Development Programme) with UN Country Team. 1998. *Namibia: Human Development Report 1998: Environment and Human Development in Namibia.* Windhoek.

UNDP (United Nations Development Programme), Accenture and Markle Foundation. 2001. *Digital Opportunity Initiative: Creating a Development Dynamic.* New York.

UNDP (United Nations Development Programme), UNDESA (United Nations Department of Economic and Social Affairs) and WEC (World Energy Council). 2000. *World Energy Assessment: Energy and the Challenge of Sustainability.* New York: UNDP.

UNDP (United Nations Development Programme), IAR (Institute of Applied Research), JPF (Joao Pinheiro Foundation) and BBS (Brazilian Bureau of Statistics). 2000. *Atlas of Human Development in Brazil.* Brasilia: United Nations Development Programme.

UNEP (United Nations Environment Programme). 1992a. "Convention on Biological Diversity." [www.unep.ch/bio/conv-e.html]. March 2001.

———. 1992b. "Rio Declaration on Environment and Development." [www.unep.org/Documents/Default.asp?DocumentID=78&ArticleID=1163]. 9 April 2001.

———. 1998. "The 1987 Montreal Protocol on Substances that Deplete the Ozone Layer." [www.unep.org/ozone/mont_t.shtml]. March 2001.

UNESCO (United Nations Educational, Scientific and Cultural Organization). 1998. *Statistical Yearbook 1998.* Paris.

———. 1999. *Statistical Yearbook 1999.* Paris.

———. 2000a. "The Internet in Education and Learning." Contribution to the International Telecommunication Union Focus Group on Promotion of Infrastructure and Use of the Internet in Developing Countries. Paris.

———. 2000b. *World Education Report 2000: The Right to Education—Towards Education for All throughout Life.* Paris.

———. 2001a. Correspondence on gross enrolment ratios. 21 March. Paris.

———. 2001b. Correspondence on net enrolment ratios. March. Paris.

UNFPA (United Nations Population Fund). 2001. Data files prepared by UNFPA based on data from United Nations Population Division. Sent to Human Development Report Office on 18 January. New York.

UNHCR (United Nations High Commissioner for Refugees). 2000. *Refugees and Others of Concern to UNHCR: 1999 Statistical Overview.* Geneva.

UNICEF (United Nations Children's Fund). 1991. *The State of the World's Children 1991.* New York: Oxford University Press

———. 1999. *The State of the World's Children 1999.* New York: Oxford University Press.

———. 2001a. Correspondence on infant and under five mortality rates. March. New York.

———. 2001b. Data files on education for all on CD-ROM. Sent to Human Development Report Office on 18 January. New York.

———. 2001c. Data files on under-five mortality rates. Sent to Human Development Report Office on 18 January. New York.

———. 2001d. *Education for All.* CD-ROM. New York.

———. 2001e. *The State of the World's Children 2001: Early Childhood.* New York: Oxford University Press.

UNICEF (United Nations Children's Fund), Innocenti Research Centre. 1999. "Child Domestic Work." Digest 5. Florence.

———. 2000. A League Table of Child Poverty in Rich Nations. Report Card Issue 1. Florence.

UNIFEM (United Nations Development Fund for Women). 2000. *Progress of the World's Women 2000—UNIFEM Biennial Report.* New York.

Universitiet Leiden. 1999. "Internet for Historians, History of the Internet: The Development of the Internet." [www.let.leidenuniv.nl/history/ivh/INTERNET.HTM]. 3 April 2001.

University of Sussex, Global Environmental Change Programme. 1999. "The Politics of GM Food: Risk, Science and Public Trust: Inaccurate Characterisation of Public Perceptions." [www.susx.ac.uk/Units/gec/gecko/gmbrief.htm#Inaccurate_characterisation_of_public_perceptions]. 2 April 2001.

UNOCHA (United Nations Office for the Coordination of Humanitarian Affairs). 1999. "Humanitarian Assistance and Assistance to Refugees." [www.un.org/ha/general.htm]. 15 March 2001.

UNPOP (United Nations Population Division). 2000. *World Population Prospects: The 2000 Revision.* [www.un.org/esa/population/wpp2000.htm]. April 2001. New York.

UPS (United Parcel Service). 2001. "Quick Cost Calculator." [www.ups.com/using/services/rave/rate.html]. 10 April 2001.

USAID (United States Agency for International Development). 1999. "Women as Chattel : The Emerging Global Market in Trafficking." *Gender Matters Quarterly* (1 February): 1-3.

US Census Bureau. 1999. *Statistical Abstract of the United States.* Washington, DC

US Department of the Treasury. 2000. "General Explanations of the Administration's Fiscal Year 2001 Revenue Proposals." [www.treas.gov/taxpolicy/library/grnbk00.pdf]. March 2001.

US Food and Drug Administration. 2000a. "Office of Orphan Products Development." [www.fda.gov/orphan/]. March 2001.

———. 2000b. "Second Annual Report to the Medical Devices Annex to the US/EC Mutual Recognition Agreement." [www.fda.gov/cdrh/mra/annualreport2000.pdf]. 2 April 2001.

US Internet Council and ITTA (International Technology and Trade Associates). 2000. *State of the Internet 2000.* Washington, DC.

US Patent and Trademark Office. 2000a. "Technology Assessment and Forecast Report: US Colleges and Universities—Utility Patent Grants 1969-1999." Washington, DC.

———. 2000b. "US Patent Statistics Report: Summary Table." [www.uspto.gov/web/offices/ac/ido/oeip/taf/us_stat.pdf]. March 2001.

van der Hoeven, Ralph. 2000. "Poverty and Structural Adjustment: Some Remarks on Tradeoffs between Equity and Growth." Employment Paper 2000/4. International Labour Office, Employment Sector, Geneva.

Vandermoortele, Jan. 2000. "Absorbing Social Shocks, Protecting Children and Reducing Poverty: The Role of Basic Social Services." United Nations Children's Fund Staff Working Paper, Evaluation, Policy and Planning Series EPP-00-001. New York.

Wallsten, Scott J. 2000. "An Econometric Analysis of Telecom Competition, Privatization, and Regulation in Africa and Latin America." Stanford University and the World Bank. [http://www.stanford.edu/~wallsten/telecom.pdf]. April 2001.

Wang, Bing, Zhu Qin and Zhicheng Guan. 2000. "University Technologies and Their Commercialization in China." In Pedro Conceicao, David Gibson, Manuel V. Heitor and Syed Shariq, eds., *Science, Technology and Innovation Policy: Opportunities and Challenges for the Knowledge Economy.* Westport, Conn.: Quorum Books.

Wang, Jia, Dean T. Jamison, Eduard Bos, Alexander Preker and John Peabody. 1999. *Measuring Country Performance on Health: Selected Indicators for 115 Countries.* Health, Nutrition, and Population Series. Washington, DC: World Bank.

Water Supply and Sanitation Collaborative Council. 1999. *Vision 21: A Shared Vision for Water Supply, Sanitation and Hygiene and a Framework for Future Action.* Stockholm.

Watkins, Kevin. 2000. *The Oxfam Education Report.* Oxford: Oxfam.

Weissman, Robert. 2001. "AIDS and Developing Countries: Facilitating Access to Essential Medicines." *Foreign Policy in Focus* 6 (6). [fpif.org/briefs/vol6/ v6n06aids.html]. April 2001.

Wendland, Wend. 2001. Correspondence on the World Intellectual Property Organization's initiative on intellectual property and genetic resources, traditional knowledge and folklore. 22 March. Geneva.

WHO (World Health Organization). 1997. *Health and Environment in Sustainable Development: Five Years after the Earth Summit.* Geneva.

———. 1998. *The World Health Report 1998—Life in the 21st Century: A Vision for All.* Geneva.

———. 2000a. *Health a Key to Prosperity: Success Stories in Developing Countries.* WHO/CDS/2000.4. Geneva.

———. 2000b. *The World Health Report 2000—Health Systems: Improving Performance.* Geneva.

———. 2001. "Globalisation, TRIPS and Access to Pharmaceuticals." WHO Policy Perspectives on Medicines 3. [www.who.int/medicines/pdf/trade6pager.pdf]. April 2001. Geneva.

Winch, Christopher. 1996. *Quality in Education.* Oxford: Blackwell.

WIPO (World Intellectual Property Organization). 2000. *Intellectual Property Statistics.* Publication A. Geneva.

———. 2001a. "Basic Facts about the Patent Cooperation Treaty." [www.wipo.int/pct/en/basic_facts/basic_facts.htm]. April 2001.

———. 2001b. "Intellectual Property and Genetic Resources, Traditional Knowledge and Folklore." Document PCIPD/2/7. Permanent Committee on Cooperation for Development Related to Intellectual Property, Geneva.

Wolfenbarger, L. L., and P. R. Phifer. 2000. "The Ecological Risks and Benefits of Genetically Engineered Plants." *Science* 290 (5499): 2088–93.

World Bank. 1993. *The East Asian Miracle.* New York: Oxford University Press.

———. 1999. *World Development Report 1998/1999: Knowledge for Development.* New York: Oxford University Press.

———. 2000a. *Annual Report 2000.* Washington, DC.

———. 2000b. *Republic of Korea: Transition to a Knowledge-Based Economy.* Report 20346-KO. East Asia and Pacific Region, Washington, DC.

———. 2000c. *World Development Indicators 2000.* CD-ROM. Washington, DC.

———. 2000d. *World Development Report 2000/2001: Attacking Poverty.* New York: Oxford University Press.

———. 2001a. Correspondence on GDP per capita growth rates. March. Washington, DC.

———. 2001b. Correspondence on income poverty. 15 February. Washington DC.

———. 2001c. "Global Poverty Monitoring." [http://www.worldbank.org/research/povmonitor]. April 2001.

———. 2001d. "Global Poverty Monitoring—Colombia." [www.worldbank.org/research/povmonitor/countrydetails/Colombia.htm]. 15 April 2001.

———. 2001e. "Global Poverty Monitoring—Romania." [www.worldbank.org/research/povmonitor/countrydetails/Romania.htm]. 15 April 2001.

———. 2001f. "International Development Goals: Strengthening Commitments and Measuring Progress." Background note prepared for the Westminster conference on child poverty, 26 February. HM Treasury and Department for International Development, United Kingdom.

———. 2001g. "World Bank Macro Time Series." Database. [www.worldbank.org/research/growth/GDNdata.htm]. Washington, DC.

———. 2001h. *World Development Indicators 2001.* CD-ROM. Washington, DC.

———. Forthcoming. *Global Development Finance.* Washington, DC.

World Economic Forum. 2000. "From the Global Digital Divide to the Global Digital Opportunity." Proposal submitted to the G-8 summit. Kyushu-Okinawa.

WRI (World Resources Institute). 1994. *World Resources 1994–95.* New York: Oxford University Press.

WTO (World Trade Organization). 1994. "Agreement on Trade-Related Aspects of Intellectual Property Rights." [www.wto.org/english/tratop_e/trips_e/t_agm0_e.htm]. March 2001.

W3C (World Wide Web Consortium). 2000. "A Little History of the World Wide Web." [www.w3.org/History.html]. 3 April 2001.

Yingjian, Wu. 2000. "The Construction of China's Information Infrastructure and International Cooperation." In Pedro Conceicao, David Gibson, Manuel V. Heitor and Syed Shariq, eds., *Science, Technology and Innovation Policy: Opportunities and Challenges for the Knowledge Economy.* Westport, Conn.: Quorum Books.

Yu, Q. Y. 1999. *The Implementation of China's Science and Technology Policy.* Westport, Conn.: Quorum Books.

Zakon, Robert Hobbes. 2000. "Hobbes' Internet Timeline." [info.isoc.org/guest/zakon/Internet/History/HIT.html]. 14 December 2000.

Zhang, Amei. 1997. "Poverty Alleviation in China: Commitment, Policies and Expenditures." Background paper prepared for *Human Development Report 1997.* United Nations Development Programme, Human Development Report Office, New York.

Human Development Indicators

Note on statistics in the Human Development Report

This Report's primary purpose is to assess the state of human development across the globe and provide a critical analysis of a specific theme each year. It combines thematic policy analysis with detailed country data that focus on human well-being, not just economic trends.

The indicators in the Report reflect the rich body of information available internationally. As a user of data, the Report presents statistical information that has been built up through the collective effort of many people and organizations. The Human Development Report Office gratefully acknowledges the collaboration of the many agencies that made publication of the latest data on human development possible (box 1).

To allow comparisons across countries and over time, where possible the indicator tables in the Report are based on internationally standardized data, collected and processed by sister agencies in the international system or, in a few cases, by other bodies. These organizations, whether collecting data from national sources or through their own surveys, harmonize definitions and collection methods to make their data as internationally comparable as possible. The data produced by these agencies may sometimes differ from those produced by national sources, often because of adjustments to harmonize data. In a few cases where data are not available from international organizations—particularly for the human development indices—other sources have been used. These sources are clearly referenced in the tables.

The text of the Report draws on a much wider variety of sources—commissioned papers, government documents, national human development reports, reports of international organizations, reports of nongovernmental organizations and journal articles and other scholarly publications. Where infor-mation from such sources is used in boxes or tables in the text, the source is shown and the full citation is given in the references. In addition, for each chapter a summary note outlines the major sources for the chapter, and endnotes specify the sources of statistical information not drawn from the Report's indicator tables.

CHANGES TO THE INDICATOR TABLES

The indicator tables in this year's Report reflect the continual efforts over the years to publish the best available data and to improve their presentation and transparency. While the structure of the indicator tables has been maintained, the tables have been streamlined to focus on indicators that are most reliable, meaningful and comparable across countries. This process has reduced the number of indicator tables—removing some tables altogether and consolidating others. In the important areas of health and education, however, additional space has been used to allow fuller analysis of the wealth of data on these issues.

This year's Report also makes more systematic use of purchasing power parity (PPP) rates of exchange, both in the indicator tables and in the text. For cross-country comparisons of real values where price differences matter, PPP data are more appropriate than data based on conventional exchange rates (box 2).

Improvements in this year's Report reflect the recent progress in measuring human development. One example is in the measurement of crime. In previous years the Report relied on data based on crimes reported to the police, information that depended heavily on a country's law enforcement and reporting system. Increasingly, however, data based directly on individuals' experiences with crime are available (box 3).

BOX 1

Major sources of data used in the Human Development Report

By generously sharing data, the following organizations made it possible for the *Human Development Report* to publish the important development statistics appearing in the indicator tables.

Carbon Dioxide Information Analysis Center (CDIAC) The CDIAC, a data and analysis centre of the US Department of Energy, focuses on the greenhouse effect and global climate change. It is the source of data on carbon dioxide emissions.

Food and Agriculture Organization (FAO) The FAO collects, analyses and disseminates information and data on food and agriculture. It is the source of data on food insecurity and agricultural indicators.

International Institute for Strategic Studies (IISS) An independent centre for research, information and debate on the problems of conflict, the IISS maintains an extensive military database. The data on armed forces are from its publication *The Military Balance.*

International Labour Organization (ILO) The ILO maintains an extensive statistical publication programme, with the *Yearbook of Labour Statistics* its most comprehensive collection of labour force data. The ILO is the source of wage and employment data and information on the ratification status of labour rights conventions.

International Monetary Fund (IMF) The IMF has an extensive programme for developing and compiling statistics on international financial transactions and balance of payments. Much of the financial data provided to the Human Development Report Office through other agencies originates from the IMF.

International Telecommunication Union (ITU) This specialized UN agency maintains an extensive collection of statistics on information and communications. The data on trends in telecommunications come from its database *World Telecommunication Indicators.*

Inter-Parliamentary Union (IPU) This organization provides data on trends in political participation and structures of democracy. The Report relies on the IPU for election-related data and information on women's political representation.

Joint United Nations Programme on HIV/AIDS (UNAIDS) This joint UN programme monitors the spread of HIV/AIDS and provides regular updates. Its *Report on the Global HIV/AIDS Epidemic* is the primary source of data on HIV/AIDS.

Luxembourg Income Study (LIS) A cooperative research project with 25 member countries, the LIS focuses on poverty and policy issues. It is the source of income poverty estimates for many OECD countries.

Organisation for Economic Co-operation and Development (OECD) The OECD publishes data on a variety of social and economic trends in its member countries as well as flows of aid. This year's Report presents data from the OECD on aid, employment and education.

Stockholm International Peace Research Institute (SIPRI) SIPRI conducts research on international peace and security. The *SIPRI Year-* *book: Armaments, Disarmament and International Security* is the source of data on military expenditure and arms transfers.

United Nations Children's Fund (UNICEF) UNICEF monitors the well-being of children and provides a wide array of data. Its *State of the World's Children* is an important source of data for the Report.

United Nations Conference on Trade and Development (UNCTAD) UNCTAD provides trade and economic statistics through a number of publications, including the *World Investment Report.* It is the original source of data on investment flows that the Human Development Report Office receives from other agencies.

United Nations Educational, Scientific and Cultural Organization (UNESCO) This specialized UN agency is the source of data on education-related matters. The Report relies on data published in UNESCO's *Statistical Yearbook* and *World Education Report* as well as data received directly from the agency.

United Nations High Commissioner for Refugees (UNHCR) This UN organization provides data on refugees through its publication *Refugees and Others of Concern to UNHCR: Statistical Overview.*

United Nations Interregional Crime and Justice Research Institute (UNICRI) This UN institute carries out international comparative research in support of the United Nations Crime Prevention and Criminal Justice Programme. It is the source of data on crime victims.

United Nations Multilateral Treaties Deposited with the Secretary General (UN Treaty Section) The Human Development Report Office compiles information on the status of major international human rights instruments and environmental treaties based on the database maintained by this UN office.

United Nations Population Division (UNPOP) This specialized UN office produces international data on population trends. The Human Development Report Office relies on *World Population Prospects* and *World Urbanization Prospects,* two of its main publications, for demographic estimates and projections.

United Nations Statistics Division (UNSD) The UNSD provides a wide range of statistical outputs and services. Much of the national accounts data provided to the Human Development Report Office by other agencies originates from the UNSD. This year's Report also relies on the UNSD for data on trade and energy.

World Bank The World Bank produces data on economic trends as well as a broad array of other indicators. Its *World Development Indicators* is the primary source for a number of indicators in the Report.

World Health Organization (WHO) This specialized agency maintains a large array of data series on health issues, the source for the health-related indicators in the Report.

World Intellectual Property Organization (WIPO) As a specialized UN agency, WIPO promotes the protection of intellectual property rights throughout the world through different kinds of cooperative efforts. The Report relies on WIPO for patent-related data.

BOX 2

The why's and wherefore's of purchasing power parities

This year's Report systematically uses purchasing power parity (PPP) rates of exchange for comparing economic measures across countries. It uses World Bank PPPs to provide the latest overall GDP measures covering a wide range of countries, and data based on the Penn World Tables for more detailed estimates and to facilitate consistent comparisons over long periods.

To compare economic statistics across countries, the data must first be converted into a common currency. Unlike conventional exchange rates, PPP rates of exchange allow this conversion to take account of price differences between countries. By eliminating differences in national price levels, the method facilitates comparisons of real values for income, poverty, inequality and expenditure patterns.

While the conceptual case for using PPP rates of exchange is clear, practical issues remain. World Bank PPPs have been compiled directly for 118 of the world's approximately 220 distinct national political entities. For countries for which PPPs are not directly compiled, estimates are made using econometric regression. This approach assumes that the economic characteristics and relationships commonly observed in surveyed countries also apply to the non-surveyed countries. While this assumption may not necessarily hold, fundamental economic relationships are thought to have general relevance and can be associated with independently observed variables in the non-surveyed countries.

The intricacies of the survey procedure and the need for countries to be globally and regionally linked have raised a number of issues relating to data reporting and in the past have led to significant delays in generating PPP results. As a result of these concerns, some governments and international institutions still refrain from using PPPs in regular operational policy decisions, though they use the method extensively in their analyses.

The importance of PPPs in economic analysis underlines the need for improvements in PPP data. This requires both institutional and financial support. In collaboration with Eurostat and the Organisation for Economic Co-operation and Development, the World Bank has set up an initiative to further improve the quality and availability of PPPs.

Source: Ward 2001.

BOX 3

The International Crime Victims Survey

The International Crime Victims Survey (ICVS) is a global programme of standardized surveys used to ask random samples of people about their experiences with crime and the police and their feelings of safety.

An international working group, jointly formed by the United Nations Interregional Crime and Justice Research Institute, the Dutch Ministry of Justice, the British Home Office and the Netherlands Institute for the Study of Criminality and Law Enforcement, is responsible for the conceptual and methodological development of the ICVS. The working group also coordinates with participating countries, develops and maintains the data sets, conducts analyses and disseminates the survey results.

Why is such a survey needed? There are two main reasons. First, measures of crime from other sources used in cross-country comparisons are often inadequate. Because the measures are based on police records, they can be greatly affected by differences among countries in how the police define, record and count crimes. Indeed, many developing countries have no central registry of crimes, leaving the ICVS as the only source of information. Second, the survey may prompt participating countries to conduct research on crime and victimization and to develop crime and criminal justice policies based on this research.

The project started in 14 industrial countries in 1989. Since then, 71 countries have participated at least once, for a total of 145 surveys. In most of the participating countries in Asia, Africa, Latin America and Central and Eastern Europe the surveys were conducted in the capital city through face-to-face interviews of a sample of 1,000 people. In industrial countries the surveys were done nationwide by telephone, generally with a sample of 2,000 people.

The ICVS produces data on victimization for a number of crimes, including assault, robbery, bribery, sexual assault and property crimes. Results from the most recent surveys, conducted in the 1990s, are presented in table 20.

Source: Van Kesteren 2001.

The Report also recognizes new efforts in time use, functional literacy and health statistics. While the Report has featured time use surveys in previous years, recent improvements in survey methods and country coverage have provided a wealth of new information, stepping beyond traditional economic measurement and into the lives and livelihoods of the world's people. Results from these new time use surveys are being compiled, and the Human Development Report Office hopes to include them in next year's Report (box 4). Surveys of functional literacy allow a more in-depth look at a vital area of human development than conventional literacy surveys have offered (box 5). And new efforts by the World Health Organization to develop better measures of the performance of health systems will no doubt enhance the assessment of human development in the area of health in future *Human Development Report*s (box 6).

Despite these strides in measuring human development, many gaps and problems remain. Sufficient and reliable data are still lacking in many areas of human development. Gaps throughout the tables demonstrate the pressing need for improvements in both the quantity and the quality of human development statistics.

Perhaps the starkest demonstration of these data problems is the large number of countries excluded from the human development index (HDI)—and therefore from the main indicator tables. The intent is to include all UN member countries, along with Switzerland and Hong Kong, China (SAR), in the HDI exercise. But because of a lack of reliable data, this year 12 more countries could no longer be included in the calculation of the HDI, reducing the total to 162. That leaves 29 countries excluded from the main indicator tables. What key indicators are available for these countries are presented in table 28.

DATA USED IN THE HUMAN DEVELOPMENT INDEX

The human development index is calculated using international data available at the time the Report is prepared. For a country to be included in the index, data ideally should be available from the relevant international statistical agency for all four components of the index.

BOX 4

Time use surveys in developing countries

Conventional measures of productive activity focus on paid economic activity. But for a comprehensive picture of work and employment, especially the activities performed by women, it is essential to measure subsistence agriculture and other unpaid productive activities as well as unpaid housework. Time use surveys provide a unique means to collect data on such activities.

Until recently time use data were not included in the data collection programmes of developing countries' national statistical offices. Most time use studies in these countries were case studies of one or a few localities and did not cover a 24-hour day.

Following the recommendations of the Fourth World Conference on Women (held in Beijing in 1995), however, at least 24 countries in Asia, Africa and Latin America and the Caribbean have begun work on national time use surveys. Although geographically, economically and culturally diverse, all these countries have come to consider national time use surveys an important statistical tool for measuring and valuing women's and men's paid and unpaid work and for increasing the visibility of women's work both at home and in the labour

market. Some of the surveys (such as those in Benin, Chad, India and Oman and the pilot studies in Nigeria and South Africa) also aim to improve the collection of data on women's economic activities, especially in the informal sector. In India the objectives include using the data for skills training and for designing poverty eradication programmes.

A joint project of the United Nations Statistics Division, the United Nations Development Programme and Canada's International Development Research Centre provided technical assistance to many of these countries. The project also studied methods and classifications used in national time use surveys to determine which procedures are suitable for collecting time use data in developing countries. And the United Nations Statistics Division is developing a technical guide on data collection methods and a classification of time use statistics that can be adapted to both developing and industrial countries. The Statistics Division will also compile data from the studies conducted in developing countries since 1995. These data should be available for *Human Development Report 2002*.

Source: Prepared by the United Nations Statistics Division based on UN (2000a).

When data are missing for one component, a country will still be included if a reasonable estimate can be found from another source.

As a result of revisions in data and methodology over time, the HDI values and ranks are not comparable across editions of the Report. Table 2 in this year's Report presents comparable HDI trends based on a consistent methodology and data.

LIFE EXPECTANCY AT BIRTH

The life expectancy estimates used in the Report are from the 2000 revision of the United Nations Population Division's database *World Population Prospects* (UN 2001d). The United Nations Population Division derives global demographic estimates and projections biannually. In the 2000 revision it made significant adjustments to further incorporate the demographic impact of HIV/AIDS, which has led to substantial changes in life expectancy estimates and projections for a number of countries, particularly in Sub-Saharan Africa.

The life expectancy estimates published by the United Nations Population Division are five-year averages. The life expectancy estimates for 1999 shown in table 1 (on the HDI) were obtained through linear interpolation based on these five-year averages. While the human development index requires yearly estimates, other tables showing data of this type, such as table 8 (on survival), present the unaltered five-year averages. Estimates for years after 2000 refer to medium-variant projections.

ADULT LITERACY

The adult literacy rates presented in the Report are estimates and projections from UNESCO's February 2000 literacy assessment. These estimates and projections are based on population data from the 1998 revision of the *World Population Prospects* database (UN 1998) and lit-

---

BOX 5

The International Adult Literacy Survey

The International Adult Literacy Survey (IALS) is the world's first international comparative assessment of adult literacy skills. The IALS study has combined household survey methods and educational assessment to provide comparable estimates of literacy skills for 24 countries. The survey tests representative samples of adults (aged 16–65) in their homes, asking them to undertake a range of common tasks using authentic materials from a wide range of social and cultural contexts. The IALS study is jointly sponsored by Statistics Canada, the US Center for Education Statistics and the Organisation for Economic Co-operation and Development (OECD).

While traditional measures of literacy focus primarily on the ability to decode the printed word, the IALS study defines literacy as the ability to understand and use printed information in daily activities at home, at work and in the community. It compiled the cross-country data to ensure that the results are comparable across countries with different languages and cultures and that any known sources of bias are corrected.

The IALS reports on three areas of literacy:
- *Prose literacy*—the knowledge and skills needed to understand and use information from texts, including editorials, news stories, poems and fiction.
- *Document literacy*—the knowledge and skills required to locate and use information in different formats, including maps, graphs, tables, payroll forms, job applications and transportation schedules.

- *Quantitative literacy*—the knowledge and skills required to apply arithmetic operations to numbers in printed materials, such as balancing a cheque book, figuring out a tip, completing an order form or determining the amount of interest on a loan from an advertisement.

Analysis of IALS data reveals several important facts. First, countries differ greatly in the level and social distribution of literacy skills. Second, these differences can be attributed to a handful of underlying factors, including differences among countries in the quantity and quality of initial education. The evidence also suggests, however, that several aspects of adult life, including the use of literacy skills at home and at work, transform skills after formal education. Finally, in many countries literacy skills play an important part in allocating economic opportunity, rewarding the skilled and penalizing the relatively unskilled.

The IALS will begin a new cycle of data collection in 2002 to better understand the role of literacy skills in determining economic outcomes for individuals and, by extension, for nations. A full analysis of the currently available data can be found in OECD and Statistics Canada (2000).

This Report uses the percentage of adults lacking functional literacy skills, defined on the basis of prose literacy, in the human poverty index for selected OECD countries, presented in table 4.

Source: Murray 2001.

---

eracy statistics collected through national population censuses, as well as refined estimation procedures.

COMBINED PRIMARY, SECONDARY AND TERTIARY GROSS ENROLMENT

The 1999 gross enrolment ratios presented in the Report are preliminary estimates from UNESCO based on the 1998 revision of population estimates and projections. Gross enrolment ratios are calculated by dividing the number of children enrolled in each level of schooling by the number of children in the age group corresponding to that level. Thus they are affected by the age- and sex-specific population estimates published by the United Nations Population Division and by the timing and methods of surveys by administrative registries, of population censuses and of national education surveys. Moreover, UNESCO periodically revises its methodology for estimating and projecting enrolment.

Gross enrolment ratios can hide important differences among countries because of differences in the age range corresponding to a level of education and in the duration of education programmes. Such factors as grade repetition can also lead to distortions in the data. For the HDI the preferred indicator of access to education as a proxy for knowledge would be net enrolment, for which data are collected for single years of age. Because this indicator measures enrolments only of a particular age group, the data could be more easily and reliably aggregated and used for international comparisons. But net enrolment data are available for too few countries to be used in the HDI.

GDP PER CAPITA (PPP US$)

The GDP per capita (PPP US$) data used in the HDI calculation are provided by the World Bank. The data are based on the latest International Comparison Programme (ICP) surveys, which cover 118 countries, the largest number ever in a round of ICP surveys. The World Bank has also provided estimates based on these surveys for another 44 countries and areas.

The surveys were carried out separately in different world regions. Because regional data are expressed in different currencies and may be based on different classification schemes or aggregation formulas, the data are not strictly comparable across regions. Price and expenditure data from the regional surveys were linked using a standard classification scheme to compile internationally comparable PPP data. The base year for the PPP data is 1996; data for the reference year, 1999, were extrapolated using relative price movements over time between each country and the United States, the base country. For countries not covered by the World Bank, PPP estimates are from the Penn World Tables 6.0 (Aten, Heston and Summers 2001).

DATA, METHODOLOGY AND PRESENTATION OF THE HUMAN DEVELOPMENT INDICATORS

Building on improvements made in 2000, this year's Report presents data for most key indicators with only a two-year lag between the reference date for the indicators and the date of the Report's release. The definitions of statistical terms have been revised and expanded to include all indicators for which short, meaningful definitions can be given. In addition, the transparency of sources has been further improved. When an agency provides data it has collected from another source, both sources are credited in the table notes. But when an international statistical organization has built on the work of many other contributors, only the ultimate source is given. The source notes also show the original data components used in any calculations by the Human Development Report Office to ensure that all calculations can be easily replicated.

COUNTRY CLASSIFICATIONS

The indicator tables cover UN member countries, along with Switzerland and Hong Kong, China (SAR). Countries are classified in four ways: in major world aggregates, by region, by human development level and by income (see the classification of countries). These designations do not necessarily express a judgement about the development stage of a particular country or area. Instead, they are classifications used by different organizations for operational purposes. The term *country* as used in the text and tables refers, as appropriate, to territories or areas.

Major world classifications. The three global groups are developing countries, Eastern Europe and the CIS and OECD. These groups are not mutually exclusive. (Replacing the OECD group with the high-income OECD group would produce mutually exclusive groups; see the classification of countries.) The classification *world* represents the universe of 162 countries covered in the main indicator tables.

Regional classifications. Developing countries are further classified into the following regions: Arab States, East Asia and the Pacific, Latin America and the Caribbean, South Asia, Southern Europe and Sub-Saharan Africa. These regional classifications are consistent with the Regional Bureaux of UNDP. An additional classification is least developed countries, as defined by the United Nations (and listed in UN 1996). Senegal was added to the list of least developed countries on 12 April 2001 but is not included in the aggregates for this group in this year's Report because the addition was made after the aggregates were finalized.

Human development classifications. All countries are classified into three clusters by achievement in human development: high human development (with an HDI of 0.800 or above), medium human development (0.500–0.799) and low human development (less than 0.500).

Income classifications. All countries are grouped by income using World Bank classifications: high income (GNP per capita of $9,266 or more in 1999), middle income ($756–9,265) and low income ($755 or less).

AGGREGATES AND GROWTH RATES

Aggregates. Aggregates for the classifications described above are presented at the end of most tables. Aggregates that are the total for the classification (such as for population) are indicated by a T. As a result of rounding, aggregates for subgroups may not always sum to the world total. All other aggregates are weighted averages.

Unless otherwise specified, an aggregate is shown for a classification only when data are available for two-thirds of the countries and represent two-thirds of the available weight in that classification. The Human Development Report Office does not fill in missing data for the purpose of aggregation. Therefore, aggregates for each classification represent only the countries for which data are available and are shown in the tables. Aggregates are not shown where appropriate weighting procedures were unavailable.

Aggregates for indices, for growth rates and for indicators covering more than one point in time are based only on countries for which data exist for all necessary points in time. For the world classification, which refers only to the

---

BOX 6

A composite index measuring the performance of health systems

In a bold new initiative the World Health Organization has developed a composite index measuring the performance of health systems in 191 countries. According to *World Health Report 2000* (WHO 2000b), even without new medical technologies important advances can be made in health outcomes—just by improving the way currently available health interventions are organized and delivered. Differences in health outcomes between countries often reflect differences in the performance of their health systems. And differences in outcomes among groups within countries can often be attributed to disparities in the health services available to them.

A notable feature of the composite index is that it summarizes performance in terms of both the over-

all level of goal achievement and the distribution of that achievement, giving equal weight to these two aspects. Five components make up the index: overall good health, distribution of good health, overall responsiveness, distribution of responsiveness and fairness in financial contributions. Good health is measured by disability-adjusted life expectancy, and the distribution of good health by an equality of child survival index. The overall responsiveness of the health system and the distribution of responsiveness are measured on the basis of survey responses relating to respect for patients and client orientation. And fairness in financial contributions is estimated using the ratio of households' total spending on health to their permanent income above subsistence.

Source: Based on WHO (2000b).

universe of 162 countries, aggregates are not always shown where no aggregate is shown for one or more regions.

Aggregates in the *Human Development Report* will not always conform to those in other publications because of differences in country classifications and methodology. Where indicated, aggregates are calculated by the statistical agency that provides the indicator itself.

Growth rates. Multiyear growth rates are expressed as average annual rates of change. In calculations of rates by the Human Development Report Office, only the beginning and end points are used. Year-to-year growth rates are expressed as annual percentage changes.

PRESENTATION

In the indicator tables countries and areas are ranked in descending order by their HDI value. To locate a country in the tables, refer to the key to countries on the back cover flap, which lists countries alphabetically with their HDI rank.

Short citations of sources are given at the end of each table. These correspond to full references in the statistical references, which follow the indicator tables and technical notes. Where appropriate, definitions of indicators appear in the definitions of statistical terms. All other relevant information appears in the notes at the end of each table.

Owing to lack of comparable data, not all countries have been included in the indicator tables. For UN member countries not included in the main indicator tables, basic human development indicators are presented in a separate table.

In the absence of the words *annual, annual rate* or *growth rate,* a hyphen between two years indicates that the data were collected during one of the years shown, such as 1995-99. A slash between two years indicates an average for the years shown, such as 1996/98. The following signs have been used:

.. Data not available.

(.) Less than half the unit shown.

< Less than.

– Not applicable.

T Total.

1 Human development index

HDI rank [a]		Life expectancy at birth (years) 1999	Adult literacy rate (% age 15 and above) 1999	Combined primary, secondary and tertiary gross enrolment ratio (%) [b] 1999	GDP per capita (PPP US$) 1999	Life expectancy index 1999	Education index 1999	GDP index 1999	Human development index (HDI) value 1999	GDP per capita (PPP US$) rank minus HDI rank [c]
High human development										
1	Norway	78.4	.. [d]	97	28,433	0.89	0.98	0.94	0.939	2
2	Australia	78.8	.. [d]	116 [e]	24,574	0.90	0.99	0.92	0.936	10
3	Canada	78.7	.. [d]	97	26,251	0.89	0.98	0.93	0.936	3
4	Sweden	79.6	.. [d]	101 [e]	22,636	0.91	0.99	0.90	0.936	13
5	Belgium	78.2	.. [d]	109 [e]	25,443	0.89	0.99	0.92	0.935	4
6	United States	76.8	.. [d]	95	31,872	0.86	0.98	0.96	0.934	-4
7	Iceland	79.1	.. [d]	89	27,835	0.90	0.96	0.94	0.932	-3
8	Netherlands	78.0	.. [d]	102 [e]	24,215	0.88	0.99	0.92	0.931	5
9	Japan	80.8	.. [d]	82	24,898	0.93	0.93	0.92	0.928	2
10	Finland	77.4	.. [d]	103 [e]	23,096	0.87	0.99	0.91	0.925	5
11	Switzerland	78.8	.. [d]	84	27,171	0.90	0.94	0.94	0.924	-6
12	Luxembourg	77.2	.. [d]	73 [f]	42,769 [g]	0.87	0.90	1.00	0.924	-11
13	France	78.4	.. [d]	94	22,897	0.89	0.97	0.91	0.924	3
14	United Kingdom	77.5	.. [d]	106 [e]	22,093	0.87	0.99	0.90	0.923	5
15	Denmark	76.1	.. [d]	97	25,869	0.85	0.98	0.93	0.921	-7
16	Austria	77.9	.. [d]	90	25,089	0.88	0.96	0.92	0.921	-6
17	Germany	77.6	.. [d]	94	23,742	0.88	0.97	0.91	0.921	-3
18	Ireland	76.4	.. [d]	91	25,918	0.86	0.96	0.93	0.916	-11
19	New Zealand	77.4	.. [d]	99	19,104	0.87	0.99	0.88	0.913	3
20	Italy	78.4	98.4	84	22,172	0.89	0.94	0.90	0.909	-2
21	Spain	78.3	97.6	95	18,079	0.89	0.97	0.87	0.908	6
22	Israel	78.6	95.8	83	18,440	0.89	0.91	0.87	0.893	3
23	Greece	78.1	97.1	81	15,414	0.89	0.92	0.84	0.881	10
24	Hong Kong, China (SAR)	79.4	93.3	63	22,090	0.91	0.83	0.90	0.880	-4
25	Cyprus	77.9	96.9	69 [h]	19,006	0.88	0.87	0.88	0.877	-2
26	Singapore	77.4	92.1	75	20,767	0.87	0.87	0.89	0.876	-5
27	Korea, Rep. of	74.7	97.6	90	15,712	0.83	0.95	0.84	0.875	5
28	Portugal	75.5	91.9	96	16,064	0.84	0.93	0.85	0.874	2
29	Slovenia	75.3	99.6 [d]	83	15,977	0.84	0.94	0.85	0.874	2
30	Malta	77.9	91.8	80	15,189 [i]	0.88	0.88	0.84	0.866	5
31	Barbados	76.6	97.0 [j, k]	77	14,353	0.86	0.90	0.83	0.864	5
32	Brunei Darussalam	75.7	91.0	76	17,868 [j, l]	0.85	0.86	0.87	0.857	-4
33	Czech Republic	74.7	.. [d]	70	13,018	0.83	0.89	0.81	0.844	6
34	Argentina	73.2	96.7	83	12,277	0.80	0.92	0.80	0.842	6
35	Slovakia	73.1	.. [d]	76	10,591	0.80	0.91	0.78	0.831	8
36	Hungary	71.1	99.3 [d]	81	11,430	0.77	0.93	0.79	0.829	5
37	Uruguay	74.2	97.7	79	8,879	0.82	0.92	0.75	0.828	9
38	Poland	73.1	99.7 [d]	84	8,450	0.80	0.94	0.74	0.828	11
39	Chile	75.2	95.6	78	8,652	0.84	0.90	0.74	0.825	9
40	Bahrain	73.1	87.1	80	13,688 [i]	0.80	0.85	0.82	0.824	-3
41	Costa Rica	76.2	95.5	67	8,860	0.85	0.86	0.75	0.821	6
42	Bahamas	69.2	95.7	74	15,258 [i]	0.74	0.89	0.84	0.820	-8
43	Kuwait	76.0	81.9	59	17,289 [i]	0.85	0.74	0.86	0.818	-14
44	Estonia	70.3	98.0 [j, k]	86	8,355	0.76	0.94	0.74	0.812	6
45	United Arab Emirates	74.8	75.1	68	18,162 [i]	0.83	0.73	0.87	0.809	-19
46	Croatia	73.6	98.2	68	7,387	0.81	0.88	0.72	0.803	10
47	Lithuania	71.8	99.5 [d]	80	6,656	0.78	0.93	0.70	0.803	13
48	Qatar	69.3	80.8	75	18,789 [j, l]	0.74	0.79	0.87	0.801	-24
Medium human development										
49	Trinidad and Tobago	74.1	93.5	65	8,176	0.82	0.84	0.74	0.798	4
50	Latvia	70.1	99.8 [d]	82	6,264	0.75	0.93	0.69	0.791	12

HDI rank [a]		Life expectancy at birth (years) 1999	Adult literacy rate (% age 15 and above) 1999	Combined primary, secondary and tertiary gross enrolment ratio (%) [b] 1999	GDP per capita (PPP US$) 1999	Life expectancy index 1999	Education index 1999	GDP index 1999	Human development index (HDI) value 1999	GDP per capita (PPP US$) rank minus HDI rank [c]
51	Mexico	72.4	91.1	71	8,297	0.79	0.84	0.74	0.790	0
52	Panama	73.9	91.7	74	5,875	0.81	0.86	0.68	0.784	15
53	Belarus	68.5	99.5 [d]	77	6,876	0.73	0.92	0.71	0.782	5
54	Belize	73.8	93.1	73	4,959	0.81	0.86	0.65	0.776	21
55	Russian Federation	66.1	99.5 [d]	78	7,473	0.69	0.92	0.72	0.775	0
56	Malaysia	72.2	87.0	66	8,209	0.79	0.80	0.74	0.774	-4
57	Bulgaria	70.8	98.3	72	5,071	0.76	0.90	0.66	0.772	16
58	Romania	69.8	98.0	69	6,041	0.75	0.88	0.68	0.772	6
59	Libyan Arab Jamahiriya	70.3	79.1	92	7,570 [j, l]	0.75	0.83	0.72	0.770	-5
60	Macedonia, TFYR	73.0	94.0 [j, k]	70	4,651	0.80	0.86	0.64	0.766	20
61	Venezuela	72.7	92.3	65	5,495	0.79	0.83	0.67	0.765	10
62	Colombia	70.9	91.5	73	5,749	0.76	0.85	0.68	0.765	6
63	Mauritius	71.1	84.2	63	9,107	0.77	0.77	0.75	0.765	-19
64	Suriname	70.4	93.0 [j, k]	83	4,178 [i]	0.76	0.89	0.62	0.758	23
65	Lebanon	72.9	85.6	78	4,705 [i]	0.80	0.83	0.64	0.758	13
66	Thailand	69.9	95.3	60	6,132	0.75	0.84	0.69	0.757	-3
67	Fiji	68.8	92.6	84	4,799	0.73	0.90	0.65	0.757	10
68	Saudi Arabia	71.3	76.1	61	10,815	0.77	0.71	0.78	0.754	-26
69	Brazil	67.5	84.9	80	7,037	0.71	0.83	0.71	0.750	-12
70	Philippines	69.0	95.1	82	3,805	0.73	0.91	0.61	0.749	21
71	Oman	70.8	70.3	58	13,356 [j, l]	0.76	0.66	0.82	0.747	-33
72	Armenia	72.7	98.3	80	2,215 [i]	0.80	0.92	0.52	0.745	44
73	Peru	68.5	89.6	80	4,622	0.72	0.86	0.64	0.743	8
74	Ukraine	68.1	99.6 [d]	77	3,458	0.72	0.92	0.59	0.742	22
75	Kazakhstan	64.4	99.0 [j, k]	77	4,951	0.66	0.92	0.65	0.742	1
76	Georgia	73.0	99.6 [d, j, k]	70	2,431	0.80	0.89	0.53	0.742	32
77	Maldives	66.1	96.2	77	4,423 [i]	0.68	0.90	0.63	0.739	7
78	Jamaica	75.1	86.4	62	3,561	0.84	0.78	0.60	0.738	17
79	Azerbaijan	71.3	97.0 [j, k]	71	2,850	0.77	0.88	0.56	0.738	27
80	Paraguay	69.9	93.0	64	4,384	0.75	0.83	0.63	0.738	5
81	Sri Lanka	71.9	91.4	70	3,279	0.78	0.84	0.58	0.735	19
82	Turkey	69.5	84.6	62	6,380	0.74	0.77	0.69	0.735	-21
83	Turkmenistan	65.9	98.0 [j, k]	81	3,347	0.68	0.92	0.59	0.730	16
84	Ecuador	69.8	91.0	77	2,994	0.75	0.86	0.57	0.726	19
85	Albania	73.0	84.0	71	3,189	0.80	0.80	0.58	0.725	16
86	Dominican Republic	67.2	83.2	72	5,507	0.70	0.79	0.67	0.722	-16
87	China	70.2	83.5	73	3,617	0.75	0.80	0.60	0.718	7
88	Jordan	70.1	89.2	55	3,955	0.75	0.78	0.61	0.714	2
89	Tunisia	69.9	69.9	74	5,957	0.75	0.71	0.68	0.714	-23
90	Iran, Islamic Rep. of	68.5	75.7	73	5,531	0.73	0.75	0.67	0.714	-21
91	Cape Verde	69.4	73.6	77	4,490	0.74	0.75	0.63	0.708	-9
92	Kyrgyzstan	67.4	97.0 [j, k]	68	2,573	0.71	0.87	0.54	0.707	15
93	Guyana	63.3	98.4	66	3,640	0.64	0.87	0.60	0.704	0
94	South Africa	53.9	84.9	93	8,908	0.48	0.87	0.75	0.702	-49
95	El Salvador	69.5	78.3	63	4,344	0.74	0.73	0.63	0.701	-9
96	Samoa (Western)	68.9	80.2	65	4,047	0.73	0.75	0.62	0.701	-8
97	Syrian Arab Republic	70.9	73.6	63	4,454	0.76	0.70	0.63	0.700	-14
98	Moldova, Rep. of	66.6	98.7	72	2,037	0.69	0.90	0.50	0.699	19
99	Uzbekistan	68.7	88.5	76	2,251	0.73	0.84	0.52	0.698	15
100	Algeria	69.3	66.6	72	5,063	0.74	0.69	0.66	0.693	-26

HDI rank [a]		Life expectancy at birth (years) 1999	Adult literacy rate (% age 15 and above) 1999	Combined primary, secondary and tertiary gross enrolment ratio (%) [b] 1999	GDP per capita (PPP US$) 1999	Life expectancy index 1999	Education index 1999	GDP index 1999	Human development index (HDI) value 1999	GDP per capita (PPP US$) rank minus HDI rank [c]
101	Viet Nam	67.8	93.1	67	1,860	0.71	0.84	0.49	0.682	19
102	Indonesia	65.8	86.3	65	2,857	0.68	0.79	0.56	0.677	3
103	Tajikistan	67.4	99.1 [d]	67	1,031 [j,l]	0.71	0.88	0.39	0.660	36
104	Bolivia	62.0	85.0	70	2,355	0.62	0.80	0.53	0.648	7
105	Egypt	66.9	54.6	76	3,420	0.70	0.62	0.59	0.635	-8
106	Nicaragua	68.1	68.2	63	2,279	0.72	0.66	0.52	0.635	7
107	Honduras	65.7	74.0	61	2,340	0.68	0.70	0.53	0.634	5
108	Guatemala	64.5	68.1	49	3,674	0.66	0.62	0.60	0.626	-16
109	Gabon	52.6	63.0 [j,k]	86	6,024	0.46	0.71	0.68	0.617	-44
110	Equatorial Guinea	50.6	82.2	64	4,676	0.43	0.76	0.64	0.610	-31
111	Namibia	44.9	81.4	78	5,468	0.33	0.80	0.67	0.601	-39
112	Morocco	67.2	48.0	52	3,419	0.70	0.49	0.59	0.596	-14
113	Swaziland	47.0	78.9	72	3,987	0.37	0.77	0.62	0.583	-24
114	Botswana	41.9	76.4	70	6,872	0.28	0.74	0.71	0.577	-55
115	India	62.9	56.5	56	2,248	0.63	0.56	0.52	0.571	0
116	Mongolia	62.5	62.3	58	1,711	0.62	0.61	0.47	0.569	7
117	Zimbabwe	42.9	88.0	65	2,876	0.30	0.80	0.56	0.554	-13
118	Myanmar	56.0	84.4	55	1,027 [j,l]	0.52	0.75	0.39	0.551	22
119	Ghana	56.6	70.3	42	1,881	0.53	0.61	0.49	0.542	0
120	Lesotho	47.9	82.9	61	1,854	0.38	0.75	0.49	0.541	1
121	Cambodia	56.4	68.2 [m]	62	1,361	0.52	0.66	0.44	0.541	13
122	Papua New Guinea	56.2	63.9	39	2,367	0.52	0.55	0.53	0.534	-12
123	Kenya	51.3	81.5	51	1,022	0.44	0.71	0.39	0.514	18
124	Comoros	59.4	59.2	36	1,429	0.57	0.51	0.44	0.510	7
125	Cameroon	50.0	74.8	43	1,573	0.42	0.64	0.46	0.506	2
126	Congo	51.1	79.5	63	727	0.44	0.74	0.33	0.502	29

Low human development

127	Pakistan	59.6	45.0	40	1,834	0.58	0.43	0.49	0.498	-5
128	Togo	51.6	56.3	62	1,410	0.44	0.58	0.44	0.489	5
129	Nepal	58.1	40.4	60	1,237	0.55	0.47	0.42	0.480	7
130	Bhutan	61.5	42.0 [j,k]	33 [n]	1,341	0.61	0.39	0.43	0.477	5
131	Lao People's Dem. Rep.	53.1	47.3	58	1,471	0.47	0.51	0.45	0.476	-2
132	Bangladesh	58.9	40.8	37	1,483	0.57	0.39	0.45	0.470	-4
133	Yemen	60.1	45.2	51	806	0.59	0.47	0.35	0.468	16
134	Haiti	52.4	48.8	52	1,464	0.46	0.50	0.45	0.467	4
135	Madagascar	52.2	65.7	44	799	0.45	0.59	0.35	0.462	16
136	Nigeria	51.5	62.6	45	853	0.44	0.57	0.36	0.455	11
137	Djibouti	44.0	63.4	22	2,377 [j,l]	0.32	0.50	0.53	0.447	-28
138	Sudan	55.6	56.9	34	664 [j,l]	0.51	0.49	0.32	0.439	19
139	Mauritania	51.1	41.6	41	1,609	0.43	0.41	0.46	0.437	-14
140	Tanzania, U. Rep. of	51.1	74.7	32	501	0.44	0.61	0.27	0.436	21
141	Uganda	43.2	66.1	45	1,167	0.30	0.59	0.41	0.435	-4
142	Congo, Dem. Rep. of the	51.0	60.3	32	801 [i]	0.43	0.51	0.35	0.429	8
143	Zambia	41.0	77.2	49	756	0.27	0.68	0.34	0.427	9
144	Côte d'Ivoire	47.8	45.7	38	1,654	0.38	0.43	0.47	0.426	-20
145	Senegal	52.9	36.4	36	1,419	0.47	0.36	0.44	0.423	-13
146	Angola	45.0	42.0 [j,k]	23	3,179	0.33	0.36	0.58	0.422	-44
147	Benin	53.6	39.0	45	933	0.48	0.41	0.37	0.420	-4
148	Eritrea	51.8	52.7	26	880	0.45	0.44	0.36	0.416	-3
149	Gambia	45.9	35.7	45	1,580	0.35	0.39	0.46	0.398	-23
150	Guinea	47.1	35.0 [j,k]	28	1,934	0.37	0.33	0.49	0.397	-32

HDI rank [a]	Life expectancy at birth (years) 1999	Adult literacy rate (% age 15 and above) 1999	Combined primary, secondary and tertiary gross enrolment ratio (%) [b] 1999	GDP per capita (PPP US$) 1999	Life expectancy index 1999	Education index 1999	GDP index 1999	Human development index (HDI) value 1999	GDP per capita (PPP US$) rank minus HDI rank [c]
151 Malawi	40.3	59.2	73	586	0.26	0.64	0.30	0.397	8
152 Rwanda	39.9	65.8	40	885	0.25	0.57	0.36	0.395	-8
153 Mali	51.2	39.8	28	753	0.44	0.36	0.34	0.378	0
154 Central African Republic	44.3	45.4	24	1,166	0.32	0.38	0.41	0.372	-16
155 Chad	45.5	41.0	31	850	0.34	0.38	0.36	0.359	-7
156 Guinea-Bissau	44.5	37.7	37	678	0.33	0.37	0.32	0.339	0
157 Mozambique	39.8	43.2	23	861	0.25	0.36	0.36	0.323	-11
158 Ethiopia	44.1	37.4	27	628	0.32	0.34	0.31	0.321	0
159 Burkina Faso	46.1	23.0	23	965	0.35	0.23	0.38	0.320	-17
160 Burundi	40.6	46.9	19	578	0.26	0.37	0.29	0.309	0
161 Niger	44.8	15.3	16	753	0.33	0.15	0.34	0.274	-7
162 Sierra Leone	38.3	32.0 [j, k]	27	448	0.22	0.30	0.25	0.258	0
Developing countries	64.5	72.9	61	3,530	0.66	0.69	0.59	0.647	–
Least developed countries	51.7	51.6	38	1,170	0.45	0.47	0.41	0.442	–
Arab States	66.4	61.3	63	4,550	0.69	0.62	0.64	0.648	–
East Asia and the Pacific	69.2	85.3	71	3,950	0.74	0.81	0.61	0.719	–
Latin America and the Caribbean	69.6	87.8	74	6,880	0.74	0.83	0.71	0.760	–
South Asia	62.5	55.1	53	2,280	0.63	0.54	0.52	0.564	–
Sub-Saharan Africa	48.8	59.6	42	1,640	0.40	0.54	0.47	0.467	–
Eastern Europe and the CIS	68.5	98.6	77	6,290	0.73	0.91	0.69	0.777	–
OECD	76.6	.. [o]	87	22,020	0.86	0.94	0.90	0.900 [o]	–
High-income OECD	78.0	.. [o]	94	26,050	0.88	0.97	0.93	0.928 [o]	–
High human development	77.3	.. [o]	91	23,410	0.87	0.96	0.91	0.914 [o]	–
Medium human development	66.8	78.5	67	3,850	0.70	0.75	0.61	0.684	–
Low human development	52.6	48.9	38	1,200	0.46	0.45	0.41	0.442	–
High income	78.0	.. [o]	93	25,860	0.88	0.97	0.93	0.926 [o]	–
Middle income	69.5	85.7	74	5,310	0.74	0.82	0.66	0.740	–
Low income	59.4	61.8	51	1,910	0.57	0.58	0.49	0.549	–
World	66.7	.. [o]	65	6,980	0.70	0.74	0.71	0.716 [o]	–

Note: The human development index has been calculated for UN member countries with reliable data in each of its components, as well as for two non-members, Switzerland and Hong Kong, China (SAR). For data on the remaining 29 UN member countries see table 28.

a. The HDI rank is determined using HDI values to the fifth decimal point.

b. Preliminary UNESCO estimates, subject to further revision.

c. A positive figure indicates that the HDI rank is higher than the GDP per capita (PPP US$) rank, a negative the opposite.

d. For purposes of calculating the HDI a value of 99.0% was applied.

e. For purposes of calculating the HDI a value of 100% was applied.

f. The ratio is an underestimate, as many secondary and tertiary students pursue their studies in nearby countries.

g. For purposes of calculating the HDI a value of $40,000 (PPP US$) was applied.

h. Excludes Turkish students and population.

i. Data refer to a year other than that specified.

j. Data refer to a year or period other than that specified, differ from the standard definition or refer to only part of a country.

k. UNICEF 2000.

l. Aten, Heston and Summers 2001.

m. UNESCO 2001a.

n. Human Development Report Office estimate based on national sources.

o. For purposes of calculating the HDI a value of 99.0% was applied for OECD countries for which data on adult literacy are missing. The resulting aggregates (97.5% for OECD countries, 98.8% for high-income OECD countries, 98.5% for high human development countries, 98.6% for high-income countries and 79.2% for the world) were used in obtaining the HDI aggregates.

Source: Column 1: UN 2001d; *column 2:* unless otherwise noted, UNESCO 2000a; *column 3:* UNESCO 2001b; *column 4:* unless otherwise noted, World Bank 2001b; aggregates calculated for the Human Development Report Office by the World Bank; *column 5:* calculated on the basis of data in column 1; *column 6:* calculated on the basis of data in columns 2 and 3; *column 7:* calculated on the basis of data in column 4; *column 8:* calculated on the basis of data in columns 5-7; see technical note 1 for details; *column 9:* calculated on the basis of data in columns 4 and 8.

2 Human development index trends

HDI rank	1975	1980	1985	1990	1995	1999
High human development						
1 Norway	0.856	0.875	0.887	0.899	0.924	0.939
2 Australia	0.842	0.859	0.871	0.886	0.926	0.936
3 Canada	0.867	0.882	0.904	0.925	0.930	0.936
4 Sweden	0.862	0.872	0.882	0.892	0.924	0.936
5 Belgium	0.845	0.861	0.874	0.895	0.925	0.935
6 United States	0.861	0.882	0.896	0.912	0.923	0.934
7 Iceland	0.860	0.883	0.891	0.910	0.916	0.932
8 Netherlands	0.860	0.872	0.886	0.900	0.921	0.931
9 Japan	0.851	0.876	0.891	0.907	0.920	0.928
10 Finland	0.835	0.854	0.872	0.894	0.907	0.925
11 Switzerland	0.872	0.884	0.891	0.904	0.912	0.924
12 Luxembourg	0.826	0.841	0.855	0.879	0.907	0.924
13 France	0.846	0.862	0.874	0.896	0.913	0.924
14 United Kingdom	0.839	0.846	0.856	0.876	0.914	0.923
15 Denmark	0.866	0.874	0.881	0.889	0.905	0.921
16 Austria	0.839	0.853	0.866	0.889	0.908	0.921
17 Germany	..	..	..	..	0.905	0.921
18 Ireland	0.816	0.828	0.843	0.868	0.891	0.916
19 New Zealand	0.846	0.853	0.865	0.873	0.900	0.913
20 Italy	0.827	0.845	0.855	0.878	0.895	0.909
21 Spain	0.817	0.837	0.853	0.875	0.893	0.908
22 Israel	0.804	0.825	0.843	0.859	0.879	0.893
23 Greece	0.800	0.821	0.841	0.857	0.867	0.881
24 Hong Kong, China (SAR)	0.754	0.793	0.820	0.857	0.875	0.880
25 Cyprus	..	0.800	0.819	0.843	0.864	0.877
26 Singapore	0.719	0.753	0.779	0.816	0.855	0.876
27 Korea, Rep. of	0.687	0.729	0.771	0.814	0.851	0.875
28 Portugal	0.735	0.758	0.785	0.818	0.853	0.874
29 Slovenia	..	..	..	0.843	0.850	0.874
30 Malta	..	..	..	..	..	0.866
31 Barbados	..	..	..	..	..	0.864
32 Brunei Darussalam	..	..	..	..	..	0.857
33 Czech Republic	..	..	..	0.833	0.841	0.844
34 Argentina	0.784	0.798	0.804	0.807	0.829	0.842
35 Slovakia	..	..	0.811	0.818	0.816	0.831
36 Hungary	0.775	0.791	0.803	0.803	0.807	0.829
37 Uruguay	0.755	0.775	0.779	0.800	0.813	0.828
38 Poland	..	..	..	0.790	0.807	0.828
39 Chile	0.700	0.735	0.752	0.779	0.809	0.825
40 Bahrain	..	..	..	..	..	0.824
41 Costa Rica	0.745	0.769	0.770	0.789	0.807	0.821
42 Bahamas	..	..	..	..	..	0.820
43 Kuwait	..	..	..	..	..	0.818
44 Estonia	..	..	..	..	..	0.812
45 United Arab Emirates	..	..	..	..	..	0.809
46 Croatia	..	..	..	0.794	0.787	0.803
47 Lithuania	..	..	..	0.814	0.780	0.803
48 Qatar	..	..	..	..	..	0.801
Medium human development						
49 Trinidad and Tobago	0.719	0.752	0.771	0.778	0.784	0.798
50 Latvia	..	0.788	0.801	0.803	0.761	0.791

HDI rank		1975	1980	1985	1990	1995	1999
51	Mexico	0.688	0.732	0.750	0.759	0.772	0.790
52	Panama	0.711	0.730	0.745	0.746	0.769	0.784
53	Belarus	..	..	..	0.808	0.774	0.782
54	Belize	..	0.710	0.718	0.751	0.769	0.776
55	Russian Federation	..	0.809	0.826	0.823	0.778	0.775
56	Malaysia	0.614	0.657	0.691	0.720	0.758	0.774
57	Bulgaria	..	0.760	0.781	0.783	0.775	0.772
58	Romania	0.753	0.787	0.793	0.775	0.771	0.772
59	Libyan Arab Jamahiriya	..	..	..	..	..	0.770
60	Macedonia, TFYR	..	..	..	..	..	0.766
61	Venezuela	0.715	0.730	0.737	0.756	0.764	0.765
62	Colombia	0.657	0.686	0.700	0.720	0.746	0.765
63	Mauritius	0.628	0.655	0.685	0.721	0.745	0.765
64	Suriname	..	..	..	..	..	0.758
65	Lebanon	..	..	..	..	..	0.758
66	Thailand	0.603	0.645	0.675	0.713	0.749	0.757
67	Fiji	0.656	0.679	0.693	0.719	0.740	0.757
68	Saudi Arabia	0.587	0.647	0.669	0.706	0.736	0.754
69	Brazil	0.641	0.676	0.690	0.710	0.734	0.750
70	Philippines	0.649	0.683	0.687	0.716	0.733	0.749
71	Oman	..	..	..	..	..	0.747
72	Armenia	..	..	..	..	..	0.745
73	Peru	0.639	0.668	0.691	0.702	0.729	0.743
74	Ukraine	..	..	..	0.793	0.744	0.742
75	Kazakhstan	..	..	..	..	..	0.742
76	Georgia	..	..	..	..	..	0.742
77	Maldives	..	..	..	..	..	0.739
78	Jamaica	0.688	0.692	0.694	0.722	0.735	0.738
79	Azerbaijan	..	..	..	..	..	0.738
80	Paraguay	0.663	0.698	0.704	0.716	0.733	0.738
81	Sri Lanka	0.614	0.648	0.674	0.695	0.717	0.735
82	Turkey	0.592	0.616	0.653	0.684	0.716	0.735
83	Turkmenistan	..	..	..	..	..	0.730
84	Ecuador	0.623	0.669	0.690	0.700	0.715	0.726
85	Albania	..	0.672	0.689	0.700	0.701	0.725
86	Dominican Republic	0.616	0.645	0.667	0.675	0.696	0.722
87	China	0.522	0.553	0.590	0.624	0.679	0.718
88	Jordan	..	0.637	0.659	0.677	0.704	0.714
89	Tunisia	0.512	0.564	0.611	0.644	0.680	0.714
90	Iran, Islamic Rep. of	0.556	0.563	0.607	0.645	0.688	0.714
91	Cape Verde	..	..	0.584	0.624	0.676	0.708
92	Kyrgyzstan	..	..	..	..	..	0.707
93	Guyana	0.678	0.681	0.670	0.676	0.699	0.704
94	South Africa	0.648	0.661	0.681	0.712	0.722	0.702
95	El Salvador	0.585	0.584	0.604	0.642	0.681	0.701
96	Samoa (Western)	..	0.555	0.646	0.661	0.685	0.701
97	Syrian Arab Republic	0.551	0.593	0.627	0.647	0.677	0.700
98	Moldova, Rep. of	..	..	..	0.758	0.704	0.699
99	Uzbekistan	..	..	..	0.693	0.683	0.698
100	Algeria	0.507	0.555	0.605	0.641	0.664	0.693

HDI rank		1975	1980	1985	1990	1995	1999
101	Viet Nam	..	..	0.581	0.604	0.647	0.682
102	Indonesia	0.467	0.529	0.581	0.622	0.662	0.677
103	Tajikistan	..	..	..	..	..	0.660
104	Bolivia	0.512	0.546	0.572	0.596	0.628	0.648
105	Egypt	0.433	0.481	0.531	0.573	0.603	0.635
106	Nicaragua	0.569	0.580	0.588	0.596	0.618	0.635
107	Honduras	0.517	0.565	0.596	0.614	0.627	0.634
108	Guatemala	0.505	0.541	0.554	0.577	0.608	0.626
109	Gabon	..	..	..	..	..	0.617
110	Equatorial Guinea	..	..	0.486	0.507	0.535	0.610
111	Namibia	..	0.530	0.545	0.551	0.624	0.601
112	Morocco	0.428	0.472	0.506	0.539	0.568	0.596
113	Swaziland	0.507	0.538	0.565	0.611	0.615	0.583
114	Botswana	0.495	0.558	0.615	0.654	0.621	0.577
115	India	0.406	0.433	0.472	0.510	0.544	0.571
116	Mongolia	..	..	0.535	0.554	0.545	0.569
117	Zimbabwe	0.545	0.570	0.621	0.598	0.563	0.554
118	Myanmar	..	..	..	..	..	0.551
119	Ghana	0.436	0.466	0.480	0.505	0.524	0.542
120	Lesotho	0.478	0.516	0.545	0.572	0.569	0.541
121	Cambodia	..	..	..	..	..	0.541
122	Papua New Guinea	0.420	0.442	0.463	0.481	0.521	0.534
123	Kenya	0.442	0.488	0.511	0.531	0.521	0.514
124	Comoros	..	0.467	0.490	0.498	0.506	0.510
125	Cameroon	0.407	0.453	0.502	0.511	0.497	0.506
126	Congo	0.411	0.461	0.510	0.504	0.505	0.502

Low human development

HDI rank		1975	1980	1985	1990	1995	1999
127	Pakistan	0.343	0.370	0.403	0.441	0.476	0.498
128	Togo	0.400	0.446	0.443	0.466	0.474	0.489
129	Nepal	0.292	0.329	0.370	0.415	0.451	0.480
130	Bhutan	..	..	..	..	..	0.477
131	Lao People's Dem. Rep.	..	..	0.372	0.402	0.443	0.476
132	Bangladesh	0.332	0.350	0.383	0.414	0.443	0.470
133	Yemen	..	..	..	0.407	0.436	0.468
134	Haiti	..	0.430	0.444	0.449	0.456	0.467
135	Madagascar	0.398	0.431	0.425	0.432	0.439	0.462
136	Nigeria	0.326	0.386	0.402	0.423	0.447	0.455
137	Djibouti	..	..	..	..	..	0.447
138	Sudan	..	..	..	..	..	0.439
139	Mauritania	0.336	0.364	0.382	0.392	0.420	0.437
140	Tanzania, U. Rep. of	..	..	..	0.422	0.427	0.436
141	Uganda	..	..	0.384	0.386	0.402	0.435
142	Congo, Dem. Rep. of the	..	..	..	..	..	0.429
143	Zambia	0.448	0.462	0.479	0.466	0.431	0.427
144	Côte d'Ivoire	0.368	0.402	0.411	0.414	0.414	0.426
145	Senegal	0.311	0.329	0.354	0.378	0.398	0.423
146	Angola	..	..	..	..	..	0.422
147	Benin	0.286	0.323	0.351	0.359	0.392	0.420
148	Eritrea	..	..	..	..	0.398	0.416
149	Gambia	0.271	0.275	0.295	0.314	0.374	0.398
150	Guinea	..	..	..	..	..	0.397

HDI rank		1975	1980	1985	1990	1995	1999
151	Malawi	0.318	0.343	0.356	0.363	0.401	0.397
152	Rwanda	0.334	0.378	0.394	0.344	0.333	0.395
153	Mali	0.251	0.277	0.291	0.310	0.344	0.378
154	Central African Republic	0.332	0.349	0.371	0.370	0.368	0.372
155	Chad	0.255	0.255	0.296	0.321	0.334	0.359
156	Guinea-Bissau	0.251	0.254	0.285	0.306	0.334	0.339
157	Mozambique	..	0.303	0.290	0.311	0.313	0.323
158	Ethiopia	..	..	0.272	0.294	0.305	0.321
159	Burkina Faso	0.236	0.263	0.286	0.294	0.301	0.320
160	Burundi	0.282	0.308	0.338	0.344	0.315	0.309
161	Niger	0.234	0.253	0.244	0.254	0.260	0.274
162	Sierra Leone	..	..	..	..	..	0.258

Note: As a result of revisions to data, the HDI values in this table are not strictly comparable to those in table 7 of *Human Development Report 2000*.

Source: Columns 1-5: calculated on the basis of data on life expectancy from UN (2001d); data on adult literacy rates from UNESCO (2000a); data on combined primary, secondary and tertiary gross enrolment ratios from UNESCO (2001b); and data on GDP at market prices (constant 1995 US$), population and GDP per capita (PPP US$) from World Bank (2001b); *column 6:* column 8 of table 1.

3 Human and income poverty
Developing countries

HDI rank	Human poverty index (HPI-1) Rank	Value (%)	Probability at birth of not surviving to age 40 (% of cohort) 1995-2000 [a]	Adult illiteracy rate (% age 15 and above) 1999	Population not using improved water sources (%) 1999	Underweight children under age five (%) 1995-2000 [b]	Population below income poverty line (%) $1 a day (1993 PPP US$) 1983-99 [b]	National poverty line 1984-99 [b]	HPI-1 rank minus income poverty rank [c]
High human development									
24 Hong Kong, China (SAR)	..	..	2.0	6.7	..	..	..	..	..
25 Cyprus	..	..	3.1	3.1	0	..	..	..	..
26 Singapore	..	..	2.3	7.9	0	..	..	..	..
27 Korea, Rep. of	..	..	1.0	2.4	8	..	<2.0	..	..
31 Barbados	..	..	3.0	..	0	5 [d]	..	..	..
32 Brunei Darussalam	..	..	3.2	9.0	..	..	..	..	..
34 Argentina	..	..	5.6	3.3	21	..	..	17.6	..
37 Uruguay	1	4.0	5.1	7.3	2	5	<2.0	..	0
39 Chile	3	4.2	4.5	4.4	6	1	<2.0	20.5	2
40 Bahrain	..	..	4.7	12.9	..	9	..	..	..
41 Costa Rica	2	4.0	4.0	4.5	2	5	6.9	..	-10
42 Bahamas	..	..	11.8	4.3	4	..	..	..	..
43 Kuwait	..	..	3.0	18.1	..	6 [d]	..	..	..
45 United Arab Emirates	..	..	5.4	24.9	..	14	..	..	..
48 Qatar	..	..	4.8	19.2	..	6	..	..	..
Medium human development									
49 Trinidad and Tobago	5	7.9	4.1	6.5	14	7 [d]	12.4	21.0	-17
51 Mexico	10	9.5	8.3	8.9	14	8	12.2	10.1	-10
52 Panama	6	8.5	6.4	8.3	13	7	10.3	37.3	-11
54 Belize	14	11.0	6.8	6.9	24	6 [d]	..	..	..
56 Malaysia	13	10.9	5.0	13.0	5	18	..	15.5	..
59 Libyan Arab Jamahiriya	27	16.7	6.4	20.9	28	5	..	..	..
61 Venezuela	8	8.6	6.5	7.7	16	5 [d]	18.7	31.3	-19
62 Colombia	9	9.1	10.1	8.5	9	8	11.0	17.7	-9
63 Mauritius	16	11.5	5.4	15.8	0	16	..	10.6	..
64 Suriname	..	..	7.4	..	5	..	..	..	..
65 Lebanon	11	10.2	5.0	14.4	0	3	..	..	..
66 Thailand	21	14.0	9.0	4.7	20	19 [d]	<2.0	13.1	14
67 Fiji	37	21.3	6.3	7.4	53	8 [d]	..	..	..
68 Saudi Arabia	29	17.0	6.4	23.9	5	14	..	..	..
69 Brazil	18	12.9	11.3	15.1	17	6	9.0	22.0	-2
70 Philippines	23	14.7	8.9	4.9	13	28	..	36.8	..
71 Oman	52	32.2	6.8	29.7	61	23	..	..	..
73 Peru	17	12.9	11.6	10.4	23	8	15.5	49.0	-12
77 Maldives	25	15.8	12.5	3.8	0	43	..	..	..
78 Jamaica	20	13.6	5.4	13.6	29	5	3.2	34.2	5
80 Paraguay	12	10.2	8.7	7.0	21	5	19.5	21.8	-17
81 Sri Lanka	31	18.0	5.8	8.6	17	34	6.6	25.0	9
82 Turkey	19	12.9	9.6	15.4	17	8	2.4	..	6
84 Ecuador	28	16.8	11.1	9.0	29	17 [d]	20.2	35.0	-10
86 Dominican Republic	22	14.4	11.9	16.8	21	6	3.2	20.6	6
87 China	24	15.1	7.9	16.5	25	10	18.5	4.6	-8
88 Jordan	7	8.5	7.9	10.8	4	5	<2.0	11.7	5
89 Tunisia	..	..	7.8	30.1	..	4	<2.0	14.1	..
90 Iran, Islamic Rep. of	30	17.3	9.3	24.3	5	11	..	..	..
91 Cape Verde	36	20.9	10.4	26.4	26	14 [d]	..	..	..
93 Guyana	15	11.4	15.4	1.6	6	12	..	..	..
94 South Africa	33	18.7	24.4	15.1	14	9	11.5	..	4
95 El Salvador	32	18.3	10.9	21.7	26	12	26.0	48.3	-9
96 Samoa (Western)	..	..	7.8	19.8	1	..	..	..	..
97 Syrian Arab Republic	34	19.8	6.9	26.4	20	13	..	..	..

HDI rank		Human poverty index (HPI-1)		Probability at birth of not surviving to age 40 (% of cohort) 1995-2000 [a]	Adult illiteracy rate (% age 15 and above) 1999	Population not using improved water sources (%) 1999	Underweight children under age five (%) 1995-2000 [b]	Population below income poverty line (%)		HPI-1 rank minus income poverty rank [c]
		Rank	Value (%)					$1 a day (1993 PPP US$) 1983-99 [b]	National poverty line 1984-99 [b]	
100	Algeria	40	23.5	10.5	33.4	6	13	<2	22.6	24
101	Viet Nam	45	29.1	12.8	6.9	44	39	..	50.9	..
102	Indonesia	38	21.3	12.8	13.7	24	34	7.7	27.1	11
104	Bolivia	26	16.4	18.4	15.0	21	10	29.4	..	-18
105	Egypt	50	31.7	10.3	45.4	5	12	3.1	22.9	22
106	Nicaragua	39	23.3	11.5	31.8	21	12	..	50.3	..
107	Honduras	35	20.8	16.0	26.0	10	25	40.5	53.0	-22
108	Guatemala	41	23.8	15.6	31.9	8	24	10.0	57.9	11
109	Gabon	..	..	32.0	..	30	..	..	..	..
110	Equatorial Guinea	..	..	33.7	17.8	57	..	..	..	..
111	Namibia	56	34.5	46.7	18.6	23	26 [d]	34.9	..	-5
112	Morocco	62	36.4	11.8	52.0	18	9 [d]	<2	19.0	36
113	Swaziland	..	..	36.3	21.1	..	10 [d]	..	..	..
114	Botswana	..	..	49.5	23.6	..	17	33.3	..	..
115	India	55	34.3	16.7	43.5	12	53 [d]	44.2	35.0	-14
116	Mongolia	44	28.9	15.0	37.7	40	10	13.9	36.3	6
117	Zimbabwe	61	36.2	51.6	12.0	15	15	36.0	25.5	-5
118	Myanmar	43	28.0	26.0	15.6	32	39	..	..	..
119	Ghana	46	29.1	27.0	29.7	36	25	38.8	31.4	-15
120	Lesotho	42	25.8	35.4	17.1	9	16	43.1	49.2	-19
121	Cambodia	78	45.0	24.4	31.8 [e]	70	52	..	36.1	..
122	Papua New Guinea	60	36.2	21.6	36.1	58	30 [d]	..	..	..
123	Kenya	51	31.8	34.6	18.5	51	22	26.5	42.0	-2
124	Comoros	47	29.9	20.6	40.8	4	26	..	..	..
125	Cameroon	49	31.1	36.2	25.2	38	22	..	40.0	..
126	Congo	48	30.7	34.8	20.5	49	17 [d]	..	..	..

Low human development

HDI rank		Human poverty index (HPI-1)		Probability at birth of not surviving to age 40 (% of cohort) 1995-2000 [a]	Adult illiteracy rate (% age 15 and above) 1999	Population not using improved water sources (%) 1999	Underweight children under age five (%) 1995-2000 [b]	Population below income poverty line (%)		HPI-1 rank minus income poverty rank [c]
		Rank	Value (%)					$1 a day (1993 PPP US$) 1983-99 [b]	National poverty line 1984-99 [b]	
127	Pakistan	65	39.2	20.1	55.0	12	26 [d]	31.0	34.0	2
128	Togo	63	38.3	34.1	43.7	46	25	..	32.3	..
129	Nepal	77	44.2	22.5	59.6	19	47	37.7	42.0	4
130	Bhutan	..	..	20.2	..	38	38 [d]	..	..	..
131	Lao People's Dem. Rep.	66	39.9	30.5	52.7	10	40 [d]	26.3	46.1	8
132	Bangladesh	73	43.3	21.4	59.2	3	56	29.1	35.6	9
133	Yemen	70	42.5	20.0	54.8	31	46	15.7	19.1	18
134	Haiti	71	42.8	31.6	51.2	54	28	..	..	..
135	Madagascar	64	38.6	31.6	34.3	53	40	63.4	70.0	-12
136	Nigeria	59	36.1	33.7	37.4	43	31	70.2	34.1	-18
137	Djibouti	57	34.7	42.3	36.6	0	18	..	..	..
138	Sudan	58	34.8	27.3	43.1	25	34 [d]	..	..	..
139	Mauritania	82	47.2	33.1	58.4	63	23	28.6	57.0	15
140	Tanzania, U. Rep. of	53	32.4	33.3	25.3	46	27	19.9	51.1	4
141	Uganda	69	41.0	48.4	33.9	50	26	..	44.4	..
142	Congo, Dem. Rep. of the	67	40.0	34.7	39.7	55	34	..	..	..
143	Zambia	68	40.0	53.6	22.8	36	24	63.7	86.0	-10
144	Côte d'Ivoire	72	42.9	40.2	54.3	23	24 [d]	12.3	..	23
145	Senegal	80	45.9	28.5	63.6	22	22	26.3	..	16
146	Angola	..	..	41.6	..	62	42	..	..	..
147	Benin	79	45.8	29.7	61.0	37	29	..	33.0	..
148	Eritrea	75	44.0	31.7	47.3	54	44	..	..	..
149	Gambia	85	49.6	40.5	64.3	38	26	53.7	64.0	4
150	Guinea	..	..	38.3	..	52	..	..	40.0	..

HDI rank	Human poverty index (HPI-1)		Probability at birth of not surviving to age 40 (% of cohort) 1995-2000 [a]	Adult illiteracy rate (% age 15 and above) 1999	Population not using improved water sources (%) 1999	Underweight children under age five (%) 1995-2000 [b]	Population below income poverty line (%)		HPI-1 rank minus income poverty rank [c]
	Rank	Value (%)					$1 a day (1993 PPP US$) 1983-99 [b]	National poverty line 1984-99 [b]	
151 Malawi	74	43.4	50.4	40.8	43	30	..	54.0	..
152 Rwanda	76	44.2	51.9	34.2	59	27	35.7	51.2	5
153 Mali	83	47.8	38.5	60.2	35	40	72.8	..	-4
154 Central African Republic	81	46.1	45.3	54.6	40	27	66.6	..	-4
155 Chad	87	53.1	41.0	59.0	73	39	..	64.0	..
156 Guinea-Bissau	86	49.6	42.2	62.3	51	23 [d]	..	..	..
157 Mozambique	84	48.3	49.2	56.8	40	26	37.9	..	8
158 Ethiopia	88	57.2	43.6	62.6	76	47	31.3	..	15
159 Burkina Faso	..	..	43.0	77.0	..	36	61.2	..	..
160 Burundi	..	..	50.1	53.1	..	37 [d]	..	36.2	..
161 Niger	90	63.6	41.4	84.7	41	50	61.4	63.0	5
162 Sierra Leone	..	..	51.6	..	72	29 [d]	57.0	68.0	..

Note: As a result of revisions in data and methodology, the HPI-1 results in this table are not comparable to those in *Human Development Report 2000*. For further details see technical note 1. The human poverty index has been calculated for UN member countries with reliable data in each of its components, which include Afghanistan (HPI-1 value, 60.2%; HPI-1 rank, 89) and Cuba (HPI-1 value, 4.6%; HPI-1 rank, 4).

a. Data refer to the probability at birth of not surviving to age 40, times 100. Data refer to estimates for the period specified.

b. Data refer to the most recent year available during the period specified.

c. Income poverty refers to the percentage of the population living on less than $1 (PPP US$) a day. The rankings are based on countries with available data for both indicators. A positive figure indicates that the country performs better in income poverty than in human poverty, a negative the opposite.

d. Data refer to a year or period other than that specified, differ from the standard definition or refer to only part of a country.

e. UNESCO 2001a.

Source: Column 1: determined on the basis of the HPI-1 values in column 2; *column 2:* calculated on the basis of data in columns 3-6; see technical note 1 for details; *column 3:* UN 2001d; *column 4:* unless otherwise noted, UNESCO 2000a; *column 5:* calculated on the basis of data on population using improved water sources from UNICEF (2000); *column 6:* UNICEF 2000, *columns 7 and 8:* World Bank 2001b; *column 9:* calculated on the basis of data in columns 1 and 7.

HPI-1 ranks for 90 developing countries

1	Uruguay	19	Turkey	37	Fiji	55	India	73	Bangladesh
2	Costa Rica	20	Jamaica	38	Indonesia	56	Namibia	74	Malawi
3	Chile	21	Thailand	39	Nicaragua	57	Djibouti	75	Eritrea
4	Cuba	22	Dominican Republic	40	Algeria	58	Sudan	76	Rwanda
5	Trinidad and Tobago	23	Philippines	41	Guatemala	59	Nigeria	77	Nepal
6	Panama	24	China	42	Lesotho	60	Papua New Guinea	78	Cambodia
7	Jordan	25	Maldives	43	Myanmar	61	Zimbabwe	79	Benin
8	Venezuela	26	Bolivia	44	Mongolia	62	Morocco	80	Senegal
9	Colombia	27	Libyan Arab Jamahiriya	45	Viet Nam	63	Togo	81	Central African Republic
10	Mexico	28	Ecuador	46	Ghana	64	Madagascar	82	Mauritania
11	Lebanon	29	Saudi Arabia	47	Comoros	65	Pakistan	83	Mali
12	Paraguay	30	Iran, Islamic Rep. of	48	Congo	66	Lao People's Dem. Rep.	84	Mozambique
13	Malaysia	31	Sri Lanka	49	Cameroon	67	Congo, Dem. Rep. of the	85	Gambia
14	Belize	32	El Salvador	50	Egypt	68	Zambia	86	Guinea-Bissau
15	Guyana	33	South Africa	51	Kenya	69	Uganda	87	Chad
16	Mauritius	34	Syrian Arab Republic	52	Oman	70	Yemen	88	Ethiopia
17	Peru	35	Honduras	53	Tanzania, U. Rep. of	71	Haiti	89	Afghanistan
18	Brazil	36	Cape Verde	54	Iraq	72	Côte d'Ivoire	90	Niger

4 Human and income poverty
OECD countries, Eastern Europe and the CIS

HDI rank		Human poverty index (HPI-2) Rank	Human poverty index (HPI-2) Value (%)	Probability at birth of not surviving to age 60 (% of cohort) 1995-2000 [a]	People lacking functional literacy skills (% age 16-65) 1994-98 [b]	Long-term unemployment (as % of labour force) [c] 1999	Population below income poverty line (%) 50% of median income [d] 1987-97 [e]	Population below income poverty line (%) $11 a day (1994 PPP US$) [f] 1994-95 [e]	Population below income poverty line (%) $4 a day (1990 PPP US$) 1993-95 [e]	HPI-2 rank minus income poverty rank [g]
High human development										
1	Norway	2	7.5	9.1	8.5	0.2	6.9	4	..	0
2	Australia	14	12.9	9.1	17.0	2.1	14.3	18	..	-2
3	Canada	11	12.1	9.5	16.6	0.9	11.9	7	..	1
4	Sweden	1	6.8	8.0	7.5	2.8 [h]	6.6	6	..	-3
5	Belgium	13	12.5	10.5	18.4 [i]	5.5	5.2	..	..	..
6	United States	17	15.8	12.8	20.7	0.3	16.9	14	..	2
7	Iceland	..	..	8.7	..	..	..	..	..	..
8	Netherlands	3	8.5	9.2	10.5	1.4	8.1	7	..	-2
9	Japan	9	11.2	8.2	.. [j]	1.1	11.8 [k]	..	..	..
10	Finland	4	8.8	11.3	10.4	3.0	5.2	5	..	1
11	Switzerland	..	..	9.6	..	1.2	9.3	..	..	..
12	Luxembourg	7	10.7	11.4	.. [j]	0.8	3.9	(.)	..	5
13	France	8	11.1	11.4	.. [j]	4.5	8.0	10	..	-1
14	United Kingdom	15	15.1	9.9	21.8	1.8	13.4	16	..	0
15	Denmark	5	9.1	12.0	9.6	1.1	7.2	..	..	..
16	Austria	..	..	10.6	..	1.2	10.6	..	..	..
17	Germany	6	10.5	10.6	14.4	4.5	7.5	7	..	-1
18	Ireland	16	15.3	10.4	22.6	5.6 [l]	11.1	..	..	..
19	New Zealand	..	..	10.7	18.4	1.4	..	..	..	..
20	Italy	12	12.3	9.1	.. [j]	7.0	14.2	..	..	..
21	Spain	10	11.5	10.3	.. [j]	8.1	10.1	..	..	..
22	Israel	..	..	8.0	..	..	13.5	..	..	..
23	Greece	..	..	9.4	..	5.9 [h]	..	..	..	..
28	Portugal	..	..	13.1	48.0	1.9	..	..	..	..
29	Slovenia	..	..	13.8	42.2	..	..	..	<1	..
30	Malta	..	..	8.4	..	..	..	..	..	..
33	Czech Republic	..	..	13.7	15.7	3.3	2.3	..	<1	..
35	Slovakia	..	..	16.6	..	..	2.1	..	<1	..
36	Hungary	..	..	21.9	33.8	3.5	10.1	..	4	..
38	Poland	..	..	17.5	42.6	4.0 [h]	11.6	..	20	..
44	Estonia	..	..	23.8	..	..	..	..	37	..
46	Croatia	..	..	15.8	..	..	..	..	..	..
47	Lithuania	..	..	21.6	..	..	..	..	30	..
Medium human development										
50	Latvia	..	..	23.7	..	..	..	..	22	..
53	Belarus	..	..	26.0	..	..	..	..	22	..
55	Russian Federation	..	..	30.1	..	..	20.1	..	50	..
57	Bulgaria	..	..	18.8	..	..	..	..	15	..
58	Romania	..	..	21.6	..	..	..	..	59	..
60	Macedonia, TFYR	..	..	14.5	..	..	..	..	..	..
72	Armenia	..	..	14.7	..	..	..	..	..	..
74	Ukraine	..	..	26.3	..	..	..	..	63	..
75	Kazakhstan	..	..	31.6	..	..	..	..	65	..
76	Georgia	..	..	17.5	..	..	..	..	..	..

HDI rank		Human poverty index (HPI-2)		Probability at birth of not surviving to age 60 (% of cohort) 1995-2000 [a]	People lacking functional literacy skills (% age 16-65) 1994 98 [b]	Long-term unemployment (as % of labour force) [c] 1999	Population below income poverty line (%)			HPI-2 rank minus income poverty rank [g]
		Rank	Value (%)				50% of median income [d] 1987-97 [c]	$11 a day (1994 PPP US$) [f] 1994-95 [e]	$4 a day (1990 PPP US$) 1993-95 [e]	
79	Azerbaijan	..	..	20.4	..	..	..	..	..	..
83	Turkmenistan	..	..	27.6	..	..	..	..	61	..
85	Albania	..	..	12.4	..	..	..	..		..
92	Kyrgyzstan	..	..	26.4	..	..	..	..	88	..
98	Moldova, Rep. of	..	..	27.4	..	..	..	..	66	..
99	Uzbekistan	..	..	23.9	..	..	..	..	63	..
103	Tajikistan	..	..	25.3	..	..	..	..	..	..

Note: This table includes Israel and Malta, which are not OECD member countries, but excludes the Republic of Korea, Mexico and Turkey, which are. For the human poverty index and related indicators for these countries see table 3.

a. Data refer to the probability at birth of not surviving to age 60, times 100. Data refer to estimates for the period specified.

b. Based on scoring at level 1 on the prose literacy scale of the International Adult Literacy Survey (see box 5 in the note on statistics). Data refer to the most recent year available during 1994-98.

c. Data refer to unemployment lasting 12 months or longer.

d. Poverty line is measured at 50% of equivalent median disposable household income.

e. Data refer to the most recent year available during the period specified.

f. Based on the US poverty line, $11 (1994 PPP US$) a day per person for a family of three.

g. Income poverty refers to the percentage of the population living on less than $11 (1994 PPP US$) a day per person for a family of three. A positive figure indicates that the country performs better in income poverty than in human poverty, a negative the opposite.

h. Data refer to 1998.

i. Data refer to Flanders.

j. For purposes of calculating the HPI-2 an estimate of 15.1%, the unweighted average for countries with available data, was applied.

k. Smeeding 1997.

l. Data refer to 1997.

Source: Column 1: determined on the basis of the HPI-2 values in column 2; *column 2:* calculated on the basis of data in columns 3-6; see technical note 1 for details; *column 3:* UN 2001d; *column 4:* unless otherwise noted, OECD and Statistics Canada 2000; *column 5:* OECD 2000c; *column 6:* unless otherwise noted, LIS 2001; *column 7:* Smeeding, Rainwater and Burtless 2000; *column 8:* Milanovic 1998; *column 9:* calculated on the basis of data in columns 1 and 7.

HPI-2 ranks for 17 selected OECD countries

1	Sweden	7	Luxembourg	13	Belgium
2	Norway	8	France	14	Australia
3	Netherlands	9	Japan	15	United Kingdom
4	Finland	10	Spain	16	Ireland
5	Denmark	11	Canada	17	United States
6	Germany	12	Italy		

5 Demographic trends

HDI rank	Total population (millions)			Annual population growth rate (%)		Urban population (as % of total) [a]			Population under age 15 (as % of total)		Population aged 65 and above (as % of total)		Total fertility rate (per woman)	
	1975	1999	2015[b]	1975-99	1999-2015	1975	1999	2015[b]	1999	2015[b]	1999	2015[b]	1970-75[c]	1995-2000[c]
High human development														
1 Norway	4.0	4.4	4.7	0.4	0.3	68.2	75.1	80.1	19.8	15.8	15.5	18.2	2.2	1.8
2 Australia	13.9	18.9	21.9	1.3	0.9	85.9	84.7	86.0	20.7	18.0	12.2	15.2	2.5	1.8
3 Canada	23.1	30.5	34.4	1.1	0.8	75.6	77.0	79.9	19.4	15.9	12.5	16.1	2.0	1.6
4 Sweden	8.2	8.9	8.6	0.3	-0.2	82.7	83.3	85.2	18.5	12.4	17.4	22.3	1.9	1.5
5 Belgium	9.8	10.2	10.3	0.2	0.0	94.9	97.3	98.0	17.5	13.9	16.8	19.9	1.9	1.5
6 United States	220.2	280.4	321.2	1.0	0.8	73.7	77.0	81.0	21.9	18.7	12.3	14.4	2.0	2.0
7 Iceland	0.2	0.3	0.3	1.0	0.6	86.7	92.4	94.6	23.5	18.7	11.6	14.1	2.8	2.0
8 Netherlands	13.7	15.8	16.4	0.6	0.2	88.4	89.3	90.8	18.4	14.7	13.6	17.8	2.1	1.5
9 Japan	111.5	126.8	127.5	0.5	0.0	75.7	78.6	81.5	14.9	13.3	16.7	25.8	2.1	1.4
10 Finland	4.7	5.2	5.2	0.4	0.0	58.3	66.7	74.2	18.3	14.2	14.8	20.7	1.6	1.7
11 Switzerland	6.3	7.2	7.0	0.5	-0.2	55.8	67.7	70.9	16.8	12.1	15.8	22.1	1.8	1.5
12 Luxembourg	0.4	0.4	0.5	0.8	1.1	73.8	91.0	95.0	18.7	17.4	14.3	16.2	2.0	1.7
13 France	52.7	59.0	61.9	0.5	0.3	73.0	75.4	79.4	18.9	17.4	15.8	18.6	2.3	1.7
14 United Kingdom	56.2	59.3	60.6	0.2	0.1	88.7	89.4	90.8	19.1	15.1	15.7	18.9	2.0	1.7
15 Denmark	5.1	5.3	5.4	0.2	0.1	81.8	85.3	86.8	18.1	15.2	15.0	19.4	2.0	1.7
16 Austria	7.6	8.1	7.8	0.3	-0.2	65.2	64.6	68.5	16.9	11.8	15.4	20.0	2.0	1.4
17 Germany	78.7	82.0	80.7	0.2	-0.1	81.2	87.3	89.9	15.8	12.1	16.1	21.0	1.6	1.3
18 Ireland	3.2	3.8	4.4	0.7	1.0	53.6	58.8	64.0	22.0	21.8	11.3	13.1	3.8	1.9
19 New Zealand	3.1	3.7	4.1	0.8	0.6	82.8	85.7	87.7	23.1	18.8	11.6	14.5	2.8	2.0
20 Italy	55.4	57.5	55.2	0.2	-0.3	65.6	66.9	70.7	14.4	12.0	17.8	22.4	2.3	1.2
21 Spain	35.6	39.9	39.0	0.5	-0.1	69.6	77.4	81.3	15.0	12.5	16.7	19.8	2.9	1.2
22 Israel	3.4	5.9	7.7	2.4	1.7	86.7	91.1	92.5	28.4	24.3	9.9	11.5	3.8	2.9
23 Greece	9.0	10.6	10.5	0.7	-0.1	55.3	59.9	65.1	15.3	12.7	17.2	21.2	2.3	1.3
24 Hong Kong, China (SAR)	4.4	6.7	8.0	1.8	1.1	89.7	100.0	100.0	16.8	13.9	10.4	13.4	2.9	1.2
25 Cyprus	0.6	0.8	0.9	1.0	0.7	43.3	56.2	64.5	23.6	19.1	11.4	14.9	2.5	2.0
26 Singapore	2.3	3.9	4.8	2.3	1.2	100.0	100.0	100.0	22.1	14.0	7.0	12.9	2.6	1.6
27 Korea, Rep. of	35.3	46.4	50.6	1.1	0.5	48.0	81.1	88.2	21.2	17.2	6.8	11.6	4.3	1.5
28 Portugal	9.1	10.0	10.0	0.4	0.0	27.7	62.7	77.5	16.8	15.3	15.4	18.0	2.7	1.5
29 Slovenia	1.7	2.0	1.9	0.6	-0.2	42.4	50.3	55.2	16.4	11.9	13.6	18.6	2.2	1.2
30 Malta	0.3	0.4	0.4	1.0	0.4	80.6	90.3	92.6	20.5	16.8	12.2	18.0	2.1	1.9
31 Barbados	0.2	0.3	0.3	0.3	0.3	38.6	49.5	58.3	21.1	16.8	10.5	11.0	2.7	1.5
32 Brunei Darussalam	0.2	0.3	0.4	2.9	1.6	62.1	71.7	78.5	32.4	23.0	3.1	6.5	5.4	2.8
33 Czech Republic	10.0	10.3	10.0	0.1	-0.2	63.7	74.7	77.4	16.8	12.8	13.7	18.7	2.2	1.2
34 Argentina	26.0	36.6	43.5	1.4	1.1	80.7	89.6	92.6	27.9	24.5	9.7	10.7	3.1	2.6
35 Slovakia	4.7	5.4	5.4	0.5	0.0	46.3	57.3	62.1	20.1	14.9	11.3	13.7	2.5	1.4
36 Hungary	10.5	10.0	9.3	-0.2	-0.5	52.8	63.8	68.5	17.2	13.3	14.6	17.4	2.1	1.4
37 Uruguay	2.8	3.3	3.7	0.7	0.6	83.0	91.0	93.6	24.8	22.6	12.8	13.5	3.0	2.4
38 Poland	34.0	38.6	38.0	0.5	-0.1	55.4	65.2	71.4	19.9	14.6	11.9	14.8	2.2	1.5
39 Chile	10.3	15.0	17.9	1.6	1.1	78.4	85.4	88.7	28.7	23.6	7.1	9.7	3.6	2.4
40 Bahrain	0.3	0.6	0.8	3.5	1.5	79.0	91.8	95.0	28.8	20.3	2.8	6.1	5.9	2.6
41 Costa Rica	2.0	3.9	5.2	2.9	1.8	41.4	47.6	53.4	32.8	27.2	5.0	7.1	4.3	2.8
42 Bahamas	0.2	0.3	0.4	1.9	1.1	73.5	87.9	91.5	29.9	24.5	5.2	7.8	3.4	2.4
43 Kuwait	1.0	1.8	2.8	2.5	2.5	83.8	97.4	98.2	33.5	25.9	2.0	6.6	6.9	2.9
44 Estonia	1.4	1.4	1.2	-0.1	-1.1	67.6	68.8	69.3	18.3	13.7	14.1	17.0	2.1	1.2
45 United Arab Emirates	0.5	2.6	3.2	6.8	1.5	65.3	85.5	88.8	26.7	21.1	2.5	9.3	6.4	3.2
46 Croatia	4.3	4.7	4.6	0.4	0.0	45.1	57.3	64.4	18.3	16.9	13.8	16.9	2.0	1.7
47 Lithuania	3.3	3.7	3.5	0.5	-0.3	55.7	68.4	71.4	20.0	13.0	13.1	16.6	2.3	1.4
48 Qatar	0.2	0.6	0.7	4.9	1.4	83.0	92.3	94.3	26.8	22.8	1.4	5.6	6.8	3.7
Medium human development														
49 Trinidad and Tobago	1.0	1.3	1.4	1.0	0.5	62.9	73.6	79.3	26.1	19.4	6.6	9.6	3.4	1.7
50 Latvia	2.5	2.4	2.2	0.0	-0.6	65.4	69.0	71.4	18.1	12.6	14.5	17.8	2.0	1.1

HDI rank		Total population (millions)			Annual population growth rate (%)		Urban population (as % of total) [a]			Population under age 15 (as % of total)		Population aged 65 and above (as % of total)		Total fertility rate (per woman)	
		1975	1999	2015 [b]	1975-99	1999-2015	1975	1999	2015 [b]	1999	2015 [b]	1999	2015 [b]	1970-75 [c]	1995-2000 [c]
51	Mexico	59.1	97.4	119.2	2.1	1.3	62.8	74.2	77.9	33.6	26.3	4.6	6.8	6.5	2.8
52	Panama	1.7	2.8	3.5	2.0	1.3	49.0	56.0	61.7	31.7	24.9	5.5	7.9	4.9	2.6
53	Belarus	9.4	10.2	9.7	0.4	-0.4	50.3	70.7	77.2	19.4	14.3	13.1	14.0	2.2	1.3
54	Belize	0.1	0.2	0.3	2.1	1.6	50.0	53.6	64.2	39.0	27.9	4.2	4.9	6.3	3.4
55	Russian Federation	134.2	146.2	133.3	0.4	-0.6	66.4	77.3	82.0	18.7	13.6	12.3	13.8	2.0	1.2
56	Malaysia	12.3	21.8	27.9	2.4	1.5	37.7	56.7	66.4	34.5	26.7	4.1	6.2	5.2	3.3
57	Bulgaria	8.7	8.0	6.8	-0.3	-1.0	57.5	69.3	74.5	16.2	12.2	16.0	17.9	2.2	1.1
58	Romania	21.2	22.5	21.4	0.2	-0.3	46.2	55.9	62.0	18.7	15.2	13.1	14.6	2.6	1.3
59	Libyan Arab Jamahiriya	2.4	5.2	7.1	3.1	1.9	60.9	87.2	90.3	34.7	30.4	3.3	5.1	7.6	3.8
60	Macedonia, TFYR	1.7	2.0	2.1	0.8	0.2	50.5	61.6	68.5	23.1	15.1	9.7	12.9	3.0	1.9
61	Venezuela	12.7	23.7	30.9	2.6	1.7	75.7	86.6	90.0	34.5	27.6	4.4	6.5	4.9	3.0
62	Colombia	25.4	41.4	52.6	2.0	1.5	60.7	73.5	79.1	33.1	27.0	4.7	6.4	5.0	2.8
63	Mauritius	0.9	1.2	1.3	1.1	0.8	43.5	41.1	48.5	26.0	21.1	6.2	8.5	3.2	2.0
64	Suriname	0.4	0.4	0.4	0.5	0.3	49.5	73.5	81.4	31.2	23.1	5.4	6.6	5.3	2.2
65	Lebanon	2.8	3.4	4.2	0.9	1.3	67.0	89.3	92.6	31.7	23.8	6.0	6.5	4.9	2.3
66	Thailand	41.1	62.0	72.5	1.7	1.0	15.1	21.2	29.3	27.0	22.0	5.1	7.8	5.0	2.1
67	Fiji	0.6	0.8	0.9	1.4	0.9	36.8	48.6	60.0	33.7	28.1	3.4	5.7	4.2	3.2
68	Saudi Arabia	7.3	19.6	31.7	4.2	3.0	58.4	85.1	89.7	43.4	38.6	2.9	4.4	7.3	6.2
69	Brazil	108.1	168.2	201.4	1.8	1.1	61.2	80.7	86.5	29.3	24.3	5.0	7.3	4.7	2.3
70	Philippines	42.0	74.2	95.9	2.4	1.6	35.6	57.7	67.8	37.9	29.6	3.5	4.9	6.0	3.6
71	Oman	0.9	2.5	4.1	4.3	3.2	19.7	82.2	92.7	44.5	41.5	2.5	3.7	7.2	5.9
72	Armenia	2.8	3.8	3.8	1.2	0.0	63.0	69.7	75.0	24.8	14.0	8.4	10.3	3.0	1.4
73	Peru	15.2	25.2	31.9	2.1	1.5	61.5	72.4	77.9	33.9	26.7	4.7	6.5	6.0	3.0
74	Ukraine	49.0	50.0	43.3	0.1	-0.9	58.3	67.9	71.5	18.5	12.8	13.7	15.7	2.2	1.3
75	Kazakhstan	14.1	16.3	16.0	0.6	-0.1	52.2	56.4	60.6	27.6	22.2	6.8	8.1	3.5	2.1
76	Georgia	4.9	5.3	4.8	0.3	-0.6	49.6	60.2	67.7	21.1	14.8	12.6	15.0	2.6	1.6
77	Maldives	0.1	0.3	0.5	3.0	3.0	18.2	26.1	31.4	44.1	40.6	3.5	3.1	7.0	5.8
78	Jamaica	2.0	2.6	3.0	1.0	0.9	44.1	55.6	63.5	31.9	25.4	7.2	7.7	5.0	2.5
79	Azerbaijan	5.7	8.0	8.7	1.4	0.6	51.5	56.9	64.0	30.0	17.5	6.5	8.1	4.3	1.9
80	Paraguay	2.7	5.4	7.8	2.9	2.3	39.0	55.3	65.0	40.0	34.1	3.5	4.3	5.7	4.2
81	Sri Lanka	13.5	18.7	21.5	1.4	0.8	22.0	23.3	32.0	26.9	22.5	6.2	8.8	4.1	2.1
82	Turkey	40.0	65.7	79.0	2.1	1.2	41.6	74.1	84.5	30.3	24.1	5.6	7.2	5.2	2.7
83	Turkmenistan	2.5	4.6	6.1	2.5	1.7	47.5	44.7	49.9	38.2	28.4	4.2	4.5	6.2	3.6
84	Ecuador	6.9	12.4	15.9	2.4	1.6	42.4	64.3	75.8	34.3	27.1	4.6	6.2	6.0	3.1
85	Albania	2.4	3.1	3.4	1.1	0.6	32.8	41.0	50.8	30.4	22.7	5.8	8.1	4.7	2.6
86	Dominican Republic	5.0	8.2	10.1	2.0	1.3	45.3	64.4	72.6	34.1	28.4	4.2	6.2	5.6	2.9
87	China	927.8 [d]	1,264.8 [d]	1,410.2 [d]	1.3 [d]	0.7 [d]	17.4	31.6	40.7	25.3	19.4	6.7	9.3	4.9	1.8
88	Jordan	1.9	4.8	7.2	3.8	2.5	55.3	73.6	79.8	40.2	36.4	2.7	3.6	7.8	4.7
89	Tunisia	5.7	9.4	11.3	2.1	1.2	49.8	64.8	73.5	30.5	24.8	5.8	6.2	6.2	2.3
90	Iran, Islamic Rep. of	33.5	69.2	87.1	3.0	1.4	45.8	61.1	68.8	38.7	27.2	3.3	5.0	6.4	3.2
91	Cape Verde	0.3	0.4	0.6	1.7	1.9	21.6	60.4	73.4	39.7	31.9	4.6	3.0	7.0	3.6
92	Kyrgyzstan	3.3	4.8	5.8	1.6	1.2	37.9	33.6	35.0	34.6	25.0	6.0	6.0	4.7	2.9
93	Guyana	0.7	0.8	0.7	0.1	-0.1	30.0	37.6	48.0	31.0	25.7	4.9	6.4	4.9	2.5
94	South Africa	25.8	42.8	44.6	2.1	0.3	48.0	50.1	56.3	34.3	30.5	3.5	5.4	5.4	3.1
95	El Salvador	4.1	6.2	8.0	1.7	1.6	40.4	46.3	53.6	35.9	29.5	4.9	6.1	6.1	3.2
96	Samoa (Western)	0.2	0.2	0.2	0.2	0.8	21.2	21.5	26.7	41.4	36.3	4.5	5.0	5.7	4.5
97	Syrian Arab Republic	7.4	15.8	23.2	3.1	2.4	45.1	54.0	62.1	41.7	34.3	3.1	3.4	7.7	4.0
98	Moldova, Rep. of	3.8	4.3	4.2	0.5	-0.2	35.8	46.2	50.3	23.9	16.7	9.2	10.2	2.6	1.6
99	Uzbekistan	14.0	24.5	30.6	2.3	1.4	39.1	37.2	38.6	37.1	25.9	4.6	5.0	6.3	2.9
100	Algeria	16.0	29.8	38.0	2.6	1.5	40.3	59.5	68.5	35.5	26.8	4.1	4.9	7.4	3.3

HDI rank		Total population (millions)			Annual population growth rate (%)		Urban population (as % of total) [a]			Population under age 15 (as % of total)		Population aged 65 and above (as % of total)		Total fertility rate (per woman)	
		1975	1999	2015 [b]	1975-99	1999-2015	1975	1999	2015 [b]	1999	2015 [b]	1999	2015 [b]	1970-75 [c]	1995-2000 [c]
101	Viet Nam	48.0	77.1	94.4	2.0	1.3	18.8	19.7	24.3	34.2	25.1	5.3	5.5	6.7	2.5
102	Indonesia	134.6	209.3	250.1	1.8	1.1	19.4	39.8	54.8	31.3	24.7	4.7	6.4	5.2	2.6
103	Tajikistan	3.4	6.0	7.1	2.3	1.0	35.5	27.5	29.5	40.2	27.1	4.5	4.6	6.8	3.7
104	Bolivia	4.8	8.1	11.2	2.2	2.0	41.5	61.9	70.1	39.8	33.7	4.0	4.9	6.5	4.4
105	Egypt	38.8	66.7	84.4	2.3	1.5	43.5	45.0	51.2	36.0	26.9	4.1	5.2	5.5	3.4
106	Nicaragua	2.5	4.9	7.2	2.8	2.4	48.9	55.8	62.6	43.1	35.2	3.0	3.7	6.8	4.3
107	Honduras	3.0	6.3	8.7	3.0	2.1	32.1	51.6	64.3	42.2	33.7	3.3	4.2	7.1	4.3
108	Guatemala	6.0	11.1	16.3	2.5	2.4	36.7	39.4	46.2	43.9	37.3	3.5	3.8	6.5	4.9
109	Gabon	0.6	1.2	1.8	2.9	2.4	40.0	80.3	88.9	39.9	40.8	5.9	5.5	4.3	5.4
110	Equatorial Guinea	0.2	0.4	0.7	2.8	2.8	27.1	46.9	61.4	43.6	43.5	3.9	3.5	5.7	5.9
111	Namibia	0.9	1.7	2.3	2.7	1.8	20.7	30.4	39.4	43.8	39.0	3.7	3.9	6.5	5.3
112	Morocco	17.3	29.3	37.7	2.2	1.6	37.7	55.3	65.6	35.1	28.1	4.1	4.9	6.9	3.4
113	Swaziland	0.5	0.9	1.0	2.6	0.7	13.9	26.1	32.7	41.8	38.6	3.4	4.3	6.5	4.8
114	Botswana	0.8	1.5	1.7	2.9	0.7	12.0	49.7	58.4	42.4	36.8	2.7	3.9	6.6	4.4
115	India	620.7	992.7	1,230.5	2.0	1.3	21.3	28.1	35.9	33.9	26.9	4.9	6.4	5.4	3.3
116	Mongolia	1.4	2.5	3.1	2.3	1.3	48.7	63.0	70.5	36.1	25.9	3.8	4.2	7.3	2.7
117	Zimbabwe	6.1	12.4	16.4	3.0	1.7	19.6	34.6	45.9	45.4	39.8	3.2	3.1	7.4	5.0
118	Myanmar	30.2	47.1	55.3	1.9	1.0	23.9	27.3	36.7	33.5	25.3	4.6	6.0	5.8	3.3
119	Ghana	9.9	18.9	26.4	2.7	2.1	30.1	37.9	47.8	41.4	36.1	3.2	4.0	6.9	4.6
120	Lesotho	1.2	2.0	2.1	2.1	0.4	10.8	27.1	38.9	39.4	36.7	4.1	5.5	5.7	4.8
121	Cambodia	7.1	12.8	18.6	2.4	2.3	10.3	15.6	22.8	44.6	38.5	2.8	3.4	5.5	5.3
122	Papua New Guinea	2.6	4.7	6.6	2.5	2.2	11.9	17.1	23.7	40.4	36.0	2.4	2.9	6.1	4.6
123	Kenya	13.6	30.0	40.0	3.3	1.8	12.9	32.1	44.5	44.0	38.3	2.8	3.0	8.1	4.6
124	Comoros	0.3	0.7	1.1	3.2	2.8	21.3	32.7	42.6	43.4	39.8	2.6	3.0	7.1	5.4
125	Cameroon	7.5	14.6	20.2	2.7	2.1	26.9	48.0	58.9	43.4	39.5	3.6	3.8	6.3	5.1
126	Congo	1.4	2.9	4.7	2.9	3.0	34.8	61.7	70.1	46.1	46.0	3.3	3.1	6.3	6.3
Low human development															
127	Pakistan	70.3	137.6	204.3	2.8	2.5	26.4	36.5	46.7	42.0	38.4	3.7	4.0	6.3	5.5
128	Togo	2.3	4.4	6.6	2.8	2.5	16.3	32.7	42.5	44.4	41.2	3.1	3.3	7.1	5.8
129	Nepal	13.1	22.5	32.1	2.2	2.2	5.0	11.6	18.1	41.1	37.2	3.7	4.2	5.8	4.8
130	Bhutan	1.2	2.0	3.1	2.3	2.6	3.5	6.9	11.6	43.1	38.8	4.2	4.5	5.9	5.5
131	Lao People's Dem. Rep.	3.0	5.2	7.3	2.2	2.2	11.4	22.9	32.7	43.0	37.3	3.5	3.7	6.2	5.3
132	Bangladesh	75.6	134.6	183.2	2.4	1.9	9.8	23.9	33.9	39.1	32.9	3.1	3.7	6.4	3.8
133	Yemen	7.0	17.6	33.1	3.9	3.9	16.6	24.5	31.2	49.7	48.9	2.3	2.0	7.6	7.6
134	Haiti	4.9	8.0	10.2	2.0	1.5	21.7	35.1	45.6	41.2	35.1	3.7	4.1	5.8	4.4
135	Madagascar	7.9	15.5	24.1	2.8	2.7	16.1	29.0	39.7	44.8	41.9	3.0	3.1	6.6	6.1
136	Nigeria	54.9	110.8	165.3	2.9	2.5	23.4	43.1	55.4	45.2	41.4	3.0	3.3	6.9	5.9
137	Djibouti	0.2	0.6	0.7	4.5	0.8	68.3	83.0	86.3	43.5	41.5	3.1	5.3	6.7	6.1
138	Sudan	16.7	30.4	42.4	2.5	2.1	18.9	35.1	48.7	40.3	35.4	3.4	4.3	6.7	4.9
139	Mauritania	1.4	2.6	4.1	2.6	2.9	20.3	56.4	68.6	44.2	43.5	3.2	3.0	6.5	6.0
140	Tanzania, U. Rep. of	16.2	34.3	49.3	3.1	2.3	10.1	31.6	46.1	45.2	40.4	2.4	3.0	6.8	5.5
141	Uganda	10.8	22.6	38.7	3.1	3.4	8.3	13.8	20.7	49.1	49.3	2.5	2.2	7.1	7.1
142	Congo, Dem. Rep. of the	23.1	49.6	84.0	3.2	3.3	29.5	30.0	39.3	48.5	48.0	2.9	2.8	6.3	6.7
143	Zambia	5.0	10.2	14.8	3.0	2.3	34.8	39.5	45.2	46.5	44.2	2.9	2.9	7.8	6.1
144	Côte d'Ivoire	6.8	15.7	21.5	3.5	2.0	32.1	45.7	55.5	42.6	38.5	3.0	3.8	7.4	5.1
145	Senegal	4.8	9.2	13.5	2.7	2.4	34.2	46.7	57.4	44.5	40.1	2.5	2.7	7.0	5.6
146	Angola	6.2	12.8	20.8	3.0	3.1	17.8	33.5	44.1	48.1	48.5	2.9	2.6	6.6	7.2
147	Benin	3.0	6.1	9.4	2.9	2.7	21.9	41.5	53.0	46.7	42.8	2.8	2.8	7.1	6.1
148	Eritrea	2.1	3.5	5.7	2.2	3.0	12.3	18.4	26.2	44.1	40.4	2.9	3.5	6.5	5.7
149	Gambia	0.5	1.3	1.8	3.5	2.1	17.0	31.8	42.5	40.4	36.8	3.1	4.0	6.5	5.2
150	Guinea	4.1	8.0	11.3	2.8	2.1	16.3	32.0	42.9	44.2	41.6	2.8	3.0	7.0	6.3

HDI rank	Total population (millions)			Annual population growth rate (%)		Urban population (as % of total) [a]			Population under age 15 (as % of total)		Population aged 65 and above (as % of total)		Total fertility rate (per woman)	
	1975	1999	2015[b]	1975-99	1999-2015	1975	1999	2015[b]	1999	2015[b]	1999	2015[b]	1970-75[c]	1995-2000[c]
151 Malawi	5.2	11.0	15.7	3.1	2.2	7.7	23.5	44.1	46.4	44.2	2.9	3.3	7.4	6.8
152 Rwanda	4.4	7.1	10.5	2.0	2.5	4.0	6.1	8.9	44.6	42.8	2.6	2.8	8.3	6.2
153 Mali	6.2	11.0	17.7	2.4	2.9	16.2	29.4	40.1	46.1	46.3	4.0	3.8	7.1	7.0
154 Central African Republic	2.1	3.6	4.9	2.4	1.8	33.7	40.8	49.7	43.0	40.5	4.0	4.0	5.7	5.3
155 Chad	4.1	7.6	12.4	2.6	3.0	15.6	23.5	30.9	46.4	46.4	3.2	2.8	6.7	6.7
156 Guinea-Bissau	0.6	1.2	1.7	2.6	2.4	15.9	23.3	31.7	43.4	43.5	3.6	3.4	6.0	6.0
157 Mozambique	10.3	17.9	23.5	2.3	1.7	8.6	38.9	51.5	43.9	41.8	3.2	3.4	6.6	6.3
158 Ethiopia	32.8	61.4	89.8	2.6	2.4	9.5	17.2	25.8	45.1	44.4	2.9	3.2	6.8	6.8
159 Burkina Faso	6.2	11.2	18.5	2.5	3.1	6.4	17.9	27.4	48.7	47.7	3.3	2.6	7.8	6.9
160 Burundi	3.7	6.3	9.8	2.2	2.8	3.2	8.7	14.5	47.7	45.0	2.9	2.4	6.8	6.8
161 Niger	4.8	10.5	18.5	3.2	3.6	10.6	20.1	29.1	49.8	49.7	2.0	1.9	8.1	8.0
162 Sierra Leone	2.9	4.3	7.1	1.6	3.2	21.4	35.9	46.7	44.1	45.0	2.9	2.9	6.5	6.5
Developing countries	2,898.3 T	4,609.8 T	5,759.1 T	1.9	1.4	25.9	38.9	47.6	33.1	28.1	5.0	6.4	5.4	3.1
Least developed countries	327.2 T	608.8 T	891.9 T	2.6	2.4	14.3	25.4	35.1	43.2	40.4	3.1	3.4	6.6	5.4
Arab States	126.4 T	240.7 T	332.7 T	2.7	2.0	40.4	54.0	61.9	38.1	32.2	3.7	4.6	6.5	4.1
East Asia and the Pacific	1,292.9 T	1,839.8 T	2,106.8 T	1.5	0.8	19.7	34.5	44.0	27.3	21.3	6.1	8.4	5.0	2.1
Latin America and the Caribbean	308.0 T	494.0 T	611.7 T	2.0	1.3	61.1	74.9	79.9	32.3	26.5	5.2	7.0	5.1	2.7
South Asia	828.0 T	1,377.6 T	1,762.1 T	2.1	1.5	21.4	29.9	38.2	35.5	29.0	4.5	5.7	5.6	3.6
Sub-Saharan Africa	302.4 T	591.3 T	866.0 T	2.8	2.4	20.8	33.5	43.3	44.7	42.4	3.0	3.2	6.8	5.8
Eastern Europe and the CIS	353.8 T	398.3 T	383.3 T	0.5	-0.2	57.7	65.9	69.6	21.4	15.9	11.5	12.9	2.5	1.5
OECD	925.4 T	1,122.0 T	1,209.2 T	0.8	0.5	70.4	77.2	81.3	20.6	17.3	12.9	16.2	2.5	1.8
High-income OECD	731.7 T	848.3 T	897.7 T	0.6	0.4	74.9	78.4	81.8	18.5	15.7	14.7	18.5	2.1	1.7
High human development	891.7 T	1,053.8 T	1,123.0 T	0.7	0.4	72.6	78.3	82.1	19.3	16.3	13.7	17.3	2.3	1.7
Medium human development	2,671.4 T	3,990.6 T	4,707.7 T	1.7	1.0	29.4	41.4	49.6	30.3	24.2	5.8	7.5	4.9	2.6
Low human development	424.4 T	818.2 T	1,217.5 T	2.7	2.5	17.5	30.4	40.6	43.8	40.9	3.1	3.4	6.7	5.6
High income	746.1 T	873.2 T	928.4 T	0.7	0.4	75.0	78.7	82.2	18.6	15.8	14.5	18.3	2.1	1.7
Middle income	1,843.1 T	2,632.6 T	3,018.6 T	1.5	0.9	34.8	49.5	57.6	27.8	22.2	6.5	8.5	4.6	2.2
Low income	1,398.2 T	2,356.9 T	3,101.2 T	2.2	1.7	21.9	31.2	40.2	37.2	32.3	4.4	5.2	5.7	4.0
World	3,987.4 T	5,862.7 T	7,048.2 T	1.6	1.2	37.8	46.5	53.2	30.2	25.8	6.9	8.3	4.5	2.8

Note: The estimates and projections in columns 1-5 and 9-14 are based on the 2000 revision of the database *World Population Prospects 1950-2050* (UN 2001d), which explicitly incorporates the impact of HIV/AIDS in 45 highly affected countries, up from 34 in the 1998 revision (UN 1998). These 45 countries are Angola, the Bahamas, Benin, Botswana, Brazil, Burkina Faso, Burundi, Cambodia, Cameroon, the Central African Republic, Chad, Congo, the Democratic Republic of the Congo, Côte d'Ivoire, Djibouti, the Dominican Republic, Eritrea, Ethiopia, Gabon, Gambia, Ghana, Guinea-Bissau, Guyana, Haiti, Honduras, India, Kenya, Lesotho, Liberia, Malawi, Mali, Mozambique, Myanmar, Namibia, Nigeria, Rwanda, Sierra Leone, South Africa, Swaziland, the United Republic of Tanzania, Thailand, Togo, Uganda, Zambia and Zimbabwe.

a. Because data are based on national definitions of what constitutes a city or metropolitan area, cross country comparisons should be made with caution.

b. Data refer to medium-variant projections.

c. Data refer to estimates for the period specified.

d. Population estimates include Taiwan, province of China.

Source: Columns 1-3, 13 and 14: UN 2001d; column 4: calculated on the basis of data in columns 1 and 2; column 5: calculated on the basis of data in columns 2 and 3; columns 6 and 8: UN 2000b; column 7: calculated on the basis of data on urban and total population from UN (2000b); columns 9 and 10: calculated on the basis of data on population under age 15 and total population from UN (2001d); columns 11 and 12: calculated on the basis of data on population aged 65 and above and total population from UN (2001d).

6 Commitment to health: access, services and resources

HDI rank	Population using adequate sanitation facilities (%) 1999	Population using improved water sources (%) 1999	Population with access to essential drugs (%) [a] 1999	One-year-olds fully immunized		Oral rehydration therapy use rate (%) 1995-2000 [b]	Contraceptive prevalence (%) [c] 1995-2000 [b]	Births attended by skilled health staff (%) 1995-99 [d]	Physicians (per 100,000 people) 1990-99 [b]	Health expenditure		
				Against tuberculosis (%) 1997-99 [b]	Against measles (%) 1997-99 [b]					Public (as % of GDP) 1998	Private (as % of GDP) 1998	Per capita (PPP US$) 1998
High human development												
1 Norway	..	100	100	..	93	..	..	..	413	7.4	1.5	2,467
2 Australia	100	100	100	..	89	..	..	..	240	5.9	2.6	1,980
3 Canada	100	100	100	..	96	..	75	..	229	6.3 [e]	2.8 [e]	2,391 [e]
4 Sweden	100	100	99	12 [f]	96	..	..	..	311	6.7	1.3	1,707
5 Belgium	..	..	99	..	64	..	..	..	395	7.9	1.0	2,172
6 United States	100	100	99	..	91	..	76	99	279	5.8 [e]	7.3 [e]	4,180 [e]
7 Iceland	..	..	100	98 [f]	98	..	..	..	326	7.2 [e]	1.3 [e]	2,358 [e]
8 Netherlands	100	100	100	..	96	..	..	..	251	6.0	2.5	1,974
9 Japan	..	..	100	91 [f]	94	..	..	..	193	5.9	1.6	1,844
10 Finland	100	100	98	99	98	..	..	..	299	5.2	1.6	1,502
11 Switzerland	100	100	100	..	..	..	82 [g]	..	323	7.6	2.8	2,739
12 Luxembourg	..	..	99	58	91	..	..	..	272	5.4	0.5	2,327
13 France	..	..	99	83 [f]	97	..	..	..	303	7.3	2.3	2,102
14 United Kingdom	100	100	99	99	95	..	..	100	164	5.9 [e]	1.1 [e]	1,532 [e]
15 Denmark	..	100	99	..	84	..	..	..	290	6.7 [e]	1.5 [e]	2,141 [e]
16 Austria	100	100	100	..	90	..	51	..	302	5.8	2.4	1,978
17 Germany	..	..	100	..	88	..	..	..	350	7.9 [e]	2.6 [e]	2,488 [e]
18 Ireland	..	..	99	..	..	..	..	..	219	4.5 [e]	1.3 [e]	1,505 [e]
19 New Zealand	..	..	100	..	82	..	75	..	218	6.2	1.8	1,454
20 Italy	..	..	99	..	55	..	..	..	554	5.6 [e]	2.6 [e]	1,830 [e]
21 Spain	..	..	100	..	78	..	81	..	424	5.4	1.6	1,202
22 Israel	..	..	99	..	94	..	..	..	385	6.0	3.6	1,730
23 Greece	..	..	100	70	90	..	..	..	392	4.7	3.6	1,207
24 Hong Kong, China (SAR)	..	..	..	..	..	..	..	..	..	..	..	..
25 Cyprus	100	100	100	..	90	..	..	..	255	..	..	..
26 Singapore	100	100	100	98	86	..	..	100	163	1.2	2.1	777
27 Korea, Rep. of	63	92	99	99	96	..	81	..	136	2.3	2.8	720
28 Portugal	..	..	100	88	96	..	..	100	312	5.2	..	..
29 Slovenia	..	100	100	98	93	..	..	..	228	6.6	0.9	1,126
30 Malta	100	100	99	96 [f]	60	..	..	..	261	..	..	..
31 Barbados	100	100	100	..	86	..	..	..	125	4.5	2.2	938
32 Brunei Darussalam	..	..	99	98	94	..	..	..	85	..	..	..
33 Czech Republic	..	..	88	99	95	..	..	..	303	6.7	0.6	928
34 Argentina	85	79	70	68	97	..	..	..	268	4.9	5.4	1,291
35 Slovakia	100	100	100	92	99	..	..	..	353	5.7	1.5	728
36 Hungary	99	99	100	100	100	..	..	..	357	5.2	..	..
37 Uruguay	95	98	66	99	93	..	..	..	370	1.9	7.2	823
38 Poland	..	..	88	94 [f]	91	..	..	..	236	4.7	1.7	510
39 Chile	97	94	88	96	93	..	..	..	110	2.7	3.1	511
40 Bahrain	..	..	100	72	100	39	62	98	100	2.6	1.6	585
41 Costa Rica	96	98	100	87	86	31 [f]	..	..	141	5.2	1.5	509
42 Bahamas	93	96	80	..	93	..	..	..	152	2.5	1.8	658
43 Kuwait	..	..	99	..	96	..	..	98	189	..	..	..
44 Estonia	..	..	100	100	89	..	..	..	297	..	1.4	..
45 United Arab Emirates	..	..	99	98	95	42	28	99	181	0.8	7.4	1,495
46 Croatia	100	95	100	96	92	(.)	..	..	229	..	1.5	..
47 Lithuania	..	..	88	99	97	..	59 [g]	..	395	4.8	1.5	429
48 Qatar	..	..	99	100	90	54 [f]	43	..	126	..	..	..
Medium human development												
49 Trinidad and Tobago	88	86	77	..	89	..	..	99	79	2.5	1.8	323
50 Latvia	..	..	90	100	97	..	48	..	282	4.2	2.6	410

HDI rank		Population using adequate sanitation facilities (%) 1999	Population using improved water sources (%) 1999	Population with access to essential drugs (%) [a] 1999	One-year-olds fully immunized		Oral rehydration therapy use rate (%) 1995-2000 [b]	Contraceptive prevalence (%) [c] 1995-2000 [b]	Births attended by skilled health staff (%) 1995-99 [d]	Physicians (per 100,000 people) 1990-99 [b]	Health expenditure		
					Against tuberculosis (%) 1997-99 [b]	Against measles (%) 1997-99 [b]					Public (as % of GDP) 1998	Private (as % of GDP) 1998	Per capita (PPP US$) 1998
51	Mexico	73	86	92	100	98	80	67	..	186	..	..	..
52	Panama	94	87	80	99	96	94 [f]	..	..	167	4.9	2.3	410
53	Belarus	..	100	70	99	98	..	50	..	443	4.9	1.1	387
54	Belize	42	76	80	93	84	..	..	..	55	2.2	0.5	132
55	Russian Federation	..	99	66	100	97	..	..	99	421	..	1.2	..
56	Malaysia	98	95	70	98	88	..	..	..	66	1.4	1.0	189
57	Bulgaria	100	100	88	98	95	..	86	..	345	3.8	0.8	230
58	Romania	53	58	85	100	98	..	64	..	184	..	1.5	..
59	Libyan Arab Jamahiriya	97	72	100	100	92	..	40	..	128	..	..	..
60	Macedonia, TFYR	93	99	66	99	92	19	..	..	204	5.5	1.0	288
61	Venezuela	74	84	90	95	78	..	..	..	236	2.6	1.6	248
62	Colombia	85	91	88	80	77	53	77	85	116	5.2	4.2	553
63	Mauritius	99	100	100	87	80	..	..	..	85	1.8	1.6	302
64	Suriname	83	95	100	..	85	..	..	..	25	..	..	..
65	Lebanon	99	100	88	..	81	82 [f]	61	95	210	2.2	7.6	..
66	Thailand	96	80	95	98	94	95	72	95	24	1.9	4.1	349
67	Fiji	43	47	100	95	75	..	..	..	48	2.9	1.4	196
68	Saudi Arabia	100	95	99	92	92	53	32	91	166	..	..	..
69	Brazil	72	83	40	99	96	54	77	88	127	2.9	3.7	453
70	Philippines	83	87	66	91	71	64	46	56	123	1.7	2.0	136
71	Oman	92	39	90	98	99	61	24	..	133	2.9	0.6	..
72	Armenia	67	84	40	93	84	30	..	96	316	3.1	4.2	..
73	Peru	76	77	60	72	92	60	64	56	93	2.4	3.7	278
74	Ukraine	..	..	66	99	99	..	68	..	299	3.6	1.5	169
75	Kazakhstan	99	91	66	99	87	32	66	98	353	3.5	2.4	273
76	Georgia	99	76	30	92	73	14	41	..	436	0.5	1.7	73
77	Maldives	56	100	50	98	97	18	..	..	40	5.1	5.5	472
78	Jamaica	84	71	95	89	82	..	66	95	140	3.2	2.6	202
79	Azerbaijan	..	..	66	91	87	..	..	99	360	..	0.6	..
80	Paraguay	95	79	44	87	72	33	57	61	110	1.7	3.6	233
81	Sri Lanka	83	83	95	97	95	34 [f]	..	95	37	1.4	1.7	95
82	Turkey	91	83	99	78	80	27	64	81	121	..	..	..
83	Turkmenistan	100	58	66	99	97	98	..	..	300	4.1	1.1	146
84	Ecuador	59	71	40	100	75	60	66	..	170	1.7	2.0	115
85	Albania	..	..	60	93	85	..	..	..	129	3.5	0.5	116
86	Dominican Republic	71	79	66	90	94	39	64	96	216	1.9	3.0	246
87	China	38	75	85	85	85	85 [f]	..	..	162	..	..	..
88	Jordan	99	96	100	..	83	29	53	97	166	5.3	3.8	..
89	Tunisia	..	..	51	99	93	81	..	82	70	2.2	2.9	287
90	Iran, Islamic Rep. of	81	95	85	99	99	48	73	..	85	1.7	2.5	229
91	Cape Verde	71	74	80	75	61	83 [f]	53	..	17	1.8	1.0	119
92	Kyrgyzstan	100	77	66	98	97	44	60	98	301	2.9	1.6	109
93	Guyana	87	94	44	91	86	..	..	..	18	4.5	0.8	186
94	South Africa	86	86	80	97	82	58	56	84	56	3.3	3.8	623
95	El Salvador	83	74	80	72	75	57	60	90	107	2.6	4.6	298
96	Samoa (Western)	99	99	100	99	91	..	..	..	34	4.8	..	..
97	Syrian Arab Republic	90	80	80	100	97	61	..	..	144	0.8	1.6	90
98	Moldova, Rep. of	..	100	66	100	99	..	74	..	350	6.4	2.1	177
99	Uzbekistan	100	85	66	97	96	37	56	98	309	3.4	0.6	87
100	Algeria	73	94	95	97	78	98 [f]	52	..	85	2.6	1.0	..

HDI rank		Population using adequate sanitation facilities (%) 1999	Population using improved water sources (%) 1999	Population with access to essential drugs (%)[a] 1999	One-year-olds fully immunized Against tuberculosis (%) 1997-99[b]	One-year-olds fully immunized Against measles (%) 1997-99[b]	Oral rehydration therapy use rate (%) 1995-2000[b]	Contraceptive prevalence (%)[c] 1995-2000[b]	Births attended by skilled health staff (%) 1995-99[d]	Physicians (per 100,000 people) 1990-99[b]	Health expenditure Public (as % of GDP) 1998	Health expenditure Private (as % of GDP) 1998	Health expenditure Per capita (PPP US$) 1998
101	Viet Nam	73	56	85	95	94	51	75	77	48	0.8	4.0	81
102	Indonesia	66	76	80	97	71	70	57	47	16	0.7	0.8	44
103	Tajikistan	..	..	44	98	95	..	..	..	201	5.2	0.9	63
104	Bolivia	66	79	70	95	100	48	48	59	130	4.1	2.4	150
105	Egypt	94	95	88	99	97	37	47	56	202	..	..	..
106	Nicaragua	84	79	46	100	71	58	60	65	86	8.3	3.9	266
107	Honduras	77	90	40	93	98	30	50	55	83	3.9	4.7	210
108	Guatemala	85	92	50	88	81	34	38	35	93	2.1	2.3	155
109	Gabon	21	70	30	60	30	39	..	..	..	2.1	1.0	198
110	Equatorial Guinea	53	43	44	99	82	..	..	..	25	..	..	..
111	Namibia	41	77	80	80	65	..	..	..	30	4.1	3.7	417
112	Morocco	75	82	66	90	93	29	50	..	46	1.2	3.2	..
113	Swaziland	..	..	100	94	72	99 [f]	..	..	15	2.7	1.0	148
114	Botswana	..	..	90	98	74	43	..	..	24	2.5	1.6	267
115	India	31	88	35	72	55	67 [f]	48	..	48	..	4.2	..
116	Mongolia	30	60	60	97	86	80	..	..	243	..	..	..
117	Zimbabwe	68	85	70	88	79	68	54	84	14	..	..	..
118	Myanmar	46	68	60	90	86	96 [f]	33	..	30	0.2	1.6	..
119	Ghana	63	64	44	88	73	36	22	44	6	1.8	2.9	85
120	Lesotho	92	91	80	68	55	84 [f]	..	..	5	..	..	..
121	Cambodia	18	30	30	78	63	21	13	31	30	0.6	6.3	90
122	Papua New Guinea	82	42	90	70	57	35	26	53	7	2.5	0.7	75
123	Kenya	86	49	36	96	79	69	39	44	13	2.4	5.4	79
124	Comoros	98	96	90	84	67	32	21	52	7	..	..	..
125	Cameroon	92	62	66	66	46	34	19	55	7	1.0	..	..
126	Congo	..	51	61	39	23	41 [f]	..	..	25	2.0	3.8	46
Low human development													
127	Pakistan	61	88	65	73	54	48	24	..	57	0.9	3.1	71
128	Togo	34	54	70	63	47	23	24	51	8	1.3	1.3	36
129	Nepal	27	81	20	86	73	29	29	32	4	1.3	4.2	66
130	Bhutan	69	62	85	90	77	85 [f]	..	..	16	3.2	3.7	87
131	Lao People's Dem. Rep.	46	90	66	63	71	32	..	..	24	1.2	1.3	35
132	Bangladesh	53	97	65	95	66	74	54	14	20	1.7	1.9	51
133	Yemen	45	69	50	78	74	35	21	22	23	..	..	..
134	Haiti	28	46	30	59	84	41	28	20	8	1.4	2.8	61
135	Madagascar	42	47	65	66	46	23	19	47	11	1.1	1.0	16
136	Nigeria	63	57	10	27	26	32	..	..	19	0.8	2.0	23
137	Djibouti	91	100	80	26	23	..	..	..	14	..	..	..
138	Sudan	62	75	15	100	88	31	..	..	9	..	..	..
139	Mauritania	33	37	66	76	56	51	..	58	14	1.4	3.4	74
140	Tanzania, U. Rep. of	90	54	66	93	78	55	24	35	4	1.3	1.8	15
141	Uganda	75	50	70	83	53	49	15	38	..	1.9	4.1	65
142	Congo, Dem. Rep. of the	20	45	..	22	15	90 [f]	..	..	7	..	..	..
143	Zambia	78	64	66	87	72	57	25	47	7	3.6	3.4	52
144	Côte d'Ivoire	..	77	80	84	66	29	..	47	9	1.2	2.6	62
145	Senegal	70	78	66	90	60	39	13	..	8	2.6	1.9	61
146	Angola	44	38	20	65	49	..	..	..	8	..	..	..
147	Benin	23	63	77	100	92	75 [f]	16	60	6	1.6	1.6	29
148	Eritrea	13	46	57	64	55	38	5	21	3	..	..	..
149	Gambia	37	62	90	97	88	99 [f]	..	..	4	1.9	1.9	56
150	Guinea	58	48	93	76	52	40	6	35	13	2.2	1.4	68

6 Commitment to health: access, services and resources

HDI rank	Population using adequate sanitation facilities (%) 1999	Population using improved water sources (%) 1999	Population with access to essential drugs (%) a 1999	One-year-olds fully immunized Against tuberculosis (%) 1997-99 b	One-year-olds fully immunized Against measles (%) 1997-99 b	Oral rehydration therapy use rate (%) 1995-2000 b	Contraceptive prevalence (%) c 1995-2000 b	Births attended by skilled health staff (%) 1995-99 d	Physicians (per 100,000 people) 1990-99 b	Health expenditure Public (as % of GDP) 1998	Health expenditure Private (as % of GDP) 1998	Health expenditure Per capita (PPP US$) 1998
151 Malawi	77	57	44	92	90	70	22	..	..	2.8	3.5	36
152 Rwanda	8	41	44	94	78	47 f	14	..	..	2.0	2.1	34
153 Mali	69	65	60	84	57	16	7	24	5	2.1	2.2	30
154 Central African Republic	31	60	50	55	40	35	15 g	46	4	2.0	1.0	33
155 Chad	29	27	46	57	49	29	4	11	3	2.3	0.6	25
156 Guinea-Bissau	47	49	44	25	19	..	..	..	17	..	..	..
157 Mozambique	43	60	50	100	90	49	6	44	..	2.8	0.7	28
158 Ethiopia	15	24	66	80	53	19	8	..	..	1.7	2.4	25
159 Burkina Faso	29	..	60	72	46	18	12	27	3	1.2	2.7	36
160 Burundi	..	..	20	71	47	38 f	..	..	..	0.6	3.0	21
161 Niger	20	59	66	36	25	21	8	18	4	1.2	1.4	20
162 Sierra Leone	28	28	44	55	29	..	..	..	7	0.9	4.5	27

a. The data on access to essential drugs are based on statistical estimates received from World Health Organization (WHO) country and regional offices and regional advisers and through the World Drug Situation Survey carried out in 1998-99. These estimates represent the best information available to the WHO Department of Essential Drugs and Medicines Policy to date and are currently being validated by WHO member states. The department assigns the estimates to four groupings: very low access (0-49%), low access (50-79%), medium access (80-94%) and good access (95% or more). These groupings are often used by the WHO in interpreting the data, as the percentage estimates may suggest a higher level of accuracy than the data afford.

b. Data refer to the most recent year available during the period specified.

c. Data refer to married women aged 15-49, but the age range covered may vary across countries.

d. Definitions of skilled health staff may vary across countries. Data refer to the most recent year available during the period specified or to a running average for a series of years surrounding that period.

e. Data refer to 1999.

f. Data refer to a year or period other than that specified, differ from the standard definition or refer to only part of a country.

g. Data refer to the survey period 1994-95.

Source: Columns 1, 2 and 4-6: UNICEF 2000; column 3: WHO 2001a; column 7: UN 2001c; column 8: WHO 2001d; column 9: WHO 2001c; columns 10-12: World Bank 2001b.

... TO LEAD A LONG AND HEALTHY LIFE ...

HDI rank	Under-nourished people (as % of total population) 1996/98	Children under-weight for age (% under age 5) 1995-2000 [a]	Children under height for age (% under age 5) 1995-2000 [a]	Infants with low birth-weight (%) 1995-99 [a]	People living with HIV/AIDS			Malaria cases (per 100,000 people) 1997 [c]	Tuberculosis cases (per 100,000 people) [d] 1998	Cigarette consumption per adult (annual average) 1992-98 [e]
					Adults (% age 15-49) 1999 [b]	Women (age 15-49) 1999 [b]	Children (age 0-14) 1999 [b]			
High human development										
1 Norway	..	..	..	4 [f]	0.07	360	<100	..	5	760
2 Australia	..	..	..	6 [f]	0.15	900	140	..	5	1,950
3 Canada	..	..	..	6 [f]	0.30	5,600	500	..	6 [g]	1,989
4 Sweden	..	..	..	5 [f]	0.08	800	<100	..	5	1,014
5 Belgium	..	..	..	6 [f]	0.15	2,600	300	..	10	1,794 [h]
6 United States	..	1 [f]	2	7 [f]	0.61	170,000	10,000	..	7	2,372
7 Iceland	..	..	..	..	0.14	<100	<100	..	6	2,241
8 Netherlands	..	..	..	..	0.19	3,000	100	..	8	2,044
9 Japan	..	..	..	7 [f]	0.02	1,300	<100	..	35	2,857
10 Finland	..	..	..	4 [f]	0.05	300	<100	..	10	1,222
11 Switzerland	..	..	..	5 [f]	0.46	5,500	<100	..	10	2,846
12 Luxembourg	..	..	..	..	0.16	..	..	..	10	..
13 France	..	..	..	5 [f]	0.44	35,000	1,000	..	12 [i]	1,785
14 United Kingdom	..	..	..	7 [f]	0.11	6,700	500	..	10	1,833
15 Denmark	..	..	..	6 [f]	0.17	900	<100	..	10	1,962
16 Austria	..	..	..	6 [f]	0.23	2,000	<100	..	16	1,908
17 Germany	..	..	..	..	0.10	7,400	500	..	13	1,748
18 Ireland	..	..	..	4 [f]	0.10	600	170	..	10	2,412
19 New Zealand	..	..	..	6 [f]	0.06	180	<100	..	10	1,223
20 Italy	..	..	..	5 [f]	0.35	30,000	700	..	10	1,855
21 Spain	..	..	..	4 [f]	0.58	25,000	<100	..	23	2,428
22 Israel	..	..	..	7 [f]	0.08	700	<100	..	10	2,137
23 Greece	..	..	..	6 [f]	0.16	1,600	<100	..	10	3,923
24 Hong Kong, China (SAR)	..	..	..	..	0.06	630	<100	..	115	761
25 Cyprus	..	..	..	..	0.10	<100	<100	..	6	..
26 Singapore	..	..	..	7 [f]	0.19	790	<100	..	61	2,835
27 Korea, Rep. of	..	..	..	9 [f]	0.01	490	<100	4	65	2,898
28 Portugal	..	..	..	5 [f]	0.74	7,000	500	..	53	2,077
29 Slovenia	3	..	..	..	0.02	<100	<100	..	21	..
30 Malta	..	..	..	..	0.12	..	..	..	4	..
31 Barbados	..	5 [f]	7	10	1.17	570	<100	..	3	512
32 Brunei Darussalam	..	..	..	..	0.20 [j]	..	..	..	52 [i]	..
33 Czech Republic	..	1 [f]	2	6 [f]	0.04	500	<100	..	17	2,504
34 Argentina	..	..	..	7	0.69	27,000	4,400	2	34	1,555
35 Slovakia	4	..	..	..	<0.01	<100	<100	..	21	2,178
36 Hungary	..	2 [f]	3	9 [f]	0.05	270	<100	..	34	2,500
37 Uruguay	4	5	8	8 [f]	0.33	1,500	<100	..	20	1,453
38 Poland	..	..	..	..	0.07	..	..	..	34	3,143
39 Chile	4	1	2	5	0.19	2,600	260	..	25	1,152
40 Bahrain	..	9	10	6 [f]	0.15 [j]	..	..	..	36	2,819
41 Costa Rica	6	5	6	7	0.54	2,800	290	126	18	873
42 Bahamas	..	..	..	..	4.13	2,200	150	..	25	435
43 Kuwait	4	6 [f]	12	7 [f]	0.12 [j]	..	..	..	31	2,525
44 Estonia	6	..	..	..	0.04	<100	<100	..	57	1,989
45 United Arab Emirates	..	14	17	6 [f]	0.18 [j]	..	..	4	33	..
46 Croatia	12	1	1	5	0.02 [j]	<100	<100	..	47	2,632
47 Lithuania	..	..	..	..	0.02	<100	<100	..	82	..
48 Qatar	..	6	8	..	0.09 [j]	..	..	..	44	..
Medium human development										
49 Trinidad and Tobago	13	7 [f]	5	10 [f]	1.05	2,500	180	..	15	684
50 Latvia	4	..	..	..	0.11	250	<100	..	81	..

HDI rank		Under-nourished people (as % of total population) 1996/98	Children under-weight for age (% under age 5) 1995-2000 [a]	Children under height for age (% under age 5) 1995-2000 [a]	Infants with low birth-weight (%) 1995-99 [a]	People living with HIV/AIDS			Malaria cases (per 100,000 people) 1997 [c]	Tuberculosis cases (per 100,000 people) [d] 1998	Cigarette consumption per adult (annual average) 1992-98 [e]
						Adults (% age 15-49) 1999 [b]	Women (age 15-49) 1999 [b]	Children (age 0-14) 1999 [b]			
51	Mexico	5	8	18	7	0.29	22,000	2,400	5	8	821
52	Panama	16	7	14	10	1.54	9,400	670	19	53	271
53	Belarus	..	..	..	..	0.28	3,500	<100	..	60	1,434
54	Belize	..	6 [f]	..	4	2.01	590	<100	1,790	40 [i]	1,092
55	Russian Federation	6	3	13	7	0.18	32,500	1,800	..	82	1,594
56	Malaysia	..	18	..	9	0.42	1,800	550	127	66	998
57	Bulgaria	13	..	..	6 [f]	0.01 [j]	..	..	..	55	2,362
58	Romania	..	6 [f]	8	7 [f]	0.02	750	5,000	..	114	1,681
59	Libyan Arab Jamahiriya	..	5	15	7 [f]	0.05 [j]	..	..	..	29	..
60	Macedonia, TFYR	7	..	..	..	<0.01	<100	<100	..	31	..
61	Venezuela	16	5 [f]	13	9 [f]	0.49	9,200	580	98	27	1,104
62	Colombia	13	8	15	9	0.31	10,000	900	452	22	339
63	Mauritius	6	16	10	13	0.08 [j]	..	..	6	12	1,634
64	Suriname	10	..	..	13 [f]	1.26	950	110	2,748	17 [i]	2,080
65	Lebanon	..	3	12	10 [f]	0.09 [j]	..	..	..	23	..
66	Thailand	21	19 [f]	16	6	2.15	305,000	13,900	163	26	1,120
67	Fiji	..	8 [f]	3	12 [f]	0.07	..	..	..	21	1,021
68	Saudi Arabia	3	14	20	7 [f]	0.01	..	..	106	16	1,259
69	Brazil	10	6	11	8	0.57	130,000	9,900	240	51	826
70	Philippines	21	28	30	9 [f]	0.07	11,000	1,300	59	219	1,844
71	Oman	..	23	23	8	0.11 [j]	..	..	45	9	..
72	Armenia	21	3	8	9	0.01	<100	<100	24	39	1,016
73	Peru	18	8	26	11 [f]	0.35	12,000	640	754	176	208
74	Ukraine	5	..	..	..	0.96	70,000	7,500	..	62	1,247
75	Kazakhstan	5	8	16	9	0.04	<100	<100	..	126	1,622
76	Georgia	23	..	..	..	<0.01	<100	<100	..	96	..
77	Maldives	..	43	27	13	0.05 [j]	..	..	4	65	1,488
78	Jamaica	10	5	6	11	0.71	3,100	230	..	5	745
79	Azerbaijan	32	10	22	6	<0.01	<100	<100	130	61	1,105
80	Paraguay	13	5	11	5	0.11	520	<100	11	36	..
81	Sri Lanka	25	34	18	25 [f]	0.07	2,200	200	1,196	38	399
82	Turkey	..	8	16	8	0.01	..	..	56	35	2,304
83	Turkmenistan	10	..	..	5 [f]	0.01	<100	<100	..	89	2,323
84	Ecuador	5	17 [f]	34	13 [f]	0.29	2,700	330	137	75	268
85	Albania	3	..	..	7 [f]	<0.01	..	..	..	22	..
86	Dominican Republic	28	6	11	13	2.80	59,000	3,800	10	52	775
87	China	11	10	17	6	0.07	61,000	4,800	2	36	1,818
88	Jordan	5	5	8	10	0.02 [j]	..	..	..	6	1,315
89	Tunisia	..	4	8	8 [f]	0.04 [j]	..	..	..	24	1,573
90	Iran, Islamic Rep. of	6	11	15	10	<0.01 [j]	..	..	60	18	785
91	Cape Verde	..	14 [f]	16	9 [f]	..	..	..	5	50	..
92	Kyrgyzstan	17	11	25	6	<0.01	<100	<100	..	123	1,927
93	Guyana	18	12	10	15	3.01	4,900	140	3,806	37	..
94	South Africa	..	9	23	..	19.94	2,300,000	95,000	75 [f]	326	1,448
95	El Salvador	11	12	23	13	0.60	4,800	560	..	28	..
96	Samoa (Western)	..	..	..	6 [f]	..	..	..	..	13	1,412
97	Syrian Arab Republic	..	13	21	7	0.01 [j]	..	..	1	35	1,318
98	Moldova, Rep. of	11	..	..	4 [f]	0.20	1,000	100	..	60	1,386
99	Uzbekistan	11	19	31	..	<0.01	<100	<100	..	62	1,274
100	Algeria	5	13	18	9 [f]	0.07 [j]	..	..	1	51	1,033

HDI rank	Under-nourished people (as % of total population) 1996/98	Children under-weight for age (% under age 5) 1995-2000 [a]	Children under height for age (% under age 5) 1995-2000 [a]	Infants with low birth-weight (%) 1995-99 [a]	People living with HIV/AIDS			Malaria cases (per 100,000 people) 1997 [c]	Tuberculosis cases (per 100,000 people) [d] 1998	Cigarette consumption per adult (annual average) 1992-98 [e]
					Adults (% age 15-49) 1999 [b]	Women (age 15-49) 1999 [b]	Children (age 0-14) 1999 [b]			
101 Viet Nam	22	39	34	17 [f]	0.24	20,000	2,500	86	113	891
102 Indonesia	6	34	42	8	0.05	13,000	680	79	20	1,389
103 Tajikistan	32	..	..	..	<0.01	<100	<100	507	41	..
104 Bolivia	23	10	26	5	0.10	680	<100	662	127	270
105 Egypt	4	12	25	10 [f]	0.02 [j]	..	..	(.)	19	1,214
106 Nicaragua	31	12	25	9	0.20	1,200	<100	915	54	889
107 Honduras	22	25	39	9 [f]	1.92	29,000	4,400	1,101	80	689
108 Guatemala	24	24	46	15	1.38	28,000	1,600	305	26	303
109 Gabon	8	..	..	..	4.16	12,000	780	3,152	118	540
110 Equatorial Guinea	..	..	..	..	0.51	560	<100	..	97	..
111 Namibia	31	26 [f]	28	16 [f]	19.54	85,000	6,600	26,217	480	..
112 Morocco	5	9 [f]	23	9 [f]	0.03 [j]	..	..	1	106	827
113 Swaziland	14	10 [f]	30	10 [f]	25.25	67,000	3,800	..	433 [g]	..
114 Botswana	27	17	29	11	35.80	150,000	10,000	..	303	..
115 India	21	53 [f]	52	33 [f]	0.70	1,300,000	160,000	275	115	119
116 Mongolia	45	10	22	7	<0.01	..	..	..	113	..
117 Zimbabwe	37	15	32	10	25.06	800,000	56,000	..	416	311
118 Myanmar	7	39	..	24 [f]	1.99	180,000	14,000	256	33	..
119 Ghana	10	25	26	8	3.60	180,000	14,000	11,941	53	169
120 Lesotho	29	16	44	11 [f]	23.57	130,000	8,200	..	272 [i]	..
121 Cambodia	33	52	56	..	4.04	71,000	5,400	1,096	158	..
122 Papua New Guinea	29	30 [f]	43	23 [f]	0.22	2,600	220	847	245	..
123 Kenya	43	22	33	16 [f]	13.95	1,100,000	78,000	..	169	339
124 Comoros	..	26	34	8 [f]	0.12 [j]	..	..	2,422 [f]	23 [g]	..
125 Cameroon	29	22	29	13 [f]	7.73	290,000	22,000	4,613	35	671
126 Congo	32	17 [f]	21	16 [f]	6.43	45,000	4,000	350	139	..
Low human development										
127 Pakistan	20	26 [f]	23	25 [f]	0.10	15,000	1,600	54	60	562
128 Togo	18	25	22	20 [f]	5.98	66,000	6,300	..	28	453
129 Nepal	28	47	54	..	0.29	10,000	930	29	106	628
130 Bhutan	..	38 [f]	56	..	<0.01	..	..	464	64	..
131 Lao People's Dem. Rep.	29	40 [f]	47	18 [f]	0.05	650	<100	1,076	42	..
132 Bangladesh	38	56	55	30	0.02	1,900	130	56	58	237
133 Yemen	35	46	52	19 [f]	0.01 [j]	..	..	8,560	73	..
134 Haiti	62	28	32	15 [f]	5.17	67,000	5,200	..	124	..
135 Madagascar	40	40	48	5	0.15	5,800	450	..	97	..
136 Nigeria	8	31	34	16 [f]	5.06	1,400,000	120,000	593	19	..
137 Djibouti	..	18	26	11 [f]	11.75	19,000	1,500	700	597	..
138 Sudan	18	34 [f]	33	15 [f]	0.99 [j]	..	..	5,283	80	..
139 Mauritania	13	23	44	11 [f]	0.52	3,500	260	..	154 [i]	327
140 Tanzania, U. Rep. of	41	27	42	14 [f]	8.09	670,000	59,000	3,602	160	196
141 Uganda	30	26	38	13	8.30	420,000	53,000	..	142	173
142 Congo, Dem. Rep. of the	61	34	45	15 [f]	5.07	600,000	53,000	..	120	137
143 Zambia	45	24	42	13 [f]	19.95	450,000	40,000	37,458 [f]	482 [g]	..
144 Côte d'Ivoire	14	24 [f]	24	12 [f]	10.76	400,000	32,000	6,990	104	593
145 Senegal	23	22	23	4	1.77	40,000	3,300	..	94	..
146 Angola	43	42	53	19 [f]	2.78	82,000	7,900	..	102	464
147 Benin	14	29	25	..	2.45	37,000	3,000	11,918	41	..
148 Eritrea	65	44	38	13 [f]	2.87 [j]	..	..	..	218	..
149 Gambia	16	26	30	..	1.95	6,600	520	27,369	114 [i]	331
150 Guinea	29	..	29	13	1.54	29,000	2,700	10,951	65	..

HDI rank	Under-nourished people (as % of total population) 1996/98	Children under-weight for age (% under age 5) 1995-2000 [a]	Children under height for age (% under age 5) 1995-2000 [a]	Infants with low birth-weight (%) 1995-99 [a]	People living with HIV/AIDS			Malaria cases (per 100,000 people) 1997 [c]	Tuberculosis cases (per 100,000 people) [d] 1998	Cigarette consumption per adult (annual average) 1992-98 [e]
					Adults (% age 15-49) 1999 [b]	Women (age 15-49) 1999 [b]	Children (age 0-14) 1999 [b]			
151 Malawi	32	30	48	20 [f]	15.96	420,000	40,000	..	220	176
152 Rwanda	39	27	42	17 [f]	11.21	210,000	22,000	20,310	93	..
153 Mali	32	40	30	16	2.03	53,000	5,000	3,688	39	..
154 Central African Republic	41	27	34	15 [f]	13.84	130,000	8,900	..	140	..
155 Chad	30	39	40	..	2.69	49,000	4,000	4,843	38	158
156 Guinea-Bissau	..	23 [f]	..	20 [f]	2.50	7,300	560	..	156 [g]	82
157 Mozambique	58	26	36	12	13.22	630,000	52,000	..	104	..
158 Ethiopia	49	47	51	16 [f]	10.63	1,600,000	150,000	..	116	..
159 Burkina Faso	32	36	31	21 [f]	6.44	180,000	20,000	..	18	..
160 Burundi	68	37 [f]	43	..	11.32	190,000	19,000	..	101	..
161 Niger	46	50	41	15 [f]	1.35	34,000	3,300	10,026	34	..
162 Sierra Leone	43	29 [f]	35	11 [f]	2.99	36,000	3,300	..	72	..
Developing countries	18	27	31	..	1.3	15,362,000 T	1,252,000 T	..	71	..
Least developed countries	38	41	46	..	4.3	6,389,000 T	590,000 T	..	97	..
Arab States	..	16	24	..	0.2	19,000 T	1,500 T	..	47	..
East Asia and the Pacific	12	16	22	..	0.2	671,000 T	43,000 T	..	47	..
Latin America and the Caribbean	12	8	16	..	0.7	434,000 T	37,000 T	..	45	..
South Asia	22	48	47	..	0.5	1,329,000 T	163,000 T	..	98	..
Sub-Saharan Africa	34	30	37	..	8.7	12,909,000 T	1,008,000 T	..	121	..
Eastern Europe and the CIS	8	..	..	..	0.2	109,000 T	14,000 T	..	70	..
OECD	..	..	..	..	0.3	330,000 T	17,000 T	..	18	..
High-income OECD	..	..	..	..	0.4	307,000 T	14,000 T	..	14	..
High human development	..	..	..	..	0.3	347,000 T	20,000 T	..	19	..
Medium human development	14	24	28	..	0.8	7,569,000 T	543,000 T	..	70	..
Low human development	32	36	39	..	4.6	7,863,000 T	719,000 T	..	82	..
High income	..	..	..	..	0.3	311,000 T	15,000 T	..	15	..
Middle income	11	10	17	..	1.0	3,422,000 T	177,000 T	..	52	..
Low income	23	43	45	..	1.3	12,045,000 T	1,090,000 T	..	92	..
World	..	24	28	..	1.1	15,778,000 T	1,281,000 T	..	63	..

a. Data refer to the most recent year available during the period specified.

b. Data refer to the end of 1999. Aggregates are rounded estimates; regional totals may not sum to the world total.

c. Data refer to malaria cases reported to the World Health Organization and may represent only a fraction of the true number in a country because of incomplete reporting systems or incomplete health service coverage, or both. Because of the diversity of case detection and reporting systems, country comparisons should be made with caution. Data refer to the end of 1997.

d. Data refer to tuberculosis cases notified to the World Health Organization and may represent only a fraction of the true number in a country because of incomplete coverage by health services, inaccurate diagnosis or deficient recording and reporting.

e. Data refer to estimates of apparent consumption based on data on cigarette production, imports and exports. Such estimates may under- or overstate true consumption in countries where tobacco products are illegally imported or exported, where there is significant stockpiling of cigarettes or where there are large transient populations. Estimates of apparent consumption cannot provide insights into smoking patterns in a population. Data refer to the most recent three-year moving average available during the period specified.

f. Data refer to a year or period other than that specified, differ from the standard definition or refer to only part of a country.

g. Data refer to 1996.

h. Includes Luxembourg.

i. Data refer to 1997.

j. Data refer to estimates produced using the 1994 prevalence rate published by the World Health Organization's Global Programme on AIDS (WHO 1995).

Source: Column 1: FAO 2000; *columns 2-4:* UNICEF 2000; *columns 5-7:* UNAIDS 2000; aggregates calculated for the Human Development Report Office by UNAIDS; *column 8:* WHO 1999; *column 9:* WHO 2000a; *column 10:* WHO 2001b.

8 Survival: progress and setbacks

HDI rank	Life expectancy at birth (years)		Infant mortality rate (per 1,000 live births)		Under-five mortality rate (per 1,000 live births)		Probability at birth of surviving to age 65 [a]		Maternal mortality ratio reported (per 100,000 live births)
							Female (% of cohort)	Male (% of cohort)	
	1970-75 [b]	1995-2000 [b]	1970	1999	1970	1999	1995-2000 [b]	1995-2000 [b]	1980-99 [c]
High human development									
1 Norway	74.4	78.1	13	4	15	4	90.0	82.2	6
2 Australia	71.7	78.7	17	5	20	5	90.2	83.1	..
3 Canada	73.2	78.5	19	6	23	6	89.3	82.3	..
4 Sweden	74.7	79.3	11	3	15	4	90.8	84.8	5
5 Belgium	71.4	77.9	21	6	29	6	89.5	80.7	..
6 United States	71.5	76.5	20	7	26	8	85.7	77.4	8
7 Iceland	74.3	78.9	13	5	14	5	90.0	84.4	..
8 Netherlands	74.0	77.9	13	5	15	5	89.1	82.7	7
9 Japan	73.3	80.5	14	4	21	4	92.1	84.0	8
10 Finland	70.7	77.2	13	4	16	5	90.3	77.9	6
11 Switzerland	73.8	78.6	15	3	18	4	90.5	82.2	5
12 Luxembourg	70.7	77.0	19	5	26	5	88.4	80.1	(.)
13 France	72.4	78.1	18	5	24	5	90.1	78.0	10
14 United Kingdom	72.0	77.2	18	6	23	6	88.3	81.5	7
15 Denmark	73.6	75.9	14	4	19	5	85.5	78.3	10
16 Austria	70.6	77.7	26	4	33	5	89.9	79.7	..
17 Germany	71.0	77.3	22	5	26	5	89.3	79.2	8
18 Ireland	71.3	76.1	20	6	27	7	87.7	80.0	6
19 New Zealand	71.7	77.2	17	6	20	6	87.6	80.9	15
20 Italy	72.1	78.2	30	6	33	6	90.9	81.6	7
21 Spain	72.9	78.1	27	6	34	6	91.4	79.8	6
22 Israel	71.6	78.3	24	6	27	6	89.7	85.1	5
23 Greece	72.3	78.0	38	6	54	7	91.4	81.6	1
24 Hong Kong, China (SAR)	72.0	79.1	..	..	..	..	91.6	83.1	..
25 Cyprus	71.4	77.8	29	7	33	8	90.3	83.2	(.)
26 Singapore	69.5	77.1	22	4	27	4	86.6	79.6	6
27 Korea, Rep. of	62.6	74.3	43	5	54	5	87.5	72.1	20
28 Portugal	68.0	75.2	53	5	62	6	88.4	75.3	8
29 Slovenia	69.8	75.0	25	5	29	6	87.3	72.8	11
30 Malta	70.6	77.6	25	6	32	7	89.7	84.2	..
31 Barbados	69.4	76.4	40	14	54	16	88.1	80.6	(.)
32 Brunei Darussalam	68.3	75.5	58	8	78	9	87.8	79.4	(.)
33 Czech Republic	70.1	74.3	21	5	24	5	87.0	72.0	9
34 Argentina	67.1	72.9	59	19	71	22	84.1	70.6	38
35 Slovakia	70.0	72.8	25	9	29	10	85.4	66.4	9
36 Hungary	69.3	70.7	36	9	39	10	81.1	59.0	15
37 Uruguay	68.7	73.9	48	15	57	17	84.7	71.4	26
38 Poland	70.5	72.8	32	9	36	10	85.1	65.8	8
39 Chile	63.4	74.9	77	11	96	12	85.4	75.6	20
40 Bahrain	63.5	72.9	55	13	75	16	84.0	75.5	46
41 Costa Rica	67.9	76.0	58	13	77	14	87.2	80.1	29
42 Bahamas	66.5	69.1	38	18	49	21	76.0	57.4	..
43 Kuwait	67.3	75.9	49	11	59	12	86.2	80.7	5
44 Estonia	70.5	70.0	21	17	26	21	81.9	54.8	50
45 United Arab Emirates	62.5	74.6	61	8	83	9	83.6	75.8	3
46 Croatia	69.6	73.3	34	8	42	9	85.3	69.5	6
47 Lithuania	71.3	71.4	23	18	28	22	83.6	59.7	18
48 Qatar	62.6	68.9	45	12	65	16	75.7	69.4	10
Medium human development									
49 Trinidad and Tobago	65.9	73.8	49	17	57	20	82.4	73.9	..
50 Latvia	70.1	69.6	21	17	26	21	79.8	56.9	45

HDI rank		Life expectancy at birth (years)		Infant mortality rate (per 1,000 live births)		Under-five mortality rate (per 1,000 live births)		Probability at birth of surviving to age 65 [a]		Maternal mortality ratio reported (per 100,000 live births)
								Female (% of cohort)	Male (% of cohort)	
		1970-75 [b]	1995-2000 [b]	1970	1999	1970	1999	1995-2000 [b]	1995-2000 [b]	1980-99 [c]
51	Mexico	62.4	72.2	79	27	110	33	80.8	69.9	55
52	Panama	66.2	73.6	46	21	68	27	83.5	76.0	70
53	Belarus	71.5	68.5	22	23	27	28	80.0	51.3	28
54	Belize	67.6	73.6	56	35	77	43	82.1	77.4	140
55	Russian Federation	69.7	66.1	29	18	36	22	77.0	46.5	50
56	Malaysia	63.0	71.9	46	8	63	9	82.0	70.8	39
57	Bulgaria	71.0	70.8	28	14	32	17	83.5	64.2	15
58	Romania	69.2	69.8	46	21	57	24	79.9	62.5	41
59	Libyan Arab Jamahiriya	52.9	70.0	105	19	160	22	76.0	68.3	75
60	Macedonia, TFYR	67.5	72.7	85	22	120	26	82.5	74.2	3
61	Venezuela	65.7	72.4	47	20	61	23	82.3	71.6	60
62	Colombia	61.6	70.4	70	26	113	31	79.1	67.6	80
63	Mauritius	62.9	70.7	64	19	86	23	80.6	63.0	50
64	Suriname	64.0	70.1	51	27	68	34	77.7	66.4	110
65	Lebanon	65.0	72.6	45	28	54	32	81.8	75.7	100
66	Thailand	59.5	69.6	74	26	102	30	78.8	66.5	44
67	Fiji	60.6	68.4	50	18	61	22	72.8	63.7	38
68	Saudi Arabia	53.9	70.9	118	20	185	25	78.4	73.4	..
69	Brazil	59.5	67.2	95	34	135	40	75.4	59.3	160
70	Philippines	58.1	68.6	60	31	90	42	75.7	67.2	170
71	Oman	49.0	70.5	126	14	200	16	78.1	72.1	19
72	Armenia	72.5	72.4	24	25	30	30	85.1	70.8	35
73	Peru	55.4	68.0	115	42	178	52	75.2	66.2	270
74	Ukraine	70.1	68.1	22	17	27	21	79.0	51.8	27
75	Kazakhstan	64.4	64.1	50	35	66	42	72.7	47.6	70
76	Georgia	69.2	72.7	36	19	46	23	84.5	67.1	70
77	Maldives	51.4	65.4	157	60	255	83	65.4	66.8	350
78	Jamaica	69.0	74.8	47	10	62	11	84.1	77.5	120
79	Azerbaijan	69.0	71.0	41	35	53	45	79.8	65.0	43
80	Paraguay	65.9	69.6	57	27	76	32	78.2	69.4	190
81	Sri Lanka	65.1	71.6	65	17	100	19	82.8	71.8	60
82	Turkey	57.9	69.0	150	40	201	48	78.6	68.7	130
83	Turkmenistan	60.7	65.4	82	52	120	71	71.7	56.9	65
84	Ecuador	58.8	69.5	87	27	140	35	77.3	69.0	160
85	Albania	67.7	72.8	68	29	82	35	87.0	78.6	..
86	Dominican Republic	59.7	67.3	91	43	128	49	74.5	64.9	230
87	China	63.2	69.8	85	33	120	41	79.4	70.9	55
88	Jordan	56.6	69.7	77	29	107	35	74.4	68.9	41
89	Tunisia	55.6	69.5	135	24	201	30	75.8	70.6	70
90	Iran, Islamic Rep. of	53.9	68.0	122	37	191	46	74.3	68.9	37
91	Cape Verde	57.5	68.9	87	54	123	73	76.2	64.6	55
92	Kyrgyzstan	63.1	66.9	111	55	146	65	75.3	57.8	65
93	Guyana	60.0	63.7	81	56	101	76	70.2	54.1	180
94	South Africa	53.7	56.7	80	54	115	69	53.7	40.2	..
95	El Salvador	58.2	69.1	111	35	162	42	75.9	65.6	120
96	Samoa (Western)	56.1	68.5	106	21	160	26	75.8	62.0	..
97	Syrian Arab Republic	57.0	70.5	90	25	129	30	77.4	72.5	110
98	Moldova, Rep. of	64.8	66.6	46	27	61	34	72.5	53.7	42
99	Uzbekistan	64.2	68.3	66	45	90	58	75.0	62.9	21
100	Algeria	54.5	68.9	123	36	192	41	75.4	72.2	220

HDI rank		Life expectancy at birth (years)		Infant mortality rate (per 1,000 live births)		Under-five mortality rate (per 1,000 live births)		Probability at birth of surviving to age 65 [a]		Maternal mortality ratio reported (per 100,000 live births)
								Female (% of cohort)	Male (% of cohort)	
		1970-75 [b]	1995-2000 [b]	1970	1999	1970	1999	1995-2000 [b]	1995-2000 [b]	1980-99 [c]
101	Viet Nam	50.3	67.2	112	31	157	40	74.1	65.6	160
102	Indonesia	49.2	65.1	104	38	172	52	69.5	61.7	450
103	Tajikistan	63.4	67.2	78	54	111	74	73.6	62.7	65
104	Bolivia	46.7	61.4	144	64	243	83	63.9	57.0	390
105	Egypt	52.1	66.3	157	41	235	52	72.8	63.9	170
106	Nicaragua	55.1	67.7	113	38	165	47	72.7	63.9	150
107	Honduras	53.8	65.6	116	33	170	42	70.5	59.3	110
108	Guatemala	53.7	64.0	115	45	168	60	67.9	56.2	190
109	Gabon	45.0	52.4	140	85	232	143	48.7	43.5	600
110	Equatorial Guinea	40.5	50.0	165	105	281	160	47.0	41.0	..
111	Namibia	49.4	45.1	104	56	155	70	31.3	28.0	230
112	Morocco	52.9	66.6	119	45	184	53	74.1	66.3	230
113	Swaziland	47.3	50.8	140	62	209	90	45.1	39.2	230
114	Botswana	53.2	44.4	99	46	142	59	29.6	24.5	330
115	India	50.3	62.3	127	70	202	98	64.7	59.9	410
116	Mongolia	53.8	61.9	..	63	..	80	64.0	53.9	150
117	Zimbabwe	56.0	42.9	86	60	138	90	23.7	22.1	400
118	Myanmar	49.3	55.8	122	79	179	112	55.9	46.6	230
119	Ghana	49.9	56.3	111	63	186	101	53.8	48.0	210
120	Lesotho	49.5	51.2	125	93	190	134	46.9	42.5	..
121	Cambodia	40.3	56.5	..	86	..	122	55.8	46.3	470
122	Papua New Guinea	44.7	55.6	90	79	130	112	48.0	41.4	370
123	Kenya	51.0	52.2	96	76	156	118	43.6	38.5	590
124	Comoros	48.9	58.8	159	64	215	86	58.6	52.1	500
125	Cameroon	45.7	50.0	127	95	215	154	42.6	38.4	430
126	Congo	46.7	50.9	100	81	160	108	45.4	37.9	..
Low human development										
127	Pakistan	49.0	59.0	117	84	181	112	58.8	56.9	..
128	Togo	45.5	51.3	128	80	216	143	45.3	40.1	480
129	Nepal	43.3	57.3	165	75	250	104	53.7	52.4	540
130	Bhutan	43.2	60.7	156	80	267	107	62.3	57.2	380
131	Lao People's Dem. Rep.	40.4	52.5	145	93	218	111	50.0	44.9	650
132	Bangladesh	44.9	58.1	145	58	239	89	55.4	53.2	440
133	Yemen	42.1	59.4	194	86	303	119	58.9	53.4	350
134	Haiti	48.5	52.0	148	83	221	129	46.3	34.2	..
135	Madagascar	44.9	51.6	184	95	285	156	48.7	43.8	490
136	Nigeria	44.0	51.3	120	112	201	187	44.6	42.1	700
137	Djibouti	41.0	45.5	160	104	241	149	39.1	32.9	..
138	Sudan	43.7	55.0	104	67	172	109	53.9	48.3	550
139	Mauritania	43.5	50.5	150	120	250	183	47.7	41.6	550
140	Tanzania, U. Rep. of	46.5	51.1	129	90	218	141	43.2	37.9	530
141	Uganda	46.4	41.9	110	83	185	131	28.1	24.9	510
142	Congo, Dem. Rep. of the	46.0	50.5	147	128	245	207	44.9	39.4	..
143	Zambia	47.2	40.5	109	112	181	202	22.8	21.7	650
144	Côte d'Ivoire	45.4	47.7	158	102	239	171	37.3	35.4	600
145	Senegal	41.8	52.3	164	68	279	118	51.0	39.4	560
146	Angola	38.0	44.6	180	172	300	295	38.1	32.9	..
147	Benin	44.0	53.5	149	99	252	156	51.4	44.8	500
148	Eritrea	44.3	51.5	150	66	225	105	47.1	40.7	1,000
149	Gambia	37.0	45.4	183	61	319	75	39.6	34.2	..
150	Guinea	37.3	46.5	197	115	345	181	40.6	37.7	670

HDI rank	Life expectancy at birth (years)		Infant mortality rate (per 1,000 live births)		Under-five mortality rate (per 1,000 live births)		Probability at birth of surviving to age 65 [a]		Maternal mortality ratio reported (per 100,000 live births)
							Female (% of cohort)	Male (% of cohort)	
	1970-75 [b]	1995-2000 [b]	1970	1999	1970	1999	1995-2000 [h]	1995-2000 [b]	1980-99 [c]
151 Malawi	41.0	40.7	189	132	330	211	30.4	28.2	620
152 Rwanda	44.6	39.4	124	110	210	180	26.3	22.9	..
153 Mali	42.9	50.9	221	143	391	235	48.5	45.5	580
154 Central African Republic	43.0	44.3	149	113	248	172	34.4	28.5	1,100
155 Chad	39.0	45.7	149	118	252	198	38.6	33.6	830
156 Guinea-Bissau	36.5	44.1	186	128	316	200	37.8	32.5	910
157 Mozambique	42.5	40.6	163	127	278	203	31.0	26.3	1,100
158 Ethiopia	41.8	44.5	160	118	239	176	35.6	31.4	..
159 Burkina Faso	41.5	45.3	163	106	290	199	34.8	29.7	..
160 Burundi	44.0	40.6	135	106	228	176	28.5	23.5	..
161 Niger	38.2	44.2	197	162	330	275	37.1	34.9	590
162 Sierra Leone	35.0	37.3	206	182	363	316	28.2	23.4	..
Developing countries	55.5	64.1	109	61	167	89	68.3	61.2	..
Least developed countries	44.2	51.3	149	100	243	159	46.0	41.7	..
Arab States	51.9	65.9	129	44	198	59	71.1	64.9	..
East Asia and the Pacific	60.4	68.8	87	34	126	44	77.2	68.5	..
Latin America and the Caribbean	60.8	69.3	87	32	125	39	77.5	64.9	..
South Asia	49.9	61.9	128	69	203	97	63.8	59.4	..
Sub-Saharan Africa	45.3	48.8	138	107	226	172	41.4	36.6	..
Eastern Europe and the CIS	69.2	68.4	37	25	47	31	79.0	55.3	..
OECD	70.4	76.4	40	13	52	15	87.2	77.3	..
High-income OECD	72.1	77.8	20	6	26	6	88.8	80.0	..
High human development	71.3	77.0	25	7	32	8	88.2	78.2	..
Medium human development	58.4	66.5	99	46	149	62	72.9	63.7	..
Low human development	44.6	52.2	142	99	231	156	47.0	43.8	..
High income	72.0	77.8	21	6	26	6	88.8	80.0	..
Middle income	62.6	69.2	85	32	121	39	78.2	67.1	..
Low income	49.6	59.0	126	80	202	120	59.0	53.6	..
World	59.9	66.4	96	56	147	80	72.2	63.5	..

a. Data refer to the probability at birth of surviving to age 65, times 100.

b. Data refer to estimates for the period specified.

c. The maternal mortality data are those reported by national authorities. UNICEF and the World Health Organization periodically evaluate these data and make adjustments to account for the well-documented problems of underreporting and misclassification of maternal deaths and to develop estimates for countries with no data (for details on the most recent estimates see Hill, AbouZahr and Wardlaw 2001). Data refer to the most recent year available during the period specified.

Source: Columns 1, 2, 7 and 8: UN 2001d; columns 3 and 5: UNICEF 2001; columns 4, 6 and 9: UNICEF 2000.

9 Commitment to education: public spending

HDI rank		Public education expenditure [a]				Public education expenditure by level (as % of all levels) [b]					
		As % of GNP		As % of total government expenditure		Pre-primary and primary		Secondary		Tertiary	
		1985-87 [c]	1995-97 [c]	1985-87 [c]	1995-97 [c]	1985-86 [c]	1995-97 [c]	1985-86 [c]	1995-97 [c]	1985-86 [c]	1995-97 [c]
High human development											
1	Norway	6.5	7.7 [d]	14.7	16.8 [d]	45.2	38.7 [e]	28.3	23.0 [e]	13.5	27.9 [e]
2	Australia	5.1	5.5 [d]	12.5	13.5 [d]	..	30.6 [e]	61.9 [f]	38.9 [e]	30.5	30.5 [e]
3	Canada	6.7	6.9 [d, g]	14.1	12.9 [d, g]	..	..	63.6 [f]	64.7 [e, f, g, h]	28.7	35.3 [e, g, h]
4	Sweden	7.3	8.3 [d]	12.8	12.2 [d]	48.0	34.1 [e, h]	20.1	38.7 [e, h]	13.1	27.2 [e, h]
5	Belgium	5.1 [i]	3.1 [d, j]	14.3 [i]	6.0 [d, j]	24.7 [i]	29.9 [e, j]	46.4 [i]	45.5 [e, j]	16.7 [i]	21.5 [e, j]
6	United States	5.0	5.4 [d, g]	11.9	14.4 [d, g]	44.7	38.7 [e, g, h]	30.3	36.1 [e, g, h]	25.1	25.2 [e, g, h]
7	Iceland	4.8	5.4 [d]	14.0	13.6 [d]	..	35.9 [e]	..	41.9 [e]	..	17.7 [e]
8	Netherlands	6.9	5.1 [d]	..	9.8 [d]	22.6	30.9 [e]	35.9	39.8 [e]	26.4	29.3 [e]
9	Japan [g]	..	3.6 [d]	..	9.9 [d]	..	39.3 [e, h]	..	41.8 [e, h]	..	12.1 [e, h]
10	Finland	5.5	7.5 [d]	11.6	12.2 [d]	30.8	33.0 [e]	41.6	36.2 [e]	18.7	28.9 [e]
11	Switzerland	4.7	5.4 [d]	18.8	15.4 [d]	..	30.6 [e]	73.6	48.1 [e]	18.1	19.3 [e]
12	Luxembourg	4.1	4.0 [d]	9.5 [i]	11.5 [g, i]	43.5	51.9 [e]	42.7	43.4 [e]	3.3	4.7 [e]
13	France	5.5	6.0 [d]	18.0 [g]	10.9 [d]	29.4	31.4 [e]	40.8	49.5 [e]	12.9	17.9 [e]
14	United Kingdom	4.8	5.3 [d]	11.3 [g]	11.6 [d]	26.7	32.3 [e, h]	45.9	44.0 [e, h]	19.8	23.7 [e, h]
15	Denmark	7.2	8.1 [d]	13.7	13.1 [d]	..	33.6 [e]	..	39.3 [e]	..	22.0 [e]
16	Austria	5.9	5.4 [d]	7.8	10.4 [d]	23.1	28.1 [e]	46.9	49.0 [e]	16.6	21.2 [e]
17	Germany	..	4.8 [d]	..	9.6 [d]	..	..	..	72.2 [e, f]	..	22.5 [e]
18	Ireland	6.7	6.0 [d]	9.5	13.5 [d]	39.4	32.2 [e]	39.7	41.5 [e]	17.7	23.8 [e]
19	New Zealand	5.4	7.3 [d]	20.9	17.1 [d, g]	38.3	28.7 [e]	28.5	40.3 [e]	28.3	29.1 [e]
20	Italy	5.0	4.9 [d]	8.3	9.1 [d]	30.1	32.0 [e]	35.5	49.2 [e]	10.2	15.1 [e]
21	Spain	3.7	5.0 [d]	8.8	11.0 [d]	..	33.3 [e]	..	47.9 [e]	..	16.6 [e]
22	Israel	6.7	7.6 [d, g]	10.0	12.3 [d, g]	42.8	42.3 [e, g]	30.8	31.2 [e, g]	18.9	18.2 [e, g]
23	Greece	2.2	3.1 [d]	6.1	8.2 [d]	37.6	35.3 [e, h]	41.3	38.0 [e, h]	20.1	25.0 [e, h]
24	Hong Kong, China (SAR)	2.5	2.9	19.8	17.0 [g]	31.5 [g]	21.9	37.9 [g]	35.0	25.1 [g]	37.1
25	Cyprus [k]	3.6	4.5	11.9	13.2	37.6	36.7	50.7	50.8	4.2	6.5
26	Singapore	3.9	3.0	11.5	23.3	30.5	25.7	36.9	34.6	27.9	34.8
27	Korea, Rep. of	3.8	3.7 [d]	..	17.5 [d]	47.0	45.3 [e, h]	36.7	36.6 [e, h]	10.9	8.0 [e, h]
28	Portugal	3.8 [i]	5.8 [d]	..	11.7 [d]	51.0	34.2 [e]	30.6	41.6 [e]	12.7	16.4 [e]
29	Slovenia	..	5.7	..	12.6	..	29.9	..	48.4	..	16.9
30	Malta	3.4	5.1	7.4	10.8	31.0	22.6 [g]	43.3	32.0 [g]	8.2	10.9 [g]
31	Barbados [g]	6.2	7.2	17.2	19.0	31.0	..	32.5	..	22.3	..
32	Brunei Darussalam	..	..	..	..	..	..	..	..	..	..
33	Czech Republic	..	5.1 [d]	..	13.6 [d]	..	31.3 [e]	..	50.2 [e]	..	15.8 [e]
34	Argentina	1.4 [i]	3.5	8.9 [i]	12.6	37.7 [g]	45.7	27.4 [g]	34.8	19.2 [g]	19.5
35	Slovakia	..	4.7	..	14.6	..	40.5	..	28.0	..	12.7
36	Hungary	5.6	4.6 [d]	6.3	6.9 [g]	51.1	36.8 [e]	19.9	46.3 [e]	16.9	15.5 [e]
37	Uruguay	3.2	3.3	15.0	15.5	37.7	32.6	28.4	29.0	22.4	19.6
38	Poland	4.6	7.5 [d]	12.5	24.8 [d]	44.2	37.6 [e, h]	17.9	15.1 [e, h]	18.2	11.1 [e, h]
39	Chile	3.3	3.6	15.3	15.5	57.0	58.3	19.5	18.8	20.3	16.1
40	Bahrain	5.2	4.4	12.3	12.0	..	30.1 [h]	..	34.5 [h]	..	..
41	Costa Rica	4.5	5.4	21.6	22.8	35.1	40.2	22.3	24.3	41.4	28.3
42	Bahamas	4.0	..	18.9	13.2	..	..	..	..	..	..
43	Kuwait	4.8	5.0	13.4	14.0	..	..	..	69.8 [f, h]	..	30.2 [h]
44	Estonia	..	7.2	..	25.5	..	18.5	..	50.7	..	17.9
45	United Arab Emirates	2.1	1.7	13.2	20.3	..	..	..	..	..	..
46	Croatia	..	5.3	..	..	..	..	..	..	..	..
47	Lithuania	5.3 [g]	5.9	12.9	22.8	..	15.1	..	50.9	..	18.3
48	Qatar	4.7	3.4 [g]	..	..	..	..	..	..	..	..
Medium human development											
49	Trinidad and Tobago	6.3	4.4 [g]	14.0	..	47.5	40.5 [g]	36.8	33.1 [g]	8.9	13.3 [g]
50	Latvia	3.4	6.5	12.4	16.5	15.8	12.1	56.2	58.9	10.3	12.2

HDI rank	Public education expenditure [a] As % of GNP		As % of total government expenditure		Public education expenditure by level (as % of all levels) [b] Pre-primary and primary		Secondary		Tertiary	
	1985-87 [c]	1995-97 [c]	1985-87 [c]	1995-97 [c]	1985-86 [c]	1995-97 [c]	1985-86 [c]	1995-97 [c]	1985-86 [c]	1995-97 [c]
51 Mexico	3.5	4.9 [d]	..	23.0 [d]	31.5 [i]	50.3 [e]	26.8 [i]	32.5 [e]	17.6 [i]	17.2 [e]
52 Panama	4.8	5.1	14.3	16.3	38.3	31.1	25.2	19.8	20.4	26.1
53 Belarus	5.0	5.9	..	17.8	..	..	74.8 [f]	72.5 [f]	14.0	11.1
54 Belize	4.7	5.0	15.4	19.5	55.7	62.8	27.7	25.8	2.3	6.9
55 Russian Federation	3.4	3.5 [d]	..	9.6 [g]	..	23.2 [e, h]	..	57.4 [e, h]	..	19.3 [e, h]
56 Malaysia	6.9	4.9	18.8	15.4	37.8	32.7	37.1	30.6	14.6	25.5
57 Bulgaria	5.4	3.2	..	7.0	..	..	65.3 [f]	73.8 [f]	12.4	18.0
58 Romania	2.2	3.6	7.5 [g]	10.5	..	42.7 [h]	..	23.8 [h]	..	16.0 [h]
59 Libyan Arab Jamahirlya	9.6	..	20.8	..	..	..	..	..	..	..
60 Macedonia, TFYR	..	5.1	..	20.0	..	54.4	..	23.6	..	22.0
61 Venezuela	5.0	5.2 [g]	19.6	22.4 [g]	..	..	..	29.5 [f, g]	..	34.7 [g]
62 Colombia [i]	2.6	4.1	22.4	16.6	42.0	40.5	32.5	31.5	21.2	19.2
63 Mauritius	3.3	4.6	10.0	17.4	45.2	31.0	37.6	36.3	5.6	24.7
64 Suriname	10.2	3.5 [g]	22.8	..	63.7	..	13.5	..	7.7	..
65 Lebanon [i]	..	2.5	11.7	8.2	..	..	..	68.9 [f, h]	..	16.2 [h]
66 Thailand	3.4	4.8	17.9	20.1	58.4	50.4	21.1	20.0	13.2	16.4
67 Fiji	6.0	..	..	..	..	..	..	..	..	..
68 Saudi Arabia	7.4	7.5	13.6	22.8	..	..	72.9 [f]	84.4 [f]	27.1	15.6
69 Brazil	4.7	5.1	17.7	..	45.9 [h]	53.5	7.7 [h]	20.3	19.6 [h]	26.2
70 Philippines	2.1	3.4	11.2	15.7	63.9	56.1	10.1	23.3	22.5	18.0
71 Oman	4.1	4.5	15.0	16.4	..	40.9	..	51.3	..	7.0
72 Armenia	..	2.0	..	10.3	..	15.8	..	63.0	..	13.2
73 Peru	3.6	2.9	15.7	19.2	39.5	35.2	20.5	21.2	2.7	16.0
74 Ukraine	5.3	5.6	21.2	14.8	..	..	74.2 [f]	73.5 [f]	13.5	10.7
75 Kazakhstan	3.4	4.4	19.8	17.6	..	7.2 [h]	..	63.0 [h]	..	13.9 [h]
76 Georgia [g]	..	5.2	..	6.9	..	22.0	..	45.1	..	18.5
77 Maldives	5.2	6.4	8.5	10.5	..	..	..	..	..	..
78 Jamaica	4.9	7.5	11.0	12.9	31.9	31.3	34.0	37.4	19.4	22.4
79 Azerbaijan	5.8	3.0	29.3	18.8	..	14.6	..	63.9	..	7.5
80 Paraguay	1.1 [i]	4.0 [i]	14.3 [i]	19.8 [i]	36.6	50.0 [h, i]	29.7	18.1 [h, i]	23.8	19.7 [h, i]
81 Sri Lanka	2.7	3.4	7.8	8.9	..	..	90.2 [f]	74.8 [f]	9.8	9.3
82 Turkey	1.2 [l]	2.2 [d]	..	14.7 [d, g]	45.9	43.3 [e, h]	22.4	22.0 [e, h]	23.9	34.7 [e, h]
83 Turkmenistan	4.1	..	29.3	..	..	..	..	..	..	..
84 Ecuador	3.5	3.5	21.3	13.0	45.5	38.4	35.8	36.0	17.8	21.3
85 Albania	..	..	11.2	..	..	63.9 [g]	..	20.6 [g]	..	10.3 [g]
86 Dominican Republic	1.3	2.3	10.0	13.8	47.3	49.5	19.7	12.5	20.8	13.0
87 China	2.3	2.3	11.1	12.2 [g]	29.5 [m]	37.4	33.2 [m]	32.2	21.8 [m]	15.6
88 Jordan	6.8	7.9	15.8	19.8	..	..	62.9 [f]	64.5 [f]	34.1	33.0
89 Tunisia	6.2	7.7	14.8	19.9	44.0 [i]	42.5	37.0 [i]	37.2	18.2 [i]	18.5
90 Iran, Islamic Rep. of	3.7	4.0	18.1	17.8	42.0	29.0	37.9	33.9	10.7	22.9
91 Cape Verde	2.9	..	14.8		61.5	..	15.9	..	..	..
92 Kyrgyzstan	9.7	5.3	22.4	23.5	10.9	6.6	60.4	68.0	8.8	14.1
93 Guyana	8.5	5.0	7.3	10.0	38.8	..	23.8	71.3 [f]	17.8	7.7
94 South Africa	6.1	7.6	..	22.0	..	43.5	73.1 [f]	29.5	24.8	14.3
95 El Salvador	3.1 [g]	2.5	12.5 [g]	16.0	..	63.5	..	6.5	..	7.2
96 Samoa (Western)	..	..	..	..	..	..	..	..	..	..
97 Syrian Arab Republic	4.8	4.2	14.0	13.6	38.4	41.9	25.3	29.8	33.6 [h]	25.9 [h]
98 Moldova, Rep. of	3.6	10.6	..	28.1	..	24.5	..	52.9	..	13.3
99 Uzbekistan	9.2 [g]	7.7	25.1	21.1	..	..	..	..	..	..
100 Algeria	9.8	5.1 [l]	27.8	16.4 [l]	..	..	..	95.3 [f, l]	..	..

HDI rank	Public education expenditure [a]				Public education expenditure by level (as % of all levels) [b]					
	As % of GNP		As % of total government expenditure		Pre-primary and primary		Secondary		Tertiary	
	1985-87 [c]	1995-97 [c]	1985-87 [c]	1995-97 [c]	1985-86 [c]	1995-97 [c]	1985-86 [c]	1995-97 [c]	1985-86 [c]	1995-97 [c]
101 Viet Nam	..	3.0	..	7.4 [g]	..	43.0	..	26.0	..	22.0
102 Indonesia	0.9 [g,i]	1.4 [n]	4.3 [g,i]	7.9 [n]	..	..	..	73.5 [f,i]	..	24.4 [i]
103 Tajikistan	..	2.2	29.5	11.5	9.2	14.9	55.7	71.2	7.7	7.1
104 Bolivia	2.1	4.9	20.1 [g]	11.1	..	50.7	..	9.8	..	27.7
105 Egypt	4.5	4.8	..	14.9	..	..	..	66.7 [f]	..	33.3
106 Nicaragua	5.4	3.9 [i]	12.0	8.8 [i]	45.6	68.6 [i]	16.7	13.9 [i]	23.2	..
107 Honduras	4.8	3.6	19.5	16.5	49.1	52.5	16.7	21.5	21.3	16.6
108 Guatemala [i]	1.9	1.7	13.8	15.8	..	63.0	..	12.1	..	15.2
109 Gabon	5.8	2.9 [i]	9.4	..	..	..	..	..	..	..
110 Equatorial Guinea [g]	1.7	1.7	3.9	5.6	..	..	..	..	..	..
111 Namibia	..	9.1	..	25.6	..	58.0	..	28.9	..	13.1
112 Morocco [i]	6.2	5.3	21.5	24.9	35.3	34.6	47.6	48.8	17.1	16.5
113 Swaziland	5.6	5.7	20.6	18.1	39.4	35.8	29.6	27.1	19.5	26.6
114 Botswana	7.3	8.6	15.9	20.6	36.3	..	40.7	..	17.2	..
115 India	3.2	3.2	8.5	11.6	38.0	39.5	25.3	26.5	15.3	13.7
116 Mongolia	11.7	5.7	17.1	15.1	10.7 [h]	19.9 [h]	51.2 [h]	56.0 [h]	17.3 [h]	14.3 [h]
117 Zimbabwe	7.7	7.1 [g]	15.0	..	..	51.7 [g]	..	26.4 [g]	..	17.3 [g]
118 Myanmar [i]	1.9	1.2 [g]	..	14.4 [g]	..	47.7 [g]	..	40.3 [g]	..	11.7 [g]
119 Ghana	3.4	4.2	24.3	19.9	24.5 [g]	..	29.5 [g]	..	12.5 [g]	..
120 Lesotho	4.1	8.4	13.4	..	39.1 [g]	41.2	32.7 [g]	29.2	22.3 [g]	28.7
121 Cambodia	..	2.9	..	..	..	..	..	..	..	..
122 Papua New Guinea	..	..	..	..	..	..	..	..	..	..
123 Kenya	7.1	6.5	14.8 [g]	16.7	59.9	..	17.7	..	12.4	..
124 Comoros	..	..	..	..	..	36.6 [i]	..	35.1 [i]	..	17.2 [i]
125 Cameroon	2.8	..	16.4	..	..	..	72.6 [f]	86.8 [f]	27.4	13.2
126 Congo	4.9 [g]	6.1	9.8 [g]	14.7	30.0 [g]	50.4	35.6 [g]	11.6	34.4 [g]	28.0
Low human development										
127 Pakistan	3.1	2.7	8.8	7.1	36.0	51.8	33.3	27.9	18.2	13.0
128 Togo	4.9	4.5	19.7	24.6	34.0	45.9	29.1	26.9	22.8	24.7
129 Nepal	2.2	3.2	10.4	13.5	35.7	45.1	19.9	19.0	33.4	19.0
130 Bhutan	3.7	4.1	..	7.0	..	44.0	..	35.6	..	20.4
131 Lao People's Dem. Rep.	0.5	2.1	6.6	8.7	..	48.3	..	30.7	..	7.4
132 Bangladesh [i]	1.4	2.2	9.9	13.8	46.1	44.8	34.7	43.8	10.4	7.9
133 Yemen	..	7.0	..	21.6 [g]	..	..	..	..	..	..
134 Haiti	1.9	..	20.6	..	51.0	..	18.1	..	10.8	..
135 Madagascar	1.9 [i]	1.9	..	16.1 [g]	42.3	30.0	26.5	33.4	27.2	21.1
136 Nigeria [n]	1.7	0.7	12.0	11.5	..	..	..	..	..	..
137 Djibouti	..	..	..	..	..	..	..	..	..	..
138 Sudan	..	1.4	..	..	..	..	..	..	..	..
139 Mauritania [i]	..	5.1	..	16.2	32.6	39.4	36.2	35.3	27.4	21.2
140 Tanzania, U. Rep. of	..	..	9.9	..	57.5	..	20.5	..	12.7	..
141 Uganda	3.5 [g,i]	2.6	..	..	44.5 [g,i]	..	33.4 [g,i]	..	13.2 [g,i]	..
142 Congo, Dem. Rep. of the	1.0	..	8.2	..	..	..	71.3 [f]	..	28.7	..
143 Zambia	3.1	2.2	9.8	7.1	43.9	41.5	26.9	18.4	18.3	23.2
144 Côte d'Ivoire	..	5.0	..	24.9	40.2	45.2	42.7	36.2	17.1	18.6
145 Senegal	..	3.7	..	33.1	50.1	34.2	25.1	42.5	19.0	23.2
146 Angola	6.2	..	13.8	..	..	..	86.8 [f,i]	..	5.0 [i]	..
147 Benin	..	3.2	..	15.2	..	59.1	..	21.7	..	18.8
148 Eritrea [i]	..	1.8	..	..	..	44.5	..	17.6	..	..
149 Gambia	3.7	4.9	8.8 [g]	21.2	49.0	48.9	21.3	31.6	13.8	12.9
150 Guinea	1.8	1.9	13.0	26.8	30.8 [g]	35.1 [h]	36.9 [g]	29.6 [h]	23.5 [g]	26.1 [h]

HDI rank	Public education expenditure [a]				Public education expenditure by level (as % of all levels) [b]					
	As % of GNP		As % of total government expenditure		Pre-primary and primary		Secondary		Tertiary	
	1985-87 [c]	1995-97 [c]	1985-87 [c]	1995-97 [c]	1985-86 [c]	1995-97 [c]	1985-86 [c]	1995-97 [c]	1985-86 [c]	1995-97 [c]
151 Malawi	3.5	5.4	9.0	18.3 [g]	41.3	58.8	15.2	8.9	23.3	20.5
152 Rwanda	3.5	..	22.9	..	67.6	..	15.3	..	11.5	..
153 Mali	3.2	2.2	17.3	..	48.4	45.9	22.6	21.6	13.4	17.7
154 Central African Republic	2.6	..	16.8	..	55.2 [i]	53.2 [i]	17.6 [i]	16.5 [i]	18.8 [i]	24.0 [i]
155 Chad	..	2.2	,,	..	..	43.5	..	24.2	..	9.0
156 Guinea-Bissau	1.8	..	..	..	..	..	..	,,	..	..
157 Mozambique	2.1	..	5.6	,,	..	..	..	..	..	..
158 Ethiopia	3.1	4.0	9.3	13.7	51.5	46.2 [h]	28.3	23.7 [h]	14.4	15.9 [h]
159 Burkina Faso	2.3	3.6 [g]	14.9	11.1 [g]	38.1	56.6	20.3	25.1	30.7	18.3
160 Burundi	3.1	4.0	18.1	18.3	45.0	42.7	32.2	36.7	19.8	17.1
161 Niger [l]	..	2.3	..	12.8	..	59.7 [h]	..	32.3 [h]	..	..
162 Sierra Leone	1.7	..	12.4	..	33.2	..	29.3	..	24.2	..

Note: As a result of a number of limitations in the data, comparisons of education expenditure data over time and across countries should be made with caution. For detailed notes on the data see UNESCO (1999).

a. Data refer to total public expenditure on education, including current and capital expenditures. See the definitions of statistical terms.

b. Data refer to current public expenditures on education. Expenditures by level may not sum to 100 as a result of rounding or the omission of the categories "other types" and "not distributed".

c. Data refer to the most recent year available during the period specified.

d. Data may not be strictly comparable to those for earlier years as a result of methodological changes.

e. Expenditures previously classified as "other types" have been distributed across the different education levels.

f. Data refer to combined expenditures for pre-primary, primary and secondary levels.

g. Data refer to a year or period other than that specified.

h. Data include capital expenditures.

i. Data refer to the ministry of education only.

j. Data refer to the Flemish community only.

k. Data refer to the Office of Greek Education only.

l. Data do not include expenditures on tertiary education.

m. Data do not include expenditures on mid-level specialized colleges and technical schools.

n. Data refer to the central government only.

Source: Columns 1-4: UNESCO 2000b; *columns 5-10:* UNESCO 1999.

... TO ACQUIRE KNOWLEDGE ...

HDI rank	Adult literacy Rate (% age 15 and above) 1999	Adult literacy Index (1985 = 100) 1999	Youth literacy Rate (% age 15-24) 1999	Youth literacy Index (1985 = 100) 1999	Net primary enrolment Ratio (%) 1995-97 [a]	Net primary enrolment Index (1984-87 = 100) [b] 1995-97 [a]	Net secondary enrolment Ratio (%) 1995-97 [a]	Net secondary enrolment Index (1984-87 = 100) [b] 1995-97 [a]	Children reaching grade 5 (%) 1995-97 [a]	Tertiary students in science, math and engineering (as % of all tertiary students) 1994-97 [a]
High human development										
1 Norway	..	..	..	..	100	103	97	115	..	18
2 Australia	..	..	..	..	95	98	89	112	..	32
3 Canada	..	..	..	..	95	100	91	102	..	..
4 Sweden	..	..	..	..	100	102	99	..	97	31
5 Belgium	..	..	..	..	98	102	88	99	..	..
6 United States	..	..	..	..	95	100	90	99	..	..
7 Iceland	..	..	..	..	98	..	87	..	..	20
8 Netherlands	..	..	..	..	100	105	91	105	..	20
9 Japan	..	..	..	..	..	..	..	..	..	23
10 Finland	..	..	..	..	98	..	93	..	100	37
11 Switzerland	..	..	..	..	..	..	..	..	..	31
12 Luxembourg	..	..	..	..	..	..	68	112	..	..
13 France	..	..	..	..	100	100	95	116	..	25
14 United Kingdom	..	..	..	..	100	102	91	115	..	29
15 Denmark	..	..	..	..	100	101	94	111	..	21
16 Austria	..	..	..	..	..	..	88	..	..	28
17 Germany	..	..	..	..	88	..	88	..	..	31
18 Ireland	..	..	..	..	92	102	86	106	..	30
19 New Zealand	..	..	..	..	100	100	90	108	..	21
20 Italy	98.4	101	99.8	100	100	104	..	..	99	28
21 Spain	97.6	102	99.8	100	100	100	..	..	..	31
22 Israel	95.8	104	99.6	101	..	..	..	..	..	..
23 Greece	97.1	104	99.8	100	93	95	87	106	..	..
24 Hong Kong, China (SAR)	93.3	106	99.2	102	90	94	69	106	..	..
25 Cyprus	96.9	105	99.8	100	81	84	..	..	100	17
26 Singapore	92.1	107	99.7	102	93	94	..	..	..	..
27 Korea, Rep. of	97.6	103	99.8	100	93	97	97	114	98	34
28 Portugal	91.9	109	99.8	101	..	..	..	..	..	31
29 Slovenia	99.6	100	99.8	100	95	..	89	..	..	29
30 Malta	91.8	107	98.5	102	100	105	79	107	100	13
31 Barbados	..	..	..	..	..	..	..	..	..	21
32 Brunei Darussalam	91.0	112	99.3	103	93	116	..	..	..	6
33 Czech Republic	..	..	..	..	89	..	87	..	..	34
34 Argentina	96.7	102	98.5	101	100	104	..	..	..	30
35 Slovakia	..	..	..	..	..	..	..	..	..	43
36 Hungary	99.3	100	99.8	100	82	84	86	130	..	32
37 Uruguay	97.7	102	99.3	101	93	104	..	..	98	24
38 Poland	99.7	100	99.8	100	97	98	..	..	..	..
39 Chile	95.6	103	98.7	101	89	100	58	..	100	43
40 Bahrain	87.1	113	98.2	105	96	99	84	103	95	..
41 Costa Rica	95.5	103	98.3	101	89	104	41	118	90	18
42 Bahamas	95.7	102	97.4	101	..	..	..	..	..	..
43 Kuwait	81.9	112	92.1	109	67	82	58	..	..	23
44 Estonia	..	..	..	..	93	..	88	..	..	32
45 United Arab Emirates	75.1	110	89.7	113	79	89	69	..	..	27
46 Croatia	98.2	102	99.8	100	84	..	79	..	..	38
47 Lithuania	99.5	100	99.8	100	94	..	85	..	..	38
48 Qatar	80.8	109	94.4	109	87	95	69	105	..	..
Medium human development										
49 Trinidad and Tobago	93.5	104	97.4	102	88	95	..	..	97	41
50 Latvia	99.8	100	99.8	100	93	..	82	..	..	29

HDI rank		Adult literacy		Youth literacy		Net primary enrolment		Net secondary enrolment		Children reaching grade 5	Tertiary students in science, math and engineering
		Rate (% age 15 and above) 1999	Index (1985 = 100) 1999	Rate (% age 15 24) 1999	Index (1985 = 100) 1999	Ratio (%) 1995-97 [a]	Index (1984-87 = 100) [b] 1995-97 [a]	Ratio (%) 1995-97 [a]	Index (1984-87 = 100) [b] 1995-97 [a]	(%) 1995-97 [a]	(as % of all tertiary students) 1994-97 [a]
51	Mexico	91.1	107	96.8	103	100	101	51	111	86	31
52	Panama	91.7	105	96.7	102	..	..	..	..	..	27
53	Belarus	99.5	101	99.8	100	..	..	..	..	..	33
54	Belize	93.1	108	97.8	103	..	..	..	..	..	..
55	Russian Federation	99.5	100	99.8	100	..	..	..	..	..	49
56	Malaysia	87.0	114	97.3	105	..		..	..		..
57	Bulgaria	98.3	102	99.6	100	93	95	80	102	..	25
58	Romania	98.0	102	99.6	100	97	..	74	..	..	32
59	Libyan Arab Jamahiriya	79.1	130	96.2	111	..	..	..	..	..	..
60	Macedonia, TFYR	..	..	..	..	95	..	56	..	95	38
61	Venezuela	92.3	106	97.8	103	84	97	22	127	89	..
62	Colombia	91.5	106	96.8	103	85	130	46	143	73	31
63	Mauritius	84.2	109	93.8	105	98	98	58	..	99	17
64	Suriname	..	..	..	..	..	..	..	..	..	..
65	Lebanon	85.6	112	94.8	105	76	..	66	..	..	17
66	Thailand	95.3	105	98.8	101	..	..	..	..	..	21
67	Fiji	92.6	108	99.0	102	..	..	..	..	..	..
68	Saudi Arabia	76.1	126	92.6	115	60	114	48	166	89	18
69	Brazil	84.9	108	92.3	104	..	..	..	..	..	23
70	Philippines	95.1	105	98.5	102	100	102	59	115	..	..
71	Oman	70.3	155	97.4	132	67	98	57	..	96	31
72	Armenia	98.3	102	99.7	100	..	..	..	..	..	33
73	Peru	89.6	108	96.6	104	91	95	55	113	..	..
74	Ukraine	99.6	100	99.9	100	..	..	..	..	..	..
75	Kazakhstan	..	..	..	..	..	..	..	..	..	42
76	Georgia	..	..	..	..	87	..	74	..	..	48
77	Maldives	96.2	104	99.1	102	..	..	..	..	..	..
78	Jamaica	86.4	109	93.8	105	..	..	..	..	..	20
79	Azerbaijan	..	..	..	..	..	..	..	..	..	..
80	Paraguay	93.0	105	96.9	102	91	102	38	152	78	22
81	Sri Lanka	91.4	105	96.7	103	..	..	..	..	..	29
82	Turkey	84.6	114	96.2	106	99	105	51	134	..	22
83	Turkmenistan	..	..	..	..	..	..	..	..	..	..
84	Ecuador	91.0	107	96.9	103	97	..	..	..	85	..
85	Albania	84.0	116	97.8	105	100	..	..	..	..	22
86	Dominican Republic	83.2	108	90.7	107	84	..	29	..	..	25
87	China	83.5	116	97.5	105	100	107	..	..	94	53
88	Jordan	89.2	119	99.4	105	..	..	..	..	..	27
89	Tunisia	69.9	133	92.7	119	100	107	54	169	91	27
90	Iran, Islamic Rep. of	75.7	133	93.7	115	90	105	71	..	..	36
91	Cape Verde	73.6	129	88.4	114	..	..	48	413	..	..
92	Kyrgyzstan	..	..	..	..	95	..	..	..	..	..
93	Guyana	98.4	102	99.8	100	87	..	66	..	91	25
94	South Africa	84.9	108	91.0	105	96	..	56	..	..	18
95	El Salvador	78.3	113	88.0	108	78	106	22	143	77	20
96	Samoa (Western)	80.2	108	86.6	106	96	..	..	..	85	..
97	Syrian Arab Republic	73.6	124	86.6	115	91	91	38	74	94	31
98	Moldova, Rep. of	98.7	103	99.8	100	..	..	..	..	..	44
99	Uzbekistan	88.5	111	96.5	104	..	..	..	..	..	..
100	Algeria	66.6	143	88.2	127	94	106	56	112	..	50

| HDI rank | Adult literacy | | Youth literacy | | Net primary enrolment | | Net secondary enrolment | | Children reaching grade 5 | Tertiary students in science, math and engineering |
	Rate (% age 15 and above) 1999	Index (1985 = 100) 1999	Rate (% age 15-24) 1999	Index (1985 = 100) 1999	Ratio (%) 1995-97 [a]	Index (1984-87 = 100) [b] 1995-97 [a]	Ratio (%) 1995-97 [a]	Index (1984-87 = 100) [b] 1995-97 [a]	(%) 1995-97 [a]	(as % of all tertiary students) 1994-97 [a]
101 Viet Nam	93.1	105	96.8	102	..	..	54	..	..	..
102 Indonesia	86.3	115	97.5	105	95	96	..	..	88	28
103 Tajikistan	99.1	102	99.8	100	..	..	..	..	..	23
104 Bolivia	85.0	115	95.6	106	..	..	..	..	..	..
105 Egypt	54.6	126	69.2	121	93	..	67	..	..	15
106 Nicaragua	68.2	108	73.4	107	77	107	33	149	51	31
107 Honduras	74.0	114	82.9	109	..	..	..	..	..	26
108 Guatemala	68.1	119	78.9	113	72	..	..	..	50	..
109 Gabon	..	..	..	..	..	..	..	..	..	..
110 Equatorial Guinea	82.2	123	96.6	108	..	..	..	..	..	..
111 Namibia	81.4	115	91.3	108	93	..	38	..	86	4
112 Morocco	48.0	143	66.5	138	75	131	..	..	75	29
113 Swaziland	78.9	119	90.0	110	91	112	38	..	76	22
114 Botswana	76.4	121	87.8	112	81	88	48	200	90	27
115 India	56.5	125	71.8	120	..	..	..	..	..	25
116 Mongolia	62.3	132	78.7	123	84	89	54	..	..	25
117 Zimbabwe	88.0	116	97.0	107	..	..	..	..	79	23
118 Myanmar	84.4	108	90.7	105	..	..	..	..	..	37
119 Ghana	70.3	138	90.2	121	..	..	..	..	..	..
120 Lesotho	82.9	111	90.2	106	66	90	18	136	..	13
121 Cambodia	..	..	..	..	100	..	22	..	49	23
122 Papua New Guinea	63.9	119	75.4	115	..	..	..	..	..	..
123 Kenya	81.5	128	94.7	111	..	..	..	..	..	..
124 Comoros	59.2	117	66.9	113	..	..	..	..	..	..
125 Cameroon	74.8	136	93.4	114	..	..	..	..	..	..
126 Congo	79.5	135	97.1	111	..	..	..	..	..	..
Low human development										
127 Pakistan	45.0	142	62.7	147	..	..	..	..	..	..
128 Togo	56.3	138	72.3	127	83	116	21	..	..	11
129 Nepal	40.4	151	58.5	146	..	..	..	..	..	14
130 Bhutan	..	..	..	..	..	..	..	..	..	..
131 Lao People's Dem. Rep.	47.3	154	69.0	145	76	106	24	..	55	..
132 Bangladesh	40.8	127	50.2	125	..	..	..	..	..	..
133 Yemen	45.2	175	63.7	157	..	..	..	..	..	6
134 Haiti	48.8	139	63.5	127	56	229	..	..	..	..
135 Madagascar	65.7	124	79.3	117	61	..	..	..	..	20
136 Nigeria	62.6	153	85.8	133	..	..	..	..	..	41
137 Djibouti	63.4	136	83.1	125	32	99	12	117	79	..
138 Sudan	56.9	141	76.2	132	..	..	..	..	..	..
139 Mauritania	41.6	124	50.6	119	61	185	..	..	64	..
140 Tanzania, U. Rep. of	74.7	131	90.6	117	48	90	..	..	81	39
141 Uganda	66.1	130	78.2	120	..	..	..	..	..	15
142 Congo, Dem. Rep. of the	60.3	149	80.8	131	..	..	..	..	..	..
143 Zambia	77.2	122	87.5	114	75	85	..	..	..	..
144 Côte d'Ivoire	45.7	161	63.6	148	55	..	..	..	75	..
145 Senegal	36.4	149	49.8	143	60	123	..	..	87	..
146 Angola	..	..	..	..	34	..	..	..	..	..
147 Benin	39.0	169	56.7	153	64	126	..	..	..	18
148 Eritrea	52.7	139	70.1	132	30	..	16	..	70	..
149 Gambia	35.7	174	56.0	159	65	104	..	..	..	..
150 Guinea	..	..	..	..	42	157	..	..	..	42

| | Adult literacy | | Youth literacy | | Net primary enrolment | | Net secondary enrolment | | Children reaching grade 5 | Tertiary students in science, math and engineering |
| | Rate (% age 15 and above) 1999 | Index (1985 = 100) 1999 | Rate (% age 15-24) 1999 | Index (1985 = 100) 1999 | Ratio (%) 1995-97 [a] | Index (1984-87 = 100) [b] 1995-97 [a] | Ratio (%) 1995-97 [a] | Index (1984-87 = 100) [b] 1995-97 [a] | (%) 1995-97 [a] | (as % of all tertiary students) 1994-97 [a] |
HDI rank										
151 Malawi	59.2	123	70.3	119	..	..	..	..	..	..
152 Rwanda	65.8	141	82.6	125	..	..	..	..	..	..
153 Mali	39.8	208	64.5	185	31	175	..	..	84	..
154 Central African Republic	45.4	163	65.8	146	..	..	..	..	..	..
155 Chad	41.0	188	64.8	166	52	141	7	..	59	14
156 Guinea-Bissau	37.7	159	56.3	142	..	..	..	..	..	..
157 Mozambique	43.2	150	59.5	138	40	83	6	..	..	16
158 Ethiopia	37.4	158	52.7	142	35	115	..	..	51	36
159 Burkina Faso	23.0	172	33.5	160	33	133	..	..	..	19
160 Burundi	46.9	140	62.0	135	29	59	..	..	..	..
161 Niger	15.3	160	22.3	157	25	100	5	..	73	..
162 Sierra Leone	..	..	..	..	..	..	..	..	..	..
Developing countries	73.1 [c]	117	84.4	108	..	..	..	..	..	..
Least developed countries	51.9 [c]	132	65.2	125	..	..	..	..	..	..
Arab States	61.3	133	78.4	124	..	..	..	..	..	..
East Asia and the Pacific	85.3	114	97.2	104	..	..	..	..	..	..
Latin America and the Caribbean	87.8	107	93.8	104	..	..	..	..	..	..
South Asia	55.1	126	69.8	121	..	..	..	..	..	..
Sub-Saharan Africa	60.5 [c]	136	76.9	124	..	..	..	..	..	..
Eastern Europe and the CIS	98.6	101	99.5	100	..	..	..	..	..	..
OECD	..	..	..	..	..	..	..	..	..	..
High-income OECD	..	..	..	..	..	..	..	..	..	..
High human development	..	..	..	..	..	..	..	..	..	..
Medium human development	78.3 [c]	113	89.1	106	..	..	..	..	..	..
Low human development	49.3 [c]	142	65.8	134	..	..	..	..	..	..
High income	..	..	..	..	..	..	..	..	..	..
Middle income	85.5 [c]	111	95.3	104	..	..	..	..	..	..
Low income	61.7 [c]	122	75.1	117	..	..	..	..	..	..
World	..	..	..	..	..	..	..	..	..	..

a. Data refer to the most recent year available during the period specified.
b. Index is calculated on the basis of the latest data available during the period specified.
c. Aggregates differ slightly from those in table 1, as only literary data from UNESCO are presented in this table.

Source: Column 1: UNESCO 2000a; column 2: calculated on the basis of data on adult literacy rates from UNESCO (2000a); column 3: UNESCO 2000c; column 4: calculated on the basis of data on youth literacy rates from UNESCO (2000c); columns 5 and 7: UNESCO 2001c; column 6: calculated on the basis of data on net primary enrolment ratios from UNESCO (2001c); column 8: calculated on the basis of data on net secondary enrolment ratios from UNESCO (2001c); column 9: UNESCO 1999; column 10: calculated on the basis of data on tertiary students from UNESCO (1999).

... TO HAVE ACCESS TO THE RESOURCES NEEDED FOR A DECENT STANDARD OF LIVING ...

		GDP		GDP per capita	GDP per capita annual growth rate (%)		GDP per capita Highest value during 1975-99 [a] (PPP US$)	Year of highest value	Average annual change in consumer price index (%)	
HDI rank		US$ billions 1999	PPP US$ billions 1999	(PPP US$) 1999	1975-99	1990-99			1990-99	1998-99
High human development										
1	Norway	152.9	126.8	28,433	2.7	3.2	28,433	1999	2.1	2.3
2	Australia	404.0	466.1	24,574	1.9	2.9	24,574	1999	2.0	1.5
3	Canada	634.9	800.4	26,251	1.4	1.7	26,251	1999	1.7	1.7
4	Sweden	238.7	200.5	22,636	1.2	1.2	22,636	1999	2.1	0.5
5	Belgium	248.4	260.2	25,443	1.8	1.4	25,443	1999	2.0	1.1
6	United States	9,152.1	8,867.7 [b]	31,872	2.0	2.0	31,872	1999	2.7	2.2
7	Iceland	8.8	7.7	27,835	1.8	1.8	27,835	1999	2.6	3.2
8	Netherlands	393.7	382.7	24,215	1.7	2.1	24,215	1999	2.4	2.2
9	Japan	4,346.9	3,151.3	24,898	2.8	1.1	25,584	1997	0.9	-0.3
10	Finland	129.7	119.3	23,096	1.9	2.0	23,096	1999	1.5	1.2
11	Switzerland	258.6	193.9	27,171	1.0	-0.1	27,443	1990	1.7	0.7
12	Luxembourg	19.3	18.5	42,769	3.8	3.8	42,769	1999	2.1	1.0
13	France	1,432.3	1,342.2	22,897	1.7	1.1	22,897	1999	1.7	0.5
14	United Kingdom	1,441.8	1,314.6	22,093	2.0	2.1	22,093	1999	2.9	1.6
15	Denmark	174.3	137.8	25,869	1.6	2.0	25,869	1999	2.0	2.5
16	Austria	208.2	203.0	25,089	2.0	1.4	25,089	1999	2.4	0.6
17	Germany	2,111.9	1,949.2	23,742	..	1.0 [c]	23,742	1999	2.4	0.6
18	Ireland	93.4	97.2	25,918	3.8	6.1	25,918	1999	2.1	1.6
19	New Zealand	54.7	72.8	19,104	0.8	1.8	19,104	1999	1.9	-0.1
20	Italy	1,171.0	1,278.1	22,172	2.1	1.2	22,172	1999	3.9	1.7
21	Spain	595.9	712.5	18,079	2.1	2.0	18,079	1999	3.9	2.3
22	Israel	100.8	112.6	18,440	2.0	2.3	18,471	1998	10.5	5.2
23	Greece	125.1	162.4	15,414	1.4	1.8	15,414	1999	9.8	2.6
24	Hong Kong, China (SAR)	158.9	148.5	22,090	4.8	1.9	23,389	1997	6.8	-4.0
25	Cyprus	9.0	14.5	19,006	4.9	2.8	19,006	1999	3.8	1.6
26	Singapore	84.9	82.1	20,767	5.3	4.7	20,767	1999	1.8	(.)
27	Korea, Rep. of	406.9	736.3	15,712	6.5	4.7	15,712	1999	5.3	0.8
28	Portugal	113.7	160.5	16,064	2.9	2.3	16,064	1999	4.8	2.3
29	Slovenia	20.0	31.7	15,977	..	2.5	15,977	1999	28.0 [c]	6.6
30	Malta	3.5 [d]	5.7 [d]	15,189 [d]	4.8 [c]	4.2 [c]	..	..	3.1	2.1
31	Barbados	2.5	3.8	14,353	1.2	1.5	14,353	1999	2.6	1.6
32	Brunei Darussalam	4.8 [d]	..	..	-2.1 [c]	-0.5 [c]	..	..	..	..
33	Czech Republic	53.1	133.8	13,018	..	0.9	13,434	1996	8.5 [c]	2.1
34	Argentina	283.2	449.1	12,277	0.3	3.6	12,844	1998	10.6	-1.2
35	Slovakia	19.7	57.1	10,591	-0.4 [c]	1.6	10,782	1989	13.0	10.6
36	Hungary	48.4	115.1	11,430	0.8	1.4	11,430	1999	21.5	10.0
37	Uruguay	20.8	29.4	8,879	1.4	3.0	9,241	1998	38.2	5.7
38	Poland	155.2	326.6	8,450	..	4.4	8,450	1999	27.8	7.3
39	Chile	67.5	129.9	8,652	4.1	5.6	8,863	1998	9.7	3.3
40	Bahrain	5.3 [d]	8.8 [d]	13,688 [d]	-0.5 [c]	0.8 [c]	..	..	1.2 [c]	..
41	Costa Rica	15.1	31.8	8,860	1.1	3.0	8,860	1999	16.2	10.0
42	Bahamas	..	4.5 [d]	15,258 [d]	1.6	-0.1	..	..	2.3	1.3
43	Kuwait	29.6	..	..	-1.5 [c]	..	..	..	2.0	3.0
44	Estonia	5.2	12.1	8,355	-1.3 [c]	-0.3	10,159	1989	25.3 [c]	3.3
45	United Arab Emirates	47.2 [d]	49.5 [d]	18,162 [d]	-3.7 [c]	-1.6 [c]	..	..	..	..
46	Croatia	20.4	33.0	7,387	..	1.0	8,239	1990	105.4	3.7
47	Lithuania	10.6	24.6	6,656	-3.6 [c]	-3.9	10,087	1990	40.2 [c]	0.8
48	Qatar	..	..	..	..	..	..	..	2.8	2.2
Medium human development										
49	Trinidad and Tobago	6.9	10.6	8,176	0.4	2.0	8,524	1982	5.9	3.4
50	Latvia	6.3	15.2	6,264	-0.9	-3.7	9,929	1989	34.6 [c]	2.4

		GDP		GDP per capita (PPP US$) 1999	GDP per capita annual growth rate (%)		GDP per capita Highest value during 1975-99 [a] (PPP US$)	Year of highest value	Average annual change in consumer price index (%)	
HDI rank		US$ billions 1999	PPP US$ billions 1999		1975-99	1990-99			1990-99	1998-99
51	Mexico	483.7	801.3	8,297	0.8	1.0	8,297	1999	19.9	16.6
52	Panama	9.6	16.5	5,875	0.7	2.4	5,875	1999	1.1	1.3
53	Belarus	26.8	69.0	6,876	-2.7 [c]	-2.9	8,429	1989	383.7 [c]	293.7
54	Belize	0.7	1.2	4,959	2.6	0.7	4,959	1999	2.3	-1.2
55	Russian Federation	401.4	1,092.6	7,473	-1.2	-5.9 [c]	12,832	1989	116.1 [c]	85.7
56	Malaysia	79.0	186.4	8,209	4.2	4.7	8,779	1997	4.0	2.7
57	Bulgaria	12.4	41.6	5,071	-0.2 [c]	-2.1	6,799	1988	129.3	2.6
58	Romania	34.0	135.7	6,041	-0.5	-0.5	8,822	1986	108.9	45.8
59	Libyan Arab Jamahiriya	..	..	..	..	..	..	..	..	..
60	Macedonia, TFYR	3.5	9.4	4,651	..	-1.5	5,340	1990	91.4	-1.3
61	Venezuela	102.2	130.3	5,495	-1.0	-0.5	7,642	1977	51.8	23.6
62	Colombia	86.6	238.8	5,749	1.7	1.4	6,201	1997	21.7	11.2
63	Mauritius	4.2	10.7	9,107	4.0	3.9	9,107	1999	7.0	6.9
64	Suriname	0.8 [d]	1.7 [d]	4,178 [d]	-0.2	3.3	..	..	88.0	98.9
65	Lebanon	17.2 [d]	19.8 [d]	4,705 [d]	..	5.7 [c]	..	..	..	..
66	Thailand	124.4	369.4	6,132	5.7	3.8	6,810	1996	5.1	0.3
67	Fiji	1.8	3.8	4,799	0.7	1.2	4,799	1999	3.4	2.0
68	Saudi Arabia	139.4	218.4	10,815	-2.2	-1.1	18,604	1980	1.2	-1.4
69	Brazil	751.5	1,182.0	7,037	0.8	1.5	7,172	1997	253.5	4.9
70	Philippines	76.6	282.6	3,805	0.1	0.9	3,956	1982	8.5	6.7
71	Oman	15.0 [d]	..	..	2.8 [c]	0.3 [c]	..	..	0.2	0.4
72	Armenia	1.8	8.4 [d]	2,215 [d]	..	-3.9	..	..	97.8 [c]	0.7
73	Peru	51.9	116.6	4,622	-0.8	3.2	5,287	1981	31.6	3.5
74	Ukraine	38.7	172.7	3,458	-9.2 [c]	-10.3	8,748	1989	413.4 [c]	..
75	Kazakhstan	15.8	73.9	4,951	-5.3 [c]	-4.9	8,131	1988	87.2 [c]	8.3
76	Georgia	2.7	13.3	2,431	..	..	..	..	1.0 [c]	19.1
77	Maldives	0.4 [d]	1.2 [d]	4,423 [d]	5.2 [c]	3.9 [c]	..	..	8.0	3.0
78	Jamaica	6.9	9.3	3,561	0.1	-0.6	4,146	1975	26.1	6.0
79	Azerbaijan	4.0	22.8	2,850	-11.8 [c]	-10.7	8,605	1987	224.9 [c]	-8.6
80	Paraguay	7.7	23.5	4,384	0.8	-0.2	5,023	1981	13.8	6.8
81	Sri Lanka	16.0	62.2	3,279	3.2	4.0	3,279	1999	10.3	4.7
82	Turkey	185.7	410.8	6,380	2.1	2.2	6,834	1998	81.5	64.9
83	Turkmenistan	3.2	16.0	3,347	-8.7 [c]	-9.6	7,427	1988	..	..
84	Ecuador	19.0	37.2	2,994	0.3	(.)	3,344	1997	34.5	52.2
85	Albania	3.7	10.8	3,189	-1.4 [c]	2.8	3,518	1982	32.1 [c]	0.4
86	Dominican Republic	17.4	46.3	5,507	1.4	3.9	5,507	1999	9.0	6.5
87	China	989.5	4,534.9	3,617	8.1	9.5	3,617	1999	9.9	-1.4
88	Jordan	8.1	18.7	3,955	0.4	1.1	4,904	1986	3.9	0.6
89	Tunisia	20.9	56.3	5,957	1.9	2.9	5,957	1999	4.6	2.7
90	Iran, Islamic Rep. of	110.8	348.3	5,531	-0.9	1.9	7,777	1976	27.1	20.1
91	Cape Verde	0.6	1.9	4,490	2.9 [c]	3.2	4,490	1999	6.0 [c]	..
92	Kyrgyzstan	1.3	12.5	2,573	-5.3 [c]	-6.4	4,507	1990		35.9
93	Guyana	0.7	3.1	3,640	-0.5	5.2	3,816	1976	6.4 [c]	7.5
94	South Africa	131.1	375.1	8,908	-0.8	0.2	11,109	1981	9.1	5.2
95	El Salvador	12.5	26.7	4,344	-0.2	2.8	4,846	1978	9.4	0.5
96	Samoa (Western)	0.2	0.7	4,047	0.2 [c]	1.4	4,183	1979	4.1	0.3
97	Syrian Arab Republic	19.4	70.0	4,454	0.8	2.7	4,454	1999	7.8	-2.7
98	Moldova, Rep. of	1.2	8.7	2,037	..	-10.8	5,996	1989	16.0 [c]	45.9
99	Uzbekistan	17.7	54.9	2,251	-3.0 [c]	-3.1	2,920	1990	..	..
100	Algeria	47.9	151.6	5,063	-0.4	-0.5	5,998	1985	19.5	2.6

		GDP		GDP per capita	GDP per capita annual growth rate (%)		GDP per capita Highest value during 1975-99 [a] (PPP US$)	Year of highest value	Average annual change in consumer price index (%)	
HDI rank		US$ billions 1999	PPP US$ billions 1999	(PPP US$) 1999	1975-99	1990-99			1990-99	1998-99
101	Viet Nam	28.7	144.2	1,860	4.8 [c]	6.2	1,860	1999	..	..
102	Indonesia	142.5	591.5	2,857	4.6	3.0	3,383	1997	13.1	20.5
103	Tajikistan	1.9	..	..	..	..	..	..	..	..
104	Bolivia	8.3	19.2	2,355	-0.6	1.8	2,632	1978	9.3	2.2
105	Egypt	89.1	214.3	3,420	2.9	2.4	3,420	1999	9.6	3.1
106	Nicaragua	2.3	11.2	2,279	-3.8	0.4	5,165	1977	35.1	11.2
107	Honduras	5.4	14.8	2,340	0.1	0.3	2,558	1979	19.5	11.7
108	Guatemala	18.2	40.7	3,674	(.)	1.5	3,798	1980	10.7	4.9
109	Gabon	4.4	7.3	6,024	-1.7	0.6	11,732	1976	5.7 [c]	..
110	Equatorial Guinea	0.7	2.1	4,676	8.4 [c]	16.3	4,676	1999	..	..
111	Namibia	3.1	9.3	5,468	(.)	0.8	5,772	1980	9.9	8.6
112	Morocco	35.0	96.5	3,419	1.4	0.4	3,500	1998	4.2	0.7
113	Swaziland	1.2	4.1	3,987	2.0	-0.2	4,135	1990	9.5	6.1
114	Botswana	6.0	10.9	6,872	5.1	1.8	6,872	1999	10.7	7.1
115	India	447.3	2,242.0	2,248	3.2	4.1	2,248	1999	9.5	4.7
116	Mongolia	0.9	4.1	1,711	-0.5 [c]	-0.6	2,051	1989	53.7 [c]	7.6
117	Zimbabwe	5.6	34.2	2,876	0.6	0.6	2,932	1991	25.4 [c]	..
118	Myanmar	..	..	..	..	..	..	..	27.1	18.4
119	Ghana	7.8	35.3	1,881	(.)	1.6	1,922	1978	29.2	12.4
120	Lesotho	0.9	3.9	1,854	2.4	2.1	1,992	1997	10.5 [c]	..
121	Cambodia	3.1	16.0	1,361	1.9 [c]	1.9	1,368	1996	7.1 [c]	4.0
122	Papua New Guinea	3.6	11.1	2,367	0.9	2.3	2,667	1994	8.7	14.9
123	Kenya	10.6	30.1	1,022	0.4	-0.3	1,078	1990	16.7	2.6
124	Comoros	0.2	0.8	1,429	-1.5 [c]	-3.1	2,007	1984	..	..
125	Cameroon	9.2	23.1	1,573	-0.6	-1.5	2,465	1986	7.3	5.3
126	Congo	2.2	2.1	727	0.3	-3.3	1,170	1984	10.0 [c]	5.4
Low human development										
127	Pakistan	58.2	247.3	1,834	2.9	1.3	1,834	1999	10.3	4.1
128	Togo	1.4	6.4	1,410	-1.3	-0.5	1,936	1980	9.3	-0.1
129	Nepal	5.0	28.9	1,237	1.8	2.3	1,237	1999	9.0	8.0
130	Bhutan	0.4	1.0	1,341	4.1 [c]	3.4	1,341	1999	10.1 [c]	..
131	Lao People's Dem. Rep.	1.4	7.5	1,471	3.2 [c]	3.8	1,471	1999	24.1	125.1
132	Bangladesh	46.0	189.4	1,483	2.3	3.1	1,483	1999	5.5	6.2
133	Yemen	6.8	13.7	806	..	-0.4	888	1990	32.6 [c]	..
134	Haiti	4.3	11.4	1,464	-2.0	-3.4	2,399	1980	23.2	8.7
135	Madagascar	3.7	12.0	799	-1.8	-1.2	1,203	1975	19.8	9.9
136	Nigeria	35.0	105.7	853	-0.8	-0.5	1,122	1977	36.2	6.6
137	Djibouti	0.5 [d]	..	..	..	-5.1 [c]	..	..	..	..
138	Sudan	9.7	..	..	..	..	..	..	81.1	16.0
139	Mauritania	1.0	4.2	1,609	-0.2	1.3	1,688	1976	6.3	4.1
140	Tanzania, U. Rep. of	8.8	16.5	501	..	-0.1	502	1990	22.6	7.9
141	Uganda	6.4	25.1	1,167	2.5 [c]	4.0	1,167	1999	11.6	6.4
142	Congo, Dem. Rep. of the	5.6 [d]	38.6 [d]	801 [d]	-4.7 [c]	-8.1 [c]	..	..	2,089.0 [c]	..
143	Zambia	3.1	7.5	756	-2.4	-2.4	1,359	1976	80.8 [c]	..
144	Côte d'Ivoire	11.2	25.7	1,654	-2.1	0.6	2,598	1978	7.8	0.8
145	Senegal	4.8	13.2	1,419	-0.3	0.6	1,535	1976	6.0	0.8
146	Angola	8.5	39.3	3,179	-2.1 [c]	-2.8	4,480	1988	787.0	286.2
147	Benin	2.4	5.7	933	0.4	1.8	933	1999	9.9 [c]	0.3
148	Eritrea	0.6	3.5	881	..	2.2 [c]	899	1998	..	..
149	Gambia	0.4	2.0	1,580	-0.3	-0.6	1,708	1984	4.3	3.8
150	Guinea	3.5	14.0	1,934	1.4 [c]	1.5	1,934	1999	..	..

	GDP		GDP per capita	GDP per capita annual growth rate (%)		GDP per capita		Average annual change in consumer price index (%)	
HDI rank	US$ billions 1999	PPP US$ billions 1999	(PPP US$) 1999	1975-99	1990-99	Highest value during 1975-99 [a] (PPP US$)	Year of highest value	1990-99	1998-99
151 Malawi	1.8	6.3	586	-0.2	0.9	618	1979	33.8	44.9
152 Rwanda	2.0	7.4	885	-1.4	-3.0	1,254	1983	18.0 [c]	-2.4
153 Mali	2.6	8.0	753	-0.7	1.1	878	1979	5.8	1.2
154 Central African Republic	1.1	4.1	1,166	-1.6	-0.3	1,596	1977	6.7 [c]	..
155 Chad	1.5	6.4	850	(.)	-0.9	998	1977	8.7	-6.8
156 Guinea-Bissau	0.2	0.8	678	0.3	-1.9	912	1997	37.6	-0.7
157 Mozambique	4.0	14.9	861	1.3 [c]	3.8	861	1999	34.9	2.0
158 Ethiopia	6.4	39.4	628	-0.3 [c]	2.4	675	1983	6.0 [c]	..
159 Burkina Faso	2.6	10.6	965	1.0	1.4	965	1999	6.1	-1.1
160 Burundi	0.7	3.9	578	-0.5	-5.0	852	1991	15.8	3.4
161 Niger	2.0	7.9	753	-2.2	-1.0	1,249	1979	6.6	-2.3
162 Sierra Leone	0.7	2.2	448	-2.5	-7.0	964	1982	31.4	34.1
Developing countries	5,826.7 T	16,201.9 T	3,530	2.3	3.2	..	..	..	..
Least developed countries	169.4 T	693.8 T	1,170	0.2 [c]	0.8	..	..	..	..
Arab States	531.2 T	1,071.7 T	4,550	0.3	0.7	..	..	..	..
East Asia and the Pacific	2,122.0 T	7,193.3 T	3,950	6.0	5.9	..	..	..	..
Latin America and the Caribbean	1,989.8 T	3,391.1 T	6,880	0.6	1.7	..	..	..	..
South Asia	684.0 T	3,120.5 T	2,280	2.3	3.4	..	..	..	..
Sub-Saharan Africa	309.8 T	984.2 T	1,640	-1.0	-0.4	..	..	..	..
Eastern Europe and the CIS	909.1 T	2,498.2 T	6,290	..	-3.4	..	..	..	..
OECD	24,863.1 T	24,606.5 T	22,020	2.0	1.5	..	..	..	..
High-income OECD	23,510.3 T	22,025.5 T	26,050	2.2	1.6	..	..	..	..
High human development	25,099.7 T	24,617.0 T	23,410	2.2	1.7	..	..	..	..
Medium human development	4,997.5 T	15,250.1 T	3,850	1.6	1.7	..	..	..	..
Low human development	254.4 T	977.0 T	1,200	0.4	0.7	..	..	..	..
High income	23,981.8 T	22,518.3 T	25,860	2.1	1.6	..	..	..	..
Middle income	5,367.9 T	13,834.9 T	5,310	1.8	2.3	..	..	..	..
Low income	1,002.4 T	4,499.0 T	1,910	1.7	1.2	..	..	..	..
World	30,351.4 T	40,733.3 T	6,980	1.3	1.1	..	..	..	..

a. Data may refer to a period shorter than that specified where data are not available for all years.

b. In theory, for the United States the value of GDP in PPP US dollars should be the same as that in US dollars, but practical issues arising in the creation of the PPP US dollar GDP series prevent this.

c. Data refer to a period other than that specified.

d. Data refer to 1998.

Source: Columns 1-3: World Bank 2001b; aggregates calculated for the Human Development Report Office by the World Bank; columns 4 and 5: World Bank 2001a; aggregates calculated for the Human Development Report Office by the World Bank; columns 6 and 7: calculated on the basis of data on GDP at market prices (constant 1995 US$), population and GDP per capita (PPP US$) from World Bank (2001b); column 8: calculated for the Human Development Report Office by the World Bank on the basis of data on the consumer price index from World Bank (2001b); column 9: calculated on the basis of data on the consumer price index from World Bank (2001b).

12 Inequality in income or consumption

			Survey based on income (I) or consumption (C) [a]	Share of income or consumption (%)				Inequality measures		
HDI rank		Survey year		Poorest 10%	Poorest 20%	Richest 20%	Richest 10%	Richest 10% to poorest 10% [b]	Richest 20% to poorest 20% [b]	Gini index [c]
High human development										
1	Norway	1995	I	4.1	9.7	35.8	21.8	5.3	3.7	25.8
2	Australia	1994	I	2.0	5.9	41.3	25.4	12.5	7.0	35.2
3	Canada	1994	I	2.8	7.5	39.3	23.8	8.5	5.2	31.5
4	Sweden	1992	I	3.7	9.6	34.5	20.1	5.4	3.6	25.0
5	Belgium	1992	I	3.7	9.5	34.5	20.2	5.5	3.6	25.0
6	United States	1997	I	1.8	5.2	46.4	30.5	16.6	9.0	40.8
7	Iceland	..	..	..	..	..	..	..	..	..
8	Netherlands	1994	I	2.8	7.3	40.1	25.1	9.0	5.5	32.6
9	Japan	1993	I	4.8	10.6	35.7	21.7	4.5	3.4	24.9
10	Finland	1991	I	4.2	10.0	35.8	21.6	5.1	3.6	25.6
11	Switzerland	1992	I	2.6	6.9	40.3	25.2	9.9	5.8	33.1
12	Luxembourg	1994	I	4.0	9.4	36.5	22.0	5.4	3.9	26.9
13	France	1995	I	2.8	7.2	40.2	25.1	9.1	5.6	32.7
14	United Kingdom	1991	I	2.6	6.6	43.0	27.3	10.4	6.5	36.1
15	Denmark	1992	I	3.6	9.6	34.5	20.5	5.7	3.6	24.7
16	Austria	1987	I	4.4	10.4	33.3	19.3	4.4	3.2	23.1
17	Germany	1994	I	3.3	8.2	38.5	23.7	7.1	4.7	30.0
18	Ireland	1987	I	2.5	6.7	42.9	27.4	11.0	6.4	35.9
19	New Zealand	..	..	..	..	..	..	..	..	..
20	Italy	1995	I	3.5	8.7	36.3	21.8	6.2	4.2	27.3
21	Spain	1990	I	2.8	7.5	40.3	25.2	9.0	5.4	32.5
22	Israel	1992	I	2.8	6.9	42.5	26.9	9.6	6.2	35.5
23	Greece	1993	I	3.0	7.5	40.3	25.3	8.5	5.3	32.7
24	Hong Kong, China (SAR)	..	..	..	..	..	..	..	..	..
25	Cyprus	..	..	..	..	..	..	..	..	..
26	Singapore	..	..	..	..	..	..	..	..	..
27	Korea, Rep. of	1993	C	2.9	7.5	39.3	24.3	8.4	5.3	31.6
28	Portugal	1994-95	I	3.1	7.3	43.4	28.4	9.3	5.9	35.6
29	Slovenia	1998	I	3.9	9.1	37.7	23.0	5.8	4.1	28.4
30	Malta	..	..	..	..	..	..	..	..	..
31	Barbados	..	..	..	..	..	..	..	..	..
32	Brunei Darussalam	..	..	..	..	..	..	..	..	..
33	Czech Republic	1996	I	4.3	10.3	35.9	22.4	5.2	3.5	25.4
34	Argentina	..	..	..	..	..	..	..	..	..
35	Slovakia	1992	I	5.1	11.9	31.4	18.2	3.6	2.6	19.5
36	Hungary	1998	C	4.1	10.0	34.4	20.5	5.0	3.5	24.4
37	Uruguay	1989	I	2.1	5.4	48.3	32.7	15.4	8.9	42.3
38	Poland	1998	C	3.2	7.8	39.7	24.7	7.8	5.1	31.6
39	Chile	1996	I	1.4	3.4	62.0	46.9	33.7	18.2	57.5
40	Bahrain	..	..	..	..	..	..	..	..	..
41	Costa Rica	1997	I	1.7	4.5	51.0	34.6	20.7	11.5	45.9
42	Bahamas	..	..	..	..	..	..	..	..	..
43	Kuwait	..	..	..	..	..	..	..	..	..
44	Estonia	1998	I	3.0	7.0	45.1	29.8	10.0	6.5	37.6
45	United Arab Emirates	..	..	..	..	..	..	..	..	..
46	Croatia	1998	I	3.7	8.8	38.0	23.3	6.3	4.3	29.0
47	Lithuania	1996	C	3.1	7.8	40.3	25.6	8.3	5.2	32.4
48	Qatar	..	..	..	..	..	..	..	..	..
Medium human development										
49	Trinidad and Tobago	1992	I	2.1	5.5	45.9	29.9	14.4	8.3	40.3
50	Latvia	1998	I	2.9	7.6	40.3	25.9	8.9	5.3	32.4

HDI rank	Survey year	Survey based on income (I) or consumption (C) [a]	Share of income or consumption (%)				Inequality measures		
			Poorest 10%	Poorest 20%	Richest 20%	Richest 10%	Richest 10% to poorest 10% [b]	Richest 20% to poorest 20% [h]	Gini index [c]
51 Mexico	1996	I	1.6	4.0	56.7	41.1	26.4	14.3	51.9
52 Panama	1997	C	1.2	3.6	52.8	35.7	29.0	14.8	48.5
53 Belarus	1998	C	5.1	11.4	33.3	20.0	3.9	2.9	21.7
54 Belize	..	..	..	..	..	..	..	..	..
55 Russian Federation	1998	C	1.7	4.4	53.7	38.7	23.3	12.2	48.7
56 Malaysia	1997	I	1.7	4.4	54.3	38.4	22.1	12.4	49.2
57 Bulgaria	1997	I	4.5	10.1	36.8	22.8	5.0	3.6	26.4
58 Romania	1994	I	3.7	8.9	37.3	22.7	6.1	4.2	28.2
59 Libyan Arab Jamahiriya	..	..	..	..	..	..	..	..	..
60 Macedonia, TFYR	..	..	..	..	..	..	..	..	..
61 Venezuela	1997	C	1.6	4.1	53.7	37.6	24.3	13.0	48.8
62 Colombia	1996	I	1.1	3.0	60.9	46.1	42.7	20.3	57.1
63 Mauritius	..	..	..	..	..	..	..	..	..
64 Suriname	..	..	..	..	..	..	..	..	..
65 Lebanon	..	..	..	..	..	..	..	..	..
66 Thailand	1998	C	2.8	6.4	48.4	32.4	11.6	7.6	41.4
67 Fiji	..	..	..	..	..	..	..	..	..
68 Saudi Arabia	..	..	..	..	..	..	..	..	..
69 Brazil	1997	I	1.0	2.6	63.0	46.7	48.7	24.4	59.1
70 Philippines	1997	C	2.3	5.4	52.3	36.6	16.1	9.8	46.2
71 Oman	..	..	..	..	..	..	..	..	..
72 Armenia	1996	C	2.3	5.5	50.6	35.2	15.3	9.2	44.4
73 Peru	1996	I	1.6	4.4	51.2	35.4	22.3	11.7	46.2
74 Ukraine	1999	C	3.7	8.8	37.8	23.2	6.4	4.3	29.0
75 Kazakhstan	1996	C	2.7	6.7	42.3	26.3	9.8	6.3	35.4
76 Georgia	1996	I	2.3	6.1	43.6	27.9	12.0	7.1	37.1
77 Maldives	..	..	..	..	..	..	..	..	..
78 Jamaica	1996	C	2.9	7.0	43.9	28.9	10.0	6.3	36.4
79 Azerbaijan	1995	I	2.8	6.9	43.3	27.8	9.8	6.3	36.0
80 Paraguay	1998	I	0.5	1.9	60.7	43.8	91.1	31.8	57.7
81 Sri Lanka	1995	C	3.5	8.0	42.8	28.0	7.9	5.3	34.4
82 Turkey	1994	C	2.3	5.8	47.7	32.3	14.2	8.2	41.5
83 Turkmenistan	1998	C	2.6	6.1	47.5	31.7	12.3	7.7	40.8
84 Ecuador	1995	C	2.2	5.4	49.7	33.8	15.4	9.2	43.7
85 Albania	..	..	..	..	..	..	..	..	..
86 Dominican Republic	1998	I	2.1	5.1	53.3	37.9	17.7	10.5	47.4
87 China	1998	I	2.4	5.9	46.6	30.4	12.7	8.0	40.3
88 Jordan	1997	C	3.3	7.6	44.4	29.8	9.1	5.9	36.4
89 Tunisia	1995	C	2.3	5.7	47.9	31.8	13.8	8.5	41.7
90 Iran, Islamic Rep. of	..	..	..	..	..	..	..	..	..
91 Cape Verde	..	..	..	..	..	..	..	..	..
92 Kyrgyzstan	1997	I	2.7	6.3	47.4	31.7	11.9	7.5	40.5
93 Guyana	1993	C	2.4	6.3	46.9	32.0	13.3	7.4	40.2
94 South Africa	1993-94	C	1.1	2.9	64.8	45.9	42.5	22.6	59.3
95 El Salvador	1997	I	1.4	3.7	55.3	39.3	28.5	14.8	50.8
96 Samoa (Western)	..	..	..	..	..	..	..	..	..
97 Syrian Arab Republic	..	..	..	..	..	..	..	..	..
98 Moldova, Rep. of	1997	I	2.2	5.6	46.8	30.7	13.7	8.3	40.6
99 Uzbekistan	1993	I	3.1	7.4	40.9	25.2	8.2	5.5	33.3
100 Algeria	1995	C	2.8	7.0	42.6	26.8	9.6	6.1	35.3

HDI rank		Survey year	Survey based on income (I) or consumption (C) [a]	Share of income or consumption (%)				Inequality measures		
				Poorest 10%	Poorest 20%	Richest 20%	Richest 10%	Richest 10% to poorest 10% [b]	Richest 20% to poorest 20% [b]	Gini index [c]
101	Viet Nam	1998	C	3.6	8.0	44.5	29.9	8.4	5.6	36.1
102	Indonesia	1999	C	4.0	9.0	41.1	26.7	6.6	4.6	31.7
103	Tajikistan	..	..	..	..	..	..	..	..	..
104	Bolivia	1997	I	0.5	1.9	61.8	45.7	91.4	32.0	58.9
105	Egypt	1995	C	4.4	9.8	39.0	25.0	5.7	4.0	28.9
106	Nicaragua	1998	C	0.7	2.3	63.6	48.8	70.7	27.9	60.3
107	Honduras	1997	I	0.4	1.6	61.8	44.3	119.8	38.1	59.0
108	Guatemala	1998	I	1.6	3.8	60.6	46.0	29.1	15.8	55.8
109	Gabon	..	..	..	..	..	..	..	..	..
110	Equatorial Guinea	..	..	..	..	..	..	..	..	..
111	Namibia	..	..	..	..	..	..	..	..	..
112	Morocco	1998-99	C	2.6	6.5	46.6	30.9	11.7	7.2	39.5
113	Swaziland	1994	I	1.0	2.7	64.4	50.2	49.7	23.8	60.9
114	Botswana	..	..	..	..	..	..	..	..	..
115	India	1997	C	3.5	8.1	46.1	33.5	9.5	5.7	37.8
116	Mongolia	1995	C	2.9	7.3	40.9	24.5	8.4	5.6	33.2
117	Zimbabwe	1990-91	C	1.8	4.0	62.3	46.9	26.1	15.6	56.8
118	Myanmar	..	..	..	..	..	..	..	..	..
119	Ghana	1998	C	2.4	5.9	45.9	29.5	12.3	7.8	39.6
120	Lesotho	1986-87	C	0.9	2.8	60.1	43.4	48.2	21.5	56.0
121	Cambodia	1997	C	2.9	6.9	47.6	33.8	11.6	6.9	40.4
122	Papua New Guinea	1996	C	1.7	4.5	56.5	40.5	23.8	12.6	50.9
123	Kenya	1994	C	1.8	5.0	50.2	34.9	19.3	10.0	44.5
124	Comoros	..	..	..	..	..	..	..	..	..
125	Cameroon	..	..	..	..	..	..	..	..	..
126	Congo	..	..	..	..	..	..	..	..	..
Low human development										
127	Pakistan	1996-97	C	4.1	9.5	41.1	27.6	6.7	4.3	31.2
128	Togo	..	..	..	..	..	..	..	..	..
129	Nepal	1995-96	C	3.2	7.6	44.8	29.8	9.3	5.9	36.7
130	Bhutan	..	..	..	..	..	..	..	..	..
131	Lao People's Dem. Rep.	1997	C	3.2	7.6	45.0	30.6	9.7	6.0	37.0
132	Bangladesh	1995-96	C	3.9	8.7	42.8	28.6	7.3	4.9	33.6
133	Yemen	1998	C	3.0	7.4	41.2	25.9	8.6	5.6	33.4
134	Haiti	..	..	..	..	..	..	..	..	..
135	Madagascar	1997	C	2.2	5.4	52.0	37.3	17.2	9.6	46.0
136	Nigeria	1996-97	C	1.6	4.4	55.7	40.8	24.9	12.8	50.6
137	Djibouti	..	..	..	..	..	..	..	..	..
138	Sudan	..	..	..	..	..	..	..	..	..
139	Mauritania	1995	C	2.5	6.4	44.1	28.4	11.2	6.9	37.3
140	Tanzania, U. Rep. of	1993	C	2.8	6.8	45.5	30.1	10.8	6.7	38.2
141	Uganda	1996	C	3.0	7.1	44.9	29.8	9.9	6.4	37.4
142	Congo, Dem. Rep. of the	..	..	..	..	..	..	..	..	..
143	Zambia	1998	C	1.1	3.3	56.6	41.0	36.6	17.3	52.6
144	Côte d'Ivoire	1995	C	3.1	7.1	44.3	28.8	9.4	6.2	36.7
145	Senegal	1995	C	2.6	6.4	48.2	33.5	12.8	7.5	41.3
146	Angola	..	..	..	..	..	..	..	..	..
147	Benin	..	..	..	..	..	..	..	..	..
148	Eritrea	..	..	..	..	..	..	..	..	..
149	Gambia	1992	C	1.5	4.4	52.8	37.6	24.9	12.1	47.8
150	Guinea	1994	C	2.6	6.4	47.2	32.0	12.3	7.3	40.3

HDI rank	Survey year	Survey based on income (I) or consumption (C) [a]	Share of income or consumption (%)				Inequality measures		
			Poorest 10%	Poorest 20%	Richest 20%	Richest 10%	Richest 10% to poorest 10% [b]	Richest 20% to poorest 20% [b]	Gini index [c]
151 Malawi	..	..	..	..	..	..	..	..	..
152 Rwanda	1983-85	C	4.2	9.7	39.1	24.2	5.8	4.0	28.9
153 Mali	1994	C	1.8	4.6	56.2	40.4	23.1	12.2	50.5
154 Central African Republic	..	..	..	..	..	..	..	..	..
155 Chad	..	..	..	..	..	..	..		..
156 Guinea-Bissau	1991	C	0.5	2.1	58.9	42.4	84.8	28.0	56.2
157 Mozambique	1996-97	C	2.5	6.5	46.5	31.7	12.5	7.2	39.6
158 Ethiopia	1995	C	3.0	7.1	47.7	33.7	11.4	6.7	40.0
159 Burkina Faso	1994	C	2.2	5.5	55.0	39.5	17.6	10.0	48.2
160 Burundi	1992	C	3.4	7.9	41.6	26.6	7.8	5.2	33.3
161 Niger	1995	C	0.8	2.6	53.3	35.4	46.0	20.7	50.5
162 Sierra Leone	..	..	..	..	..	..	..	..	..

Note: Because data come from surveys covering different years and using different methodologies, comparisons between countries must be made with caution.

a. The distribution of income is typically more unequal than the distribution of consumption, as poor people generally consume a greater proportion of their income than rich people do.

b. Data show the ratio of the income or consumption share of the richest group to that of the poorest. Because of rounding, results may differ from ratios calculated using the income or consumption shares in columns 3-6.

c. The Gini index measures inequality over the entire distribution of income or consumption. A value of 0 represents perfect equality, and a value of 100 perfect inequality.

Source: Columns 1-6 and 9: World Bank 2001b; *columns 7 and 8:* calculated on the basis of income or consumption data from World Bank (2001b).

13 The structure
of trade

. . . TO HAVE ACCESS TO THE RESOURCES NEEDED FOR A DECENT STANDARD OF LIVING . . .

HDI rank	Imports of goods and services (as % of GDP)		Exports of goods and services (as % of GDP)		Primary exports (as % of merchandise exports)		Manufactured exports (as % of merchandise exports)		High-technology exports (as % of manufactured exports)		Terms of trade (1980 = 100)[a]
	1990	1999	1990	1999	1990	1999	1990	1999	1990	1999	1998
High human development											
1 Norway	34	33	41	39	67	67	33	27	12	18	86 [b]
2 Australia	17	21 [c]	17	19 [c]	64	66	16	29	15	16	78 [b]
3 Canada	26	41	26	44	36	27	59	67	14	16	88 [b]
4 Sweden	29	38	30	44	16	12	83	83	18	31	111 [b]
5 Belgium	70	72	71	76	18 [d]	16 [c, d]	77 [d]	78 [c, d]	..	..	..
6 United States	11	13 [c]	10	11 [c]	22	13	74	83	34	36	116 [b]
7 Iceland	33	38	34	34	91	87	8	13	11	15	98 [e]
8 Netherlands	55	56	58	61	37	29	59	70	22	32	..
9 Japan	10	9	11	10	3	3	96	94	28	32	197 [b]
10 Finland	24	29	23	37	17	14	83	85	12	31	115 [e]
11 Switzerland	36	36 [c]	36	40 [c]	6	8	94	92	18	28	..
12 Luxembourg	109	97	113	113	..	..	..	..	..	..	..
13 France	22	24	21	26	23	17	77	81	19	27	118
14 United Kingdom	27	27	24	26	19	14	79	83	25	34	100 [b]
15 Denmark	31	33	36	37	35	28	60	66	19	28	110 [b]
16 Austria	39	46	40	45	12	12	88	83	14	14	..
17 Germany	..	28	..	29	10	8	89	84	15	21	111
18 Ireland	52	74	57	88	26	11	70	85	40	49	98
19 New Zealand	27	30 [c]	28	31 [c]	75	66	23	33	5	16	109 [b]
20 Italy	20	24	20	26	11	10	88	89	11	12	134
21 Spain	20	28	16	28	24	20	75	78	11	13	126 [b]
22 Israel	45	45	35	36	13	7	87	93	19	31	128 [b]
23 Greece	28	25	19	19	46	49	54	50	3	10	101 [e]
24 Hong Kong, China (SAR)	126	128	134	133	4	4	95	95	7	3	102
25 Cyprus	57	49	52	44	45	48	55	52	4	9	82
26 Singapore	195	..	202	..	27	13	72	86	51	67	82
27 Korea, Rep. of	30	35	29	42	6	8	94	91	22	36	99
28 Portugal	40	40 [c]	33	31 [c]	19	13	80	87	6	8	..
29 Slovenia	..	57	..	53	..	10	..	90	..	13	..
30 Malta	99	94 [c]	85	88 [c]	4	3 [c]	96	97	44	56	..
31 Barbados	52	55	49	50	55	44	43	55	13	15	89
32 Brunei Darussalam	..	..	..	..	100	89 [c]	(.)	11 [c]	..	..	49
33 Czech Republic	43	65	45	64	..	12	..	88	..	13	..
34 Argentina	5	11	10	10	71	67	29	32	6	9	78
35 Slovakia	36	67	27	62	..	14	..	82	..	8	..
36 Hungary	29	55	31	53	35	13	63	85	..	28	..
37 Uruguay	18	20	24	18	61	62	39	38	2	4	121
38 Poland	21	32	28	26	36	21	59	77	11	10	115 [b]
39 Chile	31	27	35	29	87	81 [c]	11	17 [c]	5	..	86
40 Bahrain	100	..	122	..	91	..	9	..	..	..	..
41 Costa Rica	41	47	35	54	66	32	27	68	12	62	133
42 Bahamas	..	..	..	..	..	..	..	..	..	..	..
43 Kuwait	58	37	45	47	94	80	6	20	6	2	57
44 Estonia	..	83	..	77	..	31	..	69	..	25	..
45 United Arab Emirates	40	..	65	..	54	..	46	..	(.)	..	27
46 Croatia	..	48	..	41	..	24	..	76	..	11	..
47 Lithuania	61	50	52	40	..	31	..	67	..	11	..
48 Qatar	..	..	..	..	84	..	16	..	..	..	41
Medium human development											
49 Trinidad and Tobago	29	44	45	50	73	63	27	37	5	3	51
50 Latvia	49	58	48	47	..	43	..	57	..	11	..

HDI rank		Imports of goods and services (as % of GDP)		Exports of goods and services (as % of GDP)		Primary exports (as % of merchandise exports)		Manufactured exports (as % of merchandise exports)		High-technology exports (as % of manufactured exports)		Terms of trade (1980 = 100)[a]
		1990	1999	1990	1999	1990	1999	1990	1999	1990	1999	1998
51	Mexico	20	32	19	31	56	15	43	85	7	32	30
52	Panama	34	41	38	33	78	83	21	17	14	13	94
53	Belarus	44	65	46	62	..	21	..	75	..	6	..
54	Belize	62	58	64	49	..	..	15	13	..	0 c	..
55	Russian Federation	18	28	18	46	..	57	..	25	..	14	..
56	Malaysia	72	97	75	122	46	19	54	80	49	64	53
57	Bulgaria	37	52	33	44	..	..	..	..	..	..	..
58	Romania	26	34	17	30	26	21	73	78	5	6	..
59	Libyan Arab Jamahiriya	..	..	..	..	95	..	5	..	(.)	..	41
60	Macedonia, TFYR	36	56	26	41	..	28 c	..	72 c	..	3 c	..
61	Venezuela	20	15	39	22	90	88	10	12	2	4	36
62	Colombia	15	19	21	18	74	69	25	31	2	7	80
63	Mauritius	72	69	65	64	34	25	66	75	1	1	102
64	Suriname	27	25 c	28	21 c	26	84 c	74	16 c	..	7 c	71
65	Lebanon	100	51 c	18	11 c	..	..	..	..	..	..	85
66	Thailand	42	45	34	57	36	23	63	74	24	40	71
67	Fiji	66	63	64	68	63	..	36	..	7	..	78
68	Saudi Arabia	36	28	46	40	93	87 c	7	13 c	(.)	(.) c	30
69	Brazil	7	12	8	11	47	44	52	54	8	16	156
70	Philippines	33	50	28	51	31	7	38	41	23	60	102
71	Oman	31	..	53	..	94	82	5	17	15	13	58
72	Armenia	46	50	35	21	..	34	..	63	..	6	..
73	Peru	14	17	16	15	82	79	18	21	2	3	45
74	Ukraine	29	52	28	53	..	..	..	..	..	..	..
75	Kazakhstan	..	40	..	45	..	74	..	25	..	11	..
76	Georgia	..	46	..	27	..	..	..	..	..	..	..
77	Maldives	94	..	36	..	..	..	..	..	..	..	..
78	Jamaica	56	59	52	49	31	..	69	..	1	..	84
79	Azerbaijan	..	51	..	34	..	87 c	..	13 c	..	..	..
80	Paraguay	39	37	33	23	..	85	10	15	(.)	7	197
81	Sri Lanka	38	43	30	35	42	23	54	75	7	4	125
82	Turkey	18	27	13	23	32	20	68	78	4	9	..
83	Turkmenistan	..	62	..	42	..	..	..	..	..	..	..
84	Ecuador	27	26	33	37	98	91	2	9	10	11	38
85	Albania	23	30	15	11	..	32 c	..	68 c	..	3 c	..
86	Dominican Republic	44	39	34	30	..	..	..	..	..	..	61
87	China	14	19	18	22	27	12	72	88	7	23	110
88	Jordan	93	62	62	44	..	44 c	51	56 c	11	..	136
89	Tunisia	51	44	44	42	31	20	69	80	4	4	83
90	Iran, Islamic Rep. of	24	16	22	21	..	..	..	..	..	..	27
91	Cape Verde	44	50	13	23	..	..	..	..	..	..	..
92	Kyrgyzstan	50	57	29	42	..	40	..	20	..	19	..
93	Guyana	80	107	63	99	..	..	..	..	..	..	76
94	South Africa	19	23	24	25	30 f	44 f	22 f	55 f	..	7 f	103
95	El Salvador	31	37	19	25	62	50	38	50	9	12	135
96	Samoa (Western)	65	..	31	..	..	..	4	..	..	..	..
97	Syrian Arab Republic	27	40	28	29	64	89	36	7	2	3	41
98	Moldova, Rep. of	..	65	..	50	..	73	..	27	..	8	..
99	Uzbekistan	48	19	29	19	..	..	..	..	..	..	..
100	Algeria	25	23	23	28	97	97	3	3	3	5	40

HDI rank	Imports of goods and services (as % of GDP)		Exports of goods and services (as % of GDP)		Primary exports (as % of merchandise exports)		Manufactured exports (as % of merchandise exports)		High-technology exports (as % of manufactured exports)		Terms of trade (1980 = 100) [a]
	1990	1999	1990	1999	1990	1999	1990	1999	1990	1999	1998
101 Viet Nam	33	..	26	..	..	..	..	..	..	..	..
102 Indonesia	24	27	25	35	65	43	35	54	3	13	48
103 Tajikistan	..	63	..	68	..	..	..	..	..	..	..
104 Bolivia	24	27	23	17	95	59	5	41	(.)	70	52
105 Egypt	33	24	20	16	57	58	42	37	2	4	45
106 Nicaragua	46	89	25	34	92	91	8	9	1	3	80
107 Honduras	40	57	36	43	91	68	9	32	1	2	101
108 Guatemala	25	27	21	19	76	66	24	34	21	13	120
109 Gabon	31	38	46	45	..	..	..	..	..	..	37
110 Equatorial Guinea	70	86	32	102	..	..	..	..	..	..	..
111 Namibia	68	64	52	53	..	..	..	..	..	..	..
112 Morocco	32	34	26	30	48	..	52	..	6	..	109
113 Swaziland	76	99	77	107	..	..	..	..	..	..	72
114 Botswana	50	33	55	28	..	..	..	..	..	..	..
115 India	10	15	7	12	28	22 c	71	76 c	6	7 c	157
116 Mongolia	42	55 c	21	50 c	..	..	..	..	..	..	..
117 Zimbabwe	23	46	23	45	68	73	31	27	1	3	120
118 Myanmar	5	1 c	3	(.) c	..	..	..	..	..	..	62
119 Ghana	26	50	17	34	..	79	..	20	..	8	48
120 Lesotho	121	109 c	17	27 c	..	..	..	..	..	..	96
121 Cambodia	13	44 c	6	34 c	..	..	..	..	..	..	..
122 Papua New Guinea	49	42	41	45	89	91 c	10	9 c	31	..	..
123 Kenya	31	31	26	24	71	77	29	23	7	6	110
124 Comoros	37	41	14	26	..	..	..	..	..	..	35
125 Cameroon	17	25	20	24	91	..	9	..	10	..	112
126 Congo	46	70	54	78	..	..	..	..	..	..	48
Low human development											
127 Pakistan	23	20	16	15	21	16	79	84	(.)	1	105
128 Togo	45	40	33	30	89	88 c	9	18	2	(.)	110
129 Nepal	21	30	11	23	..	..	83	90 c	(.)	(.) c	..
130 Bhutan	32	42	28	33	..	..	..	..	..	..	..
131 Lao People's Dem. Rep.	25	49 c	11	37 c	..	..	..	..	..	..	..
132 Bangladesh	14	19	6	13	..	9 c	77	91 c	(.)	(.) c	70
133 Yemen	27	45	16	39	..	99 c	..	1 c	..	..	..
134 Haiti	29	28	16	12	15	..	85	..	15	..	53
135 Madagascar	27	33	17	25	85	48	14	50	7	..	116
136 Nigeria	29	42	43	37	..	99	..	1	..	27	26
137 Djibouti	..	..	..	..	44	..	8	..	36	..	..
138 Sudan	..	..	..	..	..	..	..	3 c	..	5 c	71
139 Mauritania	61	49	46	39	..	..	..	..	..	..	139
140 Tanzania, U. Rep. of	37	28	13	13	..	84	..	16	..	15	57
141 Uganda	19	23	7	11	..	97	..	3	..	12	27
142 Congo, Dem. Rep. of the	29	..	30	..	..	..	..	..	..	..	66
143 Zambia	37	41	36	22	..	..	..	..	..	..	62
144 Côte d'Ivoire	27	38	32	44	..	..	..	..	..	..	84
145 Senegal	30	39	25	33	77	43	23	57	6	5	102
146 Angola	21	48 c	39	57 c	100	..	(.)	..	..	..	56
147 Benin	26	28	14	17	..	97 c	..	3 c	..	..	117
148 Eritrea	..	79	..	10	..	..	..	..	..	..	..
149 Gambia	72	67	60	51	..	94 c	..	5 c	..	..	51
150 Guinea	31	23	31	21	..	..	..	..	..	..	73

HDI rank	Imports of goods and services (as % of GDP)		Exports of goods and services (as % of GDP)		Primary exports (as % of merchandise exports)		Manufactured exports (as % of merchandise exports)		High-technology exports (as % of manufactured exports)		Terms of trade (1980 = 100) [a]
	1990	1999	1990	1999	1990	1999	1990	1999	1990	1999	1998
151 Malawi	35	43	25	27	95	..	5	..	1	..	86
152 Rwanda	14	21	6	6	..	..	..	..	..	..	188
153 Mali	34	36	17	25	..	..	?	..	51	..	94
154 Central African Republic	28	24	15	17	..	..	..	..	..	..	47
155 Chad	29	30	13	17	..	..	..	..	..	..	88
156 Guinea-Bissau	37	44	10	26	..	..	..	..	..	..	71 [e]
157 Mozambique	36	38	8	12	..	..	..	..	..	..	47
158 Ethiopia	12	29	8	14	..	..	..	..	..	..	..
159 Burkina Faso	26	29	13	11	..	..	..	..	..	..	182
160 Burundi	28	18	8	9	..	..	..	..	..	..	55
161 Niger	22	22	15	16	..	97 [c]	..	2 [c]	..	..	79
162 Sierra Leone	25	20	24	14	..	..	..	..	..	..	82
Developing countries	26	27	26	29	38	24	60	75	..	..	..
Least developed countries	22	28	13	18	..	..	..	..	..	..	..
Arab States	40	30	40	34	81	..	19	..	..	..	..
East Asia and the Pacific	40	39	41	45	24	13	75	85	..	..	..
Latin America and the Caribbean	12	18	14	16	66	49	34	51	..	..	..
South Asia	15	17	11	15	24	..	71	..	..	..	..
Sub-Saharan Africa	26	31	27	29	..	61	..	39	..	..	..
Eastern Europe and the CIS	25	39	25	44	..	36	..	55	..	..	..
OECD	18	..	17	..	20	15	78	82	..	..	..
High-income OECD	17	..	17	..	19	15	78	81	..	..	..
High human development	19	..	19	..	20	15	78	82	..	..	..
Medium human development	19	25	20	27	49	34	48	62	..	..	..
Low human development	24	28	20	21	..	..	..	..	..	..	..
High income	19	..	18	..	19	15	78	82	..	..	..
Middle income	20	26	21	29	43	29	54	68	..	..	..
Low income	20	26	17	24	..	..	..	..	..	..	..
World	19	25	19	27	24	18	73	79	..	..	..

a. The ratio of the export price index to the import price index measured relative to the base year 1980. A value of more than 100 implies that the price of exports has risen relative to the price of imports.
b. Data refer to 1999.
c. Data refer to 1998.
d. Data include Luxembourg.
e. Data refer to 1997.
f. Data refer to the South African Customs Union, which comprises Botswana, Lesotho, Namibia, South Africa and Swaziland.

Source: Columns 1-4, 7 and 8: World Bank 2001b; aggregates calculated for the Human Development Report Office by the World Bank; *columns 5 and 6:* calculated on the basis of data on merchandise trade and exports of food, agricultural raw materials, fuels, ores and metals from World Bank (2001b); aggregates calculated for the Human Development Report Office by the World Bank; *columns 9 and 10:* calculated on the basis of data on high-technology exports from UN (2001a) and data on manufactured and merchandise exports from World Bank (2001b); *column 11:* calculated on the basis of data on terms of trade from World Bank (2001b).

14 Flows of aid from DAC member countries

HDI rank	Net official development assistance (ODA) disbursed			ODA per capita of donor country (1998 US$)		ODA to least developed countries (as % of total) [b]		Net grants by NGOs (as % of GNP) [c]	
	Total (US$ millions) [a]	As % of GNP							
	1999	1990	1999	1990	1999	1990	1999	1990	1999
1 Norway	1,370	1.17	0.91	269	298	43	33	0.13	0.11
2 Australia	982	0.34	0.26	50	50	18	17	0.02	0.02
3 Canada	1,699	0.44	0.28	78	55	28	18	0.05	0.02
4 Sweden	1,630	0.91	0.70	215	190	38	25	0.06	0.03
5 Belgium	760	0.46	0.30	98	77	40	22	0.03	0.03
6 United States	9,145	0.21	0.10	55	33	18	16	0.05	0.04
8 Netherlands	3,134	0.92	0.79	183	203	32	20	0.09	0.07
9 Japan	15,323	0.31	0.35	84	106	18	17	(.)	0.01
10 Finland	416	0.65	0.33	142	84	37	25	0.03	(.)
11 Switzerland	969	0.32	0.35	124	140	41	27	0.05	..
12 Luxembourg	119	0.21	0.66	73	281	31	25	(.)	0.03
13 France	5,637	0.60	0.39	134	99	28	16	0.02	..
14 United Kingdom	3,401	0.27	0.23	55	57	31	21	0.03	0.03
15 Denmark	1,733	0.94	1.01	248	331	39	32	0.02	0.02
16 Austria	527	0.25	0.26	57	67	26	14	0.02	0.04
17 Germany	5,515	0.42	0.26	112	69	26	20	0.05	0.05
18 Ireland	245	0.16	0.31	18	66	36	37	0.07	0.01
19 New Zealand	134	0.23	0.27	29	36	19	24	0.03	0.03
20 Italy	1,806	0.31	0.15	58	33	39	22	(.)	(.)
21 Spain	1,363	0.20	0.23	24	35	19	11	0.01	..
23 Greece	194	..	0.15	..	19	..	2	..	..
28 Portugal	276	0.24	0.26	19	28	70	45	(.)	..
DAC [d]	56,378 T	0.34	0.24	77	66	26	19	0.03	0.03

Note: DAC is the Development Assistance Committee of the Organisation for Economic Co-operation and Development (OECD). Greece joined DAC in December 1999.

a. Some non-DAC countries and areas also provide ODA. According to OECD, Development Assistance Committee (2001c), net ODA disbursed in 1999 by the Czech Republic, Estonia, the Republic of Korea, Kuwait, Poland, Saudi Arabia, Turkey and the United Arab Emirates totalled $777 million. China also provides aid but does not disclose the amount.

b. Including imputed multilateral flows that make allowance for contributions through multilateral organizations. These are calculated using the geographic distribution of disbursements for the year of reference.

c. Does not include disbursements from non-governmental organizations (NGOs) that originate from official sources and are already included in ODA.

d. Aggregates are from OECD, Development Assistance Committee (2001a and 2001c).

Source: Columns 1-7: OECD, Development Assistance Committee 2001c; *columns 8 and 9:* OECD, Development Assistance Committee 2001a.

15 Flows of aid, private capital and debt

		Official development assistance (ODA) received (net disbursements) [a]				Net foreign direct investment flows (as % of GDP) [b]		Other private flows (as % of GDP) [b, c]		Total debt service			
		Total (US$ millions)	Per capita (US$)	As % of GDP						As % of GDP		As % of exports of goods and services	
HDI rank		1999	1999	1990	1999	1990	1999	1990	1999	1990	1999	1990	1999
High human development													
22	Israel	905.7 [d]	148.3 [d]	..	0.9 [d]	0.3	2.3	..	..	..	..	..	..
24	Hong Kong, China (SAR)	3.7 [d]	0.6 [d]	..	(.) [d]	..	..	..	..	..	..	..	..
25	Cyprus	49.9 [d]	65.6 [d]	..	0.6 [d]	2.3	0.7	..	..	..	..	..	..
26	Singapore	-1.1 [d]	-0.3 [d]	..	(.) [d]	15.2	8.2	..	..	..	..	..	..
27	Korea, Rep. of	-55.2	-1.2	(.)	(.)	0.3	2.3	0.1	-0.7	3.3	10.6	10.8	24.6
29	Slovenia	31.0	15.6	..	0.2	..	0.9	..	..	..	..	..	..
30	Malta	25.1	66.2	0.2	..	2.0	0.0 [e]	0.0	9.9 [e]	2.0	16.2 [e]	2.0	17.9
31	Barbados	-2.1	-7.9	0.2	-0.1	0.6	0.7	-0.8	-1.2	8.2	3.9	15.1	6.8
32	Brunei Darussalam	1.4 [d]	4.4 [d]	..	..	..	..	..	..	..	..	..	..
33	Czech Republic	318.1 [d]	30.9 [d]	(.) [d]	0.6 [d]	0.6	9.6	1.9	-0.5	3.0	6.8	..	10.3
34	Argentina	91.3	2.5	0.1	(.)	1.3	8.5	-1.4	3.0	4.4	9.1	37.0	75.9
35	Slovakia	318.3 [d]	59.0 [d]	(.) [d]	1.6 [d]	0.0	1.8	1.8	-0.4	2.1	8.7	..	13.9
36	Hungary	247.6 [d]	24.6 [d]	0.2 [d]	0.5 [d]	0.0	4.0	-0.9	6.2	12.8	15.5	34.3	26.6
37	Uruguay	21.7	6.5	0.6	0.1	0.0	1.1	-2.1	-0.8	10.6	5.1	40.8	25.0
38	Poland	983.8 [d]	25.5 [d]	2.2 [d]	0.6 [d]	0.1	4.7	(.)	2.1	1.6	5.4	4.9	20.4
39	Chile	69.1	4.6	0.3	0.1	1.9	13.7	5.0	3.9	9.1	7.7	25.9	25.4
40	Bahrain	4.0	6.0	3.4	..	..	..	..	..	..	..	..	..
41	Costa Rica	-9.8	-2.7	3.2	-0.1	2.3	4.4	-2.0	1.7	7.0	3.6	23.9	6.4
42	Bahamas	11.6 [d]	38.8 [d]	..	..	-0.6	..	..	..	..	..	..	..
43	Kuwait	7.2 [d]	3.8 [d]	..	(.) [d]	..	0.2	..	..	..	..	..	..
44	Estonia	82.7 [d]	57.3 [d]	..	1.6 [d]	0.0	5.8	..	5.0	..	10.3	..	13.2
45	United Arab Emirates	4.2 [d]	1.5 [d]	..	..	..	..	..	..	..	..	..	..
46	Croatia	48.2	10.8	..	0.2	..	6.9	..	4.8	..	8.4	..	19.4
47	Lithuania	128.9 [d]	34.9 [d]	..	1.2 [d]	0.0	4.6	..	6.2	..	2.6	..	6.3
48	Qatar	4.9 [d]	8.7 [d]	..	..	..	..	..	..	..	..	..	..
Medium human development													
49	Trinidad and Tobago	26.2	20.3	0.4	0.4	2.2	9.2	-3.5	1.2	8.9	6.6	19.3	13.1
50	Latvia	96.4 [d]	39.7 [d]	..	1.5 [d]	0.0	5.6	..	-0.7	..	7.4	..	15.0
51	Mexico	34.5	0.4	0.1	(.)	1.0	2.4	2.1	3.1	4.3	8.3	20.7	25.1
52	Panama	13.6	4.8	1.9	0.1	2.5	0.2	-0.1	6.9	6.5	7.8	6.2	8.8
53	Belarus	24.0 [d]	2.4 [d]	..	0.1 [d]	0.0	0.8	..	0.6	..	0.8	..	3.2
54	Belize	46.0	186.3	7.5	6.3	4.2	0.5	1.4	1.7	5.0	5.9	7.5	11.2
55	Russian Federation	1,816.3 [d]	12.4 [d]	(.) [d]	0.5 [d]	0.0	0.8	1.0	0.1	2.0	2.9	..	13.5
56	Malaysia	142.6	6.3	1.1	0.2	5.3	2.0	-3.6	2.1	9.8	5.9	12.6	4.8
57	Bulgaria	264.8 [d]	32.3 [d]	0.1 [d]	2.1 [d]	(.)	6.5	-0.3	2.5	6.6	9.3	19.4	19.1
58	Romania	373.4 [d]	16.6 [d]	0.6 [d]	1.1 [d]	0.0	3.1	(.)	-1.0	(.)	9.2	0.3	31.3
59	Libyan Arab Jamahiriya	7.3	1.3	..	..	..	..	..	..	..	..	..	..
60	Macedonia, TFYR	273.0	135.1	..	7.9	..	0.9	..	0.6	..	13.3	..	29.9
61	Venezuela	43.5	1.8	0.2	(.)	0.9	3.1	-1.2	-0.1	10.3	5.5	23.2	23.2
62	Colombia	301.3	7.3	0.2	0.3	1.2	1.3	-0.4	2.9	9.7	7.6	40.9	42.9
63	Mauritius	41.5	35.3	3.4	1.0	1.6	1.2	1.7	1.2	5.9	6.2	8.8	9.7
64	Suriname	36.0	87.0	19.4	..	..	..	..	..	..	..	..	..
65	Lebanon	193.9	45.4	9.1	..	0.2	1.2 [e]	0.2	8.9 [e]	3.5	3.1 [e]	3.3	9.6 [e]
66	Thailand	1,003.3	16.7	0.9	0.8	2.9	5.0	2.3	-3.0	6.2	13.2	16.9	22.0
67	Fiji	34.2	42.7	3.6	1.9	6.7	-1.9	-1.1	-0.4	7.7	2.2	12.0	3.5
68	Saudi Arabia	28.8	1.4	(.)	(.)	..	..	..	..	..	..	..	..
69	Brazil	183.6	1.1	(.)	(.)	0.2	4.3	-0.1	-1.3	1.8	9.0	22.2	110.9
70	Philippines	690.3	9.3	2.9	0.9	1.2	0.7	0.2	5.7	8.1	8.8	27.0	14.3
71	Oman	39.9	17.0	0.6	..	1.3	0.7 [e]	-3.8	-2.1 [e]	7.0	4.2 [e]	12.3	9.7

HDI rank	Official development assistance (ODA) received (net disbursements) [a] Total (US$ millions) 1999	Per capita (US$) 1999	As % of GDP 1990	As % of GDP 1999	Net foreign direct investment flows (as % of GDP) [b] 1990	1999	Other private flows (as % of GDP) [b, c] 1990	1999	Total debt service As % of GDP 1990	1999	As % of exports of goods and services 1990	1999
72 Armenia	208.5	54.7	..	11.3	0.0	6.6	..	0.0	..	3.2	..	11.9
73 Peru	452.2	17.9	1.5	0.9	0.2	3.8	0.1	2.3	1.8	5.7	10.8	32.7
74 Ukraine	479.9 [d]	9.6 [d]	0.3 [d]	1.2 [d]	0.0	1.3	..	-0.3	..	7.2	..	16.3
75 Kazakhstan	161.0	10.8	..	1.0	0.0	10.0	..	-0.7	..	8.6	..	19.4
76 Georgia	238.6	43.8	..	8.7	..	3.0	..	0.2	..	3.9	..	11.4
77 Maldives	30.7	113.9	14.5	..	4.1	3.1 [e]	0.8	2.9 [e]	6.0	4.3 [e]	4.8	3.9
78 Jamaica	-22.6	-8.7	6.4	-0.3	3.3	7.6	-1.1	-1.4	15.6	10.6	26.9	17.4
79 Azerbaijan	162.0	20.3	..	4.0	0.0	12.7	..	2.1	..	2.1	..	6.5
80 Paraguay	77.6	14.5	1.1	1.0	1.4	0.9	-0.2	0.5	6.2	3.0	12.2	6.6
81 Sri Lanka	251.4	13.2	9.1	1.6	0.5	1.1	0.1	-0.4	4.8	3.3	13.7	7.9
82 Turkey	-9.7	-0.2	0.8	(.)	0.5	0.4	0.7	4.2	4.9	7.4	29.4	26.2
83 Turkmenistan	20.9	4.4	..	0.7	..	2.5	..	-4.2	..	14.5	..	31.1
84 Ecuador	145.6	11.7	1.5	0.8	1.2	3.6	0.5	1.3	10.1	8.7	32.5	25.7
85 Albania	479.7	142.1	0.5	13.0	0.0	1.1	1.5	-0.1	0.1	1.0	0.9	3.7
86 Dominican Republic	194.7	23.2	1.4	1.1	1.9	7.7	(.)	0.4	3.3	2.2	10.4	3.9
87 China	2,323.8	1.9	0.6	0.2	1.0	3.9	1.3	0.2	2.0	2.1	11.7	9.0
88 Jordan	430.0	90.7	22.1	5.3	0.9	2.0	5.4	-0.6	15.5	8.0	20.3	11.8
89 Tunisia	244.5	25.9	3.2	1.2	0.6	1.7	-1.6	1.9	11.6	7.3	24.5	15.9
90 Iran, Islamic Rep. of	161.4	2.6	0.1	0.1	-0.3	0.1	(.)	-1.3	0.5	4.2	3.2	22.6
91 Cape Verde	136.4	318.8	31.8	23.5	0.0	2.6	(.)	0.1	1.7	3.8	4.8	10.6
92 Kyrgyzstan	266.6	54.8	..	21.3	..	2.8	..	-4.1	..	9.4	..	21.8
93 Guyana	26.6	31.1	42.6	3.9	0.0	7.1	-4.1	-0.8	74.5	15.5	..	19.5 [e]
94 South Africa	539.3	12.8	..	0.4	-0.1	1.0	..	2.4	..	3.7	..	13.9
95 El Salvador	182.7	29.7	7.2	1.5	(.)	1.9	0.1	1.0	4.3	2.8	15.3	7.6
96 Samoa (Western)	22.9	136.1	32.6	13.0	4.8	1.1	0.0	0.0	3.8	3.7	5.8	5.1
97 Syrian Arab Republic	228.2	14.5	5.6	1.2	0.6	0.5	-0.4	(.)	10.3	1.9	23.2	6.4
98 Moldova, Rep. of	102.1	23.8	..	8.8	0.0	2.9	..	-1.9	..	15.1	..	24.9
99 Uzbekistan	133.9	5.5	..	0.8	..	0.6	..	3.1	..	3.1	..	17.6
100 Algeria	88.9	3.0	0.4	0.2	0.0	(.)	-0.7	-3.1	14.2	11.1	63.4	37.8
101 Viet Nam	1,420.6	18.3	2.9	5.0	0.2	5.6	0.0	-2.7	2.7	4.9	8.9	9.8
102 Indonesia	2,206.3	10.7	1.5	1.5	1.0	-1.9	1.9	-4.0	8.7	12.5	33.3	30.3
103 Tajikistan	122.0	19.6	..	6.5	..	1.3	..	-0.8	..	2.6	..	6.5
104 Bolivia	568.6	69.9	11.2	6.8	0.6	12.2	-0.5	0.0	7.9	5.9	38.6	32.0
105 Egypt	1,579.1	25.2	12.6	1.8	1.7	1.2	-0.1	0.6	7.1	1.9	22.3	9.0
106 Nicaragua	674.7	137.2	32.9	29.8	0.0	13.2	2.0	3.6	1.6	8.3	3.9	16.1
107 Honduras	816.9	129.3	14.7	15.2	1.4	4.3	1.0	0.4	12.8	6.8	35.3	13.5
108 Guatemala	292.9	26.4	2.6	1.6	0.6	0.8	-0.1	-0.3	2.8	2.3	12.6	10.3
109 Gabon	47.6	39.3	2.2	1.1	1.2	4.6	0.5	0.2	3.0	12.4	6.4	19.3
110 Equatorial Guinea	20.2	45.6	46.0	2.9	8.3	17.3	0.0	0.0	3.9	0.7	12.1	0.8
111 Namibia	177.6	104.4	5.2	5.8	..	..	..	..	..	..	..	..
112 Morocco	678.0	24.0	4.1	1.9	0.6	(.)	0.7	-0.3	6.9	8.9	21.5	24.4
113 Swaziland	28.9	28.4	6.3	2.4	3.5	2.7	-0.2	0.0	5.5	2.5	5.7	2.6
114 Botswana	60.9	38.3	3.9	1.0	2.5	0.6	-0.5	(.)	2.8	1.4	4.4	2.4
115 India	1,484.4	1.5	0.4	0.3	0.1	0.5	0.5	-0.1	2.6	2.3	32.7	15.0
116 Mongolia	218.6	91.9	..	23.9	..	3.3	..	-0.3	..	2.9	..	4.8
117 Zimbabwe	244.2	20.5	3.9	4.4	-0.1	1.1	1.1	0.2	5.4	11.6	23.1	25.3
118 Myanmar	73.2	1.6	..	..	..	..	..	..	..	..	9.0	7.9
119 Ghana	607.5	32.3	9.6	7.8	0.3	0.2	-0.3	-0.4	6.3	6.7	36.9	19.9
120 Lesotho	31.1	14.8	22.8	3.6	2.7	18.7	(.)	0.5	3.7	5.8	4.2	9.4

15 Flows of aid, private capital and debt

HDI rank		Official development assistance (ODA) received (net disbursements) [a]				Net foreign direct investment flows (as % of GDP) [b]		Other private flows (as % of GDP) [b, c]		Total debt service			
		Total (US$ millions)	Per capita (US$)	As % of GDP						As % of GDP		As % of exports of goods and services	
		1999	1999	1990	1999	1990	1999	1990	1999	1990	1999	1990	1999
121	Cambodia	278.9	23.7	3.7	8.9	0.0	4.0	0.0	-0.1	2.7	1.1	..	2.9
122	Papua New Guinea	215.7	45.8	12.8	6.0	4.8	8.3	1.5	5.7	17.2	5.9	37.2	9.6
123	Kenya	308.0	10.5	13.9	2.9	0.7	0.1	0.8	-0.6	9.3	6.7	35.4	26.7
124	Comoros	21.5	39.4	18.1	11.1	-0.4	0.5	0.0	0.0	0.4	4.0	2.3	16.1
125	Cameroon	433.8	29.5	4.0	4.7	-1.0	0.4	-0.1	-0.6	4.7	6.0	22.5	24.3
126	Congo	140.3	49.1	7.8	6.3	0.0	0.2	-3.6	0.0	19.0	1.1	35.3	1.4
Low human development													
127	Pakistan	732.0	5.4	2.8	1.3	0.6	0.9	-0.2	-1.0	4.8	5.2	23.0	30.5
128	Togo	71.3	15.6	16.0	5.1	0.0	2.1	(.)	0.0	5.3	2.8	11.9	7.7
129	Nepal	343.7	14.7	11.7	6.9	0.2	0.1	-0.4	-0.3	1.9	2.1	13.4	7.9
130	Bhutan	66.6	85.2	16.5	15.1	0.0	0.0	-0.9	0.0	1.8	1.6	5.5	4.8
131	Lao People's Dem. Rep.	293.8	57.7	17.3	20.5	0.7	5.5	0.0	0.0	1.1	2.6	8.7	7.7
132	Bangladesh	1,203.1	9.4	7.0	2.6	(.)	0.4	0.2	(.)	2.6	1.7	28.4	10.1
133	Yemen	456.4	26.8	8.7	6.7	-2.8	-2.2	3.5	0.0	3.6	2.3	5.6	4.0
134	Haiti	262.8	33.7	5.6	6.1	0.3	0.7	0.0	0.0	1.1	1.4	10.1	10.0
135	Madagascar	358.2	23.8	12.9	9.6	0.7	1.6	-0.5	-0.2	7.2	4.5	45.5	17.1
136	Nigeria	151.6	1.2	0.9	0.4	2.1	2.9	-0.4	-0.4	11.7	2.6	22.6	6.0
137	Djibouti	75.0	115.8	45.6	..	0.0	1.2 [e]	-0.1	0.0 [e]	3.5	1.0 [e]	..	..
138	Sudan	242.9	8.4	6.2	2.5	0.0	3.8	0.0	0.0	0.4	0.6	7.5	6.5
139	Mauritania	218.5	84.1	23.3	22.8	0.7	0.2	-0.1	-0.2	14.3	11.0	29.9	28.4
140	Tanzania, U. Rep. of	989.6	30.1	27.5	11.3	0.0	2.1	0.1	-0.1	4.2	2.2	32.9	15.6
141	Uganda	589.8	27.5	15.5	9.2	0.0	3.5	0.4	(.)	3.4	2.9	58.9	23.7
142	Congo, Dem. Rep. of the	132.3	2.7	9.6	..	-0.1	(.) [e]	-0.1	0.0 [e]	3.7	0.3 [e]	13.5	1.2 [e]
143	Zambia	623.4	63.1	14.6	19.8	6.2	5.2	-0.3	-0.4	6.2	13.9	14.9	46.6
144	Côte d'Ivoire	447.0	28.8	6.4	4.0	0.4	3.1	0.1	-2.5	11.7	12.9	35.4	26.2
145	Senegal	534.3	57.5	14.4	11.2	1.0	1.3	-0.3	-0.1	5.7	5.0	20.0	16.1
146	Angola	387.5	31.4	2.6	4.5	-3.3	28.9	5.6	-1.2	3.2	13.4	8.1	21.1
147	Benin	210.8	34.5	14.5	8.9	0.1	1.3	(.)	0.0	2.1	3.0	8.2	10.9
148	Eritrea	148.5	37.2	..	23.0	..	0.0	..	0.0	..	0.6	..	1.9
149	Gambia	33.1	26.5	31.3	8.4	0.0	3.6	-2.4	0.0	11.9	5.4	22.2	8.5
150	Guinea	237.6	32.8	10.4	6.8	0.6	1.8	0.7	(.)	6.0	3.8	20.0	16.1
151	Malawi	445.8	41.3	27.9	24.6	0.0	3.3	0.1	(.)	7.4	3.8	29.3	11.4
152	Rwanda	372.9	44.9	11.3	19.1	0.3	0.1	-0.1	0.0	0.8	1.6	14.0	29.6
153	Mali	354.0	33.4	19.9	13.8	-0.3	0.7	(.)	0.0	2.8	4.1	12.3	14.3
154	Central African Republic	117.2	33.1	16.8	11.1	0.1	1.2	(.)	(.)	2.0	1.8	13.2	12.1
155	Chad	187.8	25.1	18.0	12.3	0.0	1.0	(.)	-0.1	0.7	2.1	4.4	10.3
156	Guinea-Bissau	52.4	44.2	52.7	24.0	0.8	1.4	(.)	0.0	3.4	4.4	31.0	16.4
157	Mozambique	118.4	6.8	39.9	3.0	0.4	9.7	1.0	-0.3	3.1	3.1	26.2	20.0
158	Ethiopia	633.4	10.1	14.8	9.8	0.2	1.4	-0.8	-0.2	3.4	2.5	34.9	16.8
159	Burkina Faso	398.1	36.2	12.0	15.4	0.0	0.4	(.)	0.0	1.2	2.4	6.8	15.7
160	Burundi	74.2	11.1	23.3	10.4	0.1	(.)	-0.5	(.)	3.7	4.0	43.4	45.6
161	Niger	187.1	17.8	16.0	9.3	(.)	0.7	0.4	-1.1	4.0	2.5	17.4	16.8
162	Sierra Leone	73.5	14.9	6.8	11.0	3.6	0.1	0.4	0.0	2.4	3.2	10.1	29.9

	Official development assistance (ODA) received (net disbursements) [a]				Net foreign direct investment flows (as % of GDP) [b]		Other private flows (as % of GDP) [b, c]		Total debt service			
	Total (US$ millions)	Per capita (US$)	As % of GDP						As % of GDP		As % of exports of goods and services	
HDI rank	1999	1999	1990	1999	1990	1999	1990	1999	1990	1999	1990	1999
Developing countries	33,025.9 T	7.2	1.4	0.6	0.9	2.9	0.4	0.4	4.0	5.8	18.7	22.3
Least developed countries	10,574.7 T	17.8	11.6	7.0	(.)	3.0	0.5	-0.1	2.7	2.8	15.5	13.0
Arab States	4,313.2 T	18.3	..	..	0.7	0.3	-0.1	0.3	5.5	3.6	14.7	11.4
East Asia and the Pacific	8,873.2 T	4.9	0.8	0.5	1.6	3.0	0.7	-0.2	3.8	5.2	15.7	15.8
Latin America and the Caribbean	4,539.0 T	9.2	0.4	0.2	0.7	4.5	0.3	1.1	4.0	8.1	23.6	41.6
South Asia	4,273.3 T	3.1	1.1	0.6	(.)	0.5	0.4	-0.3	2.6	2.8	20.0	16.6
Sub-Saharan Africa	10,986.9 T	18.3	..	..	0.3	2.4	0.2	0.8	3.9	4.6	19.7	14.3
Eastern Europe and the CIS	7,381.7 T	18.6	..	..	(.)	2.9	..	0.9	1.8	5.1	..	16.5
OECD	..	..	..	..	..	..	..	..	..	..	..	..
High-income OECD	..	..	..	..	..	..	..	..	..	..	..	..
High human development	..	..	..	..	..	..	..	..	..	..	..	..
Medium human development	26,223.7 T	6.6	0.9	0.5	0.6	2.4	0.6	0.4	3.4	5.5	18.9	20.4
Low human development	11,824.7 T	14.5	8.1	4.6	0.4	2.5	..	-0.4	5.0	3.9	20.6	15.3
High income	..	..	..	..	..	..	..	..	..	..	..	..
Middle income	18,692.7 T	7.2	0.7	0.3	0.6	3.3	0.5	0.8	3.6	6.3	16.9	21.8
Low income	21,627.3 T	9.2	3.0	2.1	0.3	1.0	..	-0.8	3.7	4.6	26.6	18.8
World	41,338.4 T	8.3	..	..	..	..	..	..	..	..	..	..

Note: This table presents data for countries included in Parts I and II of DAC's list of aid recipients (OECD, Development Assistance Committee 2001d). The denominator conventionally used when comparing official development assistance and total debt service with the size of the economy is GNP, not GDP (see the definitions of statistical terms). GDP is used here, however, to allow comparability throughout the table. With few exceptions, the denominators produce similar results.

a. ODA receipts are total net ODA flows from DAC countries, multilateral organizations and Arab states. A negative value indicates that the repayment of ODA loans exceeds the amount of ODA received.
b. A negative value indicates that the capital flowing out of the country exceeds that flowing in.
c. Other private flows combine non-debt-creating portfolio equity investment flows, portfolio debt flows and bank and trade-related lending. See the definitions of statistical terms.
d. Data refer to net official aid. See the definitions of statistical terms.
e. Data refer to 1998.

Source: Column 1: OECD, Development Assistance Committee 2001b; *column 2:* calculated on the basis of data on ODA from OECD, Development Assistance Committee (2001b) and data on population from World Bank (2001b); *columns 3 and 4:* calculated on the basis of data on ODA from OECD, Development Assistance Committee (2001b) and data on GDP from World Bank (2001b); *columns 5 and 6:* calculated on the basis of data on foreign direct investment and GDP from World Bank (2001b); aggregates calculated for the Human Development Report Office by the World Bank; *columns 7 and 8:* calculated on the basis of data on portfolio investment (bonds and equity), bank and trade-related lending and GDP from World Bank (2001b); aggregates calculated for the Human Development Report Office by the World Bank; *columns 9 and 10:* calculated on the basis of data on total debt service and GDP from World Bank (2001b); aggregates calculated for the Human Development Report Office by the World Bank; *columns 11 and 12:* World Bank 2001b; aggregates calculated for the Human Development Report Office by the World Bank.

16 Priorities in public spending

HDI rank	Public expenditure on education (as % of GNP)		Public expenditure on health (as % of GDP)		Military expenditure (as % of GDP) [a]		Total debt service (as % of GDP) [b]	
	1985-87 [c]	1995-97 [c]	1990	1998	1990	1999	1990	1999
High human development								
1 Norway	6.5	7.7 [d]	6.5	7.4	2.9	2.2	..	..
2 Australia	5.1	5.5 [d]	5.3	5.9	2.2	1.9	..	..
3 Canada	6.7	6.9 [d, e]	6.8	6.3 [f]	2.0	1.3	..	..
4 Sweden	7.3	8.3 [d]	7.6	6.7	2.6	2.1	..	..
5 Belgium	5.1 [g]	3.1 [d, h]	6.6	7.9	2.4	1.4	..	..
6 United States	5.0	5.4 [d, e]	4.9	5.8 [f]	5.3	3.0	..	..
7 Iceland	4.8	5.4 [d]	6.9	7.2 [f]	0.0	0.0	..	..
8 Netherlands	6.9	5.1 [d]	5.8	6.0	2.6	1.8	..	..
9 Japan	..	3.6 [d, e]	4.7	5.9	1.0	1.0	..	..
10 Finland	5.5	7.5 [d]	6.4	5.2	1.6	1.2	..	..
11 Switzerland	4.7	5.4 [d]	5.7	7.6	1.8	1.1	..	..
12 Luxembourg	4.1	4.0 [d]	5.8	5.4	0.9	0.8	..	..
13 France	5.5	6.0 [d]	6.5	7.3	3.6	2.7	..	..
14 United Kingdom	4.8	5.3 [d]	5.0	5.9 [f]	4.0	2.5	..	..
15 Denmark	7.2	8.1 [d]	7.0	6.7 [f]	2.1	1.6	..	..
16 Austria	5.9	5.4 [d]	5.2	5.8	1.0	0.9	..	..
17 Germany	..	4.8 [d]	..	7.9 [f]	2.8 [i]	1.5	..	..
18 Ireland	6.7	6.0 [d]	4.7	4.5 [f]	1.3	0.8	..	..
19 New Zealand	5.4	7.3 [d]	5.8	6.2	1.8	1.1	..	..
20 Italy	5.0	4.9 [d]	6.3	5.6 [f]	2.1	2.0	..	..
21 Spain	3.7	5.0 [d]	5.2	5.4	1.8	1.3	..	..
22 Israel	6.7	7.6 [d, e]	3.8	6.0	12.3	8.1	..	..
23 Greece	2.2	3.1 [d]	3.4	4.7	4.7	4.9	..	..
24 Hong Kong, China (SAR)	2.5	2.9	1.6	..	..	..	..	..
25 Cyprus	3.6 [j]	4.5 [j]	..	..	5.0	3.4	..	..
26 Singapore	3.9	3.0	1.0	1.2	4.8	5.3	..	..
27 Korea, Rep. of	3.8	3.7 [d]	2.1	2.3	3.7	2.8	3.3	10.6
28 Portugal	3.8 [g]	5.8 [d]	4.1	5.2	2.7	2.2	..	..
29 Slovenia	..	5.7	..	6.6	..	1.4	..	..
30 Malta	3.4	5.1	..	..	0.9	0.8	2.0	16.2 [k]
31 Barbados	6.2 [e]	7.2 [e]	5.0	4.5	..	..	8.2	3.9
32 Brunei Darussalam	..	..	1.6	..	6.7 [i]	7.6 [k]	..	..
33 Czech Republic	..	5.1 [d]	4.8	6.7	..	2.0	3.0	6.8
34 Argentina	1.4 [g]	3.5	4.2	4.9	1.3	1.5	4.4	9.1
35 Slovakia	..	4.7	5.0	5.7	..	1.7	2.1	8.7
36 Hungary	5.6	4.6 [d]	..	5.2	2.5	1.4	12.8	15.5
37 Uruguay	3.2	3.3	1.9	1.9	2.1	1.2 [k]	10.6	5.1
38 Poland	4.6	7.5 [d]	..	4.7	2.7	2.0	1.6	5.4
39 Chile	3.3	3.6	2.2	2.7	3.6	3.1	9.1	7.7
40 Bahrain	5.2	4.4	..	2.6	5.1	5.0 [k]	..	..
41 Costa Rica	4.5	5.4	5.3	5.2	0.4	..	7.0	3.6
42 Bahamas	4.0	..	2.8	2.5	..	..	..	..
43 Kuwait	4.8	5.0	4.0	..	48.5	8.3	..	..
44 Estonia	..	7.2	1.9	..	..	1.4	..	10.3
45 United Arab Emirates	2.1	1.7	0.8	0.8	4.7	3.2	..	..
46 Croatia	..	5.3	9.5	..	..	4.2	..	8.4
47 Lithuania	5.3 [e]	5.9	3.0	4.8	..	1.0	..	2.6
48 Qatar	4.7	3.4 [e]	..	..	..	..	..	..
Medium human development								
49 Trinidad and Tobago	6.3	4.4 [e]	2.5	2.5	..	..	8.9	6.6
50 Latvia	3.4	6.5	2.7	4.2	..	0.9	..	7.4

HUMAN DEVELOPMENT INDICATORS

HDI rank	Public expenditure on education (as % of GNP)		Public expenditure on health (as % of GDP)		Military expenditure (as % of GDP) [a]		Total debt service (as % of GDP) [b]	
	1985-87 [c]	1995-97 [c]	1990	1998	1990	1999	1990	1999
51 Mexico	3.5	4.9 [d]	2.1	..	0.5	0.6	4.3	8.3
52 Panama	4.8	5.1	4.6	4.9	1.4	1.4 [m]	6.5	7.8
53 Belarus	5.0	5.9	2.5	4.9	..	1.3	..	0.8
54 Belize	4.7	5.0	2.2	2.2	1.2	1.5 [m]	5.0	5.9
55 Russian Federation	3.4	3.5 [d]	2.5	..	12.3 [n]	3.8	2.0	2.9
56 Malaysia	6.9	4.9	1.5	1.4	2.6	2.3	9.8	5.9
57 Bulgaria	5.4	3.2	4.1	3.8	4.5	2.8	6.6	9.3
58 Romania	2.2	3.6	2.8	..	3.5	1.6	(.)	9.2
59 Libyan Arab Jamahiriya	9.6	..	..	..	..	..	..	..
60 Macedonia, TFYR	..	5.1	9.2	5.5	..	2.5	..	13.3
61 Venezuela	5.0	5.2 [e]	2.4	2.6	2.0	1.4	10.3	5.5
62 Colombia	..	4.1 [g]	1.2	5.2	2.6	2.5	9.7	7.6
63 Mauritius	3.3	4.6	..	1.8	0.3	0.2	5.9	6.2
64 Suriname	10.2	3.5 [e]	3.5	..	..	..	..	..
65 Lebanon	..	2.5 [g]	..	2.2	5.0	3.6	3.5	3.1 [k]
66 Thailand	3.4	4.8	1.0	1.9	2.2	1.8	6.2	13.2
67 Fiji	6.0	..	2.0	2.9	2.2	1.6	7.7	2.2
68 Saudi Arabia	7.4	7.5	..	..	12.8	13.2	..	..
69 Brazil	4.7	5.1	3.0	2.9	1.9	1.3	1.8	9.0
70 Philippines	2.1	3.4	1.5	1.7	1.4	1.2	8.1	8.8
71 Oman	4.1	4.5	2.0	2.9	18.3	10.1	7.0	4.2 [k]
72 Armenia	..	2.0	..	3.1	..	3.6	..	3.2
73 Peru	3.6	2.9	1.3	2.4	2.4	..	1.8	5.7
74 Ukraine	5.3	5.6	3.0	3.6	..	3.1	..	7.2
75 Kazakhstan	3.4	4.4	3.2	3.5	..	0.9	..	8.6
76 Georgia	..	5.2 [e]	3.0	0.5	..	1.2	..	3.9
77 Maldives	5.2	6.4	4.9	5.1	..	..	6.0	4.3 [k]
78 Jamaica	4.9	7.5	2.6	3.2	..	..	15.6	10.6
79 Azerbaijan	5.8	3.0	2.6	..	..	2.6	..	2.1
80 Paraguay	1.1 [g]	4.0 [g]	0.7	1.7	1.2	1.1	6.2	3.0
81 Sri Lanka	2.7	3.4	1.5	1.4	2.1	3.6	4.8	3.3
82 Turkey	1.2 [o]	2.2 [d]	2.2	..	3.5	5.0	4.9	7.4
83 Turkmenistan	4.1	..	3.9	4.1	..	3.4	..	14.5
84 Ecuador	3.5	3.5	1.5	1.7	1.9	..	10.1	8.7
85 Albania	..	..	3.3	3.5	..	1.4	0.1	1.0
86 Dominican Republic	1.3	2.3	1.6	1.9	..	..	3.3	2.2
87 China	2.3	2.3	2.1	..	2.7	2.1	2.0	2.1
88 Jordan	6.8	7.9	3.6	5.3	11.1	10.0	15.5	8.0
89 Tunisia	6.2	7.7	3.0	2.2	2.0	1.7	11.6	7.3
90 Iran, Islamic Rep. of	3.7	4.0	1.5	1.7	2.8	2.7	0.5	4.2
91 Cape Verde	2.9	..	..	1.8	..	0.9	1.7	3.8
92 Kyrgyzstan	9.7	5.3	4.7	2.9	..	1.7	..	9.4
93 Guyana	8.5	5.0	2.9	4.5	0.9	..	74.5	15.5
94 South Africa	6.1	7.6	3.1	3.3	3.8	1.3	..	3.7
95 El Salvador	3.1 [e]	2.5	1.4	2.6	2.7	0.9	4.3	2.8
96 Samoa (Western)	..	..	3.9	4.8	..	..	3.8	3.7
97 Syrian Arab Republic	4.8	4.2	0.4	0.8	6.9	5.6	10.3	1.9
98 Moldova, Rep. of	3.6	10.6	4.4	6.4	..	0.5	..	15.1
99 Uzbekistan	9.2 [e]	7.7	4.6	3.4	..	1.7	..	3.1
100 Algeria	9.8	5.1 [o]	3.0	2.6	1.5	3.8	14.2	11.1

HDI rank		Public expenditure on education (as % of GNP)		Public expenditure on health (as % of GDP)		Military expenditure (as % of GDP) [a]		Total debt service (as % of GDP) [b]	
		1985-87 [c]	1995-97 [c]	1990	1998	1990	1999	1990	1999
101	Viet Nam	..	3.0	0.9	0.8	7.9	..	2.7	4.9
102	Indonesia	0.9 [e, g]	1.4 [p]	0.6	0.7	1.3	1.1	8.7	12.5
103	Tajikistan	..	2.2		5.2	..	1.4	..	2.6
104	Bolivia	2.1	4.9	2.1	4.1	2.5	1.8	7.9	5.9
105	Egypt	4.5	4.8	1.8	..	3.5	2.7	7.1	1.9
106	Nicaragua	5.4	3.9 [o]	7.0	8.3	2.1	1.1	1.6	8.3
107	Honduras	4.8	3.6	3.3	3.9	..	0.6	12.8	6.8
108	Guatemala	1.9 [g]	1.7 [g]	1.8	2.1	1.6	0.6	2.8	2.3
109	Gabon	5.8	2.9 [o]	2.0	2.1	..	0.3 [k]	3.0	12.4
110	Equatorial Guinea	1.7 [e]	1.7 [e]	1.0	..	..	..	3.9	0.7
111	Namibia	..	9.1	4.0	4.1	..	3.6	..	..
112	Morocco	6.2 [g]	5.3 [g]	0.9	1.2	4.1	..	6.9	8.9
113	Swaziland	5.6	5.7	1.9	2.7	1.5	1.7	5.5	2.5
114	Botswana	7.3	8.6	1.7	2.5	4.2	3.4	2.8	1.4
115	India	3.2	3.2	0.9	..	2.9	2.4	2.6	2.3
116	Mongolia	11.7	5.7	6.0	..	5.7	2.1	..	2.9
117	Zimbabwe	7.7	7.1 [e]	3.1	..	4.5	3.4	5.4	11.6
118	Myanmar	1.9 [g]	1.2 [e, g]	1.0	0.2	4.1	3.3 [k]	..	..
119	Ghana	3.4	4.2	1.3	1.8	0.4	0.8	6.3	6.7
120	Lesotho	4.1	8.4	2.6	..	4.1	3.2 [k]	3.7	5.8
121	Cambodia	..	2.9	..	0.6	2.4	2.5	2.7	1.1
122	Papua New Guinea	..	..	3.1	2.5	2.1	1.0	17.2	5.9
123	Kenya	7.1	6.5	2.4	2.4	2.9	1.9	9.3	6.7
124	Comoros	..	..	2.9	..	..	..	0.4	4.0
125	Cameroon	2.8	..	0.9	1.0	1.5	1.5	4.7	6.0
126	Congo	4.9 [e]	6.1	1.5	2.0	..	..	19.0	1.1
Low human development									
127	Pakistan	3.1	2.7	1.1	0.9	5.7	4.4	4.8	5.2
128	Togo	4.9	4.5	1.3	1.3	3.2	..	5.3	2.8
129	Nepal	2.2	3.2	0.8	1.3	0.9	0.9	1.9	2.1
130	Bhutan	3.7	4.1	1.7	3.2	..	..	1.8	1.6
131	Lao People's Dem. Rep.	0.5	2.1	0.0	1.2	..	2.4 [m]	1.1	2.6
132	Bangladesh	1.4 [g]	2.2 [g]	0.7	1.7	1.3	1.6	2.6	1.7
133	Yemen	..	7.0	1.2	..	8.5	5.6	3.6	2.3
134	Haiti	1.9	..	1.2	1.4	..	..	1.1	1.4
135	Madagascar	1.9 [o]	1.9	..	1.1	1.2	1.4	7.2	4.5
136	Nigeria	1.7 [p]	0.7 [p]	1.0	0.8	0.7	1.4	11.7	2.6
137	Djibouti	..	..	..	..	6.3	4.4 [k]	3.5	1.0 [k]
138	Sudan	..	1.4	0.7	..	3.6	2.6	0.4	0.6
139	Mauritania	..	5.1 [g]	..	1.4	3.8	2.3 [m]	14.3	11.0
140	Tanzania, U. Rep. of	..	..	1.6	1.3	..	1.3	4.2	2.2
141	Uganda	3.5 [e, g]	2.6	..	1.9	2.5	2.1	3.4	2.9
142	Congo, Dem. Rep. of the	1.0	..	..	..	..	..	3.7	0.3 [k]
143	Zambia	3.1	2.2	2.6	3.6	3.7	1.0	6.2	13.9
144	Côte d'Ivoire	..	5.0	1.5	1.2	1.5	0.9 [m]	11.7	12.9
145	Senegal	..	3.7	0.7	2.6	2.0	1.5	5.7	5.0
146	Angola	6.2	..	1.4	..	5.8 [q]	23.5 [q]	3.2	13.4
147	Benin	..	3.2	1.6	1.6	1.8	..	2.1	3.0
148	Eritrea	..	1.8 [o]	..	..	..	22.9	..	0.6
149	Gambia	3.7	4.9	2.2	1.9	1.1	0.8	11.9	5.4
150	Guinea	1.8	1.9	2.0	2.2	..	1.4 [k]	6.0	3.8

HDI rank	Public expenditure on education (as % of GNP)		Public expenditure on health (as % of GDP)		Military expenditure (as % of GDP) [a]		Total debt service (as % of GDP) [b]	
	1985-87 [c]	1995-97 [c]	1990	1998	1990	1999	1990	1999
151 Malawi	3.5	5.4	..	2.8	1.3	0.8 [m]	7.4	3.8
152 Rwanda	3.5	..	1.7	2.0	3.7	4.2	0.8	1.6
153 Mali	3.2	2.2	1.6	2.1	2.1	2.2	2.8	4.1
154 Central African Republic	2.6	..	..	2.0	1.6 [l]	..	2.0	1.8
155 Chad	..	2.2	..	2.3	..	1.2 [k]	0.7	2.1
156 Guinea-Bissau	1.8	..	1.1	..	..	1.3 [k]	3.4	4.4
157 Mozambique	2.1	..	3.6	2.8	10.1	2.4	3.1	3.1
158 Ethiopia	3.1	4.0	0.9	1.7	4.9	9.0	3.4	2.5
159 Burkina Faso	2.3	3.6 [e]	1.0	1.2	3.0	1.6	1.2	2.4
160 Burundi	3.1	4.0	1.1	0.6	3.4	6.1	3.7	4.0
161 Niger	..	2.3 [o]	..	1.2	1.9	..	4.0	2.5
162 Sierra Leone	1.7	..	..	0.9	0.9	1.6	2.4	3.2

Note: The denominator conventionally used when comparing expenditures and debt with the size of the economy is GNP, not GDP (see the definitions of statistical terms). GDP is used here wherever possible, however, to allow comparability throughout the table. With few exceptions the denominators produce similar results.

a. As a result of a number of limitations in the data, comparisons of military expenditure data over time and across countries should be made with caution. For detailed notes on the data see SIPRI (2000).

b. For aggregates see table 15.

c. Data refer to the most recent year available during the period specified.

d. Data are not strictly comparable to those for earlier years as a result of methodological changes in surveys.

e. Data refer to a year or period other than that specified.

f. Data refer to 1999.

g. Data refer to the ministry of education only.

h. Data refer to the Flemish community only.

i. Data refer to the Federal Republic of Germany before unification.

j. Data refer to the Office of Greek Education only.

k. Data refer to 1998.

l. Data refer to 1991.

m. Data refer to 1997.

n. Data refer to the former Soviet Union.

o. Data do not include expenditure on tertiary education.

p. Data refer to the central government only.

q. These data should be interpreted in the light of the highly uncertain economic statistics resulting from the impact of war on the Angolan economy.

Source: Columns 1 and 2: UNESCO 2000b; *columns 3 and 4:* World Bank 2001b; *column 5:* SIPRI 2001; *column 6:* SIPRI 2000; *columns 7 and 8:* calculated on the basis of data on total debt service and GDP from World Bank (2001b).

17 Unemployment in OECD countries

HDI rank		Unemployed people (thousands) 1999	Unemployment			Youth unemployment		Long-term unemployment (as % of total unemployment) [a]	
			Rate (% of labour force) 1999	Average annual rate (% of labour force) 1990-98	Female rate as % of male rate 1999	Rate (% of labour force aged 15-24) [b] 1999	Female rate as % of male rate 1999	Female 1999	Male 1999
High human development									
1	Norway	75.0	3.2	5.0	88	9.6	99	6.3	7.3
2	Australia	680.5	7.2	9.0	96	13.9	91	25.8	31.8
3	Canada	1,188.9	7.6	9.8	92	14.0	82	10.2	12.8
4	Sweden	240.8	5.6	6.3	89	14.2	92	30.1 [c]	36.3 [c]
5	Belgium	385.8	9.0	8.7	137	22.6	99	60.9	60.1
6	United States	5,878.9	4.2	5.9	107	9.9	92	6.2	7.4
7	Iceland	2.6	1.9	3.5	179	4.4	100	15.2	6.6
8	Netherlands	221.5	3.2	6.0	181	7.4	124	40.4	47.7
9	Japan	3,171.5	4.7	2.9	94	9.3	80	14.8	27.4
10	Finland	261.0	10.2	12.1	110	21.5	106	26.2	33.1
11	Switzerland	98.6	2.7	3.5	133	5.6	102	39.0	40.7
12	Luxembourg	5.4	2.9	2.4	194	6.8	119	27.2 [d]	38.6 [d]
13	France	2,924.1	11.1	11.2	133	26.6	123	41.6	39.0
14	United Kingdom	1,779.1	6.0	8.1	75	12.3	72	21.6	34.8
15	Denmark	148.9	5.2	7.6	131	10.0	111	20.1	20.9
16	Austria	221.8	5.2	5.1	102	5.9	116	36.1	28.1
17	Germany	3,428.0	8.3	7.6	112	8.5	85	54.0 [c]	49.9
18	Ireland	95.5	5.6	12.7	90	8.5	97	46.9 [e]	63.3 [e]
19	New Zealand	127.3	6.8	8.1	93	13.7	88	17.9	23.0
20	Italy	2,669.4	11.5	10.6	182	32.9	134	60.7	62.1
21	Spain	2,604.9	15.9	20.0	209	28.5	172	55.5	45.4
23	Greece	532.6	12.0	9.3	233 [c]	29.7 [c]	184 [c]	61.5 [b]	44.7 [c]
27	Korea, Rep. of	1,353.0	6.3	2.9	73	14.2	66	1.9	4.7
28	Portugal	214.8	4.5	5.8	133	8.7	154	42.9	39.5
33	Czech Republic	454.1	8.8	4.7	144	17.0	116	40.9	32.7 [b]
36	Hungary	284.8	7.1	10.1	84	12.4	86	47.9	50.6
38	Poland	2,390.5	13.9	12.7	133 [c]	23.2 [c]	117 [c]	41.8 [c]	32.5 [c]
Medium human development									
51	Mexico	493.6	2.6	3.8	150	3.4	167	0.4	2.7
82	Turkey	1,738.5	7.3	7.3	86	14.6	77	44.1	29.8
OECD [f]		33,671.3 T	6.7 [g]	7.0 [g]	115	11.8	102	32.3	30.3

Note: This table does not include Slovakia, which joined the OECD in 2000.
a. Data refer to unemployment lasting 12 months or longer.
b. The age range for the labour force may be 16-24 for some countries.
c. Data refer to 1998.
d. Data are based on a small sample and must be treated with caution.
e. Data refer to 1997.
f. Aggregates are from OECD (2000a, 2000b, 2001a and 2001b).
g. Does not include the Czech Republic and Hungary.

Source: Column 1: OECD 2001a; column 2: OECD 2000a; column 3: OECD 2001b; columns 4 and 6: calculated on the basis of data on male and female unemployment rates from OECD (2000b); columns 5, 7 and 8: OECD 2000b.

18 Energy and the environment

HDI rank	Traditional fuel consumption (as % of total energy use)		Electricity consumption per capita (kilowatt-hours)		GDP per unit of energy use (PPP US$ per kg of oil equivalent)		Carbon dioxide emissions Share of world total (%)	Per capita (metric tons)	Ratification of environmental treaties [a] Framework Convention on Climate Change	Kyoto Protocol to the Framework Convention on Climate Change [b]	Vienna Convention for the Protection of the Ozone Layer	Convention on Biological Diversity
	1980	1997	1980	1998	1980	1998	1997	1997				
High human development												
1 Norway	0.4	1.1	18,289	24,607	2.4	4.8	..	..	●	○	●	●
2 Australia	3.8	4.4	5,393	8,717	2.1	4.1	1.3	17.3	●	○	●	●
3 Canada	0.4	4.7	12,329	15,071	1.5	3.2	2.0	16.2	●	○	●	●
4 Sweden	7.7	17.9	10,216	13,955	2.1	3.6	0.2	5.4	●	○	●	●
5 Belgium	0.2	1.6	4,402	7,249	2.4	4.3	0.4	10.2	●	○	●	●
6 United States	1.3	3.8	8,914	11,832	1.6	3.8	22.6	20.1	●	○	●	○
7 Iceland	..	..	12,553	20,150	1.9	2.8	(.)	7.7	●		●	●
8 Netherlands	0.0	1.1	4,057	5,908	2.2	4.9	0.7	10.4	●	○	●	●
9 Japan	0.1	1.6	4,395	7,322	3.3	6.0	4.8	9.2	●	○	●	●
10 Finland	4.3	6.5	7,779	14,129	1.8	3.4	0.2	10.9	●	○	●	●
11 Switzerland	0.9	6.0	5,579	6,981	4.4	7.0	0.2	5.6	●	○	●	●
12 Luxembourg	0.0	..	9,803	12,400	1.0	5.1	(.)	18.9	●	○	●	●
13 France	1.3	5.7	3,881	6,287	2.9	5.0	1.4	5.8	●	○	●	●
14 United Kingdom	0.0	3.3	4,160	5,327	..	5.4	2.2	8.9	●	○	●	●
15 Denmark	0.4	5.9	4,222	6,033	..	6.4	0.2	10.7	●	○	●	●
16 Austria	1.2	4.7	4,371	6,175	3.5	6.7	0.3	7.5	●	○	●	●
17 Germany	0.3	1.3	5,005	5,681	..	5.5	3.4	10.2	●	○	●	●
18 Ireland	0.0	0.2	2,528	4,760	2.3	6.4	0.2	10.0	●	○	●	●
19 New Zealand	0.2	0.8	6,269	8,215	..	4.0	0.1	8.3	●	○	●	●
20 Italy	0.8	1.0	2,831	4,431	3.9	7.4	1.7	7.1	●	○	●	●
21 Spain	0.4	1.3	2,401	4,195	3.8	5.9	1.0	6.2	●	○	●	●
22 Israel	0.0	0.0	2,826	5,475	3.6	5.7	0.2	9.7	●	○	●	●
23 Greece	3.0	4.5	2,064	3,739	4.2	5.7	0.3	7.6	●	○	●	●
24 Hong Kong, China (SAR)	0.9	0.7	2,167	5,244	6.4	8.5	0.1	3.5	–	–	–	–
25 Cyprus	0.0	..	1,494	3,468	3.5	6.1	(.)	7.1	●	●	●	●
26 Singapore	0.4	0.0	2,280	6,771	2.3	3.1	0.3	23.4	●		●	●
27 Korea, Rep. of	4.0	2.4	859	4,497	2.8	4.0	1.8	9.4	●	○	●	●
28 Portugal	1.2	0.9	1,469	3,396	5.6	7.0	0.2	5.0	●	○	●	●
29 Slovenia	..	1.5	..	5,096	..	4.4	0.1	7.5	●	○	●	●
30 Malta	..	..	1,363	3,719	3.7	6.0	(.)	4.6	●	○	●	●
31 Barbados	25.0	..	..	..	..	..	(.)	3.4	●	●	●	●
32 Brunei Darussalam	0.8	..	1,523	7,676	..	..	(.)	17.5			●	
33 Czech Republic	0.6	1.6	3,701	4,748	..	3.2	0.5	11.9	●	○	●	●
34 Argentina	5.9	4.0	1,171	1,891	4.7	7.3	0.6	3.9	●	○	●	●
35 Slovakia	..	0.5	3,817	3,899	..	3.2	0.2	6.9	●	○	●	●
36 Hungary	2.0	1.6	2,389	2,888	2.0	4.3	0.2	5.7	●	●	●	●
37 Uruguay	11.1	21.0	948	1,788	5.0	9.9	(.)	1.6	●	●	●	●
38 Poland	0.4	0.8	2,390	2,458	..	3.2	1.4	9.0	●	○	●	●
39 Chile	12.3	11.3	876	2,082	3.1	5.4	0.2	4.0	●	○	●	●
40 Bahrain	0.0	..	4,970	7,645	1.0	1.4	0.1	25.5	●		●	●
41 Costa Rica	26.3	54.2	860	1,450	5.7	9.5	(.)	1.3	●	○	●	●
42 Bahamas	0.0	..	..	..	..	..	(.)	6.0	●	●	●	●
43 Kuwait	0.0	0.0	5,793	13,800	1.3	..	0.2	28.9	●		●	○
44 Estonia	..	13.8	..	3,531	..	2.5	0.1	13.0	●	○	●	●
45 United Arab Emirates	..	..	5,320	9,892	4.4	1.8	0.3	34.5	●		●	●
46 Croatia	..	3.2	..	2,463	..	3.9	0.1	4.2	●	○	●	●
47 Lithuania	..	6.3	..	1,909	..	2.7	0.1	4.0	●	○	●	●
48 Qatar	0.0	..	9,489	13,912	..	..	0.2	66.7	●		●	●
Medium human development												
49 Trinidad and Tobago	1.4	0.8	1,584	3,478	1.3	1.1	0.1	17.2	●	●	●	●
50 Latvia	..	26.2	..	1,879	19.6	3.4	(.)	3.3	●	○	●	●

18 Energy and the environment

HDI rank		Traditional fuel consumption (as % of total energy use)		Electricity consumption per capita (kilowatt-hours)		GDP per unit of energy use (PPP US$ per kg of oil equivalent)		Carbon dioxide emissions — Share of world total (%)	Per capita (metric tons)	Ratification of environmental treaties [a] — Framework Convention on Climate Change	Kyoto Protocol to the Framework Convention on Climate Change [b]	Vienna Convention for the Protection of the Ozone Layer	Convention on Biological Diversity
		1980	1997	1980	1998	1980	1998	1997	1997				
51	Mexico	5.0	4.5	846	1,513	3.1	5.2	1.5	3.9	●	●	●	●
52	Panama	26.6	14.4	828	1,211	3.2	6.5	(.)	2.8	●	●	●	●
53	Belarus	..	0.8	..	2,762	..	2.5	0.3	5.9	●		●	●
54	Belize	50.0	..	..	..	..	..	(.)	1.7	●		●	●
55	Russian Federation	..	0.8	..	3,937	..	1.7	5.9	9.7	●	○	●	●
56	Malaysia	15.7	5.5	631	2,554	2.7	3.9	0.5	6.2	●	○	●	●
57	Bulgaria	0.5	1.3	3,349	3,166	0.9	2.0	0.3	5.9	●	○	●	●
58	Romania	1.3	5.7	2,434	1,626	1.6	3.5	0.4	4.8	●	●	●	●
59	Libyan Arab Jamahiriya	2.3	0.9	1,588	3,677	..	..	0.2	8.0	●		●	○
60	Macedonia, TFYR	..	6.1	..	..	..	..	(.)	5.4	●		●	●
61	Venezuela	0.9	0.7	1,823	2,566	1.7	2.4	0.8	8.2	●		●	●
62	Colombia	15.9	17.7	561	866	4.1	7.9	0.3	1.7	●		●	●
63	Mauritius	59.1	36.1	..	..	..	..	(.)	1.5	●		●	●
64	Suriname	2.4	..	..	..	..	..	(.)	5.1	●		●	●
65	Lebanon	2.4	2.5	789	1,820	..	3.7	0.1	5.0	●		●	●
66	Thailand	40.3	24.6	279	1,345	3.0	5.1	0.9	3.5	●	○	●	○
67	Fiji	45.0	..	..	..	..	..	(.)	1.0	●	●	●	●
68	Saudi Arabia	0.0	0.0	1,356	4,692	3.0	2.1	(.)	(.)	●		●	
69	Brazil	35.5	28.7	974	1,793	4.4	6.5	1.2	1.8	●	○	●	●
70	Philippines	37.0	26.9	353	451	5.6	7.0	0.3	1.0	●	○	●	●
71	Oman	..	..	614	2,828	..	..	0.1	7.7	●		●	●
72	Armenia	..	0.0	..	930	..	4.3	(.)	0.8	●		●	●
73	Peru	15.2	24.6	502	642	4.6	7.8	0.1	1.2	●	○	●	●
74	Ukraine	..	0.5	..	2,350	..	1.2	1.5	7.2	●	○	●	●
75	Kazakhstan	..	0.2	..	2,399	..	1.8	0.5	7.5	●	○	●	●
76	Georgia	..	1.0	..	1,257	..	5.0	(.)	0.9	●	●	●	●
77	Maldives	..	..	..	..	..	..	(.)	1.2	●	●	●	●
78	Jamaica	5.0	6.0	482	2,252	1.9	2.2	(.)	4.3	●	●	●	●
79	Azerbaijan	..	0.0	..	1,584	..	1.5	0.1	4.2	●	●	●	●
80	Paraguay	62.0	49.6	245	756	4.2	5.4	(.)	0.7	●	●	●	●
81	Sri Lanka	53.5	46.5	96	244	3.5	8.0	(.)	0.4	●		●	●
82	Turkey	20.5	3.1	439	1,353	3.6	5.8	0.8	3.1			●	●
83	Turkmenistan	..	..	..	859	..	1.2	0.1	7.3	●	●	●	●
84	Ecuador	26.7	17.5	361	625	3.0	4.3	0.1	1.7	●	●	●	●
85	Albania	13.1	7.3	1,083	678	..	10.3	(.)	0.5	●		●	●
86	Dominican Republic	27.5	14.3	433	627	3.7	7.5	0.1	1.6	●		●	●
87	China	8.4	5.7	264	746	0.8	4.0	13.9	2.7	●	○	●	●
88	Jordan	0.0	0.0	387	1,205	3.3	3.6	0.1	2.3	●		●	●
89	Tunisia	16.1	12.4	379	824	4.0	6.9	0.1	1.8	●		●	●
90	Iran, Islamic Rep. of	0.4	0.7	515	1,343	2.9	3.3	1.2	4.5	●		●	●
91	Cape Verde	..	..	..	..	..	..	(.)	0.3	●			●
92	Kyrgyzstan	..	0.0	..	1,431	..	4.0	(.)	1.4	●		●	●
93	Guyana	24.1	..	..	..	..	..	(.)	1.2	●		●	●
94	South Africa	4.9	43.4	3,213	3,832	2.7	3.3	1.3	8.2	●		●	●
95	El Salvador	52.9	34.5	274	559	4.3	6.5	(.)	0.9	●	●	●	●
96	Samoa (Western)	50.0	..	..	..	..	..	(.)	0.8	●	●	●	●
97	Syrian Arab Republic	0.0	0.0	354	838	2.9	3.3	0.2	3.2	●		●	●
98	Moldova, Rep. of	..	0.5	..	689	..	2.2	(.)	2.4	●		●	●
99	Uzbekistan	..	0.0	..	1,618	..	1.1	0.4	4.4	●	●	●	●
100	Algeria	1.9	1.5	265	563	5.0	5.4	0.4	3.2	●		●	●

HDI rank		Traditional fuel consumption (as % of total energy use)		Electricity consumption per capita (kilowatt-hours)		GDP per unit of energy use (PPP US$ per kg of oil equivalent)		Carbon dioxide emissions — Share of world total (%)	Carbon dioxide emissions — Per capita (metric tons)	Ratification of environmental treaties [a] — Framework Convention on Climate Change	Kyoto Protocol to the Framework Convention on Climate Change [b]	Vienna Convention for the Protection of the Ozone Layer	Convention on Biological Diversity
		1980	1997	1980	1998	1980	1998	1997	1997				
101	Viet Nam	49.1	37.8	50	232	..	4.0	0.2	0.6	●	○	●	●
102	Indonesia	51.5	29.3	44	320	2.2	4.6	1.0	1.2	●	○	●	●
103	Tajikistan	..	..	..	2,046	..	..	(.)	0.9	●		●	●
104	Bolivia	19.3	14.0	226	409	3.4	4.0	(.)	1.4	●	●	●	●
105	Egypt	4.7	3.2	380	861	3.5	4.7	0.5	1.7	●	○	●	●
106	Nicaragua	49.2	42.2	303	281	3.6	4.0	(.)	0.7	●	●	●	●
107	Honduras	55.3	54.8	215	446	2.9	4.5	(.)	0.7	●	●	●	●
108	Guatemala	54.6	62.0	241	322	4.1	6.1	(.)	0.7	●	●	●	●
109	Gabon	30.8	32.9	618	749	1.9	4.5	(.)	2.9	●		●	●
110	Equatorial Guinea	80.0	..	..	..	..	..	(.)	1.5	●	●	●	●
111	Namibia	..	..	..	..	..	..	..	..	●		●	●
112	Morocco	5.2	4.0	223	443	6.8	10.2	0.1	1.2	●		●	●
113	Swaziland	..	..	..	..	..	..	(.)	0.4	●		●	●
114	Botswana	35.7	..	..	..	..	..	(.)	2.2	●		●	●
115	India	31.5	20.7	130	384	1.9	4.3	4.2	1.1	●		●	●
116	Mongolia	14.4	4.3	..	..	..	..	(.)	3.0	●	●	●	●
117	Zimbabwe	27.6	25.2	990	896	1.5	3.3	0.1	1.6	●		●	●
118	Myanmar	69.3	60.5	31	64	..	..	(.)	0.2	●		●	●
119	Ghana	43.7	78.1	424	289	2.9	4.6	(.)	0.2	●		●	●
120	Lesotho	..	..	..	..	..	..	..	..	●	●	●	●
121	Cambodia	100.0	89.3	..	..	..	..	(.)	(.)	●		●	●
122	Papua New Guinea	65.4	62.5	..	..	..	..	(.)	0.5	●	○	●	●
123	Kenya	76.8	80.3	93	129	1.1	2.0	(.)	0.2	●		●	●
124	Comoros	..	..	..	..	..	..	(.)	0.1	●		●	●
125	Cameroon	51.7	69.2	156	185	2.8	3.5	(.)	0.2	●		●	●
126	Congo	77.8	53.0	66	83	0.8	1.8	(.)	0.1	●		●	●
Low human development													
127	Pakistan	24.4	29.5	125	337	2.1	4.0	0.4	0.7	●		●	●
128	Togo	35.7	71.9	..	..	..	..	(.)	0.2	●		●	●
129	Nepal	94.2	89.6	12	47	1.5	3.5	(.)	0.1	●		●	●
130	Bhutan	100.0	..	..	..	..	..	(.)	0.2	●			●
131	Lao People's Dem. Rep.	72.3	88.7	..	..	..	..	(.)	0.1	●		●	●
132	Bangladesh	81.3	46.0	16	81	4.5	8.9	0.1	0.2	●		●	●
133	Yemen	..	1.4	59	96	..	3.7	0.1	1.0	●		●	●
134	Haiti	80.7	74.7	41	33	3.7	5.3	(.)	0.2	●		●	●
135	Madagascar	78.4	84.3	..	..	..	..	(.)	0.1	●		●	●
136	Nigeria	66.8	67.8	68	85	0.8	1.2	0.3	0.8	●		●	●
137	Djibouti	..	..	..	..	..	..	(.)	0.6	●		●	●
138	Sudan	86.9	75.1	35	47	..	..	(.)	0.1	●		●	●
139	Mauritania	0.0	0.0	..	..	..	..	(.)	1.2	●		●	●
140	Tanzania, U. Rep. of	92.0	91.4	37	54	..	1.1	(.)	0.1	●		●	●
141	Uganda	93.6	89.7	..	..	..	..	(.)	0.1	●		●	●
142	Congo, Dem. Rep. of the	73.9	91.7	147	110	3.5	2.8	(.)	(.)	●		●	●
143	Zambia	37.4	72.7	1,016	539	0.9	1.2	(.)	0.3	●	○	●	●
144	Côte d'Ivoire	52.8	91.5	..	..	..	..	0.1	0.9	●		●	●
145	Senegal	50.8	56.2	95	111	2.3	4.4	(.)	0.4	●		●	●
146	Angola	64.9	69.7	67	60	..	3.8	(.)	0.4	●		●	●
147	Benin	85.4	89.2	30	46	1.3	2.4	(.)	0.1	●		●	●
148	Eritrea	..	96.0	..	..	..	..	..	..	●			●
149	Gambia	72.7	78.6	..	..	..	..	(.)	0.2	●		●	●
150	Guinea	71.4	74.2	..	..	..	..	(.)	0.1	●	●	●	●

	Traditional fuel consumption (as % of total energy use)		Electricity consumption per capita (kilowatt-hours)		GDP per unit of energy use (PPP US$ per kg of oil equivalent)		Carbon dioxide emissions		Ratification of environmental treaties [a]			
							Share of world total (%)	Per capita (metric tons)	Framework Convention on Climate Change	Kyoto Protocol to the Framework Convention on Climate Change [b]	Vienna Convention for the Protection of the Ozone Layer	Convention on Biological Diversity
HDI rank	1980	1997	1980	1998	1980	1998	1997	1997				
151 Malawi	90.6	88.6	..	..	..	..	(.)	0.1	●		●	●
152 Rwanda	89.8	88.3	..	..	..	..	(.)	0.1	●		●	●
153 Mali	86.7	88.9	..	..	..	..	(.)	(.)	●	○	●	●
154 Central African Republic	88.9	87.5	..	..	..	..	(.)	0.1	●		●	●
155 Chad	95.9	97.6	..	..	..	..	(.)	(.)	●		●	●
156 Guinea-Bissau	80.0	57.1	..	..	..	..	(.)	0.2	●			●
157 Mozambique	43.7	91.4	34	54	0.6	2.0	(.)	0.1	●		●	●
158 Ethiopia	89.6	95.9	16	22	..	2.1	(.)	(.)	●		●	●
159 Burkina Faso	91.3	87.1	..	..	..	..	(.)	0.1	●		●	●
160 Burundi	97.0	94.2	..	..	..	..	(.)	(.)	●		●	●
161 Niger	79.5	80.6	..	..	..	..	(.)	0.1	●	○	●	●
162 Sierra Leone	90.0	86.1	..	..	..	..	(.)	0.1	●			●
Developing countries	21.1	16.7	318	757	2.2	4.3	35.5	1.9	–	–	–	–
Least developed countries	76.1	75.1	58	76	..	3.7	0.4	0.2	–	–	–	–
Arab States	8.0	5.6	491	1,312	3.3	3.4	2.5	2.6	–	–	–	–
East Asia and the Pacific	14.8	9.4	261	818	1.3	4.2	19.0	2.6	–	–	–	–
Latin America and the Caribbean	18.0	15.7	845	1,464	3.7	5.7	5.2	2.6	–	–	–	–
South Asia	30.2	20.3	133	387	2.1	4.3	6.0	1.1	–	–	–	–
Sub-Saharan Africa	45.5	62.9	463	480	1.8	2.4	2.0	0.9	–	–	–	–
Eastern Europe and the CIS	..	1.2	..	2,893	..	2.1	12.4	7.5	–	–	–	–
OECD	1.3	3.3	4,916	6,969	2.2	4.6	49.9	11.0	–	–	–	–
High-Income OECD	1.0	3.4	5,932	8,451	2.1	4.6	43.5	12.6	–	–	–	–
High human development	1.1	3.3	5,216	7,482	2.2	4.6	50.2	11.7	–	–	–	–
Medium human development	..	10.8	352	944	..	3.7	40.3	2.5	–	–	–	–
Low human development	64.5	63.3	76	132	1.7	2.9	1.1	0.3	–	–	–	–
High income	1.0	3.4	5,875	8,406	2.2	4.6	45.0	12.7	–	–	–	–
Middle income	..	7.3	588	1,370	..	3.9	37.6	3.5	–	–	–	–
Low income	46.4	29.8	106	362	1.9	3.4	9.1	1.0	–	–	–	–
World	7.3	8.2	1,449	2,074	2.1	4.2	91.6 [c]	3.9	–	–	–	–

● Ratification, acceptance, approval, accession or succession.

○ Signature.

a. Information is as of 30 March 2001. The United Nations Framework Convention on Climate Change was signed in New York in 1992, the Kyoto Protocol to the United Nations Framework Convention on Climate Change in Kyoto in 1997, the Vienna Convention for the Protection of the Ozone Layer in Vienna in 1985 and the Convention on Biological Diversity in Rio de Janeiro in 1992.

b. Has not yet entered into force.

c. The world total is less than 100% because of the omission of data for countries not reported on and because the global total used in this calculation includes other emissions not included in national totals, such as emissions from bunker fuels and oxidation of non-fuel hydrocarbon products.

Source: Columns 1 and 2: World Bank 2001b, based on data from the United Nations Statistics Division; aggregates calculated for the Human Development Report Office by the World Bank; *columns 3-6:* World Bank 2001b; aggregates calculated for the Human Development Report Office by the World Bank; *column 7:* calculated on the basis of data on carbon dioxide emissions from CDIAC (2000); *column 8:* calculated on the basis of data on carbon dioxide emissions from CDIAC (2000) and data on population from UN (1998); *columns 9-12:* UN 2001b.

HDI rank	Internally displaced people (thousands) 1999[c]	Refugees[a] By country of asylum (thousands) 1999	Refugees[a] By country of origin (thousands)[d] 1999	Conventional arms transfers[b] (1990 prices) Imports US$ millions 1999	Imports Index (1991=100) 1999	Exports US$ millions 1999	Exports Share (%)[e] 1995-99	Total armed forces Thousands 1999	Total armed forces Index (1985=100) 1999
High human development									
1 Norway	–	48	..	170	52	..	0.1	31	83
2 Australia	–	60	..	341	235	298	0.6	55	78
3 Canada	–	123	..	33	5	168	1.0	61	73
4 Sweden	–	160	..	79	343	157	0.6	53	81
5 Belgium	–	18	..	37	42	28	0.5	42	46
6 United States	–	513	..	111	31	10,442	48.0	1,372	64
7 Iceland	–	(.)	..	..	..	..	..	..	..
8 Netherlands	–	139	..	225	110	329	2.0	56	53
9 Japan	–	4	..	1,089	74	..	(.)	243	100
10 Finland	–	13	..	821	1,346	16	(.)	32	87
11 Switzerland	–	82	..	508	134	58	0.3	28	139
12 Luxembourg	–	1	..	..	..	..	..	1	114
13 France	–	130	..	105	11	1,701	10.5	317	68
14 United Kingdom	–	137	..	155	17	1,078	6.6	212	65
15 Denmark	–	69	..	137	120	..	(.)	24	82
16 Austria	–	83	..	48	1,600	37	0.1	41	74
17 Germany	–	976	(.)	126	17	1,334	5.5	333	70
18 Ireland	–	1	..	30	273	..	..	12	84
19 New Zealand	–	5	..	337	1,021	..	(.)	10	77
20 Italy	–	23	..	..	..	533	1.8	266	69
21 Spain	–	6	..	289	318	43	0.9	187	58
22 Israel	–	(.)	..	1,205	98	144	1.0	174	122
23 Greece	–	6	..	633	135	1	0.1	166	82
24 Hong Kong, China (SAR)	–	1	..	..	..	..	..	..	..
25 Cyprus	–	(.)	..	242	233	..	(.)	10	100
26 Singapore	–	..	..	163	56	1	0.1	73	133
27 Korea, Rep. of	–	(.)	..	1,245	141	..	0.1	672	112
28 Portugal	–	(.)	..	1	(.)	..	..	50	68
29 Slovenia	–	4	3	19	..	..	..	10	..
30 Malta	–	(.)	..	..	..	..	..	2	238
31 Barbados	–	..	..	..	..	..	..	1	60
32 Brunei Darussalam	–	..	..	..	..	..	..	5	122
33 Czech Republic	–	1	(.)	..	..	124	0.5	58	..
34 Argentina	–	2	..	223	..	..	(.)	71	65
35 Slovakia	–	(.)	..	..	..	..	0.2	45	..
36 Hungary	–	5	1	56	181	..	0.1	43	41
37 Uruguay	–	(.)	..	13	18	..	..	26	80
38 Poland	–	1	2	1	1	51	0.3	241	75
39 Chile	–	(.)	1	177	199	3	(.)	93	92
40 Bahrain	–	..	(.)	..	..	..	..	11	393
41 Costa Rica	–	23	..	..	..	..	..	..	..
42 Bahamas	–	(.)	..	54	2,700	..	..	1	180
43 Kuwait	–	4	(.)	126	21	..	0.1	15	128
44 Estonia	–	..	(.)	..	..	..	(.)	5	..
45 United Arab Emirates	–	1	..	595	209	..	0.1	65	150
46 Croatia	52	28	340	..	..	..	..	61	..
47 Lithuania	–	(.)	(.)	4	..	..	..	12	..
48 Qatar	–	(.)	..	117	900	..	(.)	12	197
Medium human development									
49 Trinidad and Tobago	–	..	..	..	..	..	..	3	129
50 Latvia	–	(.)	1	4	..	..	(.)	6	..

19 Refugees and armaments

		Internally displaced people (thousands) 1999 [c]	Refugees [a]		Conventional arms transfers [b] (1990 prices)				Total armed forces	
			By country of asylum (thousands) 1999	By country of origin (thousands) [d] 1999	Imports		Exports		Thousands 1999	Index (1985 = 100) 1999
HDI rank					US$ millions 1999	Index (1991 = 100) 1999	US$ millions 1999	Share (%) [e] 1995-99		
51	Mexico	–	25	..	14	67	..	..	179	138
52	Panama	–	1	..		..	..	..	..	..
53	Belarus	–	(.)	(.)	..	..	38	0.7	81	..
54	Belize	–	3	..	..	..	..	..	1	183
55	Russian Federation	498	80	16	..	..	3,125	13.1	1,004	..
56	Malaysia	–	51	..	916	2,349		(.)	105	95
57	Bulgaria	–	1	1	6	1	89	0.1	81	54
58	Romania	–	1	3	35	81	19	(.)	207	109
59	Libyan Arab Jamahiriya	–	11	(.)	..	..	..	(.)	65	89
60	Macedonia, TFYR	–	21	4	95	..	..	..	16	..
61	Venezuela	–	(.)	..	142	55	..	..	56	114
62	Colombia	–	(.)	3	40	83	..	..	144	218
63	Mauritius	–	(.)	..	..	..	..	..	..	..
64	Suriname	–	..	..	12	..	..	..	2	90
65	Lebanon	–	4	4	..	..	..	..	68	390
66	Thailand	–	100	..	185	43	..	..	306	130
67	Fiji	–	..	..	..	..	..	..	4	130
68	Saudi Arabia	–	6	..	1,231	104	..	(.)	163	260
69	Brazil	–	2	..	221	201	..	0.1	291	105
70	Philippines	–	(.)	45	..	..	..	..	110	96
71	Oman	–	..	..	..	..	..	(.)	44	149
72	Armenia	–	296	190	..	..	..	..	53	..
73	Peru	–	1	3	108	114	..	..	115	90
74	Ukraine	–	3	1	..	..	429	1.8	311	..
75	Kazakhstan	–	15	8	259	..	155	0.2	66	..
76	Georgia	279	5	28	60	..	..	0.1	26	..
77	Maldives	–	..	..	..	..	..	..	..	..
78	Jamaica	–	(.)	..	5	..	..	..	3	133
79	Azerbaijan	570	222	309	..	..	..	..	70	..
80	Paraguay	–	(.)	..	..	..	..	..	20	140
81	Sri Lanka	613	(.)	93	26	25	..	..	115	532
82	Turkey	–	3	36	1,134	146	46	(.)	639	101
83	Turkmenistan	–	19	1	..	..	..	..	19	..
84	Ecuador	–	(.)	..	24	12	..	..	57	134
85	Albania	–	4	1	..	..	..	..	54	134
86	Dominican Republic	–	1	..	3	..	..	..	25	110
87	China	–	293	121	1,688	734	79	2.0	2,820	72
88	Jordan	–	1	(.)	44	126	..	(.)	104	148
89	Tunisia	–	(.)	1	..	..	..	..	35	100
90	Iran, Islamic Rep. of	–	1,836	53	67	4	..	(.)	545	89
91	Cape Verde	–	..	..	..	..	..	..	1	14
92	Kyrgyzstan	6	11	4	..	..	..	0.1	9	..
93	Guyana	–	..	..	..	..	..	..	2	24
94	South Africa	–	15	..	14	70	14	0.1	70	66
95	El Salvador	–	(.)	10	..	..	..	..	25	59
96	Samoa (Western)	–	..	..	..	..	..	..	..	..
97	Syrian Arab Republic	–	7	3	20	5	..	(.)	316	79
98	Moldova, Rep. of	8	(.)	1	..	..	..	0.3	11	..
99	Uzbekistan	–	1	44	..	..	..	..	74	..
100	Algeria	–	165	2	..	..	..	..	122	72

HDI rank	Internally displaced people (thousands) 1999 [c]	Refugees [a] By country of asylum (thousands) 1999	Refugees [a] By country of origin (thousands) [d] 1999	Conventional arms transfers [b] (1990 prices) Imports US$ millions 1999	Conventional arms transfers [b] (1990 prices) Imports Index (1991 = 100) 1999	Conventional arms transfers [b] (1990 prices) Exports US$ millions 1999	Conventional arms transfers [b] (1990 prices) Exports Share (%) [e] 1995-99	Total armed forces Thousands 1999	Total armed forces Index (1985 = 100) 1999
101 Viet Nam	–	15	322	154	..	..	..	484	47
102 Indonesia	–	163	(.)	213	2,663	66	0.1	299	108
103 Tajikistan	–	5	45	..	..	..	..	9	..
104 Bolivia	–	(.)	..	..	..	..	..	33	118
105 Egypt	–	7	(.)	748	106	..	(.)	450	101
106 Nicaragua	–	(.)	19	..	..	..	(.)	16	25
107 Honduras	–	(.)	(.)	..	..	..	..	8	50
108 Guatemala	–	1	23	..	..	..	..	31	99
109 Gabon	–	15	..	..	..	..	..	5	196
110 Equatorial Guinea	–	..	(.)	..	..	..	..	1	59
111 Namibia	–	7	1	..	..	..	..	9	..
112 Morocco	–	1	(.)	..	..	..	..	196	132
113 Swaziland	–	1	..	..	..	..	..	..	..
114 Botswana	–	1	..	34	1,133	..	..	9	225
115 India	–	180	(.)	566	43	..	(.)	1,173	93
116 Mongolia	–	..	..	..	..	..	..	9	28
117 Zimbabwe	–	2	..	..	..	..	..	39	95
118 Myanmar	–	..	128	27	16	..	..	344	185
119 Ghana	–	13	12	..	..	..	..	7	46
120 Lesotho	–	..	..	..	..	..	..	2	100
121 Cambodia	–	(.)	37	2	..	..	(.)	139	397
122 Papua New Guinea	–	..	..	..	..	..	..	4	134
123 Kenya	–	224	5	..	..	..	..	24	177
124 Comoros	–	(.)	..	..	..	..	..	..	..
125 Cameroon	–	49	(.)	..	..	..	..	13	179
126 Congo	–	40	27	..	..	..	..	10	115
Low human development									
127 Pakistan	–	1,202	1	839	183	..	(.)	587	122
128 Togo	–	12	3	..	..	..	..	7	194
129 Nepal	–	128	..	..	..	..	..	50	200
130 Bhutan	–	..	108	..	..	..	..	6	200
131 Lao People's Dem. Rep.	–	..	14	..	..	..	..	29	54
132 Bangladesh	–	22	1	130	277	..	..	137	150
133 Yemen	–	61	2	53	68	..	..	66	103
134 Haiti	–	..	2	..	..	..	..	..	..
135 Madagascar	–	(.)	..	..	..	..	..	21	100
136 Nigeria	–	7	1	..	..	..	..	94	100
137 Djibouti	–	23	2	..	..	..	..	8	280
138 Sudan	–	391	468	10	26	..	..	95	167
139 Mauritania	–	(.)	28	..	..	..	..	16	185
140 Tanzania, U. Rep. of	–	622	..	..	..	..	..	34	84
141 Uganda	–	218	10	32	..	..	..	40	200
142 Congo, Dem. Rep. of the	–	285	248	..	..	..	..	56	116
143 Zambia	–	206	..	..	..	..	..	22	133
144 Côte d'Ivoire	–	138	..	..	..	..	..	8	64
145 Senegal	–	22	11	..	..	..	..	11	109
146 Angola	–	13	351	..	..	..	..	113	227
147 Benin	–	4	..	..	..	..	..	5	107
148 Eritrea	–	3	346	..	..	..	..	200	..
149 Gambia	–	17	(.)	..	..	..	..	1	160
150 Guinea	–	502	(.)	..	..	..	..	10	98

	Internally displaced people (thousands) 1999 [c]	Refugees [a] By country of asylum (thousands) 1999	Refugees [a] By country of origin (thousands) [d] 1999	Conventional arms transfers [b] (1990 prices) Imports US$ millions 1999	Imports Index (1991 = 100) 1999	Exports US$ millions 1999	Exports Share (%) [e] 1995 99	Total armed forces Thousands 1999	Total armed forces Index (1985 = 100) 1999
HDI rank									
151 Malawi	–	2	..	..	..	..	..	5	94
152 Rwanda	–	34	86	29	..	..	..	47	904
153 Mali	–	8	(.)	..	..	..	..	7	151
154 Central African Republic	–	49	(.)	..	..	..	..	3	117
155 Chad	–	24	58	..	..	..	..	30	249
156 Guinea-Bissau	–	7	3	..	..	..	..	7	85
157 Mozambique	–	(.)	..	..	..	..	..	6	55
158 Ethiopia	–	258	54	8	13	..	..	326	150
159 Burkina Faso	–	1	..	..	..	..	..	6	145
160 Burundi	50	22	526	..	..	..	..	40	769
161 Niger	–	(.)	..	..	..	..	..	5	241
162 Sierra Leone	500	7	487	6	..	..	..	3	97
Developing countries	..	7,563 T	..	..	..	..	..	13,011 T	97
Least developed countries	..	2,920 T	..	..	..	..	..	1,887 T	181
Arab States	..	681 T	..	..	..	..	..	1,834 T	112
East Asia and the Pacific	..	623 T	..	..	..	..	..	5,403 T	81
Latin America and the Caribbean	..	61 T	..	..	..	..	..	1,200 T	101
South Asia	..	3,368 T	..	..	..	..	..	2,613 T	105
Sub-Saharan Africa	..	2,829 T	..	..	..	..	..	1,312 T	157
Eastern Europe and the CIS	..	723 T	..	..	..	..	..	2,572 T	..
OECD	..	2,631 T	..	..	..	..	..	5,465 T	75
High-income OECD	..	2,596 T	..	..	..	..	..	3,588 T	68
High human development	..	2,669 T	..	..	..	..	..	5,291 T	75
Medium human development	..	3,926 T	..	..	..	..	..	11,955 T	71
Low human development	..	4,289 T	..	..	..	..	..	2,100 T	149
High income	..	2,607 T	..	..	..	..	..	3,951 T	71
Middle income	..	2,764 T	..	..	..	..	..	10,161 T	67
Low income	..	5,512 T	..	..	..	..	..	5,234 T	120
World	..	11,676 T [f]	..	..	..	..	..	19,346 T	77

a. Data refer to the end of 1999. They do not include Palestinian refugees.

b. Figures are trend indicator values, which are an indicator only of the volume of international arms transfers, not of the actual financial value of such transfers. Published reports of arms transfers provide partial information, as not all transfers are fully reported. The estimates presented are conservative and may understate actual transfers of conventional weapons.

c. Includes only those to whom the United Nations High Commissioner for Refugees (UNHCR) extends assistance in pursuance to a special request by a competent organ of the United Nations

d. The country of origin for many refugees is unavailable or unreported. These data may therefore be underestimates.

e. Calculated using the 1995-99 totals for all countries and non-state actors with exports of major conventional weapons as defined in SIPRI (2000).

f. The aggregate is from UNHCR (2000).

Source: Columns 1-3: UNHCR 2000; columns 4 and 6: SIPRI 2000; columns 5 and 7: calculated on the basis of data on weapons transfers from SIPRI (2000); column 8: IISS 2000; column 9: calculated on the basis of data on armed forces from IISS (2000).

20 Victims of crime

		People victimized by crime (as % of total population) [a]					
	Year [b]	Total crime [c]	Property crime [d]	Robbery	Sexual assault [e]	Assault	Bribery (corruption) [f]
National							
Australia	1999	30.1	13.9	1.2	1.0	2.4	0.3
Austria	1995	18.8	3.1	0.2	1.2	0.8	0.7
Belgium	1999	21.4	7.7	1.0	0.3	1.2	0.3
Canada	1999	23.8	10.4	0.9	0.8	2.3	0.4
Czech Republic	1995	33.3	13.6	1.5	1.3	1.3	7.9
Denmark	1999	23.0	7.6	0.7	0.4	1.4	0.3
England and Wales	1999	26.4	12.2	1.2	0.9	2.8	0.1
Estonia	1994	30.1	14.8	3.4	1.0	2.2	3.8 [g]
Finland	1999	19.1	4.4	0.6	1.1	2.1	0.2
France	1999	21.4	8.7	1.1	0.7	1.4	1.3
Georgia	1995	24.2	13.1	2.5	0.9	1.0	21.9
Italy	1991	24.6	12.7	1.3	0.6	0.2	..
Japan	1999	15.2	3.4	0.1	0.1	0.1	(.)
Lithuania	1995	28.0	12.9	2.0	0.5	1.5	11.0
Malta	1996	23.1	10.9	0.4	0.1	1.1	4.0
Netherlands	1999	25.2	7.4	0.8	0.8	1.0	0.4
New Zealand	1991	29.4	14.8	0.7	1.3	2.4	..
Northern Ireland	1999	15.0	6.2	0.1	0.1	2.1	0.2
Poland	1999	22.7	9.0	1.8	0.2	1.1	5.1
Portugal	1999	15.5	7.5	1.1	0.2	0.4	1.4
Scotland	1999	23.2	7.6	0.7	0.3	3.0	..
Slovakia	1991	22.9	8.3	1.6	0.7	1.3	..
Slovenia	1996	23.3	8.3	0.9	1.2	1.6	1.2
Sweden	1999	24.7	8.4	0.9	1.1	1.2	0.1
Switzerland	1999	18.2	4.5	0.7	0.6	1.0	0.2 [g]
United States	1999	21.1	10.0	0.6	0.4	1.2	0.2
Major city							
Asunción (Paraguay)	1995	34.4	16.7	6.3	1.7	0.9	13.3
Beijing (China)	1991	19.0	2.2	0.5	0.6	0.6	..
Bishkek (Kyrgyzstan)	1995	27.8	11.3	1.6	2.2	2.1	19.3
Bogotá (Colombia)	1996	54.6	27.0	11.5	4.8	2.5	19.5
Bratislava (Slovakia)	1996	36.0	20.8	1.2	0.4	0.5	13.5
Bucharest (Romania)	1995	26.9	9.3	0.8	0.8	2.9	11.4
Budapest (Hungary)	1995	23.4	11.5	0.7	(.)	0.5	3.3
Buenos Aires (Argentina)	1995	61.1	30.8	6.4	6.4	2.3	30.2
Cairo (Egypt)	1991	28.7	12.1	2.2	1.8	1.1	..
Dar es Salaam (Tanzania)	1991	..	23.1	8.2	6.1	1.7	..
Gaborone (Botswana)	1996	31.7	19.7	2.0	0.7	3.2	2.8
Jakarta (Indonesia)	1995	20.9	9.4	0.7	1.3	0.5	29.9
Johannesburg (South Africa)	1995	38.0	18.3	4.7	2.7	4.6	6.9
Kampala (Uganda)	1995	40.9	20.6	2.3	5.1	1.7	19.5
La Paz (Bolivia)	1995	39.8	18.1	5.8	1.5	2.0	24.4
Manila (Philippines)	1995	10.6	3.3	1.5	0.1	0.1	4.3
Minsk (Belarus)	1996	20.7	6.2	1.6	1.1	1.3	13.1
Moscow (Russian Federation)	1995	36.9	16.8	4.3	1.5	2.7	18.0
Mumbai (India)	1995	31.8	6.7	1.3	3.5	0.8	22.9
Riga (Latvia)	1995	31.3	13.4	2.6	0.6	1.0	12.6

	Year [b]	**People victimized by crime** (as % of total population) [a]					
		Total crime [c]	Property crime [d]	Robbery	Sexual assault [e]	Assault	Bribery (corruption) [f]
Rio de Janeiro (Brazil)	1995	44.0	14.7	12.2	7.5	3.4	17.1
San José (Costa Rica)	1995	40.4	21.7	8.9	3.5	1.7	9.2
Skopje (Macedonia, TFYR)	1995	21.1	9.4	1.1	0.3	0.7	7.4
Sofia (Bulgaria)	1996	36.7	20.7	2.5	0.6	2.2	17.8
Tirana (Albania)	1995	26.0	9.9	1.6	2.0	0.8	12.8
Tunis (Tunisia)	1991	37.5	20.1	5.4	1.5	0.4	..
Ulaanbaatar (Mongolia)	1995	41.0	18.3	3.3	0.5	2.4	4.6
Zagreb (Croatia)	1996	19.0	6.8	1.1	0.5	1.5	14.7

Note: Data are from the International Crime Victims Survey (see box 3 in the note on statistics).

a. Data refer to reported victimization.

b. Surveys were conducted in 1992, 1995, 1996/97 and 2000. Data refer to the year preceding the survey.

c. Data refer to 11 crimes recorded in the survey: robbery, burglary, attempted burglary, car theft, car vandalism, bicycle theft, sexual assault, theft from car, theft of personal property, assault and threats and theft of motorcycle or moped.

d. Includes car theft, theft from car, burglary with entry and attempted burglary.

e. Data refer to female population only.

f. Data refer to people who have been asked or expected to pay a bribe by a government official.

g. Data refer to 1995.

Source: Columns 1-7: UNICRI 2001.

... AND ACHIEVING EQUALITY FOR ALL WOMEN AND MEN

HDI rank		Gender-related development index (GDI)		Life expectancy at birth (years) 1999		Adult literacy rate (% age 15 and above) 1999		Combined primary, secondary and tertiary gross enrolment ratio (%) 1999 [a]		Estimated earned income (PPP US$) 1999 [b]		HDI rank minus GDI rank [c]
		Rank	Value	Female	Male	Female	Male	Female	Male	Female	Male	
High human development												
1	Norway	1	0.937	81.3	75.4	.. [d]	.. [d]	99	95	22,037 [e]	34,960 [e]	0
2	Australia	2	0.935	81.7	76.0	.. [d]	.. [d]	118 [f]	114 [f]	19,721	29,469	0
3	Canada	3	0.934	81.4	75.9	.. [d]	.. [d]	98	96	20,016 [e]	32,607 [e]	0
4	Sweden	5	0.931	82.1	77.0	.. [d]	.. [d]	107 [f]	95	18,302 [e]	27,065 [e]	-1
5	Belgium	7	0.928	81.3	75.0	.. [d]	.. [d]	111 [f]	107 [f]	15,510	35,798	-2
6	United States	4	0.932	79.7	73.9	.. [d]	.. [d]	99	91	24,302 [e]	39,655 [e]	2
7	Iceland	6	0.930	81.4	76.8	.. [d]	.. [d]	91	86	21,297	34,335	1
8	Netherlands	8	0.926	80.7	75.3	.. [d]	.. [d]	100	104 [f]	16,405	32,170	0
9	Japan	11	0.921	84.1	77.3	.. [d]	.. [d]	81	83	15,187	35,018	-2
10	Finland	9	0.923	81.0	73.7	.. [d]	.. [d]	108 [f]	99	18,405 [e]	28,023 [e]	1
11	Switzerland	14	0.919	82.0	75.6	.. [d]	.. [d]	81	87	17,977	36,569	-3
12	Luxembourg	19	0.907	80.4	73.9	.. [d]	.. [d]	74 [g]	71 [g]	22,733	63,473 [h]	-7
13	France	10	0.922	82.3	74.5	.. [d]	.. [d]	96	93	17,525	28,554	3
14	United Kingdom	12	0.920	80.0	75.0	.. [d]	.. [d]	112 [f]	100	16,753	27,611	2
15	Denmark	13	0.920	78.6	73.6	.. [d]	.. [d]	101 [f]	94	21,274	30,565	2
16	Austria	16	0.915	80.9	74.7	.. [d]	.. [d]	89	90	16,445 [e]	34,182 [e]	0
17	Germany	15	0.916	80.6	74.3	.. [d]	.. [d]	93	95	15,846	31,994	2
18	Ireland	18	0.908	79.1	73.8	.. [d]	.. [d]	93	89	14,347 [e]	37,641 [e]	0
19	New Zealand	17	0.910	80.1	74.8	.. [d]	.. [d]	103 [f]	95	15,119	23,209	2
20	Italy	20	0.903	81.6	75.2	98.0	98.8	87	81	13,632 [e]	31,238 [e]	0
21	Spain	21	0.901	81.9	74.8	96.7	98.5	99	91	10,741 [e]	25,747 [e]	0
22	Israel	22	0.888	80.4	76.6	93.9	97.8	84	82	12,360 [e]	24,687 [e]	0
23	Greece	24	0.874	80.8	75.5	95.8	98.5	81	80	9,401 [e]	21,595 [e]	-1
24	Hong Kong, China (SAR)	23	0.877	82.2	76.7	89.7	96.4	66	61	15,547	28,396	1
25	Cyprus	25	0.872	80.2	75.7	95.1	98.7	70 [i]	67 [i]	12,511	25,524	0
26	Singapore	26	0.871	79.6	75.2	88.0	96.2	75	76	13,693	27,739	0
27	Korea, Rep. of	29	0.868	78.4	70.9	96.2	99.1 [d]	85	95	9,667	21,676	-2
28	Portugal	28	0.870	79.1	71.9	89.5	94.5	99	94	11,163	21,348	0
29	Slovenia	27	0.871	78.9	71.5	99.6 [d]	99.7 [d]	85	80	12,232 [e]	19,942 [e]	2
30	Malta	31	0.850	80.4	75.2	92.4	91.1	79	82	6,526 [e]	24,017 [e]	-1
31	Barbados	..	..	78.9	73.9	..	..	77	77	..	..	..
32	Brunei Darussalam	30	0.853	78.3	73.6	87.3	94.3	77	76	10,865 [e,j]	24,163 [e,j]	1
33	Czech Republic	32	0.842	78.0	71.2	.. [d]	.. [d]	70	69	10,214 [e]	15,980 [e]	0
34	Argentina	33	0.833	77.0	69.9	96.7	96.8	86	80	6,319 [e]	18,467 [e]	0
35	Slovakia	34	0.829	77.0	69.1	.. [d]	.. [d]	77	74	8,393 [e]	12,912 [e]	0
36	Hungary	35	0.826	75.4	66.8	99.2 [d]	99.5 [d]	83	79	8,381	14,769	0
37	Uruguay	37	0.825	78.3	70.8	98.1	97.3	83	76	5,963 [e]	11,974 [e]	-1
38	Poland	36	0.826	77.3	69.0	99.7 [d]	99.7 [d]	86	83	6,453 [e]	10,561 [e]	1
39	Chile	39	0.817	78.5	72.5	95.4	95.8	77	78	4,613 [e]	12,772 [e]	-1
40	Bahrain	41	0.814	75.6	71.4	82.2	90.5	83	77	6,194	19,228	-2
41	Costa Rica	42	0.813	79.2	74.5	95.5	95.4	66	67	4,518	13,080	-2
42	Bahamas	38	0.819	73.6	64.9	96.4	94.9	77	72	12,138 [e]	18,457 [e]	3
43	Kuwait	40	0.815	78.4	74.3	79.4	84.0	61	57	10,563 [e]	22,086 [e]	2
44	Estonia	..	..	75.8	64.8	..	..	89	84	..	..	..
45	United Arab Emirates	45	0.798	77.8	73.5	78.0	73.8	71	65	5,954 [e]	24,392 [e]	-2
46	Croatia	44	0.799	77.6	69.6	97.1	99.3 [d]	69	68	5,300 [e]	9,612 [e]	0
47	Lithuania	43	0.801	77.0	66.5	99.5 [d]	99.6 [d]	83	77	5,406	8,055	2
48	Qatar	48	0.788	71.0	68.5	82.6	80.1	75	75	5,831 [e,j]	25,753 [e,j]	-2
Medium human development												
49	Trinidad and Tobago	47	0.789	76.5	71.8	91.7	95.4	65	65	4,510 [e]	11,878 [e]	0
50	Latvia	46	0.789	75.6	64.3	99.8 [d]	99.8 [d]	83	80	5,021 [e]	7,716 [e]	2

21 Gender-related development index

HDI rank		Gender-related development index (GDI)		Life expectancy at birth (years) 1999		Adult literacy rate (% age 15 and above) 1999		Combined primary, secondary and tertiary gross enrolment ratio (%) 1999 [a]		Estimated earned income (PPP US$) 1999 [b]		HDI rank minus GDI rank [c]
		Rank	Value	Female	Male	Female	Male	Female	Male	Female	Male	
51	Mexico	49	0.782	75.8	69.8	89.1	93.1	70	71	4,486	12,184	0
52	Panama	50	0.782	76.6	72.0	91.0	92.3	76	73	3,821	7,892	0
53	Belarus	51	0.781	74.4	62.8	99.4 [d]	99.7 [d]	79	75	5,373 [e]	8,599 [e]	0
54	Belize	59	0.755	75.3	72.6	92.9	93.7	72	73	1,858 [e]	7,972 [e]	-7
55	Russian Federation	52	0.774	72.5	60.1	99.4 [d]	99.7 [d]	82	75	5,877 [e]	9,283 [e]	1
56	Malaysia	55	0.768	74.8	69.9	82.8	91.1	67	64	5,153 [e]	11,183 [e]	-1
57	Bulgaria	53	0.770	74.8	67.1	97.7	98.9	76	69	3,951	6,251	2
58	Romania	54	0.769	73.3	66.5	97.1	99.0	70	68	4,441 [e]	7,711 [e]	2
59	Libyan Arab Jamahiriya	61	0.748	72.5	68.6	66.9	90.2	92	92	2,771 [e,j]	12,024 [e,j]	-4
60	Macedonia, TFYR	..	..	75.1	70.9	..	..	70	70	..	..	..
61	Venezuela	57	0.759	76.0	70.2	91.8	92.9	66	64	3,104 [e]	7,855 [e]	1
62	Colombia	56	0.760	74.6	67.8	91.5	91.5	73	73	3,587 [e]	7,965 [e]	3
63	Mauritius	60	0.754	75.1	67.3	80.8	87.6	64	62	4,789 [e]	13,452 [e]	0
64	Suriname	..	..	73.0	67.8	..	..	86	80	..	..	..
65	Lebanon	66	0.741	74.4	71.3	79.8	91.8	81	76	2,160 [e]	7,364 [e]	-5
66	Thailand	58	0.755	72.9	67.0	93.5	97.0	61	60	4,634	7,660	4
67	Fiji	63	0.744	70.7	67.1	90.5	94.7	83	84	2,322 [e]	7,193 [e]	0
68	Saudi Arabia	75	0.719	72.7	70.3	65.9	83.5	60	62	2,715 [e]	17,857 [e]	-11
69	Brazil	64	0.743	71.8	63.9	84.9	84.8	80	79	4,067	10,077	1
70	Philippines	62	0.746	71.1	67.0	94.9	95.3	84	80	2,684	4,910	4
71	Oman	77	0.715	72.4	69.5	59.6	79.1	56	59	3,554 [e,j]	22,001 [e,j]	-10
72	Armenia	65	0.742	75.6	69.6	97.5	99.2 [d]	77	82	1,775 [e]	2,685 [e]	3
73	Peru	73	0.724	71.3	66.3	84.9	94.4	79	81	1,835	7,455	-4
74	Ukraine	67	0.739	73.5	62.7	99.5 [d]	99.7 [d]	78	77	2,488	4,576	3
75	Kazakhstan	..	..	70.2	58.9	..	..	81	73	..	..	..
76	Georgia	..	..	77.0	68.8	..	..	71	69	..	..	..
77	Maldives	69	0.735	65.3	66.9	96.2	96.3	77	77	3,256 [e]	5,531 [e]	2
78	Jamaica	68	0.736	77.1	73.1	90.3	82.4	62	63	2,746 [e]	4,400 [e]	4
79	Azerbaijan	..	..	74.8	67.7	..	..	72	70	..	..	..
80	Paraguay	72	0.725	72.3	67.8	91.9	94.2	64	64	2,105	6,625	1
81	Sri Lanka	70	0.732	75.0	69.3	88.6	94.3	71	68	2,193	4,305	4
82	Turkey	71	0.726	72.1	67.0	75.9	93.2	55	68	3,937 [e]	8,772 [e]	4
83	Turkmenistan	..	..	69.3	62.5	..	..	81	81	..	..	..
84	Ecuador	79	0.711	72.8	67.6	89.1	92.8	74	80	1,331 [e]	4,643 [e]	-3
85	Albania	74	0.721	76.1	70.2	76.9	90.9	71	71	2,248 [e]	4,088 [e]	3
86	Dominican Republic	78	0.712	70.0	65.0	83.2	83.2	75	69	2,794 [e]	8,133 [e]	0
87	China	76	0.715	72.5	68.3	75.5	91.2	73	73	2,841 [e]	4,350 [e]	3
88	Jordan	81	0.698	71.5	68.9	83.4	94.5	57	53	1,728	6,008	-1
89	Tunisia	80	0.700	71.2	68.8	59.3	80.4	72	75	3,055 [e]	8,802 [e]	1
90	Iran, Islamic Rep. of	83	0.696	69.4	67.7	68.7	82.7	69	76	2,331 [e]	8,581 [e]	-1
91	Cape Verde	84	0.696	71.8	66.0	65.1	84.5	76	79	2,687 [e]	6,560 [e]	-1
92	Kyrgyzstan	..	..	71.4	63.4	..	..	70	65	..	..	..
93	Guyana	88	0.693	67.5	59.3	97.9	98.8	66	65	1,949 [e]	5,435 [e]	-4
94	South Africa	85	0.695	56.2	51.6	84.2	85.7	96	89	5,473 [e]	12,452 [e]	0
95	El Salvador	87	0.694	72.9	66.8	75.6	81.3	64	63	2,399	6,363	-1
96	Samoa (Western)	..	..	72.5	65.9	78.8	81.4	67	63	..	..	..
97	Syrian Arab Republic	90	0.677	72.1	69.8	59.3	87.7	61	65	1,881 [e]	6,960 [e]	-3
98	Moldova, Rep. of	82	0.696	70.3	62.8	98.1	99.5 [d]	75	70	1,618 [e]	2,495 [e]	6
99	Uzbekistan	86	0.695	71.7	65.8	84.0	93.1	74	79	1,769 [e]	2,740 [e]	3
100	Algeria	91	0.673	70.8	67.9	55.7	77.4	69	75	2,169 [e]	7,882 [e]	-1

HDI rank		Gender-related development index (GDI)		Life expectancy at birth (years) 1999		Adult literacy rate (% age 15 and above) 1999		Combined primary, secondary and tertiary gross enrolment ratio (%) 1999 [a]		Estimated earned income (PPP US$) 1999 [b]		HDI rank minus GDI rank [c]
		Rank	Value	Female	Male	Female	Male	Female	Male	Female	Male	
101	Viet Nam	89	0.680	70.2	65.5	91.0	95.4	64	69	1,552 [e]	2,170 [e]	2
102	Indonesia	92	0.671	67.7	63.9	81.3	91.5	61	68	1,929 [e]	3,780 [e]	0
103	Tajikistan	93	0.656	70.4	64.5	98.7	99.5 [d]	63	72	769 [e, j]	1,295 [e, j]	0
104	Bolivia	94	0.640	63.8	60.4	78.6	91.7	67	73	1,446 [e]	3,272 [e]	0
105	Egypt	97	0.620	68.5	65.3	42.8	66.1	72	80	1,847	4,954	-2
106	Nicaragua	95	0.628	70.8	66.1	69.8	66.6	65	61	1,338 [e]	3,231 [e]	1
107	Honduras	96	0.623	68.8	63.2	74.1	73.9	63	60	1,202 [e]	3,462 [e]	1
108	Guatemala	98	0.610	67.7	61.9	60.5	75.6	45	53	1,691 [e]	5,622 [e]	0
109	Gabon	..	..	53.8	51.4	..	..	87	85	..	..	..
110	Equatorial Guinea	99	0.598	52.2	49.0	73.3	91.9	59	68	2,659 [e]	6,749 [e]	0
111	Namibia	100	0.594	44.9	44.7	80.4	82.4	80	77	3,676 [e]	7,308 [e]	0
112	Morocco	101	0.579	69.1	65.4	35.1	61.1	46	58	1,930 [e]	4,903 [e]	0
113	Swaziland	102	0.575	48.0	46.0	77.9	80.0	70	74	2,424 [e]	5,594 [e]	0
114	Botswana	103	0.571	41.9	41.6	78.9	73.8	70	70	5,183 [e]	8,638 [e]	0
115	India	105	0.553	63.3	62.4	44.5	67.8	49	62	1,195 [e]	3,236 [e]	-1
116	Mongolia	104	0.566	64.5	60.5	52.1	72.6	64	51	1,363 [e]	2,058 [e]	1
117	Zimbabwe	106	0.548	42.6	43.2	83.8	92.3	63	67	2,159 [e]	3,593 [e]	0
118	Myanmar	107	0.547	58.4	53.6	80.1	88.8	55	55	746 [e, j]	1,311 [e, j]	0
119	Ghana	108	0.538	57.9	55.3	61.5	79.4	39	45	1,618 [e]	2,145 [e]	0
120	Lesotho	111	0.528	48.0	47.8	93.3	71.7	65	57	1,127 [e]	2,594 [e]	-2
121	Cambodia	109	0.534	58.6	54.1	57.7 [k]	80.1 [k]	54	71	1,190 [e]	1,541 [e]	1
122	Papua New Guinea	110	0.530	57.3	55.4	56.0	71.4	35	42	1,742 [e]	2,941 [e]	1
123	Kenya	112	0.512	52.2	50.4	74.8	88.3	51	52	966	1,078	0
124	Comoros	113	0.503	60.8	58.0	52.1	66.3	33	38	996 [e]	1,861 [e]	0
125	Cameroon	114	0.496	50.8	49.1	68.6	81.2	39	47	964 [e]	2,189 [e]	0
126	Congo	115	0.495	53.3	49.0	73.0	86.6	56	69	516 [e]	946 [e]	0
Low human development												
127	Pakistan	117	0.466	59.5	59.8	30.0	58.9	28	51	826 [e]	2,787 [e]	-1
128	Togo	116	0.468	52.8	50.4	39.6	73.6	49	76	908 [e]	1,918 [e]	1
129	Nepal	120	0.461	57.8	58.3	22.8	58.0	52	67	849 [e]	1,607 [e]	-2
130	Bhutan	..	..	62.8	60.3	..	..	..	..	..	..	..
131	Lao People's Dem. Rep.	119	0.463	54.4	51.9	31.7	63.0	52	65	1,169 [e]	1,774 [e]	0
132	Bangladesh	121	0.459	59.0	58.9	29.3	51.7	33	41	1,076 [e]	1,866 [e]	-1
133	Yemen	131	0.410	61.2	59.0	23.9	66.6	29	72	345 [e]	1,272 [e]	-10
134	Haiti	118	0.463	55.4	49.4	46.8	51.1	51	53	1,030 [e]	1,916 [e]	4
135	Madagascar	122	0.456	53.4	51.1	58.8	72.8	43	46	595 [e]	1,005 [e]	1
136	Nigeria	123	0.443	51.7	51.3	54.2	71.3	41	49	520 [e]	1,182 [e]	1
137	Djibouti	..	..	45.3	42.6	52.8	74.9	18	26	..	..	..
138	Sudan	129	0.413	57.0	54.2	44.9	68.9	31	36	308 [e, j]	1,016 [e, j]	-4
139	Mauritania	126	0.428	52.7	49.5	31.4	52.2	37	44	1,163 [e]	2,062 [e]	0
140	Tanzania, U. Rep. of	124	0.432	52.2	50.0	65.7	84.0	32	33	418 [e]	585 [e]	3
141	Uganda	125	0.428	43.8	42.5	55.5	76.8	41	49	942 [e]	1,393 [e]	3
142	Congo, Dem. Rep. of the	128	0.418	52.3	49.7	48.7	72.4	26	37	575 [e]	1,031 [e]	1
143	Zambia	127	0.420	40.6	41.4	70.2	84.6	46	52	577 [e]	934 [e]	3
144	Côte d'Ivoire	132	0.409	48.1	47.5	37.2	53.8	30	46	892 [e]	2,379 [e]	-1
145	Senegal	130	0.413	54.8	51.1	26.7	46.4	31	40	996 [e]	1,844 [e]	2
146	Angola	..	..	46.3	43.6	..	..	21	25	..	..	..
147	Benin	134	0.402	55.4	52.0	23.6	55.4	34	57	769 [e]	1,102 [e]	-1
148	Eritrea	133	0.403	53.2	50.4	39.4	66.5	24	29	601	1,164	1
149	Gambia	136	0.390	47.3	44.5	28.5	43.1	37	53	1,181 [e]	1,987 [e]	-1
150	Guinea	..	..	47.6	46.6	..	..	20	37	..	..	..

HDI rank		Gender-related development index (GDI)		Life expectancy at birth (years) 1999		Adult literacy rate (% age 15 and above) 1999		Combined primary, secondary and tertiary gross enrolment ratio (%) 1999[a]		Estimated earned income (PPP US$) 1999[b]		HDI rank minus GDI rank[c]
		Rank	Value	Female	Male	Female	Male	Female	Male	Female	Male	
151	Malawi	137	0.386	40.2	40.4	45.3	73.8	69	78	485 [e]	689 [e]	-1
152	Rwanda	135	0.391	40.6	39.1	59.1	72.9	39	41	719 [e]	1,054 [e]	2
153	Mali	138	0.370	52.2	50.2	32.7	47.3	22	34	582 [e]	928 [e]	0
154	Central African Republic	139	0.361	46.0	42.7	33.3	58.6	20	29	894 [e]	1,452 [e]	0
155	Chad	140	0.346	46.7	44.2	37.3	50.1	20	42	629 [e]	1,077 [e]	0
156	Guinea-Bissau	143	0.308	45.9	43.1	18.3	58.3	27	47	442 [e]	921 [e]	-2
157	Mozambique	141	0.309	40.8	38.8	27.9	59.3	19	26	713 [e]	1,013 [e]	1
158	Ethiopia	142	0.308	44.9	43.3	31.8	42.8	19	34	414 [e]	844 [e]	1
159	Burkina Faso	144	0.306	47.0	45.1	13.3	33.0	18	28	766 [e]	1,177 [e]	0
160	Burundi	145	0.302	41.5	39.6	39.0	55.6	16	21	472 [e]	690 [e]	0
161	Niger	146	0.260	45.1	44.5	7.9	23.0	12	20	561 [e]	941 [e]	0
162	Sierra Leone	..	..	39.6	37.0	..	..	21	32	..	..	..

a. Preliminary UNESCO estimates, subject to further revision.

b. Because of the lack of gender-disaggregated income data, female and male earned income are crudely estimated on the basis of data on the ratio of the female non-agricultural wage to the male non-agricultural wage, the female and male shares of the economically active population, the total female and male population and GDP per capita (PPP US$) (see technical note 1). Unless otherwise specified, estimates are based on data for the latest year available during 1994-99.

c. The HDI ranks used in this column are those recalculated for the 146 countries with a GDI value. A positive figure indicates that the GDI rank is higher than the HDI rank, a negative the opposite.

d. For purposes of calculating the GDI a value of 99.0% was applied.

e. No wage data available. For purposes of calculating the estimated female and male earned income, an estimate of 75%, the unweighted average for the countries with available data, was used for the ratio of the female non-agricultural wage to the male non-agricultural wage.

f. For purposes of calculating the GDI a value of 100.0% was applied.

g. The ratio is an underestimate, as many secondary and tertiary students pursue their studies in nearby countries.

h. For purposes of calculating the GDI a value of $40,000 (PPP US$) was applied.

i. Excludes Turkish students and population.

j. Calculated on the basis of GDP per capita (PPP US$) data from Aten, Heston and Summers 2001.

k. UNESCO 2001a.

Source: Column 1: determined on the basis of the GDI values in column 2; column 2: calculated on the basis of data in columns 3-10; see technical note 1 for details; columns 3 and 4: UN 2001d; columns 5 and 6: unless otherwise noted, UNESCO 2000a; columns 7 and 8: UNESCO 2001b; columns 9 and 10: unless otherwise noted, calculated on the basis of data on GDP per capita (PPP US$) from World Bank (2001b), data on wages from ILO (2001c), data on the economically active population from ILO (1996) and data on population from UN (2001d); column 11: determined on the basis of the recalculated HDI ranks and the GDI ranks in column 1.

GDI ranks for 146 countries

1	Norway	26	Singapore	51	Belarus	76	China	101	Morocco	126	Mauritania
2	Australia	27	Slovenia	52	Russian Federation	77	Oman	102	Swaziland	127	Zambia
3	Canada	28	Portugal	53	Bulgaria	78	Dominican Republic	103	Botswana	128	Congo, Dem. Rep. of the
4	United States	29	Korea, Rep. of	54	Romania	79	Ecuador	104	Mongolia	129	Sudan
5	Sweden	30	Brunei Darussalam	55	Malaysia	80	Tunisia	105	India	130	Senegal
6	Iceland	31	Malta	56	Colombia	81	Jordan	106	Zimbabwe	131	Yemen
7	Belgium	32	Czech Republic	57	Venezuela	82	Moldova, Rep. of	107	Myanmar	132	Côte d'Ivoire
8	Netherlands	33	Argentina	58	Thailand	83	Iran, Islamic Rep. of	108	Ghana	133	Eritrea
9	Finland	34	Slovakia	59	Belize	84	Cape Verde	109	Cambodia	134	Benin
10	France	35	Hungary	60	Mauritius	85	South Africa	110	Papua New Guinea	135	Rwanda
11	Japan	36	Poland	61	Libyan Arab Jamahiriya	86	Uzbekistan	111	Lesotho	136	Gambia
12	United Kingdom	37	Uruguay	62	Philippines	87	El Salvador	112	Kenya	137	Malawi
13	Denmark	38	Bahamas	63	Fiji	88	Guyana	113	Comoros	138	Mali
14	Switzerland	39	Chile	64	Brazil	89	Viet Nam	114	Cameroon	139	Central African Republic
15	Germany	40	Kuwait	65	Armenia	90	Syrian Arab Republic	115	Congo	140	Chad
16	Austria	41	Bahrain	66	Lebanon	91	Algeria	116	Togo	141	Mozambique
17	New Zealand	42	Costa Rica	67	Ukraine	92	Indonesia	117	Pakistan	142	Ethiopia
18	Ireland	43	Lithuania	68	Jamaica	93	Tajikistan	118	Haiti	143	Guinea-Bissau
19	Luxembourg	44	Croatia	69	Maldives	94	Bolivia	119	Lao People's Dem. Rep.	144	Burkina Faso
20	Italy	45	United Arab Emirates	70	Sri Lanka	95	Nicaragua	120	Nepal	145	Burundi
21	Spain	46	Latvia	71	Turkey	96	Honduras	121	Bangladesh	146	Niger
22	Israel	47	Trinidad and Tobago	72	Paraguay	97	Egypt	122	Madagascar		
23	Hong Kong, China (SAR)	48	Qatar	73	Peru	98	Guatemala	123	Nigeria		
24	Greece	49	Mexico	74	Albania	99	Equatorial Guinea	124	Tanzania, U. Rep. of		
25	Cyprus	50	Panama	75	Saudi Arabia	100	Namibia	125	Uganda		

... AND ACHIEVING EQUALITY FOR ALL WOMEN AND MEN

HDI rank		Gender empowerment measure (GEM)		Seats in parliament held by women (as % of total) [a]	Female legislators, senior officials and managers (as % of total) [b]	Female professional and technical workers (as % of total) [b]	Ratio of estimated female to male earned income [c]
		Rank	Value				
High human development							
1	Norway	1	0.836	36.4	31 [d]	58 [d]	0.63
2	Australia	9	0.738	25.4	25	47	0.67
3	Canada	5	0.763	23.6	35	53	0.61
4	Sweden	3	0.809	42.7	29	49	0.68
5	Belgium	14	0.692	24.9	19 [d]	50 [d]	0.43
6	United States	10	0.738	13.8	45 [d]	53 [d]	0.61
7	Iceland	2	0.815	34.9	25	53	0.62
8	Netherlands	7	0.755	32.9	23	46	0.51
9	Japan	31	0.520	10.8	9 [d]	44 [d]	0.43
10	Finland	4	0.783	36.5	29 [d]	62 [d]	0.66
11	Switzerland	13	0.696	22.4	20	40	0.49
12	Luxembourg	..	..	16.7	..	..	..
13	France	..	..	9.1	..	..	..
14	United Kingdom	16	0.671	17.0	33	45	0.61
15	Denmark	12	0.705	37.4	3	50	0.70
16	Austria	11	0.723	25.1	26	49	0.48
17	Germany	8	0.749	30.4	26	50	0.50
18	Ireland	18	0.644	13.7	34	50	0.38
19	New Zealand	6	0.756	30.8	37	52	0.65
20	Italy	29	0.536	10.0	19	43	0.44
21	Spain	15	0.688	26.6	31	44	0.42
22	Israel	24	0.569	12.5	25	54	0.50
23	Greece	39	0.502	8.7	25	46	0.44
24	Hong Kong, China (SAR)	..	..	–	22	38	..
25	Cyprus	..	..	7.1	..	..	..
26	Singapore	35	0.509	6.5	21	42	0.49
27	Korea, Rep. of	61	0.358	5.9	5	31	0.45
28	Portugal	20	0.629	18.7	32	51	0.52
29	Slovenia	22	0.574	12.2	31	51	0.61
30	Malta	..	..	9.2	..	..	..
31	Barbados	17	0.648	20.4	39 [d]	51 [d]	0.60
32	Brunei Darussalam	..	..	..	..	..	..
33	Czech Republic	26	0.546	14.2	23	54	0.64
34	Argentina	..	..	21.3	..	..	..
35	Slovakia	27	0.546	14.0	32	60	0.65
36	Hungary	41	0.493	8.3	34	62	0.57
37	Uruguay	42	0.491	11.5	28 [d]	61 [d]	0.50
38	Poland	32	0.518	12.7	34	60	0.61
39	Chile	49	0.445	8.9	22 [d]	51 [d]	0.36
40	Bahrain	..	..	..	9 [d]	20 [d]	..
41	Costa Rica	23	0.571	19.3	30	45	0.35
42	Bahamas	19	0.639	19.6	31	51	0.66
43	Kuwait	..	..	0.0	..	..	..
44	Estonia	25	0.552	17.8	35	67	0.63
45	United Arab Emirates	..	..	0.0	..	..	..
46	Croatia	30	0.527	16.2	26	52	0.55
47	Lithuania	45	0.474	10.6	39	69	0.67
48	Qatar	..	..	..	..	..	..
Medium human development							
49	Trinidad and Tobago	21	0.599	20.9	40	51	0.38
50	Latvia	28	0.540	17.0	39	65	0.65

HDI rank		Gender empowerment measure (GEM)		Seats in parliament held by women (as % of total) [a]	Female legislators, senior officials and managers (as % of total) [b]	Female professional and technical workers (as % of total) [b]	Ratio of estimated female to male earned income [c]
		Rank	Value				
51	Mexico	37	0.507	15.9	23	40	0.37
52	Panama	44	0.475	9.9	33 [d]	46 [d]	0.48
53	Belarus	..	..	18.4	..	..	..
54	Belize	40	0.496	13.5	37 [d]	39 [d]	0.23
55	Russian Federation	53	0.434	5.6	37	64	0.63
56	Malaysia	38	0.503	14.5	21 [d]	44 [d]	0.46
57	Bulgaria	..	..	10.8	..	..	..
58	Romania	48	0.449	9.3	26	56	0.58
59	Libyan Arab Jamahiriya	..	..	..	..	..	..
60	Macedonia, TFYR	..	..	6.7	..	..	..
61	Venezuela	51	0.439	9.7	24 [d]	58 [d]	0.40
62	Colombia	36	0.507	12.2	40 [d]	48 [d]	0.45
63	Mauritius	59	0.403	5.7	23	38	0.36
64	Suriname	52	0.438	17.6	13 [d]	69 [d]	0.36
65	Lebanon	..	..	2.3	..	..	..
66	Thailand	..	..	..	22 [d]	55 [d]	..
67	Fiji	..	..	..	48 [d]	10 [d]	..
68	Saudi Arabia	..	..	..	..	..	..
69	Brazil	..	..	5.9	..	61 [d]	..
70	Philippines	46	0.470	11.8	33 [d]	63 [d]	0.55
71	Oman	..	..	..	..	..	..
72	Armenia	..	..	3.1	..	..	..
73	Peru	33	0.516	20.0	23	41	0.25
74	Ukraine	54	0.428	7.8	38	63	0.54
75	Kazakhstan	..	..	11.2	..	..	..
76	Georgia	..	..	7.2	..	..	..
77	Maldives	..	..	6.0	..	..	..
78	Jamaica	..	..	16.0	..	..	..
79	Azerbaijan	..	..	10.5	..	..	..
80	Paraguay	57	0.407	8.0	23 [d]	54 [d]	0.32
81	Sri Lanka	56	0.409	4.0	50	50	0.51
82	Turkey	63	0.308	4.2	9 [d]	36 [d]	0.45
83	Turkmenistan	..	..	26.0	..	..	..
84	Ecuador	43	0.482	14.6	28 [d]	47 [d]	0.29
85	Albania	..	..	5.2	..	..	..
86	Dominican Republic	34	0.510	14.5	31	49	0.34
87	China	..	..	21.8	..	..	..
88	Jordan	..	..	2.5	..	..	..
89	Tunisia	..	..	11.5	..	..	..
90	Iran, Islamic Rep. of	..	..	3.4	..	..	..
91	Cape Verde	..	..	11.1	..	..	..
92	Kyrgyzstan	..	..	6.7	..	..	..
93	Guyana	..	..	18.5	..	..	..
94	South Africa	..	..	27.9 [e]	..	..	..
95	El Salvador	50	0.440	9.5	28	47	0.38
96	Samoa (Western)	..	..	..	..	..	..
97	Syrian Arab Republic	..	..	10.4	..	..	..
98	Moldova, Rep. of	..	..	8.9	..	..	..
99	Uzbekistan	..	..	7.2	..	..	..
100	Algeria	..	..	4.0	..	..	..

HDI rank		Gender empowerment measure (GEM)		Seats in parliament held by women (as % of total) [a]	Female legislators, senior officials and managers (as % of total) [b]	Female professional and technical workers (as % of total) [b]	Ratio of estimated female to male earned income [c]
		Rank	Value				
101	Viet Nam	..	..	26.0	..	..	..
102	Indonesia	..	..	8.0	..	..	..
103	Tajikistan	..	..	12.4	..	..	..
104	Bolivia	55	0.425	10.2	25	43	0.44
105	Egypt	64	0.258	2.4	11	29	0.37
106	Nicaragua	..	..	9.7	..	..	..
107	Honduras	47	0.449	9.4	36 [d]	51 [d]	0.35
108	Guatemala	..	..	8.8	..	..	..
109	Gabon	..	..	10.9	..	..	..
110	Equatorial Guinea	..	..	5.0	..	..	..
111	Namibia	..	..	20.4	..	..	..
112	Morocco	..	..	0.7	..	..	..
113	Swaziland	60	0.385	6.3	24 [d]	61 [d]	0.43
114	Botswana	..	..	17.0	..	..	..
115	India	..	..	..	..	..	..
116	Mongolia	..	..	10.5	..	..	..
117	Zimbabwe	..	..	9.3	..	..	..
118	Myanmar	..	..	..	..	..	..
119	Ghana	..	..	9.0	..	..	..
120	Lesotho	..	..	10.7	..	..	..
121	Cambodia	..	..	9.3	..	..	..
122	Papua New Guinea	..	..	1.8	..	..	..
123	Kenya	..	..	3.6	..	..	..
124	Comoros	..	..	..	..	..	..
125	Cameroon	..	..	5.6	..	..	..
126	Congo	..	..	12.0	..	..	..
Low human development							
127	Pakistan	..	..	..	8 [d]	25 [d]	..
128	Togo	..	..	4.9	..	..	..
129	Nepal	..	..	7.9	..	..	..
130	Bhutan	..	..	9.3	..	..	..
131	Lao People's Dem. Rep.	..	..	21.2	..	..	..
132	Bangladesh	62	0.309	9.1	5 [d]	35 [d]	0.58
133	Yemen	..	..	0.7	..	..	..
134	Haiti	..	..	..	..	..	..
135	Madagascar	..	..	8.0	..	..	..
136	Nigeria	..	..	3.3	..	..	..
137	Djibouti	..	..	0.0	..	..	..
138	Sudan	..	..	9.7	..	..	..
139	Mauritania	..	..	3.0	..	..	..
140	Tanzania, U. Rep. of	..	..	22.2	..	..	..
141	Uganda	..	..	17.8	..	..	..
142	Congo, Dem. Rep. of the	..	..	..	..	..	..
143	Zambia	..	..	10.1	..	..	..
144	Côte d'Ivoire	..	..	8.5	..	..	..
145	Senegal	..	..	14.0	..	..	..
146	Angola	..	..	15.5	..	..	..
147	Benin	..	..	6.0	..	..	..
148	Eritrea	58	0.404	14.7	17	30	0.52
149	Gambia	..	..	2.0	..	..	..
150	Guinea	..	..	8.8	..	..	..

HDI rank	Gender empowerment measure (GEM)		Seats in parliament held by women (as % of total) [a]	Female legislators, senior officials and managers (as % of total) [b]	Female professional and technical workers (as % of total) [h]	Ratio of estimated female to male earned income [c]
	Rank	Value				
151 Malawi	..	..	9.3	..	..	..
152 Rwanda	..	..	25.7	..	..	..
153 Mali	..	..	12.2	..	..	..
154 Central African Republic	..	..	7.3	..	..	..
155 Chad	..	..	2.4	..	..	..
156 Guinea-Bissau	..	..	7.8	..	..	..
157 Mozambique	..	..	30.0	..	..	..
158 Ethiopia	..	..	7.8	..	..	..
159 Burkina Faso	..	..	11.0	..	..	..
160 Burundi	..	..	14.4	..	..	..
161 Niger	..	..	1.2	..	..	..
162 Sierra Leone	..	..	8.8	..	..	..

a. Data are as of 8 March 2001.

b. Data refer to the latest year available during the period 1990-99.

c. Calculated on the basis of data in columns 9 and 10 in table 21. Estimates are based on data for the latest year available during the period 1994-99.

d. Data are based on the International Standard Classification of Occupations (ISCO-68) as defined in ILO (2001c).

e. Calculated on the basis of the 54 permanent seats (that is, excluding the 36 special rotating delegates appointed on an ad hoc basis).

Source: Column 1: determined on the basis of the GEM values in column 2; *column 2:* calculated on the basis of data in columns 3-5 in this table and in columns 9 and 10 in table 21 (see technical note 1 for details); *column 3:* calculated on the basis of data on parliamentary seats from IPU (2001c); *columns 4 and 5:* calculated on the basis of occupational data from ILO (2001c); *column 6:* calculated on the basis of data in columns 9 and 10 in table 21.

GEM ranks for 64 countries

1 Norway	17 Barbados	33 Peru	49 Chile
2 Iceland	18 Ireland	34 Dominican Republic	50 El Salvador
3 Sweden	19 Bahamas	35 Singapore	51 Venezuela
4 Finland	20 Portugal	36 Colombia	52 Suriname
5 Canada	21 Trinidad and Tobago	37 Mexico	53 Russian Federation
6 New Zealand	22 Slovenia	38 Malaysia	54 Ukraine
7 Netherlands	23 Costa Rica	39 Greece	55 Bolivia
8 Germany	24 Israel	40 Belize	56 Sri Lanka
9 Australia	25 Estonia	41 Hungary	57 Paraguay
10 United States	26 Czech Republic	42 Uruguay	58 Eritrea
11 Austria	27 Slovakia	43 Ecuador	59 Mauritius
12 Denmark	28 Latvia	44 Panama	60 Swaziland
13 Switzerland	29 Italy	45 Lithuania	61 Korea, Rep. of
14 Belgium	30 Croatia	46 Philippines	62 Bangladesh
15 Spain	31 Japan	47 Honduras	63 Turkey
16 United Kingdom	32 Poland	48 Romania	64 Egypt

... AND ACHIEVING EQUALITY FOR ALL WOMEN AND MEN

HDI rank	Adult literacy		Youth literacy		Net primary enrolment		Net secondary enrolment		Gross tertiary enrolment [a]	
	Female rate (% age 15 and above) 1999	Female rate as % of male rate 1999	Female rate (% age 15-24) 1999	Female rate as % of male rate 1999	Female ratio (%) 1995-97 [b]	Female ratio as % of male ratio 1995-97 [b]	Female ratio (%) 1995-97 [b]	Female ratio as % of male ratio 1995-97 [b]	Female ratio (%) 1994-97 [b]	Male ratio (%) 1994-97 [b]
High human development										
1 Norway	..	..	..	..	100	100	98	101	71	53
2 Australia	..	..	..	..	95	100	89	101	83	77
3 Canada	..	..	..	..	94	98	90	99	95	81
4 Sweden	..	..	..	..	100	100	99	100	57	43
5 Belgium	..	..	..	..	98	100	87	98	57	55
6 United States	..	..	..	..	95	100	90	100	92	71
7 Iceland	..	..	..	..	98	100	88	102	45	30
8 Netherlands	..	..	..	..	99	99	91	101	46	48
9 Japan	..	..	..	..	..	..	..	..	36	44
10 Finland	..	..	..	..	98	100	94	101	80	68
11 Switzerland	..	..	..	..	..	..	..	..	25	40
12 Luxembourg	..	..	..	..	..	..	70	108	7 [c]	12 [c]
13 France	..	..	..	..	100	100	95	101	57	45
14 United Kingdom	..	..	..	..	100	100	93	103	56	49
15 Denmark	..	..	..	..	100	100	..	..	53	43
16 Austria	..	..	..	..	..	..	89	101	49	48
17 Germany	..	..	..	..	89	102	89	100	44	50
18 Ireland	..	..	..	..	93	102	88	105	43	39
19 New Zealand	..	..	..	..	98	101	91	102	73	53
20 Italy	98.0	99	99.8	100	100	100	..	..	52	42
21 Spain	96.7	98	99.8	100	100	100	..	..	56	47
22 Israel	93.9	96	99.6	100	..	..	..	..	41	36
23 Greece	95.8	97	99.8	100	93	100	88	103	46	47
24 Hong Kong, China (SAR)	89.7	93	99.8	101	91	103	71	107	..	..
25 Cyprus	95.1	96	99.8	100	81	101	..	..	25 [d]	20 [d]
26 Singapore	88.0	92	99.8	100	..	..	..	..	31	37
27 Korea, Rep. of	96.2	97	99.8	100	93	101	97	100	52	82
28 Portugal	89.5	95	99.8	100	..	..	..	..	44	33
29 Slovenia	99.6	100	99.8	100	94	99	90	103	41	31
30 Malta	92.4	101	99.8	103	100	100	79	100	32	27
31 Barbados	..	..	..	..	..	..	..	..	34	23
32 Brunei Darussalam	87.3	93	99.8	101	93	100	..	..	8	5
33 Czech Republic	..	..	..	..	89	100	89	103	23	24
34 Argentina	96.7	100	98.8	100	..	..	..	..	..	..
35 Slovakia	..	..	..	..	..	..	..	..	23	22
36 Hungary	99.2	100	99.8	100	82	99	87	102	26	22
37 Uruguay	98.1	101	99.6	101	93	101	..	..	..	..
38 Poland	99.7	100	99.8	100	96	100	..	..	28	21
39 Chile	95.4	100	99.0	100	88	97	60	108	29	34
40 Bahrain	82.2	91	98.3	100	98	103	88	108	..	..
41 Costa Rica	95.5	100	98.6	101	89	101	43	113	28	33
42 Bahamas	96.4	102	98.3	102	..	..	..	..	..	..
43 Kuwait	79.4	95	92.8	101	67	98	58	100	24	15
44 Estonia	..	..	..	..	92	98	90	105	46	38
45 United Arab Emirates	78.0	106	94.5	111	79	98	71	106	21	5
46 Croatia	97.1	98	99.8	100	84	99	80	102	29	27
47 Lithuania	99.5	100	99.8	100	93	99	85	101	38	25
48 Qatar	82.6	103	96.8	105	82	90	70	102	41	14
Medium human development										
49 Trinidad and Tobago	91.7	96	97.1	99	88	100	..	..	7	9
50 Latvia	99.8	100	99.8	100	91	96	83	100	40	27

23 Gender inequality in education

HDI rank		Adult literacy Female rate (% age 15 and above) 1999	Adult literacy Female rate as % of male rate 1999	Youth literacy Female rate (% age 15-24) 1999	Youth literacy Female rate as % of male rate 1999	Net primary enrolment Female ratio (%) 1995-97 [b]	Net primary enrolment Female ratio as % of male ratio 1995 97 [b]	Net secondary enrolment Female ratio (%) 1995-97 [b]	Net secondary enrolment Female ratio as % of male ratio 1995-97 [b]	Gross tertiary enrolment [a] Female ratio (%) 1994-97 [b]	Gross tertiary enrolment [a] Male ratio (%) 1994-97 [b]
51	Mexico	89.1	96	96.2	99	100	100	..	..	15	17
52	Panama	91.0	99	96.3	99	..	..	..	..	..	..
53	Belarus	99.4	100	99.8	100	..	..	..	..	49	39
54	Belize	92.9	100	98.5	101	..	..	..	..	..	..
55	Russian Federation	99.4	100	99.8	100	..	..	..	..	49	37
56	Malaysia	82.8	91	97.4	100	..	..	..	..	..	..
57	Bulgaria	97.7	99	99.5	100	91	97	69	73	52	31
58	Romania	97.1	98	99.7	100	97	99	75	102	24	21
59	Libyan Arab Jamahiriya	66.9	74	92.6	93	..	..	..	..	..	..
60	Macedonia, TFYR	..	..	..	..	94	98	55	97	22	17
61	Venezuela	91.8	99	98.5	101	85	102	27	153	..	..
62	Colombia	91.5	100	97.5	101	..	..	49	115	17	16
63	Mauritius	80.8	92	94.3	101	98	100	61	110	6	6
64	Suriname	..	..	..	..	..	..	..	..	..	..
65	Lebanon	79.8	87	92.6	95	..	..	71	115	27	27
66	Thailand	93.5	96	98.3	99	..	..	..	..	..	..
67	Fiji	90.5	96	99.0	100	..	..	..	..	..	..
68	Saudi Arabia	65.9	79	89.8	94	58	94	41	76	15	17
69	Brazil	84.9	100	94.1	104	..	..	..	..	..	..
70	Philippines	94.9	100	98.7	100	..	..	..	..	33	25
71	Oman	59.6	75	95.3	96	66	98	57	99	7	9
72	Armenia	97.5	98	99.7	100	..	..	..	..	14	11
73	Peru	84.9	90	95.1	97	..	..	..	..	..	..
74	Ukraine	99.5	100	99.9	100	..	..	..	..	..	..
75	Kazakhstan	..	..	..	..	..	..	..	..	37	29
76	Georgia	..	..	..	..	87	99	74	98	44	40
77	Maldives	96.2	100	99.3	100	..	..	..	..	..	..
78	Jamaica	90.3	110	97.2	108	..	..	..	..	7	9
79	Azerbaijan	..	..	..	..	..	..	..	..	18	17
80	Paraguay	91.9	98	96.9	100	91	101	39	107	11	10
81	Sri Lanka	88.6	94	96.4	99	..	..	..	..	4	6
82	Turkey	75.9	81	93.6	95	96	96	43	73	15	27
83	Turkmenistan	..	..	..	..	..	..	..	..	..	..
84	Ecuador	89.1	96	96.4	99	97	101	..	..	..	..
85	Albania	76.9	85	96.9	98	100	100	..	..	14	10
86	Dominican Republic	83.2	100	91.5	102	85	102	33	135	27	19
87	China	75.5	83	96.0	97	100	100	..	..	4	7
88	Jordan	83.4	88	99.6	100	..	..	..	..	..	..
89	Tunisia	59.3	74	88.2	91	98	98	54	101	12	15
90	Iran, Islamic Rep. of	68.7	83	91.3	95	88	96	68	92	13	22
91	Cape Verde	65.1	77	85.4	93	..	..	48	102	..	..
92	Kyrgyzstan	..	..	..	..	93	96	..	..	13	11
93	Guyana	97.9	99	99.8	100	87	100	68	106	12	11
94	South Africa	84.2	98	91.0	100	96	101	67	149	16	18
95	El Salvador	75.6	93	87.1	98	78	101	23	113	18	18
96	Samoa (Western)	78.8	97	87.2	101	95	99	..	..	..	..
97	Syrian Arab Republic	59.3	68	77.8	82	87	93	36	90	13	18
98	Moldova, Rep. of	98.1	99	99.8	100	..	..	..	..	29	24
99	Uzbekistan	84.0	90	94.9	97	..	..	..	..	..	..
100	Algeria	55.7	72	83.8	91	91	93	54	94	10	14

HDI rank		Adult literacy		Youth literacy		Net primary enrolment		Net secondary enrolment		Gross tertiary enrolment [a]	
		Female rate (% age 15 and above) 1999	Female rate as % of male rate 1999	Female rate (% age 15-24) 1999	Female rate as % of male rate 1999	Female ratio (%) 1995-97 [b]	Female ratio as % of male ratio 1995-97 [b]	Female ratio (%) 1995-97 [b]	Female ratio as % of male ratio 1995-97 [b]	Female ratio (%) 1994-97 [b]	Male ratio (%) 1994-97 [b]
101	Viet Nam	91.0	95	97.0	100	..	..	..	..	..	..
102	Indonesia	81.3	89	96.8	99	93	97	..	..	8	15
103	Tajikistan	98.7	99	99.8	100	..	..	..	..	13	27
104	Bolivia	78.6	86	93.5	96	..	..	..	..	..	..
105	Egypt	42.8	65	61.7	81	88	89	64	90	16	24
106	Nicaragua	69.8	105	76.1	108	78	103	35	118	12	11
107	Honduras	74.1	100	84.5	104	..	..	..	..	9	11
108	Guatemala	60.5	80	72.4	85	68	89	..	..	..	..
109	Gabon	..	..	..	..	..	..	..	..	..	..
110	Equatorial Guinea	73.3	80	94.9	97	..	..	..	..	..	..
111	Namibia	80.4	98	93.0	104	97	108	44	134	10	6
112	Morocco	35.1	57	57.0	75	67	80	..	..	9	13
113	Swaziland	77.9	97	90.8	102	91	101	41	119	6	6
114	Botswana	78.9	107	91.9	110	83	105	52	117	5	6
115	India	44.5	66	63.8	81	..	..	..	..	5	8
116	Mongolia	52.1	72	73.0	87	86	105	61	133	24	10
117	Zimbabwe	83.8	91	95.5	97	..	..	..	..	4	9
118	Myanmar	80.1	90	90.2	99	..	..	..	..	7	4
119	Ghana	61.5	77	87.3	94	..	..	..	..	..	..
120	Lesotho	93.3	130	98.4	120	71	117	24	185	3	2
121	Cambodia	..	..	..	..	92	92	16	55	1	2
122	Papua New Guinea	56.0	78	70.4	88	..	..	..	..	2	4
123	Kenya	74.8	85	93.7	98	..	..	..	..	..	..
124	Comoros	52.1	79	61.1	84	..	..	..	..	(.)	1
125	Cameroon	68.6	84	93.1	99	..	..	..	..	..	..
126	Congo	73.0	84	96.3	98	..	..	..	..	..	..
Low human development											
127	Pakistan	30.0	51	48.4	64	..	..	..	..	..	..
128	Togo	39.6	54	57.6	66	72	77	13	44	1	6
129	Nepal	22.8	39	40.7	54	..	..	..	..	..	..
130	Bhutan	..	..	..	..	..	..	..	..	..	..
131	Lao People's Dem. Rep.	31.7	50	56.1	69	72	91	21	79	2	4
132	Bangladesh	29.3	57	39.4	65	..	..	..	..	..	..
133	Yemen	23.9	36	43.8	53	..	..	..	..	1	7
134	Haiti	46.8	92	63.6	100	55	98	..	..	..	..
135	Madagascar	58.8	81	75.6	91	62	104	..	..	2	2
136	Nigeria	54.2	76	82.5	93	..	..	..	..	..	..
137	Djibouti	52.8	71	78.1	89	27	75	10	68	(.)	(.)
138	Sudan	44.9	65	70.0	85	..	..	..	..	..	..
139	Mauritania	31.4	60	40.4	67	58	92	..	..	1	6
140	Tanzania, U. Rep. of	65.7	78	87.8	94	49	103	..	..	(.)	1
141	Uganda	55.5	72	71.3	84	..	..	..	..	1	3
142	Congo, Dem. Rep. of the	48.7	67	73.5	83	..	..	..	..	..	..
143	Zambia	70.2	83	84.6	94	74	98	..	..	1	4
144	Côte d'Ivoire	37.2	69	58.1	84	47	75	..	..	3	9
145	Senegal	26.7	57	40.7	69	55	85	..	..	..	..
146	Angola	..	..	..	..	35	109	..	..	..	..
147	Benin	23.6	43	36.9	48	48	61	..	..	1	5
148	Eritrea	39.4	59	60.7	76	29	90	14	85	(.)	2
149	Gambia	28.5	66	47.6	74	57	79	..	..	1	2
150	Guinea	..	..	..	..	33	65	..	..	(.)	2

23 Gender inequality in education

HDI rank		Adult literacy		Youth literacy		Net primary enrolment		Net secondary enrolment		Gross tertiary enrolment [a]	
		Female rate (% age 15 and above) 1999	Female rate as % of male rate 1999	Female rate (% age 15 24) 1999	Female rate as % of male rate 1999	Female ratio (%) 1995-97 [b]	Female ratio as % of male ratio 1995-97 [b]	Female ratio (%) 1995-97 [b]	Female ratio as % of male ratio 1995-97 [b]	Female ratio (%) 1994-97 [b]	Male ratio (%) 1994-97 [b]
151	Malawi	45.3	61	59.9	74	..	..	..	..	(.)	1
152	Rwanda	59.1	81	80.5	95	..	..	..	..	..	..
153	Mali	32.7	69	58.1	82	25	66	..	..	1	2
154	Central African Republic	33.3	57	56.9	76	..	..	..	..	..	..
155	Chad	32.3	65	57.7	80	38	58	3	30	(.)	1
156	Guinea-Bissau	18.3	31	32.5	40	..	..	..	..	..	..
157	Mozambique	27.9	47	44.8	60	34	76	5	67	(.)	1
158	Ethiopia	31.8	74	51.8	97	27	62	..	..	(.)	1
159	Burkina Faso	13.3	40	22.2	50	27	67	..	..	(.)	1
160	Burundi	39.0	70	59.9	93	28	88	..	..	..	..
161	Niger	7.9	34	13.2	42	19	63	4	61	..	..
162	Sierra Leone	..	..	..	..	..	..	..	..	..	..
Developing countries		65.3	81	80.3	91	..	..	..	..	..	..
Least developed countries		41.9	68	57.7	79	..	..	..	..	..	..
Arab States		49.0	67	71.5	84	..	..	..	..	..	..
East Asia and the Pacific		78.7	86	96.1	98	..	..	..	..	..	..
Latin America and the Caribbean		86.9	98	94.2	101	..	..	..	..	..	..
South Asia		43.2	65	61.0	78	..	..	..	..	..	..
Sub-Saharan Africa		52.6	77	72.5	89	..	..	..	..	..	..
Eastern Europe and the CIS		98.2	99	99.3	100	..	..	..	..	..	..
OECD		..	..	..	..	..	..	..	..	..	..
High-income OECD		..	..	..	..	..	..	..	..	..	..
High human development		..	..	..	..	..	..	..	..	..	..
Medium human development		71.6	84	86.2	94	..	..	..	..	..	..
Low human development		38.2	63	57.2	77	..	..	..	..	..	..
High income		..	..	..	..	..	..	..	..	..	..
Middle income		80.2	88	94.0	97	..	..	..	..	..	..
Low income		52.2	74	68.6	84	..	..	..	..	..	..
World		..	..	..	..	..	..	..	..	..	..

a. Tertiary enrolment is generally calculated as a gross ratio.

b. Data refer to the most recent year available during the period specified.

c. The ratio is an underestimate, as many students pursue their studies in nearby countries.

d. Excludes Turkish institutions.

Source: Column 1: UNESCO 2000a; *column 2:* calculated on the basis of data on adult literacy rates from UNESCO (2000a); *column 3:* UNESCO 2000c; *column 4:* calculated on the basis of data on youth literacy rates from UNESCO (2000c); *columns 5 and 7:* UNESCO 2001c; *column 6:* calculated on the basis of data on net primary enrolment ratios from UNESCO (2001c); *column 8:* calculated on the basis of data on net secondary enrolment ratios from UNESCO (2001c); *columns 9 and 10:* UNESCO 1999.

24 Gender inequality in economic activity

		Female economic activity rate (age 15 and above)			Employment by economic activity (%)						Contributing family workers	
					Agriculture		Industry		Services		Female (as % of total)	Male (as % of total)
HDI rank		Rate (%) 1999	Index (1985 = 100) 1999	As % of male rate 1999	Female 1994-97 [a]	Male 1994-97 [a]	Female 1994-97 [a]	Male 1994-97 [a]	Female 1994-97 [a]	Male 1994-97 [a]	1994-99 [a]	1994-99 [a]
High human development												
1	Norway	58.9	114	84	2	7	10	35	87	59	67	33
2	Australia	55.6	114	76	4	6	11	31	85	63	62	38
3	Canada	59.8	110	81	2	5	12	32	86	63	66	34
4	Sweden	63.0	109	89	1	4	12	39	87	57	64	36
5	Belgium	39.8	113	65	..	..	..	..	..	..	85	15
6	United States	58.4	110	80	1	4	13	34	85	63	67	33
7	Iceland	67.6	103	85	4	12	15	35	81	53	50	50
8	Netherlands	45.3	120	66	2	4	9	31	85	62	84	16
9	Japan	51.1	106	67	6	5	24	39	69	55	82	18
10	Finland	57.4	101	86	5	9	14	39	81	52	44	56
11	Switzerland	51.6	112	66	4	5	15	35	82	59	..	..
12	Luxembourg	37.6	109	57	..	..	..	..	..	..	..	..
13	France	48.1	107	76	..	..	..	..	..	..	..	..
14	United Kingdom	52.6	110	74	1	3	13	38	86	59	65	35
15	Denmark	61.9	104	84	2	5	15	36	83	58	..	..
16	Austria	44.5	104	65	8	6	14	42	78	52	68	32
17	Germany	48.4	105	69	3	3	19	46	79	51	75	25
18	Ireland	36.4	117	51	3	15	15	34	79	49	56	44
19	New Zealand	56.9	122	78	6	11	13	33	81	56	64	36
20	Italy	38.4	111	58	7	7	22	38	72	55	57	43
21	Spain	37.3	120	55	6	10	14	39	80	52	62	38
22	Israel	48.3	120	67	1	3	14	38	84	58	78	22
23	Greece	37.5	119	57	23	18	13	28	63	54	71	29
24	Hong Kong, China (SAR)	49.1	103	63	(.)	(.)	15	31	85	69	..	..
25	Cyprus	49.1	110	62	10	11	18	30	71	58	..	..
26	Singapore	50.2	105	64	(.)	(.)	25	34	75	66	75	25
27	Korea, Rep. of	53.0	110	69	13	10	21	38	66	52	88	12
28	Portugal	50.8	106	70	16	12	21	40	64	48	59	41
29	Slovenia	53.8	96	80	13	12	31	49	57	38	59	41
30	Malta	25.3	119	36	..	..	..	..	..	..	..	..
31	Barbados	58.7	108	76	4	6	13	25	71	60	..	..
32	Brunei Darussalam	49.0	130	61	..	..	..	..	..	..	..	..
33	Czech Republic	62.4	102	84	4	7	29	50	66	43	78	22
34	Argentina	35.0	120	45	(.)	2	12	32	88	65	..	..
35	Slovakia	62.9	103	84	6	11	27	49	67	40	74	26
36	Hungary	48.5	99	72	4	11	25	40	71	50	64	36
37	Uruguay	47.9	125	66	2	7	17	34	82	59	..	..
38	Poland	57.2	98	80	20	21	21	41	59	38	59	41
39	Chile	37.1	126	48	4	19	14	34	81	47	..	..
40	Bahrain	32.1	135	37	(.)	1	32	57	67	41	..	..
41	Costa Rica	36.6	126	45	6	27	17	26	76	46	46	54
42	Bahamas	68.4	113	85	1	8	6	22	93	69	..	..
43	Kuwait	40.7	129	52	..	..	..	..	..	..	..	..
44	Estonia	61.6	95	82	8	16	27	39	65	44	61	39
45	United Arab Emirates	32.0	129	37	..	..	..	..	..	..	..	..
46	Croatia	48.4	103	72	..	..	..	..	..	..	73	27
47	Lithuania	57.8	94	79	18	23	21	35	61	42	55	45
48	Qatar	35.9	140	40	..	..	..	..	..	..	..	..
Medium human development												
49	Trinidad and Tobago	43.7	115	58	5	14	13	33	82	54	77	23
50	Latvia	61.0	95	81	18	23	20	33	62	44	56	44

HDI rank		Female economic activity rate (age 15 and above)			Employment by economic activity (%)						Contributing family workers	
		Rate (%) 1999	Index (1985 = 100) 1999	As % of male rate 1999	Agriculture		Industry		Services		Female (as % of total) 1994-99 [a]	Male (as % of total) 1994-99 [a]
					Female 1994-97 [a]	Male 1994-97 [a]	Female 1994-97 [a]	Male 1994-97 [a]	Female 1994-97 [a]	Male 1994-97 [a]		
51	Mexico	38.9	120	47	13	30	19	24	68	46	47	53
52	Panama	43.0	116	54	3	29	11	21	86	49	27	73
53	Belarus	58.9	96	82	..	..	..	..	..	..	..	..
54	Belize	27.1	122	31	5	38	10	20	84	40	..	..
55	Russian Federation	59.1	96	81	..	..	..	..	..	..	42	58
56	Malaysia	47.8	111	60	14	19	30	36	56	45	..	..
57	Bulgaria	57.2	96	86	..	..	..	..	..	..	..	..
58	Romania	51.0	92	76	43	35	24	36	33	29	76	24
59	Libyan Arab Jamahiriya	24.7	116	32	..	..	..	..	..	..	..	..
60	Macedonia, TFYR	50.2	109	71	6	10	41	53	51	32	..	..
61	Venezuela	42.6	123	53	2	19	14	28	84	53	..	..
62	Colombia	47.7	134	60	(.)	1	21	32	76	66	67	33
63	Mauritius	37.7	122	48	13	15	43	39	45	46	54	46
64	Suriname	35.5	128	48	2	8	6	33	90	53	..	..
65	Lebanon	29.1	132	38	..	..	..	..	..	..	..	..
66	Thailand	72.9	97	84	51	49	17	22	32	28	66	34
67	Fiji	35.4	155	44	..	..	..	..	..	..	..	..
68	Saudi Arabia	20.7	166	26	..	..	..	..	..	..	..	..
69	Brazil	43.9	110	52	22	28	9	26	68	45	..	..
70	Philippines	49.4	107	61	28	48	13	19	59	33	..	..
71	Oman	18.6	175	24	..	..	..	..	..	..	..	..
72	Armenia	62.1	100	86	..	..	..	..	..	..	..	..
73	Peru	34.0	124	43	5	10	12	27	83	63	68	32
74	Ukraine	55.3	94	79	..	..	..	..	..	..	64	36
75	Kazakhstan	60.6	99	81	..	..	..	..	..	..	..	..
76	Georgia	55.7	95	77	..	..	..	..	..	..	..	..
77	Maldives	65.9	104	79	..	..	..	..	..	..	..	..
78	Jamaica	69.3	103	86	11	31	12	27	77	42	66	34
79	Azerbaijan	54.3	97	74	..	..	..	..	..	..	..	..
80	Paraguay	36.6	110	43	1	6	13	37	87	57	..	..
81	Sri Lanka	42.2	118	55	40	33	24	22	34	41	56	44
82	Turkey	49.3	111	60	65	30	13	29	21	40	..	..
83	Turkmenistan	62.0	101	81	..	..	..	..	..	..	..	..
84	Ecuador	32.3	128	38	2	10	16	26	83	64	63	37
85	Albania	59.6	105	73	..	..	..	..	..	..	..	..
86	Dominican Republic	39.9	124	47	..	..	..	..	..	..	23	77
87	China	73.0	102	86	..	..	..	..	..	..	..	..
88	Jordan	25.8	160	33	..	..	..	..	..	..	..	..
89	Tunisia	36.8	112	46	20	22	40	32	38	44	..	..
90	Iran, Islamic Rep. of	28.3	136	36	..	..	..	..	..	..	..	..
91	Cape Verde	45.8	115	52	..	..	..	..	..	..	..	..
92	Kyrgyzstan	60.7	102	83	48	48	7	12	38	31	..	..
93	Guyana	41.3	126	49	..	..	..	..	..	..	..	..
94	South Africa	46.3	104	59	..	..	..	..	..	..	..	..
95	El Salvador	45.5	132	54	7	38	21	25	72	37	33	67
96	Samoa (Western)	..	..	..	..	..	..	..	..	..	..	..
97	Syrian Arab Republic	28.2	121	36	..	..	..	..	..	..	..	..
98	Moldova, Rep. of	60.0	94	83	..	..	..	..	..	..	..	..
99	Uzbekistan	62.0	102	84	..	..	..	..	..	..	..	..
100	Algeria	28.6	153	38	..	..	..	..	..	..	..	..

		Female economic activity rate (age 15 and above)			Employment by economic activity (%)						Contributing family workers	
					Agriculture		Industry		Services		Female (as % of total)	Male (as % of total)
HDI rank		Rate (%) 1999	Index (1985 = 100) 1999	As % of male rate 1999	Female 1994-97 [a]	Male 1994-97 [a]	Female 1994-97 [a]	Male 1994-97 [a]	Female 1994-97 [a]	Male 1994-97 [a]	1994-99 [a]	1994-99 [a]
101	Viet Nam	73.5	100	90	71	70	9	12	20	18	..	..
102	Indonesia	55.0	115	67	42	41	16	21	42	39	..	..
103	Tajikistan	57.1	101	78	..	..	..	..	..	..	..	..
104	Bolivia	47.8	112	57	2	2	16	40	82	58	67	33
105	Egypt	34.5	118	44	42	32	9	25	48	43	35	65
106	Nicaragua	46.9	125	55	..	..	..	..	..	..	..	..
107	Honduras	39.8	122	46	7	53	27	19	66	28	40	60
108	Guatemala	35.3	128	41	..	..	..	..	..	..	..	..
109	Gabon	62.8	98	75	..	..	..	..	..	..	..	..
110	Equatorial Guinea	45.6	99	51	..	..	..	..	..	..	..	..
111	Namibia	54.0	101	67	..	..	..	..	..	..	..	..
112	Morocco	41.2	109	52	..	..	..	..	..	..	..	..
113	Swaziland	42.1	106	52	..	..	..	..	..	..	..	..
114	Botswana	64.5	95	77	..	..	..	..	..	..	..	..
115	India	42.0	98	50	..	..	..	..	..	..	..	..
116	Mongolia	73.2	101	87	..	..	..	..	..	..	..	..
117	Zimbabwe	66.6	100	78	38	22	10	32	52	46	..	..
118	Myanmar	65.8	98	75	..	..	..	..	..	..	..	..
119	Ghana	80.6	98	98	..	..	..	..	..	..	..	..
120	Lesotho	47.3	100	56	..	..	..	..	..	..	..	..
121	Cambodia	81.5	99	96	..	..	..	..	..	..	..	..
122	Papua New Guinea	67.0	98	78	..	..	..	..	..	..	..	..
123	Kenya	74.6	100	84	..	..	..	..	..	..	..	..
124	Comoros	62.4	96	73	..	..	..	..	..	..	..	..
125	Cameroon	49.3	103	58	..	..	..	..	..	..	..	..
126	Congo	58.5	101	71	..	..	..	..	..	..	..	..
Low human development												
127	Pakistan	35.0	126	41	67	44	11	20	22	36	..	..
128	Togo	53.5	100	62	..	..	..	..	..	..	..	..
129	Nepal	56.9	101	67	..	..	..	..	..	..	..	..
130	Bhutan	58.0	100	65	..	..	..	..	..	..	..	..
131	Lao People's Dem. Rep.	74.6	100	84	..	..	..	..	..	..	..	..
132	Bangladesh	65.8	99	76	78	54	8	11	11	34	74	26
133	Yemen	30.1	108	36	..	..	..	..	..	..	..	..
134	Haiti	56.7	95	69	..	..	..	..	..	..	..	..
135	Madagascar	69.1	98	78	..	..	..	..	..	..	..	..
136	Nigeria	48.1	100	56	..	..	..	..	..	..	..	..
137	Djibouti	..	..	..	..	..	..	..	..	..	..	..
138	Sudan	34.3	112	40	..	..	..	..	..	..	..	..
139	Mauritania	63.2	94	74	..	..	..	..	..	..	..	..
140	Tanzania, U. Rep. of	81.9	98	93	..	..	..	..	..	..	..	..
141	Uganda	80.0	98	88	..	..	..	..	..	..	..	..
142	Congo, Dem. Rep. of the	60.9	97	72	..	..	..	..	..	..	..	..
143	Zambia	65.3	98	76	..	..	..	..	..	..	..	..
144	Côte d'Ivoire	43.9	100	51	..	..	..	..	..	..	..	..
145	Senegal	61.3	100	72	..	..	..	..	..	..	..	..
146	Angola	72.9	98	82	..	..	..	..	..	..	..	..
147	Benin	73.8	98	90	..	..	..	..	..	..	..	..
148	Eritrea	74.7	98	87	..	..	..	..	..	..	10	90
149	Gambia	69.6	100	78	..	..	..	..	..	..	..	..
150	Guinea	77.5	97	89	..	..	..	..	..	..	..	..

HDI rank		Female economic activity rate (age 15 and above)			Employment by economic activity (%)						Contributing family workers	
		Rate (%) 1999	Index (1985 = 100) 1999	As % of male rate 1999	Agriculture		Industry		Services		Female (as % of total) 1994-99 [a]	Male (as % of total) 1994-99 [a]
					Female 1994-97 [a]	Male 1994-97 [a]	Female 1994-97 [a]	Male 1994-97 [a]	Female 1994-97 [a]	Male 1994-97 [a]		
151	Malawi	78.2	98	90	..	..	..	..	..	..	..	..
152	Rwanda	83.1	99	89	..	..	..	..	..	..	..	..
153	Mali	71.7	98	80	..	..	..	..	..	..	..	..
154	Central African Republic	68.0	94	79	..	..	..	..	..	..	..	..
155	Chad	67.1	102	76	..	..	..	..	..	..	..	..
156	Guinea-Bissau	56.9	100	63	..	..	..	..	.	..	..	..
157	Mozambique	82.9	98	92	..	..	..	..	..	..	..	..
158	Ethiopia	57.4	98	67	88	89	2	2	11	9	..	..
159	Burkina Faso	76.1	96	92	..	..	..	..	..	..	..	..
160	Burundi	82.6	99	89	..	..	..	..	..	..	..	..
161	Niger	69.4	98	75	..	..	..	..	..	..	..	..
162	Sierra Leone	44.4	104	53	..	..	..	..	..	..	..	..

Note: As a result of a number of limitations in the data, comparisons of labour statistics over time and across countries should be made with caution. For detailed notes on the data see ILO (1996, 1999 and 2001c). The percentage shares of employment by economic activity may not sum to 100 because of rounding or the omission of activities not classified.

a. Data refer to the most recent year available during the period specified.

Source: Columns 1-3: calculated on the basis of data on the economically active population and total population from ILO (1996); *columns 4-9:* ILO 2001a; *columns 10 and 11:* calculated on the basis of data on contributing family workers from ILO (2001c).

25 Women's political participation

HDI rank	Year women received right [a]		Year first woman elected (E) or appointed (A) to parliament	Women in government at ministerial level (as % of total) [b] 1999	Seats in parliament held by women (as % of total) [c]	
	To vote	To stand for election			Lower house or single house	Upper house or senate
High human development						
1 Norway	1907, 1913	1907, 1913	1911 A	42.1	36.4	–
2 Australia	1902, 1962	1902, 1962	1943 E	19.5	23.0	30.3
3 Canada	1917, 1950	1920, 1960	1921 E	24.3	20.6	32.4
4 Sweden	1861, 1921	1907, 1921	1921 E	55.0	42.7	–
5 Belgium	1919, 1948	1921, 1948	1921 A	18.5	23.3	28.2
6 United States	1920, 1960	1788 [d]	1917 E	31.8	14.0	13.0
7 Iceland	1915	1915	1922 E	33.3	34.9	–
8 Netherlands	1919	1917	1918 E	31.0	36.0	26.7
9 Japan	1945, 1947	1945, 1947	1946 E	5.7	7.3	17.8
10 Finland	1906	1906	1907 E	44.4	36.5	–
11 Switzerland	1971	1971	1971 E	28.6	23.0	19.6
12 Luxembourg	1919	1919	1919 E	28.6	16.7	–
13 France	1944	1944	1945 E	37.9	10.9	5.9
14 United Kingdom	1918, 1928	1918, 1928	1918 E	33.3	18.4	15.6
15 Denmark	1915	1915	1918 E	45.0	37.4	–
16 Austria	1918	1918	1919 E	31.3	26.8	20.3
17 Germany	1918	1918	1919 E	35.7	30.9	24.6
18 Ireland	1918, 1928	1918, 1928	1918 E	18.8	12.0	18.3
19 New Zealand	1893	1919	1933 E	44.0	30.8	–
20 Italy	1945	1945	1946 E	17.6	11.1	8.0
21 Spain	1931	1931	1931 E	17.6	28.3	24.3
22 Israel	1948	1948	1949 E	6.1	12.5	–
23 Greece	1927, 1952	1927, 1952	1952 E	7.1	8.7	–
24 Hong Kong, China (SAR)	–	–	–	–	–	–
25 Cyprus	1960	1960	1963 E	..	7.1	–
26 Singapore	1947	1947	1963 E	5.7	6.5	–
27 Korea, Rep. of	1948	1948	1948 E	6.5	5.9	–
28 Portugal	1931, 1976	1931, 1976	1934 E	9.7	18.7	–
29 Slovenia	1945	1945	1992 E [e]	15.0	12.2	–
30 Malta	1947	1947	1966 E	5.3	9.2	–
31 Barbados	1950	1950	1966 A	14.3	10.7	33.3
32 Brunei Darussalam	– [f]	– [f]	– [f]	0.0	– [f]	– [f]
33 Czech Republic	1920	1920	1992 E [e]	..	15.0	12.3
34 Argentina	1947	1947	1951 E	7.3	26.5	2.8
35 Slovakia	1920	1920	1992 E [e]	19.0	14.0	–
36 Hungary	1918	1918	1920 E	35.9	8.3	–
37 Uruguay	1932	1932	1942 E	..	12.1	9.7
38 Poland	1918	1918	1919 E	18.7	13.0	11.0
39 Chile	1931, 1949	1931, 1949	1951 E	25.6	10.8	4.2
40 Bahrain	1973 [g]	1973 [g]	– [g]	..	..	..
41 Costa Rica	1949	1949	1953 E	28.6	19.3	–
42 Bahamas	1961, 1964	1961, 1964	1977 A	16.7	15.0	31.3
43 Kuwait	– [f]	– [f]	– [f]	0.0	0.0	–
44 Estonia	1918	1918	1919 E	14.3	17.8	–
45 United Arab Emirates	– [f]	– [f]	– [f]	..	0.0	–
46 Croatia	1945	1945	1992 E [e]	16.2	20.5	6.2
47 Lithuania	1921	1921	1920 A	18.9	10.6	–
48 Qatar	– [f]	– [f]	– [f]	0.0	– [f]	– [f]
Medium human development						
49 Trinidad and Tobago	1946	1946	1962 E + A	8.7	11.1	32.3
50 Latvia	1918	1918	–	6.7	17.0	–

HDI rank		Year women received right[a]		Year first woman elected (E) or appointed (A) to parliament	Women in government at ministerial level (as % of total)[b] 1999	Seats in parliament held by women (as % of total)[c]	
		To vote	To stand for election			Lower house or single house	Upper house or senate
51	Mexico	1947	1953	1952 A	11.1	16.0	15.6
52	Panama	1941, 1946	1941, 1946	1946 E	20.0	9.9	
53	Belarus	1919	1919	1990 E [e]	25.7	10.3	31.1
54	Belize	1954	1954	1984 E + A	11.1	6.9	37.5
55	Russian Federation	1918	1918	1993 E [e]	..	7.6	0.6
56	Malaysia	1957	1957	1959 E		10.4	26.1
57	Bulgaria	1944	1944	1945 E	18.8	10.8	–
58	Romania	1929, 1946	1929, 1946	1946 E	20.0	10.7	5.7
59	Libyan Arab Jamahiriya	1964	1964	..	12.5	..	–
60	Macedonia, TFYR	1946	1946	1990 E [e]	10.9	6.7	–
61	Venezuela	1946	1946	1948 E	0.0	9.7	–
62	Colombia	1954	1954	1954 A	47.4	11.8	12.7
63	Mauritius	1956	1956	1976 E	9.1	5.7	–
64	Suriname	1948	1948	1975 E	..	17.6	–
65	Lebanon	1952	1952	1991 A	0.0	2.3	–
66	Thailand	1932	1932	1948 A	5.7	..	10.5
67	Fiji	1963	1963	1970 A	20.7	..	..
68	Saudi Arabia	– [f]	– [f]	– [f]	..	– [f]	– [f]
69	Brazil	1934	1934	1933 E	0.0	5.7	7.4
70	Philippines	1937	1937	1941 E	..	11.3	17.4
71	Oman	– [f]	– [f]	– [f]	..	– [f]	– [f]
72	Armenia	1921	1921	1990 E [e]	..	3.1	–
73	Peru	1955	1955	1956 E	16.2	20.0	–
74	Ukraine	1919	1919	1990 E [e]	..	7.8	–
75	Kazakhstan	1924, 1993	1924, 1993	1990 E [e]	17.5	10.4	12.8
76	Georgia	1918, 1921	1918, 1921	1992 E [e]	9.7	7.2	–
77	Maldives	1932	1932	1979 E	..	6.0	–
78	Jamaica	1944	1944	1944 E	12.5	13.3	23.8
79	Azerbaijan	1921	1921	1990 E [e]	2.6	10.5	–
80	Paraguay	1961	1961	1963 E	..	2.5	17.8
81	Sri Lanka	1931	1931	1947 E	..	4.0	–
82	Turkey	1930	1934	1935 A	0.0	4.2	–
83	Turkmenistan	1927	1927	1990 E [e]	..	26.0	–
84	Ecuador	1929, 1967	1929, 1967	1956 E	20.0	14.6	–
85	Albania	1920	1920	1945 E	15.0	5.2	–
86	Dominican Republic	1942	1942	1942 E	..	16.1	6.7
87	China	1949	1949	1954 E	5.1	21.8	–
88	Jordan	1974	1974	1989 A	0.0	0.0	7.5
89	Tunisia	1957, 1959	1957, 1959	1959 E	10.0	11.5	–
90	Iran, Islamic Rep. of	1963	1963	1963 E + A	9.4	3.4	–
91	Cape Verde	1975	1975	1975 E	35.0	11.1	–
92	Kyrgyzstan	1918	1918	1990 E [e]	..	10.0	2.2
93	Guyana	1953	1945	1968 E	..	18.5	–
94	South Africa	1930, 1994	1930, 1994	1933 E	38.1	29.8	31.5 [h]
95	El Salvador	1939	1961	1961 E	15.4	9.5	–
96	Samoa (Western)	1990	1990	1976 A	7.7	..	–
97	Syrian Arab Republic	1949, 1953	1953	1973 E	11.1	10.4	–
98	Moldova, Rep. of	1978, 1993	1978, 1993	1990 E	..	8.9	–
99	Uzbekistan	1938	1938	1990 E [e]	4.4	7.2	–
100	Algeria	1962	1962	1962 A	0.0	3.4	5.6

HDI rank	Year women received right [a] To vote	To stand for election	Year first woman elected (E) or appointed (A) to parliament	Women in government at ministerial level (as % of total) [b] 1999	Seats in parliament held by women (as % of total) [c] Lower house or single house	Upper house or senate
101 Viet Nam	1946	1946	1976 E	..	26.0	–
102 Indonesia	1945	1945	1950 A	5.9	8.0	–
103 Tajikistan	1924	1924	1990 E [e]	..	12.7	11.8
104 Bolivia	1938, 1952	1938, 1952	1966 E	..	11.5	3.7
105 Egypt	1956	1956	1957 E	6.1	2.4	–
106 Nicaragua	1955	1955	1972 E	23.1	9.7	–
107 Honduras	1955	1955	1957 [i]	33.3	9.4	–
108 Guatemala	1946	1946	1956 E	7.1	8.8	–
109 Gabon	1956	1956	1961 E	12.1	9.2	13.2
110 Equatorial Guinea	1963	1963	1968 E	..	5.0	–
111 Namibia	1989	1989	1989 E	16.3	25.0	7.7
112 Morocco	1963	1963	1993 E	4.9	0.6	0.7
113 Swaziland	1968	1968	1972 E + A	12.5	3.1	13.3
114 Botswana	1965	1965	1979 E	26.7	17.0	–
115 India	1950	1950	1952 E	10.1	8.8	..
116 Mongolia	1924	1924	1951 E	10.0	10.5	–
117 Zimbabwe	1957	1978	1980 E + A	36.0	9.3	–
118 Myanmar	1935	1946	1947 E	..	..	..
119 Ghana	1954	1954	1960 A [i]	8.6	9.0	–
120 Lesotho	1965	1965	1965 A	..	3.8	27.3
121 Cambodia	1955	1955	1958 E	7.1	7.4	13.1
122 Papua New Guinea	1964	1963	1977 E	0.0	1.8	–
123 Kenya	1919, 1963	1919, 1963	1969 E + A	1.4	3.6	–
124 Comoros	1956	1956	1993 E	..	..	..
125 Cameroon	1946	1946	1960 E	5.8	5.6	–
126 Congo	1963	1963	1963 E	..	12.0	–
Low human development						
127 Pakistan	1947	1947	1973 E	..	..	..
128 Togo	1945	1945	1961 E	7.4	4.9	–
129 Nepal	1951	1951	1952 A	14.8	5.9	15.0
130 Bhutan	1953	1953	1975 E	..	9.3	–
131 Lao People's Dem. Rep.	1958	1958	1958 E	10.2	21.2	–
132 Bangladesh	1972	1972	1973 E	9.5	9.1	–
133 Yemen	1967 [j]	1967 [j]	1990 E [i]	..	0.7	–
134 Haiti	1950	1950	1961 E	18.2	..	..
135 Madagascar	1959	1959	1965 E	12.5	8.0	–
136 Nigeria	1958	1958	..	22.6	3.4	2.8
137 Djibouti	1946	1986	– [k]	5.0	0.0	–
138 Sudan	1964	1964	1964 E	5.1	9.7	–
139 Mauritania	1961	1961	1975 E	13.6	3.8	1.8
140 Tanzania, U. Rep. of	1959	1959	..	..	22.2	–
141 Uganda	1962	1962	1962 A	27.1	17.8	–
142 Congo, Dem. Rep. of the	1967	1970	1970 E	..	..	..
143 Zambia	1962	1962	1964 E + A	6.2	10.1	–
144 Côte d'Ivoire	1952	1952	1965 E	9.1	8.5	–
145 Senegal	1945	1945	1963 E	15.6	12.1	18.3
146 Angola	1975	1975	1980 E	14.7	15.5	–
147 Benin	1956	1956	1979 E	10.5	6.0	–
148 Eritrea	1955	1955	1994 E	11.8	14.7	–
149 Gambia	1960	1960	1982 E	30.8	2.0	–
150 Guinea	1958	1958	1963 E	11.1	8.8	–

		Year women received right [a]		Year first woman elected (E) or appointed (A) to parliament	Women in government at ministerial level (as % of total) [b] 1999	Seats in parliament held by women (as % of total) [c]	
HDI rank		To vote	To stand for election			Lower house or single house	Upper house or senate
151	Malawi	1961	1961	1964 E	11.8	9.3	–
152	Rwanda	1961	1961	1965 [i]	13.0	25.7	–
153	Mali	1956	1956	1964 E	33.3	12.2	–
154	Central African Republic	1986	1986	1987 E	..	7.3	–
155	Chad	1958	1958	1962 E	..	2.4	–
156	Guinea-Bissau	1977	1977	1972 A	8.3	7.8	–
157	Mozambique	1975	1975	1977 E	..	30.0	–
158	Ethiopia	1955	1955	1957 E	22.2	7.7	8.3
159	Burkina Faso	1958	1958	1978 E	8.6	8.1	13.0
160	Burundi	1961	1961	1982 E	4.5	14.4	–
161	Niger	1948	1948	1989 E	10.0	1.2	–
162	Sierra Leone	1961	1961	..	8.1	8.8	–

a. Data refer to the year in which the right to vote or stand for election on a universal and equal basis was recognized. Where two years are shown, the first refers to the first partial recognition of the right to vote or stand for election.

b. Data were provided by states based on their definition of national executive and may therefore include women serving as ministers and vice ministers and those holding other ministerial positions, including parliamentary secretaries.

c. Data are as of 8 March 2001.

d. No information is available on the year all women received the right to stand for election. However, the constitution does not mention gender with regard to this right.

e. Refers to the year women were elected to the current parliamentary system.

f. Women's right to vote and to stand for election has not been recognized. Brunei Darussalam, Oman, Qatar and Saudi Arabia have never had a parliament.

g. According to the constitution in force (1973), all citizens are equal before the law; however, women were not able to exercise electoral rights in the only legislative elections held in Bahrain, in 1973. The first legislature of Bahrain was dissolved by decree of the emir on 26 August 1975. Women were allowed to vote in the referendum of 14-15 February 2001, however, which approved the National Action Charter.

h. Calculated on the basis of the 54 permanent seats (that is, excluding the 36 special rotating delegates appointed on an ad hoc basis).

i. No information or confirmation available.

j. Refers to the former People's Democratic Republic of Yemen.

k. The country has not yet elected or appointed a woman to the national parliament.

Source: Columns 1-3: IPU 1995 and 2001b; column 4: IPU 2001a; columns 5 and 6: calculated on the basis of data on parliamentary seats from IPU (2001c).

26 Status of major international human rights instruments

HUMAN AND LABOUR RIGHTS INSTRUMENTS

HDI rank	International Convention on the Elimination of All Forms of Racial Discrimination 1965	International Covenant on Civil and Political Rights 1966	International Covenant on Economic, Social and Cultural Rights 1966	Convention on the Elimination of All Forms of Discrimination Against Women 1979	Convention Against Torture and Other Cruel, Inhuman or Degrading Treatment or Punishment 1984	Convention on the Rights of the Child 1989
High human development						
1 Norway	●	●	●	●	●	●
2 Australia	●	●	●	●	●	●
3 Canada	●	●	●	●	●	●
4 Sweden	●	●	●	●	●	●
5 Belgium	●	●	●	●	●	●
6 United States	●	●	○	○	●	○
7 Iceland	●	●	●	●	●	●
8 Netherlands	●	●	●	●	●	●
9 Japan	●	●	●	●	●	●
10 Finland	●	●	●	●	●	●
11 Switzerland	●	●	●	●	●	●
12 Luxembourg	●	●	●	●	●	●
13 France	●	●	●	●	●	●
14 United Kingdom	●	●	●	●	●	●
15 Denmark	●	●	●	●	●	●
16 Austria	●	●	●	●	●	●
17 Germany	●	●	●	●	●	●
18 Ireland	●	●	●	●	○	●
19 New Zealand	●	●	●	●	●	●
20 Italy	●	●	●	●	●	●
21 Spain	●	●	●	●	●	●
22 Israel	●	●	●	●	●	●
23 Greece	●	●	●	●	●	●
24 Hong Kong, China (SAR)	–	–	–	–	–	–
25 Cyprus	●	●	●			
26 Singapore				●		●
27 Korea, Rep. of	●	●	●	●	●	●
28 Portugal	●	●	●	●	●	●
29 Slovenia	●	●	●	●	●	●
30 Malta	●	●	●	●	●	●
31 Barbados	●	●	●	●		●
32 Brunei Darussalam						●
33 Czech Republic	●	●	●	●	●	●
34 Argentina	●	●	●	●	●	●
35 Slovakia	●	●	●	●	●	●
36 Hungary	●	●	●	●	●	●
37 Uruguay	●	●	●	●	●	●
38 Poland	●	●	●	●	●	●
39 Chile	●	●	●	●		●
40 Bahrain	●				●	●
41 Costa Rica	●	●	●	●		●
42 Bahamas	●			●		●
43 Kuwait	●		●	●	●	●
44 Estonia	●	●	●	●	●	●
45 United Arab Emirates	●					●
46 Croatia	●	●	●	●	●	●
47 Lithuania	●	●	●	●	●	●
48 Qatar	●				●	●
Medium human development						
49 Trinidad and Tobago	●	●	●	●		●
50 Latvia	●	●	●	●	●	●

HDI rank	International Convention on the Elimination of All Forms of Racial Discrimination 1965	International Covenant on Civil and Political Rights 1966	International Covenant on Economic, Social and Cultural Rights 1966	Convention on the Elimination of All Forms of Discrimination Against Women 1979	Convention Against Torture and Other Cruel, Inhuman or Degrading Treatment or Punishment 1984	Convention on the Rights of the Child 1989
51 Mexico	●	●	●	●	●	●
52 Panama	●	●	●	●	●	●
53 Belarus	●	●	●	●	●	●
54 Belize	○	●	○	●	●	●
55 Russian Federation	●	●	●	●	●	●
56 Malaysia				●		●
57 Bulgaria	●	●	●	●	●	●
58 Romania	●	●	●	●	●	●
59 Libyan Arab Jamahiriya	●	●	●	●	●	●
60 Macedonia, TFYR	●	●	●	●	●	●
61 Venezuela	●	●	●	●	●	●
62 Colombia	●	●	●	●	●	●
63 Mauritius	●	●	●	●	●	●
64 Suriname	●	●	●	●		●
65 Lebanon	●	●	●	●	●	●
66 Thailand		●	●	●		●
67 Fiji	●			●		●
68 Saudi Arabia	●			●	●	●
69 Brazil	●	●	●	●	●	●
70 Philippines	●	●	●	●	●	●
71 Oman						●
72 Armenia	●	●	●	●	●	●
73 Peru	●	●	●	●	●	●
74 Ukraine	●	●	●	●	●	●
75 Kazakhstan	●			●	●	●
76 Georgia	●	●	●	●	●	●
77 Maldives	●			●		●
78 Jamaica	●	●	●	●		●
79 Azerbaijan	●	●	●	●	●	●
80 Paraguay	○	●	●	●	●	●
81 Sri Lanka	●	●	●	●		●
82 Turkey	○	○	○	●	●	●
83 Turkmenistan	●	●	●	●		●
84 Ecuador	●	●	●	●	●	●
85 Albania	●	●	●	●	●	●
86 Dominican Republic	●	●	●	●	○	●
87 China	●	○	●	●	●	●
88 Jordan	●	●	●	●	●	●
89 Tunisia	●	●	●	●	●	●
90 Iran, Islamic Rep. of	●	●	●			●
91 Cape Verde	●	●	●	●	●	●
92 Kyrgyzstan	●	●	●	●	●	●
93 Guyana	●	●	●	●		●
94 South Africa	●	●	○	●	●	●
95 El Salvador	●	●	●	●		●
96 Samoa (Western)				●		●
97 Syrian Arab Republic	●	●	●			●
98 Moldova, Rep. of	●	●	●	●	●	●
99 Uzbekistan	●	●	●	●	●	●
100 Algeria	●	●	●	●	●	●

HDI rank	International Convention on the Elimination of All Forms of Racial Discrimination 1965	International Covenant on Civil and Political Rights 1966	International Covenant on Economic, Social and Cultural Rights 1966	Convention on the Elimination of All Forms of Discrimination Against Women 1979	Convention Against Torture and Other Cruel, Inhuman or Degrading Treatment or Punishment 1984	Convention on the Rights of the Child 1989
101 Viet Nam	●	●	●	●		●
102 Indonesia	●			●	●	●
103 Tajikistan	●	●	●	●	●	●
104 Bolivia	●	●	●	●	●	●
105 Egypt	●	●	●	●	●	●
106 Nicaragua	●	●	●	●	○	●
107 Honduras		●	●	●	●	●
108 Guatemala	●	●	●	●	●	●
109 Gabon	●	●	●	●	●	●
110 Equatorial Guinea		●	●	●	●	●
111 Namibia	●	●	●	●	●	●
112 Morocco	●	●	●	●	●	●
113 Swaziland	●					●
114 Botswana	●	●		●	●	●
115 India	●	●	●	●	○	●
116 Mongolia	●	●	●	●		●
117 Zimbabwe	●	●	●	●		●
118 Myanmar				●		●
119 Ghana	●	●	●	●	●	●
120 Lesotho	●	●	●	●		●
121 Cambodia	●	●	●	●	●	●
122 Papua New Guinea	●			●		●
123 Kenya		●	●	●	●	●
124 Comoros	○			●	○	●
125 Cameroon	●	●	●	●	●	●
126 Congo	●	●	●	●		●
Low human development						
127 Pakistan	●			●		●
128 Togo	●	●	●	●	●	●
129 Nepal	●	●	●	●	●	●
130 Bhutan	○			●		●
131 Lao People's Dem. Rep.	●	○	○	●		●
132 Bangladesh	●	●	●	●	●	●
133 Yemen	●	●	●	●	●	●
134 Haiti	●	●		●		●
135 Madagascar	●	●	●	●		●
136 Nigeria	●	●	●	●	○	●
137 Djibouti				●		●
138 Sudan	●	●	●		○	●
139 Mauritania	●			●		●
140 Tanzania, U. Rep. of	●	●	●	●		●
141 Uganda	●	●	●	●	●	●
142 Congo, Dem. Rep. of the	●	●	●	●	●	●
143 Zambia	●	●	●	●	●	●
144 Côte d'Ivoire	●	●	●	●	●	●
145 Senegal	●	●	●	●	●	●
146 Angola		●	●	●		●
147 Benin	○	●	●	●	●	●
148 Eritrea				●		●
149 Gambia	●	●	●	●	○	●
150 Guinea	●	●	●	●		●

HDI rank	International Convention on the Elimination of All Forms of Racial Discrimination 1965	International Covenant on Civil and Political Rights 1966	International Covenant on Economic, Social and Cultural Rights 1966	Convention on the Elimination of All Forms of Discrimination Against Women 1979	Convention Against Torture and Other Cruel, Inhuman or Degrading Treatment or Punishment 1984	Convention on the Rights of the Child 1989
151 Malawi	●	●	●	●	●	●
152 Rwanda	●	●	●	●		●
153 Mali	●	●	●	●	●	●
154 Central African Republic	●	●	●	●		●
155 Chad	●	●	●	●	●	●
156 Guinea-Bissau	○	○	●	●	○	●
157 Mozambique	●	●		●	●	●
158 Ethiopia	●	●	●	●	●	●
159 Burkina Faso	●	●	●	●	●	●
160 Burundi	●	●	●	●	●	●
161 Niger	●	●	●	●	●	●
162 Sierra Leone	●	●	●	●	○	●
Others [a]						
Afghanistan	●	●	●	○	●	●
Andorra						●
Antigua and Barbuda	●			●	●	●
Bosnia and Herzegovina	●	●	●	●	●	●
Cook Islands						●
Cuba	●			●	●	●
Dominica		●	●	●		●
Grenada	○	●	●	●		●
Holy See	●					●
Iraq	●	●	●	●		●
Kiribati						●
Korea, Dem. Rep. of		●	●	●		●
Liberia	●	○	○	●		●
Liechtenstein	●	●	●	●	●	●
Marshall Islands						●
Micronesia, Fed. Sts.						●
Monaco	●	●	●		●	●
Nauru						●
Niue						●
Palau						●
Saint Kitts and Nevis				●		●
Saint Lucia	●			●		●
Saint Vincent and the Grenadines	●	●	●	●		●
San Marino		●	●			●
São Tomé and Principe	○	○	○	○	○	●
Seychelles	●	●	●	●	●	●
Solomon Islands	●		●			●
Somalia	●	●	●		●	●
Tonga	●					●
Tuvalu				●		●
Vanuatu				●		●
Yugoslavia	●	●	●	●	●	●
Total states parties [b]	157	147	144	167	123	191
Signatures not yet followed by ratification	9	6	7	3	11	1

● Ratification, accession or succession.

○ Signature not yet followed by ratification.

Note: Information is as of 30 March 2001.

a. These are the countries or areas, in addition to the 162 countries or areas included in the main indicator tables, that have signed or ratified at least one of the six human rights instruments.

b. Refers to ratification, accession or succession.

Source: Columns 1-6: UN 2001b.

27 Status of fundamental labour rights conventions

HDI rank	Freedom of association and collective bargaining		Elimination of forced and compulsory labour		Elimination of discrimination in respect of employment and occupation		Abolition of child labour	
	Convention 87 [a]	Convention 98 [b]	Convention 29 [c]	Convention 105 [d]	Convention 100 [e]	Convention 111 [f]	Convention 138 [g]	Convention 182 [h]
High human development								
1 Norway	●	●	●	●	●	●	●	●
2 Australia	●	●	●	●	●	●		
3 Canada	●			●	●	●		●
4 Sweden	●	●	●	●	●	●	●	
5 Belgium	●	●	●	●	●	●	●	
6 United States				●				●
7 Iceland	●	●	●	●	●	●	●	●
8 Netherlands	●	●	●	●	●	●	●	
9 Japan	●	●	●		●		●	
10 Finland	●	●	●	●	●	●	●	●
11 Switzerland	●	●	●	●	●	●	●	●
12 Luxembourg	●	●	●	●	●	●	●	
13 France	●	●	●	●	●	●	●	
14 United Kingdom	●	●	●	●	●	●	●	●
15 Denmark	●	●	●	●	●	●	●	●
16 Austria	●	●	●	●	●	●	●	
17 Germany	●	●	●	●	●	●	●	
18 Ireland	●	●	●	●	●	●		●
19 New Zealand			●	●	●	●		
20 Italy	●	●	●	●	●	●		●
21 Spain	●	●	●	●	●	●	●	
22 Israel	●	●	●	●	●	●	●	
23 Greece	●	●	●	●	●	●	●	
24 Hong Kong, China (SAR)	–	–	–	–	–	–	–	–
25 Cyprus	●	●	●	●	●	●	●	●
26 Singapore		●	●	○				
27 Korea, Rep. of					●	●	●	
28 Portugal	●	●	●	●	●	●	●	●
29 Slovenia	●	●	●	●	●	●	●	
30 Malta	●	●	●	●	●	●	●	
31 Barbados	●	●	●	●	●		●	●
32 Brunei Darussalam								
33 Czech Republic	●	●	●	●	●	●		
34 Argentina	●	●	●	●	●	●	●	
35 Slovakia	●	●	●	●	●	●	●	
36 Hungary	●	●	●	●	●	●	●	●
37 Uruguay	●	●	●	●	●	●	●	
38 Poland	●	●	●	●	●	●	●	
39 Chile	●	●	●	●	●	●	●	●
40 Bahrain			●	●		●		
41 Costa Rica	●	●	●	●	●		●	
42 Bahamas		●	●	●				
43 Kuwait	●		●	●		●	●	●
44 Estonia	●	●	●	●	●			
45 United Arab Emirates			●	●	●		●	
46 Croatia	●	●	●	●	●	●		
47 Lithuania	●	●	●	●	●	●		
48 Qatar			●			●		●
Medium human development								
49 Trinidad and Tobago	●	●	●	●	●	●		
50 Latvia	●	●		●	●	●		

HDI rank		Freedom of association and collective bargaining		Elimination of forced and compulsory labour		Elimination of discrimination in respect of employment and occupation		Abolition of child labour	
		Convention 87[a]	Convention 98[b]	Convention 29[c]	Convention 105[d]	Convention 100[e]	Convention 111[f]	Convention 138[g]	Convention 182[h]
51	Mexico	●		●	●	●	●		●
52	Panama	●	●	●	●	●	●	●	●
53	Belarus	●	●	●	●	●	●	●	●
54	Belize	●	●	●	●	●	●	●	●
55	Russian Federation	●	●	●	●	●	●	●	
56	Malaysia		●	●	○	●			●
57	Bulgaria	●	●	●	●	●	●	●	●
58	Romania	●	●	●	●	●	●	●	●
59	Libyan Arab Jamahiriya	●	●	●	●	●	●	●	●
60	Macedonia, TFYR	●	●	●		●	●	●	
61	Venezuela	●	●	●	●	●	●	●	
62	Colombia	●	●	●	●	●	●		
63	Mauritius		●	●	●			●	●
64	Suriname	●	●	●	●				
65	Lebanon		●	●	●	●	●		
66	Thailand			●	●	●			
67	Fiji		●	●	●				
68	Saudi Arabia			●	●	●	●		
69	Brazil		●	●	●	●	●		●
70	Philippines	●	●		●	●	●	●	●
71	Oman			●					
72	Armenia					●	●		
73	Peru	●	●	●	●	●	●		
74	Ukraine	●	●	●	●	●	●	●	●
75	Kazakhstan	●					●		
76	Georgia	●	●	●	●	●	●	●	
77	Maldives								
78	Jamaica	●	●	●	●	●	●		
79	Azerbaijan	●	●	●	●	●	●	●	
80	Paraguay	●	●	●	●	●	●		
81	Sri Lanka	●	●	●		●	●	●	
82	Turkey	●	●	●		●	●	●	
83	Turkmenistan	●	●	●	●	●	●		
84	Ecuador	●	●	●	●	●	●	●	●
85	Albania	●	●	●	●	●	●	●	
86	Dominican Republic	●	●	●	●	●	●	●	●
87	China					●		●	
88	Jordan		●	●	●	●	●	●	●
89	Tunisia	●	●	●	●	●	●	●	●
90	Iran, Islamic Rep. of			●	●	●	●		
91	Cape Verde	●	●	●	●	●	●		
92	Kyrgyzstan	●	●	●	●	●	●	●	
93	Guyana	●	●	●	●	●	●	●	●
94	South Africa	●	●	●	●	●	●	●	●
95	El Salvador			●	●	●	●	●	●
96	Samoa (Western)								
97	Syrian Arab Republic	●	●	●	●	●	●		
98	Moldova, Rep. of	●	●	●	●	●	●	●	
99	Uzbekistan		●	●	●	●	●		
100	Algeria	●	●	●	●	●	●	●	

HDI rank	Freedom of association and collective bargaining		Elimination of forced and compulsory labour		Elimination of discrimination in respect of employment and occupation		Abolition of child labour	
	Convention 87[a]	Convention 98[b]	Convention 29[c]	Convention 105[d]	Convention 100[e]	Convention 111[f]	Convention 138[g]	Convention 182[h]
101 Viet Nam					●	●		●
102 Indonesia	●	●	●	●	●	●	●	●
103 Tajikistan	●	●	●		●	●	●	
104 Bolivia	●	●		●	●	●	●	
105 Egypt	●	●	●	●	●	●		
106 Nicaragua	●	●	●	●	●	●	●	●
107 Honduras	●	●	●	●	●	●	●	
108 Guatemala	●	●	●	●	●	●	●	
109 Gabon	●	●	●	●	●	●		
110 Equatorial Guinea					●		●	
111 Namibia	●	●	●	●			●	●
112 Morocco		●	●	●	●	●	●	●
113 Swaziland	●	●	●	●	●	●	●	●
114 Botswana	●	●	●	●	●	●	●	●
115 India			●	●	●	●		
116 Mongolia	●	●			●	●		
117 Zimbabwe		●	●	●	●	●	●	●
118 Myanmar	●		●					
119 Ghana	●	●	●	●	●	●		●
120 Lesotho	●	●	●		●	●		
121 Cambodia	●	●	●	●	●	●	●	
122 Papua New Guinea	●	●	●	●	●	●		●
123 Kenya		●	●	●			●	
124 Comoros	●	●	●	●	●			
125 Cameroon	●	●	●	●	●	●		
126 Congo	●	●	●	●	●	●	●	
Low human development								
127 Pakistan	●	●	●	●		●		
128 Togo	●	●	●	●	●	●	●	●
129 Nepal		●			●	●	●	
130 Bhutan								
131 Lao People's Dem. Rep.			●					
132 Bangladesh	●	●	●	●	●	●		
133 Yemen	●	●	●	●	●	●	●	●
134 Haiti	●	●	●	●	●	●		
135 Madagascar	●	●	●		●	●	●	
136 Nigeria	●	●	●	●	●	●		
137 Djibouti	●	●	●	●	●			
138 Sudan		●	●	●	●	●		
139 Mauritania	●		●	●		●		
140 Tanzania, U. Rep. of	●	●	●	●			●	
141 Uganda		●	●	●				
142 Congo, Dem. Rep. of the		●	●		●			
143 Zambia	●	●	●	●	●	●	●	
144 Côte d'Ivoire	●	●	●	●	●	●		
145 Senegal	●	●	●	●	●	●	●	●
146 Angola		●	●	●	●	●		
147 Benin	●	●	●	●	●	●		
148 Eritrea	●	●	●	●	●	●	●	
149 Gambia								
150 Guinea	●	●	●	●	●	●		

HDI rank	Freedom of association and collective bargaining		Elimination of forced and compulsory labour		Elimination of discrimination in respect of employment and occupation		Abolition of child labour	
	Convention 87 [a]	Convention 98 [b]	Convention 29 [c]	Convention 105 [d]	Convention 100 [e]	Convention 111 [f]	Convention 138 [g]	Convention 182 [h]
151 Malawi	●	●	●	●	●	●	●	●
152 Rwanda	●	●		●	●	●	●	●
153 Mali	●	●	●	●	●	●		●
154 Central African Republic	●	●	●	●	●	●	●	●
155 Chad	●	●	●	●	●	●		●
156 Guinea-Bissau		●	●	●	●	●		
157 Mozambique	●	●		●	●	●		
158 Ethiopia	●	●		●	●	●	●	
159 Burkina Faso	●	●	●	●	●	●	●	
160 Burundi	●	●	●	●	●	●	●	
161 Niger	●	●	●	●	●	●	●	●
162 Sierra Leone	●	●	●	●	●	●		
Others [i]								
Afghanistan				●	●	●		
Antigua and Barbuda	●	●	●	●	●	●	●	
Bosnia and Herzegovina	●	●	●	●	●	●	●	
Cuba	●	●	●	●	●	●	●	
Dominica	●	●	●	●	●	●	●	●
Grenada	●	●	●	●	●			
Iraq		●	●	●	●	●	●	
Liberia	●	●	●	●		●		
Saint Kitts and Nevis	●	●	●	●	●	●		●
Saint Lucia	●	●	●	●	●	●		●
Saint Vincent and the Grenadines		●	●	●				
San Marino	●	●	●	●	●	●	●	●
São Tomé and Principe	●	●			●	●		
Seychelles	●	●	●	●	●	●	●	●
Solomon Islands			●					
Somalia			●	●		●		
Total ratifications	132	146	154	150	148	144	102	60

● Convention ratified.

○ Ratification denounced.

Note: Information is as of 1 February 2001.

a. Freedom of Association and Protection of the Right to Organize Convention (1948).

b. Right to Organize and Collective Bargaining Convention (1949).

c. Forced Labour Convention (1930).

d. Abolition of Forced Labour Convention (1957).

e. Equal Remuneration Convention (1951).

f. Discrimination (Employment and Occupation) Convention (1958).

g. Minimum Age Convention (1973).

h. Worst Forms of Child Labour Convention (1999).

i. These are the countries or areas, in addition to the 162 countries or areas included in the main indicator tables, that have ratified at least one of the eight fundamental labour rights conventions.

Source: Columns 1-8: ILO 2001b.

	Total population (thousands) 1999	Total fertility rate (per woman) 1995-2000 [a]	Life expectancy at birth (years) 1995-2000 [a]	Infant mortality rate (per 1,000 live births) 1999	Under-five mortality rate (per 1,000 live births) 1999	Adults living with HIV/AIDS (% age 15-49) 1999 [b]	Adult literacy rate (% age 15 and above) 1999	Combined primary, secondary and tertiary gross enrolment ratio (%) 1999	GDP per capita (PPP US$) 1999	Under-nourished people (as % of total population) 1996-98 [c]	Population using improved water sources (%) 1999
Afghanistan	21,202	6.9	42.5	165	257	<0.01 [d]	36	30	..	70	13
Andorra	82	..	..	6	7	..	..	..	..	..	100
Antigua and Barbuda	65	..	..	17	20	..	..	..	10,225	..	91
Bosnia and Herzegovina	3,846	1.4	73.3	15	18	0.04 [d]	..	..	..	10	..
Cuba	11,158	1.6	75.7	6	8	0.03	97	76	..	19	95
Dominica	71	..	..	16	18	..	..	..	5,425	..	97
Grenada	93	..	..	22	27	..	..	..	6,817	..	94
Iraq	22,335	5.3	58.7	104	128	<0.01 [d]	55	49	..	17	85
Kiribati	82	..	..	53	72	..	..	..	..	..	47
Korea, Dem. Rep. of	22,110	2.1	63.1	23	30	<0.01 [d]	..	..	..	57	100
Liberia	2,709	6.8	48.1	157	235	2.80	53	16	..	46	..
Liechtenstein	32	..	..	10	11	..	..	..	..	..	..
Marshall Islands	50	..	..	63	92	..	..	..	..	..	..
Micronesia, Fed. Sts.	120	4.3	71.8	20	24	..	..	..	..	..	..
Monaco	33	..	..	5	5	..	..	..	..	..	100
Nauru	12	..	..	25	30	..	..	..	..	..	..
Palau	19	..	..	28	34	..	..	..	..	..	79
Saint Kitts and Nevis	39	..	..	24	29	..	..	..	11,596	..	98
Saint Lucia	146	2.7	73.0	17	19	..	..	..	5,509	..	98
Saint Vincent and the Grenadines	113	..	..	21	25	..	..	..	5,309	..	93
San Marino	26	..	..	6	6	..	..	..	..	..	..
São Tomé and Principe	135	..	..	59	76	..	..	..	1,977 [e]	..	..
Seychelles	79	..	..	13	17	..	..	..	9,974 [e]	..	..
Solomon Islands	432	5.6	67.4	22	26	..	..	..	1,975	..	71
Somalia	8,418	7.3	46.9	125	211	..	..	7	..	75	..
Tonga	99	..	..	18	22	..	..	..	..	..	100
Tuvalu	10	..	..	40	56	..	..	..	..	..	100
Vanuatu	192	4.6	67.2	37	46	..	..	..	3,108	..	88
Yugoslavia	10,567	1.8	72.2	20	23	0.10 [d]	..	..	..	3	..

Note: The table presents data for UN member countries not included in the main indicator tables.

a. Data refer to estimates for the period specified.

b. Data refer to the end of 1999.

c. Data refer to the most recent year available during the period specified.

d. Data refer to estimates produced using the 1994 prevalence rate published by the World Health Organization's Global Programme on AIDS (WHO 1995).

e. Aten, Heston and Summers 2001. Data refer to a year other than that specified.

Source: Columns 1-3: UN 2001d; *columns 4, 5 and 11:* UNICEF 2000; *column 6:* UNAIDS 2000; *column 7:* UNESCO 2000a; *column 8:* UNESCO 2001b; *column 9:* World Bank 2001b; *column 10:* FAO 2000.

CALCULATING THE HUMAN DEVELOPMENT INDICES

The diagrams here offer a clear overview of how the five human development indices used in the *Human Development Report* are constructed, highlighting both their similarities and their differences. The text on the following pages provides a detailed explanation.

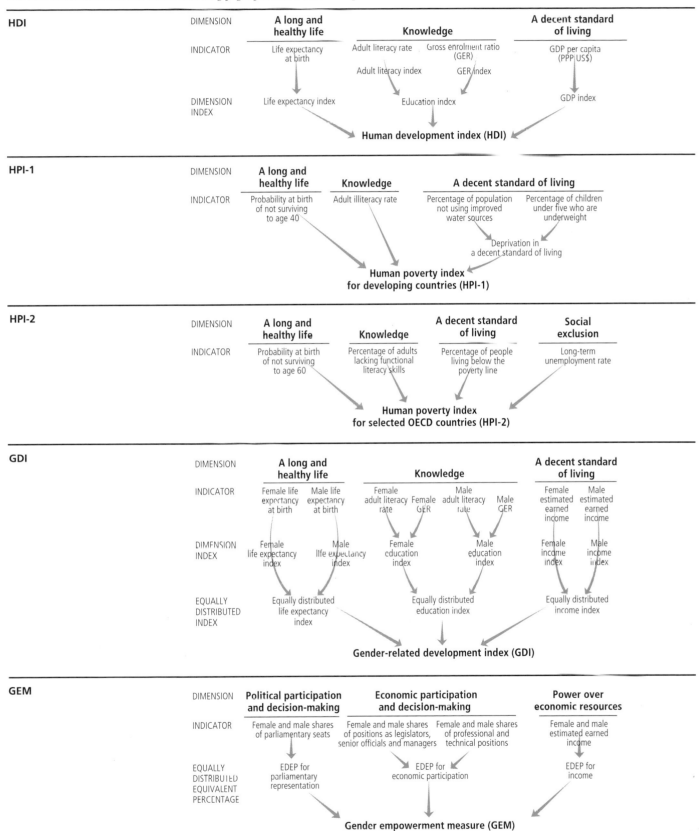

The human development index (HDI)

The HDI is a summary measure of human development. It measures the average achievements in a country in three basic dimensions of human development:

- A long and healthy life, as measured by life expectancy at birth.
- Knowledge, as measured by the adult literacy rate (with two-thirds weight) and the combined primary, secondary and tertiary gross enrolment ratio (with one-third weight).
- A decent standard of living, as measured by GDP per capita (PPP US$).

Before the HDI itself is calculated, an index needs to be created for each of these dimensions. To calculate these dimension indices —the life expectancy, education and GDP indices—minimum and maximum values (goalposts) are chosen for each underlying indicator.

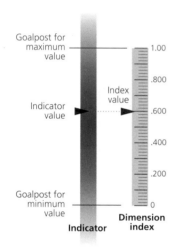

Performance in each dimension is expressed as a value between 0 and 1 by applying the following general formula:

$$\text{Dimension index} = \frac{\text{actual value} - \text{minimum value}}{\text{maximum value} - \text{minimum value}}$$

The HDI is then calculated as a simple average of the dimension indices. The box at right illustrates the calculation of the HDI for a sample country.

Goalposts for calculating the HDI

Indicator	Maximum value	Minimum value
Life expectancy at birth (years)	85	25
Adult literacy rate (%)	100	0
Combined gross enrolment ratio (%)	100	0
GDP per capita (PPP US$)	40,000	100

Calculating the HDI

This illustration of the calculation of the HDI uses data for Armenia.

1. Calculating the life expectancy index

The life expectancy index measures the relative achievement of a country in life expectancy at birth. For Armenia, with a life expectancy of 72.7 years in 1999, the life expectancy index is 0.795.

$$\text{Life expectancy index} = \frac{72.7 - 25}{85 - 25} = \mathbf{0.795}$$

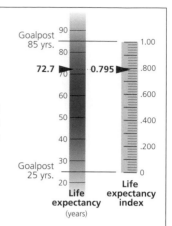

2. Calculating the education index

The education index measures a country's relative achievement in both adult literacy and combined primary, secondary and tertiary gross enrolment. First, an index for adult literacy and one for combined gross enrolment are calculated. Then these two indices are combined to create the education index, with two-thirds weight given to adult literacy and one-third weight to combined gross enrolment. For Armenia, with an adult literacy rate of 98.3% and a combined gross enrolment ratio of 79.9% in 1999, the education index is 0.922.

$$\text{Adult literacy index} = \frac{98.3 - 0}{100 - 0} = 0.983$$

$$\text{Gross enrolment index} = \frac{79.9 - 0}{100 - 0} = 0.799$$

$$\text{Education index} = 2/3 \text{ (adult literacy index)} + 1/3 \text{ (gross enrolment index)}$$
$$= 2/3 \text{ (0.983)} + 1/3 \text{ (0.799)} = \mathbf{0.922}$$

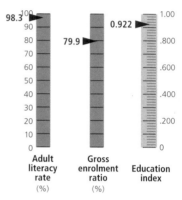

3. Calculating the GDP index

The GDP index is calculated using adjusted GDP per capita (PPP US$). In the HDI income serves as a surrogate for all the dimensions of human development not reflected in a long and healthy life and in knowledge. Income is adjusted because achieving a respectable level of human development does not require unlimited income. Accordingly, the logarithm of income is used. For Armenia, with a GDP per capita of $2,215 (PPP US$) in 1998, the GDP index is 0.517.

$$\text{GDP index} = \frac{\log (2,215) - \log (100)}{\log (40,000) - \log (100)} = \mathbf{0.517}$$

4. Calculating the HDI

Once the dimension indices have been calculated, determining the HDI is straightforward. It is a simple average of the three dimension indices.

$$\text{HDI} = 1/3 \text{ (life expectancy index)} + 1/3 \text{ (education index)}$$
$$+ 1/3 \text{ (GDP index)}$$
$$= 1/3 \text{ (0.795)} + 1/3 \text{ (0.922)} + 1/3 \text{ (0.517)} = \mathbf{0.745}$$

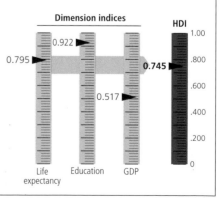

The human poverty index for developing countries (HPI-1)

While the HDI measures average achievement, the HPI-1 measures *deprivations* in the three basic dimensions of human development captured in the HDI:

• A long and healthy life—vulnerability to death at a relatively early age, as measured by the probability at birth of not surviving to age 40.
• Knowledge—exclusion from the world of reading and communications, as measured by the adult illiteracy rate.
• A decent standard of living—lack of access to overall economic provisioning, as measured by the percentage of the population not using improved water sources and the percentage of children under five who are underweight.

Calculating the HPI-1 is more straightforward than calculating the HDI. The indicators used to measure the deprivations are already normalized between 0 and 100 (because they are expressed as percentages), so there is no need to create dimension indices as for the HDI.

In this year's Report, because reliable data on access to health services are lacking for recent years, deprivation in a decent standard of living is measured by two rather than three indicators—the percentage of the population not using improved water sources and the percentage of children under five who are underweight. An unweighted average of the two is used as an input to the HPI-1.

The human poverty index for selected OECD countries (HPI-2)

The HPI-2 measures deprivations in the same dimensions as the HPI-1 and also captures social exclusion. Thus it reflects deprivations in four dimensions:

• A long and healthy life—vulnerability to death at a relatively early age, as measured by the probability at birth of not surviving to age 60.
• Knowledge—exclusion from the world of reading and communications, as measured by the percentage of adults (aged 16–65) lacking functional literacy skills.
• A decent standard of living—as measured by the percentage of people living below the income poverty line (50% of the median disposable household income).
• Social exclusion—as measured by the rate of long-term unemployment (12 months or more).

Calculating the HPI-1

1. Measuring deprivation in a decent standard of living
An unweighted average of two indicators is used to measure deprivation in a decent standard of living.

$$\text{Unweighted average} = 1/2 \ (\text{population not using improved water sources}) + 1/2 \ (\text{underweight children under five})$$

A sample calculation: the Dominican Republic
Population not using improved water sources = 21%
Underweight children under five = 6%

$$\text{Unweighted average} = 1/2 \ (21) + 1/2 \ (6) = 13.5\%$$

2. Calculating the HPI-1
The formula for calculating the HPI-1 is as follows:

$$\text{HPI-1} = [1/3 \ (P_1^{\alpha} + P_2^{\alpha} + P_3^{\alpha})]^{1/\alpha}$$

Where:
P_1 = Probability at birth of not surviving to age 40 (times 100)
P_2 = Adult illiteracy rate
P_3 = Unweighted average of population not using improved water sources and underweight children under age five
$\alpha = 3$

A sample calculation: the Dominican Republic
$P_1 = 11.9\%$
$P_2 = 16.8\%$
$P_3 = 13.5\%$

$$\text{HPI-1} = [1/3 \ (11.9^3 + 16.8^3 + 13.5^3)]^{1/3} = \textbf{14.4}$$

Calculating the HPI-2

The formula for calculating the HPI-2 is as follows:

$$\text{HPI-2} = [1/4 \ (P_1^{\alpha} + P_2^{\alpha} + P_3^{\alpha} + P_4^{\alpha})]^{1/\alpha}$$

Where:
P_1 = Probability at birth of not surviving to age 60 (times 100)
P_2 = Adults lacking functional literacy skills
P_3 = Population below income poverty line (50% of median disposable household income)
P_4 = Long-term unemployment rate (lasting 12 months or more)
$\alpha = 3$

A sample calculation: Australia
$P_1 = 9.1\%$
$P_2 = 17.0\%$
$P_3 = 2.1\%$
$P_4 = 14.3\%$

$$\text{HPI-2} = [1/4 \ (9.1^3 + 17.0^3 + 2.1^3 + 14.3^3)]^{1/3} = \textbf{12.9}$$

Why $\alpha = 3$ in calculating the HPI-1 and HPI-2

The value of α has an important impact on the value of the HPI. If $\alpha = 1$, the HPI is the average of its dimensions. As α rises, greater weight is given to the dimension in which there is the most deprivation. Thus as α increases towards infinity, the HPI will tend towards the value of the dimension in which deprivation is greatest (for the Dominican Republic, the example used for calculating the HPI-1, it would be 16.8%, equal to the adult illiteracy rate).

In this Report the value 3 is used to give additional but not overwhelming weight to areas of more acute deprivation. For a detailed analysis of the HPI's mathematical formulation see Sudhir Anand and Amartya Sen's "Concepts of Human Development and Poverty: A Multidimensional Perspective" and the technical note in *Human Development Report 1997* (see the list of selected readings at the end of this technical note).

The gender-related development index (GDI)

While the HDI measures average achievement, the GDI adjusts the average achievement to reflect the *inequalities* between men and women in the following dimensions:

- A long and healthy life, as measured by life expectancy at birth.
- Knowledge, as measured by the adult literacy rate and the combined primary, secondary and tertiary gross enrolment ratio.
- A decent standard of living, as measured by estimated earned income (PPP US$).

The calculation of the GDI involves three steps. First, female and male indices in each dimension are calculated according to this general formula:

$$\text{Dimension index} = \frac{\text{actual value} - \text{minimum value}}{\text{maximum value} - \text{minimum value}}$$

Second, the female and male indices in each dimension are combined in a way that penalizes differences in achievement between men and women. The resulting index, referred to as the equally distributed index, is calculated according to this general formula:

Equally distributed index
= {[female population share (female index$^{1-\epsilon}$)]
+ [male population share (male index$^{1-\epsilon}$)]}$^{1/1-\epsilon}$

ϵ measures the aversion to inequality. In the GDI $\epsilon = 2$. Thus the general equation becomes:

Equally distributed index
= {[female population share (female index^{-1})]
+ [male population share (male index^{-1})]}$^{-1}$

which gives the harmonic mean of the female and male indices.

Third, the GDI is calculated by combining the three equally distributed indices in an unweighted average.

Goalposts for calculating the GDI

Indicator	Maximum value	Minimum value
Female life expectancy at birth (years)	87.5	27.5
Male life expectancy at birth (years)	82.5	22.5
Adult literacy rate (%)	100	0
Combined gross enrolment ratio (%)	100	0
Estimated earned income (PPP US$)	40,000	100

Note: The maximum and minimum values (goalposts) for life expectancy are five years higher for women to take into account their longer life expectancy.

Calculating the GDI

This illustration of the calculation of the GDI uses data for Israel.

1. Calculating the equally distributed life expectancy index

The first step is to calculate separate indices for female and male achievements in life expectancy, using the general formula for dimension indices.

FEMALE
Life expectancy: 80.4 years

$$\text{Life expectancy index} = \frac{80.4 - 27.5}{87.5 - 27.5} = 0.882$$

MALE
Life expectancy: 76.6 years

$$\text{Life expectancy index} = \frac{76.6 - 22.5}{82.5 - 22.5} = 0.902$$

Next, the female and male indices are combined to create the equally distributed life expectancy index, using the general formula for equally distributed indices.

FEMALE
Population share: 0.507
Life expectancy index: 0.882

MALE
Population share: 0.493
Life expectancy index: 0.902

Equally distributed life expectancy index = {[0.507 (0.882^{-1})] + [0.493 (0.902^{-1})]}$^{-1}$ = **0.891**

2. Calculating the equally distributed education index

First, indices for the adult literacy rate and the combined primary, secondary and tertiary gross enrolment ratio are calculated separately for females and males. Calculating these indices is straightforward, since the indicators used are already normalized between 0 and 100.

FEMALE
Adult literacy rate: 93.9%
Adult literacy index: 0.939
Gross enrolment ratio: 83.5%
Gross enrolment index: 0.835

MALE
Adult literacy rate: 97.8%
Adult literacy index: 0.978
Gross enrolment ratio: 82.1%
Gross enrolment index: 0.821

Second, the education index, which gives two-thirds weight to the adult literacy index and one-third weight to the gross enrolment index, is computed separately for females and males.

Education index = 2/3 (adult literacy index) + 1/3 (gross enrolment index)

Female education index = 2/3 (0.939) + 1/3 (0.835) = 0.905

Male education index = 2/3 (0.978) + 1/3 (0.821) = 0.926

Finally, the female and male education indices are combined to create the equally distributed education index:

FEMALE
Population share: 0.507
Education index: 0.905

MALE
Population share: 0.493
Education index: 0.926

Equally distributed education index = {[0.507 (0.905^{-1})] + [0.493 (0.926^{-1})]}$^{-1}$ = **0.915**

3. Calculating the equally distributed income index

First, female and male earned income (PPP US$) are estimated (for details on this calculation see the addendum to this technical note). Then the income index is calculated for each gender. As for the HDI, income is adjusted by taking the logarithm of estimated earned income (PPP US$):

$$\text{Income index} = \frac{\log(\text{actual value}) - \log(\text{minimum value})}{\log(\text{maximum value}) - \log(\text{minimum value})}$$

FEMALE
Estimated earned income (PPP US$): 12,360

MALE
Estimated earned income (PPP US$): 24,687

$$\text{Income index} = \frac{\log(12,360) - \log(100)}{\log(40,000) - \log(100)} = 0.804$$

$$\text{Income index} = \frac{\log(24,687) - \log(100)}{\log(40,000) - \log(100)} = 0.919$$

Calculating the GDI continues on next page

Second, the female and male income indices are combined to create the equally distributed income index:

FEMALE
Population share: 0.507
Income index: 0.804

MALE
Population share: 0.493
Income index: 0.919

$$\text{Equally distributed income index} = \{[0.507\ (0.804^{-1})] + [0.493\ (0.919^{-1})]\}^{-1} = \mathbf{0.857}$$

4. Calculating the GDI

Calculating the GDI is straightforward. It is simply the unweighted average of the three component indices—the equally distributed life expectancy index, the equally distributed education index and the equally distributed income index.

$$\text{GDI} = 1/3\ (\text{life expectancy index}) + 1/3\ (\text{education index}) + 1/3\ (\text{income index})$$
$$= 1/3\ (0.891) + 1/3\ (0.915) + 1/3\ (0.857) = \mathbf{0.888}$$

Why $\epsilon = 2$ in calculating the GDI

The value of ϵ is the size of the penalty for gender inequality. The larger the value, the more heavily a society is penalized for having inequalities.

If $\epsilon = 0$, gender inequality is not penalized (in this case the GDI would have the same value as the HDI). As ϵ increases towards infinity, more and more weight is given to the lesser achieving group.

The value 2 is used in calculating the GDI (as well as the GEM). This value places a moderate penalty on gender inequality in achievement.

For a detailed analysis of the GDI's mathematical formulation see Sudhir Anand and Amartya Sen's "Gender Inequality in Human Development: Theories and Measurement," Kalpana Bardhan and Stephan Klasen's "UNDP's Gender-Related Indices: A Critical Review" and the technical notes in *Human Development Report 1995* and *Human Development Report 1999* (see the list of selected readings at the end of this technical note).

The gender empowerment measure (GEM)

Focusing on women's opportunities rather than their capabilities, the GEM captures gender inequality in three key areas:

• Political participation and decision-making power, as measured by women's and men's percentage shares of parliamentary seats.
• Economic participation and decision-making power, as measured by two indicators—women's and men's percentage shares of positions as legislators, senior officials and managers and women's and men's percentage shares of professional and technical positions.
• Power over economic resources, as measured by women's and men's estimated earned income (PPP US$).

For each of these three dimensions, an equally distributed equivalent percentage (EDEP) is calculated, as a population-weighted average, according to the following general formula:

$$\text{EDEP} = \{[\text{female population share (female index}^{1-\epsilon})] + [\text{male population share (male index}^{1-\epsilon})]\}^{1/1-\epsilon}$$

ϵ measures the aversion to inequality. In the GEM (as in the GDI) $\epsilon = 2$, which places a moderate penalty on inequality. The formula is thus:

$$\text{EDEP} = \{[\text{female population share (female index}^{-1})] + [\text{male population share (male index}^{-1})]\}^{-1}$$

For political and economic participation and decision-making, the EDEP is then indexed by dividing it by 50. The rationale for this indexation: in an ideal society, with equal empowerment of the sexes, the GEM variables would equal 50%—that is, women's share would equal men's share for each variable.

Finally, the GEM is calculated as a simple average of the three indexed EDEPs.

Female and male earned income

Despite the importance of having gender-disaggregated data on income, direct measures are unavailable. For this Report crude estimates of female and male earned income have therefore been derived.

Income can be seen in two ways: as a resource for consumption and as earnings by individuals. The use measure is difficult to disaggregate between men and women because they share resources within a family unit. By contrast, earnings are separable because different members of a family tend to have separate earned incomes.

The income measure used in the GDI and the GEM indicates a person's capacity to earn income. It is used in the GDI to capture the disparities between men and women in command over resources and in the GEM to capture women's economic independence. (For conceptual and methodological issues relating to this approach see Sudhir Anand and Amartya Sen's "Gender Inequality in Human Development" and, in *Human Development Report 1995*, chapter 3 and technical notes 1 and 2; see the list of selected readings at the end of this technical note.)

Female and male earned income (PPP US$) are estimated using the following data:

- Ratio of the female non-agricultural wage to the male non-agricultural wage.
- Male and female shares of the economically active population.
- Total female and male population.
- GDP per capita (PPP US$).

Key

W_f / W_m = ratio of female non-agricultural wage to male non-agricultural wage
EA_f = female share of economically active population
EA_m = male share of economically active population
S_f = female share of wage bill
Y = total GDP (PPP US$)
N_f = total female population
N_m = total male population
Y_f = estimated female earned income (PPP US$)
Y_m = estimated male earned income (PPP US$)

Note

Calculations based on data in the technical note may yield results that differ from those in the indicator tables because of rounding.

Estimating female and male earned income

This illustration of the estimation of female and male earned income uses 1999 data for Israel.

1. Calculating total GDP (PPP US$)
Total GDP (PPP US$) is calculated by multiplying the total population by GDP per capita (PPP US$).

Total population: 5,910 (thousand)
GDP per capita (PPP US$): 18,440
Total GDP (PPP US$) = 5,910 (18,440) = 108,980,400 (thousand)

2. Calculating the female share of the wage bill
Because data on wages in rural areas and in the informal sector are rare, the Report has used non-agricultural wages and assumed that the ratio of female wages to male wages in the non-agricultural sector applies to the rest of the economy. The female share of the wage bill is calculated using the ratio of the female non-agricultural wage to the male non-agricultural wage and the female and male percentage shares of the economically active population. Where data on the wage ratio are not available, a value of 75%, the unweighted average (rounded value) for countries with available data, is used.

Ratio of female to male non-agricultural wage (W_f/W_m) = 0.75
Female percentage share of economically active population (EA_f) = 40.7%
Male percentage share of economically active population (EA_m) = 59.3%

$$\text{Female share of wage bill } (S_f) = \frac{W_f/W_m (EA_f)}{[W_f/W_m (EA_f)] + EA_m} = \frac{0.75 (40.7)}{[0.75 (40.7)] + 59.3} = \mathbf{0.340}$$

3. Calculating female and male earned income (PPP US$)
An assumption has to be made that the female share of the wage bill is equal to the female share of GDP.

Female share of wage bill (S_f) = 0.340
Total GDP (PPP US$) (Y) = 108,980,400 (thousand)
Female population (N_f) = 2,995 (thousand)

$$\text{Estimated female earned income (PPP US$) } (Y_f) = \frac{S_f(Y)}{N_f} = \frac{0.340 (108,980,400)}{2,995} = \mathbf{12,372}$$

Male population (N_m) = 2,915 (thousand)

$$\text{Estimated male earned income (PPP US$) } (Y_m) = \frac{Y - S_f(Y)}{N_m} = \frac{108,980,400 - [0.340 (108,980,400)]}{2,915} = \mathbf{24,675}$$

Selected readings

Anand, Sudhir, and Amartya Sen. 1994. "Human Development Index: Methodology and Measurement." Occasional Paper 12. United Nations Development Programme, Human Development Report Office, New York. (HDI)

———. 1995. "Gender Inequality in Human Development: Theories and Measurement." Occasional Paper 19. United Nations Development Programme, Human Development Report Office, New York. (GDI, GEM)

———. 1997. "Concepts of Human Development and Poverty: A Multi-dimensional Perspective." In United Nations Development Programme, *Human Development Report 1997 Papers: Poverty and Human Development*. New York. (HPI-1, HPI-2)

Bardhan, Kalpana, and Stephan Klasen. 1999. "UNDP's Gender-Related Indices: A Critical Review." *World Development* 27(6): 985–1010. (GDI, GEM)

United Nations Development Programme. 1995. *Human Development Report 1995*. New York: Oxford University Press. Technical notes 1 and 2 and chapter 3. (GDI, GEM)

———. 1997. *Human Development Report 1997*. New York: Oxford University Press. Technical note 1 and chapter 1. (HPI-1, HPI-2)

———. 1999. *Human Development Report 1999*. New York: Oxford University Press. Technical note. (HDI)

CALCULATING THE TECHNOLOGY ACHIEVEMENT INDEX

The technology achievement index (TAI) is a composite index designed to capture the performance of countries in creating and diffusing technology and in building a human skills base. The index measures achievements in four dimensions:

- Technology creation, as measured by the number of patents granted to residents per capita and by receipts of royalties and license fees from abroad per capita.
- Diffusion of recent innovations, as measured by the number of Internet hosts per capita and the share of high- and medium-technology exports in total goods exports.
- Diffusion of old innovations, as measured by telephones (mainline and cellular) per capita and electricity consumption per capita.
- Human skills, as measured by mean years of schooling in the population aged 15 and above and the gross tertiary science enrolment ratio.

For each of the indicators in these dimensions the observed minimum and maximum values (among all countries with data) are chosen as "goalposts". Performance in each indicator is expressed as a value between 0 and 1 by applying the following general formula:

$$\text{Indicator index} = \frac{\text{actual value} - \text{observed minimum value}}{\text{observed maximum value} - \text{observed minimum value}}$$

The index for each dimension is then calculated as the simple average of the indicator indices in that dimension. The TAI, in turn, is the simple average of these four dimension indices.

Goalposts for calculating the TAI

Indicator	Observed maximum value	Observed minimum value
Patents granted to residents (per million people)	994	0
Royalties and license fees received (US$ per 1,000 people)	272.6	0
Internet hosts (per 1,000 people)	232.4	0
High- and medium-technology exports (as % of total goods exports)	80.8	0
Telephones (mainline and cellular, per 1,000 people)	901[a]	1
Electricity consumption (kilowatt-hours per capita)	6,969[a]	22
Mean years of schooling (age 15 and above)	12.0	0.8
Gross tertiary science enrolment ratio (%)	27.4	0.1

a. OECD average.

Note
Calculations based on data in the technical note may yield results that differ from those in annex table A2.1 in chapter 2 because of rounding.

Calculating the TAI

This illustration of the calculation of the TAI uses data for New Zealand for various years in 1997–2000.

1. Calculating the technology creation index
Patents and receipts of royalties and license fees are used to approximate the level of technology creation. Indices for the two indicators are calculated according to the general formula.

$$\text{Patent index} = \frac{103 - 0}{994 - 0} = 0.104$$

$$\text{Royalty and license fee index} = \frac{13.0 - 0.0}{272.6 - 0.0} = 0.048$$

The technology creation index is the simple average of these two indices:

$$\text{Technology creation index} = \frac{0.104 + 0.048}{2} = \mathbf{0.076}$$

2. Calculating the diffusion of recent innovations index
Using Internet hosts and the share of high- and medium-technology exports in total goods exports, the same formula is applied to calculate the diffusion of recent innovations index.

$$\text{Internet host index} = \frac{146.7 - 0.0}{232.4 - 0.0} = 0.631$$

$$\text{High- and medium-technology export index} = \frac{15.4 - 0.0}{80.8 - 0.0} = 0.191$$

$$\text{Diffusion of recent innovations index} = \frac{0.631 + 0.191}{2} = \mathbf{0.411}$$

3. Calculating the diffusion of old innovations index
The two indicators used to represent the diffusion of old innovations are telephones (mainline and cellular) and electricity consumption per capita. For these, the indices are calculated using the logarithm of the value, and the upper goalpost is the OECD average. For a detailed discussion see annex 2.1.

$$\text{Telephony index} = \frac{\log(720) - \log(1)}{\log(901) - \log(1)} = 0.967$$

For electricity consumption New Zealand's value is capped at 6,969, since it exceeds the goalpost.

$$\text{Electricity index} = \frac{\log(6,969) - \log(22)}{\log(6,969) - \log(22)} = 1.000$$

$$\text{Diffusion of old innovations index} = \frac{0.967 + 1.000}{2} = \mathbf{0.984}$$

4. Calculating the human skills index
The human skills index is calculated according to the general formula, using mean years of schooling and the gross tertiary science enrolment ratio.

$$\text{Mean years of schooling index} = \frac{11.7 - 0.8}{12.0 - 0.8} = 0.973$$

$$\text{Gross tertiary science enrolment index} = \frac{13.1 - 0.1}{27.4 - 0.1} = 0.476$$

$$\text{Human skills index} = \frac{0.973 + 0.476}{2} = \mathbf{0.725}$$

5. Calculating the technology achievement index
A simple average of the four dimension indices gives us the technology achievement index.

$$\text{TAI} = \frac{0.076 + 0.411 + 0.984 + 0.725}{4} = \mathbf{0.549}$$

ASSESSING PROGRESS TOWARDS THE MILLENNIUM DECLARATION GOALS FOR DEVELOPMENT AND POVERTY ERADICATION

This year's *Human Development Report* assesses the progress by countries towards specific targets outlined in the Millennium Declaration goals for development and poverty eradication. Each target has been set for 2015, with 1990 as the reference year. So achieving a target of, say, halving a rate or ratio by 2015 would mean reducing its 1990 value by 50% by 2015. Assessing the achievements of countries between 1990 and 1999 reveals whether they are progressing fast enough to meet the targets.

Monitoring progress at the global level requires data that are comparable. Yet data are missing or unreliable for some targets and for many countries. Countries at higher levels of development are more likely to have data, so those included in the assessment are likely to be among the better performers. High-income OECD countries have been excluded from the assessment. The number of countries whose progress has been assessed for each target ranges from 58 to 159 (technical note table 3.1).

The assessment of countries' achievements in 1999 is based on the following criteria:

- *Achieved:* The country has already achieved the target.
- *On track:* The country has attained the rate of progress needed to achieve the target by 2015 or has attained 90% of that rate of progress.
- *Lagging:* The country has achieved 70–89% of the rate of progress required to achieve the target by 2015.
- *Far behind:* The country has achieved less than 70% of the required rate of progress.
- *Slipping back:* The country's level of achievement is at least 5 percentage points worse in 1999 than in 1990.

The rate of progress required to meet the target is determined by the achievement that would be required by 1999, assuming a linear path of progress. Where data are not available for 1990 or 1999, data for the closest available year have been used. All countries within 10 percentage points of the universal goal (such as 100% school enrolment) in 1999 are considered to be on track.

The preferred indicator for assessing progress towards halving the proportion of people in extreme poverty is the share of the population living on less than $1 (PPP US$) a day, but country time series based on this poverty line are not widely available. A proxy approach has therefore been used, employing growth rate estimates from a study by Hanmer and

Naschold (2000). This study developed growth rates for two scenarios: business as usual (assuming no change in growth patterns) and pro-poor conditions (in which the benefits of growth reach poor people faster).

In each scenario the growth rate required for a country to meet the target of halving poverty by 2015 depends on whether that country has low or high inequality, as measured by the Gini index. Countries with high inequality (defined as a Gini index of 43 or higher) require faster growth to reach the target (technical note table 3.2). Given these growth rates, each country's progress has been assessed by the extent to which it has attained the required rate of growth.

For several other indicators—the maternal mortality ratio, the percentage of people with access to improved water sources and the percentage of children reaching grade 5—reliable data are difficult to obtain and time series are unavailable, so rates of progress are unknown. Proxy assessments have been made based on performance in the most recent year for which reasonably reliable data are available (technical note table 3.3).

Technical note table 3.1
Indicators used in assessment of progress towards Millennium Declaration goals

	Indicator	Countries assessed[a]	Source
Extreme poverty	Average annual GDP per capita growth rate, 1990–99, and Gini index, 1990–99[b]	85 (77)	World Bank 2001a and 2001b
Hunger	Percentage of people undernourished, 1990/92 and 1996/98	86 (73)	FAO 2000
Safe water	Percentage of people with access to improved water sources, 1999	133 (82)	UNICEF 2000
Universal education	Net primary enrolment ratio, 1990 and 1995–97[b]	58 (39)	UNESCO 2001c
	Percentage of children reaching grade 5, 1995 cohort	83 (39)	UNESCO 2000d
Gender equality	Ratio of girls to boys in school (girls' gross enrolment ratio to boys'), 1990 and 1995–97[b]		
	Primary level	88 (63)	UNESCO 1999
	Secondary level	85 (64)	UNESCO 1999
Maternal mortality	Maternal mortality ratio (per 100,000 live births), 1995	145 (85)	Hill, AbouZahr and Wardlaw 2001
Infant and child mortality	Infant mortality rate (per 1,000 live births), 1990 and 1999[c]	159 (85)	UNICEF 2001
	Under-five mortality rate (per 1,000 live births), 1990 and 1999	159 (85)	UNICEF 2001

a. Figures in parentheses refer to the percentage of the world population covered by the assessment.
b. Data refer to the most recent year available during the period specified.
c. International development goal.

Technical note table 3.2
Annual GDP per capita growth rate needed to halve poverty by 2015
Percent

	Business as usual	Pro-poor conditions
High-inequality countries (Gini index ≥ 43)	7.1	3.7
Low-inequality countries (Gini index < 43)	3.7	1.5

Source: Hanmer and Naschold 2000.

Technical note table 3.3
Criteria for assessing progress in maternal mortality, access to improved water sources and completion of primary schooling

Assessment	Maternal mortality ratio (per 100,000 live births) 1995	People with access to improved water sources (%) 1999	Children reaching grade 5 (%) 1995 cohort
Achieved	< 20	100	100
On track	21–99	90–99	90–99
Lagging	100–599	70–89	70–89
Far behind	600 or more	<70	<70

Statistical references

Aten, Bettina, Alan Heston and Robert Summers. 2001. "Penn World Tables 6.0." University of Pennsylvania, Center for International and Interarea Comparisons, Philadelphia.

CDIAC (Carbon Dioxide Information Analysis Center). 2000. *Trends: A Compendium of Data on Global Change.* [cdiac.esd.ornl.gov/trends/trends.htm]. December 2000.

FAO (Food and Agriculture Organization of the United Nations). 2000. "State of Food Insecurity 2000." [www.fao.org/focus/e/sofi00/sofi001-e.htm]. January 2001.

Hanmer, Lucia, and Felix Naschold. 2000. "Attaining the International Development Target: Will Growth Be Enough?" *Development Policy Review* 18 (March): 11–36.

Hill, Kenneth, Carla AbouZahr and Tessa Wardlaw. 2001. "Estimates of Maternal Mortality for 1995." *Bulletin of the World Health Organization* 79 (3): 182–93.

IISS (International Institute for Strategic Studies). 2000. *The Military Balance 2000–2001.* Oxford: Oxford University Press.

ILO (International Labour Organization). 1996. *Estimates and Projections of the Economically Active Population, 1950–2010.* 4th ed. Diskette. Geneva.

——. 1999. *Key Indicators of the Labour Market 1999.* Geneva.

——. 2001a. Correspondence on employment by sector. March. Geneva.

——. 2001b. *ILO Database on International Labour Standards (ILOLEX).* [ilolex.ilo.ch]. February 2001.

——. 2001c. *Laboursta Database.* [laborsta.ilo.org]. February 2001.

IPU (Inter-Parliamentary Union). 1995. *Women in Parliaments 1945–1995: A World Statistical Survey.* Geneva.

——. 2001a. Correspondence on women in government at the ministerial level. March. Geneva.

——. 2001b. Correspondence on year women received the right to vote and to stand for election and year first woman was elected or appointed to parliament. March. Geneva.

——. 2001c. *Parline Database.* [www.ipu.org/wmn-e/classif.htm]. March 2001.

LIS (Luxembourg Income Study). 2001. "Population below Income Poverty Line." [lisweb.ceps.lu/keyfigures/povertytable.htm]. February 2001.

Milanovic, Branko. 1998. *Income, Inequality and Poverty during the Transition from Planned to Market Economy.* Washington, DC: World Bank.

Murray, Scott. 2001. Correspondence on functional literacy. Statistics Canada. March. Ottawa.

OECD (Organisation for Economic Co-operation and Development). 2000a. *Economic Outlook.* Paris.

——. 2000b. *Employment Outlook 2000.* Paris.

——. 2000c. *Quarterly Labour Force Statistics.* No.1. Paris.

——. 2001a. Correspondence on total unemployed. February. Paris.

——. 2001b. Correspondence on unemployment rates. February. Paris.

OECD (Organisation for Economic Co-operation and Development), Development Assistance Committee. 2001a. Correspondence on net grants by non-governmental organizations. February. New York.

——. 2001b. Correspondence on net official development assistance receipts and net official aid receipts. February. Paris.

——. 2001c. Correspondence on official development assistance disbursed. February. New York.

——. 2001d. *Geographical Distribution of Financial Flows to Aid Recipients: 1995–1999.* Paris.

OECD (Organisation for Economic Co-operation and Development) and Statistics Canada. 2000. *Literacy in the Information Age: Final Report on the IALS.* Paris.

SIPRI (Stockholm International Peace Research Institute). 2000. *SIPRI Yearbook 2000: Armaments, Disarmament and International Security.* Oxford: Oxford University Press.

——. 2001. Correspondence on military expenditure data. March. Stockholm.

Smeeding, Timothy M. 1997. "Financial Poverty in Developed Countries: The Evidence from the Luxembourg Income Study." In United Nations Development Programme, *Human Development Report 1997 Papers: Poverty and Human Development.* New York.

Smeeding, Timothy M., Lee Rainwater and Gary Burtless. 2000. "United States Poverty in a Cross-National Context." Working Paper 244. Luxembourg Income Study, New York.

UN (United Nations). 1996. "Committee for Development Planning Report on the Thirtieth Session." E/1996/76. [www.un.org/documents/ecosoc/docs/1996/e1996-76.htm]. March 2001.

——. 1998. *World Population Prospects 1950–2050: The 1998 Revision.* Database. Department of Economic and Social Affairs, Population Division. New York.

——. 2000a. *The World's Women 2000: Trends and Statistics.* Department of Economic and Social Affairs, Statistics Division. New York.

——. 2000b. *World Urbanization Prospects: The 1999 Revision.* Department of Economic and Social Affairs, Population Division. New York.

——. 2001a. Correspondence on export data. Department of Economic and Social Affairs, Statistics Division. January. New York.

——. 2001b. "Multilateral Treaties Deposited with the Secretary-General." [untreaty.un.org]. March 2001.

——. 2001c. *United Nations Population Division Database on Contraceptive Use.* Department of Economic and Social Affairs, Population Division. February. New York.

——. 2001d. *World Population Prospects 1950–2050: The 2000 Revision.* Database. Department of Economic and Social Affairs, Population Division. New York.

UNAIDS (Joint United Nations Programme on HIV/AIDS). 2000. *Report on the Global HIV/AIDS Epidemic, June 2000.* [www.unaids.org/epidemic_update/]. December 2000.

UNESCO (United Nations Educational, Scientific and Cultural Organization). 1999. *Statistical Yearbook 1999.* Paris.

——. 2000a. Correspondence on adult literacy rates. January. Paris.

——. 2000b. Correspondence on education expenditures. December. Paris.

——. 2000c. Correspondence on youth literacy rates. January. Paris.

——. 2000d. *World Education Report 2000: The Right to Education—Towards Education for All throughout Life.* Paris.

———.2001a. Correspondence on adult literacy rates. March. Paris.

———.2001b. Correspondence on gross enrolment ratios. March. Paris.

———.2001c. Correspondence on net enrolment ratios. March. Paris.

UNHCR (United Nations High Commissioner for Refugees). 2000. *Refugees and Others of Concern to UNHCR: 1999 Statistical Overview.* Geneva.

UNICEF (United Nations Children's Fund). 2000. *The State of the World's Children 2001.* New York: Oxford University Press.

———. 2001. Correspondence on infant and under-five mortality rates. March. New York.

UNICRI (United Nations Interregional Crime and Justice Research Institute). 2001. Correspondence on data on crime victims. February. Turin.

Van Kesteren, John. 2001. Correspondence on the International Crime Victims Survey (ICVS). United Nations Interregional Crime and Justice Research Institute. March. Turin.

Ward, Michael. 2001. "Purchasing Power Parity and International Comparisons." Background paper for *Human Development Report 2001.* United Nations Development Programme, Human Development Report Office, New York.

WHO (World Health Organization). 1995. *Weekly Epidemiological Record* 70: 353–60. [www.who.int/wer/]. December 2000.

———. 1999. *Weekly Epidemiological Record* 74: 265–72. [www.who.int/wer/]. January 2001.

———.2000a. *Global Tuberculosis Control: WHO Report 2000.* [www.who.int/gtb/publications/globrep00/]. January 2001.

———. 2000b. *World Health Report 2000: Health Systems—Improving Performance.* Geneva.

———. 2001a. Correspondence on access to essential drugs. Department of Essential Drugs and Medicines Policy. February. Geneva.

———. 2001b. Correspondence on cigarette consumption data. January. Geneva.

———. 2001c. "WHO Estimates of Health Personnel." [www.who.int/whosis/]. January 2001.

———.2001d. *WHO Global Database on Coverage of Maternity Care.* Department of Reproductive Health and Research. January. Geneva.

World Bank. 2001a. Correspondence on GDP per capita growth rates. March. Washington, DC.

———.2001b. *World Development Indicators 2001.* CD-ROM. Washington, DC.

Definitions of statistical terms

Armed forces, total Strategic, land, naval, air, command, administrative and support forces. Also included are paramilitary forces such as the gendarmerie, customs service and border guard, if these are trained in military tactics.

Arms transfers, conventional Refers to the voluntary transfer by the supplier (and thus excludes captured weapons and weapons obtained through defectors) of weapons with a military purpose destined for the armed forces, paramilitary forces or intelligence agencies of another country. These include major conventional weapons or systems in six categories: ships, aircraft, missiles, artillery, armoured vehicles and guidance and radar systems (excluded are trucks, services, ammunition, small arms, support items, components and component technology and towed or naval artillery under 100-millimetre calibre).

Births attended by skilled health staff The percentage of deliveries attended by a doctor (a specialist, a non-specialist or a person with midwifery skills who can diagnose and manage obstetrical complications as well as normal deliveries), nurse or midwife (a person who has successfully completed the prescribed course of midwifery and is able to give the necessary supervision, care and advice to women during pregnancy, labour and the postpartum period and to care for newborns and infants) or trained traditional birth attendant (a person who initially acquired his or her ability by delivering babies or through apprenticeship to other traditional birth attendants and who has undergone subsequent extensive training and is now integrated in the formal health care system).

Birth-weight, infants with low The percentage of infants with a birth-weight of less than 2,500 grams.

Carbon dioxide emissions Anthropogenic (human-originated) carbon dioxide emissions stemming from the burning of fossil fuels and the production of cement. Emissions are calculated from data on the consumption of solid, liquid and gaseous fuels and gas flaring.

Cellular mobile subscribers People subscribing to a communications service in which voice or data are transmitted by radio frequencies.

Children reaching grade 5 The percentage of children starting primary school who eventually attain grade 5 (grade 4 if the duration of primary school is four years). The estimate is based on the reconstructed cohort method, which uses data on enrolment and repeaters for two consecutive years.

Cigarette consumption per adult, annual average The sum of production and imports minus exports of cigarettes divided by the population aged 15 and above.

Consumer price index Reflects changes in the cost to the average consumer of acquiring a basket of goods and services that may be fixed or change at specified intervals.

Contraceptive prevalence The percentage of married women aged 15–49 who are using, or whose partners are using, any form of contraception, whether modern or traditional.

Contributing family worker Defined according to the International Classification by Status in Employment (ICSE) as a person who works without pay in an economic enterprise operated by a related person living in the same household.

Crime, people victimized by The percentage of the population who perceive that they have been victimized by certain types of crime in the preceding year, based on responses to the International Crime Victims Survey. For further information see box 3 in the note on statistics.

Crime, total Refers to 11 crimes recorded in the International Crime Victims Survey: robbery, burglary, attempted burglary, car theft, car vandalism, bicycle theft, sexual assault, theft from car, theft of personal property, assault and threats and theft of motorcycle or moped. See *crime, people victimized by*.

Debt service, total The sum of principal repayments and interest actually paid in foreign currency, goods or services on long-term debt, interest paid on short-term debt and repayments to the International Monetary Fund.

Earned income (PPP US$), estimated (female and male) Roughly derived on the basis of the ratio of the female non-agricultural wage to the male non-agricultural wage, the female and male shares of the economically active population, total female and male population and GDP per capita (PPP US$). For details on this estimation see technical note 1.

Earned income, ratio of estimated female to male The ratio of estimated female earned income to estimated male earned income. See *earned income (PPP US$), estimated (female and male)*.

Economic activity rate The proportion of the specified group supplying labour for the production of economic goods and services during a specified period.

Education expenditure, public Public spending on public education plus subsidies to private education at the primary, secondary and tertiary levels. It includes expenditure at every level of administration—central, regional and local. See *education levels*.

Education index One of the three indices on which the human development index is built. It is based on the adult literacy rate and the combined primary, secondary and tertiary gross enrolment ratio. For details on how the index is calculated see technical note 1.

Education levels Categorized as pre-primary, primary, secondary or tertiary in accordance with the International Standard Classification of Education (ISCED). *Pre primary education* (ISCED level 0) is provided at such schools as kindergartens and nursery and infant schools and is intended for children not old enough to enter school at the primary level. *Primary education* (ISCED level 1) provides the basic elements of education at such establishments as primary and elementary schools. *Secondary education* (ISCED levels 2 and 3) is based on at least four years of previous instruction at the first level and provides general or specialized instruction, or both, at such institutions as middle school, secondary school, high school, teacher training school at this level and vocational or technical school. *Tertiary education* (ISCED levels 5-7) refers to education at such institutions as universities, teachers colleges and higher-level professional schools—requiring as a minimum condition of admission the successful completion of education at the second level or evidence of the attainment of an equivalent level of knowledge.

Electricity consumption per capita Refers to gross production, in per capita terms, which includes consumption by station auxiliaries and any losses in the transformers that are considered integral parts of the station. Included also is total electric energy produced by pumping installations without deduction of electric energy absorbed by pumping.

Employment by economic activity Employment in industry, agriculture or services as defined according to the International Standard Industrial Classification (ISIC) system (revisions 2 and 3). *Industry* refers to mining and quarrying, manufacturing, construction and public utilities (gas, water and electricity). *Agriculture* refers to agriculture, hunting, forestry and fishing. *Services* refer to wholesale and retail trade; restaurants and hotels; transport, storage and communications; finance, insurance, real estate and business services; and community, social and personal services.

Energy use, GDP per unit of The ratio of GDP (PPP US$) to commercial energy use, measured in kilograms of oil equivalent. This ratio provides a measure of energy efficiency by showing comparable and consistent estimates of real GDP across countries relative to physical inputs (units of energy use). See *GDP (gross domestic product)* and *PPP (purchasing power parity)*.

Enrolment ratio, gross The number of students enrolled in a level of education, regardless of age, as a percentage of the population of official school age for that level. See *education levels*.

Enrolment ratio, gross tertiary science The number of students enrolled in tertiary education in science, regardless of age, as a percentage of the population of the relevant age range. *Science* refers to natural sciences; engineering; mathematics and computer sciences; architecture and town planning; transport and communications; trade, craft and industrial programmes; and agriculture, forestry and fisheries. See also *education levels* and *enrolment ratio, gross*.

Enrolment ratio, net The number of students enrolled in a level of education who are of official school age for that level, as a percentage of the population of official school age for that level. See *education levels*.

Essential drugs, population with access to The percentage of the population for whom a minimum of 20 of the most essential drugs are continuously and affordably available at public or private health facilities or drug outlets within one hour's travel from home.

Exports, high and medium technology See *exports, high technology;* and *exports, medium technology.*

Exports, high technology Includes exports of electronics and electrical products such as turbines, transistors, televisions, power generating equipment and data processing and telecommunications equipment, as well as other high-technology exports such as cameras, pharmaceuticals, aerospace equipment and optical and measuring instruments.

Exports, low technology Includes exports of textiles, paper, glassware and basic steel and iron products (such as sheets, wires and unworked casting).

Exports, manufactured Includes exports of chemicals, basic manufactures, machinery and transport equipment and other miscellaneous manufactured goods, based on the Standard International Trade Classification.

Exports, medium technology Includes exports of automotive products, manufacturing equipment (such as agricultural, textile and food processing machinery), some forms of steel (tubes and primary forms) and chemical products such as polymers, fertilizers and explosives.

Exports, merchandise Goods provided to the rest of the world, including primary exports, manufactured exports and other transactions. See *exports, manufactured;* and *exports, primary.*

Exports, primary Defined according to the Standard International Trade Classification to include exports of food, agricultural raw materials, fuels and ores and metals.

Exports of goods and services The value of all goods and other market services provided to the rest of the world, including the value of merchandise, freight, insurance, transport, travel, royalties, license fees and other services. Labour and property income (formerly called factor services) is excluded.

Fertility rate, total The average number of children a woman would bear if age-specific fertility rates remained unchanged during her lifetime.

Fertilizer consumption The amount of manufactured fertilizer—nitrogen (N), phosphate (P_2O_5) and potassium (K_2O)—consumed per year per hectare of arable and permanently cropped land.

Foreign direct investment, net flows Net inflows of investment to acquire a lasting management interest (10% or more of voting stock) in an enterprise operating in an economy other than that of the investor. It is the sum of equity capital, reinvestment of earnings, other long-term capital and short-term capital.

Fuel consumption, traditional Estimated consumption of fuel wood, charcoal, bagasse and animal and vegetable wastes. Traditional fuel use and commercial energy use together make up total energy use.

Functional literacy skills, people lacking The proportion of the adult population aged 16–65 scoring at level 1 on the prose literacy scale of the International Adult Literacy Survey (IALS). Most tasks at this level require the reader to locate a piece of information in the text that is identical to or synonymous with the information given in the directive.

GDP (gross domestic product) The total output of goods and services for final use produced by an economy, by both residents and non-residents, regardless of the allocation to domestic and foreign claims. It does not include deductions for depreciation of physical capital or depletion and degradation of natural resources.

GDP index One of the three indices on which the human development index is built. It is based on GDP per capita (PPP US$). For details on how the index is calculated see technical note 1.

GDP per capita (PPP US$) See *GDP (gross domestic product)* and *PPP (purchasing power parity).*

GDP per capita annual growth rate Least squares annual growth rate, calculated from constant price GDP per capita in local currency units.

Gender empowerment measure (GEM) A composite index measuring gender inequality in three basic dimensions of empowerment—economic participation and decision-making, political participation and decision-making and power over economic resources. For details on how the index is calculated see technical note 1.

Gender-related development index (GDI) A composite index measuring average achievement in the three basic dimensions captured in the human development index—a long and healthy life, knowledge and a decent standard of living—adjusted to account for inequalities between men and women. For details on how the index is calculated see technical note 1.

Gini index Measures the extent to which the distribution of income (or consumption) among individuals or households within a country deviates from a perfectly equal distribution. A value of 0 represents perfect equality, a value of 100 perfect inequality.

GNP (gross national product) Comprises GDP plus net factor income from abroad, which is the income residents receive from abroad for factor services (labour and capital), less similar payments made to non-residents who contribute to the domestic economy.

Grants by NGOs, net Resource transfers by national non-governmental organizations (private non-profit-making agencies) to developing countries or territories identified in part I of the Development Assistance Committee (DAC) list of recipient countries. Calculated as gross outflows from NGOs minus resource transfers received from the official sector (which are already counted in official development assistance). See *official development assistance (ODA), net.*

Health expenditure per capita (PPP US$) The sum of public and private expenditure (in PPP US$), divided by the population. Health expenditure includes the provision of health services (preventive and curative), family planning activities, nutrition activities and emergency aid designated for health (but does not include provision of water and sanitation). See *health expenditure, private; health expenditure, public;* and *PPP (purchasing power parity).*

Health expenditure, private Direct household (out-of-pocket) spending, private insurance, charitable donations and direct service payments by private corporations. Together with public health expenditure, it makes up total health expenditure. See *health expenditure per capita (PPP US$)* and *health expenditure, public.*

Health expenditure, public Recurrent and capital spending from government (central and local) budgets, external borrowings and grants (including donations from international agencies and non-governmental organizations) and social (or compulsory) health insurance funds. Together with private health expenditure, it makes up total health expenditure. See *health expenditure per capita (PPP US$)* and *health expenditure, private.*

HIV/AIDS, people living with The estimated number of people living with HIV/AIDS at the end of the year specified.

Human development index (HDI) A composite index measuring average achievement in three basic dimensions of human development—a long and healthy life, knowledge and a decent standard of living. For details on how the index is calculated see technical note 1.

Human poverty index (HPI-1) for developing countries A composite index measuring deprivations in the three basic dimensions captured in the human development index—longevity, knowledge and standard of living. For details on how the index is calculated see technical note 1.

Human poverty index (HPI-2) for selected OECD countries A composite index measuring deprivations in the three basic dimensions captured in the human development index—longevity, knowledge and standard of living—and also capturing social exclusion. For details on how the index is calculated see technical note 1.

Illiteracy rate, adult Calculated as 100 minus the adult literacy rate. See *literacy rate, adult.*

Imports of goods and services The value of all goods and other market services purchased from the rest of the world, including the value of merchandise, freight, insurance, transport, travel, royalties, license fees and other services. Labour and property income (formerly called factor services) is excluded.

Income or consumption, shares of Based on national household surveys covering various years. Consumption surveys produce lower levels of inequality between poor and rich than do income surveys, as poor people generally consume a greater share of their income. Because data come from surveys covering different years and using different methodologies, comparisons between countries must be made with caution.

Income poverty line, population below Refers to the percentage of the population living below the specified poverty line:
- $1 a day—at 1985 international prices (equivalent to $1.08 at 1993 international prices), adjusted for purchasing power parity.
- $4 a day—at 1990 international prices, adjusted for purchasing power parity.
- $11 a day (per person for a family of three)—at 1994 international prices, adjusted for purchasing power parity.
- National poverty line—the poverty line deemed appropriate for a country by its authorities.
- 50% of median income—50% of the median disposable household income.

Infant mortality rate The probability of dying between birth and exactly one year of age expressed per 1,000 live births.

Internally displaced people Refers to people who are displaced within their own country and to whom the United Nations High Commissioner for Refugees

(UNHCR) extends protection or assistance, or both, in pursuance to a special request by a competent organ of the United Nations.

Internet host A computer system connected to the Internet—either a single terminal directly connected or a computer that allows multiple users to access network services through it.

Labour force All those employed (including people above a specified age who, during the reference period, were in paid employment, at work, with a job but not at work, or self-employed) and unemployed (including people above a specified age who, during the reference period, were without work, currently available for work and seeking work).

Legislators, senior officials and managers, female Women's share of positions defined according to the International Standard Classification of Occupations (ISCO-88) to include legislators, senior government officials, traditional chiefs and heads of villages, senior officials of special interest organizations, corporate managers, directors and chief executives, production and operations department managers and other department and general managers.

Life expectancy at birth The number of years a newborn infant would live if prevailing patterns of age-specific mortality rates at the time of birth were to stay the same throughout the child's life.

Life expectancy index One of the three indices on which the human development index is built. For details on how the index is calculated see technical note 1.

Literacy rate, adult The percentage of people aged 15 and above who can, with understanding, both read and write a short, simple statement on their everyday life.

Literacy rate, youth The percentage of people aged 15–24 who can, with understanding, both read and write a short, simple statement on their everyday life.

Malaria cases The total number of malaria cases reported to the World Health Organization by countries in which malaria is endemic. Many countries report only laboratory-confirmed cases, but many in Sub-Saharan Africa report clinically diagnosed cases as well.

Maternal mortality ratio reported Reported annual number of deaths of women from pregnancy-related causes per 100,000 live births, not adjusted for the well-documented problems of underreporting and misclassification.

Military expenditure All expenditures of the defence ministry and other ministries on recruiting and training military personnel as well as on construction and purchase of military supplies and equipment. Military assistance is included in the expenditures of the donor country.

Official aid Grants or loans that meet the same standards as for official development assistance (ODA) except that recipients do not qualify as recipients of ODA. Part II of the Development Assistance Committee (DAC) list of recipient countries identifies these countries.

Official development assistance (ODA), net Grants or loans to qualifying countries or territories, net of repayments, identified in part I of the Development Assistance Committee (DAC) list of recipient countries, that are undertaken by the official sector with promotion of economic development and welfare as the main objective, on concessional financial terms.

Official development assistance (ODA) to least developed countries See *official development assistance (ODA), net* and country classifications for least developed countries.

Oral rehydration therapy use rate The percentage of all cases of diarrhoea in children under age five treated with oral rehydration salts or recommended home fluids, or both.

Patents granted to residents Patents are documents, issued by a government office, that describe an invention and create a legal situation in which the patented invention can normally be exploited (made, used, sold, imported) only by or with the authorization of the patentee. The protection of inventions is generally limited to 20 years from the filing date of the application for the grant of a patent.

Physicians Includes graduates of a faculty or school of medicine in any medical field (including teaching, research and administration).

Population growth rate, annual Refers to the annual exponential growth rate for the period indicated. See *population, total*.

Population, total Refers to the de facto population, which includes all people actually present in a given area at a given time.

PPP (purchasing power parity) A rate of exchange that accounts for price differences across countries, allowing international comparisons of real output and incomes. At the PPP US$ rate (as used in this Report), PPP US$1 has the same purchasing power in the domestic economy as $1 has in the United States. For details on conceptual and practical issues relating to PPPs see box 2 in the note on statistics.

Private flows, other A category combining non-debt-creating portfolio equity investment flows (the sum of country funds, depository receipts and direct purchases of shares by foreign investors), portfolio debt flows (bond issues purchased by foreign investors) and bank and trade-related lending (commercial bank lending and other commercial credits).

Probability at birth of not surviving to a specified age Calculated as 1 minus the probability of surviving to a specified age for a given cohort. See *probability at birth of surviving to a specified age.*

Probability at birth of surviving to a specified age The probability of a newborn infant surviving to a specified age, if subject to prevailing patterns of age-specific mortality rates.

Professional and technical workers, female Women's share of positions defined according to the International Standard Classification of Occupations (ISCO-88) to include physical, mathematical and engineering science professionals (and associate professionals), life science and health professionals (and associate professionals), teaching professionals (and associate professionals) and other professionals and associate professionals.

Refugees People who have fled their country because of a well-founded fear of persecution for reasons of their race, religion, nationality, political opinion or membership in a particular social group and who cannot or do not want to return.

Research and development expenditures Current and capital expenditures (including overhead) on creative, systematic activity intended to increase the stock of knowledge. Included are fundamental and applied research and experimental development work leading to new devices, products or processes.

Royalties and license fees, receipts of Receipts by residents from non-residents for the authorized use of intangible, non-produced, non-financial assets and proprietary rights (such as patents, trademarks, copyrights, franchises and industrial processes) and for the use, through licensing agreements, of produced originals of prototypes (such as films and manuscripts). Data are based on the balance of payments.

Sanitation facilities, population using adequate The percentage of the population using adequate sanitation facilities, such as a connection to a sewer or septic tank system, a pour-flush latrine, a simple pit latrine or a ventilated improved pit latrine. An excreta disposal system is considered adequate if it is private or shared (but not public) and if it hygienically separates human excreta from human contact.

Schooling, mean years of The average number of years of school attained by the population aged 15 and above.

Science, math and engineering, tertiary students in The share of tertiary students enrolled in natural sciences; engineering; mathematics and computer sciences; architecture and town planning; transport and communications; trade, craft and industrial programmes; and agriculture, forestry and fisheries. See *education levels.*

Scientists and engineers in R&D People trained to work in any field of science who are engaged in professional research and development (R&D) activity. Most such jobs require the completion of tertiary education.

Seats in parliament held by women Refers to seats held by women in a lower or single house or an upper house or senate, where relevant.

Technology achievement index A composite index based on eight indicators in four dimensions: technology creation, diffusion of recent innovations, diffusion of old innovations and human skills. For more details on how the index is calculated see technical note 2.

Telephone mainline A telephone line connecting a subscriber to the telephone exchange equipment.

Terms of trade The ratio of the export price index to the import price index measured relative to a base year. A value of more than 100 implies that the price of exports has risen relative to the price of imports.

Tractors in use The number of tractors in use per hectare of arable and permanently cropped land.

Tuberculosis cases The total number of tuberculosis cases notified to the World Health Organization. A tuberculosis case is defined as a patient in whom tuberculosis has been bacteriologically confirmed or diagnosed by a clinician.

Under-five mortality rate The probability of dying between birth and exactly five years of age expressed per 1,000 live births.

Under height for age, children under age five Includes moderate and severe stunting, which is defined as below two standard deviations from the median height for age of the reference population.

Undernourished people People whose food intake is insufficient to meet their minimum energy requirements on a chronic basis.

Underweight for age, children under age five Includes moderate and severe underweight, which is defined as below two standard deviations from the median weight for age of the reference population.

Unemployment All people above a specified age who are not in paid employment or self-employed, but are available for work and have taken specific steps to seek paid employment or self-employment.

Unemployment, long-term Unemployment lasting 12 months or longer. See *unemployment*.

Unemployment, youth Refers to unemployment between the ages of 15 (or 16) and 24, depending on national definitions. See *unemployment*.

Urban population The midyear population of areas defined as urban in each country, as reported to the United Nations. See *population, total*.

Waiting list for mainlines Unmet applications for connection to the telephone network that have had to be held over owing to a lack of technical facilities (equipment, lines and the like).

Water sources, population not using improved Calculated as 100 minus the percentage of the population using improved water sources. See *water sources, population using improved*.

Water sources, population using improved The percentage of the population with reasonable access to an adequate amount of drinking water from improved sources. Reasonable access is defined as the availability of at least 20 litres per person per day from a source within one kilometre of the user's dwelling. Improved sources include household connections, public standpipes, boreholes with handpumps, protected dug wells, protected springs and rainwater collection (not included are vendors, tanker trucks and unprotected wells and springs).

Women in government at ministerial level Defined according to each state's definition of a national executive and may include women serving as ministers and vice-ministers and those holding other ministerial positions, including parliamentary secretaries.

Classification of countries

Countries in the human development aggregates

High human development (HDI 0.800 and above)

Argentina
Australia
Austria
Bahamas
Bahrain
Barbados
Belgium
Brunei Darussalam
Canada
Chile
Costa Rica
Croatia
Cyprus
Czech Republic
Denmark
Estonia
Finland
France
Germany
Greece
Hong Kong, China (SAR)
Hungary
Iceland
Ireland
Israel
Italy
Japan
Korea, Rep. of
Kuwait
Lithuania
Luxembourg
Malta
Netherlands
New Zealand
Norway
Poland
Portugal
Qatar
Singapore
Slovakia
Slovenia
Spain
Sweden
Switzerland
United Arab Emirates
United Kingdom
United States
Uruguay

(48 countries and areas)

Medium human development (HDI 0.500–0.799)

Albania
Algeria
Armenia
Azerbaijan
Belarus
Belize
Bolivia
Botswana
Brazil
Bulgaria
Cambodia
Cameroon
Cape Verde
China
Colombia
Comoros
Congo
Dominican Republic
Ecuador
Egypt
El Salvador
Equatorial Guinea
Fiji
Gabon
Georgia
Ghana
Guatemala
Guyana
Honduras
India
Indonesia
Iran, Islamic Rep. of
Jamaica
Jordan
Kazakhstan
Kenya
Kyrgyzstan
Latvia
Lebanon
Lesotho
Libyan Arab Jamahiriya
Macedonia, TFYR
Malaysia
Maldives
Mauritius
Mexico
Moldova, Rep. of
Mongolia

Morocco
Myanmar
Namibia
Nicaragua
Oman
Panama
Papua New Guinea
Paraguay
Peru
Philippines
Romania
Russian Federation
Samoa (Western)
Saudi Arabia
South Africa
Sri Lanka
Suriname
Swaziland
Syrian Arab Republic
Tajikistan
Thailand
Trinidad and Tobago
Tunisia
Turkey
Turkmenistan
Ukraine
Uzbekistan
Venezuela
Viet Nam
Zimbabwe

(78 countries and areas)

Low human development (HDI below 0.500)

Angola
Bangladesh
Benin
Bhutan
Burkina Faso
Burundi
Central African Republic
Chad
Congo, Dem. Rep. of the
Côte d'Ivoire
Djibouti
Eritrea
Ethiopia
Gambia
Guinea
Guinea-Bissau
Haiti
Lao People's Dem. Rep.
Madagascar
Malawi
Mali
Mauritania
Mozambique
Nepal
Niger
Nigeria
Pakistan
Rwanda
Senegal
Sierra Leone
Sudan
Tanzania, U. Rep. of
Togo
Uganda
Yemen
Zambia

(36 countries and areas)

Countries in the income aggregates [a]

High income
(GNP per capita of $9,266 or more in 1999)

Australia
Austria
Bahamas
Belgium
Brunei Darussalam
Canada
Cyprus
Denmark
Finland
France
Germany
Greece
Hong Kong, China (SAR)
Iceland
Ireland
Israel
Italy
Japan
Kuwait
Luxembourg
Netherlands
New Zealand
Norway
Portugal
Qatar
Singapore
Slovenia
Spain
Sweden
Switzerland
United Arab Emirates
United Kingdom
United States
(33 countries and areas)

Middle income
(GNP per capita of $756–9,265 in 1999)

Albania
Algeria
Argentina
Bahrain
Barbados
Belarus
Belize
Bolivia
Botswana
Brazil
Bulgaria
Cape Verde
Chile
China
Colombia
Costa Rica
Croatia
Czech Republic
Djibouti
Dominican Republic
Ecuador
Egypt
El Salvador
Equatorial Guinea
Estonia
Fiji
Gabon
Guatemala
Guyana
Honduras
Hungary
Iran, Islamic Rep. of
Jamaica
Jordan
Kazakhstan
Korea, Rep. of

Latvia
Lebanon
Libyan Arab Jamahiriya
Lithuania
Macedonia, TFYR
Malaysia
Maldives
Malta
Mauritius
Mexico
Morocco
Namibia
Oman
Panama
Papua New Guinea
Paraguay
Peru
Philippines
Poland
Romania
Russian Federation
Samoa (Western)
Saudi Arabia
Slovakia
South Africa
Sri Lanka
Suriname
Swaziland
Syrian Arab Republic
Thailand
Trinidad and Tobago
Tunisia
Turkey
Uruguay
Venezuela
(71 countries and areas)

Low income
(GNP per capita of $755 or less in 1999)

Angola
Armenia
Azerbaijan
Bangladesh
Benin
Bhutan
Burkina Faso
Burundi
Cambodia
Cameroon
Central African Republic
Chad
Comoros
Congo
Congo, Dem. Rep. of the
Côte d'Ivoire
Eritrea
Ethiopia
Gambia
Georgia
Ghana
Guinea
Guinea-Bissau
Haiti
India
Indonesia
Kenya
Kyrgyzstan
Lao People's Dem. Rep.
Lesotho
Madagascar
Malawi
Mali
Mauritania
Moldova, Rep. of
Mongolia

Mozambique
Myanmar
Nepal
Nicaragua
Niger
Nigeria
Pakistan
Rwanda
Senegal
Sierra Leone
Sudan
Tajikistan
Tanzania, U. Rep. of
Togo
Turkmenistan
Uganda
Ukraine
Uzbekistan
Viet Nam
Yemen
Zambia
Zimbabwe
(58 countries and areas)

a. Based on World Bank classifications (effective as of 1 July 2000).

Developing countries

Algeria	Iran, Islamic Rep. of	Tunisia	Uganda	Iceland
Angola	Jamaica	Turkey	Yemen	Ireland
Argentina	Jordan	Uganda	Zambia	Italy
Bahamas	Kenya	United Arab Emirates	*(40 countries and areas)*	Japan
Bahrain	Korea, Rep. of	Uruguay		Korea, Rep. of
Bangladesh	Kuwait	Venezuela	**Eastern Europe and**	Luxembourg
Barbados	Lao People's Dem. Rep.	Viet Nam	*the Commonwealth*	Mexico
Belize	Lebanon	Yemen	*of Independent States*	Netherlands
Benin	Lesotho	Zambia	*(CIS)*	New Zealand
Bhutan	Libyan Arab Jamahiriya	Zimbabwe		Norway
Bolivia	Madagascar	*(112 countries and areas)*	Albania	Poland
Botswana	Malawi		Armenia	Portugal
Brazil	Malaysia	**Least developed**	Azerbaijan	Slovakia
Brunei Darussalam	Maldives	**countries** [a]	Belarus	Spain
Burkina Faso	Mali	Angola	Bulgaria	Sweden
Burundi	Mauritania	Bangladesh	Croatia	Switzerland
Cambodia	Mauritius	Benin	Czech Republic	Turkey
Cameroon	Mexico	Bhutan	Estonia	United Kingdom
Cape Verde	Mongolia	Burkina Faso	Georgia	United States
Central African Republic	Morocco	Burundi	Hungary	*(30 countries and areas)*
Chad	Mozambique	Cambodia	Kazakhstan	
Chile	Myanmar	Cape Verde	Kyrgyzstan	**High-income**
China	Namibia	Central African Republic	Latvia	**OECD countries** [b]
Colombia	Nepal	Chad	Lithuania	Australia
Comoros	Nicaragua	Comoros	Macedonia, TFYR	Austria
Congo	Niger	Congo, Dem. Rep. of the	Moldova, Rep. of	Belgium
Congo, Dem. Rep. of the	Nigeria	Djibouti	Poland	Canada
Costa Rica	Oman	Equatorial Guinea	Romania	Denmark
Côte d'Ivoire	Pakistan	Eritrea	Russian Federation	Finland
Cyprus	Panama	Ethiopia	Slovakia	France
Djibouti	Papua New Guinea	Gambia	Slovenia	Germany
Dominican Republic	Paraguay	Guinea	Tajikistan	Greece
Ecuador	Peru	Guinea-Bissau	Turkmenistan	Iceland
Egypt	Philippines	Haiti	Ukraine	Ireland
El Salvador	Qatar	Lao People's Dem. Rep.	Uzbekistan	Italy
Equatorial Guinea	Rwanda	Lesotho	*(25 countries and areas)*	Japan
Eritrea	Samoa (Western)	Madagascar		Luxembourg
Ethiopia	Saudi Arabia	Malawi	## OECD countries	Netherlands
Fiji	Senegal	Maldives		New Zealand
Gabon	Sierra Leone	Mali		Norway
Gambia	Singapore	Mauritania	Australia	Portugal
Ghana	South Africa	Mozambique	Austria	Spain
Guatemala	Sri Lanka	Myanmar	Belgium	Sweden
Guinea	Sudan	Nepal	Canada	Switzerland
Guinea-Bissau	Suriname	Niger	Czech Republic	United Kingdom
Guyana	Swaziland	Rwanda	Denmark	United States
Haiti	Syrian Arab Republic	Samoa (Western)	Finland	*(23 countries and areas)*
Honduras	Tanzania, U. Rep. of	Sierra Leone	France	
Hong Kong, China (SAR)	Thailand	Sudan	Germany	
India	Togo	Tanzania, U. Rep. of	Greece	
Indonesia	Trinidad and Tobago	Togo	Hungary	

a. The classification *least developed countries* is based on the UN definition that went into effect in 1994 (with the countries as listed in UN 1996). Senegal was added to the list of least developed countries on 12 April 2001 but is not included in the aggregates for this group in this year's Report because the addition was made after the aggregates were finalized.
b. Excludes the Czech Republic, Hungary, the Republic of Korea, Mexico, Poland, Slovakia and Turkey.

Developing countries in the regional aggregates

Arab States

Algeria
Bahrain
Djibouti
Egypt
Jordan
Kuwait
Lebanon
Libyan Arab Jamahiriya
Morocco
Oman
Qatar
Saudi Arabia
Sudan
Syrian Arab Republic
Tunisia
United Arab Emirates
Yemen
(17 countries and areas)

Asia and the Pacific

East Asia and the Pacific
Brunei Darussalam
Cambodia
China
Fiji
Hong Kong, China (SAR)
Indonesia
Korea, Rep. of
Lao People's Dem. Rep.
Malaysia
Mongolia
Myanmar
Papua New Guinea
Philippines
Samoa (Western)
Singapore
Thailand
Viet Nam
(17 countries and areas)

South Asia
Bangladesh
Bhutan
India
Iran, Islamic Rep. of
Maldives
Nepal
Pakistan
Sri Lanka
(8 countries and areas)

Latin America and the Caribbean

Argentina
Bahamas
Barbados
Belize
Bolivia
Brazil
Chile
Colombia
Costa Rica
Dominican Republic
Ecuador
El Salvador
Guatemala
Guyana
Haiti
Honduras
Jamaica
Mexico
Nicaragua
Panama
Paraguay
Peru
Suriname
Trinidad and Tobago
Uruguay
Venezuela
(26 countries and areas)

Southern Europe

Cyprus
Turkey
(2 countries and areas)

Sub-Saharan Africa

Angola
Benin
Botswana
Burkina Faso
Burundi
Cameroon
Cape Verde
Central African Republic
Chad
Comoros
Congo
Congo, Dem. Rep. of the
Côte d'Ivoire
Equatorial Guinea
Eritrea
Ethiopia
Gabon
Gambia
Ghana
Guinea
Guinea-Bissau
Kenya
Lesotho
Madagascar
Malawi
Mali
Mauritania
Mauritius
Mozambique
Namibia
Niger
Nigeria
Rwanda
Senegal
Sierra Leone
South Africa
Swaziland
Tanzania, U. Rep. of
Togo
Uganda
Zambia
Zimbabwe
(42 countries and areas)

Indicator	Indicator tables
A	
Armed forces	
index	19
total	19
Arms transfers, conventional	
exports	
share of total	19
total	19
imports	
index	19
total	19
B	
Births attended by skilled health staff	6
Birth-weight, infants with low	7
C	
Carbon dioxide emissions	
per capita	18
share of world total	18
Children reaching grade 5	10
Cigarette consumption per adult, annual average	7
Consumer price index, average annual change in	11
Contraceptive prevalence	6
Contributing family workers	
female	24
male	24
Crime, people victimized by	
assault	20
bribery (corruption)	20
property crime	20
robbery	20
sexual assault	20
total crime	20
D	
Debt service	
as % of exports of goods and services	15
as % of GDP	15, 16
Displaced people, internally	19
E	
Earned income, estimated	
ratio of female to male	22
female	21
male	21
Economic activity rate, female	24
as % of male rate	24
index	24
Education expenditure, public	

Indicator	Indicator tables
as % of GNP	9, 16
as % of total government expenditure	9
pre-primary and primary	9
secondary	9
tertiary	9
Education index	1
Electricity consumption per capita	18
Employment by economic activity	
agriculture	
female	24
male	24
industry	
female	24
male	24
services	
female	24
male	24
Energy use, GDP per unit of	18
Enrolment ratio, gross	
combined primary, secondary and tertiary	1, 28
female	21
male	21
tertiary	
female	23
male	23
Enrolment ratio, net	
primary	10
female	23
female as % of male	23
index	10
secondary	10
female	23
female as % of male	23
index	10
Environmental treaties, ratification of	18
Essential drugs, population with access to	6
Exports	
of goods and services	13
high technology	13
manufactured	13
primary	13
F	
Fertility rate, total	5, 28
Fuel consumption, traditional	18
Functional literacy skills, people lacking	4
G	
GDP index	1
GDP per capita (PPP US$)	1, 11, 28
annual growth rate	11
highest value during 1975–99	11
year of highest value	11
GDP, total	

Indicator	Indicator tables
in PPP US$ billions	11
in US$ billions	11
Gender empowerment measure (GEM)	22
Gender-related development index (GDI)	21

H

Indicator	Indicator tables
Health expenditure	
per capita (PPP US$)	6
private	6
public	6, 16
HIV/AIDS	
adult rate of	7, 28
children living with	7
women living with	7
Human development index (HDI)	1
trends in	2
Human poverty index (HPI-1) for developing countries	3
Human poverty index (HPI-2) for selected OECD countries	4
Human rights instruments, status of major international	26

I

Indicator	Indicator tables
Illiteracy rate, adult	3
Immunization of one-year-olds	
against measles	6
against tuberculosis	6
Imports of goods and services	13
Income inequality measures	
Gini index	12
income ratio, richest 10% to poorest 10%	12
income ratio, richest 20% to poorest 20%	12
Income or consumption, share of	
poorest 10%	12
poorest 20%	12
richest 10%	12
richest 20%	12
Infant mortality rate	8, 28
Investment flows, net foreign direct	15

L

Indicator	Indicator tables
Labour rights conventions, status of fundamental	27
Life expectancy at birth	1, 8, 28
female	21
male	21
Life expectancy index	1
Literacy rate, adult	1, 10, 28
female	21, 23
female as % of male	23
index	10
male	21
Literacy rate, youth	10

Indicator	Indicator tables
female	23
female as % of male	23
index	10

M

Indicator	Indicator tables
Malaria cases	7
Maternal mortality ratio reported	8
Military expenditure	16

O

Indicator	Indicator tables
Official development assistance (ODA) disbursed, net	
as % of GNP	14
net grants by NGOs as % of GNP	14
per capita of donor country	14
to least developed countries	14
total (US$ millions)	14
Official development assistance (ODA) received (net disbursements)	
as % of GDP	15
per capita	15
total	15
Oral rehydration therapy use rate	6

P

Indicator	Indicator tables
Physicians	6
Population	
annual growth rate	5
aged 65 and above	5
total	5, 28
under age 15	5
urban	5
Poverty, income	
population living below $1 a day	3
population living below $4 a day	4
population living below $11 a day	4
population living below 50% of median income	4
population living below national poverty line	3
Private flows, other	15

R

Indicator	Indicator tables
Refugees	
by country of asylum	19
by country of origin	19

S

Indicator	Indicator tables
Sanitation, adequate facilities, population using	6
Science, math and engineering, tertiary students in	10

Indicator	Indicator tables
Survival	
probability at birth of not surviving to age 40	3
probability at birth of not surviving to age 60	4
probability at birth of surviving to age 65	
female	8
male	8

T

Indicator	Indicator tables
Terms of trade	13
Tuberculosis cases	7

U

Indicator	Indicator tables
Under-five mortality rate	8, 28
Under height for age, children under age five	7
Undernourished people	7, 28
Underweight for age, children under age five	3, 7
Unemployed people	17
Unemployment rate	17
average annual	17
female as % of male	17

Indicator	Indicator tables
youth	17
youth, female as % of male	17
Unemployment, long-term	4
female	17
male	17

W

Indicator	Indicator tables
Water, improved sources	
population not using	3
population using	6, 28
Women's economic participation	
female legislators, senior officials and managers	22
female professional and technical workers	22
Women's political participation	
female legislators, senior officials and managers	22
seats in parliament held by women	22, 25
women in government at ministerial level	25
year first woman elected or appointed to parliament	25
year women received right to stand for election	25
year women received right to vote	25

Countries and regions that have produced human development reports

Arab States

Algeria, *1998, 2000**
Bahrain, *1998*
Djibouti, *2000*
Egypt, *1994, 1995, 1996, 1997–98*
Iraq, *1995*
Jordan, *2000, 2001**
Kuwait, *1997, 1998–99, 2000**
Lebanon, *1997, 1998, 2000**
Libyan Arab Jamahiriya, *1999*
Morocco, *1997, 1998–99, 2001**
Occupied Palestinian territory, *1996–97*
Saudi Arabia, *2000**
Somalia, *1998*
Tunisia, *1999*
United Arab Emirates, *1997*
Yemen, *1998, 2000**

Asia and the Pacific

Bangladesh, *1992, 1993, 1994, 1995, 1996, 1998, 2000*
Bhutan, *1999*
Cambodia, *1997, 1998, 1999, 2000, 2001**
China, *1997, 1999, 2001**
East Timor, *2001**
India, *2001**
India, Arunachal Pradesh, *2001**
India, Assam, *2001**
India, Himachal Pradesh, *2001**
India, Karnataka, *1999, 2001**
India, Madhya Pradesh, *1995, 1998, 2001**
India, Maharashtra, *2001**
India, Orissa, *2001**
India, Punjab, *2001**
India, Rajasthan, *1999, 2000**
India, Sikkim, *2001**
India, Tamil Nadu, *2001**
India, Uttar Pradesh, *2001**
Indonesia, *2001**
Iran, Islamic Rep. of, *1999*
Korea, Rep. of, *1998*
Lao People's Dem. Rep., *1998, 2001**
Maldives, *2000**
Mongolia, *1997, 2000*
Myanmar, *1998*
Nepal, *1998, 2000**
Pakistan, *2001**
Palau, *1999*
Papua New Guinea, *1998*
Philippines, *1994, 1997, 2000, 2001**
Singapore, *2001**
Solomon Islands, *2001**
Sri Lanka, *1998, 2001**
Thailand, *1999*
Tuvalu, *1999*
Vanuatu, *1996*

Europe and the CIS

Albania, *1995, 1996, 1998, 2000*
Armenia, *1995, 1996, 1997, 1998, 1999, 2000*
Azerbaijan, *1995, 1996, 1997, 1998, 1999, 2000*
Belarus, *1995, 1996, 1997, 1998, 1999, 2000*
Bosnia and Herzegovina, *1998, 1999, 2000*
Bulgaria, *1995, 1996, 1997, 1998, 1999, 2000*
Bulgaria, Sofia, *1997*
Croatia, *1997, 1998, 1999*
Czech Republic, *1996, 1997, 1998, 1999, 2000**
Estonia, *1995, 1996, 1997, 1998, 1999, 2000*
Georgia, *1995, 1996, 1997, 1998, 1999, 2000, 2001**
Hungary, *1995, 1996, 1998, 1999*
Kazakhstan, *1995, 1996, 1997, 1998, 1999, 2000**
Kyrgyzstan, *1995, 1996, 1997, 1998, 1999, 2000*
Latvia, *1995, 1996, 1997, 1998, 1999, 2000**
Lithuania, *1995, 1996, 1997, 1998, 1999, 2000*
Macedonia, TFYR, *1997, 1998, 1999*
Malta, *1996*
Moldova, Rep. of, *1995, 1996, 1997, 1998, 1999, 2000*
Poland, *1995, 1996, 1997, 1998, 1999, 2000, 2001**
Romania, *1995, 1996, 1997, 1998, 1999, 2000*
Russian Federation, *1995, 1996, 1997, 1998, 1999, 2000**
Saint Helena, *1999*
Slovakia, *1995, 1997, 1998, 1999, 2000*
Slovenia, *1998, 1999, 2000*
Tajikistan, *1995, 1996, 1997, 1998, 1999*
Turkey, *1995, 1996, 1997, 1998, 1999, 2000**
Turkmenistan, *1995, 1996, 1997, 1998, 1999, 2000**
Ukraine, *1995, 1996, 1997, 1998, 1999*
Uzbekistan, *1995, 1996, 1997, 1998, 1999*
Yugoslavia, *1996, 1997*

Latin America and the Caribbean

Argentina, *1995, 1996, 1997, 1998, 1999*
Argentina, Province of Buenos Aires, *1996, 1997, 1998, 1999*
Argentina, Province of Catamarca, *1996*
Argentina, Province of Entre Ríos, *1996*
Argentina, Province of Mendoza, *1996*
Argentina, Province of Neuquén, *1996*
Belize, *1997, 1998*
Bolivia, *1998, 2000*
Bolivia, Cochabamba, *1995*
Bolivia, La Paz, *1995*
Bolivia, Santa Cruz, *1995*
Brazil, *1996, 1998*
Chile, *1996, 1998, 2000*
Colombia, *1998, 1999, 2000*
Costa Rica, *1994, 1995, 1996, 1997, 1998, 1999*
Cuba, *1996, 1999*
Dominican Republic, *1997, 1999*
Ecuador, *1999*
El Salvador, *1997, 1999*
Guatemala, *1998, 1999, 2000*
Guyana, *1996, 1999–2000**
Honduras, *1998, 1999*
Jamaica, *2000*
Nicaragua, *2000*
Panama, *2001**
Paraguay, *1995, 1996*
Peru, *1997*
Trinidad and Tobago, *2000*
Uruguay, *1999*
Venezuela, *1995, 1996, 1997, 1998, 1999*

Sub-Saharan Africa

Angola, *1997, 1998, 1999*
Benin, *1997, 1998, 1999, 2000*
Botswana, *1997, 2000*
Burkina Faso, *1997, 1998*
Burundi, *1997, 1999*
Cameroon, *1992, 1993, 1996, 1998*
Cape Verde, *1997, 1998*
Central African Republic, *1996*
Chad, *1997*
Comoros, *1997, 1998, 2001**
Côte d'Ivoire, *1997, 2000*
Equatorial Guinea, *1996, 1997*
Ethiopia, *1997, 1998*
Gabon, *1998, 1999*
Gambia, *1997, 2000*
Ghana, *1997, 1998, 1999, 2000*
Guinea, *1997*
Guinea-Bissau, *1997*
Kenya, *1999*
Lesotho, *1998, 2001**
Liberia, *1999*
Madagascar, *1997, 1999*
Malawi, *1997, 1998*
Mali, *1995, 1998, 1999, 2000*
Mauritania, *1996, 1997, 1998, 2000*
Mozambique, *1998, 1999, 2000**
Namibia, *1996, 1997, 1998*
Niger, *1997, 1998, 1999, 2000**
Nigeria, *1996, 1998, 2000**
São Tomé and Principe, *1998*
Senegal, *1998*
Sierra Leone, *1996*
South Africa, *1998, 2000*
Swaziland, *1997, 1998*
Tanzania, U. Rep. of, *1997, 1999, 2001**
Togo, *1995, 1997, 1999*
Uganda, *1996, 1997, 1998*
Zambia, *1997, 1998, 1999–2000*
Zimbabwe, *1998*

Regional reports

Africa, *1995*
Arab States, *2001**
Central America, *1999, 2001**
Eastern Europe and the CIS, *1995, 1996, 1997, 1999*
Latin America and the Caribbean, *2001**
Pacific Islands, *1994, 1999*
South Asia, *1997, 1998, 1999, 2000, 2001**
South-East Asia, *2001**
Southern African Development Community, *1998, 2001**
West and Central Africa, *2001**

* Under preparation as of March 2001.

Note: Information as of March 2001.

Source: Prepared by the Human Development Report Office.